The Ancient Cities and Global Trade of Palestine

The Ancient Cities and Global Trade of Palestine

A 7,000-Year History

Nur Masalha

BLOOMSBURY ACADEMIC
LONDON • NEW YORK • OXFORD • NEW DELHI • SYDNEY

BLOOMSBURY ACADEMIC
Bloomsbury Publishing Plc, 50 Bedford Square, London, WC1B 3DP, UK
Bloomsbury Publishing Inc, 1359 Broadway, New York, NY 10018, USA
Bloomsbury Publishing Ireland, 29 Earlsfort Terrace, Dublin 2, D02 AY28, Ireland

BLOOMSBURY, BLOOMSBURY ACADEMIC and the Diana logo are
trademarks of Bloomsbury Publishing Plc

First published in Great Britain 2026

Cover design by Namkwan Cho
Cover image: Buy Jaffa Oranges, 1929, by Frank Newbould. Yale Center
for British Art, Gift of Henry S. Hacker, Yale BA 1965

A catalogue record for this book is available from the British Library.

A catalog record for this book is available from the Library of Congress.

ISBN: HB: 978-0-7556-5970-8
PB: 978-0-7556-5969-2
ePDF: 978-0-7556-5972-2
eBook: 978-0-7556-5971-5

Typeset by Integra Software Services Pvt. Ltd.
Printed and bound in Great Britain

For product safety related questions contact productsafety@bloomsbury.com.

Contents

Acknowledgements

Many colleagues and friends have contributed with ideas, materials and expert knowledge to the completion of this work and are sincerely acknowledged. Also a number of diligent and independent anonymous reviewers offered their time and expertise to review the manuscript and this greatly benefited the work. I am hugely indebted to all. However, any shortcomings and deficiencies that remain are entirely mine.

Introduction

Ancient Palestine as a transit country: Global trade routes and the commercial geography of ancient Palestine

The ancient cities of Palestine were built on layers and layers of history and culture and their wealth and prosperity were partly derived from the geo-political location of the country. Transit trade, in particular, was an important source of revenue for Palestine and for millennia the wealth of Palestine and the flourishing of its ancient city-states and civilizations came from being at the centre of both international trade and being a hub of local industries. Located at the crossroads of three continents, Asia, Europe and Africa, Palestine, despite its relative small size, produced a large number of manufactured commodities for the international market and global distribution in Antiquity, the Middle Ages and throughout the modern period. Focusing on the ancient trading and industrial cities of Palestine, this book is the third in my trilogy which explores the long history of Palestine. This trilogy began with *Palestine: A Four Thousand Year History* (2018), which was followed by *Palestine Across Millennia: A History of Literacy, Learning and Educational Revolutions* (2022). The book focuses on the international trade of, and local industries in, Palestine and how these two economic forces shaped the urban social, economic and cultural life in the country. It is an ambitious work about the historic evolution of the towns and cities in Palestine over the last 7,000 years. This long history of global trade, traditional industries and urbanism in Palestine unites powerful economic forces and social movements across multiple historical periods for the first time, presenting them as part of a cumulative and incremental advancement of urbanism in the country rather than disconnected periods of commercial-economic and social-urban history. Furthermore, this work focuses on the *longue durée* of Palestine's ancient commercial and urban history across millennia, and within the wider study of ancient global trade and urbanism in the Near East, which is often overlooked in most writings on Palestine.

The *Neolithic Revolution* in the Near East, one of humanity's most important milestones, was the transition from a society of hunting and gathering to a society of agricultural life, food production and the establishment of permanent village and town life; this agricultural revolution ultimately set the stage for subsequent urban human development in the Near East and globally (Simmons 2007). Food production and the establishment of permanent villages and market towns combined with regional trade were fundamental to the emergence of early urban life in ancient Palestine and the wider Middle East. Involved in regional trade and international distribution networks, ancient Palestine began developing an agricultural economy in the Neolithic age, about 10,000–12,000 years ago, and its strong *agricultural industries* are millennia old whereas in Ireland and many parts of Europe farming began at around 4,000 BCE. Furthermore three metallic revolutions were at the centre of the early cities and the rise of urbanism in ancient Palestine: copper, bronze and iron corresponding to the *Chalcolithic Age*, *Bronze Age* and *Iron Age*. Through the management and control of the rise and growth of regional trade during the Bronze Age, the most common type of *states* in Palestine and the Levant during this period became the *city-states*. The roots of these early urban centres in Palestine go back to the *Copper Age* (Chalcolithic Age: *χαλκός λίθος*), and urban centres and city-states experienced a sharp rise in the early and middle Bronze Age.

Located within the Jordan Rift Valley, the Timna valley, north of the Gulf of Aqaba, is the site of one of the most extensive industrial activities of ancient mineral and copper mining and smelting in Palestine. The early mining industry of Timna in southern Palestine dates back to the late Neolithic Age; extensive archaeological excavations at the Timna valley discovered hundreds of copper mines and smelting camps with furnaces, rock drawings, geological features, an ancient Egyptian mining sanctuary, jewellery, and other artefacts (Levin 2020: 487). However with the beginning of the metallic revolutions of the Chalcolithic Age and Bronze Age, with the rise of complex society in Palestine and with the subsequent recorded history and written records in Bronze Age Palestine, the story of 'civilization' in Palestine (whether pastoral, agricultural or urban) was always complex and multi-layered and with multiple beginnings. City-states were a common feature in Bronze Age Palestine. Moreover ancient cities also went through spectacular rise, decline and some even disappeared completely. Moreover, ancient urbanism in Palestine cannot be understood as a linear process. For instance, the Chalcolithic Age saw early urbanism in the country, a process that accelerated during the early Bronze Age and the country saw '750-years of a spectacular urban age' characterized by phenomenal urban growth and rise of cities at the outset of the Bronze Age, followed by a period characterized by regression and urban decline and even (according to some historians) 'urban collapse' at the end of this period (Richard 1987: 22–43) caused partly by foreign invasions. Located at the intersection of three continents and ancient global trade routes, Palestine was particularly coveted by foreign powers and vulnerable to foreign invasions. Moreover, the middle Bronze Age (1750–1550 BCE) saw again the dramatic rise of 'city-states' and 'centres of ancient polities' in Palestine – city-states that were ruled by kings or local chieftains and possessed armies – as seen by the archaeological excavations *Tell al-Mutasallim* (*Tell Megiddo*), *Tell Hazor* and *Tell Kabri, Tell al-Safi and Tell Balata* (Cline, Ratzlaff and Yasur-Landau 2023; Taha and van der Kooij 2014), the late Bronze Age saw the first recorded name of *Palestine* in Egyptian sources (Masalha 2018). Furthermore, urbanism in late Bronze Age Palestine is well documented through a rich collection of written Egyptian documents, as well as through extensive archaeological excavations. The strength of urbanization in Palestine is evident from the Egyptian documents: the list of seventy-nine entries of villages, towns and cities in Palestine in the list of Thutmosis III and twenty-four or twenty-five entries – some with their own kings – also on Palestine in the al-Amarna lettersas well as other place names cited in New Kingdom documents give the impression of a chain of strong, fortified towns and cities in Palestine (Gonen 1984: 61–73).

Overall Palestine saw the rise of market towns – to be followed later by the developmentn of cities and sophisticated urban civilization – 7,000 years ago at the end of the Copper Age and at the outset of the early Bronze Age, at around 3,200 BCE. Despite having one of the longest histories of civilization in the world, the overwhelming majority of publications on Palestine focus on the modern period and overlooks the long history of Palestine, its ancient cities and civilizations.

Ancient international 'transit trade routes' through Palestine, the ancient spice and incense trade and the rise of local Palestinian industries were at the heart of the growth of urbanism in Palestine and the prosperity of its towns and cities. The spice trade, based on efficient and lucrative cooperation of merchants from multiple nationalities, was known from the earliest Antiquity. Spices: pepper, cinnamon, ginger, cardamom from Asia and aromatics from south Arabia have long been luxury products and used for dining or in medicine. The high value and the extraordinary profits derived from the international commerce passing through were sufficient to stimulate the entrepreneurial spirit of Palestinian, Syrian, Egyptian, Arab, Greek and Roman merchants at an early stage. In Antiquity Arab merchants, in particular, were for a long time the obligatory intermediaries between the Far East and the Christian West, because they were in contact with the civilizations that controlled the production of spices (India, China, Indonesia), and mastered the art of navigation in the Indian Ocean to seek spices as close as possible to the spice markets in India and other countries in Asia. The rise and decline of the ancient 'spice and perfume cities' of the southern region of Palestine, the Naqab (the Negev) was a case in point: these historic 'spice cities' of southern Palestine flourished for more than one and a half millennia along the *incense routes* from the ancient Nabataean city of Petra to the two harbours within the territorial domain of the Gaza city (*Constantia Maiumas Neapolis* and *Anthedon*), then from these two harbours of Gaza the commodities were shipped to the Mediterranean world and Europe. On the return journey from Gaza and Damascus the Nabataean caravans were bulging with olive oil, henna, storax, asbestos, clothes, glass, gold coins and silver items – silver which provided a model for the creation of silver currency in the region in Antiquity.

Palestinian heritage and Israel's cultural genocide in Gaza: Evidence of thriving ancient urban trading centres in Palestine

Given the continuing destruction of archaeological and cultural heritage of Palestine in recent years, especially in the ongoing genocidal war in Gaza, underscores the urgency and relevance of the study. This work was completed two years into the ongoing Israeli genocidal war on Gaza – which followed the Hamas attacks of 7 October 2023. Applying scorched earth policy in the past two years, and the destruction of buildings, hospitals, schools, mosques, urban infrastructure, crops, heritage sites and ancient ports and monasteries, Israel has sought to destroy everything to make life unliveable in the Gaza Strip. In the process the Israeli army systematically destroyed hundreds of Palestinian archaeological sites and heritage centres across the Gaza region. Although much of the discussion in this work focuses on historical Gaza and the long history of this great Palestinian city before the 1948 Nakba, the current Israeli war on Gaza was described by an Israeli Holocaust historian, Professor Raz Segal as 'A Textbook Case of Genocide'.[1] Two years later, in September 2025 a UN commission of inquiry, citing statements by Israeli leaders, and the pattern of strikes by Israeli forces as evidence of genocidal intent, concluded that Israel committed genocide against the Palestinians in Gaza.[2] Combined with a 'cultural genocide', nearly 200 sites of historical importance were destroyed or badly damaged in Israeli air strikes on the Gaza Strip in the first 100 days of the Israeli war on Gaza.[3] Palestinian archaeologists working with British archaeologists estimate that more than two-thirds of heritage, cultural and archaeological and heritage sites and museums, with hundreds of priceless historical artefacts, in Gaza city have been destroyed or badly damaged during the war so far. Many of these heritage sites appear to have been directly targeted by Israeli forces in attacks that could constitute war crimes. The 800-year-old Mamluk period Pasha Palace and the nearby Hamam al-Samara, a 700-year-old bath house and the historic al-Omari Mosque were among the most important of Gaza city's monuments; together with dozens of major heritage sites in the Gaza Strip have been deliberately targeted for destruction by the Israeli strikes on Gaza, together with hospitals, schools, universities, museums, roads and much of the urban infrastructure in the Gaza Strip. Originally a Byzantine church, the al-Omari mosque, which was converted and expanded 1,400 years ago under Islam, home to rare Islamic manuscripts along with a major ancient harbour daring back to 800 BCE, one of the world's oldest Christian monasteries other heritage sites in the Gaza Strip, were important evidence of the importance of Gaza city as a thriving trading centre in Palestine for several millennia.[4] Wiping out the cultural heritage of the Palestinian people was one of the many war crimes South Africa cited against Israel in its lawsuit that was heard at the International Court of Justice in the Hague in January 2024.[5]

One of the most important trading hubs in ancient Palestine and an international emporium in Antiquity, the city of Gaza has been inhabited continuously for over 4,000 years and for millennia the city prospered as a key centre of regional and international routes. Ancient Gaza was a large and well-fortified city in Antiquity. Mentioned in the written sources nearly 4,000 years ago, the name of the city of Gaza was first mentioned in the Egyptian records at Karnak in the annals of Thutmose III (1568 BCE). From the text it is clear that at the time Gaza was controlled by the Egyptian authorities and the city functioned as the capital of Egyptian-governed Palestine.

In classical and late Antiquity Gaza became one of the best-known and most developed cities in the Mediterranean region and also became known retrospectively as one of the most powerful 'five city-states' (*Pentapolis*) of the ancient Palestinians or Philistines, who created a distinct material, commercial and spectacular urban culture in Palestine during the late Bronze Age and Iron Age (1200–600 BCE). Furthermore, in Antiquity Gaza was described by Greek historians as the most important trading city in Syria. The Greek historian Plutarch (*c*.46–119 CE) describes Gaza as the 'greatest city of Syria'. At the time Gaza, because of the enormous volume of its Mediterranean maritime trade, was the only city in Palestine and Syria that was served by *two harbours* on the Mediterranean shore. Earlier in the twelfth century BCE Gaza was of the five great cities of the *Philistines*, ruled by autonomous kings. Located strategically at the ancient global crossroads, Gaza gained importance as a commercial link between Egypt and Syria and as the gateway to the Mediterranean Sea. Located at the heart of long-distance international trade routes, for millennia merchants followed an international route known as *Via Maris* along the Palestinian coast, carrying goods to and from Egypt; Gaza, the southernmost city in ancient Palestine, was the first way-station along this international trade route, and its abundant water supply made it the most welcome after the long trek through the parched Sinai Peninsula.

Gaza's close proximity to ancient Egypt also played an important role in its ancient trade and spectacular urban development. From 320-317 BCE under the Ptolemies of Egypt, Gaza was the most important urban and trading centre for Egypt in Palestine. According to the Ptolemies' Zeno archive – produced by a senior state official in charge of taxation and the frankincense trade – the south Arabia global commerce through Palestine and Gaza – the city of Gaza was an essential hub with the Trans-Arabian trade with the Yemen (known in Antiquity as *Arabia Felix*), the Red Sea coast and the coast of Somalia and Land of Punt, all of which produced commodities such as resin, dyes, aromatic essences, ginger, pepper and balsam. The harbour of Gaza is also mentioned in some Egyptian papyri ('Gaza' in Ameling et al. 2014, Vol. III: 412). The evidence shows that Gaza was a very prosperous trading city and important urban centre in the third and second centuries BCE ('Gaza' in Ameling et al. 2014: 414). In 63 BCE Gaza and Idumaea, 'rich in palm trees' are listed among the countries that sent help to Pompey and in the fourth century CE the *Onomasticon* of Eusebius of Caesarea Maritima (the capital of Byzantine Palestine) says: 'Even today it [Gaza] is an important city in Palestine' ('Gaza' in Ameling et al. 2014, Vol. III: 415–18). Because of centrality to Roman trade, the emperor Hadrian's visit to Gaza in 129-130 CE is said to have resulted for Gaza in the establishment of a festival in honour of him ('Gaza' in Ameling et al. 2014, Vol. III: 418). The Nessana archive of Byzantine Palestine mentions Gaza frequently and places the city at the heart of the international trade system of Antiquity ('Gaza' in Ameling et al. 2014, Vol. III: 419).

7,000-year-old archaeological mounds and the birth of urban life in Palestine: Internationally exchanged goods and ancient cities from the Chalcolithic Age to Antiquity

Up until today research on urbanism in Palestine has centred on the Bronze Age (*c*.3300–*c*.1200 BC) or has begun with existing cities in Palestine and seeks to trace their early history to the Bronze Age. This work argues that the archaeological evidence points to an earlier urbanism in Palestine that began with the first metal production revolution of the *Chalcolithic Age* 7,000 years ago. The *Chalcolithic or Copper Age* was an archaeological period in the ancient Near East, beginning 7,000 years ago in the fifth millennium BCE and lasting for a millennium and a half. Technologically the Chalcolithic Age was a revolutionary period in Palestine. This age witnessed major formative socio-economic changes in the country and the emergence of early urban towns in Palestine. The beginnings of the metallic revolution stimulated craft production in towns using materials such as flint, ivory, ceramics and basalt. New burial practices, elaborate iconography and the establishment of cultic sanctuaries occurred during this period. Crucially the extensive trade regional networks transformed early urbanism and the first Palestinian towns. The period characterized was by the increasing use of smelted copper and the emergence of early trade systems Palestine and the wider the ancient Near East. These long-distance trade systems centred on the production and exchange of copper and obsidian (natural glass; see Chapter 2), trade systems which were serviced by, and estimated the early rise of towns in Palestine as attested by the excavations of 7,000 year-old archaeological mounds (*tells*) in the country.

In fact long-distance obsidian trade through Palestine preceded the copper trade system of the Chalcolithic Age and goes back to the Neolithic Age. Archaeological excavations show the most commonly found items were obsidian items (including obsidian blades) at Neolithic sites in Palestine, and that the main source of obsidian during the Neolithic Age in Palestine was located in central Anatolia (Forbes 1964: 124; Meyers 1997: 124; Rast 1992: 58). The Chalcolithic Age metallic revolution was followed by a second metal production revolution during the Bronze Age and this was another revolutionary period characterized primarily by the use of more sophisticated bronze tools and the accelerated development of complex urban societies and major cities in the Near East, as well as the invention and adoption of writing in the region (Masalha 2018, 2022). Practical necessities and the requirements of regional trade, money and accounting were key drivers behind the invention of the early Sumerian writing in ancient Iraq (Mesopotamia) during the Bronze Age and the spread of writing throughout the urban centres of the ancient Middle East, Palestine included (Masalha 2022).

There are very few sites in the world with continuous human settlements from the Chalcolithic Age until the modern period. Archaeological excavations at *Tell al-Safi* – located on the southern banks of Wadi 'Ajjur, 35 km northwest of the Palestinian city of al-Khalil (Hebron) – since 1996 show that the site (a tell or archaeological mound) was continuously inhabited since the fifth millennium BCE. The site of a Palestinian village depopulated by Israel in 1948, Tell al-Safi was settled 7,000 years ago and remained 'virtually continuously inhabited from the Chalcolithic Age until the modern periods' (Negev and Gibson 2005: 445).

From the Bronze Age onwards the archaeological evidence is supplemented by documentary evidence. During the late Bronze Age the city-state of Gath developed strong relations with the Egyptian state, then the superpower of the Near East and correspondence of local leaders in Palestine with Egypt was common. From the correspondence of the *Tell al-Amarna* letters of Egypt in 1250–1335 BCE the king of Gath was called Suwardata (or *Shuwardata*); Suwardata was the author of eight al-Amarna letters to the Egyptian pharaoh. In one letter Suwardata complained about the conduct of another ruler of a Palestinian city-state named Lebaya (or Abdi

Heba), who ruled the city of Sichem (*Tell Balata*), near modern Nablus, a Bronze Age city-state which at the time of al-Amarna letters dominated central Palestine, the city of Jerusalem included. One of the Amarna letters was from Abdi-Ḫeba himself to the Egyptian Pharaoh Amenhotep III seeking a military training for his son in Egypt (Moran 1992; 324; Redford 1992: 270). In one letter addressed to the Pharaoh, Suwardata writes seeking military support from Egypt and saying, perhaps with some deliberate exaggeration, that '30 cities' (and city-states) were waging war against his own city-state:

> May the king, my lord, be informed that 30 cities have waged war against me. I am alone! The war against me is severe. The king, my lord, has cast me from his hand. May the king, my lord, send archers.

The massive archaeological evidence for the numerous city-states in Bronze Age and Iron Age Palestine lies in the numerous archaeological mounds excavated. *Tell* is the commonly used Arabic term by archaeologists for ancient man-made mounds in Palestine and for mounded accretion due to long-term human settlement since the Chalcolithic Age in Palestine some 7,000 years ago. Originally a market town in the Chalcolithic Age, Tell al-Safi evolved into a major ancient city-state in Bronze Age Palestine ruled by a king; in the early Bronze Age the size of the inhabited area of the city was estimated at twenty-four hectares, growing to thirty-four hectares by the late Bronze Age. This Palestinian city, presumed to be the ancient Philistine city-state of Gath – one of the famous *pentapolis* (five cities) of ancient Philistia (Palestine) located in north-eastern Philistia – continued to flourish through the Iron Age and archaeological finds of manufactured items and vessels on the site from this period included a cylinder seal, showing circular lamellae typical of hippopotamus ivory found inside a holemouth jar in a well-stratified EB III (*c.* 2700/2600–2350 BCE) context. The motif was that of a crouching male lion (Maeir et al. 2011: 12–31; Ross et al. 2020: 74–89; Wimmer and Maeir 2007: 37–48). A large city in the Iron Age, Gath was 'enclosed on three sides by a large man-made' defensive moat (Wigoder 2005: 348–9).

Other archaeological finds dated to both the Neolithic Age and Chalcolithic Age in Palestine yielded astonishing discoveries about the earliest civilizations in the country. These finds show that the city of Jericho, whose beginnings are in the Neolithic Age, is one of the oldest cities in the world. During the Chalcolithic Age the town of Jericho (excavated at *Tell Jericho* or *Tell al-Sultan* or *Tell Jericho*), recognized today as unique UNSECO Heritage Site in Palestine, developed a complex urban society and became a major regional trading town in Palestine and the town was the oldest fortified city in the world.[6] The archaeological finds from Copper Age from either sites in Palestine show that Jericho was not an isolated urban locality in Chalcolithic Palestine, but was closely related to the development of complex urban society during the Chalcolithic Age.

These astonishing Chalcolithic Age archaeological finds, including the earliest known textile fibre and cotton production and exchange in the Near East, were uncovered by archaeologists in Palestine, and dated to the early and middle

Chalcolithic Age, some 7,000 year ago. They were uncovered at the archaeological mound in the central Jordan valley of Palestine when the initiation excavations were carried out on the sites such as *Tell al-Sufouh*. In recent decades Israeli archaeologists have been excavating this site and have given the site a biblical sounding name: *Tel Tsaf*. Other important indigenous Palestinian archaeological mounds such as *Tell al-Duweir* – which was also inhabited from the Chalcolithic Age and developed into a city in the early Bronze Age (3300–3000 BCE) – were retrospectively 'Hebrewfied to the biblically-sounding *Tel Lachish*.[7] Located to the south of the city of Beisan in the central Jordan valley of Palestine, and dated to *c*.5200–4700 BCE (Liu et al. 2022), *Tell al-Sufouh* has been excavated since the 1940s. Important finds from the Chalcolithic Age were unearthed at the site, including 7,200-year-old pottery vessels and a rich assemblage of imported exotic manufactured artefacts of beads and obsidian imported via the regional Chalcolithic Age trade system from Syria and central Anatolia. The excavations on the site revealed the evolution of a complex urban society in Palestine during the middle Chalcolithic Age with the construction of new techniques and exchange, and significant technological advancements related to urban culture with regional trade connections and trade exchange (Rosenberg 2024). Crucially the archaeological finds from *Tell al-Sufouh*, which revealed grain silos, pottery and extensive evidence of the domestication of olive trees as well as cotton fibre, point to the 'beginning' of two of the most important Palestinian 'historic industries': the cotton industry and olive oil industry 7,000 years ago. An important part of the industrial heritage of the country, olive oil production, in particular, is among the oldest and most important ancient trading industries in Palestine and tools for olive oil production and olive kernels, which were excavated in the Carmel mountains area, were dated back to the seventh millennium BCE.[8]

Olive Presses in Palestine (2009), by Palestinian archaeologist and historian Khaled Nashif, was an important contribution to the growing archaeological scholarship on the ancient olive industry of the country by indigenous Palestinian scholars.

The urban revolution in Palestine, which began with the Chalcolithic Age and metallic revolution and regional copper, and was the accelerated during the second metallic revolution of Bronze Age, can be seen from the proliferation of archaeological mounds and sites of ancient cities in Palestine and from the archaeological excavations of a large number of ancient mounds (known in Palestine by their Arabic names as *tells*) across the country. During this period a number of urban centres and city-states in the country – city-states and ancient polities which dominated their regional trade routes and large parts of the Palestinian countryside – began to emerge, especially in the middle Bronze Age. Archaeological excavations of Palestinian urban sites from the early and middle Bronze Age have progressed immensely since the 1930s during the British Mandatory period and these excavations have yielded a great deal of archaeological treasures, artefacts and material history. In 1932 tombs belonging to the early Bronze Age were uncovered on the *Tell Megiddo*. Other sites in Beisan and Jericho were excavated in the 1930s also reached early Bronze Age deposits and uncovered tombs belonging to the early Bronze Age (De Vaux 1966; 2008: 208–37). By excavating several large well-stratified archaeological mounds, and by the application of scientific and comparative methods to better classified material, particularly pottery, obsidian glass objects and a variety of household vessels, the picture that has emerged gives us an insight into a complex urban society trading widely and interacting commercially, culturally and architecturally with a wide range of civilizations from the Minoan civilization in Crete to the ancient civilizations of Egypt and Iraq.

Archaeological excavations of these *tells* have accelerated since the 1930s and have yielded important findings especially about the middle Bronze Age, including estimate the populations of some of the large cities of the middle Bronze age at around 5,000 inhabitants, earning their living from both agriculture and international trade in merchandise with the countries of the Levant as well as with what is now known as modern Turkey and Armenia. The average size of each of these Bronze Age cities was about 100–400 *dunums* (25–100 *acres*).

Necessity is the mother of all inventions and the requirements of regional trade, money and payments were key factors behind the invention of the proto-Canaanite alphabet in the growing urban centres and city-states of Bronze Age Palestine (Masalha 2022). The rise of these city-states of Bronze Age Palestine was accompanied with the expansion of the Palestine's international trade and the development of the Semitic (proto-Canaanite) alphabet, which was essential for trade, money and accounting, and the development of complex stratified society, with elite groups of scribes serving organized religion, temples, palaces and ruling elites. Bronze Age temples themselves were often involved in regional trade. In addition to the construction of large temples and palaces for ruling elites, the growing city-states and cities saw the constructions of large public buildings whose construction was by regional styles of architecture and regional trade; some of the Bronze Age palaces had large wine cellars, temples, scribal schools, watchtowers and formidable fortification systems. The overall population of Palestine during the middle Bronze Age was estimated at 150,000; this population continued to grow during Antiquity and was estimated at about 1,000,000 in late Antiquity (late Roman and Byzantine periods) (Broshi and Gophna 1985: 73–90).

Furthermore, Palestine (a relatively small country in size) has a large number of archaeological *tells*, mounds created by the accumulation of remains of ancient urban centres and city-states, many of them dated to the Bronze Age. Extensively excavated in modern times, especially in the last 150 years, many of these ancient urban centres that emerged in early and middle Bronze Age Palestine were in cities and city-states and represented by well-known modern archaeological sites and archaeological *tells* such as Gezer (*Tell a-Jazzar*), *Tell Kabri* (upper western Galilee), Jericho, *Tell al-Ajjul, Tell al-Sakan* (in the southern vicinity of Gaza city), *Tell Yubna* (Byzantine period), *Tell al-Tell, Tell Dothan, Tell Taannek, Tell Umm al-'Amr* (the archaeological site of Saint Hilarion Monastery in the Gaza Strip) and *Tell al-Mutasallim (Tell Megiddo)* – the latter being the archaeological site of the powerful city-state of Megiddo (*Tell al-Mutasallim*) which emerged during the early and middle Bronze Age (De Vaux 1966; 2008: 208–37; Taha 2017: 6–11) – whose early urban culture and 'Great Temple' of the early Bronze Age (3500–2200 BC) had a marked impact on the development of urban culture of the Levant (Wiener 2016).

Another major early urban site in ancient Palestine is the archaeological site at *Tell Taannek*, a mound approximately 14 acres (60 dunum) in size. The site is located eight kilometres south of *Tell al-Mutasallim* (Megiddo). The modern Palestinian village *Taannek*, located on the south-eastern slope of *Tell Taannek*, still bears the ancient name Taannach. In ancient times the city of *Tell Taannek* occupied a strategic location on the border between the mountainous area and the plains on the main route between the cities of Jenin and Haifa. The city was mentioned around 1350 BCE in the Egyptian Amarna letters. Later Taannek was mentioned as a town in the fourth century CE by Eusebius of Caesarea Maritima. Another city-state Gezer (*Tell al-Jezari*) is an archaeological site roughly midway between Jerusalem and Jaffa, whose early settlement dates to the Chalcolithic Age at the end of the fourth millennium BCE. It became a major fortified Canaanite city-state during the Bronze Age in the first half of the second millennium BCE. The Amarna letters mention the kings of Gezer swearing loyalty to the rulers of ancient Egypt, then the superpower of the ancient Near East.

Often these highly fortified early Palestinian city-states and kingdoms rose along ancient regional trade routes and became renowned for their strategic location. For instance, the importance of the city-state of 'Gezer' (the site of *Tell al-Jazar*, *Tell Gezer*) – the site of the Palestinian village of Abu Shosha, destroyed by Israel in 1948 – in Bronze Age Palestine was due in part to the strategic position it held and its position at the crossroads of the ancient Palestinian coastal trade routes linking Syria, Anatolia, Egypt and Iraq (Mesopotamia) as well as the trade route linking the international coastal highway to Jerusalem and Jericho.

The 4,000-year-old wine industry of the city-state of Kabri (Galilee)

Another major archaeological *tell* was the site of the middle Bronze Age Palestinian city-state at Tell Kabri (Arabic: *Tell al-Qahwa*, literally 'mound of coffee') in upper western Palestine. *Tell Kabri* was excavated in 2013-19. The excavated site, carried out by a joint Israeli-American team of archaeologists, uncovered a large Bronze Age city, whose residents (estimated at 5,000) earned their living through agriculture and international commerce. The relatively large city (by the standards of the Bronze Age) was built around the year 2500 BCE and its territory ranged over seventy-nine acres (360 *dunums*), which were surrounded by dirt embankments seven metres high and thirty-five metres thick, on which were built guard towers. At its height of its power in the middle Bronze Age this city-state controlled much of the surrounding region and the northern-southern international copper and obsidian trade through Palestine, and the remains of pieces of merchandise, including obsidian, were uncovered whose origins lay modern Turkey, Egypt and Crete. This inland city-state was connected to a trading seaport on the Mediterranean coast, apparently at Akhziv. The excavations uncovered one of the largest middle Bronze Age (1750–1550 BCE) Canaanite palaces – a two-story palace which was decorated with colourful frescoes and ornaments in Minoan style that is found in the Bronze Age city of Knossos in Crete. The only site (and palace) to be uncovered in Bronze Age Palestine with Minoan style of architectural influences, this was the result of thriving maritime trade conducted by the rulers of the city-state with the Minoan civilization of Crete in the Bronze Age (Cline et al. 2023; Wiener 2013).

The recent Tell Kabri archaeological excavations uncovered not only a large Palestinian city by the standard of the Bronze Age, with extensive international trade links, but also the oldest and largest known palatial wine storage complex in the ancient Near East at Kabri's palace, a 3,700-year-old storeroom held 2,000 litres of strong, sweet wine (Burrows 2013; Cline et al. 2023). The Archaeological Museum at Heraklion, in Crete – which I visited in April 2024 – focuses on the Bronze Age Minoan civilization of the island and the excavations at the then capital city of Knossos, shows extensive Minoan trade links with the cites of the Levant, including Minoan import of merchandise and ivory from Palestine and Syria. Also the export-oriented wine industry of Kabri was remarkable:

> There was a time when the Canaanites made the best wines in the world. Their wines were consumed in great quantities and exported all over the Near East. They were particularly favored by the pharaohs of Egypt. One of the most exciting archaeological finds in recent years was a Canaanite palace at Tel Kabri, which housed the largest Canaanite wine cellar yet discovered. Estimates say this site dates back to 3,800 years ago.
>
> (Montefiore 2025)

This city-state of Kabri was abandoned around the year 1600 BCE for unknown reasons.

The polyculture of Bronze Age Palestine, especially the country's agricultural industries, which centred on grape (and wine), olive (and olive oil) and wheat was a major source of prosperity in the country and a major factor in the rise of its city-states; as we shall see in Chapter 6, the economy of Byzantine Palestine was also dominated by the local wine and olive oil industries. As we shall see in Chapter 15, the scale of the olive oil agro-industry in Palestine created *olive oil specialist markets* in several cities in Palestine under Islam and the olive oil industry became a major source for state taxation and revenues in Ottoman Palestine. Also, ancient Egypt and Mesopotamia were hugely indebted to their famous rivers (the Nile, the Euphrates and Tigris) for the fertility of soil that allowed them to build and feed large *imperial cities* and great empires on the basis of large-scale agriculture and great agricultural wealth. But in Palestine, at the centre of highly profitable export industries, were the wine-making and olive oil; olive oil was central to the soap-making industries of Islamic Palestine in the Middle Ages and the modern period. Interestingly grapes, olives and wheat (bread), which were a big part of the staples of Palestine for millennia and were a major source of prosperity in the country, became associated with the sacred and spiritualism in Christianity (*wine* and *bread*) and in Islam (*olive* and *bread*). Highlighting the centrality of bread in Palestinian diet and its sanctity in the country's shared ancient religious traditions, in his encyclopaedic work *Bread in Palestine*, Palestinian scholar Shukri 'Arraf

> takes us on a rich journey in the history of bread in the Palestinian land, from the dawn of history to modern times, by shedding light on the relationship of man and woman and their efforts with the land and the natural landscape in Palestine, in the process of bread production, planting, harvesting and storing, until the production of the loaf of bread, as a basic material in the life of the people of this land.
>
> ('Arraf 2024)

Many Middle Eastern religious temples in Antiquity became economic power houses and economic and manufacturing hubs attracting pilgrims, merchants, craftsmen and local industrialists leading to the influx of people causing the growth of local markets and the economic and urban development of surrounding areas. This was a global phenomenon that can be seen in the case of ancient temples in Egypt, India, Ethiopia and elsewhere. As we shall see in Chapter 2, temples in the ancient Middle East were heavily involved with the merchant communities of the cities and in the lucrative long-distance trade from the Bronze Age onwards. Although *organized religion* (with priesthood, temples and formal rituals) in ancient Palestine had its head in the clouds, the centrality of essential produce such as wheat (bread), wine (grape) and olive oil – a 7,000-year-old important produce in Palestine used in sacred ceremonies to anoint kings in ancient Palestine – shows that organized religion, which was heavily involved in lucrative long-distance trade, marched on its stomach. Moreover, in Arabic the ancient city of Jerusalem, the religious capital of Palestine, is called *Al-Quds*, literally the *Sacred*. Religion and power often went hand-in-hand with the construction of the *sacred* such as the creation of famous *sacred cities* such as ancient Jerusalem and Rome. However despite the synonymous association of Palestine with the *Holy Land* (Terra Sancta), the comparatively smaller scale agriculture in ancient Palestine – compared with ancient Italy, Egypt and Mesopotamia – could not support the creation of *mega imperial* and *sacred cities* such as Rome, or the creation of *mega imperial cities* such as those of Egypt and Mesopotamia. Consequently, the centrality of trade and international trade routes in a transit country such as Palestine – as well as the importance of the maritime port cities of Palestine – became central to the rise and growth of famous cities in Bronze Age and Iron Age Palestine and the subsequent rise of two leading *sacred cities* in Palestine: Jerusalem (Al-Quds) and al-Khalil (Hebron), two famous *cities of pilgrimage* and trade since Antiquity.

Agriculture was an important part of the economy of Palestine since the Neolithic Age and this also became evident in the agricultural calendars of Palestine during the Bronze Age. Ancient calendars were created by people who used various methods of timekeeping and to serve cultural, agricultural and day-to-day practical purposes. The early historically attested calendars in the ancient Middle East were created by the Sumerians in the Bronze Age with the development of early writing; the early Sumerian writing and calendar, which was used in Palestine, divided the year into twelve lunar months, but with people living with a degree of uncertainty about the beginning of the month. During the Bronze Age many inhabitants of the villages and towns of Palestine earned their living through agriculture – and this can be seen in *the agricultural calendar* of the city-state of Gezer[9] – international commerce began to emerge as a key source of income during the Bronze Age. However, the growth of regional trade, especially in copper and other metals, accelerated urbanization processes in the country during the middle Bronze Age. Also, a large number of calendars emerged in the ancient Near East during the Iron Age and in Antiquity reflecting the evolving political, economic and urban development in the region; there was a famous local 'Calendar of Gaza and Ascalon' during the late Ptolemaic and early Roman period reflecting a degree of local and fiscal autonomy and the powerful economic and commercial centrality of these two twin Palestinian cities in Antiquity (Al-'Arif 1943; Stern 2012: 289).

Also, unlike the enormous scale of agriculture in Mesopotamia and Egypt, the agricultural scale of Palestine, and agriculture for local consumption on its own, could not have supported the creation of powerful Bronze Age city-states, which maintained relatively strong armies, and controlled international trade routes through powerful city-states such as those of Gezer and Megiddo. Other sources of income needed for these early powerful city-states, such as involvement in international trade systems and regional trade routes, were created to generate significant revenues and maintain powerful local armies. Another well-known example from the modern era in Palestine of the centrality of the revenues gained from foreign trade is the case of powerful Palestinian leader Dhaher al-'Umar (1689–1775 CE) and his monopoly on the export of raw cotton to European markets as a way of financing a local powerful army in the eighteenth century, an army which was capable of defeating the larger Ottoman army and created a Galilee-based Palestinian statehood.

In fact, the impact of international trade on both ancient and modern Palestine as a whole was radical and transformative. Take the story of the cotton industry in Palestine. The English word 'cotton' has Arabic origins derived from the medieval Arabic word *qutn* or *qutun*. The cotton industry played an important role in the history, economy and the textile and linen industries of Palestine since the Middle Ages. The Old City of Jerusalem boasts a well-known *Cotton Market* (*Souq al-Qattatin* – along with the gate known as *Bab al-Qattanin*, Cotton Gate) – which dates back to the Mamluk period, established in 1336–37. Generally the Mamluk period was a period of urban building boom programme and commercial boom in Jerusalem, as evidenced by the ninety remaining structures from this great period of trade, urbanization and magnificent Islamic architecture in the city. These urban buildings included merchant caravanserais, *madrasas* and colleges, hospitals, libraries, charitable foundations, public baths and public drinking fountains (*sabils*), all of which became central to advanced urban life in Palestine under Islam.

However, it was the international trade in raw cotton export to Europe in the eighteenth century that played a key transformative role on the economy and urban environment in Palestine. In the mid-eighteenth century, Palestinian leader Dhaher al-'Umar shifted the centre of power in Galilee from the hinterland of the ancient city of Safad – which had functioned as the capital of the Galilee and northern Palestine for several centuries under the Mamluks (Drory 2004: 163–90) – to the Mediterranean seaport city of Acre and with its focus on exporting Palestinian raw cotton to Europe (see Chapter 14), and revenues were reinvested in Acre, Tiberias, Nazareth and other urban and rural localities in Galilee. As a result, Acre itself was radically transformed from a backwater town into one of the biggest, wealthiest and most developed cities in Palestine and the Levant region. As we shall see in Chapter 14, this Palestinian raw cotton export also played a part in the modern industrial and textile revolutions in Britain. Acre also attracted many Greek and Italian merchants who settled in the city.

In the process of translation from the Bronze Age to the Iron Age, the growth of towns and cities in Palestine and the emergence of new city-states accelerated along the country's major international trade routes, the most important of which during this period was the route running from Lower Egypt and along the Palestinian Mediterranean coast. During this age the powerful city-states of Philistia, with their iron industries, expanded demographically and developed technologically and financially - and developed the first monetary system in Palestine - and became among the most important trading cities of the ancient world.

During the Iron Age, the five city-states of the ancient Philistines (ancient Palestinians) became economically and commercially powerful and geo-politically distinct polities. They became collectively known as the *Philistine Pentapolis* (from Greek *πεντα penta*, 'five' and *πόλις polis*, 'city'). Described retrospectively in Antiquity as the *Philistine Pentapolis,* these five Palestinian city-states were strategically and commercially located along the highways of international trade routes. They also developed collectively as a political institutional and trading confederation of five city-states of the ancient Philistines. Four of these city-states were maritime city-states, with international trading connections: Gaza, Ascalon, Isdud (Ashdod) and Ekron. The fifth city-state was an inland state. Together the *Philistine Pentapolis* were among the most materially developed polities of the ancient world. During this period, the international south-Arabian/Palestine/Mediterranean trade in spices, aromatics and cosmetics ensured that a hybrid *Palestinian-Arabian* currency of the *Philistine Pentapolis* - city-states - flourishes in the sixth-fifth centuries BCE. These Palestinian city-states and kingdoms of the coastal region became Hellenized during the Ptolemaic period which began with the invasion of Egypt and later Palestine by Alexander the Great who invaded Gaza in 332 BC and looted its frankincense warehouses (see below).

Indeed, the strategic location of these rich trading cities of coastal Palestine and the lucrative regional and long-distance trade of Palestine also attracted the attention and ambitions of military conquers imperial generals: from the 'Napoleon of ancient Egypt', Thutmose III, who besieged and destroyed the powerful Canaanite city-state of Megiddo in the early middle of the Bronze Age, to Alexander the Great who besieged Gaza in 332 BCE and looted its frankincense warehouses, to Napoleon whose unsuccessful siege of Acre in 1799 became one of the turning points of his failed invasion of Egypt and Palestine.

Indeed, it was the desire to control the pivotal and highly lucrative Palestinian-Syrian trade routes of the middle Bronze Age that drove Thutmose III's Palestine campaign; also it was this famed wealth and global cotton trade of Acre that attracted the attention of Napoleon (and a failed siege) and attempts to occupy this port city in 1799, in the same way the Trans-Arabian frankincense trade of Gaza attracted the attention of another famous military conquer, Alexander the Great, who took the port city of Gaza in 332 BCE, after a long siege, a city which was at the centre of Trans-

Arabian incense trade, and looted its frankincense and myrrh houses (Conan 2007: 25; Retso 2003). When Alexander the Great later conquered Gaza, he sent great quantities of frankincense and myrrh to his tutor in Macedonia and instructed him to use it lavishly. Gaza was a major Mediterranean port for the Arabian trade in frankincense and myrrh (Pearlstine 2022: 22). Knowing the high value of their products, traders in frankincense and myrrh often guarded their secrets with legends about this highly profitable trade in elite products.

Historic continuities: Arts and crafts, ancient textile cities and modern Palestinian embroidery

The ancient Palestine textile industry shows how the traditional industries of Palestine were dominated by the development of skilled craft industries. The earliest known cotton production and distribution in the Near East was uncovered by archaeologists in Palestine, and dated to the Chalcolithic Age, some 7,000 year ago. For thousands of years the production, application and exchange of fibre technology (cordage and textiles) have played an important role in Palestine and this process has deep roots in prehistory. Micro-botanical analysis on soils from anthropogenic sediments in activity areas at the archaeological mound of *Tell al-Sufouh* – renamed by Israeli archaeologists as *Tel Tsaf* – located to the south of Beisan in the Jordan valley of Palestine, dated to *c*.5200–4700 BCE recovered micro fibre remains and included at least two types of the best fibres in Palestine and the earliest evidence of cotton in the Near East; some of these ancient Palestinian cotton fibres were dyed in various colours. Some of these fibres also represent the remnants of ancient clothing, fabric containers, cordage and other belongings (Liu et al. 2022). Other archaeological excavations at another Chalcolithic Age mound in Palestine, Tell al-Safi, northwest of the city of al-Khalil (Hebron), show that this site of a major Palestinian city from the early Bronze Age through the Iron Age was continuously inhabited for 7,000 years since the fifth millennium BCE (Negev and Gibson 2005: 445).

As we shall see in Chapter 5, in Antiquity the Palestinian city of Beisan (Schythopolis) produced the finest and most expensive linen fabrics in the Roman world, an export-oriented industry that employed a large number of women. In modern times Palestinian women, using linen, silk and traditional cultural practices known as *tatreez* (embroidery), decorated their *thobe* (or dress) with symbols of Palestinian history, memory, cities and communities telling the story of the maker's urban life and her deep connection to the land of Palestine through colourfully stitched motifs. As we shall see in Chapter 5, a series of closely related textile industries developed in the cities of Palestine and Syria in Antiquity. Also, the expertise and the processes of the production of Tyrian purple dye, as a *royal purple fabric*, were then passed over from neighbouring Tyre to cities in Palestine. Purple is a secondary colour created by mixing red and blue. During the Roman and Byzantine periods, this purple (royal) dye was combined with Chinese silk and linen cloth industries of the Palestinian cities of Gaza, Caesarea Maritima (*Caesarea Palaestina*), Lydda Neapolis

(Nablus) and Scythopolis (Beisan) and both Palestine and Syria became closely associated with export-oriented extensive silk industries in Antiquity. As shall see in Chapter 8, the export-oriented textile, silk and linen industries of Palestine continued to flourish throughout the Middle Ages and into the modern period. The city of al-Ramla hosted Egyptian *textile* merchants throughout early Islam; and the Palestinian cotton-producing cities of Lydda, Ramla and Acre hosted Venetian communities of cotton merchants during the late Mamluk period (Ashtor 2014: 253–61) and Italian and French cotton merchants resided in Acre the late eighteenth and early nineteenth centuries.

The copper revolution and the birth of urbanism: The regional copper trade and city-states in Bronze Age Palestine

Archaeological research has shown that the early Bronze Age Palestine (3200–2000 BCE) experienced a dramatic growth in urban civilization, especially at the outset of this period, But the same research has also uncovered a period of decline and regression in urbanism as a result of outside invasions and internal political instability towards the end of this early Bronze Age at around 2000 BCE (Richard 1987: 22–43).

But in fact, urbanism in Palestine has its earliest roots in the late Chalcolithic Age (*c*.4500–3600 BCE) with the emergence of regional trade. The term Chalcolithic Age is derived from the term copper. Copper mining and smelting in the ancient Near East and the transit copper trade in Palestine and through Palestine gave birth to the cities of ancient Palestine at the end of the Chalcolithic period and early Bronze Age, although the construction of the early city-state (and small kingdoms) began in the Near East about 6,000 years ago, in the Chalcolithic Age.

Necessity is the mother of all technological inventions and social innovations and the two types of early cities in the Near East (Palestine included) during the late Chalcolithic Age and early Bronze Age: the *market town* and the *city-state* (the latter often kingdoms with social hierarchy, ruling elites, organized religion, temples, scribal schools, and forces of law and order). These early cities and civilizations of the Near East were born out of necessity rather than high-minded idealism. Civilizations, long-distance trade and the construction of early cities in the ancient Near East and Palestine often went hand-in-hand. Although early urbanism in the Near East had multiple beginnings and was driven by multiple factors, long-distance trade was often at the heart of the construction of early market towns, cities and *entrepôt* in Palestine, where local produce and merchandise can be imported from distance regions, guarded and stored and traded locally or exported again to other regions beyond Palestine.

While indigenous Palestinian collective memory and writing often portrayed historic Palestine as an agricultural country inhabited by *unchanging Palestinian peasantry*, using *unchanging* ancient agricultural tools, in fact important recent studies by indigenous Palestinian scholars who engage a wide range of archaeological, textual and historical sources in multiple languages have highlighted important aspects of the rich and varied heritage of Palestine. For instance, *Atlas of Palestinian Rural*

Heritage (2015) discusses the remarkable evolution of a variety of crafts, agricultural tools, industries and trade in pre-modern culture of rural Palestine (Al-Hroub 2015). Furthermore, the early city-states (small kingdoms) and civilizations in Palestine were dominated by the rise of the regional copper trade and copper industries. The growth of the great ancient cities of Palestine was spurred by regional trade and the industrial production of metals such as copper and the industrial blending of metals such as copper and tin, to create bronze, and industries of Bronze Age metal production became central to urban expansion. Although copper was mined in significant quantities in the Palestinian Naqab (Negev) since the Chalcolithic Age, tin, copper alloys, ore and obsidian were imported to Palestine from distant regions in central and southern Anatolia and Armenia (Rosen 2019).

As we shall see in Chapter 2, copper mining in the southern region of Palestine, the Naqab (Negev), became a major industry in ancient times. Inevitably the pursuit of profitable regional trade and the construction of early cities in the Near East (Palestine included) also meant the emergence of social stratification and social hierarchies, with different social groups and classes engaged in specific types of economic activity and social life. Indeed, two key features of early urbanism in Palestine are the rise of social stratification and powerful social elites that dominated these cities. While in Neolithic Palestine, the agricultural revolution created early *village settlements* 10,000–12,000 years ago, the Chalcolithic Age in Palestine (7,000 years ago) was closely connected with the metal production revolution, regional trade and the emergence of early urban centres – urban centres that were characterized by social, economic and political stratifications and the rise of powerful urban social elites that controlled and regulated the new copper industry and the regional trade in metal goods.

This early urbanization began in the northern Naqab of southern Palestine and was closely linked to the copper trade and copper production on sites in southern Palestine dating back to the late Chalcolithic Age when copper production was carried out near large corporate buildings within village settlements found primarily in the Palestinian northern Naqab. The early Bronze Age metallic revolution and copper manufacturing were also linked to the emergence of the first chiefdom organizations in this part of Palestine and this metal production and trade seems to have been controlled by social elites (Levy et al. 2002; Ornit and Sebbane 1989: 139–62). In addition to copper production in the south of Palestine (the Naqab) evidence for cotton and olive tree domestication and cultivation were also uncovered on archaeological sites near the town of Beisan in the Jordan valley of Palestine, all dated to the sixth and early fifth millennia of the Chalcolithic Age.

Trade and increasing urbanization processes in Palestine also led to the creation of the early *city-states* in the country – city-states whose social elites controlled the regional copper trade and other trade routes through Palestine. This process can be seen much in evidence in the early Bronze Age at around 3200 BCE, an age associated with the dramatic rise of great urban centres in Palestine – as well as highly stratified urban social spaces. In comparison the agricultural villages of the Neolithic Age and the somewhat smaller market towns of the Chalcolithic Age localities (4000–3200 BCE) were considerably more egalitarian localities in the country.

Ancient city-states in Bronze Age and Iron Age Palestine

Ancient city-states governed by kings and maintaining local armies were the most common type of *cities* in the 'civilization' of Bronze Age and Iron Age Palestine. Although the overarching term 'civilization', in both English and Arabic, is also derived from the term 'city' (in Arabic: *madaniyya* and *nadina*), civilizations, like all ancient city-states and all types of modern states, were not born out of ideas and principles, but depended on their ability to create and maintain law and order by organizing and paying for armed forces. Moreover, as we shall see below, civilizations and the ancient city-states marched on their stomach, and there was more to the civilizations of ancient Palestine and Phoenicia than what English historian Edward Gibbon was prepared to credit them (Gibbon 1875, Vol. 1: 27–8). To begin with the merchants of the Phoenician city-states – whose inhabitants were a Semitic-speaking people closely related to the coastal people and inhabitants of port cities of ancient Palestine – were the most celebrated traders and maritime sailors and skippers of Antiquity and the first to create navies and a maritime trading empire around the Mediterranean.

Neither the 'Palestinians' of the Bronze Age nor the 'Phoenicians' of the late Bronze Age and Iron Age called themselves 'Canaanites' or 'Phoenicians' respectively – these two terms were coined subsequently by others during classical Antiquity – the first by biblical authors (Masalha 2018) and the recorded by Greek authors of classical Antiquity; these Greek authors also coined the toponyms Mesopotamia and Phoenicia and popularized the names Palestine, Egypt and Persia. The ancient independent city-states of what the Greek authors called the 'Phoenicians' were effectively and directly successors to the Bronze Age ancient city-states of Palestine and these Phoenician city-states continued the cultural and religious traditions of Bronze Age 'Palestinians' and famously created a chain of highly developed independent coastal city-states including Byblos, Tyre, Sidon, Sarepta, Tripoli, and Berytus (Beirut), all located today in modern Lebanon. The influence of these city-states (of southern Lebanon) extended to northern Palestine and to the cities and towns of Acre; *Al-Zeib*; Kabri (*Tell Kabri*) and Dor (Tantur), located to the south of modern-day Haifa. Aided by a ship-construction industry and timbers from the famous Lebanese cedar wood; because of their famous ancient global trade in purple dye these coastal city-states became known to the ancient Greeks as the 'Phoenicians' or the 'people of purple'.[10] Evidently, however, in Antiquity the purple dye industry itself was shared by the ancient coastal cities of ancient Phoenicia and Palestine.

The purple dye became an iconic colour and elite fashion in the Levant in Antiquity. Purple dyed textiles had a striking colour and natural beauty and were resistant to fading. The colour became a symbol of social status and economic wealth in Antiquity, first in the Levant and gradually throughout the Mediterranean region. Developed initially by the independent city-states of Tyre, Byblos and Sidon – city-states that had inherited and developed further many of the cultural traditions and commercial practices of the earlier Bronze Age independent city-states of Palestine. The colour purple became closely associated with the Phoenician maritime and commercial empire across the Mediterranean of classical Antiquity, an empire that lasted for a millennium. The focus of the city-states of Tyre and Sidon was on international commerce, which they expanded primarily by means of sea routes. The country's famed cedars were ideal for shipbuilding. These city-states also adapted existing technology to colour cloths: blue with indigo, whereas red came from the kermes, a parasitic insect that lives in oak trees. Indigo dying had been used in the ancient Middle East as far back as 3000 BCE. During the Middle Ages under Islam Egypt, Palestine became the main source of indigo dying in the region.

The Phoenician city-states of the Mediterranean and their neighbouring Palestinian coastal cities and city-states were among the most influential and inventive peoples of ancient times. They become merchants and explorers and spreaders of the *pro-Canaanite alphabet* and the facilitators of a network cultural exchanges among major cradles of civilizations. Phoenician sea travellers and merchants used the Mediterranean superhighway, to trade and settled the southern, northern and western Mediterranean and beyond. As we shall see below, both Syrian and Palestinian merchants in Antiquity followed in the footsteps of these merchants of the Phoenician city-states in Antiquity. The spread of the Proto-Canaanite alphabet (proto-Sinaitic script, see Chapter 3) and the *Tyrian purple dye*, with its expansive high-chrome pigments, was then spread to, and used by the ruling elites of the Greek and Roman Empires and became known to the Romans and Byzantines as royal dye and royal colour and was worn exclusively by Roman and Byzantine emperors and their senior magistrates and officials. Being expensive to produce, Murex purple dye and purple fabric became closely associated with wealth and power.

Powerful symbols and representations of urban Palestine in Classical and Late Antiquity: The *Expositio Totius Mundi et Gentium* and the *Madaba Mosaic Floor Map*

The commercial centrality of ancient Palestine and its famous cities to the ancient global trade systems was singled out by a well-known treatise of Antiquity entitled: *Expositio Totius Mundi et Gentium: A Commercial-Geographical Description of the World and Its People.*[11] Compiled in the mid-fourth century CE by a textile merchant, who was probably a native of either Palestine or Syria (Grüll 2014: 629–42), according to Jean Rougé the author of *Expositio Totius Mundi et Gentium*: first lived in the Palestinian city of Nablus (Neapolis) afterwards he moved to Tyre (Rougé 1966: 27–38). The commercial treatise was originally written in koinē Greek, then the language of learning, philosophy, arts and commerce in the Mediterranean world. The survey describes in detail, *inter alia*, the economic and commercial geography of the Levant and Palestine and the closely related flourishing urban centres of Syria and Palestine and the cities of what is known today as modern Lebanon. Generally, classical sources used the terms Phoenicia, Palestine and Syria interchangeably and presented a picture different from the modern racialized and ideological obsession with

'Phoenicianism' (Gualtieri 2009: 22–3). As we shall see below, the terms *Palestinian*, *Phoenician* and *Syrian* were used interchangeably in many classical sources and the same tendency continued in modern European sources.

The real significance of the *Expositio Totius Mundi et Gentium* lays in the fact that it provides very important information on the industries and commercial geography of Palestine and its key cities – information that cannot be obtained from any other source from the middle of the fourth century. Also of great significance is the fact that out of the sixty-one internally important trading cities of Antiquity mentioned by the *Expositio*, twenty cities belong to Syria and *Palaestina* (i.e. one-third of the whole), compared with only sixteen belong to the western part of the Roman Empire. There are twenty-seven different goods listed in the text, which are exported from all the cities mentioned. Focusing on the great urban centres of the Levant, the author of the *Expositio* provides a detailed list of the most important commercial and manufacturing cities of '*Syria-Phoenicia*' and *Palaestina* including: eleven cities from Syria and 'Phoenicia' (modern Lebanon): Antiochia, Berytus (Beirut), Byblos, Damascus, Heliopolis (Baalbek), Laodicea, Sarepta, Seleucia, Sidon, Tyrus (Tyre), Tripolis, and eight cities from *Palaestina*: Ascalon, Caesarea Maritima, Gaza, Jericho, Lydda, Nablus (Neapolis), Beisan (Scythopolis) and Acre (Ptolemais). Clearly the author of *Expositio* was bilingual (Greek and Latin) and he was fully aware that the ancient cities of Lebanon and Palestine possessed sophisticated legal systems that were central to the conduct of commercial activities; The city of Caesarea Maritima and its bilingual School of Caesarea were a major centre for bilingual legal studies in Palestine in late Antiquity, but Justinian's prohibition of 533 of teaching there, the famous School of Law of Berytus (Beirut) with its emphasis on homogenizing the Byzantine legal system – remained easily accessible to Palestinian law students who learned Latin as an important aspect of the study of legal Latin texts at the time (Geiger 2010; Masalha 2022); while several Palestinian lawyers and authors of late Antique Palestine were then known as *scholastikos* and *gramáticos* who were often bilingual or trilingual (Geiger 2010; Masalha 2022).

After commenting on the commercial environment of dozens of cities of Antiquity in the Levant, the author of *Expositio* provides intimate details on his native region:

> Now there is the land of Syria. It is divided into three Syrias: Phoenicia, Palestine, and Coela [Coele-Syria].[12] These have many different excellent and great cities; by mentioning just a little about these I shall surely delight my audience. First of all there is the prosperous, royal city of Antioch, where the ruler of the world has his seat… It is a fine city, outstanding in its public works. The other cities are like Tyre which is quite well off in that it carries on a thriving business with many people (indeed, no eastern city is more crowded with people or more avid in its business) … After that there is the very delightful city of Berytus which possesses legal institutions; indeed the Roman judicial system seem to rest largely on this city … Next there is the city of Caesarea [Maritima]. It too is very delightful and abounds in all things, and the disposition of the city is outstanding. Its *tetrapylon*, a singular and famous sight, is spoken off everywhere. It is necessary to name

> part of the other cities and that singular things each possess. … Now here are all the other cities. Ascalon and Gaza are outstanding, "boiling" in business, and abound in all things. They export fine wine to all of Syria and Egypt. The city of Neapolis [Nablus] is renowned and very celebrated, while Tripolis, Scythopolis [Beisan], and the city of Byblus are very busy. … Then there are the following cities: Sidon, Sarepta, Ptolemais [Acre], the excellent Eleutheropolis [Beit Jibrin], and also Damascus … Serapta, Caesarea, Nea[polis] [Nablus], and Lydda produce genuine purple dye. All the above-mentioned cities grow grain, grapes, and olives and are prosperous.
>
> (Woodman 1964: 30)

The text of the *Expositio* reveals the importance of the internationally reputable wine industries of Gaza and Ascalon, which will be discussed in detail in Chapter 6. Two centuries separate the *Expositio*, of the mid-fourth century CE, from the famous *Madaba Mosaic Floor Map*, of the mid-sixth century CE, one of the most powerful symbols of urban Palestine in Antiquity. This Byzantine period map was aimed at Christian pilgrims as well as travellers and merchants. The Madaba Map was discovered in 1884, in the course of the construction of a new Greek Orthodox church in Madaba (present-day Jordan) on the site of its Byzantine predecessor, St George's church. It is incredibly important to read the *material evidence* of the Map together with the *written evidence* of the *Expositio*. The material evidence from the Madaba Map describes the high sophistication and dynamism of the cities of Byzantine Palestine and attests to the high urban development and economic and commercial prosperity and expansion of Palestine in Antiquity. Ascalon was a bustling seaport in late Antiquity covering more than 150 acres; with a population of at least 15,000. In late Antiquity the Bishop of Caesarea Maritima, Eusebius, in *Omenestecon*, called Ascalon the most famous city in Palestine; by 536 CE Ascalon was a seat of a bishop; the city's gates and the story buildings and magnificent architecture depicted in the Madaba Floor Map add more details to what we know about Ascalon for the *Expositio*. Overall the Madaba Floor Map shows that urban development and the construction of civic buildings and churches in Palestine reached a zenith in the mid-sixth century and the Madaba Floor Map is one of the most powerful symbols of this urban economic and cultural boom in Palestine in late Antiquity. Mosaic pavements of Palestine from the Byzantine era were often uncovered by modern archaeologists, showing the large-scale of the Palestine mosaic industry of late Antiquity and the multiple uses of mosaic in urban Palestine (Avi-Yonah. 1932: 136–81; 1933: 26–47; 49–73). Also, as we shall see in Chapter 6, the city of Gaza developed an extensive mosaic industry in late Antiquity – an industry that continued into, and was further developed in the Umayyad and Ababsid periods in the city of Jerusalem – and these mosaics are also testimony to the spectacular Palestine urban mosaic industry, ancient, medieval and modern. The Madaba Floor Map is also among the oldest surviving material evidence for the official use of the name *Palaestina* in Antiquity (see also Masalha 2018). Showing the 'border of Egypt and *Palaestina*' (Greek: '*οροι Αιγυπτου και Παλαιστινης*') and the Mediterranean Sea, and featuring a detailed description of the holy city of Aelia Capitolina (Jerusalem) at its centre – as well as details of two dozen of Palestinian cities – the remaining parts of the map contain the oldest surviving original cartographical material and vivid depiction of the ancient cities of *Palaestina*.

The *Expositio,* when discussing Caesarea Maritima, the large port city of Byzantine Palestine and the capital of the province of *Palaestina Prima*, also known also as *Metropolis Palaestina* informs us that this economically affluent city had a permanent market as one of the multifaceted realms of urban life and a newly built classical *tetrapylon* (Greek: *τετράπυλον*, 'four gates'), plural *tetrapyla*, known in Latin as a *quadrifrons* ('four fronts') with a gate on each of the four sides, generally built on a crossroad and they were built as landmarks at significant geographical commercial international crossroads (including maritime routes and inland trade networks). During the late Roman and Byzantine periods urban centres and cities of Palestine expanded massively and Caesarea Maritima grew and developed to become one of the biggest and busiest harbour in the Mediterranean world; the city also had five trade roads radiating in all directions in Palestine, thus establishing the transport infrastructure not only for inland commerce to all major cities in Palestine but also for international commence between Palestine, Egypt, Syria and Arabia. Since the time of the Emperor Hadrian the city also had a steady supply of water provided by several aqueducts, and for agriculture springs, wells and rainwater were abundant. In classical Antiquity the merchants of Caesarea Maritima began importing raw Chinese silk – raw silk being one of China's most important products in Antiquity. Ancient Levant's preoccupation with dress and status symbols such as clothing dyed with Tyrian purple with its striking colour and its resistance to fading enabled trading Palestinian cities, such Caesarea Maritima, to develop a major centre for manufacturing and exporting silk textile and purple dye (see Chapter 5); the hinterland of Caesarea Maritima was also celebrated for its productivity in wine, olive oil, corn and wheat (Patrich 2011: 117–18).

This book will explore the evolution and expansion of Palestinian urbanism in ancient times and the interaction of Palestinian trading cities across history with their surrounding rural life and the wider regional context. In this respect, Henri Lefebvre's three constituents of the social production of urban spaces – perceived, conceived and lived experiences (Lefebvre 2011) – are relevant to the way multicultural urban Palestine of Antiquity – *Caesarea Palaestina* (also known as Caesarea Maritima; Arabic: Qaysariah), Gaza (Ghazzah) Ascalon ('Asqalan), Nablus, al-Ramla, Al-Quds/Jerusalem, Acre (Arabic Akka; Greek: Ptolemais) Nazareth, Jaffa, Tiberias, Beisan, Safad – evolved historically. The urbanization processes and city planning during the Philistine, Hellenistic, Roman and Byzantine periods were maintained and developed further under Islam in the Middle Ages and this planning of the urban space is still visible today in the Arab-Islamic medieval Palestine including the Old City of Jerusalem, a city whose urban planning and architecture are among the best surviving medieval cities in the world.

Palestine's geographic and strategic location made it central to the long-distance trade routes of Antiquity and to the first truly global trade systems of the ancient world. A relatively small country in size, Palestine was a 'bridge country' lying at the crossroads of great continents: Asia, Africa and Europe. As a key country at the centre of the 'transit trade' of the ancient world, the geography and physiography of Palestine played a key role in early global commercial history. Furthermore, Palestine itself produced a large number of agricultural and industrial commodities for export via global distribution networks throughout its history. As we shall see below, some of these natural agricultural and manufactured products of Palestine such as *Gaza Wine* of Antiquity or *Jaffa Orange* of the modern period became internationally and iconically celebrated and instantly recognized as key markers of Palestine and Palestinian identity.

In the opening chapter of his *Decline and Fall of the Roman Empire*, Edward Gibbon evoked, in the eighteenth century, in a few sentences the two most celebrated countries of the ancient Near East and the centrality of Phoenicia and Palestine to what he saw as 'Western civilization' and mankind:

> Phoenicia and Palestine were sometimes annexed to, and sometimes separated from, the jurisdiction of Syria. The former of these was a narrow and rocky coast; the latter was a territory scarcely superior to Wales, either in fertility or extent. Yet Phoenicia and Palestine will forever live in the memory of mankind; since America, as well as Europe, has received letters from the one, and religion from the other.
>
> (Gibbon 1875 Vol.1: 27–8; Bowersock 2019)

For millennia Palestine, or the *Holy Land*, was universally known of all countries because of its association with great world religions and the fact that the country has been packed with history and culture and civilization (Casto 1937: 235–59).

Appropriating the Palestinian past: The erasure of the name *Palestine* and its replacement with the terms *Israel*, *Syria*, *Southern Levan* and *Phoenicia* in post-1948 Western scholarship

English historian Edward Gibbon (1737–1794), the eminent historian of the Roman Empire, declared in the eighteenth century that *Palestine* was one of the most famous countries in the world (Gibbon 1875 Vol.1: 27–8), and between the eighteenth century and 1948 far more books were published by English historians on *Roman Palestine* than on Roman Britain, or the Roman province of *Britannia*. In the mountains of pre-1948 literature on ancient Palestine, we have thousands of books published in English and other European languages which used the term *Palestine* in their titles. Moreover the cities of Roman Palestine had highly *mixed populations* with Jewish, Christian, Samaritan and pagan communities living side by side; this *multicultural reality* of Palestine continued in Byzantine Palestine and Islamic Palestine. Furthermore until 1948 Western scholars clearly identified historic Palestine (and the Palestinians) as a distinct country and referred to famous cities in Palestine as *Palestinian cities*. However, in the post-1948 period, with the destruction of historic Palestine during the Palestinian Nakba, and the creation of the State of Israel, in 1948 (Masalha 1992, 2012)

– and with the disappearance of Palestine from international maps and dictionaries – Western scholars have sought to privilege one particular: the modern European Jewish settlers in Palestine; they also have sought to replace the term *Palestine* – which had been used for millennia (Masalha 2018) – with the term *Israel* and suddenly archaeological discoveries on sites and archaeological mounds from Chalcolithic Palestine or Bronze Age Palestine became headlines about *Chalcolitic Israel* and *Bronze Age Israel*. Professor Mary Beard, a renewed English classicist, of Cambridge University, specializing in ancient Rome made several documentaries for the BBC TV about the Roman Empire describing this empire 'extending from Spain to Israel' – while every classicist in the West knows that the country under the Romans was *Palestine* and mountains of books published before 1948 are found in the British Library on *Roman Palestine* and *ancient Palestine*.

Another fundamental flaw in the way the history of Palestine has been approached in the West is the centring of the history of Palestine around the Bible, claims of *biblical Jewish monotheism* and the treatment of the biblical stories as 'history' rather than myth-narratives (Masalha 2018). In fact the Old Testament talks about *Elohim*, plural for 'gods' and polytheism, a dominant feature of Palestine in Antiquity. Moreover *monotheism* in Palestine was a late development; it emerged in late Antiquity and in the early Middle Ages. Although the population of rural and urban Roman Palestine was culturally and religious mixed, until the late fourth century CE the Hellenized cities of Palestine were dominated by Hellenistic and Roman paganism combined with indigenous *polytheism*; Roman polytheism and Roman pagan temples dominated the skyline of the cities of Palestine and pagan rituals and practices shaped urban culture and everyday life in urban Palestine, as we shall see in Chapters 3, 5, 6 and 7. The patron deity of the ancient Palestinian city of Beisan (Schythopolis) was Dionysus, an eastern deity widely worshipped in Roman Palestine and the pagan nature god of wine grape harvest and orchards, who, according to ancient myths, taught humans the art of growing and cultivating plants; the city of Nablus (Neapolis) was the centre of pagan learning, the Galilee city of Sepphoris (*Eirenopolis Ειρηνούπολις*; Saffurriya) and the synagogues of the Galilee were modelled on Roman temples and pagan practices and rituals, with the god of wine, Dionysus, appearing on decorated mosaic pavements in public buildings and private homes (Rose 2010: 25–49; Weiss and Netzer 1998: 90); likewise Gaza was dominated by a large number of pagan temples, pantheons of polytheism and syncretic religion until the early fifth century (Masalha 2018, 2022). However, renowned Western historians and archaeologists are under enormous pressures from Zionist lobbies in the West to toe the line, while Israeli and Zionist historians and archaeologists have sought to erase the historic heritage of Palestine and systematically replace the historical toponyms (place names) in Palestine. Appropriating the past is a key feature of Israel's archaeological practices in Palestine.[13] Thousands of newly invented Israeli Hebrew place names and biblically imagined place names began to appear (Masalha 2023: 37–71) and Western scholars began avoiding using the term *Palestine* and *Palestinian* and replacing these ancient terms with terms *Israel* and *Syria* and *southern Levant*.

Moreover classical sources themselves clearly identified *Palestine* as a distinct entity from Phoenicia and always referred to Palestine as a distinct country within the Levant.

The social, cultural, commercial and industrial lives of Palestinian cities of Antiquity such as Gaza, Asclaon, Jaffa, Lydda, Caesarea Maritima, Aelia Capitolina (Jerusalem/Al-Quds), Nablus ('Neapolis'), Jericho, Beisan (Schythopolis) and Elusa are extensively documented in classical sources. However, as we will see in Chapter 4, this problem was confounded by the fact that even cultural organizations such as UNESCO, which were tasked with 'preserving' the historical heritage of sites of Antiquity, began to adopt the newly invented Israeli toponyms, which were designed to erase the cultural and historical heritage of Palestine.

The merchant-maritime city-states of Palestine and Phoenicia: Maritime trade and Mediterranean port cities (*Maiumas*) of Palestine

Despite the problematic modern radicalized construction of '*Phoenicians*' and '*Phoenicianism*', it is still possible, on the basis of classical sources, to speak of famous trading cities of Phoenicia and the Mediterranean coastal cities of Syria. Also some Palestinian ancient cities such as the port city of Akka (Acre) seemed to have originally flourished as a major 'Phoenician city' of merchant-mariners and the purple textile industry of the Phoenicians, the merchant-mariners of purple (whose Greek name, 'Phoenicians', seems to be derived from their trade in the purple fabric), was subsequently inherited and developed further by the Palestinian cities of Nablus and Caesarea Maritima. Not surprisingly many ancient sources conflated the ancient Palestinian merchants with the Phoenicians. Indeed Palestine's neighbouring cities and geography and geology had a huge impact on the economy and commerce of ancient Palestine, and its traditional and commercial industries, with Phoenicia and the rest of the Mediterranean region. Often because of the fame of the Phoenician merchants in ancient times, modern Western historians often confused leading Palestinian merchants in Antiquity who came from Ascalon and Gaza and traded with, or settled in, Italy in Antiquity with the Phoenician merchants (Clackson et al. 2020: 179).

The neighbouring Phoenicians of the coastal city-states of what is now modern Lebanon, often working closely with Canaanite merchants, were legendary merchants and mariners who together with Canaanite merchants founded Carthage (modern Tunis), which became one of the most important trading hubs of the ancient Mediterranean and one of the most affluent cities of the classical world. The city's location made it master of the Mediterranean's maritime trade for many centuries in Antiquity.

Maritime travel, navigation and long-distance trade by sea were far easier and much cheaper than overland travel and trade in ancient times and the Phoenicians became archetypal *merchant-mariners* of the ancient world. With their formidable expertise in maritime trade all across the Mediterranean world, the Phoenician merchant-mariners left a lasting impact on the evolution of the economy of their ancient Palestinian and Canaanite neighbours and the urban environment of ancient Palestine. In fact, in classical Antiquity the Phoenicians also provided a template for other ancient

Mediterranean *merchant-mariners* including Carthage, great city of Antiquity, now a residential suburb of the city of Tunis. Becoming a thriving port and trading Mediterranean centre, the Carthaginians developed into a major Mediterranean merchant-mariner power and a rival to Rome. Other ancient merchant-mariners who were inspired by the neighbouring Phoenician archetype included the Canaanites, Philistines (ancient Palestinians), Syrians, Greeks, Romans, Arabs as well as the *merchant-mariners* of the Italian city-states of Venice and Genoa in the high Middle Ages and early modern period. The historical Genoese merchant-mariners' quarter and port can still be seen in the modern Palestinian Mediterranean city of Acre.

Long-distance trade, navigation and adventures also provided a fertile imagination for storytelling and fictional writing. In classical Antiquity the Nabataean Arab kingdom of north Arabia and southern Palestine dominated the Trans-Arabian desert trade from Yemen to the Mediterranean. The 'Arab ethnicity' of the Nabataeans is widely accepted by archaeologists and historians and this 'Arab ethnicity' argument has been backed by evidence of the Arabic language being embodied in the Nabataeans Aramaic texts of the early Roman period in Palestine and north Arabia (Graf 2019). In classical Antiquity the Nabataean Trans-Arabian trade in frankincense, aromatics and gold with the kingdoms of Yemen may have been the background for the Old Testament's legend of the Queen of Sheba visiting Jerusalem and bringing a caravan of precious gifts to King Solomon including frankincense and myrrh (1 Kings 10:1–13 and 2 Chronicles 9: 1–12) – although modern-day archaeology of both Palestine and Yemen find no trace of King Solomon and the Queen of Sheba herself (Finkelstein 2007: 167).

In the Middle Ages among the medieval Arab mariners the *archetype of merchant-mariners* can be found in *Sinbad the Sailor* (Arabic: سندباد البحري) a fictional mariner and the hero of folk tales of an Arab mariner, described as hailing from Baghdad at the height of the Islamic Abbasid empire (eighth and ninth centuries CE). In the course of seven voyages throughout the seas India, south of Asia and east Africa, Sinbad had fantastic adventures in magical realms, encountering monsters and witnessing magical adventures. The tales of Sinbad the Sailor became an addition to the *One Thousand and One Nights* and the tales reflects the trend within the medieval realm of Arab and Muslim sailors exploring the world in a period of great economic and maritime trade growth and the opening up of new trading maritime trading routes; the tales reflected the experiences of medieval Arab and Muslim mariners who sailed to the hazards of the Indian Ocean countries and the east African coastal countries and sought new trading routes and new countries to trade with (Pinault 1998: 721–2).

Furthermore, since Antiquity the eastern Mediterranean location of Palestine, its land and maritime trade routes and the international trade systems constructed around these trade highways and superhighways of Palestine allowed the trade and economy of the country to flourish and enable ideas and religions to spread widely. The tradition associated the birth of Jesus in Bethlehem, Roman Palestine, and the *Star of Bethlehem* and the 'wise men from the East' – which modern astronomers have made several attempts to link the star to celestial events – is widely known. However, as we shall see in Chapter 2 from the Neolithic Age onwards, and long before the birth of Jesus and the rise of Christianity in Palestine and the Mediterranean region, long-distance trade through the transit highways of Palestine and night navigation between the coastal cities of ancient Egypt, Palestine and the Levant often required observation of the sky and the astronomical knowledge of the stars. This ancient observation of the stars, essential for travel and navigation, was also connected to the rise of ancient traditions of deities associated with the sky and the heaven and this led to the evolution and spread of religious ideas and shared religious traditions and shared forms of religious worship and even shared deities across the ancient Middle East.

The international transit trade routes of Palestine and the ancient global trade systems also enabled cultures and civilizations to meet, exchange ideas, create cultural montage and civilizational fusions based on cross-cultural fertilization and human flourishing. The same geographic and strategic location of Palestine along the eastern Mediterranean determined the country's international trade and trade partners. Ancient Palestine and the evolution of its international trade routes should always be seen within its wider Near Eastern context and neighbouring countries. Moreover, in ancient times the sphere of influence of the Mediterranean coastal city-states of 'Phoenicia' encompassed the Mediterranean coastal cities of northern Palestine, from Al-Zib and Acre in the north of Palestine to Dor (Tantura) in central Palestine; in fact, the Phoenicians' superhighway of the Mediterranean trade also overlapped with the Mediterranean maritime trade of the coastal cities of ancient Palestine. And the coastal city-states of Phoenicia deployed their Mediterranean maritime trade as a soft power very effectively. Subsequently in Antiquity the merchants of Palestine, Syria, Carthage (modern Tunisia), Egypt, Greece and Rome inherited this merchant's sea faring spirit of the *Phoenicians* and their effective use of the maritime superhighway of the Mediterranean for trade and speedy transport of goods. Furthermore, the coastal region of Palestine is one of the few in the Levant with an easy low-laying route inland, Marj Ibn Amer, which connected to the Sea of Galilee and the ancient city of Tiberias (founded around 20 CE), from there to Damascus and beyond.

Also, crucially, international trade of the Mediterranean world of Antiquity facilitated the spread of pro-Canaanite *alphabet*, which had emerged in and around ancient Palestine, to spread widely As a soft power, and for practical purposes, this international trade enabled both the Phoenician and Palestinian coastal cities of the Mediterranean to spread the alphabet revolution (which also became known as the *Phoenician alphabet*) through maritime trade and consequently this process democratized literacy throughout the Mediterranean region and the ancient Middle East; from this alphabet both the Greek alphabet of classical Antiquity and the early Arabic alphabet of Yemen emerged. Arab merchants and the Trans-Arabian trade also contributed to the spread of the Nabataean Arabic of classical Antiquity and generally of the Arabic language from the Arabian Peninsula to Palestine, Syria and the rest of Bilad al-Sham and Iraq centuries before the advent of Islam in the early seventh century CE. Regional and global trade not only contributed to the spread and democratization of literacy in Palestine but also enabled the creation of 'cities of learning' in the country in late Antiquity and the Middle Ages under Islam.

Not only both Phoenicia and Philistia (ancient Palestine) took part in the spread of the proto-Canaanite alphabet in Antiquity, but several Palestinian coastal cities such as Caesarea Maritima took up in Antiquity and developed further several industries, such purple dye, which historical was invented and popularized by the Phoenician city-states. Furthermore, in pre-modern Palestine leading Arab merchant families in Jerusalem and other key Palestinian cities often created and maintained large private family 'libraries' which ensured widespread literacy in Palestine (Masalha 2022).

For many centuries in Antiquity and the Middle Ages, China, India, and South Arabia and Ethiopia were the origin of trade flows through Palestine and the wider Near East – a global trade system dominated by luxury goods: frankincense, aromatics, spices, herbs, Chinese raw silk, tea and porcelain; many of these elite goods flowed from Asia westwards, while gold, silver, wines and olive oil were shipped from the eastern Mediterranean through the Red Sea in the opposite direction. As we shall see in Chapter 1, the geographic location of Palestine within the Near East influenced the construction of ancient trade systems and international highways and trading routes through and across Palestine. The evolution of Palestine as a 'transit country' for long-distance trade in precious commodities such as frankincense, aromatics, spices and (Chinese) silk from Asia, south Arabia and the African horn enabled cross-cultural fertilization, and made it possible for new ideas, technologies and religious and intellectual revolutions to spread widely; these international trade routes criss-crossing Palestine and the international trade systems associated with them will be discussed in Chapter 1.

Crucially global trade routes and trade systems caused the phenomenal rise and decline (and in some cases, disappearance as urban environment) of cities in Palestine. International and regional trade was also often greatest single driver of economic growth and demographic expansion in urban Palestine and the case study of its impact on specific Palestinian cities will be explored in this work. Furthermore, often the strategic and commercial location of Mediterranean Palestine also drew attention of occupying armies, maritime empires and colonial-settlers; occasionally trade also brought in or spread epidemics in Palestinian cities with catastrophic consequences. Also occasionally the struggle for the control of the international trade routes of Palestine led to 'trade wars' and military invasions – as we shall see in Chapter 3, the wars over the 'spice routes' of southern Palestine between the Nabataean Arab kingdom of classical Antiquity and the Hellenistic Hasmonaean Jewish kingdom of Judaea in the first century BCE. Moreover, by the middle Bronze Age (1750–1550 BCE) the struggle for the control of the copper trade system (and obsidian trade) and the key trade and strategic routes of Palestine and Syria led to the Egyptian military campaign against a coalition of Palestinian and Syrian kingdoms. Waged by the then superpower of the region, Egypt, this campaign culminated in the siege and the Battle of Megiddo of the fifteenth century BCE in which the Egyptian forces commanded by Thutmose III defeated and destroyed the Palestinian kingdom of Megiddo.[14] An important urban centre in the Levant and a powerful city-state in early and middle Bronze Age Palestine, Megiddo had dominated the Plain of Esdraelon (Marj Ibn Amer) and the strategic location at the crossing of two international military and trade routes in ancient Palestine – trade and strategic routes that had given this city-kingdom wealth and an importance far beyond its actual size. The scale of the urban and commercial development of the kingdom of Megiddo can be attested by the excavation by modern archaeologists of the 'Great Temple' of Megiddo, the largest of its kind in the Near East during the early Bronze Age (Wiener 2016).

The physical geography and topography of Palestine consisted of five distinct regions: the hilly and mountainous northern regions known since ancient times as Galilee; the southern Nagab (Negev) region – although much of it desert, its northern parts had sedentary population and land cultivation since ancient times and played a big part in the rise of Palestinian wine industries during the late Roman and Byzantine periods. Palestine's geo-political location and its physical geography and topography – with three parallel strips lying between the Mediterranean Sea and Jordan River: the Mediterranean coastal plains, the uplands or hilly central country, and the Rift Valley, much of which lies along the Jordan River – determined its international trade routes and superhighways. The Mediterranean coastal plains are connected with the Jordan River by Marj Ibn Amer (the Esdraelon plain), the most fertile plain in Palestine, and historically a vital transit route linking the Palestinian coastal highway with the ancient trade routes and trade systems connecting Palestine, Syria, Anatolia, Egypt and Mesopotamia and the entire ancient Northern Fertile Crescent from Mesopotamia (modern Iraq) to Palestine and Egypt.

In the Bronze Age the growing demands for metals by urban societies of ancient Egypt and Palestine stimulated early copper workers and miners to prospect for copper in the southern regions Sinai and Palestine, where extensive ancient mines were uncovered at Timna, in the southern Naqab of Palestine (McNeil 1990).

Having the sites of important copper mines and being a 'transit country' at the crossroads of ancient trade (and copper) systems and strategic routes, Palestine was also central to ancient regional and global trade routes that contributed to the spread copper and copper industries, some of the most important commodities of the flourishing of civilization in the Bronze Age, frankincense, technologies of writing, and the proto-Canaanite alphabet (see Chapter 2), and of technologies and cultures, of religions and civilizations, and of legal systems such as the Hammurabi code of laws.

Palestine's geographic location and strategic importance connected two *superhighways*: the Mediterranean Sea and the Red Sea, both central to the international trade of Antiquity, and key land highways of the Near East. Some of these land trade route and trade systems of the Near Eastern Northern Fertile Crescent, accommodating long-distance trade and facilitating far-reaching trade relations between different distant regions, date back to the Neolithic Age. For instance, archaeological excavations have shown that the main source of the natural glass trade known as obsidian during the late Neolithic Age in Palestine was located far away in the central Anatolia region of modern Turkey;

> The Neolithic Age was apparently one during which some far-reaching trade relations between different regions were carried on. The most commonly found items in Neolithic sites suggesting trade connections were tools made from obsidian. Research has shown that the main source for obsidian during the Neolithic in Palestine was located far away at Goellue Dagg, southwest of the modern city of Nevsehir in Turkey.
>
> (Rast 1992: 58)

The importance of this regional *obsidian* trade and obsidian as a resource contributing to the rise of urbanism cannot be overemphasized, as archaeological discoveries of central Anatolian obsidian in towns such as Jericho in Palestine in the Neolithic period have shown (Meyers 1997: 124).

The Chalcolithic and Bronze Ages saw the greatest evolutions of long-distance trade (passing through Palestine and Palestinian towns) first in copper and subsequently (in the Bronze Age) in copper alloys over a vast region from Armenia and Anatolia to the eastern Mediterranean and Egypt. Obsidian vessels and tools were uncovered in the 2013-2019 excavations at *Tell Kabri*, a middle Bronze Age Palestinian city and a palace, in upper western Galilee, were dated to 5500 BCE. The inhabitants of the Bronze Age city (their number is estimated at 5,000) earned their living through agriculture and international commerce. The excavations by a joint Israeli-American team of archaeologists uncovered remains and pieces of merchandise whose origins lay in Anatolia (modern Turkey), Egypt and Crete, and the inland Bronze Age city operated a trading Mediterranean port at Akhziv (Al-Zib). Although the Canaanite name is unknown, the name of Bronze Age site at *Tell Kabri* was taken from the name of the modern Palestinian village *Al-Kabri*, a nearby large Arab village north-east of Acre, expelled and depopulated by Israel in 1948 and replaced by the Israeli settlement/kibbutz Kabri.

The economic and commercial history of Palestine was largely determined by being 'a bridge country' on Mediterranean coast lying at the crossroads of three great continents: Asia, Africa and Europe, and linking the *Mashreq* and *Maghbrib* countries of the Arab world. This strategic location of Palestine greatly influenced its commercial geography and the long history of its involvement in the ancient regional trade and global trade systems of Antiquity.

In the ancient Near East two types of state-building and states emerged in the Bronze Age: the *city-state* with vast territories around it – such as the formidable Palestinian city-state of Megiddo, created in the fertile Marj Ibn Amer (Esdarlean valley) and the well-known Mesopotamian and Egyptian empires. Necessity was at the heart of the birth of these two types of states. Copper mining and smelting mines in southern Palestine and Sinai and the Near Eastern copper trade gave birth to ancient civilizations and the city-state in the *two* Fertile Crescents: the *Northern Fertile Crescent* from Mesopotamia to Egypt across Syria and Palestine and the *Southern Fertile Crescent* of South Arabia and Yemen, what ancient Greek historians and geographers called as *Eudaemon Arabia* (*Εὐδαίμων Ἀραβία*, flourishing Arabia), which gave the world trade system and ancient global markets one of its most precious commodities in Antiquity, frankincense, and the perfume and traditional medicine industries. The copper trade of Palestine – being a transit country at the crossroad of international trade routes in the Fertile Crescents and the Near East – fuelled the creation of its earliest Bronze Age cities.

Obsidian vessels and remains of international merchandise were excavated in 2013-19 at Tell Kabri, a middle Bronze Age Palestinian city in western upper Galilee, were dated to 5500 BCE; the remains of merchandise excavated show the city-state – which had a seaport at Akhziv – had international trade links with Egypt, Crete and areas in modern Turkey. By the Bronze Age, international trade, driven by profit and the search for precious metals such as obsidian – a naturally occurring volcanic glass formed when lava is extruded from a volcano cools rapidly with minimal crystal growth – and copper and tin, created a region joined up by international trade stitching from Armenia in the north and Afghanistan in the east to the eastern Mediterranean in the West. At the same time, during the Bronze Age, Palestine's neighbouring Mediterranean Phoenician trading cities, such as Tyre and Sidon, with their powerful navies, spread their language, settlements and culture throughout the Mediterranean world. Both the Palestinian *pro-Canaanite alphabet* as well as technologies such as *Murex purple* dye and purple fabric also spread throughout the Mediterranean region.

In Antiquity some precious commodities and monopoly elite products began to emerge in Palestinian cities and what became known as the *royal colour* of purple textile (originally developed by Phoenician Tyre) gives us a glimpse into the way in which the commercial geography of Palestine evolved and the way elite products, and international trade in these precious products, became intertwined with the rise of social stratification and organized religion with religious hierarchy within both Palestine and the wider Mediterranean region. This elite purple colour textile, which Palestinian cities produced in late Antiquity, was later adopted by the hierarchy of the various churches around the Mediterranean world and it can still be seen today among the senior hierarchy of the Catholic Church and protestant churches in Europe and even in the Armenian Church in twenty-first century Armenia.

At the heart of Palestine's and the Levant's ancient trade routes and at the Mediterranean end of the south Arabian spice trading system of Antiquity was the city of Gaza, one of the oldest cities of the world. The first-known mention of Gaza occurs on a temple wall in Karnak, Egypt dating to 1468 BCE, which listed the cities conquered by Pharaoh Thutmose III (also spelt Tuthmosis). Gaza was then a prized possession of the ancient Egyptians because of its strategic location on the 'Way of the Sea', the trunk road connecting Egypt, Palestine and Syria (Terpstra 2019: 170). The Palestine military campaigns of Thutmose III (who ruled Egypt from 1479 to 1425 BCE and conquered much of the Near East) were also a turning point in the history of Bronze Age Palestine. The powerful army of Thutmose (the 'Napoleon of ancient Egypt') defeated the army of the Canaanite city-state of Megiddo in Palestine – which had dominated the strategic and trade routes of northern Palestine – at the Battle of Megiddo, the largest battle of Thutmose's seventeen military campaigns, after a long siege of the city of Megiddo that lasted for eight months. The Egyptian victory forced the rulers of the Bronze Age city-states Palestine to pay tribute to Egypt in large quantities of wine, honey, incense and ivory (Budge 2013: 37).

In Antiquity the merchant communities of several powerful Palestinian Mediterranean cities developed *port cities* – effectively autonomous maritime cities, or 'cities within cities'; they were called *Maiumas Gaza* (also known as *Maiumas Gazae* under the Byzantines), *Maiumas Ascalon and Maiumas Asddod (Isdud).* The most famous of the three *Maiumas* (also called Maiuma) was *Gaza Maiumas*, which became an autonomous city during the early Byzantine period and remained as a separate city from Gaza for centuries. Even in the tenth century under Islam renowned Palestinian geographer al-Maqdisi Maqdisi mentioned Maiumas as one of the key cities of the

Arab province of Palestine, *Jund Filastin*, an autonomous city separate from the city of Gaza (Le Strange 1886: 11; Wa'ar 2023: 26).

These *maiumas* (port cities) of Gaza and Ascalon, in particular, would grow into administratively autonomous cities and among the most important trading posts in ancient Palestine and the whole Levant. Gaza, in particular, strategically linking three continents (Asia, Africa and Europe) and at the centre of the Trans-Arabian/Indian spice trade to Europe (the Trans-Arabian spice trade will be discussed in Chapter 3) and was placed on at the crossroad of three international trading axes: (1) a north-south axis from Syria to Egypt; (2) an east-west axis connecting the south Arabian Peninsula to the Mediterranean region; (3); a north-south axis linking Gaza with the port city of Byzantine Aelas (Arabic: Aylah, modern Aqaba) and the Indian trade via the Red Sea (Terpstra 2019: 170). The mistake many historians make is to project the modern boundaries of British Mandatory Palestine (1918-48) on the political geography of ancient and medieval Palestine and its ancient cities. In fact, the ancient cities of Aelas (modern Aqaba) and Petra (as well as Mount Sinai) were an integral part of Palestine in Antiquity and they were key international trading cities and central to the international caravan trade and Red Sea global trade of the Byzantine province of *Palaestina Salutaris*. Becoming a well-developed city in Antiquity which flourished on international competence and desert caravans and contained many spectacular buildings and extraordinary urban infrastructure, Petra, at some stage during the Byzantine period, became the administrative capital of, and a regional *religious metropolis*, *Palaestina Salutaris* (Masalha 2018). Even in the tenth century Jerusalemite Palestinian geographer al-Maqdisi included Amman, the capital of modern Jordan, among the top twelve key cities of the Arab province of Palestine, '*Jund Filastin*' (Le Strange 1886: 11).

The global commercial importance and prosperity of Palestine grew in Antiquity phenomenally and this can be seen in the *Expositio Totius Mundi et Gentium*. This document provides us with first-hand evidence about the commercial visibility of Palestinian cities within the wider context of the region in late Antiquity. The global trade involving Palestine in Antiquity dealt with the two most precious commodities at the time: the spice trade from India to the Mediterranean region and the frankincense trade from Yemen and Ethiopia to Europe, both were transported through Palestine. Generally the international maritime trading system of Antiquity was also linked the commercial geography of Palestine and fuelled the economic prosperity of Palestine and its cities.

Market cities (*Emporia*), urban markets and everyday life in Palestine: Shopping for food, spices and household goods from classical Antiquity to the modern period

Nearly 5,000 years separate the early regional trade systems in obsidian and copper of Chalcolithic Palestine and the country's incipient urbanization during the Chalcolithic Age, on the one hand, and the global trade systems of classical Antiquity and Roman

Palestine, on the other. Crucially there is something fairly 'modern' about the planned urban markets and the planned shopping malls of Roman Palestine during classical Antiquity. Indeed when it comes to the urban markets and everyday shopping, there is a great deal in common between classical Antiquity and the modern period, for millennia since classical Antiquity the vast majority of markets were located in the urban centres of Palestine and these markets shaped the cityscape and urban life in the country.

Extensive archaeological evidence uncovered in Palestine shows the impact of international trade on the urban marketplaces in Palestine, public spaces that continued to evolve and were conceptualized and reconceptualized across millennia. While *market towns* catering for local produce began to emerge in Palestine in the Chalcolithic Age, under the impact of regional and international trade, several *market cities* or *emporia* (with large markets) began to emerge in Palestine throughout Antiquity. In classical Antiquity the term used for a trading post or market in Palestine and throughout the Near East was *emporium* in both Greek (*ἐμπόριον*) and Latin. The plural *emporia* often referred to a large market. As we shall see in Chapter 3, Aelas (known throughout early Islam as Aylah, modern Aqaba) a famous *emporia* (with large markets) throughout Antiquity began minting its own currency within the Byzantine province of *Palaestina Salutaris* in late Antiquity. Aelas supplied Thebes in Egypt and Gaza in Palestine with aromatics frankincense, myrrh, bitumen from south Arabia; it also supplied Egypt with linen clothing and stone amulets from Palestine.

The urban markets and *ancient market cities* of Palestine evolved across millennia and continue to do so:

1. ***The Marketplace***: being the centre of urban life the marketplace became one of the most distinctive features of the urban landscape and public spaces of Palestine. During classical Antiquity, the marketplace of urban Palestine was influenced by the *Forum*, the multipurpose public space and buildings which included *marketplace* of Rome, which subsequently also developed into a space for social gathering and for cultural celebration, triumphal processions, criminal trials and even gladiatorial matches. In late Antiquity under the Byzantines some of the excesses of the 'pagan' Roman era were banned. However, archaeological evidence for the relative standardization of the urban public spaces and the establishment of large urban *marketplaces* in the cities of Roman Palestine and during the Byzantine period can be found everywhere; at the heart of this standardization of urban life public baths, gymnasiums, theatres, amphitheatres for mass entertainment, civic life institutions and restaurants were not only key features of urban life but also dominated urban spaces – which included Gaza, Caesarea Maritima, Ascalan, Neapolis (Nablus), Aelia Capitolina (Jerusalem), Jericho, Schythopolis (Beisan), Ptolemais (Acre), *Eirenopolis* (Sepphoris, modern Saffuriya) and *Maximianopolis* (Lajjun) – designed to entertain local social elites and ordinary inhabitants, soldiers, travellers, pilgrims, foreign merchants in transit as well as communities of foreign merchant residing in the commercial centres of Palestine. Keeping the urban masses entertained during the Roman and Byzantine periods meant that cheap wine and the numerous amphitheatres

of urban Palestine provided relatively cheap entertainment for the urban masses in the same way modern football grounds popular music venues provide cheap entertainment for modern masses.

2. ***Seasonal Food and Markets:*** seasonal fruits and vegetable were always a big part of the major urban markets of Palestine (ancient, medieval and modern). A fourth-century Roman tax collector named Theophanes who travelled from Egypt to Savia via Palestine and stopped for several days at the coastal city of Ascalon provides information about his daily shopping list and a selection of seasonal food he purchased in the thriving market of Ascalon at the end of July: 'fine loaves, grapes, fresh figs, peaches, apples, lees, reduced wine, plums, ordinary wine, fish sauce, vinegar, gourds, vegetables, eggs and *exatila* (probably fish)' (Weingarten 2015: 400).
3. ***Permanent and Planned Urban Markets:*** there is something modern about the planned urban markets of Palestine in Antiquity, and the modern equivalents are found in the global shopping malls. The growth of domestic and international trade also created permanent urban marketplaces, with permanent specialist shops, which were built in the cities of Palestine during this period of Antiquity and many of these urban market spaces survived in the medieval Islamic cities of Palestine as well as in the modern Arab cities of Palestine. Caesarea Maritima, the capital of Roman and Byzantine Palestine had a large paved permanent rectangular market – a precursor of the modern urban shopping malls – surrounded by Roman-style columns, within which stores were erected, stalls were manned and commercial transactions in wine, olive oil, spices, herbs, textile, meat and vegetables took place. In the fourth century CE the marketplace of Caesarea Maritima (then *Metropolis Palaestina*) – whose major harbour served the Mediterranean maritime trade – had a rich variety of locally manufactured industrial and agricultural products, including wheat, bread, wine, olive oil, dates, rice, cumin, grapes, figs, onion, glass, purple dye, flax growing and linen weaving and of silk textile manufactured from raw silk imported from China (Patrich 2011: 117–19). As we shall see in Chapter 5, during the Roman and Byzantine periods, although raw silk was imported from China until the late fifth and early sixth centuries, high-quality flax, which commended the highest price in Antiquity, was cultivated in Palestine, primarily in the Galilee and Marj Ibn Amer and flax processing into textile fibre centred on the Palestinian city of Beisan (Schythopolis), then one of the most important administrative and textile-making centres of ancient Palestine.
4. ***The Origins of the Urban Covered Market and Shopping Mall:*** shopping is a big part of modern urban life and interestingly the world's oldest shipping mall was constructed in Antiquity by the Syrian architect Apollodorus of Damascus in Rome; a brilliant engineer of Arad Nabataean Arab descent, Apollodorus was credited with buildings in Rome including the Forum and the nearby *Trajan's Market* complex (*Mercatus Traiani*) the world's oldest shopping mall with arcades, shops and apartments built in a multi-level structure. The structure which can still be seen today has inspired the modern shipping malls of today (see Chapter 1).

5. ***The Specialist Markets of Urban Islamic Palestine and Global Trade Systems:*** over time the urban markets of Palestine under the Romans, Byzantines and Muslims evolved and developed *specialist markets* for specific goods traded locally and globally. These specialist markets flourished in Palestine in particular under Islam, something we can still see in the names of several historic specialist markets in Islamic Jerusalem (within the walled city):
   1. *Market of Spice Traders* (*Souq al-'Attarin*); the *Market of Spice (and Perfume) preserved in its modern Arabic name: Souq Al-'Attarin,* the ancient global systems and routes through Palestine of the spices and aromatics trade from south Arabia, India and the Horn of Africa.
   2. *Market of the Cotton Merchants* (*Souq Al-Qattanin*). The historic Arab cotton trade of Jerusalem also survived in the name of one of the oldest Arab families in the city: *Al-Qattana*.
   3. *Olive Oil Market* (*Souq al-Zayt*): Olive oil merchants who specialized in the field of olive oil trade (*Jallabi al-Zyat*) unloaded, weighed and sold olive oil at as specific place in the old city: *Khan al-Zayt* (the 'Caravansarai of the Oil Merchants').
6. ***Arcaded Bazars:*** arcaded marketplaces in the middle of a Middle Eastern city and its open public spaces have been in use in architecture since Roman and Byzantine times. In the Middle Ages Middle Eastern and Arab bazaars in the cities of Palestine were often arcaded rows of shops, or arcaded walkways that provided access to shops and protection from extreme weather conditions especially the extreme summer heat of the region. Also, most Islamic mosques in the Middle Ages include arcaded courtyards. The design of modern enclosed or partially enclosed shopping centres has also been influenced by these Arab marketplaces.
7. ***Weekly Markets:*** As we shall see in Chapter 13, reshaping marketplaces within the context of Islam in the Middle Ages, and the emergence of the caravanserais within the context of seaports and urban and rural marketplaces, beginning with the Umayyad period in the early seventh century, is much in evidence. There were a variety of markets in Palestine, included covered markets and weekly markets; one historically famous weekly market was the *Market Khan* of the caravanserai (Near Mount Tabor), which for nearly three hundred years between 1581 and the late nineteenth century held its weekly market, initially on Monday, and later on Thursday, attracted thousands of merchants and shoppers from across urban and rural and even from neighbouring Arab countries. In the mid-nineteenth century, this market was described as follows:

On Monday of each week a great fair is held at the khans, when, for a few hours, the scene is very lively and picturesque. These gatherings afford an excellent opportunity to observe Syrian manners, customs, and costumes, and to become acquainted with the character and quality of Syrian productions. Thousands of people assemble from all parts of the country, either to sell, trade or purchase. Cotton is brought in bales from Nablus; barley, and wheat, and sesamum, and Indian corn from Huleh, the Hauran, and Esdraelon [Mar Ibn Amer]. From Gilead and Bashan [Transjordan], and the surrounding districts, come horses and donkeys, cattle and flocks, with cheese, *leben, semen*, honey and similar articles. Then there are miscellaneous matters, such as chicken and eggs, figs, raisins, apples, melons, grapes and all sorts of fruits and vegetables in season. The pedlars open their packages of tempting fabrics, the jeweller is there with his trinkets; the tailor with his ready-made garments; the shoemaker with his stock, from rough, hairy sandals to yellow and red Morocco boots; the farrier is there with his tools, nails, and flat iron shoes, and drives a prosperous business for a few hours; and so does the saddler, with his coarse sacks and gaily trimmed cloths. And thus it is with all the arts and occupations known to this people .... But long before sunset not a soul of this busy throng remains on the spot. All return home, or to take refuge in some neighbouring village.

(Thomson 1859, Vol.2: 152–3)

8. ***Market Superintendents and Inspectors:*** In Antiquity Hellenization processes in Palestine added another layer to the toponym of Palestine, without necessarily replacing the strong indigenous culture of the country and its manor cities. The large urban marketplaces constructed in the cities of Roman and Byzantine Palestine were called *agoras*. (*ἀγορά*), meaning 'market' or gathering place, modelled on the historic public spaces of the Greek city-state (*polis*); these marketplaces were supervised officials known as *agoranomos*, or market superintendents, who regulated goods and supervised prices. The hundreds of weights uncovered through archaeological excavations throughout Roman and Byzantine Palestine, with the seal of the *agoranomos*, serve as proof of the large-scale of economic activity in the cities of Palestine in Antiquity (Safrai 1994, 2003: 134).

   Market Overseer and regulating markets: Chapter 9 will explore the role and work of *agoranomos* (ἀγορανόμος) and *muhtasib* institutions in Byzantine and Islamic Palestine and from late Antiquity until the modern period. The *muhtasibs* were throughout medieval Islam the institution of the market inspectors of urban Palestine. They regulated market prices and ensured quality of products: this institution will be discussed in Chapter 9 within the context of the moral economy of urban commerce and market regulations in Islamic Palestine. Overall, the guiding principle of commercial urbanism marketplaces and town planning throughout the early centuries of Islamic Palestine (and Syria) followed some patterns of classical orthogonal plans of urbanism and marketplaces in late Antiquity Palestine (Pahlitzsch 2009: 125–52). But Islamic Palestine also introduced some key urban innovations that transformed the multifaceted urban life in Palestine by linking commercial activities, including urban markets and urban caravansaries to charitable *waqf* foundations in the cities of Palestine line with Islamic religious conception of moral economy and the maintenance of charitable social and religious institutions.

9. ***Great Mosques, Markets and Merchants' Carvansarais: Urban Planning and Urban Spaces in Islamic Palestine:*** Overall, the guiding principle of commercial urbanism marketplaces and town planning throughout the early centuries of

Islamic Palestine (and Syria) followed some patterns of classical orthogonal plans of urbanism and marketplaces in late Antique Palestine (Pahlitzsch 2009: 127). However Islamic Palestine also introduced some key urban innovations and urban spaces that contributed to the transformation of urban life in the country, Urban planning and spaces the cities of Nablus and al-Ramla under Islam in the Middle Ages the urban markets were not prerequisite for the Islamic towns and cities of Palestine but also went and in hand with town planning great mosques supported by these markets and the great Islamic style merchants caravans of the Middle Ages; all these innovations; the 'Great Mosques' (sacred spaces); the urban markets and merchants' caravanserais (secular spaces) – which also functioned as commercial centres in the city – were constructed in close proximity to each other and as mutually supporting multifaceted realms of urban life and were often linked to Islamic charitable (*waqfs*) institutions in the city. Moreover despite their proximity to the urban markets the Great urban mosques of Palestine were often designed as 'cities within cities' surrounded by inner walls and their sacred spaces often important public libraries and Islamic madrasas/colleges; these spaces also often functioned as tranquil spaces and as a respite from the hassle and bustle of the crowded urban markets.

10. ***The Ancient Crafts of Goldsmithing and the Gold Markets of Urban Palestine under Islam and Women's Economic Agency:*** Under the Byzantines, the *solidi* gold coins minted in the city of Gaza, became known as the *Gold Standard of Gaza* and applied to trade and payments in Palestine and beyond (see Chapter 6); under Islam in the Middle Ages 'The Arabs, as heirs to the Sassanid Empire, effectively engrossed the greater part of the world's gold production' (Blanchard, Vol. 1-2, 2001 and Vol. 3, 2005). However gold production under Islam fluctuated and alternated with silver, and the Islamic empires could only draw on intermittent gold supplies from certain critical regions in western Asia, while subsequently much of the focus of gold mining shifted to Africa and 'Sahelian Way' thus benefitting the Arab gold trade of north Africa; this route 'was characterised by an active commerce in salt, copper, slaves and above all gold, which by this pre-desert trade route was carried by Arab merchants to Egypt' (Blanchard, Vol.1, 2001: 145). In Palestine, gold coins were 'struck in Palestine' in the city of al-Ramla, for the first time in the history of the country under Islam (Masalha 2018). Under the Mamluks and Ottoman the cities of Nablus, Gaza and Jerusalem also developed *gold-smithing industries* and established specialist *gold markets*. While selling gold jewellery at these urban gold markets began to flourish in historical cities in Palestine since the Mamluk period and there is still a functioning historic goldsmithing industry and gold market in Nablus (Moors 1998: 208–23; Schaeublin 2023: 93). Another famous gold market was established in the city of Gaza in 1476. In the late thirteenth century the Mamluks had made Gaza the capital of a province in Palestine and the province bore the name of the city, *Mamlakat Ghazzah* (the Province of Gaza) (Masalha 2018); the city's gold market reflected this political and economic rise again of Gaza under the Mamluks and the importance of the city in the caravan trade routes from Damascus to medieval Cairo. A narrow covered gold *souq* in the old city of Gaza, near the

Great Umari Mosque of Gaza, the market was established by a prominent Gaza merchant, Shaykh Shams al-Din al-Hamsi. Selling gold jewel to newly engaged and wedded couples, the market survived into the modern period (Irving 2011: 264; Patel and Aburawa 2016) and purchasing gold jewellery became the premier and most reliable form of saving in pre-modern and modern Palestine. Often the inferior economic power of women is cited as the main cause for their social and political subordination to men. However historically women under Islam were not deprived of economic and commercial agency and the focus on selling and buying gold jewel in the urban gold markets of Palestine under Islam became an important commercial asset for women and an import tool in their actual social empowerment:

> to many women in Jabal Nablus [and in urban Palestine as a whole] the gold jewellery they receive as part of their dower [at the time of marriage] has been an important economic resource [for women] ... a focus on gold as a major economic asset may reveal the possibilities for women to act as an economic agent of sorts.
>
> (Moors 1998: 211; also Schaeublin 2023: 93)

Indigenous agency versus imperial chronologies and settler-colonial narratives

History is often written by the victors, the colonizer and occupiers. In modern times much of the history of Palestine is based on, or derived, from imperial chronologies and imperial conquests – beginning with the ancient Egyptian, Assyrian, Persian, Greek, Roman, Byzantine empires and through the Umayyad, Abbasid, Fatimid, Mamluk, Ottoman and British Empire – with almost complete disregard for the indigenous agency of Palestine and Palestinians. Furthermore, Palestine, being subjected to ethnic-cleansing and settler-colonial occupation over seventy-seven years, the real ancient history of the country is often erased and replaced by newly concocted myth-narratives created by European Zionist settler-colonizers. The newly invented history of Palestine is often presented as a chronology of imperial conquests and as disconnected themes and, crucially, and as a history of colonial domination with little regard to the indigenous agency of Palestine and the Palestinians. Consequently the real cultural, intellectual and historical significance of Palestine and its ancient cities and towns to the ancient world's trade systems and trade routes are silenced and replaced by mythical biblical stories and legends (Masalha 2018; 2022). This book seeks to address the lacuna in the historical writing, with special reference to the indigenous urban life and commercial geography of Palestine, its ancient global trade and its indigenous economic and industrial heritage.

Furthermore often themes such as Palestine's internationally famous Gaza Wine of Antiquity, Gaza's famous Rhetorical School of the Byzantine period, the innovative Water Clock of Gaza, the urban planning of Julian of Ascalon and his applied

Metrology, the scientific study of measurements and its economics, and, generally, the urban sophistication of Palestine under the Byzantines are treated by West and Israeli historians are separate themes of *imperial chronology* and history with no intrinsic connection between them or to the indigenous agency of Palestine and the Palestinians; this volume aims at challenging this colonial approach and exploring the historical evolution of Palestine as country and distinct geo-political entity interacting with Palestinian indigenous agency. The work will show extraordinary intellectual, material and scientific heritage of the 'cities of learning' of Byzantine Palestine, that is, Gaza, Nablus (Neapolis), *Caesarea Palaestina*, Ascalon ('Asqalan), Jerusalem (Al-Quds), Beisan (Scythopolis), provided one of the many cultural routes to the Golden Age of Islamic Palestine from the eighth to the eleventh century and during the Mamluk from 1260 to 1516 (Masalha 2022).

As we shall see in Chapters 12 to 17, the economy history of Palestine in the modern period, from the eighteenth century until the Palestine Nakba of 1948, was a product dynamic growth in, initially, international trade of Palestinian raw cotton and rapid economic expansion. The spectacular rise of three major Palestinian industries: the raw cotton industry of the eighteenth and early nineteenth centuries, the soap industry of Nablus and the citrus industry of coastal Palestine were largely oriented towards foreign exports. This work will show how periods of mercantile expansion in Palestine, both in ancient and modern Palestine, led to the phenomenal growth of Palestinian towns and cities and the country's major urban centres.

Indeed, trade (regional and international, maritime and land) did to ancient societies (as well as Palestine) what the industrial revolution did to modern societies. International trade, on land and by sea, subverted cultural conservatism and insularity and transmitted goods, ideas and key technologies across languages and to vast areas and societies which were not directly linked. The direct evidence from Palestine shows how international trade in late Antiquity expanded and transformed the urban centres of the country, and allowed for the emergence and development of local industries. For instance, the evidence for the Trans-Arabia-Red Sea trade with China, which passed through Gaza, or the size of the industrial area of Byzantine Gaza suggests high capital investment in the international famous wine industry of the city by both state and private investors, with the manufactory processing plants processing wine from the Naqab, the southern region of Palestine.

Also, as we shall see in Chapters 1 and 3, the significant profits from the Trans-Arabia-Gaza-Mediterranean trade helped finance not only the academies of Athens and Alexandria but also contributed to the financing of the Rhetorical School of Gaza during Byzantine era, an internationally famous college in the fifth to sixth centuries that transformed Gaza into the premier 'university town' of Palestine and the 'Athens of Asia' – a city within an extraordinarily relaxed setting and flourishing cultural and intellectual urban environment (Masalha 2022).

Palestine's extensive global trade allowed for the investment of revenues in buildings, commercial and public institutions and school and even higher education's institution in key cities in the countries. The Madaba Map shows the scale of urban Palestine and the expansion of urban public spaces across the country. Also global trade in high-quality agricultural produce and manufactured goods also allowed for the emergence of common trade names, and trademarks of Palestinian identity, such as Gaza Wine (*Vinum Gazetum*) in late Antiquity Palestine, or *Al-Khalil Glassware* (زجاج الخليل) in the Middle Ages, and *Nablus Soap* and *Jaffa Orange* in modern Palestine. Other famous modern Palestinian brands include the Zalatuimo's sweets manufacturers of Jerusalem (see Chapter 17).

The Roman occupation of Palestine brought about the expansion of the global trade routes of Palestine and the emergence of some 'modern-sounding' famous Palestinian trademarks. First there was the globally famous Palestinian textile brand: the linen of Schythopolis (Beisan) in the Roman and Byzantine periods. During the Roman and Byzantine periods the city of Schythopolis, the capital of the province of *Palaestina Secunda* under the Byzantines and one of the most important industrial and textile centres of ancient Palestine, whose archaeological remains began in the Chalcolithic Age, benefited from the high-quality flax of Galilee, cultivated for the production of textiles (discussed in Chapter 5). The fine linen and textile of Schythopolis was right at the top of the *of maximum prices* (Latin: *Edictum de Pretiis Rerum Venalium),* an edict concerning the sale price of goods issued by Roman Emperor Diocletian in 301 CE. This *Price Edict* criticizes monopolies and sets maximum prices (and wages) for all important goods and services during the Eastern Empire Diocletian reign. In this *Price Edict* the linen and clothing-manufacturers of Scythopolis are authorized to ask for the highest price for the high-quality of tunics and other clothes made of linen in this Palestinian city.

A high-quality Palestine textile industry was not confined to the Roman and Byzantine periods. As shall see in Chapter 12, the Palestine textile industry expanded under Islam in the Middle Ages, especially during the Fatimid and Mamluk periods, and this expansion underscored the important role Palestinian ports and port cities played in the context of foreign textile export, especially during the Fatimids' and Mamluk dominance of maritime trade in the eastern Mediterranean and the natural indigo dye industry, used in Palestinian costumes, which was made in plantations in the Jordan valley.

The spread of new radical religious ideas often accompanied periods of huge economic and commercial growth coupled with social upheavals. No less important is the fact that both Christianity and Islam (to a large extent) rose and spread historically, as we shall see in Chapters 5 and 6, to vast areas through and under the impact of the expanding Middle Eastern global trade routes and activities. The rise of both Christianity and Islam took place not during periods of economic stagnation but against the background of huge growth in international trade and economic activities coupled with social upheavals and spread of new radical ideas. Christianity, in particular, spread in Palestine and Syria, and especially in the coastal towns and cities of the eastern Mediterranean during a hugely dynamic period of economic and commercial growth and the rise of the global wine trade of Palestine and the Levant; wine production was theologically sanctified and economically encouraged by Christianity in Byzantine Palestine, partly because Palestine's international trade in wine was on the increase during the Roman period and the export of Palestinian wine became phenomenally lucrative in late Antiquity. Indeed Near Eastern (Palestinian and Syrian) Christian wine merchants during the late Roman and Byzantine eras were influential in maritime cities such as *Maiumas Gaza*, Alexandra, Ascalon and Caesarea Maritima and even in Italian cities such as Naples; it is remarkable that, with the rise of the Palestinian Mediterranean wine trade, port cities in Palestine such as *Maiumas Gaza* and *Maiuma Ascalan* (the port cities of Gaza and Ascalon) had their own separate bishops – in addition to the bishops of Gaza and Ascalan (Ring et al. 1996: 287).

Modernity and the expansion in modern transport contributed to the rise of modern Palestinian agricultural industries and agri-industrial products such the Nablus Soap industries and citrus industries, which were subsumed under the common trade name: Jaffa Orange. Moreover, since ancient times the costs of maritime shipping were always cheaper than the costs of the long-distance land trade of Palestine (and through the transit routes of Palestine) by donkeys (in Bronze Age) and by Arabian camels (in the Iron Age). More than two and a half thousands years later, in the Ottoman period, camels continued to transport Palestinian olive oil and soap manufactured in Jerusalem and Nablus to various towns and cities in Palestine and to neighbouring countries (Cohen 2002: 77–85) and in the early twentieth century, following the introduction of modern railways in Palestine in the late nineteenth century, we began to see caravans of camels involved in the Palestine citrus industry for export overseas. Camel loaded boxes of Jaffa Orange and waiting for commercial trains at Jaffa city train station to be loaded on trains to Port Said in Egypt and then shipped to international markets in Europe as Jaffa Orange was gaining wide international fame, in the same way the camel caravans were transporting luxurious spices and aromatics across southern Palestine from Petra to Gaza during the Bronze Age. Furthermore, the development of the steam engine in modern times and steamships and steam-powered vessels opened up new maritime trade routes and trade globalization by long-distance commercial steamships in the nineteenth century. These technological developments in modern maritime trade and shipping had an impact on key urban centres in Palestine. Generally speaking, the modern Mediterranean maritime trade with Europe contributed phenomenally to the expansion of the urban space and social, economic, cultural, educational and intellectual life of the coastal Mediterranean cities in Palestine, especially Jaffa, Haifa, Gaza and (to a lesser extent) Acre in the modern period, especially in the second half of the nineteenth century and first half of the twentieth century. At the time, historic Palestinian urban centres of the Galilee hinterland such as Tiberias and Safad remained lagging behind in social, economic and educational developments (Abbasi 2023).

This work further explores the commercial history of Palestine across millennia within its evolving wider social, economic and commercial environment of 'two Fertile Crescents': the northern and southern. Chapter 2 shows how the copper mining industry of Sinai and southern Palestine (the Naqab) during the Bronze Age was closely linked to the rise of the Bronze Age cities of both Egypt and Palestine. Chapter 3 shows how the Trans-Arabian Spice trade and frankincense trade from Yemen and Dhofar (in modern Oman) impacted the creation of trading ancient kingdoms of southern Palestine. The 'Petra-Gaza Road' became one of the most trading routes of the ancient Middle East (Cohen 1982: 240–7). Chapter 3 will explore the rise of *spice cities* on the 1,500-mile *incense routes* and Nabataean caravan trail that ran all the way from Yemen, through Petra, into the Naqab, finally ending at the port city of Gaza (Maimas) and the emergence of urban planning and *melting pot cities* in southern Palestine along the spice routes of Petra-Gaza.

Chapter 3 discusses the tanneries and the textile industries of the Roman province of Syria-Palestine. Chapter 6 shows how much of the rise of the viticulture and wine industries of Palestine during the Byzantine period was closely linked to Palestine's foreign export to Egypt. Other chapters also explore the development of close economic and commercial links of Palestine and specific cities in Palestine within the wider ancient Middle Eastern and Arab surroundings. Also various chapters will show how trading cities and commercial centres in Palestine which developed export-oriented economies hosted large communities of foreign merchants, and the presence of these foreign merchant communities had an impact on the demography and social and cultural diversity of these cities; Gaza city had many Egyptian *wine merchants* in classical and late Antiquity; al-Ramla hosted Egyptian *textile merchants* throughout early Islam; and the Palestinian cotton-producing towns of Lydda, Ramla and Acre hosted Venetian communities of cotton merchants during the late Mamluk period (Ashtor 2014: 253–61) and late Italian and French cotton merchants resided in Acre in the late eighteenth and early nineteenth centuries.

The work furthermore shows how specific Palestinian cities often developed strong commercial relationship with neighbouring Arab cities of the Near East. For instance, Nablus connected trade routes throughout history, became known as 'Little Damascus', for its strong commercial relations with Damascus for many centuries during the Mamluk period (1260–1516) and Ottoman period (1516–1918) in Palestine.

The famous caravanserai, the *Caravanserai of the Merchants* (*Khan al-Tujjar*) located in the old city of Nablus and at the heart the commercial centre of the city, was built in the sixteenth century at the beginning of the Ottoman rule in Palestine. The cities of Gaza and Ascalon had strong trading relationship with Egypt since the Bronze Age. And Al-Khalil (Hebron) developed strong trading relations with Al-Fustat (medieval Cairo) and exported much of its glassware products to Egypt for many centuries until the modern period. Under Islam Palestine remained an important country for transit trade, connecting both the Mashreq (East) and Maghrib (West) parts of the Islamic empire, and providing trade routes for the regional trade between Syria and Egypt. Chapter 13 will explore the establishment of numerous caravanserais (khans) and some of the most spectacular urban merchants' khans of medieval Palestine.

Archaeological discoveries and new paradigms

Much of Palestinian historical writings on the economic and commercial history of Palestine have been framed within a modern nationalist perspective that focuses on 'national' iconic trade brands such as Jaffa Orange, al-Khalil Glassware, Nablus Soap and Nablus Kunafa and Zalatimo's Sweets, trademarks which have become part of the folk tales and iconography of modern Palestine. However, there is no Palestinian social or collective memory of some of the important ancient common trade names in Palestine such as Gaza Wine or the textile industry of Beisan (Schythopolis) – iconic and famous trade brands which flourished during the Roman and Byzantine periods. Hardly any Palestinian is aware of the *Water Clock of Gaza*, a key treasure of Palestinian creativity in Antiquity and a clock which symbolized the immense technological progress of urban Palestine in late Antiquity – a water clock that had a major impact on the historical development of clocks, in general, and the water clocks of medieval classical Islam.

Equally significant is the fact that Western collective memory often associates Palestine not with highly developed ancient cities with global trade connections but with arcadia: a country of shepherds and sheep, of mountainous topography and sparse population of pastoralists with romantic New Testament landscape, while Israeli-Zionist collective memory and academic institutions have systematically weaponized the Old Testament and utilized *biblical archaeology*, a retrospective settler-colonial project, to silence the ancient history of Palestine and dispossess and disinherit the Palestinians from their ancient ancestral homeland.

Yet, in contrast to the silences of collective memory, extensive archaeological discoveries have shown that in ancient Palestine, the Roman and Byzantine eras included internationally renowned *Vinum Gazetum*, or Gaza Wine, a white sweet luxurious wine was shipped in large quantities from the port of Gaza throughout the Mediterranean and to cities in modern France, German and well as London. As we shall see in Chapter 6, Palestinian wine was also packaged in ceramic *Gaza amphorae*, an internationally famous Palestinian bag-shaped amphorae (bulging amphorae), a long, bullet-shaped transport jars made them suitable for long-distance wine transport on ships across the Mediterranean as well as land transport from and to south Arabia and Yemen (Ray and Salles 1996: 28l: Vroom 2018: 648). Archaeologists have also excavated and recovered huge numbers of these *Gaza jars* as far away as France, Spain, Germany, Britain, Crimea, Carthage (in north Africa), south Arabia, and Nubia (modern Sudan) ('Gaza' in Ameling et al. 2014, Vol. III: 421).

Ancient global trade in Palestinian wine and other locally produced merchandise was a major source of income for Palestinian, Egyptian, Phoenician, Syrian and Greek merchant communities and the inhabitants of the coastal cities of the eastern Mediterranean in Antiquity. Furthermore, the ancient seaports of Palestine, Lebanon and Syria offered merchants the services of skilled ship-owners and highly skilled port workers (Sartre 2005: 258).

Using mountains of modern archaeological discoveries, this book aims at debunking collective memory myths and recovering and reclaiming the economic and commercial history of ancient Palestine and retracing the genealogy of its commercial geography and its long-distance trade routes. Also, the archaeological discoveries of vast quantities of gold and silver coins at some historic trading urban centres in Palestine give us a new insight into the impact of the international trade and key trade routes of Palestine on the evolution of financial and urban centres in the country.

From the ancient to the modern: The concept of *Polis* and continuities of urban Palestine

In late Roman and Byzantine Palestine, with its high urban density and sophistication, twenty-five cities in the country enjoyed a municipal status within the full sense of the term *polis* – whole cities had their own walls and issued their own coins indicating a degree of autonomy (Broshi 2001: 99–100). Most of these cities of classical Antiquity also had planned colonnaded streets (Burns 2007), while some of them – such as Aelia Capitolina (Jerusalem) and the former Nabataea city of Oboda in the Negev (see Chapter 3) – also had 'akrópolis' (ἀκρόπολις from *ákros*, 'top most' and *pólis*, 'city'), an upper city (a city within a city) with great classical style temples and architecture. In the case of Jerusalem the Greek-style acropolis temple, surrounded by walls, was constructed by the Hellenized Arab-Jewish King Herod in the first century BCE. While Jerusalem was King Herod's religious capital, his administrative and political capital was Caesarea Maritima, which for centuries under the Romans and Byzantines served as *Metropolis Palaestina* and one of the greatest Palestinian *Poleis* in Antiquity (see Chapters 5 and 6).

However, there is no pure concept of the Greek term *polis* (Greek: plural *poleis* *πόλεις*) or *city*. This pure concept of the *polis* as an egalitarian democracy is a product of modern European imagination. The overwhelming majority in classical Athens, for instance, were women and slaves, who were not treated as full citizens, and at the height of its classical period the 'Athenian democracy' was confined to a minority of male voters. However, the *polis* evolved historically and spread around the Mediterranean region from the fourth century BCE onwards during the Greco-Egyptian Ptolemaic period, with its Egyptian-based hybrid culture; the term also hybridized and incorporated multi-layered indigenous cultural identities and created hybrid urban identities in both Egypt and the wider Near East. In Palestine the term *polis* represented that hybrid urban identity and incorporated Hellenistic and indigenous Palestinian, economic, monetary and cultural traditions and practices. Furthermore, barter was widespread in Ptolemaic Egypt and Palestine, and with the minting of currency and cash supplies limited, barter was aided by the use of credit and brokerage. All these economic strategies: barter, credit and currency were used to price goods and services in the ancient economy, trade and traditional industries of Palestine.

The size of the economy of ancient Palestine did not produce and could not support the creation of mega imperial cities such as Nineveh, Persepolis, Alexandria, Rome or Istanbul. For instance, it took a vast imperial such as the Roman Empire to feed an imperial city like Rome, which at its height housed one million inhabitants and, as we shall see in Chapter 6, consumed vast quantities of Palestinian wine (also known as Gaza Wine) and varieties of wine from all over the Roman Empire. But the economy of ancient Palestine, which combined local agriculture and foreign trade, produced great urban centres and cities many of which, under the impact of Hellenization, also acquired the Greek term *polis* in Antiquity and several of these cities minted local currencies – currencies whose value and style were influenced politics and cultures of regional powers.

Under the impact of Hellenization of the urban centres of Palestine in Classical and Late Antiquity, the Greek term *polis* (or city) was used widely and applied to a wide range of towns and cities in Palestine. This wide variety of designation of *poleis* included:

1. ***The Palestine Pentapolis:*** This was a retrospective collective designation in classical Antiquity of the earlier late Bronze Age and Iron Age 'five Palestinian city-states', or the *Philistines Pentapolis*. A *pentapolis* (Greek: πεντα-*penta*-, 'five' and πόλις 'city') is a geo-political and institutional grouping of five cities. The term *Palestine Pentapolis* was applied to the five cities of the ancient Philistines during the Iron Age: Gaza, Ascalon, Isdud (Ashdod), Gaza, Ekron and Gath. These *city-states* of the *Palestine Pentapolis* were a federation of five powerful *city-states* which emerged during the late Bronze Age and flourished in particular during the Iron Age. Generally, these city-states were dominated by rulers who were surrounded by powerful elite ruling over a socially stratified class society.
2. ***Metropolis Palaestinea (the Metropolis Capital of Palestine)***, or the capital city of Palestine was Caesarea Maritima, a capital city of Palestine during the Roman and Byzantine periods.
3. ***Metropolis:*** *This term* was applied to secular regional and administrative capitals in Byzantine Palestine as well as to the major cities which represented the Orthodox Church hierarchy in the three-in-one provinces of Palestine under the Byzantine: *Palaestina Prima, Palaestina Secunda* and *Palaestina Tertia* (Masalha 2018: 135–50): *Scythopolis* (Beisan), *Metropolis of Palaestinea Secunda*, Petra, *Metropolis* of *Palaestinea Tertia* under the Byzantines, and Caesarea Maritima as *Metropolis Palaestina Prima*.
4. ***Official Municipal Status and Regional Capitals:*** The term *polis* was also applied to Palestinian cities that had acquired the full and formal *municipal status* of *polis* during the late Roman and Byzantine periods. These included *Eleutheropolis* (Beit Jibrin) and *Diospolis* (Lydda) during the late Roman and Byzantine periods, and the name *Eirenopolis* ('city of peace') was given to the Palestinian Galilean city of Sepphoris (*Σέπφωρις*; the modern Arab town of Saffuriya until 1948) during the Roman period. These were relatively large cities, such as *Neapolis* (Nablus); *Scythopolis* (Beisan), *Diospolis* (Lydda), *Eleutheropolis* (Bayt Jibrin), Casearea-Maritima, Gaza, Eusa in the Nagab (in the province of *Palaestina Tertia*). In both classical and late Antiquity, the urban life of these cities acquired many of the most sophisticated public buildings and cultural institutions in Palestine: public buildings and public amenities, magnificent architecture, large urban markets, temples and churches, schools, libraries, entertainments and sport facilities, amphitheatres and racecourses, bath-houses, courtyards, mosaic floors with colourful geometric patterns, water pools, dams regular water supplies and numerous wine and olive presses. Much of the large investment in these large urban centres such as the construction of theatres, racecourses and public baths was undertaken with local initiatives and the support of the local merchant communities, with imperial support under the Romans and Byzantines

often confined to the maintenance of garrisons, military fortifications and the construction of road systems.

5. ***Akrópolis*** (ἀκρόπολις *from ákros*, 'topmost' and *pólis*, 'city'): the term *Akrópolis* was not confined to classical Athens; under the impact of Hellenization, this term was applied loosely in some cities in Palestine to describe 'topmost city' or a upper city (a city within a city) in which classical style large temples were built.
6. ***Krokodeilon Polis***: The extent of Hellenization can also be seen from the fact that an ancient stream in the centre of Palestine was called *Krokodeilon polis*, 'Crocodiles City' (also spelt *Crocodilopolis*), or 'Crocodiles Stream', known in Arabic as Tell al-Milat (lit. 'Mortar Mound'). Today this is an archaeological mound on the Mediterranean coast in the vicinity of the modern Arab town of Jisr al-Zarka.
7. ***Historic Urban Continuities of the Polis City in Palestine***: Many of these cities that had acquired the formal *municipal* title of *polis* in Antiquity continued to flourish as major trading centres in Palestine under Islam in the Middle Ages. *Maximianopolis* acquired the formal title of municipality (given in honour Roman emperor *Maximianus*; *c*.250–310 CE). The rise of the city of Maximianopolis (Greek: Μαξιμιανόπολις) – later renamed *Lajjun* under Islam – located one kilometre south of the remains of the Bronze Age city-state of Megiddo is hardly surprising. Both cities: Megiddo and Maximianopolis/Lajjun rose in the most fertile region in Palestine: Marj Ibn Amer (Esdarleon Valley) and contained key stations on the most important international trade routes in Palestine: the international highway from Syria to Egypt. Maximianopolis emerged as an important city in the Byzantine province of *Palaestina Secunda*; during the same period it was a seat of a Bishop in the All-Palestine Orthodox Church; under Islam in Palestine the important city of *Lajjun* was located sixteen kilometres northwest of the modern city of Jenin. The city continued to flourish as a key station in Palestine along the Damascus-medieval Cairo trade route and a capital of a sub-district in Palestine, thus effectively preserving the formal municipal status of the city as *polis* under the Byzantines. The Palestinian Arabic place name also preserved an early Roman legion garrison town in *Syria-Palestine* province called 'Legio'. During the Mamluk period the city served as an important station in the Arab postal service (*barid*) and during the Ottoman period Lajjun was the capital of a district that bore its name. Although the Arab village Lajjun was depopulated by Israel in 1948, Maximianopolis (Lajjun) prospered as an important urban centre and a key trade station in Palestine for nearly two millennia, only to be replaced by the nearby city of Jenin as a regional capital from the late Ottoman period onwards. After 1948 many of the Palestinian refugee inhabitants of Lajjun subsequently settled in the nearby Arab town of Umm al-Fahm.
8. ***From Garrison Towns to Commercial Urban Centres***: Some of the historic cities of Palestine began their urban life as garrison towns. This includes Maximianopolis (later the Arab town Lajjun) a Roman legion garrison town in *Syria-Palaestine* province called 'Legio' which refers to the Roman legion stationed

there. In the third century, the town was renamed *Maximianopolis* ('City of Maximian') and a Kurnub (Mampsis) an important Nabataean caravan station on the 'Incense Road' in the Naqab and later a Roman garrison town and a city under the Byzantines, which appeared on the Madaba Mosaic Floor Map (see Chapter 3). Memphis became a major urban and financial centre in Byzantine Palestine. The city of Jenin (today with a population of 60,000) began its rise as an urban centre during the Mamluk period as a major garrison town, with Mamluk emirs (military commanders) and troops defending the Galilee stationed in the city. Earlier in the 1220s, the Arab geographer Yaqut al-Hamawi described Jenin as 'a small and beautiful town, lying between [the cities] of Nablus and Beisan, in the [province] of Jund al-Urdun [of Palestine]. There is much water, and many springs are found here, and often have I visited it' (Le Strange 1890: 564). Today it serves as the administrative, commercial and financial centre for the towns and villages of the northern West Bank.

9. ***Continuities of Palestine from Ancient Metropolitan Bishoprics to Modern Palestinian Mutrans:*** Several ancient Palestinian cities – some of which were provincial capitals in Byzantine Palestine – including Caesarea Maritima, (Caesarea Palaestina), Beisan (Schythopolis), Eusa, Sebastia and Jerusalem were ecclesiastical seats of a *metropolitan* bishopric and this senior ecclesiastical position has survived in modern Palestine in the form of the term *Mutran, an Arabized* Greek term for metropolitan. One contemporary example is the Mutran (archbishop) Atallah Hanna, the Archbishop of Sebastia in the (All-Palestine) Greek Orthodox Church of Jerusalem. Found in the Bronze Age and located some twelve kilometres northwest of the ancient city of Nablus and becoming a major regional urban centre in Antiquity, the town of Sebastia (from Greek *sebastos*, 'venerable') is thought to be one of the oldest continuously inhabited ancient places in the West Bank, Palestine.

Gradually in Antiquity, we can see the phenomenal growth of urbanization by the fact that, under the impact of Hellenization from the fourth century BCE onwards, and throughout the Roman and Byzantine periods, a large number of Palestinian cities were described or named as *polis,* top of which were the *Philistine Pentapolis*: Gaza, Ascalon, Ashdod, Ekron and Gath. Another important city of ancient Philistine, which was described as *polis,* was Timna, to the west of Jerusalem. This city should not be confused, with Timna, the Bronze Age copper-smelting town in *Wadi Araba*, to the north of modern-day Aqaba.

Also the Palestine *poleis (cities)* continued to evolve during the Roman and Byzantine period, and with the growth of education, schools and commerce, the *polis* became known as a *body of citizens* (often associated with male citizens); it was often meant autonomous cities (or *city-states*) ruled by their bodies of citizens. Also, with the development of governance in classical Antiquity often the Palestine *polis* often meant a large city that dominated and incorporated in its administrative and religious jurisdiction a large number of villages either surrounding the city or located in the same district.

Like their neighbouring Phoenician trading coastal city-states, the coalition of Palestinian city-states and kingdoms, or the *Philistine Pentapolis*, with their considerable maritime trade and their shipbuilding industry and metal production workshops and their international aromatics and spice trade with south Arabia and beyond, developed as powerful entities and a Mediterranean powerhouse of commercial and economic activities in Bronze Age Palestine.

The name Palestine is found in Egyptian sources from the late Bronze Age. However, following the integration of the ancient Philistines and their coastal cities with other population groups in Palestine, the name *Peleset*, or *Philistia*, became the dominant toponym for the region as a whole and other names used for this country of the southern Levant, such as Djahi, Retenu and Cana'an, all gave way to *Palestine*, the name most commonly used in eighth and seventh - century BCE Assyrian inscriptions. Using a 'part for the whole' designation, Palestine came to refer to the greater region (Palashtu, Piliste or Philistia), literally the 'land of the Peleset', of the southern Levant. This wider conception of Palestine included not only the Mediterranean coastal cities of Philistia and the hinterland: Gaza, Ekron, Gath, Ashdod, Ascalon, Timna and Tantur, but served also for the interior of the country and gradually as a wider designation for the whole area from Lebanon to Egypt. Interestingly also, almost all the toponyms of the cities of *Philistia*: Gaza, Askelon ('Asqalan), Ashdod (Isdud), Tantur (Tantura), Gath (Jat), Ekron ('Aqir) survived into the modern era and were preserved in the modern Palestinian Arabic names and were mostly depopulated by Israel in 1948.

International trade (both maritime and land trade) was central to the rise and fame of the *Philistine Pentapolis* (mostly maritime cities or 'cities of the sea'). These cities flourished on the maritime trade and formed a geo-political entity for political, military, trading and monetary reasons. International trade contributed to the economic, monetary, political and institutional integration of much of Palestine in ancient times. And for over half a millennium in the Iron Age the federated city-states of the *Philistine Pentapolis* developed the first monetary system in Palestine and dominated much of the coastal region of Palestine from Al-Arish in the south to Tantur (modern Tantura) in the north and their hinterlands. As we shall see in Chapter 1, the geo-political location of the *Philistine Pentapolis* allowed them to benefit from the hugely lucrative Trans-Arabian and south Arabia spice trade from India and through Gaza and Ascalon to the Mediterranean world.

Subsequently the monetary and financial system of Palestine was influenced by different multiple traditions and multiple regimes; for instance, under the Egyptian Ptolemaic rule trading Palestinian cities such as Ascalon and Gaza minted silver Greek *tetradrachm* (*τετράδραχμον*). The famous *tetradrachm of Ascalon* featured the draped bust of Cleopatra VII, the famous Hellenistic pharaoh and queen of the Ptolemaic kingdom of Egypt, who ruled from 51 to 30 BCE and was one of the most important rulers of the ancient world. Ascalon, a major financial centre in Palestine under the Ptolemies, issued *tetradrachm of Ascalon* in 50/49 and 39/38 BCE by following the Ptolemaic traditions with the famous portrait of Cleopatra VII on the obverse (the head or principal design) and an eagle on the reverse (Fotopoulos 2006: 274).

Town and Gown: Regional trade, economic prosperity and *Cities of Learning* in Palestine

For millennia Palestine functioned as a transit country for people, ideas and international trade and exchanges of intellectual ideas and technologies and its transnational highways, linking three different continents, straddled the country (Masalha 2018). This transnational history of education in Palestine – which can be seen in the Sumerian-style schooling of the Bronze Age cities of Shikmu (near Nablus), Megiddo, Gezer and ancient Jericho, the Byzantine philosophical academies and libraries of Gaza and Caesarea Palaestina (often referred to under the Byzantines as *Metropolis Palaestinae*) and the Islamic law colleges of medieval Jerusalem, and the beginnings of the modern educational revolution of late Ottoman Palestine and the British Mandatory period – has left an indelible legacy and marked impact on education and schooling in Palestine.

Under the impact of Hellenization and classicization of late Antiquity, the urban centres of Palestine undergo an educational revolution and several cities in Palestine emerge as centres of classical education, an educational revolution that transforms urban life in Palestine. In my book *Palestine Across Millennia A History of Literacy, Learning and Educational Revolutions* (2022), I explore the impact of international trade on the spread of literacy and the rise of cities of learning and higher education in Palestine in Antiquity. The relations between 'Town and Gown' are complex and have been for a long time the subject of research and scholarly publications (Berkey 2014; Brockliss 1989 Vol. VIII: 238; Hadjittofi 2019: 145–63; Westberg 2019: 164–86; 2017: 394–417).

The early function of literacy and scribal schools in ancient Palestine were pragmatic, and literacy, arithmetic and accountancy were geared towards practical needs of commerce and administration. Inevitably education was focused on narrow urban ruling elites. However the economic and demographic growth of the cities of Palestine in classical and late Antiquity brought about a pedagogical revolution of late Antique Palestine and increasingly the spread of trade and economic in the country democratized and widened education and gave rise to cities of learning in Palestine – with the 'city' as a whole with its civic institutions became the focus of learning and citizenship (Masalha 2022). Moreover, for centuries in late Antiquity, industrial and commercial cities such Gaza, Caesarea Maritima, Nablus (Neapolis) as well as Islamic Jerusalem under the Mamluks and late Ottoman Jerusalem all embodied the transformation of the urban space and the rise of the idea of 'cities of learning' (see also Stenger 2019) and cosmopolitanism.

Focusing on the urban centres of Palestine, *Palestine across Millennia* explores peaks-and-troughs in advanced and higher education in the country; the work shows high levels of education in cosmopolitan Roman Neapolis, cosmopolitan Byzantine Gaza and *Caesarea Palaestina* and Mamluk Jerusalem. However, the blending of 'Gown and Town' (college and city) in the history of Palestinian education was not unique to the great learning cities of Gaza and Caesarea Maritima and under the Byzantines. *Palestine across Millennia* explores the blending of academic life and top educational institutions (*fiqh madrasas*) with the surrounding urban life in the great Islamic city of Jerusalem under the Ayyubids and Mamluks.

Commercial cities and banking centres in Palestine: Financing trade, minting currency and money changers

The global trade routes of Palestine led to the rise of some great ancient cities in the country as major financial centres. In my book *Palestine: A Four Thousand Year History* (2018) I have shown how, historically, the political, administrative and financial capitals of Palestine were not always the country's religious capitals. The same principle applies to the trading urban centres of Palestine that were not always associated with the religious centres in the country. In classical Antiquity and Late Antiquity, the city of Memphis, located on the famous spice routes between Petra and Gaza, became the financial and banking centre of southern Palestine (the Naqab), while, at the same time, the Naqab city of Elusa – also located on the same spice network of routes – was the religious capital of the same region. This can be seen in the huge quantities of gold and silver currency excavated by archaeologist from the site of Memphis.

As we shall see below, one of the most famous international bankers of Antiquity was the Palestinian merchant-banker Philostratus of Ascalon, (*Φιλόστρατος*), a native of the maritime city of Ascalon, which in Antiquity was one of the most important international centres for commerce and banking in the Mediterranean. A fabulously wealthy international merchant-banker, Philostratus traded with cities across the Mediterranean and later became a distinguished citizen of the Italian city Naples and was socially active in this city between 130 and 90 BCE; he also received many honours for his local charitable activities.

In Antiquity and the Middle Ages international trade, financial system and the minting of gold and silver often went hand-in-hand with gaining a substantial degree of independence. We know that large quantities of Hellenistic style silver coins were minted at the city of Ascalon during the Ptolemaic/Hellenistic/Seleucids periods. In the second century BCE Ascalon became a financial centre in Palestine from the Seleucids after receiving financial autonomy from them to mint silver coins and the city continued to be a financial centre and produce silver coins under both the Romans and Byzantines – which was also the basis for the city's claims to great degree of independence ('free city'), a special status obtained from imperial authorities ('Ascalon' in Ameling et al. 2014, Vol. III: 242).

Also the city of Ramla, the political and administrative capital of Palestine throughout the early four centuries of Islamic rule in Palestine, was a key centre for minting gold and silver coins in Palestine. Both Ascalon, which was a major trading and banking city in Palestine connected with the sea trade with the Ptolemaic and Hellenistic and Mediterranean world, and al-Ramla, which was established during the Umayyad period, were located at the centre of the international trade and strategic route between Damascus and medieval Cairo (al-Fustat). Al-Ramla became a key financial centre in Palestine throughout early Islam and minted a Palestinian currency with the Arabic words: '*minted in Palestine*'. Like the location of Memphis as a regional financial centre for the Arab spice trade routes between Petra and Gaza and the Mediterranean world in Antiquity, the location of al-Ramla on the key Damascus-Egypt trade route and as a regional commercial hub between Palestine and Egypt and the presence of Egyptian textile merchants in the city led its rise under Islam as a premier financial centre of Palestine, with the largest mint in the country and with local money changers:

> Coins labelled 'Ramla-Filastin' were widely circulated in Palestine and in neighbouring regions. Ramla's position as a commercial centre in Palestine is attested by a unique find of a hoard of gold coins, containing 376 coins of a wide geographical distribution from the Maghreb to Iran … the coins, minted between 761 and 979, were probably the property of a local money changer.
>
> (Avni 2014: 178)

Minting coinage, global trade and municipal autonomy in ancient Palestine

In modern times an enormous amount of ancient currency was unearthed in and around the city of Gaza. For much of its history in Antiquity Gaza city was officially recognized as an *autonomous polis* capable of minting its own coins and exercising wide influence through its own financial and monetary system, a sign of its flourishing global trade system. Gaza began minting its own coins in the Persia period, which lasted from 539 BCE until the beginning of the Hellenistic period in 322 BCE. Next Ptolemian coins were minted in Gaza, attested to Ptolemy II and III. In the second century BCE Gaza minted only bronze coinage, mostly city-coinage. A new era appears on the Gaza coins towards the end of the second century BCE, coins which testify to the city having been granted autonomous status by the last Seleucids. Gaza also struck its own coins in the mid-first century BCE – not long after its establishment as a *polis* (an officially recognized autonomous municipality) under the Romans in 61/60 CE ('Gaza' in Ameling et al. 2014, Vol. III: 245–8).

Minting its own coinage and determining its own financial system went hand-in-hand with developing its own local civic, administrative and judicial system. In the fourth century CE, Saint Jerome mentions the 'Duumvir of Gaza' in connection with the chariot races in the city. The *duumviri* (Latin for 'two men' pairs of magistrates) were joint magistrates of ancient Rome and Roman Palestine. Their chief duties were concerned with the administration of justice. The office was determined by election and lasted one year. They were also expected to deal with public finance of a city, deal with proceedings in the town council, and run the elections in the *comitium*, Latin for assembly; the latter was the open-air public meeting space of Gaza cities under the Romans and the location for much of the judicial and political and activity of the city.

Also in the fourth century Ammian Marcellinus (*c.*330, died *c.*391–400), a Byzantine soldier and historian and a native of Palestine or Syria, knew Gaza as a venerable old city, one of the splendid towns of Palestine;

> the last region of the Syria is Palestine, extending over a great extent of territory and abounding in cultivated and well-kept lands; it also has some splendid cities, nine of which yields to any of the others, but they rival one another, as it were, by plumb-line. These are Caesarea Maritima, which king Herod the Great built in honour of the emperor Octavianus, Eleutheropolis (Bei Jibrin) and Neapolis (Nablus), along with Ascalon and Gaza, built in a former age.
>
> ('Gaza' in Ameling et al. 2014, Vol. III: 219–420)

However, Gaza's strategic location was a mixed blessing (Butt 1995; Sadeq 2015: 47–54), bringing both commerce and prosperity – but also attracting aggressive foreign armies and marauding bandits and pirates both overland and by sea. Also, as we shall see below, the phenomenal economic prosperity of the ancient city of Gaza as a major urban centre in Palestine in Antiquity depended on a strategic location at the centre of international trade routes. However, the decline of this Petra-Gaza 'transit routes' for transporting armies, spices and herbs across the semi-arid and desert Nabataean region (then part of *Palaestina Tertia*) to the Mediterranean world in late Antiquity – in Palestine roughly the period between 250 and early seventh century CE – forced the city of Gaza and the Naqab cities to adjust their economies and introduce vine farming as part of the flourishing Palestine wine-making industry of the Christian Byzantine period – an export-geared industry that became famous known in Europe as Gaza Wine. This agricultural/industrial transformation of these urban centres into *cities of wine* production for international export – by adopting old Nabataean water storage technique and the building of dams developed for a semi-arid region – enabled these cities to continue flourishing for further three centuries until the advent of Islam. However, in the Middle Ages, under Islam, the dramatic decline of the Palestine wine-making industry and the dramatic decline of the Petra-Gaza *incense routes* contributed to the dramatic decline and virtual disappearance of some of these historic Palestinian 'spice cities' in the Naqab: Oboda, Sbeita, Kurnub, Elusa, Nessana – cities which had flourished as 'spice and perfume cities' for more than a millennium under the Nabataean Arabs and the Romans and for three more centuries as 'wine-making cities' under the Byzantines.

Crucially, the dramatic rise of urbanism in Palestine in the Bronze Age went hand-in-hand with the rise of the regional and international copper trade and the expansion of the regional trade routes and trade systems in the Levant. This long history of urbanism and global trade in Palestine stretches across millennia – a history packed with culture, architecture, intellectuals' schools, writing and social and religious institutions (Masalha 2018, 2022) and a history of a country which for millennia was at the heart of the ancient global trade routes and trade systems.

Concerned about the reaction from pro-Zionist lobbies in the West, the overwhelming majority of authors and documentary makers in the West avoid mentioning the word *Palestine*, when seeking to trace the ancient frankincense trade from Yemen to Europe and the ancient spice trade from India and Indonesia to the Mediterranean world. They often end their books and documentaries with the ancient city of Petra (in modern Jordan) and fail to mention that this global ancient trade in precious spices and incense had to go through Palestine, and its Mediterranean port cities of in order to reach its final destination in Europe. As a very expensive commodity, frankincense was used by social and religious elites and in royal circles in countries across the Near East and Mediterranean world. This partly explains why Alexander the Great chose to loot the frankincense stores of Gaza and ship the looted good to the great temples of ancient Greece. As a highly prized commodity with presumed miraculous health properties, frankincense is mentioned in the New Testament as one of the three gifts (with gold and myrrh) that the *magi* (or 'three kings') 'from the East' presented to Jesus as a young child in Bethlehem, Palestine (Matthew 2: 11). The frankincense tree is found in south Arabia, Dhofar in Oman and parts of East Africa and frankincense had been used since ancient times for many different applications, from medicinal uses to burning incense for worship.

State trade monopolies in ancient Palestine

The political economy of Palestine in Antiquity experienced periods of neo-liberal economics and free trade and periods that were characterized by strong state intervention and tight control of trade and even state monopolies of trade and some key traditional industries. During the three centuries of the Greco-Egyptian Ptolemaic period (roughly from 332–30 CE) of economic and intellectual expansion, Palestine was ruled from Alexandria in Egypt. Control of international trade routes and creation of 'trade monopolies' played a major part in Ptolemaic economic policies in Palestine. Competing commercially with, and fighting militarily against, the ancient trading Nabataean Arab kingdom of southern Palestine and north Arabia for the control of the long-distance trade in spices and aromatics, the Ptolemaic rulers militarily fortified many cities in Palestine, expanded the Hellenization (which often meant cultural hybridization) of the urban centres and built new garrison towns and trading posts in the country. These Ptolemaic state 'trade monopolies' – as well as tight control by the central government on the local minting and design of currency by Palestinian cities – became a template for the subsequent establishment of state trade monopolies of certain sectors of the economy in classical and late Antique Palestine.

A long tradition of libraries and learning existed in the ancient cities of the Near East. However, the rise of cities of learning in Palestine in late Antiquity was directly influenced by one of the largest and most significant libraries of the ancient world, the Great Library of Alexandria – which was part of a larger research institution called the *Mouseion of Alexandria*[15] – a universal library which acquired many papyrus scrolls in all fields of learning owing to the Ptolemaic rulers' well-funded policies for procuring texts and prompting knowledge in one of the greatest cities of learning in the ancient world. Although the Library of Alexandria declined gradually over the course of several centuries, it provided a model for the establishment and rise of the Library of Caesarea Maritima – a city of learning and the capital of Palestine during the late Roman and Byzantine periods – a library and a research institution which also amassed large collections of papyrus scrolls during late Antiquity (Masalha 2022).

As we shall see in Chapter 14, in the modern period state trade monopolies, especially of raw cotton industry and wheat export to Europe, were also introduced by the Palestinian regime Dhaher al-'Unmar in the eighteenth century. The profits from this lucrative foreign trade were used by Dhaher al-'Unmar to fund his army and expand and fortify the towns and cities of the Galilee, especially his capital the port city of Acre which he transformed into the wealthiest and most developed city in Palestine in the eighteenth century.

Thalattocracy as a soft power and maritime cities: Eusebius of Caesarea Maritima, merchant navies and the concept of *maritime power*

The maritime cities (and ancient city-states) of Palestine were a significant part of the Mediterranean maritime trade network in Antiquity and became the barometer for maritime trade trends and foreign export to Europe. The centrality of the Mediterranean maritime trade to the economy, export of goods and prosperity of Palestine in Antiquity can be seen in the fact many ancient Palestinian ports and maritime cities including Mauimas Gaza (also known as Mauima under Islam), Anthedon, Ascalon, Ashdod (Isdud), Joppa (Jaffa), Apollonia (*Arsuf*), Caesarea Maritima, Dora (*Tantura*), Ptolemais (Acre) and Akhziv developed their own shipping workshops (and some city-states had their own navies) and were busy exporting goods to the whole Mediterranean region.

Moreover, necessity is the mother of all inventions and creativity often comes from the need to solve, practically, a problem. In the ancient Near East merchant coastal elites created navies and their maritime trade was often backed by powerful political structures and local shipping industries. The profits generated from maritime trade and long-distance trade created greater social stratification and big gaps between the wealthy urban elites and the urban poor in the urban centres of Palestine, as well as a bigger gap between the urban elites and the Palestinian peasantry. Long before classical Antiquity, the merchant-mariners of the Mediterranean city-states of Phoenicia provided the best-known template by their establishment of a large shipping industry and a highly successful merchant navy. Other merchant communities in Antiquity followed suit and since then rich merchant communities have built ships and created merchant navies – the peasants and tribes, on the other hand, did not need to develop maritime trade or build large trading ships. The tribes of central and northern Arabia (unlike the Yemeni merchants in Antiquity and the Omani merchants in the Middle Ages) famously developed, during the Iron Age, the *Ship of Desert*: the camel caravans which became the main means of transport designed specifically for the arid desert environment. This long-distance desert trade via camel caravans flourished for centuries and transported precious commodities and day-to-day consumer goods all the way from south Arabia to the Mediterranean coast via the Palestinian port cities (*maiumas*) of Gaza and Ascalon. These Arabian and Nabataean Arab tribes who engaged in long-distance trade needed and knew how to rear and develop the body of a particular type of camel suitable for long-distance desert trade. During the Iron Age the Arab camel underwent various modifications that helped it to survive in the hot and dry conditions of the Arabian deserts and to become known as the *Ship of Desert*, another way of alluding to the fact the bulk of long-distance trade in Antiquity was conducted by merchant ships.

By contrast, the south Arabian merchants (of Yemen and Oman) developed sea power, extensive shipping industries and merchant ships, the most celebrated of which were boats known as *Dhows*. The latter was a generic term for a variety of traditional trading and shipping vessels operating between the seaports of south Arabia and Oman and India and the east African coasts.

With written references to the south Arabian shipping industry in Greek sources dating back to 600 BCE, the *Dhows* sailed the superhighway of the Red Sea, the Gulf of Aqaba, the Persian Gulf, the Gulf of Oman, the Indian Ocean and the East Africa coast for millennia; they carried spices, cinnamon, frankincense, myrrh, Chinese silk, fruits and other goods and, at one point, they were also used in the infamous East Africa slave trade. This type of vessel also enabled the Omanis in the Middle Ages to develop a maritime trading empire which, at its peak in the nineteenth century, included parts of the Indian Ocean and East Africa. Crucially the long-distance transport of goods by the *Dhows* was significantly cheaper and much faster than the land transport of goods.

The concept of *thalassocracy*, the political economy of maritime trading and sea power, was conceptually coined by prominent Palestinian author of the early fourth-century Eusebius of Caesarea Maritima, a city also known at the time as *Metropolis Palaestina*. Eusebius was a native and the bishop of Caesarea Maritima and one was the most influential Palestinian intellectuals of late Antiquity and one of the best-known founding fathers of the Church. Much of the Western publications on Eusebius of Caesarea Maritima focused on Eusebius's sacred geography and his theological and ecclesiastical works and on his famous 'theological library in Caesarea' (Carriker 2003; Masalha 2018, 2022) with less attention devoted to his contribution to secular knowledge and ideas of strategic knowledge, maritime trade and soft power. But why would this leading public figure Caesarea Maritima come up with the concept of *thalassocracy,* or sea power, unless he thought this concept had some relevance to the rising power of his seaport city?

Historian Eusebius must have been aware of the former archetypal maritime empire of the Phoenician city of Tyre that had dominated the Mediterranean for several centuries before the classical Greek and Roman Empires. But more likely the concept of *thalassocracy* was derived from his own context and the realities of Caesarea Maritima, at the not only *Metropolis of Palaestina*, but also the largest city in Byzantine Palestine, a maritime city with one of the largest seaports in the Mediterranean Sea. The term *Thalassokratia* was derived from the terms *θάλασσα* ('sea') and κρατεῖν ('power'), something known to Eusebius and the ancients as Mediterranean maritime empire. As we shall see in Chapter 5, at the time Caesarea Maritima was one of the most powerful trading cities in Palestine and had some of the most developed silk and textile trade and industries in the Mediterranean region. Caesarea Maritima was also linked with international superhighways for maritime and land trade in Antiquity. *Thalassokratia* also pointed to the power that described cities with large harbours and powerful merchant fleets and maritime realms and extensive sea trade. The concept fitted perfectly the maritime commerce of Caesarea Maritima at the time. The concept of *thalassocracy* was also later applied to Italian maritime trading city-states of Venice and Genoa of the Middle Ages and in the modern period to European trading empires and can simply refer to navel power in both commercial and military senses.

In Antiquity powerful merchant classes of the coastal cities of Phoenicia, Palestine, Egypt, Greece, Rome and south Arabia all concentrated on developing long-distance maritime trade and with large ships capable of transporting vast quantities of commodities and consumer goods. As we shall see, maritime archaeology shows that several powerful coastal cities of the *Philistine Pentapolis* developed large ports and large Mediterranean commercial navies in the Iron Age and Antiquity. These highly sophisticated ancient *Philistines* created some of the largest trading cities on the Mediterranean port cities (*maiumas*) of Gaza and Ascalan, backed by highly developed ship industries. Inheriting some of the trading skills of the neighbouring Phonetician cities, they created large merchant navies which traded with the whole of the Mediterranean world.

There is also some evidence to suggest that the Nabataean Arab kingdom of classical Antiquity – which occupied southern Palestine and northern Arabia and controlled the Trans-Arabian trade to Gaza and the Palestine Mediterranean coast – developed its own Red Sea ports and maritime ships. Other cases from ancient Palestine also show that often the soft power of maritime trade and merchant ships were accompanied by the hard power of a military navy. In the case of the 'autonomous', powerful and rich merchants of island-town of Iotabe – which at one point was incorporated into the Palestinian province of *Palaestina Tertia* during the Byzantine period – developed their own Red Sea navy during the Byzantine period. Crucially the profitability of the maritime shipping was shown by the fact that the costs of long-distance maritime transport was one-fifth of the costs of the long-distance land transport of goods and five to seven times faster than the land transport.

After the Assyrian conquest of Palestine in 712 BCE, the Assyrian rulers recognized the significance of naval power and merchant navies of both the (former Phoenician) maritime cities of Tyre and Sidon, Byblos and Acre and the ancient Palestinian port cities of Gaza, Ascalon, Ashdod and Dor (Tanutra). The Assyrian writers and administrators also publicized the name and coastal region of Palestine in the ninth, eighth and seventh centuries. Assyrian clay tablet and Cuneiform inscriptions refer to the Mediterranean coastal region of Palestine, which included the *maiuams* (port cities) of Gaza, Ascalon, Asdod, Dor (Tantura), with different spellings: Pilishti, Pilishte, Palashtu, Pilishtu, Pilistu, Pilisti, Pilistin (Masalha 2018: 61–2). In one inscription, dated 676 BCE, the Assyrian rulers ordered:

> If a ship belonging to Baal (the king), the first of the people from the country of Tyre, collided with (another ship) in the country of the Philistines, Or in any

> region belonging to the country of Assyria, everything inside the ship will be confiscated for the benefit of '*Esarhaddon*,' the king of Assyria.

As for the people inside these ships, the inscription says that no one should harm them; only their names should be recorded. The document goes on to say: these are the seaports and the roads which *Esarhaddon*, the king of Assyria, sent prisoners-soldiers to Baal his servant so that he would undertake to watch them: from Tyre to the port city of Acre (Akka) and the port city of Dora (Tantura in Palestine); in all the regions of the Philistines, and in the cities located within all the Mediterranean coastal areas occupied by Assyria, and in the city of Byblos, and Mount Lebanon, and all the mountainous cities.[16]

Palestinian merchant-bankers and migrant communities in Europe in classical Antiquity: Philostratus of Ascalon

There is a long tradition in Palestine and Syria, going back to Antiquity, of members of the Arab Orthodox communities taking Greek names or Arabized Greek names; today the Palestinian Arab Archbishop of Sebastia, born *Nizar Hanna* in Galilee in 1965, is called *Theodosios Atallah Hanna*, with both *Atallah* and *Theodosios* meaning 'gift of God', in Arabic and Greek respectively. In classical Antiquity assuming Greek names was common among Palestinian and Syrian/Phoenician merchants and migrants who settled in Greek and Italian cities (Demetriou 2023: 89–90).

Greek-sounding names in Antiquity did not imply Greek 'ethnicity'; in fact, many indigenous Palestinians, Syrians and Arabs were bilingual and some multilingual and many took Greek-sounding names. The Roman Arab emperor *Julius Philippus* (*c.*204–249 CE), commonly known as *Philip the Arab*, had a Greek sounding name. We also have plenty of evidence for both cross-cultural influences and for mixed marriages between Europeans, especially Italians and Greeks, and eastern Mediterranean people (Clackson et al. 2020: 179) which could result only from the increasing movement of people and goods across the Mediterranean.

The famous case of Philostratus (*Φιλόστρατος*) of Ascalon, who was not ethnically Greek, was a case in point. A successful Palestinian international merchant-banker, Philostratus lived and traded as a merchant-banker on the Greek island of Delos; Philostratus later became a distinguished citizen of the Italian city Naples and was socially active in this city between 130 and 90 BC; he also received many honours for his local charitable activities (Demetriou 2023: 89–90). Evidently all of Philostratus' charitable dedications in the city-island of Delos were on behalf of himself, or his family or on behalf of his native city of Ascalon. On Delos, Philostratus worshipped a deity from his home city of Ascalon, Ba'al, a name whom he translated into Greek as the 'Ascalonite Poseidon'; another deity he worshipped on Delos was a 'Semitic goddess', 'Palestinian Astarte' (Demetriou 2023: 89–90). The archaeological discoveries of many figurines of 'Ashira' in fourth- and third-centuries BCE Palestine not only undermine the myth-narratives of 'biblical archaeology' but also confirm the widespread cult of the veneration of the female divinity of 'Palestinian Astarte' in classical Antiquity in Palestine (Masalha 2018, 2022).

The indigenous Palestinian Bronze Age and Iron Age deity of *Astarte* had an equivalent Greek deity: *Aphrodite*, and both deities were part of the pantheon and syncretic religion of Palestine. Translating the names of indigenous Palestinian deities into Greek sounding deities was also common among migrant merchants and mariners. Earlier, a mid-400 BCE grave stele (uncovered in Athens in 1861) was for another Palestinian merchant from the coastal city of Ascalon, who had died in classical Athens. Currently in the National Archaeological Museum of Greece in Athens, the bilingual (Phoenician-Greek) inscription reads: Shem-Antipatros son of Abdashtart-Aphrodisias of Ascalon, erected by Domsaloss on of Domanos of Sidon. The Greek text of the stele amalgamates the indigenous Palestinian and Greek names and the name of the Palestinian merchant 'Abd Astarte of Ascalon', literally 'the worshipper of Astarte', the ancient deity of Ascalon, with Aphrodisias, the 'worshipper of Aphrodite', the ancient goddess of love, beauty, desires and fertility and a goddess closely associated with the Palestinian goddess Ishtar and the hedonistic life of the ancient Palestinian cities along the Mediterranean shore of Palestine. This amalgamation of two distinct deities and hybridization of religious traditions was not uncommon in throughout the ancient Mediterranean world. The migration of merchants and sailors of all nationalities through the international maritime trade across the Mediterranean contributed to this amalgamation of religious traditions and the rise of what can be described as international religious pantheon.

This international maritime trade also contributed to the spread of ancient Near Eastern religions across the Mediterranean and the movement of maritime merchants and goods, especially the frankincense and incense trade fuelled by the construction of temples (which often included scribal schools and libraries) resulted in the spread of religious ideas and the creation of 'supermarkets of religions' as well as the rise of tolerant *pantheistic spirituality* and the construction of syncretic religions and polytheistic *pantheons*: 'temples of all the gods', an urban development found in major trading urban centres of the Mediterranean. As we shall see in Chapter 3, the religion of the Nabataean Arab Kingdom of classical Antiquity – which dominated southern Palestine and flourished at the centre of the Trans-Arabian spice and aromatics trade from Yemen to Gaza and Ascalon and whose merchants and goods moved across long distances – was an earlier form of Arab syncretic religion and pantheism (polytheism). The Nabataean syncretic religion embraced and combined multiples religious traditions and divinities including Palestinian, Near Eastern and Greco-Roman deities.

Also trade and the rise of polytheistic-pantheistic spirituality of Arabia's pre-Islamic past may also be preserved in certain practices rooted in *pre-Islamic* Arabian spirituality, including the Islamic practice of pilgrimage to *Mecca* – a major trading city in pre-Islamic Arabia – to circumambulate to Kaaba, an ancient sanctuary in pre-Islamic times and the most sacred site in Islam. While in Antiquity spiritual pantheism flourished with the rise to global trade and *the movement of multiethnic merchant communities* across vast regions, while in modern times the *movement of capital and capitalism* brought about the revival of a form of spiritual pantheism. This revival took place in Palestine by the leaders of Iranian Babi (Shi'ite) merchant capitalist communities allied with global capital and trade interests of the British empire. Their leaders constructed, with British protection, Bahai temples (shrines) in the Palestinian port cities of Haifa and in Acre (Palestine) where the remains of the Iranian founders of Babism and Bahaism are buried.

The importance of the Palestinian Mediterranean maritime trade to the economy and prosperity of Palestine in Antiquity can be seen in the fact that busy ancient Palestinian ports and maritime cities, including Gaza, Ascalon, Caesarea Maritima, Jaffa, Apollonia (Arsuf), Dora (Tantura) and Ptolemais (Acre), traded with the Mediterranean world. Central to the history of this vast ancient maritime trade of the Mediterranean region were the merchant-mariners of all the coastal cities of Palestine and those of Syria and Phoenicia, which established trading posts, seaports, communities of merchants and migrants and adventurers in every corner of the ancient Mediterranean region. Less known is the fact that throughout classical and late Antiquity, and long before the rise of Islam, Palestinian, Syrian and Arabian merchants and bankers settled in Europe, on Greek islands and in the Mediterranean cities of Italy, in significant numbers. As we shall see in Chapters 5 and 6, at one point in late Antiquity, these Syrian and Palestinian merchants appear to dominate certain sectors of the foreign trade and textile industry of these Greek and Italian cities. As we shall see below, these migrant Syrian and Palestinian merchants also brought their religious traditions and cultural practices to the shores of Europe. Palestinian merchants, in particular, brought their Canaanite religious traditions and the cults of *Palaistine Aphrodite Urania* and *Ba'al*, the latter is most important deity in ancient Palestine who was associated with the sun, rain, thunder, agriculture and fertility, to the Mediterranean coastal cities of Europe.

It has already been suggested that the large volume of Asian and south Arabian foreign trade passing through Palestine prompted the cities of the Philistines (especially Gaza, Ascalon and Ashdod (Isdud)) to create the first monetary system in Palestine. These trading Palestinian maritime cities produced some of the wealthiest maritime merchant communities of Antiquity. Often Palestinian and Syrian merchants and bankers under the impact of lucrative long-distance trade and shipping industry and grew phenomenally in wealth and demography and this demographic growth prompted them develop early town planning in Palestine.

In classical Antiquity the wealthiest and most famous of all Palestinian merchant-bankers in Europe was the aforementioned Philostratus of Ascalon. An international banker, Philostratus was involved in the lucrative Palestinian trade with Italy, and received citizenship from Naples. For Philostratus, his bank and his connections and activities in Naples made him one of the most influential philanthropist and benefactors of the Italian cities of Antiquity ('Ascakon' in Ameling et al. Vol, III: 241; Leiwo 1989: 575).

Philostratus of Ascalon, while keeping his indigenous Palestinian faith, had cosmopolitan education and wide Mediterranean business and banking connections (Meyboom 2016: 347). Judging by his religious activities on the island of Delos, Philostratus subscribed to the Canaanite cult of Ba'al – a deity associated with the sun, rain, thunder, agriculture and fertility. In the second century BCE, Philostratus became the wealthiest merchant-banker on the island of Delos, then a Mediterranean commercial hub, combining trade and religion; the island had acquired the status of a holy sanctuary in the Mediterranean region, and had its own Greek Olympian mythology that made it the birthplace of Apollo and Artemis.

However, in Antiquity the Near Eastern Mediterranean trade allowed for the spread of other religious traditions on the island of Delos and for the exchange and hybridization of religious traditions across the island and beyond. In the second century BCE Delos also developed into a 'free port' and a booming cosmopolitan trade centre in the Mediterranean with merchants of multiple ethnicities, from all over the Mediterranean world, including Syrian and Palestinian merchants, meeting and exchanging ideas. The island established markets, shops, warehouses, banks and new residential quarters for wealthy merchants. Becoming a great cosmopolitan port city with cosmopolitan communities and a banking system, the island also became a 'supermarket' of religions and religious sanctuaries – with religious temples and sanctuaries from the Hellenistic world and Near East, and temples Near Eastern deities such *Ba'al*, the most famous deity of the Canaanite pantheon. Evidently Philostratus made an offering to a number of altars on Delos, the most famous of which was that of *Astarte Palaistine Aphrodite Urania* of Ascalon (Teixidor 2015: 44).

The link between international and maritime trade and syncretic religion in ancient Palestinian cities such as Ascalon, which flourished on the trade with south Arabia and the Mediterranean world, on the one hand, and the pre-Islamic Arabian pantheon, on the other, is interesting. *Palaistine Aphrodite Urania* of Ascalon was a Semitic goddess associated with the sea and seafaring whose cult and rituals originated in the eastern Mediterranean and spread across the Mediterranean world and ancient Arabia with trade in purple and other luxury goods. According to Herodotus, the Arabs called this goddess *Alitta* or *Alilat* (Ἀλίττα or Ἀλιλάτ), also known to the Arabs as *Al-Lat* and *Aphrodite Urania* (Herodotus. 1920; Smith 1870: 132). *Al-Lat* (اللات) was a pre-Islamic Arabian goddess and a key goodness in the Arabian pantheon of the worshipped under various associations throughout the entire Arabia Peninsula as well as by the Nabatean Arabs at the height of their trading empire during the classical period. The cult of *al-Lat* was also worshipped in Palestine and Syria (Healey 2001: 114) – something which bring us to a full circle connecting with *Palaistine Aphrodite Urania* of Ascalon, Jaffa and the ancient coastal cities of Palestine.

Driven by maritime trade and commercial interests of the Mediterranean world, this pragmatic approach to the 'supermarket of religions' on Delos and hybridization of religious traditions subsequently flourishing most famously throughout the Roman world, Roman Palestine included. At Delos, Philostratus contributed financially and generously to the ancient culture of religious charity, which was associated with trade and profit-making: he honoured the religious sanctuaries and the deities of his native Ascalon (in Palestine), especially *Ba'al*, whose temple was located near the summit of the island. In addition to the creation of a religious sanctuary of the gods of native Palestine on Delos, Philostratus created a sanctuary for the Palestinian gods worshipped at Ascalon on the island (Scott 2012: 70).

In addition to honouring his Palestinian homeland at Delos, Philostratus later donated a portico and an *exedra* (*ἐξέδρα*: a room in a temple) to the 'Agora of the Italians' also at Delos – something which also indicates his extensive Italian banking interests and commercial connections. The *agora* was the market and the most important gathering public space at Delos and in the classical Greek *polis* (city-state) and *Agora of the Italians* at Delos became a famous garden and a public space, with the size of some 6,000 square metres, constructed between 130–120 BCE, situated prominently in the centre of Delos, between the famous sanctuary of Apollo to the south and the Sacred Lake to the north. Philostratus himself was honoured at Delos with a public statue in the centre of the island (Meyboom 2016: 347). Philostratus of Ascalon offered and received dedication for his generous donations to the *Agora des Italiens* to the point of gaining the citizenship of Naples (Adams 2003: 787; Clackson et al. 2020: 179; Hollander 2007: 167). His grand house at Delos near Mount Cythnusa has been discovered and excavated in the modern era (Cook et al. 1930: 649). Antipater of Sidon (*Antipatros ho Sidonios*), a Greek-speaking poet of the second half of the second century BCE – praised by Cicero – and who listed in one of his poems the Seven Wonders of the world, writes about 'Philostratos, citizen of Palestine':

> O far-famed Philostratos, citizen of Palestine that (?) pays heed to the gods, you have dedicated these five gifts. For wide-ruling Zeus: a sacred incense-holder, glowing with rich myrrh and frankincense.[17]

Spice cities and perfume markets in Palestine: Global spice trade and modern Palestinian culinary culture

A popular saying in Arabic: 'if it were not for tastes, the markets would not have flourished'. This popular proverb captures the *pleasures* and historical significance, flavours, textures and aromas of the world-renowned spice markets of the Arab world. Since Antiquity, pleasure and profits were key drivers for the emergence of the global spice system and the creation of the famous spice markets of the Middle East and North Africa. These historic spice markets combined a variety of locally produced fruits and agricultural products as well as a wide range of herbs native to Palestine and the Eastern Mediterranean. The 'market of spice traders' or *Souk al-'Attarin* is an old name which has been preserved in the modern markets of the Old City of Jerusalem and in several Arab cities such as Damascus, Beirut, Tunis and Marrakech. These ancient markets of spice merchants and medicinal herbal sellers also specialized in perfumes, beauty trading products, aromatics and jasmine, rose water and *henna* to dye skin, hair and finger nails as well as fabrics. If the copper trade and copper mining and smelting give birth to the city and civilization in the two Fertile Crescents (the northern and southern), the international trade in spices, perfume products and silk all gave birth to the great urban marketplaces of Palestine and the Near East. It has already been suggested that in Antiquity *spice cities* rose along the 1,500-mile incense route and Nabataean caravan trail that ran all the way from Yemen, through Petra, into the Naqab, finally ending at the maritime port cities (*maimuas*) of Gaza and Ascalon in Palestine. The impact of this ancient spice trade system can still be seen in the cities of Palestine today.

Liquors Palaestini, Liquors Arabes and Arabian Myrrh as common trade names in Antiquity

Since ancient times the 'market of spice traders' of urban Palestine and the Near East were filled with herbs, spices and perfumes and often these spice and aromatics markets mirrored the Trans-Arabian ancient frankincense and incense and spice trade routes from South Arabia and India to the Mediterranean through Palestine. In classical Antiquity and in late Antiquity Palestine produced a range of internationally famous wines, the best-known of which was Gaza Wine (*Vinum Gazetum*) of the Byzantine period. Earlier in classical Antiquity an aromatic Palestinian wine, then known as *liquors Palaestini*, an important trade name during the Roman period, became famous around the Mediterranean region and in Rome a considerable quantities of the Palestinian bag-shaped shreds of Gaza Wine amphorae were dated to the third century CE. Earlier Publius Papinius Statius, a classical Roman poet of the first century CE, refers in the Silvae to *liquors Palaestini* (Palestinian wine) (Feldman 1996: 565; Zeiner 2005: 104), which was of fine quality and exported throughout the Roman Empire. As we shall see in Chapter 3, spices, pepper and a range of food items were widely available in the widespread and economically important markets of urban Palestine in Antiquity. The fame of *liquors Palaestini* was partly derived from the application of south Arabian spices and local herbs and the Palestinian aromatic *balsam* to wine-making in Palestine and the Arab region as a whole, something which Statius called *liquors Arabes* (Zeiner 2005: 104). Palestinian *balsam*, dates and a variety of fruits were also widely exported throughout the Near East and shipped to distant Mediterranean countries (Lapin 2001: 124).

Another ancient trade name widely marketed in Antiquity and widely available in the urban markets of Palestine through the Trans-Arabian desert routes and exported from the port cities of Palestine to the Mediterranean world was *Arabian myrrh*, extracted from a type of trees native to south Arabia and the Horn of Africa. Like frankincense, Arabian myrrh resin has been used since Antiquity in perfumery, incenses and medicine and was widely mixed with wine in ancient cultures to produce pleasurable feelings as well as used in medicine as a painkiller; modern scientists have also discovered that the ancient Egyptians also used Arabian myrrh in mummification processes.

The global ancient Near Eastern trade in aromatics and spices is not only preserved in common trade names such as in *Arabian myrrh* but also the names of modern Palestinian and Arab-specialized urban markets as well as the culinary culture of the Levant and in the names of some of the most popular Palestinian dishes. There are two terms for spices in Arabic, *tawabil* and *baharat*. The names of two of the most popular Palestinian dishes, *mutabbal* and *tabuleh*, are derived from the Arabic word for spice (*tawabil*). Also Palestinian and Arad widespread use of Indian spices in local culinary culture are found in the name *baharat* in Arabic بهارات became the Arabic; the Arabic word originated from the Indian name *Bharata*, an Indian king, featured in the literature of as India. Bharata is also the traditional name of the Indian subcontinent, a historically large producer and trader of spices with the ancient Near East. As we shall see below, since ancient times the Indian spices often arrived by the Trans-Arabian spice routes on camel caravans from south Arabia to Petra and Palestine or by the maritime Red Sea route to the island-town of Iotabe (modern Tiran) and then the port city of Aelas (modern Aqaba) and then by camel caravans through the historic *Petra-Oboda-Elusa-Gaza* Mediterranean routes. These *Baharat*, or Indian spices, and the spice trade passing through Palestine's established routes involved historical civilizations in southeast Asia, India, Sri Lanka, south Arabia and the Mediterranean world. This international trade in spices such as cinnamon, pepper, cardamom, nutmeg, ginger, turmeric, clove and star anise was known in the Near East since Antiquity.[18] *Baharat* in modern Arabic is also a spice mixture blend used in Middle Eastern cuisines and mixture of finely ground spices is often used to season lamb, fish, chicken, beef and soups. Today virtually all these spices and aromatics of the ancient trade routes and Trans-Arabian spice route: cinnamon, pepper, cardamon, nutmeg, ginger and turmeric are present in varieties of Palestinian food items and hot drinks.

Frankincense, the 'Petra-Gaza Road', and the global trans-Arabian spice trade: The creation of frontier Arab kingdoms in Southern Palestine in Antiquity

International trading routes in ancient Palestine and seafaring (through both the Mediterranean Sea and Red Sea) combined to develop an integrated Palestine in the Iron Age II (*c.*1000-600 BCE). While in the middle Bronze Age, trade helped the city-states of Megiddo and Hazor develop strong central adminitrations and armies, in the Iron Age II the trade helped the cities of Philistia to develop as a federation of a geo-political entity and to develop an autonomous monetary system in Palestine in the form of silver coins, issued in the late sixth-fourth centuries BCE. These economic and commercial developments continued into Antiquity.

Much has been written about the ancient south Arabian and Yemeni perfume factories and the 'Petra-Gaza Spice Road' (Cohen 1982: 240–7; Jung 2011: 52; Masalha 2018). The incense trade routes to the Mediterranean zones of Palestine and the spice trade of the Nabatean Arabs of north Arabian and the Palestinian Naqab were undoubtedly used by nomad caravans from very early times and it is conceivable that Arab tribes dealing in south Arabian perfume products made use of this route as far back as the eighth century BCE. Beginning with Iron Age II the Arabs of Yemen, and subsequently the Nabatean Arabs of southern Palestine, were associated with large-scale perfume industries and a global trade in frankincense and myrrh produced in southern Arabia – combined with the international trade spices imported from India and as far as the Indonesian islands. Herodotus recorded in about 450 BCE that Arabia was

> the only place that produces frankincense, myrrh, cassia, cinnamon and the gum called ladanon'.
>
> (Groom 2012: 13)

Historically the spice trade passing through Palestine's established routes involved historical civilizations in southeast Asia, India, Sri Lanka, south Arabia and the Mediterranean world. This international trade in spices is known in the Near East since Antiquity.[19] The spices found their way into the ancient Near East long before the beginning of the Christian era and the spice trade was massive during the Greco-Roman period and goods were transported by Arab and Ethiopian merchants via Red Sea maritime trade and on land by camels via the *incensce route* and Trans-Arabia spice route towards the Mediterranean world. Before and after the rise of Islam in the early seventh century, Arab traders plied these maritime and land routes and dominated the western Indian Ocean maritime routes, and Arab traders took over conveying goods via the Near East to Europe. These land and maritime spice trade routes led to tremendous growth in commercial activities between Palestine and the wider Near East and Europe.

Early on in Antiquity this global trade system transformed Palestine into a 'bridge country' between the classical Mediterranean world and south Arabia and the Southern Fertile Crescent for the international spice and aromatics trade from south Arabia and the Southern Fertile Crescent to the Mediterranean. This Southern Fertile Crescent is what is now known Yemen and Oman. It was known to ancient Greek geographers as *Eudaemon Arabia* (*Εὐδαίμων Ἀραβία*) and in Latin *as Arabia Felix*, blessed or flourishing Arabia and fertile Arabia respectively. Yemen was the best irrigated and most productive in the Arabian Peninsula and in ancient times it experienced more rainfall than any part of Arabia. Part of its wealth and importance to the ancient world was its near monopoly on the trade in Indian cinnamon and spices and both its own products and imports from India and the Horn of Africa (Harding 1965: 24-7). The economic growth of Yemen created class stratification and social professionalization. Greek geographer and historian Strabo (*c.*64 BCE–*c.*24 CE) wrote that *Arabia Felix*, or fertile Arabia, was composed of five kingdoms, each with its own social classes of rulers, warriors, farmers, craftsmen and merchants; those who engage in the mechanical arts; another, the myrrh-bearing country and another the frankincense-bearing country, although the same countries produce cassia cinnamon [produced from the Cinnamomum tree], and [aromatic] nard (Jones 1917: 365) – also called spikenard which is a class of aromatic amber-coloured essential oil which has been used over the centuries as a perfume and traditional medicine.

During classical and late Antiquity, this Trans-Arabian trade through the Nabataean Arab kingdom in and the Palestine Naqab to Gaza encouraged the migration of Ghassanid Arab population to Palestine. In the third to early seventh centuries CE, large parts of the Palestine provinces were settled by the Ghassanid Arab population that immigrated from Arabia; the Palestine ecclesia integrated these Ghassanid Arabs and large parts of these provinces were gradually transformed in the fifth to sixth centuries into Ghassanid Arab phylarchates, or 'frontier kingdoms', under Byzantine patronage and indirect imperial control. Ghassanid influence on *Provincia Palaestina* lasted for centuries, and their Christian Arab kings (supreme phylarchs) reined until the Islamic conquest of Palestine in the seventh century.

As we shall see in Chapters 1 and 3, the Trans-Arabian spice trade also created ancient kingdoms in southern Palestine. The great value of the Trans-Arabian trade meant that within a few hundred years the Nabatean Arabs developed into a major state, covering much of the area of north Arabia, parts of modern Jordan and the Palestinian Naqab. Frankincense and incense trade from Yemen and India and through southern Palestine and the port city of Gaza (*Maiumas Gaza*) and onto the Mediterranean world was instrumental in the creation and rise of the ancient Nabatean Arab kingdom of Petra in the fourth century BCE – a kingdom which encompassed the Naqab and southern Palestine and a province which became officially and administratively known during the Roman times as Petraea, and which was reorganized during the Byzantine period as the province of *Palaestina Salutaris* (*Third Palestine*) (fourth to early seventh centuries). For centuries this province remained at the centre of the Trans-Arabia spice and aromatics trade and the cities and urban centres along the long-distance trade routes of *Arabia Petraea* (which was subsequently renamed under the Byzantine *Palaestina Salutaris*) grew phenomenally during the Roman and Byzantine era, cities became a melting pot of Arab and Hellenistic cultures and civilization.

This *Third Palestine*, or the former province of *Arabia Petraea*, became an integral part of the three-in-one Palestinian provinces: *Palaestina Prima* (with its capital Caesarea Maritima), *Palaestina Seconda* (with its capital Scythopolis/Beisan) and *Palaestina Salutaris (Third Palestine)*, with its capital Petra. In his work *Third Palestine: A Regional Study in Byzantine Urbanization* (2000), Kenneth Gutwein explores the development of market towns and cities in the arid region of the Naqab (Negev) which was part of the province of *Palaestina Salutaris*. The work also describes how the Trans-Arabian and global trade transformed the urban environment of southern Palestine. The inhabitants of *Palaestina Salutaris* created *melting pot* towns and cities of Greek and Arabian influences and constructed magnificent churches and edifices and achieved an unprecedented high-level of wealth and prosperity due to the commercial role played by the myriad cities and market towns of southern Palestine. At the heart of the trading melting pot in the urban societies of southern Palestine were the port cities of Gaza and Petra. Known in Greek as *Petra* (the Rock), but to its ancient indigenous Nabataean Arabian founders as *Raqmu*, the city which was always a trading centre and a melting pot culture of Arabian and Greek influences became the capital of *Palaestina Salutaris* and played a major role in Christian Holy Land pilgrimage and the lucrative Trans-Arabian trade in spices (Gutwein 2000).

Historians who have written about the *Trans-Arabian Trade* and Red Sea have often described this international trade as a one-way trade from south Arabia and Yemen to the Mediterranean region via Palestinian port cities attached to the cities of Gaza and Ascalon. But, in fact, this was a *two-way trade* and during the Roman and Byzantine period, the archaeological evidence shows (see Chapter 6) that huge quantities of Gaza Wine and Ascalon wine were exported to south Arabia and Yemen.

The Nabataean Arab incense trade routes, maritime Gaza and Europe

As we shall see in Chapter 1, the geographic and strategic location of the city of Gaza made it the centre of one of the most important trade and military routes in the ancient world – and the centre of what became known in ancient times as both the *Via Maris* ('the Way of the Sea') and by the ancient Egyptians, the *Way of Horus*. The latter was named after the Egyptian 'God of the Sky' who was also known as 'Protector of Trade Routes'. This key trade route connected Palestine and Syria with ancient Egypt, the most powerful empire of the ancient world, on the one hand, and Palestine with south Arabia and Yemen, together with Southeast Asian trade, on the other. The city of Gaza also connected the south Arabian spice and incense trade with Europe through the Mediterranean Sea. In ancient times the name of Gaza, and generally southern Palestine, became intertwined with the lucrative frankincense trade and other precious commodities. But the goods transported on land via the Palestinian Naqab were diverse: they included spices, perfumes, medicinal herbs, incense and cosmetics, all originating either in the Tropics or in south Arabia, the Horn of Africa, and India (e.g. Amar 2003: 61–6).

The highly prized frankincense was universally used in ancient religious rituals and even in some traditional ancient medicines. Gaza and other cities such as Ascalon became pivotal to the Mediterranean frankincense trade from south Arabia and the spice trade from Asia and India as well as the Red Sea maritime silk route from China to Palestine. All these commodities were shipped to Gaza port city either through the Red Sea and or through the Trans-Arabian camel caravans through Petra and the trade posts dotted across the Palestinian Naqab. The modern romance and myths surrounding the central Asian 'Silk Road' from China have attracted many publications and museums exhibitions in the West. But in fact the inland (central Asian) silk routes were five times more expensive and much slower than the extensive silks imported in Antiquity from China via the maritime silk routes of the Indian Ocean and the Red Sea and then through both Egypt and the city of Aelas (modern Aqaba), in *Palaestina Tertia*, and then on land to Gaza port city and then to the Mediterranean world. This major Red Sea maritime silk route to the Palestinian city of Aelas has attracted little scholarly attention.

The Palestinian Naqab itself was a traditional axis of Trans-Arabian trade to the Mediterranean world; the Naqab became one of the preferred directions for the Nabataean Arab spice caravans from the mid-third century BCE onwards, during which the Nabataean Arab kingdom controlled much of southern Palestine. The Nabataean Kingdom became a powerful state of the Nabataean Arabs during classical Antiquity from the mid-third century BCE until 106 CE with its replacement by the Roman province of *Arabia Petraea* (or the Rome's *Provincia Arabia*; a frontier province of the Roman Empire at the centre of the Trans-Arabian spice caravans; the same province at the centre of the spice and aromatic caravans became known as *Palaestina Satutaris (or the Third Palestine)* under the Byzantines). In classical Antiquity the Nabataean Arab kingdom controlled the eastern trade routes to Gaza and the Mediterranean coast. Amassing large wealth from the Trans-Arabian spice trade, the kingdom stretched from the Naqab into the Hijaz and up as far north as Damascus, which it controlled for a short period in 85–71 BCE. In addition to controlling the Trans-Arabian trade, the Nabataean Arabs transported spices and aromatics to Petra from the town of Leuke Kome (Greek: λευκή κώμη, 'white village'), a port city on the Red Sea and a market town for the small vessels arriving from south Arabia (Jones 1917; Young 1997: 266–8).

The struggle for the control of the lucrative spice and aromatics trade through Palestine in classical Antiquity drew in a rising power in Judea in Palestine: the Hasmoneans. They embodied Hellenistic Judaism in Antiquity that combined Jewish religious tradition with Hellenistic culture and religion. These were the Hellenized ruling Jewish dynasty in Judea and the surrounding area in from 140 BCE to 37 CE – who were initially semi-autonomously in the Seleucid empire and became clients of Rome from 63 BCE – whose kings took the Greek title *besillleus* (βασιλεύς, Greek for 'king'). Seeking to grab the Palestine end of the Nabataean Arab spice trade, Alexander Jannaeus (103–76 BCE) of the Hasmoneans occupied Gaza in 99 BCE. This led to the interruption of the spice and aromatics' caravans to Gaza and the Mediterranean for a period of time.

However, in 106 CE the Romans sought to assert their control over the Trans-Arabian spice trade by annexing the Nabatean Arab kingdom itself into the newly created Roman Arab province of *Arabia Petraea*, a Roman frontier province in charge of the lucrative trade from south Arabia and India – in the fourth century CE *Arabia Petraea* became the Byzantine province of *Palaestina Salutaris*, whose metropolis was the city of Petra. Under the Byzantines, *Palaestina Salutaris*, like Palestine as a whole, remained at the heart of the Trans-Arabian trade to the Palestinian coastal cities of the Mediterranean Sea, and thus attesting to the millennia-age continuity of the international spice trade through Palestine's international routes.

The incense trade, frankincense and the ancient aromatics industries were born out of practical necessities, rather than the romantic images being portrayed in Western documentary of our time. Crowded with worshippers and ancient tourists, temples from Gaza of ancient Palestine to Tyre of the Phoenician to Athens and Rome of the classical world and to the ancient temples of Egypt, Mesopotamia and India were perfumed and 'purified' with frankincense and incense to rid the temples of bad odours and the stench produced by fish markets and birds and crowded city spaces. Also, bad air and foul-smelling vapour, or *miasma* (μίασμα) Greek for 'pollution', a theory which was advanced by Hippocrates in the fourth century BCE and accepted widely the Near East, China and Europe, that bad air caused the spread of contagious diseases and some epidemics that were not uncommon in crowded cities.

High ideals and the sublime were often invoked to back up human necessity for clean air and hygienic confined and crowded spaces. Rising and flourishing for centuries and then disappearing, frankincense was one of the most precious and expensive commodities of Antiquity; it was a highly sought-after commodity that became at the centre of both the aromatics industry and traditional medical treatment of Antiquity. In Antiquity the city of Gaza in Palestine traded internationally with frankincense from Yemen more than the city of Rome at the height of the Roman

Empire in the second century CE. When Alexander the Great occupied the Gaza in 332 BCE, a city at the centre of Trans-Arabian frankincense trade, he had 500 *talents* weights of frankincense and 100 *talents* of myrrh all looted from Gaza, sent to his old tutor Leonidas of Epirus in order to be used 'in his offerings to the gods' (Retso 2003; Terpstra 2019: 170).

The *talent* (τάλαντον, *talanton*) was a unit of weight used in the ancient world, and adopted by the Greeks through their trade with the Phoenicians. They were often used for weighing gold and silver; but it was also used in connection with precious imported goods such as ivory and frankincense. A Greek attic *talent* was approximately 26 kilograms; so the 600 frankincense and myrrh *talents* looted from Gaza would translate to about 15,600 kilograms, or 15 tonnes. By comparison, Rome, at its heights a city of one million people (mostly inhabited by the urban poor of all nationalities), traded about 3,000 tons of frankincense annually and it remained a famous multipurpose Forum which included marketplace.

The looting of Gaza's frankincense and myrrh by Alexander is linked to another Greek account about the Arab frankincense trade to the Mediterranean by the Nabataean Arab kingdom and its capital Petra. In the year 312 BCE, the Greek historian Diodorus Siculus (Diodorus of Sicily) recorded – on the basis of contemporary accounts by officers of Alexander – who talked about the 'land of the Arabs who are called Nabataeans' – who procured and transported frankincense, perfumes and all sorts of precious spices from south Arabia to Gaza on the Mediterranean. According to these accounts Alexander dispatched a force of 4,000 infantry and 600 cavalry with one of his officers, Athenaeus, to attack Petra. In a surprise nigh raid on Petra, the Greek forces killed some Nabateans, imprisoned others and managed to collect a substantial amount of frankincense, myrrh and silver from Petra. Departing before dawn, Athenaeus and his forces hurried back to the west in expectation of hot pursuit by the Nabateans. The Nabatean forces did pursue the Greek forces and destroyed virtually all the infantry and pursued much of the cavalry (Bowersock 1994: 13–15).

After Alexander, Gaza became central to the Ptolemaic Egyptian administration and economy in Palestine in the third century BCE. Under the Ptolemaic rule Gaza rose to become the most important trading city in Palestine, with Koinic Greek becoming the administrative and commercial language of both Egypt and Palestine. This led Apollonius, the chief finance minister of Ptolemaic Egypt between 262 and 245 BCE – also an important merchant and land-owner, who owned estates in Galilee, Palestine – to post a special agent in Gaza. Ptolemaicera documentary evidence in Koinic Greek shows the city had developed strong trading links with India and south Arabia. Apollonios' business documentation and the great amount of information in the archive of papyri kept by his assistant secretary and business agent Zenon – who travelled on a business trip through Palestine between 260 and 258 BCE, where his master had commercial interests – shows the growing international geographical range of areas sending goods to and through Gaza (Hölbl 2001: 58–9; Terpstra 2019: 170). The dossier of letters written by Zenon speak of the considerable export from Palestine to Egypt especially of wine, olive oil, wheat and cereals, and some export of slaves (Hadas 2007: 46–7). The Ptolemaic rulers of Egypt renamed several cities in Palestine and sought to promote greater urbanization in the country as a way of raising the standard of living of the population. However, much of the Palestinian exports of key produce to Egypt during the Ptolemaic period was state-administered rather than through private enterprise (Etheredge 2011: 22).

Limes Palaestinae and *Limes Arabiae*: Trade posts and military forts in southern Palestine under the Romans and Byzantines

Palestine was a distinct geo-political entity with distinct provinces under both the Romans and the Byzantines. Hence the Latin terms *Limes Palaestinae:* 'The borders of Palestine' and *Limes Arabiae*: 'The borders of the Roman province of Arabia' are terms we come across in the Latin literature of classical Antiquity in connection to both the international trade routes of southern and eastern Palestine and the military fortifications of these eastern borders of the Roman Empire. International trade routes transporting precious commodities and generally business in Antiquity were militarized and protected by a system of fortifications and the important Nabataean Spice Routes, and subsequently Roman and Byzantine trade through southern Palestine, had to be protected by fortified and well-guarded military posts – military posts which in Antiquity were known as *Limes Palaestinae* and *Limes Arabiae* and the two concepts became closely linked in classical and late Antiquity.

The two terms also originated in the Nabataean Arab Spice Route in the Naqab and the Nabataean spice routes from the Red Sea through Petra and across the Neqab to the Palestine coast cities of Gaza and Ascalon. The Nabataean Arab kingdom was the first to establish caravan routes with trade infrastructures that linked caravan trade routes with military forts, way-stations (caravanserai), stone watchtowers, road markers and cisterns. Archaeological evidence shows spacing of the Nabataean caravanserai stations through the Naqab, roughly 15–20 km between stations, suggests a day's journey. State administered stations, caravanserai themselves are equipped with rooms, open courtyards, large kitchens, and water, and suggest a defensive stance, if not truly fortified (Rosen 2019). These Nabataean military posts and trading stations became archetypal and central to the constructions of the military/trading station fortifications of the *Limes Palaestinae* and *Limes Arabiae* throughout classical and late Antiquity.

Under the Nabataeans the time taken between stations in the Palestinian Naqab – which was relatively shorter than the Eurasian silk routes' caravan distances between stops – was 18 km per day. By contrast, the speed of the Arab maritime trade voyages was much greater: the average Arabian Dhow boat covered almost 150 km per day. However, this Nabatean Arab system of trade stations and military fort infrastructure consisted of well-equipped trade stations across the Naqab trade routes.

This system, subsequently known as *Limes Palaestinae* and *Limes Arabiae,* was maintained during the Roman and Byzantine periods. During the Byzantine period Palestine Arab *phylarchs* and Arab *federate* in *Palaestina Tertia* and other frontier regions of Byzantine Palestine performed important function including collecting transit taxes at toll stations and maintaining internal and external security and as auxiliaries to the regular Roman and later Byzantine forces in a defence system of the *Limes Palaestinae* – a chain of forts, fortifications with watchtowers (equipped with rooms and caravanserais, cisterns and watering stations, watchtowers) along the southern and eastern frontier regions of Palestine and along the trade routes from Petra to Gaza and from Aelas to Gaza. The *Limes Palaestinae* in the province of *Palaestinae Tertia* and *Palaestina Secunda* were an integral part of what was known as *Limes Arabiae*, a series of forts that stretched from Aelas (Aylah) *in Palaestnae Tertia* to the Byzantine eastern frontiers in modern Jordan and Syria. In the sixth century Palestine Arab *phylarchs* and Ghassanid Arab *federate* moved into these forts and contributed to the fortifications that helped secure the border regions and trade routes of Palestine (Shahid 1995: 35).

The international transit trade routed through this system of fortified road stations in southern Palestine. Several fortified road stations – some combining caravanserai and industrial facilities for perfume production – were constructed on the Incense Road between Gaza-Elusa-Oboda-Kalgouia (Moyat Awad) – Petra. Southern Palestine also appears to have developed its own perfume industries; archaeologists have uncovered the remains of ancient perfume factories created along the Nabataean incense route of Petra-Oboda-Elusa-Gaza route.

Border trade stations and customs taxes in Ancient Palestine

In ancient times the authorities controlling Palestine's international highways or controlling provinces in Palestine often levied lucrative taxes on international goods passing through Palestine's border provinces or Palestinian port cites and at least some of the *Limes Palaestinae* and *Limes Arabiae* border stations function as taxation posts. At its height during the Hellenistic and Roman period the Nabataean Arab kingdom (with its capital Petra), which controlled much of southern Palestine, flourished on imposing considerable taxes on the Trans-Arab spice trade through the port city of Gaza and further afield.

Quality often wins. However, we do not have precise figures about the qualities of Gaza Wine consumed in Europe and outside Palestine over several centuries in late Antiquity – but judging from:

a. the vast quantities of Gaza amphorae excavated in Europe, in Istanbul, Italy, France, Spain, Germany, Britain as well as in the Crimean peninsula, Egypt and south Arabia;
b. the praise heaped on this wine by poets, authors and senior church figures in Europe and in Egypt;
c. the scale of the wine factories in Palestine during the Byzantine era and the recent discovery of the largest wine factory in the Byzantine Empire, the international quantities consumed over time must have been huge.

Chapters 4 and 6 will show scale of the wine produced in Palestine between the fourth and seventh century and the Palestinian wine exported to many countries overseas in late Antiquity must have been enormous. Along the frontiers of ancient Palestine, key permanent trading stations were created for collecting revenues from long-distance transit trade passing through Palestine. Chapter 1 shows that one of these lucrative key posts was the island-town of Iotabe (Greek *Ἰωτάβη;* Arabic: *Yotoba*), now called the island Tiran (at the entrance of the Gulf of Aqaba), which controlled much of the Indian Ocean trade and collected taxes from ships heading for the port city of Aelas (modern Aqaba); by all accounts the taxes collected were considerable. The superhighway of the Red Sea maritime trade also generated vibrant cosmopolitan ports in Palestine in late Antiquity such as Iotabe and Aylah (Aelas) (Power 2012). This island also became known in ancient times as *Iotapa in Palaestina* and was part of the Byzantine province of *Palaestina Tertia*, of late Antiquity (*La Gerarchia Catholica* 2013). As we shall see in Chapter 2, this strategic border island was an integral part of *Palaestina* and its transit trade tax collection and its commercial, monetary and fiscal system in Antiquity.

Trade and the spread of multilingualism: The *melting pot* cities of Palestine in Antiquity

Throughout much of its ancient history, Palestine and its urban centres were multilingual. The dominant paradigm of classical Palestine (under Hellenistic Ptolemies, Romans and Byzantines) among Western historians is that of that Hellenistic elites dominated urban Palestine, while Syriac, which was derived from Aramaic, was the language of the peasantry and countryside. But the picture derived from both the historical and literacy sources is far more complicated. To begin with, koinē Greek was the official language of the administration in Palestine.

As we shall see in Chapter 3, the Nabataean Arabs who established a powerful Arab kingdom and wealthy cities that prospered on the 'spice routes' in north Arabia and southern Palestine in Antiquity were multilingual and used Arabic, Aramaic and Greek – Aramaic being the language of trade in western Asia from the beginning of the first millennium BCE and into classical Antiquity. Also, archaeological discoveries and the existence of Nabataean Arabs in the south of the country and Arabic-speaking Ghassanid communities and even Ghassanid Arab *federate* inhabitants and forces of Byzantine Palestine (in the three-in-one Palestine provinces: *Palaestina Prima, Palaestina Secunda and Palaestina Tertia*, in the sixth and early seventh centuries (Masalha 2018: 135–150)) make the dominant Greek dominant paradigm untenable.

In fact, the international trade of Palestine and transit trade routes through Palestine have created *melting pot* cities and for over a millennium in Antiquity the cultural, linguistic and demographic makeup of urban Palestine became complex, and immigration and social mobility were much in evidence and the multilingualism of urban Palestine occurred: in the cities and towns the language spoken was often Greek; Syriac, Arabic (Evans 2005: 2) in addition to Arabic and Nabataean Arabic being spoken, especially in cities and market towns in the southern eastern parts of the country towns and in many urban parts of *Palaestina Prima*. Multi-culturalism and multilingualism in urban Palestine are indications of generally high rates of literacy among the social elites of the country and also the existence of a formal system of education that was common in urban Palestine.

The discovery of Greek and Arabic papyri documents at Nessana (Greek: Νιζάνα), an ancient Nabataean Arab city located in the southwest Naqab – a locality known to local modern Palestinians as Auja al-Hafir – provided evidence for the teaching of classic texts in the schools of Nessana, a city whose native language was apparently Arabic. Crucially the city of Nessana served international transit trade and pilgrims and merchants travelling through southern Palestine to Gaza, Egypt and Arabia, an international trade which was dominated by Arab merchants.

In the mid-1930s hundreds of papyri documents and letters were excavated, dating from the sixth and seventh centuries CE, revealing a wealth of information about day-to-day life trade and transaction in Palestine Nabataean Arab society in the last phases of the Byzantine rule and the earliest phases of Arab-Islamic administration. This Byzantine and Umayyad corpus (spanning the years from 500 to 700) was discovered in 1935 at al-Auja, on the frontier between the Sinai and the Naqab, which, like Petra, was part of the province of Palestine III (*Palaestina Salutaris*). The Nabataean Arab cultural and linguistic base is still visible, notably in personal names. The papyri were probably discarded, but instead of being destroyed, they were kept in rooms attached to religious establishments. These texts are essentially Greek, but some are bilingual Greek-Arabic, or entirely Arabic. Among these papyri documents were the private archive of a major family in the city of Nessana covering the years 537 to 593; these were written in Greek, but the archive also reflects a community whose native language appears to be Arabic (Crone with Silverstein 2016: 17; Shahid 1989: 143–4). One of these Arabic papyri documents was from the local Arab governor granting the Christian inhabitants of the region dhamma status and freedom of worship on payment of the appropriate Jizya tax (Colt 1962; Hoyland 2015: 51–71). The tax was historically levied in the form of a financial charge on protected non-Muslim subjects (known as dhimmi) in order to fund the public expenditures of the administration, in place of the *zakat* and *khums* taxes that Muslim subjects were obliged to pay. Another Arabic papyrus document of Nessana described the Islamic coinage struck instituted within the financial, administrative and currency reforms of the Caliph 'Abd al-Malik ibn Marwan (646–705 CE), replacing the *Byzantine-Islamic* currency of the province of Palestine (Jund Filastin) with a new Umayyad Arabic currency (Evans 2005: 22; Goodwin 2004 1-12). The multilingual (Greek, Latin, Arabic) environment of late Antiquity Palestine, in general, and that of Nessana, in particular (Greek, Latin, Arabic), were much in evidence. The native language was Arabic; the Greek papyri documents of Nessana also included official Byzantine letters, documents and private wills as well as fragmentary text from Virgil's work and a glossary of Virgil's Aeneid, in Latin and Greek (Colt 1962; Hoyland 2015: 65–6; Magness 2003; and Shahid 1989: 143), an epic poem written by Virgil in the first century BCE. This vocabulary list for the Aeneid was used by local schoolboys and read in a local Nessana school and in elementary schools in Palestine in the early sixth century (Evans 2005: 22). Furthermore, fourth-century documents and letters mention the names of sophists and rhetors who were involved in other schools of rhetoric in various cities in Palestine (including Aelia Capitolina, Gaza, Caesarea and Elusa), one of which even held a Chair in Rhetoric.

Elusa was a Nabataean Arab town in the Palestinian Naqab founded in the late fourth or early third century and flourished on the Trans-Arabian perfume trade. Its name was preserved in the modern Arab village of Al-Khalasa until 1948. It was located to the south-west of Beersheba and maintained a school and an official teacher of rhetoric (Hidary 2017: 6).

Trademarks of Palestinian identity: Global brands, common trade names and national iconography

Gaza wine, Beisan textiles, Al-Khalil glassware, Nablus soap, Jaffa orange

It has already been shown that *liquors Palaestini, Liquors Arabes* and *Arabian Myrrh* became common trade names in Antiquity. Common trade names and iconic trademarks such as *Jaffa Orange, Nablus Soap* and *Al-Khalil Glassware* are central to the national iconography of Palestine. Branding is thought to be a modern concept associated with the rise of modern industrial capitalism. In the nineteenth century, with the rise of modern mass manufactured products, in the US and Britain, branding started to become the means whereby producers of manufactured goods would emphasize qualities and reputation in their products and would use the manufacturers' name to produce such products as tea, tobacco, chocolate, etc. However, as we shall see, trade brands, or common trade names, have existed since Antiquity. In Palestine, the four most iconic brands and internationally recognized common trade names are: *Gaza Wine (Vinum) Al-Khalil Glassware, Nablus Soap* and *Jaffa Orange* – the first: *Vinum Gazetum*, emerged in Byzantine Palestine and was popularized in Europe in late Antiquity and the Middle Ages and the modern period. Other modern Palestinian brands include the Zalatimo's Sweets manufacturers of Jerusalem (see Chapter 17);

> A trademark is intended to distinguish the source of the goods of one commercial entity from those of another. For example, by placing the mark "Zalatimo" on its products, the Amman based Zalatimo's Brothers lets the customers know that Zalatimo manufacturer special oriental sweets of exceptional quality.
>
> (Khoury 2010: 14)

The international success of the Palestinian Zalatimo sweets manufactures is also evident in the fact that *ZALATIMO SWEETS SINCE 1860 AND DESIGN. ZALATIMO SWEETSCOMPANY* is listed in the *Official Gazette of the United States Patents and Trademarks.*[20]

Two brands – *Gaza Wine* in Antiquity and *Jaffa Orange* (see Chapters 6 and 17) which did not come all from Jaffa – earned their reputations from the merchants and particularly from the port from which they were shipped to Europe from *Maiumas Gaza* in Antiquity and the port city of Jaffa in the modern period. In Western Europe in Antiquity where Latin poets, writers and senior clergymen gave it a good 'press' the reputation of the Gaza Wine soared; modern economic historians and archaeologists added their findings about the rise of *Gaza amphorae* in the fourth to sixth centuries, and these amphorae have been unearthed throughout Mediterranean countries and in Europe as far north as Britain (Mayerson 1992: 76–80).

Produced largely in the fertile agricultural hinterlands of Palestine, the top brands *Gaza Wine* and *Jaffa Orange* were named after the Palestinian port cities from which they were shipped to Europe, while the third, *Nablus Soap*, was named after the city in which it was produced at high-quality and in large quantities in the late Ottoman period and British Mandatory period. No less important are the textile industry of Roman and Byzantine Palestine; for instance, the flax and *linen of Scythopolis* (Beisan) became a top brand of high-quality during the Roman and Byzantine periods.

In Palestine historically, olive oil, grape (and wine) and wheat were both *staple crops* and *cash crops*. Cash crops are marketed crops grown to sell for profit. The term is used to differentiate marketed crops from staple crops, or 'subsistence crops', which are grown as food for the farmer's family; olive, olive oil, grape, wine, wheat, honey, fish and dairy products were at the heart of the Palestinian diet of Antiquity. Cash crops (in particular olive oil and wine) were exported widely around the Mediterranean region in Antiquity and the profitable production of these cash crops were a major source of revenues for the growing population of Palestine. Also, olive oil and wine became especially important to the Palestinian diet in ancient times and local olive trees and vineyards were also major producers of olive oil and wine for regional international markets. Wine-making in ancient Palestine and the ancient Mediterranean world achieved a place as a dietary staple. As we shall see in Chapter 6, the quantity of wine recommended by some leaders of early Palestinian monasticism was up to three glasses daily and wine was included in regular diet by early Palestinian monasteries (Bitton-Ashkelony and Kofsky 2006: 183–4),

For several centuries during the Byzantine period, *Vinum Gazetum* (Latin for Gaza Wine) was probably the most famous wine produced and consumed in the ancient world and (as we shall see in Chapter 6) its high-quality was attested in numerous European documents. *Vinum Gazetum* and other Palestinian iconic trade brands (which will be discussed in Chapters 6, 10, 14 and 17) provide us with one of the most important sources of knowledge as to the significance of Palestine's global trading activities across millennia.

In fact, much research on three Palestinian international trade brands: *Gaza Wine*, *Jaffa Orange* and *Nablus Soap* have been produced. Yet works on these Palestinian common trade names have been carried out in either isolation from each other or without exploring their inter-connectedness or their significant international export dimensions and their crucial role in the prosperity and urban expansion of Palestinian cities. Furthermore, no attempt has been made to connect these major foreign exports to Europe across millennia with, say the Palestinian cotton export to Europe in the eighteenth century and with the *Jaffa Orange* export to Europe from the second half of the nineteenth century until 1948. In other words, these iconic brands: *Gaza Wine*, *Beisan Textile*, *Jaffa Orange* and *Nablus Soap*, all point to emergence of major *traditional industries* in Palestine across many millennia, industries which were not simply aimed at the internal market but primarily focused on the lucrative international market. Spurred by technological innovation in the country and capital investment, these lucrative foreign markets generated revenues that were then reinvested in the main cites of Palestine and contributed significantly to the expansion and development of urban Palestine.

Palestinian traditional industries and agro-industries and the lucrative international export of Palestinian key brands (*Gaza Wine, Schythopolis Linen, Jaffa Orange* and *Nablus Soap*) did play an important role in urbanization in both ancient and modern Palestine. Some industries such as Nablus Soap sought, in the second half of the nineteenth century and first half of the twentieth centuries, to modernize and keep up with changes and adjust its modus operandi to meet the needs of modern customers.

Modern brand name products often associated with manicured products following mass manufacturing and industrialization; pre-modern industrial brand names are quite rare in pre-industrial societies with predominantly rural and agricultural cultures. However, common name product did emerge in trading societies of Antiquity. This book, while contextualizing the rise of these iconic trade names and traditional industries, aims also at addressing the rise and expansion of urban Palestine across the ages.

The Palestinian international trade and export to the Mediterranean world and Europe, in Antiquity, the Middle Ages and modern times is often misunderstood, if we consider the common trade names conventionally assigned to three types of products: the ancient *Schythopolis Textile*, *Vinum Gazetum* (Gaza Wine) and *Jaffa Orange* in modern times, these titles often refer to seaports in Palestine from which such goods were shipped, rather than their actual places of manufacture.

The wines produced in southern Palestine (which includes the Gaza and Ascalon regions and by the towns and villages of the northern Naqab) in late Antiquity in general was referred to as 'Gazan', or *Vinum Gazetum* because it was exported through *Maiumas Gaza*, the port city of Gaza, in the same way the Palestinian silk and textile products were exported in the Middle Ages through the port of Gaza, and Palestinian citrus exported to Europe in the modern age became known as 'Jaffa Orange' because it were exported through the port of Jaffa. Gazan wine was internationally rated very highly Like Gaza Wine – which was produced throughout southern Palestine (the Ascalon and Gaza regions in particular) – 'Gauze' and the Palestine silkworm and linen industries flourished under Islam in the regions of Ascalon and Gaza.

Structurally and thematically, some of the key traditional industries of Palestine will figure prominently in the chapter titles of this book; other significant traditional industries such as sugar industry of Palestine – which was developed significantly under the Mamluks – and the quarries and the stone industry of Palestine under the Ottomans and since the Ottoman period will be discussed in Chapter 11.

Merchants and peasants: The symbiotic relations between city and country

Generally, several traditional industries in Palestine, such as the glass industry of al-Khalil, the soap industry of Jerusalem and Nablus and the linen industry of Schythopolis (Beisan), benefited from either widely available local raw materials or locally produced materials. It is important to emphasize that any discussion of the production of specialized industrial products and top brands of Palestine should not be confined the merchants of these cities but should also include the symbiotic social and economic and relations between city and country, and the merchants of the city and the peasants of the hinterlands of these cities. Also urban prosperity often depended on the rural economy of Palestine. In Antiquity 'most cities [in Palestine] developed into enterprising centres of production and retail trade', yet the 'consumer-city mode' is inappropriate for urban Palestine. In Antiquity – as in the modern period – Palestinian city economies were intricate and the production of specialist brands depended on range of activities provided by the city's hinterland (Kingsley and Decker 2015a: 44–68). For instance, as we shall see in Chapter 6, the production of Gaza Wine during the Byzantine period involved many farmers and large parts of the countryside and many villages and towns in southern Palestine, including the countryside of the city of Ascalon and many villages and towns in the Naqab. In a similar vein, Chapter 5 shows that much of the fine *linen of Schythopolis* during the Roman and Byzantine periods came from the Galilee countryside, Marj Ibn Amer (Jisreel Valley) and the countryside of the city of Tiberias.

In late Antiquity, the craft of glass-making and large-scale glass production in Palestine, which centred largely on the cities of Schythopolis (Beisan) and Caesarea Maritima – which each yield eight to tentons of glass in a single firing – was another highly specialized industrial pursuit and reflected the joint enterprise and symbiotic economic relations between town and country in Palestine (Kingsley and Decker 2015a: 44–68).

The same principle of the cities symbiotic relationship with the countryside (and with the involvement of large number of villages) applies to the soap industry of Nablus and the orange industry of Jaffa in the modern period. A good discussion of the hinterland of Nablus, its olive industry and the peasants and merchants of the area in connection with the modern city's soap factories is found in Doumani (1995: 27–33).

Social prejudices and historical misrepresentations: Contribution of the Palestinian Bedouin communities to the rise of urban industries

As we shall see in Chapter 3, the Nabataean Arab and Bedouin communities of northern Arabia and southern Palestine constructed some of the most important global trade systems of classical Antiquity and created an important kingdom and spectacular and highly developed cities from the proceeds of spice, frankincense and aromatics. These cities, the most famous of which Petra, dominated the Trans-Arabian desert incense routes and transformed the Palestinian cities of the Naqab for over a millennium – a transformation that subsequently led to the development of a flourishing agriculture and an important wine industry in the Naqab during the Byzantine period (Chapter 6). However many historians have continued to be silent on the history of the sedentarized Bedouin communities of Palestine and their important contribution to the flourishing ancient and modern villages, towns and cities in Palestine.

Many authors of the history of Palestine do credit the symbiotic relations between merchants and peasants and the role of this symbiotic relationship in the rise of some of the most spectacular industries of urban Palestine. By contrast the sedentarized and semi-sedentarized Bedouin communities of Palestine have long suffered from social prejudice, racism and outright marginalization and silencing by many modern authors. Also Arab historians who confine perception of 'civilization' to urban centres tend to project their own prejudices on Arab and Palestinian Bedouin communities as 'anti-civilization'. Furthermore many authors depict these Bedouin communities of Palestine as a constant threat to urban and 'civilized' life in the country, while totally ignoring their contribution to the spectacular rise of urban industries. Chapter 10 will show the contribution of the Bedouin communities to the spectacular rise of glassware and ceramic industries in the city of al-Khalil (Hebron) and Chapter 15 will explore an equally important contribution to the soap industry of Nablus. Trade with the Bedouin communities of central Palestine was indispensable for the soap-making industry of Nablus and glass-making industry of al-Khalil since in both cases these communities furnished the alkaline soda (*qilw*) required by these industrial process. In the case of the glass industry of al-Khalil, the Palestine Bedouin trade networks brought up minerals including sodium carbonate, from the Dead Sea – an essential local material for the success of this industry.

Guilds of urban artisans and craftsmen and professional qualifications: Skilled workers and merchants and trade associations in Ancient and Medieval Palestine

While modern capitalist industries in Europe produced modern organized labour and trade unions, traditional craft industries of medieval Europe, which were often dominated by merchants and urban craftsmen, were associated with a variety of guilds and professional associations of free artisans skilled in a particular craft and merchants involved in a particular trade who organized themselves to protect the practice of their professional skills and expert craft or their specific trade within a particular town or city. As we shall see in Chapter 15 under Islam the scale of the olive oil soap-making industry of Palestine also necessitated skilled workers with professional qualifications and produced guilds of soap makers (*Sanii al-Saboun, or sabbans*) in Jerusalem in the sixteenth century – guilds of skilled workers who formally organized themselves with teachers of the craft and head teachers and used the legal system and local judicial courts to ensure the professional regulation and protection of their rights, skills and professional expertise (Cohen 2002: 85). These guilds of craftsmen saw their responsibility as cultivating their skills and refining their products in order to achieve high-quality products and improve the social life of ordinary people and general hygiene in the teeming medieval cities of Palestine and beyond.

Although historically the professional *guild association* concept evolved in the Roman Empire, it became common in the industrial settings of Palestine in Antiquity (especially under the Romans and Byzantines) and in the urban centres of Palestine under Islam in the Middle Ages. The concept emerged in the industrial and textile towns and cities and within the wealth of expertise and technical skills created within the old-age manufacturing sectors of traditional industries like textiles, silk and linen weaving, tanneries and soap-making – export-oriented industries with high reputations in which the urban centres of Palestine excelled. Guild associations began to emerge throughout the Roman Empire and Palestine had a variety of these associations. As we shall see in Chapter 5, the large-scale textile industry of Roman Palestine, which involved several Palestinian cities, witnessed the emergence of early guild associations, or *collegia*, in the country. These were organized by textile weavers and merchants in some urban centres such as the collegial city of Diocaesarea/Sepphoris (the modern Arab town of Saffuriya), then one of the largest and most industrialized cities in the country. Reference to guilds of textile workers and linen weavers in a number of Palestinian cities are found; a guild of linen weavers in Diocaesarea/Sepphoris and inscriptions mentioning guilds of weavers have been found in Tiberias (Safrai 1994; 2003).

There were other types of merchant guild associations in urban Roman Palestine introduced by Hellenistic Judaism, which was a form of Judaism that blended Jewish religious traditions with Hellenistic culture and pagan religion of urban Palestine. Although the main centre of Hellenistic Judaism was the city of Alexandria in Egypt, powerful aspects of Hellenistic Judaism existed in the urban synagogues of ancient Palestine in classical Antiquity especially in textile cities such as Sepphoris (Saffuriya) in Galilee and Caesarea Maritima whose urban life and learning institutions and libraries were hugely influenced in classical Antiquity by Alexandria (Masalha 2022). Examples of extensive Hellenization of Jewish synagogues in urban Roman Palestine can be seen in the excavation of zodiac sun-gods on ancient synagogue mosaic floors that have been discovered by archaeological excavations of sites in the Galilee and elsewhere in Roman and early Byzantine Palestine. One of these sites of zodiac sun-gods synagogues was located in the textile city of Sepphoris in Galilee, showing the evolution of Jewish pagan culture and hybrid Jewish identity in urban Roman Palestine (Rose 2010: 25–49; Talgam and Weiss 2004).

During this period of Hellenistic Judaism and cultural hybridization in Roman Palestine, Jewish *rabbis-merchants* involved in the lucrative silk trade began to flourish. For these rabbis, with international trade connections, Greek terms such as emporia (ἐμπόριον) for *markets, trade* and *merchandise* became widely common in their rabbinical literature of classical Antiquity. For instance, in the city of Caesarea Maritima, which was one of the key centres of the pure dye tanneries and textile industry of Palestine, the influential Jewish rabbis of the city – many of whom, as we shall see in Chapter 5, were wealthy silk merchants who imported raw Chinese silk to Palestine in the third and fourth centuries CE – (Patrich 2011: 119) formed the highly developed guild associations within the Palestinian Jewish rabbinate, and they constituted a distinctive socio-economic class in Roman Palestine (Hezser 1997: 182). However, as we shall see in Chapter 6, the rise of *monks-wine-merchants* and their role in the economy and wine industries of Byzantine Palestine in the fifth and sixth centuries would soon eclipse any previous involvement of the Jewish *rabbi-silk-*

merchant in the textile industries and textile trade of Palestine in the third and fourth century AD (Patrich 2011: 119).

In Jerusalem in the early Ottoman period the scale of soap-making industries of the city facilitated the emergence of the professional experts and *guilds of soap makers* – in the way the scale of the textile of Palestine in Antiquity, and specialist expertise required in this industry encouraged the emergence of the ancient guilds of Roman and Byzantine Palestine. In the sixteenth century the entire soap production process in Jerusalem was carried out by skilled soap makers (*Sanii al-Saboun*) whose professional qualifications in soap-making and membership of the guild of soap makers had to be checked and confirmed by the head of the guild: *Shaykh al-Mu'allimin fi Tabkh al-Sabun,* who was nominated by the Muslim Qadi (city of Jerusalem judge) (Cohen 2002: 82–5).

Polyculture and the economic prosperity of Palestine: Agriculture, horticulture, viticulture and sericulture

The hawakeer and the basateen of Palestine

Chapter 6 shows how Dionysus – an eastern deity whose Roman equivalent was Bacchus, the god of the grape harvest, wine-making and fertility – was widely worshipped as a nature deity in Palestine across several centuries in Antiquity. Dionysus also became the patron deity of the Palestinian city of Schythopolis (Beisan) in Antiquity. Interestingly both *wine* and *bread* were sanctified by Jesus of Nazareth (and in the New Testament), while the sanctification of *bread* (derived from wheat) was widely maintained by the Palestinian Muslims and this tradition has survived into the modern period; the holy Quran in effect also sanctified *olive oil.* All these sacred religious traditions in Palestine are hardly surprising, when we consider the fact that grape, olive and wheat have been staples of Palestinian (and Near Eastern) diet for millennia and the heart of the prosperity of the country.

As I show in Chapter 6, grapes and the wine industry became central to the prosperity of Palestine and its polyculture and horticulture and international export in late Antiquity, and how sunny hillsides and slopes (or *hawakeer*) of Palestine were preferred over flatter terrain, which was preserved for *basateen* in Palestine: vines growing on hillsides and slopes of the *hawakeer* of Palestine received a greater intensity of the sun's rays and benefited from better drainage of soil leading to a high-quality crop of ripe grapes. Indeed the agricultural prosperity of Palestine and its polyculture in Antiquity, which was reliant on several commercial crops, most notably grapes, olives and wheat, and produced several highly lucrative agricultural industries, has long been widely acknowledged as a primary source of prosperity in the country. However, more complex issues concerning the structure of production and international trade, and how both were affected by wider macroeconomic Mediterranean international trade system have been examined in Kingsley and Decker (2015b: 44–68) – covering a period that is widely perceived to be a 'Golden Age' in Palestine history, an age of economic and agricultural boom and phenomenal demographic and cultural growth. Between the fourth and seventh centuries the ancient cities of Palestine expanded phenomenally – with twenty-five cities having a municipal status in the full sense of the *polis* – and hundreds of new Palestinian towns and villages were established in response to the pressure exerted by regional population growth (Kingsley and Decker 2015a: 1–27, 2015b: 44–68). For instance, in late Antiquity widespread wheat cultivation encouraged the development of the basalt millstone manufacturing industry in the Tiberias region within the Galilee, from where hour glass-shaped products were exported throughout Palestine and even into Cyprus (Kingsley and Decker 2015b: 44–68).

In Antiquity olive oil production and olive presses were equally pivotal to the Palestinian economy. Among the 365 known oil presses in the Byzantine era, particularly large concentrations existed in central Palestine and the Galilee: sixty presses in the Acre area; 109 installations associated with fifty-eight sites in the western central and the lower Syrian Golan heights; fifty-three presses to the south of Caesarea Maritima; and sixty around the city of Jaffa (Kingsley and Decker 2015b: 44–68).

The history of agriculture and horticulture in Palestine goes back for at least 12,000 years and its origins lie in the transition of human communities from a nomadic lifestyle to sedentary, or semi-sedentary, agricultural and horticultural communities. (von Hagen 1957). The term horticulture derives from the Latin words *hortus* and *cultura*, which mean 'garden' and 'cultivation', respectively. Horticulture is the art of cultivating plants in gardens to produce food, fruit and medicinal ingredients, and gardens for comfort and ornamental purposes. Horticulturists are agriculturalists who grow fruits and nuts, vegetables and herbs, as well as flowers and ornamental trees and, in modern times, cultivate green lawns and recreational spaces (Arteca 2015: 584; Preece and Read 2005: 4–6). Today, horticulture is divided into several categories that focus on the cultivation and processing of different types of plants and food items for specific purposes. In order to conserve the science of horticulture, multiple organizations worldwide educate, encourage and promote its advancement. Horticulture also involves plant propagation and cultivation to improve plant growth, yields, quality, nutritional value, and resistance to insects, diseases and environmental stresses.

Many non-native authors who write about the history of Palestine and who are not familiar with the indigenous Arabic terminology of the country tend to lump the complex polyculture and horticulture of the country under the term *bustans (orchards*, or agricultural fields). In fact in Palestine the two distinct categories of horticulture evolved historically and became known in Arabic as *basateen* (or *bustans*), and *hawakeer* (horticulture) also included landscape, soil management and terrace maintenance of the *hawakeer* of the hilly and mountainous region. For thousands of years the traditional domestic gardens, or *ḥawakeer*, which surrounding the hilly villages, towns and urban centres of Palestine, were widespread and were integral to households of all economic backgrounds in the country. These traditional domestic gardens also served as a space for work and socializing and constituted a focus of collective (extended family) life, and provided a wide diversity of agricultural crops and fruit tree cultivation. Historically economically central to agricultural urban and village produce of Palestine today, these spaces have been transformed into lawns and flowerbeds intended strictly for recreation and ornament (see, for instance, Mazzawi and Sa'ar. 2018: 537–55).

Historically there were many types of horticulture in Palestine including:

a. *Viticulture*: the cultivation and production of grapes, largely intended for wine-making and Palestinian wine became internationally famous during the Byzantine era (fourth to seventh century CE).
b. *Sericulture*: involves two processes. the cultivation of the silkworm from the egg stage through completion of the cocoon. The cultivation of mulberry trees that provide leaves upon which the worms feed. The production of silk begins with the cultivation of the mulberry tree and production of raw silk by means of raising caterpillars (larvae), particularly those of the domesticated silkworm (*Bombyx mori*). Raw Chinese silk was imported into Palestine until the fifth century CE, until Christian monks and Christian missionaries smuggled silkworms from China to Byzantine Palestine and Syria in the sixth century. The cultivation of the mulberry tree and silkworms flourished in southern Palestine in the Middle Ages. In the tenth century, Palestinian historian al-Maqdisi speaks of the silkworms of Ascalon as renowned (Conder 2018: 136).
c. *Horticultural oil*: olive cultivation and olive oil production and soap manufacturing; the olive gardens are famous in Palestine and throughout the Mediterranean region; olive trees in Palestine have survived for hundreds, and in some cases, thousands of years.

   As we shall see in Chapter 6, in Palestine historically olive oil was both a *staple crop* (and a crop central to the Palestinian food and diet) and a cash crop produced to sell for profit and exported widely around the Mediterranean region.

d. *Fruticulture*: the production of fruits and nuts was at the centre of the local diet in Antiquity and dried fruits and nuts were also exported to Egypt in Antiquity and the Middle Ages.

Like agriculture, horticulture can be on a large scale and small scale. In Palestine horticulture focuses on the use of small plots with a wide variety of mixed crops while agriculture focuses on one large primary crop at a time. At times lucrative and based on capital intensive industries, the foreign trade of Palestine had also major impact on the local agricultural economy of the country and on the rise of *cash crop economy*, especially in wine production in ancient times, silk, linen, cotton and wool fabrics in the Middle Ages and raw cotton and orange cultivation in the modern period.

In Palestine (ancient, medieval and modern) *cash crops* were usually crops (and their related products) that attracted demand in foreign markets in countries such as Egypt and in Europe, and hence had significant export value. However, prices for the major cash crops (and products related to them) of Palestine (wine, orange, soap, silk) were set in international trade markets. As consequence of this, Palestinian producers relying on such cash crops benefited from high prices in foreign trade markets but also suffered low prices when excess supply occurred on the global markets and prices dropped sharply.

Agricultural revolutions and technological innovations in Ancient Palestine

Western orientalists and biblical archaeologists and travellers who arrived in Palestine in the eighteenth and nineteenth centuries to authenticate the biblical stories often described the 'pastoral landscape' and 'unchanging local peasantry' since the time of Jesus of Nazareth. Many Palestinian authors, on the other hand, seeking to emphasize the *continuities* of ancient and modern Palestine often refer to the 'unchanging ploughing' methods and ancient irrigation technology of the Palestinian peasantry. In fact, one of the most enduring myths about Palestinian agriculture centres on the claim that the 'ploughing' methods of farming have changed little since Antiquity.

Nothing can be further from the truth, especially when we examine the historical developments in Palestinian agriculture. Although we should distinguish between modern *technologies* and ancient *crafts* and *traditional industries*, technological innovations took place in Palestine and the wider Near East across millennia. For instance, the significant viticulture and famous wine production of Palestine in late Antiquity not only depended on the existence of large regional and overseas markets, but also depended on the emergence of major technological developments in farming and irrigation methods in Palestine. The country, its agriculture and most of its urban centres had water in abundance and many villages and towns had perennial springs (Ziadeh 1953: 67-93).

Also, aqueducts and water canals were constructed in Antiquity and throughout the Middle Ages. Also both Palestinian estate owners and farmers rose to the challenge of the great demand for high-quality wine in lucrative foreign markets in late Antiquity by investing heavily in the land and new developments in irrigation methods. This also included the adoption of hitherto underutilized and more efficient wine presses. Accompanying these new technological methods was the use of the 'screw press' in both wine production and the olive oil industry of Palestine. This development was simultaneous with spread of the irrigation technology known as *saqiya*. The introduction of this method required significant capital investment and a significant pool of highly skilled local craftsmen. This phenomenon provides a glimpse of the pace of the technological developments in the region, and all these were partly driven by foreign and oversees market conditions and the spread of technology in the countryside (Decker 2008: 65).

Moreover, in the literature of *peasant studies* in Palestine there is a lot of confusion regarding the differences between farmers and peasants, the latter being referred to as Palestinian *fellaheen*. The Arabic term *fellaheen* is derived from the Arabic term for farming and the cultivation of the land. Farmers including any person are associated, directly or indirectly, in terms of livelihood, with farming the land. In Palestine farmers could be *fellaheen* (peasants), landlords (*effendis*) and sharecroppers; also in Palestine the peasants (whether poor or rich, owners of the land or worked on the land owned by landlords) were a type of farmer, who cultivated the land themselves and produced either for the family consumption or for profit from domestic, regional or international market.

Developments in the farming and agricultural industries and the phenomenal agrarian expansion in Palestine and the Levant in late Antiquity (especially in the fourth to sixth. centuries CE) were accompanied and underpinned by the demographic expansion of Palestinian cities and the expanding and vibrant urban culture in the cities of Palestine in late Antiquity. There is a vast and growing archaeological corpus that underpins the hypothesis that the Palestine of late Antiquity witnessed rural settlement peaks accompanied by massive urban development and expansion and economic prosperity. The economic boom period was from to the fifth into the seventh century. Technology and technological innovations played an important part in these agricultural industries and economic booms.

Overseas markets and Palestine's agricultural industries

Existing international and overseas markets were prerequisite for the creation and maintenance of long-distance trading systems. The international markets of the Mediterranean world during classical Antiquity were hugely instrumental in the flourishing Nabataean Arab trade and the Trans-Arabian spice and perfume trade through Palestine. Similarly, the large-scale international trade in Palestinian wine and other agricultural commodities in Antiquity (especially during the Roman and Byzantine periods) were mainly the result of the phenomenal expansion of foreign and overseas markets and for produce from both Palestine and Syria (Decker 2008: 66). Much of the wine exported from the East flowed from the vats of the presses in the provinces of *Palaestina I-III* and Phoenicia [modern Lebanon]. Archaeological evidence also shows the widespread use of new technological methods within the large wine production of Palestine; with large-scale production and shipment of wine to overseas markets. This combination of exports to lucrative foreign and overseas markets, technological innovations in Palestine, together with intensive capital investment, brought about the spectacular rise, rapid expansion and huge profitability of the Gaza Wine industry in Roman and Byzantine Palestine and the Nablus Soap and Jaffa Orange industries of modern Palestine, developments which were also accompanied with phenomenal urban expansion.

By the same token, the decline of key foreign and overseas markets and lack of technological innovations and capital investments brought about the sharp decline of the glassware industry of the Palestinian city of al-Khalil (Hebron) during the modern period – a city which boasted a large and hugely profitable glassware industry during the Mamluk and Ottoman periods and a glassware industry that led to the defining of a distinct Palestinian school of glassware. Furthermore, while evidently both Gaza Wine and Nablus Soap became *capital intensive industries*, the glassware industry of al-Khalil remained *labour intensive industry.*

Egypt as a key destination for Palestinian foreign export

Egypt and Palestine enjoyed millennia of association since Antiquity (Cohen 1984; Masalha 2018) and for Palestine, trading with its biggest neighbour was crucial to the Palestinian economy as Egypt became a key trading partner. Also, for millennia ancient Egypt was a superpower and had the biggest economy in the region. And for millennia Egypt was the most important commercial trader with Palestine. One of the key international highways and trading routes in ancient Palestine was known as the *Way of Horus*, named after the falcon-headed God of the Sky and one of the earliest and most important gods in the Egyptian pantheon; Horus, known as 'Protector Trade Routes', is one of the most commonly used symbols of ancient and modern Egypt.

Perhaps not surprisingly, the name *Palestine* occurs first in ancient Egyptian sources from the late Bronze Age in relation to the Egyptian struggle to control the Palestine during the reigns of Ramesses II and III and of Merneptah (1276–1178 BCE), son of Ramesses II. The name Palestine originally derives from the 3200-year-old documented name *Peleset*, used to refer to the people in southern Levant, allies of the 'Libyans', three who are mentioned in Egyptian inscriptions, including the victory Stele of Merneptah, which celebrates the Egyptian victory over ancient Libya and their allies in separate Egyptian military campaigns in ancient Palestine. These allies of the Libyans (Tjeḥenu) include a number of peoples besides the *Peleset*, some of whose names are identifiable. These names include the Shardana (Sardinia), the Ekwesh, the Teresh, the Tjekker, the Lukka, the Kheta (Hatti = Hittite), the Amor (Amurru), the Shasw (Bedouin in the Sinai), including the disputed translation of Asher or Israel of the Merneptah Stele. Discovered and originally interpreted by biblical archaeologist Flinders Petrie at Thebes in 1896, and currently housed in the Egyptian Museum in Cairo, there is actually no mention of the 'Israelites' (or 'Israelite merchants' in Egypt) in the Merneptah Stele or in any other Egyptian texts. 'No other inscription from Palestine, or from Transjordan in the Iron Age, has so far provided any specific reference to Israel' or 'Israelites' trade with Egypt (Lemche 1998: 46, 62).

Although Palestine's geo-political location at the centre of international highways and global trade routes was a key factor in its ancient economic prosperity, a significant proportion of the locally manufactured products of Palestine since ancient times went to neighbouring Egypt and Palestinian merchants also lived and settled in the cities of Lower Egypt. Also a significant number of Egyptian *wine merchants* were based in the port city of Gaza (Maiumas Gaza) during the Roman and Byzantine periods. Furthermore, as we have already seen, the famous 'Zenon Archive' – a cache of papyrus documents discovered by archaeologists in the Nile Valley in 1914 and named after Zenon, a senior public official in Ptolemaic Egypt and a secretary to the finance minister around the 250s–230s BC – shows that Palestine exported considerable amounts of wine, olive oil and cereals to Ptolemaic Egypt of the third century BCE. As we shall see in Chapter 6 the consumption of high-quality Palestinian wine (also known as Gaza Wine) by the social and political elites of ancient Egypt continued to grow throughout Antiquity and reached new heights in late Antiquity during Byzantine Palestine.

Although for the greater part of its ancient history Egypt was culturally insular, commercially Egypt was a major trading partner of ancient Palestine. Also Palestinian merchant regularly came to Egypt to work or trade. However, for a relatively short period during the middle Bronze Age a class of Palestinian traders, known to historians as the Hyksos, who had settled peacefully in the Nile Delta of Egypt and assimilated neatly into Egyptian culture adopting Egyptian customs, dress and religious beliefs – and who have been credited with introducing several technological innovations to Egypt, such as the horse and chariot and the composite bow – ruled Egypt for about one hundred years (1700–1570 BCE). But more often it was Palestine which came under the direct rule or indirect influence of the powerful ancient Egyptian empire, rather than the other way round.

Also, the material and mining resources of ancient Palestine were the target of the Pharaohs. However, the international trade between Palestine and Egypt dates back to the middle Chalcolithic Age (4000–3200 BCE), during which Palestine exported to the Delta cities of Egypt and cities in Palestine – copper which was extensively mined in the Naqab (Negev) and transported by convoys of donkeys to Lower Egypt. Furthermore, the upper classes of Egypt were the largest consumer of Gaza Wine during late Antiquity. Egypt was also a key destination for the *Linen of Asqalan* during the Mamluk period and the *Glassware of al-Khalil* (Hebron) (Mamluk and Ottoman periods) and *Nablus Soap* during the late Ottoman period and British Mandatory period (1918–48). With commerce thriving during the late Ottoman period the olive oil soap factories of Palestine pile their bars by the tens of thousands. During this period Palestinians were cultivating olives, cotton, tobacco, dura, sesame, and exporting soap and glassware to Egypt, barley to Britain, wheat to Italy and France, and Jaffa oranges around the world (Dukes and Green (n.d.)).

Global trade, world religions and Palestine: The rise of Christianity and Islam

Historically, regional and long-distance international trade contributed enormously to the spread of ideas, religions and civilizations and of course consumerism. As we shall see in Chapters 6 and 7 on Gaza Wine, the port cities of Palestine and the Eastern Mediterranean combined trade played an important role in the rise of Christianity in the Mediterranean world and its eventual triumph in late Antiquity. Also, as we shall see in Chapter 1, the Trans-Arabian spice and aromatics trade from Yemen and India and through the port city of Gaza in Palestine and on to the Mediterranean was a major contributory factor in the rise of pre-Islamic Mecca trading aristocracy in the Hijaz in the sixth century and this development subsequently led to the rise of Islam in the early seventh century. ʿAbd al-Muṭṭalib, chief of the Quraysh tribal confederation grandfather of the Prophet of Islam himself, was a long-distance merchant who traded with Palestine, Syria and Yemen, and according to one Islamic tradition he died during one of his trading missions and was buried in Gaza, Palestine.

The preachers and foot soldiers of early world religions often marched on their stomachs. Often the thriving port cities of ancient Palestine, on both the Mediterranean Sea and on the Red Sea: Gaza, Ascalon, Ashdod (Isdud), Jaffa, Caesarea Maritima, Acre and Aylah (modern Aqaba), played a key role in international trade and these port cities accommodated communities of foreign merchants (including Egyptians, Greeks and south Arabians and Indians). No less important in late Antiquity these port cities played an important part in the spread of Christianity to overseas through international trade. Christianity, in particular, spread in Palestine and Syria and then through the Mediterranean world, spread not only by Christian preachers but also by wine merchants and through the Mediterranean wine trade. Indeed during the Roman and early Byzantine periods Christian wine merchants became highly influential in port cities such as *Maiumas Gaza*; Alexandra, Ascalon and Caesarea Maritima; it is also telling that, with the rise of the Palestinian Mediterranean wine trade, port cities in Palestine such as *Maiumas Gaza* and *Maiuma Ascalan* (the port cities of Gaza and Ascalon) had their own separate autonomous Christian bishops – in addition the regular bishops of Gaza and Ascalon.

Under Christianity during the Byzantine period (fourth to early seventh centuries) the production of what became internationally famous as the Gaza Wine of Palestine, intertwined with the growth of Holy Land pilgrimage and the rise of the Palestinian monasteries, caused the golden age of the Palestine wine industries (Mayerson 1992: 76–80). In fact both *wine* and *bread* were famously sanctified by Jesus of Nazareth (in Roman Palestine); in one of his miracles (narrated in the New Testament), Jesus is said to have transformed water into wine, an act that may acknowledge the health of fermented wine versus the often-polluted nature of water and anxiety about the frequently water-transmitted epidemics in Antiquity and the Middle Ages. Jesus followers concentrated on extending measures to balance the use and abuse of wine but never supported total prohibition. Saint Paul and other fathers of early Christianity carried on such moderating attitudes. Rather than castigating wine for its effects on sobriety, they considered it a gift from God, both for its medicinal qualities and the tranquilizing characteristics that offered relief from pain and the anxiety of daily life.

Interestingly while the religious prohibition on wine under Islam in Palestine was maintained from the Abbasid period onwards (see below), the *sanctification bread* was widely maintained by the Palestinian Muslims and this tradition has survived into the modern period.

During the Byzantine period the Gaza Wine, in particular, was spread internationally by the Christian monasteries of Palestine and Christian pilgrims to the sites of the Holy Land. Both European and Byzantine Christianity celebrated Gaza Wine, which was imported in large quantities from Palestine, for several centuries in late Antiquity. Chapter 6 will also explore the ways in which Gaza Wine was treated by the various monastic schools of Palestine and their links to the world-famous wine industry of Byzantine (Christian) Palestine. The earliest known Christian monasticism appeared simultaneously in the deserts of Egypt and Palestine around the third century CE. The famous monastic developments of the Gaza region were intimately connected to both the Palestinian and the Egyptian experiences (Hevelone-Harper 2005: ix). However, by the fourth century greater Palestine effectively replaced Egypt as the centre of desert monasticism. Between the fourth and early seventh centuries, Palestine and in particular the fertile region of Gaza and the arid (desert) region east Jerusalem – which became known as the 'desert of Jerusalem' – was 'converted into a city' and became the centre of the global Christian monastic movement. The dozens of monasteries of Palestine in both the Gaza region and the region east of Jerusalem were centres for knowledge preservation and knowledge production, from the preservation of ancient technology, to the copying and archiving of ancient manuscripts to internationally famous wine-making in the region of Gaza.

The outward-looking Mediterranean *Monastic School of Gaza* interacted closely with the cities of Gaza and Ascalon and other urban centres in the south of Palestine. However, as we shall see in Chapter 6, in Palestine the monasteries evolved into two distinct types: the *Monastic School of Gaza* and *the Monastic School of Mar Saba* – 'monastery of hermits', or *lauras* (Greek: *Λαύρα*, lavra), associated with the semi-hermitical monastic communities in what became known as the 'desert monasticism' – while the *Sabaite school* and monasteries in the desert east of Jerusalem combined monastic life with cultural and music creation and translation activities from Syria and Greek into Arabic (especially in the eighth to eleventh centuries), the early monasteries in the Gaza region combined monastic life with vineyard cultivation and wine production.

These early monastic traditions of Egypt and Byzantine Palestine had a huge impact on the development of worldwide monastic traditions of Christianity as well as on religious mysticism in general. However, while scholars of the early monasticism of Egypt and Palestine, and what is often termed as *desert monasticism*, tend to homogenize these early monastic traditions of Christianity, in fact, as we shall see in Chapter 4, these early monastic traditions, like early Christianity itself, were diverse and heterogeneous. One of the most spectacular chapters in the history of late Antiquity Palestine was the monastic culture and monastic legacy of the Gaza region. An intellectual monastic community flourished in the region of Gaza in the Byzantine province of *Palaestina Prima* from the fourth to the seventh centuries, creating a distinct Palestinian monastic tradition, shaped by the Christological intellectual battles of the fifth and sixth centuries, and producing a wealth of literary works which might be termed the *Monastic School of Gaza* (Bitton-Ashkelony and Kofsky 2006).

However, the rise of Islam in the early seventh century brought about the decline of wine production and consumption in Palestine throughout the Middle Ages. By contrast, Arab merchants brought about the international commercialization of *Coffea arabica* in the late Middle Ages and early modern period – coffee which was described by early modern European Christians as the 'wine of Islam'. As we shall see in Chapter 16, *Coffea arabica*, the dominant coffee beans of the modern period, was spread by Arab merchants first among the Ottomans and later on found its way to Europe and the rest of the world.

1

Palestine as a Transit Country

International Highways, Commercial Geography and the Trade Routes of Palestine

The Way of the Sea (Via Maris) and the Way of Horus

In the Bronze Age relatively large cities began to emerge in Mesopotamia and the Levant, Palestine included, at the intersections of natural transport routes and long-distance trade routes, as dictated by commercial geography and topography (Barjamovic et al. 2019: 1455–503).

This process of urban growth, the transformation of market towns into urban centres, along major regional trade routes can be observed most distinctly in ancient Palestine. Commanding major international trade routes, ancient Palestine evolved as a 'transit country' for inter-continental and regional trades from south to north and from east to west; evolving into a bridge country at the centre of international trade systems became a major striking feature of ancient Palestine. Despite its small size, the great importance of Palestine as a juncture of international trade, industry, technology and monetarism, as well as agricultural innovation, can be illustrated by the fact that some of the most famous trade routes of the ancient world emerged in Palestine or were connected to Palestine in some form or another. These international trade routes were:

1. *Via Maris* (or the *Way of the Sea*): also known in the Iron Age as the *Way of the Philistines*; the route connected Lower Egypt with Palestine, Phoenicia and Syria;
2. *The Way of Horus*: named after the Egyptian God of the Sky and 'Protector of Trade Routes', connected Lower Egypt with Palestine and Gaza through North Sinai;
3. *Darb al-Sultan* (Arabic for *the Sultan Road*): originally the Nabataean Arab kingdom's *Incense Road* for camel caravans travelling along the Petra–Gaza *Incense Road*, the Palestine *Incense Road*: connected the South Arabian and Trans-Arabian spice route and frankincense trails with Gaza and the Mediterranean world with

south Arabia and Yemen. Being called the *Sultan Road* by the Arabs, the Arabic name has echoes of the ancient *King's Highway* connecting Upper Egypt with Damascus. For millennia this Arab *Incense Road* was one of the most important historic trading roads of southern Palestine and as we shall see in Chapter 3, several Palestinian spice and perfume cities flourished along this road throughout Antiquity and into the Middle Ages under Islam;
4. The *King's Highway*: connecting Upper Egypt with southern Palestine, Petra and Damascus;
5. The Romans constructed an extensive road system in the Near East including *The Via Traiana Nova Road*: the new Roman road that connected southern Palestine with Petra and Damascus; it was constructed at the height of the Roman Empire;
6. *The Maritime Route of Iotapa in Palaestina. The Red Sea Maritime Trade Route to Palestine: Iotabe-Aylah-Gaza.*

As we shall see in Chapter 2, beginning with the Bronze Age donkey caravans, some of which numbered 3,000 donkeys, transported a variety of goods from Damascus to Egypt, using key transit routes of Palestine such as the *Way of the Sea* and the *King's Highway* and across a vast area stretching from the Euphrates in the north to the Nile in the south (Bough 2012: 49–50).

The importance of these superhighway of Palestine, especially the *Via Maris*, also known the *Way of the Philistines*, as Palestine's most international trade and strategic route, was related to the fact that this key route linked the trade of ancient Egypt with Syria and Mesopotamia; it also connected the Mediterranean world and Europe with the South Arabian and Asian spice and textile trades from India and China respectively – the South Arabian trade linked the Palestinian port cities of the Mediterranean Sea to Petra and for several centuries in Antiquity this route was controlled by the Nabataean Arab kingdom. Historically the coastal cities of Palestine: Gaza, Ascalon, Ashdod (Isdud), Joppa (Jaffa) and Tantur (Dora, modern Tanura) and Acre benefited from and fully exploited the geo-political position of the country as a 'transit country', which served international trade routes and linked three different continents, Africa, Asia and Europe. The merchant classes of both the Phoenicians and ancient Philistines controlled much of the Levantine coast of the eastern Mediterranean in Antiquity and the key Palestinian international highway: the *Way of the Philistines*, or *Via Maris*, was described in Exodus as the '*way of the Land of the Philistines*' (Old Testament: '*derech Eretz Plishtim*': 13:17). The great Palestinian coastal trading cities: Gaza, Ascalon, Ashdod, Joppa (Jaffa) and Dora traded in the south with Egypt through the *Way of Horus*, and linked the cities of the Egyptian delta in the north with the Phoenician port cities of Byblos, Tyre and Sidon, thus creating a single integrated trade system for the whole ancient Near East.

Much of the evidence concerning the importance of international trade routes of Palestine to the ancient global trade systems comes from ancient Egyptian and Assyrian sources. For instance, the key important international trade and strategic route: *Way of Horus*, was symbolically named after Horus, one of the most significant ancient Egyptian deities, who served many functions, most importantly as god of kingship, protection, the sun and the sky and appeared in Egyptian hieroglyphs as *ḥr.w*, *Falcon*. It was the most important international trade, traffic and strategic route running through the country's coastline dating from the early Bronze Age. It was the most important historic route from ancient Egypt to the Levant – subsequently this route linked Egypt with Palestine and the Fertile Crescent throughout the Palestinian trade routes system. Along this strategic route and especially the Palestinian route *Way of the Sea*, some of the most important cities in Palestine sprang up, including ancient Gaza – which, at one point, became ancient Egypt's administrative capital of Palestine – Ashdod (Isdud), Ascalon (Asqalan), Joppa (Jaffa), Tantur (Tantura) and later Caesarea Palaestina.

Modern 'national' frontiers between Egypt and Palestine should not be projected onto ancient history. In ancient times the *Way of Horus* followed the coastal plain from Egypt to North Sinai and to southern Palestine. We also have new archaeological discoveries about the Egyptian side of this long route. On the Egyptian side (and we can also assume on the Palestinian side) the *Way of Horus* was based on the combination of trading posts backed by powerful military posts and many fortifications and a series of defensive forts surrounding by defensive walls. During the New Kingdom of ancient Egypt, 1580 to 1080 BCE the *Way of Horus* route extended 350 km, from near present-day Qantara in Egypt to the city of Rafah and beyond. This route is described in *The Inscriptions of the Ways of Horus* as follows:

> The Ways of Horus was a high road secured by a network of fortresses and provided with water reservoirs, as well as supply and custom stations that were established along the route between the Eastern Delta and South Palestine. It was a vital artery through which the military and commercial traffic between Egypt and Asia flowed.
>
> (Al-Ayedi 2006: 7)

As we have seen in the Introduction, the style of combined trade stations along international trade routes with strong military forts can be seen throughout the ancient Near East and in the Nabataean Arab trade routes in Palestine during classical Antiquity.

To the north of the *Way of Horus*, the *Way of the Sea* followed the coastal plain of Palestine until Tantur before veering north-eastwards, with alternative roads through Wadi 'Ara into Marj Ibn 'Amer (the Plain of Esdraelon), then passing by Mount Tabor and northwards towards present-day Syria. This branch also connected the Jordan Rift valley by Marj Ibn Amer, the most fertile plain in Palestine, and historically a vital transit route linking the Palestinian coastal highway with the ancient trade routes and trade systems of *Anatolia-Syria-Palestine*, and to the east, Mesopotamia. Another branch continued from the coastal city of Tantur northwards to the city of acre and along the Phoenician coastal cities of Tyre, Sidon Byblos, Berytus (modern Beirut) and Tripoli. The *Way of the Sea*, as the most international highway in Palestine, was criss-crossed by other trading routes in the country, including from Jaffa to Jerusalem, then Jericho and Transjordan.

Although developing most extensively in the Bronze Age, in fact the international trade between Palestine and Egypt dates back to the late Chalcolithic Age (4000-3200 BCE). During this Copper Age (and subsequently during the Bronze Age), Palestine both exported local copper to ancient Egypt and was, crucially, at the centre of the much bigger Anatolian-Levant-Egypt copper trade system, the first truly global trade system in the world. Furthermore, for millennia there was a steady trade between Palestine/Syria and Egypt and Egyptian merchants imported Palestinian products such as copper, wood, wine and olive oil; Palestinian trade routes also facilitated international trade to Lower Egypt originated in Syria and Anatolia (Smith 2008: 40). As we shall see in Chapter 8, a community of Egyptian textile merchants were also based in the city of al-Ramla, the capital of the province of Palestine throughout early Islam. Indeed, vast amounts of Palestinian pottery from the Bronze Age period and Antiquity were discovered in Egypt – pots manufactured in Palestine and transported to Egypt presumably primarily as containers of wine and olive oil (Grainger 2016: 27).

Not surprisingly, the name *Palestine* first occurs in Egyptian sources from the Late Bronze Age in relation to the Egyptian struggle to control the Philistines during the reigns of Ramesses II and III and of Merneptah (1276-1178 BCE). In fact, the name Palestine originally derives from the 3,200-year-old documented name *Peleset*, used to refer to the people in southern Levant, allies of the 'Libyans', three of who are mentioned in Egyptian inscriptions, including the Merneptah Stele, which celebrates the Egyptian victory over Libya. These allies of the Libyans include a number of peoples besides the *Peleset*, some of whose names are identifiable.

The extensive archaeological evidence for Palestine trading links with Lower Egypt goes back to the Bronze Age and, as we shall see in Chapter 2, during this period ancient Egypt began mining copper in the Palestine Naqab (Negev) on an industrial scale. Not surprisingly a cognate of the name Palestine, 'Peleset', is found on five inscriptions as referring to the settlement of a seafaring people along the southern Palestinian coast from the mid-twelfth century BCE during the reigns of Ramesses II and III of the nineteenth Egyptian dynasty. The 3,200-year-old documents from Ramesses III, including an inscription dated *c.*1150 BCE, at the Mortuary Temple of Ramesses III at the Medinat Habu Temple in Luxor – one of the best-preserved temples of Egypt – refer to the *Peleset* among those who fought against Ramesses III (Breasted 2001: 24; also, Bruyère 1929-30), who reigned from 1186 to 1155 BCE.

The above strategic highways, including the *Way of Horus* and the *Way of the Sea*, also served ancient Egypt's regional wars before and during the New Kingdom. Ramesses III's war against the so-called 'sea peoples' (1181-1175 BCE) placed *Peleset*, geographically in the land of Djahi, that is Palestine. In fact, new archaeological discoveries from a 3,000-year-old Philistine graveyard in Ascalon have resulted in a new paradigm on the origins of the Philistines, firmly suggesting that they were not marauding Aegean invaders of the southern Levant or 'sea peoples' that appeared in Palestine in the course of the Late Bronze Age, but an indigenous population of the Near East (Evian 2017: 267-85). Since the nineteenth century biblical Orientalist scholars have linked the Egyptian cognate *Peleset* inscriptions with the 'biblical Philistines'. Subsequently Assyrian inscriptions from the eighth and seventh centuries refer to this southern coastal region as 'Palashtu' or 'Pilistu'.[1]

The *Way of the Philistines* and the rise of ancient Philistia as a geo-political entity

Throughout much of the late Bronze and Iron Ages (*c*.1200–600 BCE), the ancient Philistines and the great city-states of Philistia dominated the coastal Mediterranean region of Palestine and flourished on strong international trade links; as we shall see below, international trade prompted these city-states to develop the first monetary system of Palestine in the late sixth–early fifth centuries BCE. Furthermore Philistia, with its powerful trading city-states, Gaza, Ascalon and Ashdod, was viewed as a geo-political entity by the ancient Egyptians and Assyrians and, subsequently, by the Persians and ancient Greeks (Masalha 2018).

Seafaring and international trade routes in ancient Palestine and the highly sophisticated great cities of Philistia, which included Gaza, Ascalon, Ashdod and Jaffa, combined to develop geo-politically as an integrated south in the course of Iron Age II (*c*.1000–600 BCE) and Philistia was the first to develop political autonomy and an autonomous monetary system in Palestine in the form of silver coins, issued in the late sixth, fifth and fourth centuries BCE. The Trans-Arabian spice trade and Mediterranean trade made this local Palestinian currency, known as the coinage of Philistia, widely circulated in the Philisto-Arabian region and beyond and became known as Philisto-Arabian coins. Underwater archaeology of shipwrecks of the Palestine Mediterranean coast and terrestrial excavations and as well archaeological discoveries and epigraphically evidence can help us read the history of Palestine through the eyes of these indigenous inhabitants of Palestine and their international trading links.

The same cities of ancient Philistia and the Philistines as a whole gave us the name *Palestine* as a geo-political entity and gave us subsequently the Arabic name *Filastin*. Since the Iron Age the most traditional and earliest toponyms for the area which became known in classical Antiquity as 'Palestine'. They were the toponyms of Retenu and Djahi, which might be seen as traditional names, as used in the fourteenth-century BCE Egyptian story of Sinuhe. Retenu was used to refer to the regions along the eastern shore of the Mediterranean and was divided into three sub-regions: Amurru, in the north, Lebanon (sometimes referred to as 'Upper Retenu'), which lay south of Amurru and north of the Litani river, and Djahi, the southernmost part of Retenu, which referred to the regions south of the Litani to Ascalon ('Asqalan, or perhaps Gaza) and as far as the Rift Valley to the east.

The traditional biblical approaches to the ancient Philistines, and *Peleset* have been constructed through the eyes of Western archaeologist and Zionist settler-colonizers. However, new archaeological discoveries in Palestine and epigraphic evidence on ancient Palestine – carved on road signs, walls, temples, memorials, gravestones, coins and Philistine graveyards uncovered recently in Ascalon, dating to about 3,000 years ago (David 2017) – have all transformed our understanding of the impact of international trade on the commercial history of ancient history of Palestine; the new scholarship has resulted in new paradigms which have revolutionized our scholarly knowledge on Palestine and its location within the ancient global trade systems.

Connecting ancient Egypt and Africa in the south with Palestine, Phoenicia, Syria, Anatolia in the north and Mesopotamia in the east, the *Way of the Philistines* became central to both the international trade systems of the ancient world and to the evolution of the idea of ancient Philistia as a geo-political entity. The *Way of the Philistines* as a distinct and famous coastal route in Palestine also found in the fact that in the Middle Ages this international route acquired in Europe a Latin name: *Via Maris*, or the *Way of the Sea*. Becoming an integral part of the extensive and expanding road systems in Roman Palestine in Antiquity, the excavated Roman milestones of the *Via Maris* confirm the importance of this route in Antiquity. The ancient traditions related to the *Via Maris* continued into the modern period and modern scholars have often used the Latin term *Via Maris* to describe this highway. For local Near Eastern merchants and pilgrims and European travellers, merchants and businessmen and for marching armies, the long *Via Maris* (Arabic: *Tariq al-Bahr*) became as important and as famous as the *Via Appia* (the *Appian Way*), one of the earliest and strategically most important Roman roads in Italy.

Already established in the Bronze Age as an international trade route for the copper trade and a strategic route for the movement of people and army legions, the *Way of the Philistines* remained the most important transit route in Palestine for millennia and one of the most important international routes in Antiquity. In the Iron Age,

> [The] integration [of the Philistines] with the indigenous population resulted in the geographically, but hardly ethnically, distinctive region of Philistia, which was tightly linked to the international trade routes. These followed the Via Maris, on the one hand, through the Jezreel [Mar Ibn Amer] and in the direction of northern Mesopotamia, and, on the other hand, continued along the coast to the Phoenician seaports of northern Palestine and southern Lebanon. (Thompson 2016: 165) ....
>
> Under Assyrian patronage, Palestine's expansive trading politics not only dominated the coastal economy but, over the course of the Iron II period, created an integrated South. Arab trade supported the processing of grains, cattle and fruits from the northern Negev and coastal plain with the sheep and wool, olives and wines from the Judean foothills and highlands. Among the southern coast's most important towns were Jaffa, 'Aphek, Ekron, Ashdod, *Gimti*[2] (Gath; *Tall al-Safi*[3]), Askelon and Gaza.
>
> (Thompson 2016: 165)

For millennia merchants and merchant-mariners of all nationalities, indigenous Philistines, Nabataean Arabs, Phoenicians, Egyptians, Syrians, Greeks, Romans, transported precious commodities from far-distant regions, followed the international route of the *Via Maris*, along the Palestinian coast, carrying goods and precious commodities from south Arabia to Europe and to and from Egypt, through the city of Gaza, the southernmost city in ancient Palestine and the first way-station along this international trade route. Gaza also had an abundant water supply that made it most welcome after the long trek through the *Way of Horus* and the relatively parched route of north Sinai.

Time-keeping also evolved with Palestine's international trade and along the major trade routes of Palestine and with the movement of people and goods across long distances. As we shall see in Chapter 6, the city of Gaza also developed the water clock in Byzantine times, one of the most advanced water-clocks in late Antiquity.

The Trans-Arabian *Incense Routes* and the economic integration of southern Palestine: The ancient cities of Petra, Oboda, Elusa and Gaza

Complementing the two key international trade routes of Palestine: *Way of the Sea* (the *Way of the Philistines*) and the *Way of Horus* were the *Incense Routes* and the frankincense trade routes. Originating in south Arabia, the *Incense Routes* centred on the Petra-Gaza road through the Naqab (Negev). The port city of Gaza was also at the centre of another desert route from the Red Sea.

From the rich ancient port city of Gaza to the wealthy trading town of Petra (originally known to its literate Nabataean Arabs as Raqmu) in the east and via the long-distance spice trade and frankincense route of south Arabia and Yemen – a region known to ancient Greek historians as *Arabia Felix* (literally: *Fertile/Happy Arabia*; *Εὐδαίμων Ἀραβία, Eudaemon Arabia*) was also the Latin name used by classical geographers to describe south Arabia and Yemen (Graf et al. 2022; Sergeant and Lewcock 1983). This highly lucrative trans-Arabia spice and frankincense trade will be discussed in detail in Chapter 3.

The much-documented trade of *incense routes* through the Palestinian Naqab to Gaza developed by the strategically located Nabataean Arabs in the second half of the first millennium BCE, partly in the wake of the rise of market demand in the classical Mediterranean for such precious goods as spices and incense:

> In controlling this land route [between north Arabia and the Mediterranean], they [the Nabateans] controlled a monopoly on the lucrative goods moving from the Tropics, South Arabia, the Horn of Africa, and India, to the markets of the developing Roman world, goods which included spices, incense, cosmetics, perfumes, and medicinal herbs.
>
> (Rosen 2019)

This network of desert trails, or the incense routes, traversed southern Palestine and the Naqab was a Gaza-dominated thoroughfare plied by Nabataean Arab caravans bringing loads of Arabian aromatics to be shipped from the port of Gaza to the Roman Mediterranean world. From the third century BCE onward the central Naqab saw a process of urbanization and a sharp increase in caravan traffic as the Nabataean Arab tribes settled down in a series of villages and major towns in the Naqab including the towns Elusa, Nessana, Oboda, Mempsis (Kurnub) and Sbeita, along or close to the Trans-Arabian Petra-Gaza spice and incense road. The port of Gaza was at the end of the Nabataean Arab spice road where trade was conducted in herbs, spices, aromatics, drapery, glass and food. Goods arrived in the port on the backs of camels from southern

Arabia through Petra and the Naqab. The Mediterranean section of the Petra-Gaza Road was a trade corridor along which incense, spices and perfumes harvested or purchased in southern Arabia were brought to the Mediterranean and Roman world.[4]

At the height of the Nabataean Arab kingdom, Hellenistic era documentary evidence from the third century BCE shows the merchants of the city of Gaza were developing strong long-distance trading links with both Yemen and the India Ocean (Hölbl 2001: 58-9; Terpstra 2019: 170).

The King's Highway

The *King's Highway* was another ancient trade route of vital importance in southern Palestine connecting Upper Egypt with Syria and Mesopotamia. It ran from Upper Egypt across the Sinai to the Gulf of Aqaba then turned northward across the Palestinian Naqab to Petra and Transjordan, then to Damascus and the Euphrates River and Mesopotamia. In Antiquity, for several centuries the trade caravans of Nabataean Arab kingdom used this superhighway effectively to transport spice and aromatic trade to ancient Egypt and Syria.

Interestingly, the annexation of the Nabataean Arab kingdom by the Roman Empire in 106 CE (after the death of its last Nabataean king Rabbel II) and its replacement by the Roman province of *Arabia Petraea* (*Έπαρχία Πετραίας Ἀραβίας*), during the reign of Emperor Trajan (who had spent a significant part of his military career in Syria while his father was governor of the province of Syria), did not lead to the shifting of the lucrative Trans-Arabian/Red Sea trade route from southern Palestine to Egypt, as some researchers have suggested. In fact, this development led to the expansion of the Roman road system in Palestine and the expansion of the Red Sea-India spice trade system through Palestine. The Romans renovated and expanded the *King's Highway* in Palestine and Transjordan and diversified the trade routes of southern Palestine, as seen by the construction of the new road: the *Via Traiana Nova* under Trajan. This road also allowed the growth and expansion of the cities of the Palestinian Naqab.

In the Middle Ages, under Islam, closely related routes for merchants and travellers – including the pilgrimage route to Mecca and the *barid* system (the 'postal service'), the state-run courier service of the Umayyad and later the Abbasid states – and a system of caravanserais were developed. And in modern times the construction of Hejaz Railway followed the Transjordan and Damascus section of the ancient *King's Highway.*

Pax Romana and road expansion under the Romans: The transformation of urban centres in southern Palestine

The Via Traiana Nova road

The Romans created the most extensive and most outstanding road and transportation system in the ancient world, with tens of thousands of kilometres of hard-surfaced highways, designed for both military, administrative and trade use. Roman roads were notable for their straightness, solid foundations and milestones. In addition to the construction of an extensive road system for the speedy movement of troops, and inns for travellers and merchants, along the main highways in the Near East in general and Palestine in particular, the Romans also employed *cursus publicus* (Latin: 'the public way') officials who were mandated by the state to maintain and supervise this extensive transportation services – a system of road signs, travellers' inns, couriers and wagon drivers. The maintenance of this system, which also applied to Roman Palestine, was charged to the local inhabitants and local towns and villages along the main routes and enforced by state appointed tax collectors who regularly travelled by *cursus publicus*.

The Roman road system made possible the Roman conquest, administration and the massive expansion of global trade and transit trade in Palestine; the same imperial Roman highways provided for the great movement of people and new ideas and the speedy transportation of commodities, and later, as a means for the diffusion of Christianity from its original birth place in Palestine to the whole Mediterranean world and beyond. During the Roman and Byzantine periods city landmarks became central to the road infrastructure of Palestine and international and domestic trading routes continued to develop. Major Palestinian cities were often served by a good road system during this period. Aelia Capitolina, the name of Jerusalem throughout the Roman and Byzantine eras, due to its religious centrality under both the Romans and later the Byzantines, served as a starting point for no fewer than seven highways. These seven highways were later broadly reflected under Islam and in the sixteenth-century Ottoman walls and gates of the Old City of Jerusalem (al-Quds). These routes out of the city of Aelia Capitolina and 'Hadrian's Column' can be seen in the Madaba Map of the sixth century. Islam inherited this classical legacy of extensive road system and developed urban spaces in Palestine. Under the Ottomans the most spectacular gate of the Old City of al-Quds, Bab al-'Amud (literally, the 'Column Gate'), also known as the Damascus Gate, the northern gate of the city reflecting direction of the route to Damascus and the centrality of the Palestinian trade with Damascus and Syria as a whole.

At its height the Roman Empire was among the largest empires of the ancient world, with an estimated fifty to ninety million inhabitants, roughly 20 per cent of the world's population at the time, and with the largest global markers and the most extensive global trade routes. Civilization under the Romans was also a tool of imperialism, and the unprecedented expansion of road infrastructure and trade routes in Palestine enabled what became known as age of *Pax Romana* ('Roman Peace') – a period of massive expansion of international 'transit trade' through Palestine and a period of new road construction and road expansion in southern Palestine and a period of urbanized commercial innovations in the country. This *Pax Romana* relied on the active collaboration of powerful local elites and powerful local merchant groups that benefited from the expansion of the Roman international trade with south Arabia, the Horn of Africa, India and China. The period is a roughly 200 year-long time span of Roman history that is identified by historians as the golden age of the Roman imperial power, relative political stability and economic prosperity. *Pax Romana* combined ruthless military might, an efficient and vast transport system created by skilful engineers and highly profitable East-West global trade. Dated from the accession of Augustus in 27 BCE to about 180 CE, Roman 'transit trade' in the Mediterranean and its long-distance travel and trade, through Palestine and Arabia, with India and China increased phenomenally during this period. Roman, Greek, Syrian, Egyptian, Palestinian-Nabataeans and Arabian merchants sailed East to acquire silks, gems, spices and onyx. Merchants of many ethnicities and nationalities (including Palestinian and Arab merchants) benefited from the profits and incomes generated in this vast empire with its large and planned urban markets; incomes raised due to the global trade in the Mediterranean region and more specifically through the Red Sea, East Africa, south Arabia and India and China were vast (Goldsworthy 2016: 392; Temin 2013: 13). This unprecedented expansion of global commerce required the maintenance of *Pax Romana* and security system and an efficient road system to guard travellers and merchants and protect the trade from highwaymen and local dissidents. And this expansion of the global trade with India and China was a major factor in the expansion of the Palestinian-Trans-Arabian trade caravans and trade routes in the first century CE.

During Roman Palestine the highly lucrative Trans-Arabian spice caravans through Petra and southern Palestine spurred the construction of new Roman road systems in the south of Palestine – an extensive road infrastructure that Palestine had not seen before. The new Roman road system came to be known as: *Via Traiana Nova,* or the *New Road of Tranjan*. An international road, it was commissioned by the Roman Emperor Trajan – emperor from 98 to 117 CE and best known for his prolific public building programmes, constructed in the newly created Roman province of *Arabia Petraea*, which had replaced the old Nabataean Arab kingdom. The new road and public building programmes transformed the urban environment of the Nagab and southern Palestine.

Trajan himself was closely familiar with Palestine, Syria and *Arabia Petrea*. As a young soldier, he had risen through the ranks of the Roman army and had served in these parts of the Roman-Arabian frontier region – a region not only strategically important but also central to the desert *incense roads* from south Arabia and the spice trade from India and the silk trade from China. Also, in 76–77 CE Trajan's father had been Governor of Syria (*Legatus pro-praetore Syriae*), where Trajan himself had served, at the same time, as military *tribunus legionis*. Both military service and the protection of the lucrative global Roman trade routes from Asia went hand in hand.

Western historians often discuss the remarkable monumental building programmes of the Roman Empire, while ignoring the impact of the building traditions of the ancient Near East on Roman engineering projects and road construction projects. This Near Eastern influence is found in the fact that Trajan's military engineer and chief civil architect was a native Syrian named Apollodorus of Damascus, the most celebrated engineer and architect of Antiquity. Living from 60 to 130 CE, Apollodorus of Damascus was closely associated with the major urban building programmes and major road constructions of the Roman Empire; many important commissions were entrusted to him by the Roman Emperors Trajan and Hadrian. A brilliant Syrian engineer and an architect associated with monumental structures, Apollodorus was credited with many of Trajan's buildings and baths in Rome including the Forum and with the nearby *Trajan's Market* complex (*Mercatus Traiani*) the world's oldest shopping mall with arcades, shops and apartments built in a multi-level structure and where it is still possible to visit several of the levels today. He was also responsible for introducing many Eastern innovations to the Roman military and civil works of architecture, such as making the dome a standard in Roman architecture. Apollodorus was driven by the belief of 'building for posterity'. He was also reportedly influenced by the monumental building traditions of Hellenistic Syria-Palestine and the Nabataean Arab building traditions and the construction of combined military forts and trade posts.

At the time it was common for the Arabs of Syria and the Roman province of Arabia to take Greek or Roman sounding names. The Roman Emperor *Marcus Julius Philippus* (Emperor from 244 to 249 CE) was an Arab ('Philip the Arab') – from an Arab district south of Damascus, which at the time was part of the Roman Province of Arabia, and formally known as the Nabataean kingdom of Petra – had a Roman sounding name. Also, both his father, Julius Marinus, and his brother, Gaius Julius Priscus, had non-Arabic sounding names. Equally, Apollodorus of Damascus, despite his Greek sounding name, was of a Nabataean Arab descent, which originated from old the Nabataean Arab kingdom; during his lifetime Apollodorus became famous for his mastery of the Nabataean Arab culture architecture filtered through Hellenistic modes of building style and thought (Farena 2003: 9) – and this partly explains his integration of market planning and the construction of urban markets space into his style of monumental urban architecture.

The highly lucrative Trans-Arabian spice and incense road from Yemen to Petra and then to Damascus had made the Nabataean city of Bosra (Greek: Βόστρα), one of the wealthiest cities of classical Antiquity and the city became the prosperous provincial capital of the Roman province of *Arabia Petraea* following the annexation of the Nabataean Arab kingdom in 106 CE. For centuries before its annexation to Rome, the Nabataean Arab kingdom had become the wealthiest and one of the most powerful Arab states of classical Antiquity. It had prospered on the Trans-Arabian spice and incense trade and had encompassed vast territories extending from north Arabia in the south to the city of Damascus in the north. These territories were affected by arid and semi-arid conditions. To overcome their semi-arid and desert environment the Nabataean Arab merchants and engineers had built *covered (shaded) markets* in their towns and devised some of the cleverest underground water systems in the ancient world. Around their capital Petra and throughout the surrounding desert in the Palestinian Naqab and in Transjordan, there are the remains of dams and cisterns created by the Nabataean engineers. There Nabataean building traditions combined Greek with indigenous Near Eastern and Arab styles. Building on these hybrid traditions of civil and engineering and architecture, Apollodorus became personally responsible for the transformation of ancient Rome, the construction of much of the magnificent buildings of the Roman capital. Although this famous monumental architecture, which became the symbol of Roman political, economic and military power and global trading empire, is widely acknowledged, Apollodorus's urban planning programmes and classical urban innovations throughout the Roman Empire had an impact on urban and commercial developments in the cities of southern Palestine during the Roman period (Chapter 3). This Arab and Nabataean engineering heritage is often ignored or erased in Western writing on classical Antiquity.

The *New Road of Trajan* ran from the Gulf of Aqaba on the Red Sea and the Palestinian city of Aelas (modern Aqaba) (then an integral part of Palestine) to Petra and then to the town of Bosra in Hauran (Syria). The construction of the new road started immediately after the annexation of *Arabia Petraea* to the Roman Empire by the Roman governor Gaiyus Caluius Severus; the road was completed under Hadrian. This new road became central to Rome's eastern trade and to the Trans-Arabian trade to the Mediterranean world and the old Incense Road from Petra to Gaza. In the first century CE, the *Roman Petra Road* was marked by milestones and was combined with great gates that served the entrance of the Roman city of Petra. Mediterranean-facing section of the *Incense Road*, the Petra–Gaza trails, remained a strong trade corridor along which aromatics, spices and perfumes harvested or purchased in southern Arabia were transported.

Crucially along the *Via Traiana Nova* and the Trans-Arabian-Palestinian spice route, several *spice cities* flourished in the first to third centuries CE – cities that combined town planning that was hugely influenced by the guiding principles of classical architecture and classical urban spaces and planned market spaces (Segal 1988: 110). The *Via Traiana Nova* road also introduced travel innovations to the road system of Palestine in the form of *milestones* as highway and road location markers. As throughout the global Roman road system, in addition to many villages, cities and mansions along the *Via Traiana Nova* emerged; there was also a sophisticated post system with hostels, or traveller stations. The Romans is Palestine set up stones every mile to indicate distance and added *milestones* to every eighteen miles; these milestones became an integral part of the road system of Palestine; travellers and merchants could also find refreshment and a place to stay for the night. Also cartographers began to draw early road maps to indicate distance and direction for travellers and merchants as well as for imperial and military movement of Roman army legions (Lawson 2004: 217).

Aelas, or Aylah (modern Aqaba) was an important Palestinian trading city during the Roman period – and its important trading position under early Islam was illustrated by the fact that the city minted its own local Islamic coinage. Aelas, with its strategic location at the north-eastern tip of the Gulf of Aqaba and the Red Sea between the continents of Asia and Africa, became an important port city for thousands of years and during the Roman and Byzantine period Aelas became the key Red Sea port for the city of Gaza and its Indian trade. Its strategic location on the Red Sea and its proximity to the ancient copper mines of the Naqab meant the city became a regional hub for Palestinian copper mining, copper production and copper trade with Egypt that had occurred since the Chalcolithic and Bronze Ages. Today Aqaba Archaeological Museum (Jordan) houses one of its most important historic exhibits: the first milestone of the Roman *Via Traiana Nova* highway. Its inscription is still clear and reads that the Emperor Trajan opened the road from Syria to the Red Sea (French 2012: 261–2).

The same tradition associated with Roman road system of milestones in Palestine was maintained in Byzantine Palestine; the same road system also re-introduced by the Umayyad caliphs in Islam who laid the milestones along the highways of Palestine and the wider Near East; travellers, merchants and pilgrims used the system as a guide to long-distance highways; the separation between one milestone and the next was one mile, exactly as in the original Roman road system (Klimscha 2011: 177–210).

The Red Sea global maritime trade and Palestine: The cities of Iotabe, Aylah, Elusa, Gaza

As the international trading links of Palestine with south Asia and East Africa expanded considerably during the Roman and Byzantine periods, huge amounts of customs charges were levied on trade passing through 'transit routes' of Palestine; the transit customs charges were collected through the collection posts dotted along the eastern and southern frontiers of Palestine and from the maritime shipping through the Red Sea to the Palestinian city of Aelas on the Gulf of Aqaba.

The rise of this highly profitable maritime shipping arriving through the Red Sea to Aelas (Aylah) and then transported through the Palestine Naqab to the cities of Elusa and Gaza during the Byzantine period will be explored in Chapter 3. Ancient maritime shipping of spices and other goods through the Red Sea to Aelas was five times cheaper than land transportation of the same goods of spices and incense through the Trans-Arabian Petra route to Palestine, hence the popularity of the global maritime routes of Palestine via both the Red Sea and Mediterranean Sea and the growing global maritime trade via the ocean trade and the Red Sea and Palestine to the Mediterranean world in late classical Antiquity. Often this Indian Ocean trade in spices, cotton and silk via the Red Sea and Aelas and then on land to Gaza is portrayed as a one-way (spices, incense and silk) trade from Asia and south Arabia to Mediterranean world via Gaza. But, in fact, the trade was in both directions, and as we shall see in Chapter 6, the famous *Gaza Wine* was also exported to Yemen and southern Arabia in large quantities via the Aelas and the Red Sea. However, the balance of this trade in Antiquity was often in favour of southeast Asia and south Arabia. Also due to the huge volume of this lucrative maritime Red Sea-India trade, the struggle for the control of this trade routes passing through the Byzantine province of *Palaestina Tertia* (*Palaestina Salutaris*) reached new heights in the fourth to sixth centuries CE.

A key trading post on the Red Sea-Indian trade route of Palestine was the island of Iotabe (Greek Ἰωτάβη), located to the south of the city of Aelas and controlling the Straits of Iotabe – currently known Straits of Tiran – and the access to Red Sea. Under the Byzantines both Iotabe and Aelas were within the jurisdiction of the province of *Palaestina Tertia*. Located at the Palestine end of Indian Ocean trade route with Europe, the port city of Gaza was with the Byzantine province of *Palestina Prima*. But the merchants of Gaza, Aelas and Iotabe were closely connected. Widely cited in documentary evidence of late Antiquity as *Iotapa in Palaestina*, today Iotape is known in Latin Church sources as *Iotapa in Palaestina*, and is listed by the Roman Catholic Church as the Titular See of *Iotapa in Palaestina* (or *Iotapensis in Palaestina*). Iotabe is thought to be what is now known as Tiran Island, located at the entrance to the Straits of Tiran, and connecting the Red Sea with the Gulf of Aqaba. Iotapa was until 2017 administered by Egypt and now a Saudi Arabian island. In late Antiquity, merchants of *Iotapa in Palaestina* played a key role in collecting transit tax revenues from the Indian trade shipping to the port city of Aelas and then the same goods were transported on land via camel caravans to Gaza, and then shipped again to the Mediterranean world.

2

Ancient Obsidian and Copper Regional Trade Systems

The Mining Industries and Urbanization in Ancient Palestine and Egypt (From the Late Neolithic Ages to the Iron Age)

The dawn of urban life in Anatolia and Palestine: Çatalhöyük, Jericho and Neolithic trade systems

Modern archaeological excavations at many sites in Palestine have shown that the main source of the natural glass trade known as obsidian during the Neolithic Age was located far away in the central Anatolia region of modern Turkey. The long-distance obsidian trade through Palestine preceded the Chalcolithic Age copper trade and goes back to the Neolithic Age. Archaeological excavations show the most commonly uncovered obsidian items and tools at Neolithic sites in Palestine originated from central Anatolia (Forbes 1964: 124; Rast 1992: 58).

> The Neolithic Age was apparently one during which some far-reaching trade relations between different regions were carried on. The most commonly found items in Neolithic sites suggesting trade connections were tools made from obsidian. Research has shown that the main source for obsidian during the Neolithic in Palestine was located far away at Goellue Dagg, southwest of the modern city of Nevsehir in Turkey.
>
> (Rast 1992: 58)

Furthermore, in the Chalcolithic Age, tin, copper alloys, ore and obsidian were imported to Palestine from distant regions in southern Anatolia (Rosen 2019).

Modern archaeological excavations have also revolutionized and transformed our understanding of early 'urban civilization' in the Middle East in the late Neolithic Age. Archaeological excavations in the late 1950s early 1960 uncovered the spectacular Neolithic town of Çatalhöyük (*Çatal Hüyük*) in southern Anatolia, which existed from approximately 7500 BCE to 5600 BCE. Supporting at its height some 7,000 inhabitants who lived on flourishing agriculture and regional trade, archaeological excavations at Çatalhöyük show the mining industry of obsidian has flourished in southern Anatolia since the Neolithic Age. This trade in obsidian contributed to the creation and the flourishing of a centre of advanced urban culture and a Neolithic civilization in southern Anatolia with regional trade connections (Gangal et al. 2014; Kucukdogan 2021; Mellaart 1962: 41–65; Renfrew 2006: 395–404). The cultural artefacts and human skulls excavated by archaeologists at Çatalhöyük plastered and painted with natural red ochre, in colour from yellow to deep orange or brown, to recreate faces, were similar to customs more characteristic of Neolithic sites in Syria and Palestine, especially the Palestinian Neolithic settlement of Jericho, a 10,000-year-old settlement and an ancient city in Palestine often associated with the inception of Neolithic agriculture in Palestine and a settlement which slightly predates Çatalhöyük. However, these similarities between Çatalhöyük and Jericho and the discovery of obsidian at many sites in Neolithic Palestine raise some intriguing questions about the impact of late Neolithic Chalcolithic trade systems and trade routes on Palestine and the possibility of late Neolithic and Chalcolithic Age 'urban civilization' in the country.

As we have already shown, the Neolithic Age saw the construction of a long-distance obsidian trade system and trading stations across Palestine and that the Chalcolithic (Copper) Age and Bronze Ages saw the greatest evolution of the long-distance trade (passing through Palestine) in copper and copper alloys in a vast region from Anatolia and Armenia to the eastern Mediterranean and ancient Egypt, then the colossus of the ancient world. Copper mining and smelting and the Near Eastern copper trade gave birth to ancient civilizations and the rise of the city in Palestine and the Levant as a whole. The mining, production and trade in copper and tin were among the main technological ingredients of the Bronze Age. Copper mining and the international trade in copper and bronze were among the key features in the evolution of complex urban societies in the ancient Near East and the eastern Mediterranean. During the third to first millennia BCE, and particularly during the late Bronze Age, this international trade in copper transformed societies in the eastern Mediterranean and the Levant, including Egypt, Syria, Palestine and Cyprus. Archaeological evidence of metallurgical activities, and finding from mining and smelting sites, and from shipwrecks in the eastern Mediterranean provide us with important sources of information about the metallurgical revolution of the Bronze Age and about how ancient technology and the trade in copper functioned (Jones 2007). Copper is a soft, malleable and ductile metal. It was the first metal to be smelted from sulphide ores, *c.*5000 BCE; it was the first metal to be discovered at some archaeological mounds in Palestine dating to the Chalcolithic Age, 7,000 years ago; and it was the first metal to be cast into a shape in a mould, *c.*4000 BCE; and the first metal to be purposely alloyed with another metal, tin, to create bronze *c.*3500 BCE; bronze was common at many urban sites in Bronze Age Palestine.

The Naqab copper mines and ancient Egypt

The earliest trade in copper between Palestine and Egypt dates back to the Chalcolithic period (4000-3200 BCE), during which copper mined in southern Palestine (the Naqab) was transported to ancient Egypt. In the fourth millennium BCE, the Egyptian city of Ma'adi, located at the base of the Nile Delta in Lower Egypt, served as the focal point for copper mined in Sinai and the Naqab. The archaeological evidence shows that the city of Ma'adi seems to have traded more with Palestine than other cities in Upper Egypt. Arriving in Ma'adi from southern Palestine and Sinai, copper and turquoise was carried on donkey caravans by local tribesmen. At the time Palestine also served as a key 'transit country' for the international trade in copper and boasted strong overland routes to Syria and Anatolia, the latter being the source of much of the ancient international trade in copper. In addition to copper, there was a steady trade between Palestine and Lower Egypt for products such as wood, wine and olive oil. Also, vast amounts of Palestinian pottery from the Bronze Age period were discovered in Lower Egypt – pots manufactured in Palestine and transported to Egypt presumably as containers of wine and olive oil (Grainger 2016: 27). Egypt was not a wine country; Herodotus ii, 77, says they had no wine, and therefore they created an artificial alcohol made of barley; and much of the Egyptian wine was imported from Palestine.

In the middle of the Bronze Age, in 1650 BCE, Palestinian merchants who had settled in Egypt, known as the Hyksos, took over the country and ruled it for about a century.

The city of Gaza was also at the centre of the transit cooper trade from Anatolia to Lower Egypt. In particular, the prosperity of Gaza during the Bronze Age depended, in part, on its trade with Egypt more than did any other Palestinian city, although this trade fluctuated and went into decline at time during the middle Bronze Age when the trade with Egypt decreased (Filfil and Louton 2008). During the reign and Palestine campaigns of Thutmose III, the city of Gaza is mentioned as a stop on the Syrian-Egyptian caravan routes and was mentioned in the fourteenth-century Amarna letters; Gaza later served as Egypt's administrative capital in Egyptian-ruled late Bronze Age Palestine (Hasel 1998: 258). Gaza remained under Egyptian control for 350 years until it was taken over by the local Philistines during the late Bronze Age in the twelfth century BCE, when Gaza became part of the rise of the *Philistine Pentapolis*, the federation of five Palestinian city-states of the late Bronze Age and Iron Age – city-states ruled by kings – a geo-political federation that included some of the most developed urban centres in Iron Age Palestine financially, commercially, politically and technologically. The high levels of development of these Philistine Pentapolis city-states and their autonomous rule can also be seen from the fact that they began, in the fifth century BCE, minting the first known indigenous Palestinian currency in Antiquity.

The urban growth and expansion of the city of Ma'adi at the base of the Nile delta in Lower (northern) Egypt was closely linked to this international trade in copper. Ma'adi (which today stands on the site of a town that has turned out to be a significant prehistoric

Egyptian site) is the oldest site in ancient Lower Egypt in which copper artefacts have been discovered in large quantities; this evidence provides the most excessive evidence for the Palestinian copper trade with Egypt, rather than Egyptians themselves going to Sinai or Palestine to mine copper. Ma'adi was an important entrepôt handling trade between the Nile Valley, Sinai and Palestine. The archaeological evidence from Ma'adi shows 'concordable body' of imported pottery from Bronze Age I Palestine and copper, which was imported from Palestine and through the transit routes of Palestine (Trigger et al. 1983: 25-6).

Located south of modern Cairo on the east bank of the Nile and one of the largest excavated towns in ancient Egypt, from the fourth millennium onwards Ma'adi served as the focal point for the obsidian and copper trade from Palestine. The towns and cities of Palestine provided focal points for the obsidian trade routes through the country and this international obsidian trade created one of the oldest trade systems in the world:

> The Neolithic Age was apparently one during which some far-reaching trade relations between different regions were carried on. The most commonly found items in Neolithic sites suggesting trade connections were tools made from obsidian. Research has shown that the main source for obsidian during the Neolithic in Palestine was located far away at Goellue Dagg, southwest of the modern city of Nevsehir in Turkey.
>
> (Rast 1992: 58)

Obsidian, copper and turquoise were transported from and across Palestine and Sinai and were carried on donkey caravans by local tribesmen and there was a steady trickle of trade with Palestine for products such as wood, wine and olive oil. At the time Palestine enjoyed overland contacts with Syria and beyond to Anatolia. Ma'adi seems to have traded more with Palestine than with Upper Egypt as witnessed by the obsidian trade: obsidian coming via the international trade routes of Palestine into Lower Egypt originated in Anatolia (Smith 2008: 40).

While during the Chalcolithic Age the copper discovered at archaeological excavations in Palestine was imported from Anatolia, very significant discoveries at the Maadi's excavation in Egypt was the presence of Palestinian smelted copper from the Bronze Age:

> Analyses of the copper suggest a Palestinian source, either the mines of Timna or at Fenan in Wadi Arabah. Raw copper may well have been Lower Egypt's major import, carried across the Sinai Peninsula by donkey caravan along with other goods: pigments, risen, bitumen, oil, cedar, flint tools and vases and spindle whorls of basalt, Some of these goods were transported in ceramic vessels. Site H in Wadi Gaza to the east (within the Gaza Strip), where many artefacts of Lower Egyptian origin have been found, may represent a trading post along the route to Palestine'.
>
> (Bard 2005: 255-8)

In the fast developing and demographically expanding Bronze Age, cities of Egypt and Palestine had multiple uses for bronze, including for household tools and ornaments, and, more importantly, as saw for stone cutting, in conjunction with sand,[1] stones being the essential item of building materials and house construction in urban Palestine.

Transported from and through Palestine in large quantities by donkey caravans, this international trade in copper was also combined with the obsidian international trade. Archaeological evidence shows that obsidian was found in significant quantity in some ancient mining sites in the western Naqab. However much of the obsidian trade passing through the transit trade routes of Palestine on to Lower Egypt originated in the volcanic regions of central Anatolia and the mountainous regions of Armenia (Smith 2008: 40).

obsidian sharp blades were used for variety of purposes, inter alia, to manufacture and polish knives and other cutting and piercing tools; obsidian was polished to create early ancient mirrors and decorative objects; obsidian knives were also used for the ritual performance of male circumcision which, according to Horodotus, was practised by the ancient Egyptians and by the 'Syrians called Palestinians' who 'confess that they learnt the custom of [male circumcision from] the Egyptians' (Herodotus 1858, Book II, Ch. 104; 1836, Vol. 1, Book II: 247). The Ma'adi excavations also uncovered a few examples of obsidian blades typical of the Palestinian blades of the early Bronze Age, as well as hundreds of Palestinian tabular scrapers. Stone tools produced in workshops and quarries and then transported to urban centre, tabular scrapers first appeared in ancient Palestine in the late Neolithic Age and reached their peak in the Chalcolithic and early Bronze Age. Suggestions for the uses of tabular scrapers by archaeologists included as a butchering tool or as wool-shearing knives or employed in ritual activities in religious temples.

The regional copper trade and the domestication of the donkey and camel

The pre-modern beasts of burden of international commerce transport in the ancient Near East included the donkey, mule and camel. The earliest long-distance trading paths from around 4000 BCE involved donkeys and the transportation of semi-precious stones and metal from mines as well as the transportation of gems and spices back to Egypt (Bough 2012: 49).

The Christian tradition of Palestine describes the donkeys as symbols of endurance, service, humility and peace and tells of the story of Jesus of Nazareth (in Galilee) entering Jerusalem riding a donkey symbolizing his arrival in peace (Matthew 21: 1-3, 6; Luke 19: 35). In the first half of the twentieth century donkeys could still be seen being used extensively in Palestinian agriculture as well as to transport produce to local markets. Also in the late nineteenth and early twentieth centuries donkeys can be seen placed in front of hotels in the urban centres of Palestine waiting to transport travellers, tourists and pilgrims to key Christian holy sites in Palestine.

But the Christian tradition borrowed from the long history of the extensive use of donkeys as a domesticated beast of service and endurance in local transport in Palestine and the key transit trade routes of Palestine – a history that precedes the Christian tradition by millennia. From the massive archaeological evidence we have from the ancient Egyptian city of Ma'adi, we also have the earliest example of domesticated donkeys in the ancient Near East. As we shall see below, in the ancient trade in copper donkey caravans and camel caravans were central. The domestication of the donkey during the Chalcolithic Age and over the course of the fourth millennium BCE and its integration into Near Eastern trade economies and overland trade transformed the nature of long-distance trade exchange systems. As well as their services as beasts of burden, the archaeological evidence show that the donkeys were valued in Ma'adi for their meat (Bard 2005).

Also donkeys were used in Assyrian trade: merchandise within the Middle East was normally transported on asses and by caravans of donkeys. As beasts of burden and endurance, donkeys could also travel along steep and mountain paths that could not be used for normal traffic, or would be uncomfortable or dangerous for camels ('Ma'adi and Wadi Digla', in Seeher 2005: 255–8). The advantages of the donkey in the hilly regions of Palestine and the Levant, and the narrow ragged and rocky mountain paths are clear and these advantages remained much in evidence into the modern period.

Evidence for early long-distance trade in copper and obsidian (from Anatolia) across Palestine can be found in the Chalcolithic Age 7,000 years ago. By the mid-third millennium in Mesopotamia, caravans of donkeys travelling between towns and cities were well established. Dating back to the fifth and early-mid fourth millennia BCE, the long-distance copper trade through Palestine was based on massive donkey caravans (Rosen 2019). Bronze Age trading posts and commercial cities in Palestine, where merchandise was transported, imported, stored, traded and exported, grew and expanded due to the long-distance overland donkey caravan trade in copper – trade that connected Anatolia and Egypt. As the economy of urban Palestine developed, the cities grew and expanded under the impact of the transit trade and the role of local merchants in long-distance trade widened. A key aspect of this transition in donkey caravans in the Bronze Age was the shift from the trade and transport of rare objects to everyday objects, that is, mass or bulk and mass trade (Rosen 2019).

In the Bronze Age long-distance trade of donkey caravans was not confined to the north-south (Syria and Anatolia to Egypt) trade but also expanded massively east-west from the great city-states of Mesopotamia to the Mediterranean city-states of Syria and Palestine 5,000–6,000 years ago. Archives of thousands of economic cuneiform tablets and records detailing trade activities and traders were unearthed from the excavations of southern Mesopotamian city-state of Ur during the third and second millennia BCE. By the early third millennium the Sumerian traders of Ur were engaged in long-distance trade with the city-states of Palestine and Syria, notably Ebla and Ugarit on the Mediterranean Sea, and they travelled by donkey caravans to all parts of the Fertile Crescent, Egypt included. They imported copper, precious stones, woods and ivory and exported woollen clothing and cloth, barley and Mesopotamian grown foodstuffs. Backed by the state these Sumerian merchants traded with the palaces and religious temples of ancient Iraq. The donkey caravans transported copper and tin, the two metals that were at the heart of the Bronze Age revolution and the two metals that were essential for the manufacturing of both domestic tools as well as weapons (Alexander and Violet 2012: 12–17).

These donkey caravans also transported silver, gold, precious stones, grain, wool and woollen goods. Silver and grain, in particular, were in use as mediums of exchange during the Bronze Age and silver served as a unit of value and commodities were often priced in silver (Alexander and Violet 2012: 12–17). This use of silver in the Bronze Age to price commodities in the ancient Middle East created a long-lasting financial model for international commerce in Antiquity and as we shall below the dominant currency of Palestine throughout Antiquity was minted in silver coins. According to the New Testament (Matthew 26:15) a disciple of Jesus, Judas Iscariot, betrayed Jesus in Roman Palestine for 'thirty pieces of silver' (*ἀργύρια, argyria* 'silver coins') – possibly the type of Ptolemaic silver tetradrachms coins minted in some cities in Palestine, Phoenicia and Syria and in common use of daily transaction in urban Palestine. Earlier, under the Ptolemais, Palestinian autonomous ('free') cities as Ascalon, which became a financial centre in Antiquity, minted its own internationally traded silver currency.

In the third and second millennia BCE, during the middle Bronze Age, the Sumerian city-states of Mesopotamia famously invented the earliest known writing known as cuneiform and this Sumerian writing and the earliest known corpus of recorded literature was known to have been taught in Bronze Age city-states in Palestine and became a useful practical language used for regional communication and trade and a practical tool for recording commercial goods and tax accounting (Masalha 2022).

Women's agency and ancient economic and commercial history

While this work centres on Palestine's role within larger trade networks, it is essential to acknowledge the contribution of urban neighbouring centres, including Bronze Age city-states of Mesopotamia and Syria, Phoenician Mediterranean trade and ancient Egyptian commercial policies to the commercial and economic history of Palestine; the experiences of all these ancient neighbouring trading powers highlight both commonalities and distinctive features of the Palestinian experience. As we have seen in the Introduction, the wider medieval Islamic context of the gold markets of urban Palestine and the selling and buying of gold jewellery in the ancient cities of Palestine under Islam became an important commercial assets for women and underlined the commercial and economic agency of women in the country (Moors 1998: 211). Back in Bronze Age Ur – long before the rise of the patriarchal Akkadian, Babylonian and Assyrian empires – these Bronze Age city-states of Mesopotamia, Palestine and Syria treated women and men on equal footing. For instance, the local temples of Bronze Age Sumerian Ur involved women in manufacturing wool clothing and textile for long-distance trade, and most of this temple textile industry of woollen cloth garments was done by thousands of women weavers. The everyday stuff of woollen garments and textiles produced in Mesopotamian temple's workshops were also exported to distant lands in the Fertile Crescent and southern Arabia in exchange for metals, such as tin and copper, precious stones, leather goods, sesame oil, barley and other natural resources (Alexander and Violet 2012: 12–17). As we shall see in Chapter 5, women also played a major role in the production of flax, which was central to the highly valued clothing industry of Palestine in Antiquity. In ancient Palestine flax, the production of which employed a large number of women, was one of the most important raw and most expensive materials for clothing and the textile industries in the Roman Empire (Peskowitz 2004: 129–45; Safrai 2003: 88, 113). This ancient economic power and agency of women and the extensive involvement of women in the various stages of production on the clothing industries of the ancient Palestine and the Middle East, industries geared towards foreign export, and consequently in the long-distance trade has been often overlooked by historians.

Levantine trade and Damascus as a 'City of Asses': Trade stations and the hybridization of super-donkeys

In the Levant, the city of Damascus, which occupied a central position on several trade routes, including two main trade routes of Palestine to ancient Egypt, including the *Way of the Sea* and the *King's Highway*, became known as the 'City of Asses'. It was the meeting point of many trade routes and the main means of transport was the donkey. Damascus became a very popular city among for merchants to trade and exchange donkeys. The donkeys travelled in great caravans across Syria and Palestine – caravans reported consisting of 3,000 donkeys, carrying a variety of goods over a vast area stretching from the Euphrates to the Nile (Bough 2012: 49).

Often long-distance ancient trade routes were protected by strong military forts and armed soldiers. DNA analysis and a genome sequencing study of 4,500 year-old skeletons burial site at Umm al-Marra in northern Syria revealed that the Sumerians of southern Mesopotamia created a super-strength donkeys by crossing female domestic donkeys with Syrian male wild asses. A type of interbred 'super donkey', called *kungas*, with a massive size became not only the backbone of the long-distance trade but also the original war horses of the Bronze Age. One of the earliest known examples of hybrid animal breeding in the ancient Middle East, and interbred to be stronger and faster so they could haul a chariot into battle, the *kungas* emerged hundreds of years before the introduction of the Arabian horses in the ancient Middle East and were partly used to transport goods and equipment and pull chariots in battles. These strong and fast *kungas* may have also been used in the defence of combined trade/military compounds on key regional trade routes in the Levant (Schwartz et al. 2006: 603–41 and 633–4). Used as draft animals in ancient Syria and Mesopotamia, these super-donkeys were implicitly mentioned in the third millennium BCE cuneiform writings from the Syrian city-state of Ebla, one of the most important trading kingdoms of Antiquity.

Another revolution in long-distance transport followed the subsequent breeding and adoption of the domestic camel by the Arabs into the economic systems of the Near East in the Iron Age; this led to further expansion of the overland north-south copper transit trade through Palestine and the rise of the Trans-Arabian camel caravans and the incense trade from Yemen to the Mediterranean port cities of Palestine. Used for riding and as a beast of burden, the advantage of the camel over the donkey lay in the fact that it could carry a much greater load, having five times the capacity of the donkey (Contenau 1954: 86) and was able to travel for extended periods of time without water, a characteristic that made it essentially invaluable for desert transportation. The camel is not only stronger and larger than the donkey, it is able to penetrate more deeply into the desert. While, a donkey can carry on its back about eighty kilograms and must be watered every day, the camel can be loaded with 200 to 300 kilograms and can travel up to three days without being watered (Rosen 2019). This made the case for the superior efficiency of pack camels in the arid and desert parts of the Middle East. Essential products of the Arabian camel included its milk and meat, which constituted a big part of the local diet.

Introduced by the north Arabian tribes in transportation in ancient Palestine, most scholars today agree that the Arabian camel was used as a pack domestic animal in the southern Levant and Palestine sometime in the early Iron Age. Archaeological evidence from copper smelting sites of the Arabah in the Naqab enable us to pinpoint the introduction of domestic camels to southern Palestine in last third of the tenth century BCE. This introduction coincided with the major reorganization of the copper industry of the region – attributed to the results of the military campaign of Pharaoh Shoshenq I – and as part of the efforts to improve efficiency by facilitating copper trade with Egypt (Sapir-Hen and Ben-Yosef 2013: 277–85).

Moreover, new political and international trade developments in the Palestinian Naqab began to make an impact on the greater use of the Arabian camel in the region at about 2,500 years ago; these developments impacted the first urbanized settlements in the Naqab by the Amorites, Nabataean Arabs and Edomite Arabs of southern Palestine. As we shall see in Chapter 3, a long list of *spice and perfume cities* began to flourish in the Palestinian Naqab during the Nabataean Arab kingdom of classical Antiquity.

Finkelstein (1988) has linked this urban rise in the Naqab in the Iron Age in the central Negev of Palestine to the domestication of the Arabian camel, also known as the dromedary (*Camelus dromedarius*)[2] or the one-humped camel, the tallest of the three species of camels and the Trans-Arabian trade across the Naqab. The word 'camel' derived from the Latin word camelus, from the Greek *kamēlos* and from the old Semitic languages that gave the Arabic word *jamal*. First domesticated and hybridized in the Arabia Peninsula by the Arabs about 4,000 years ago, by the end of the second millennium BCE the Arabian camel came into general use in the ancient Near East (Forbes 1965: 193–213).

The Arabian camel feeds on foliage and desert vegetation; several adaptations of this camel, such as its ability to tolerate losing more than 30 per cent of its total water content, allowed it to thrive in its desert habitat and flourish on the

Trans-Arabian trade. The adaption to the desert environments, coinciding with specific geo-political and tradition contexts, enabled the significant increase in the Trans-Arabian trade through Palestine, and consequent economic and urban prosperity in the Palestinian Naqab, especially in the first millennium (Finkelstein 1988: 241–52; Fritz, 1981: 61–73).

The Nabataean Arab kingdom of classical Antiquity was a key beneficiary of the domestication of the Arabian camel and the Nabataean kings used the Arabian camel effectively not only for their hugely lucrative Trans-Arabian spice and perfume trade from and to Gaza, but also as an effective cavalry at the centre of the army – an army which decisively defeated the Hellenistic Hasmonean Jewish kings of Palestine at a key battle to the east of the Sea of Galilee in the first century BCE (see Chapter 3). Interestingly, after the Roman conquest of the Nabataean Arab kingdom in 106 CE and its replacement by the Roman province of *Arabia Petraea*, the merchants of the former Nabataean spice city of Kurnub (renamed Memphis) in the Naqab started breeding Arabian horses – horses that were prized for their stamina and endurance in the harsh conditions of the Arabian deserts (Culbertson 2014; Negev 1988: 8). These Arabian horses became another major contribution of the Arabs to the revolution in transport and warfare in Late Antiquity and the Middle Ages.

Two thousand years later, in the early twentieth century, following the introduction of the modern railway system into Ottoman Palestine and the Levant, we can still see caravans of the Arabian camels loaded with luxury goods for export and carefully packed boxes of the internationally famous Jaffa oranges of Palestine, while waiting for commercial trains at Jaffa city train station, heading for Port Said in Egypt. The Jaffa orange boxes were ready to be shipped from Port Said to the international markets of Europe. In a similar fashion camels transported luxury goods of spices and aromatics across southern Palestine to be shipped from the port city of Gaza to Mediterranean and European cities in classical and late Antiquity. However, this time Jaffa oranges were the produce of Palestine (see Chapter 18).

In Iron Age Palestine, the caravans of Arabian camels continued to play a crucial role in the development of copper trade out of the Timna mines in southern Palestine, and the Arabian camel became closely associated with copper industry of Palestine and Egypt (Sapir-Hen and Ben-Yosef 2013: 277–85). However ancient Egypt is credited with introducing copper mining and smelting in both the Palestinian Naqab and Sinai and during the Bronze Age between 1400 and 1300 BC (Shahin 2005; Tebes 2008). The popularity of the Arabia camel continued to increase in the Midde Ages after the Islamic conquest of north Africa and the expansion of the Muslim trade routes in Africa. While the vast Islamic empire was accomplished largely on horseback, new trade links in the Middle East and north Africa and across the African Sahara (desert) allowed Arabian camel to be imported *en masse*. Evolving across millennia, the Arabian camel was well-suited to long desert journeys and could carry a great deal of cargo, allowing substantial trans-Saharan trade for the first time.

Copper smelting at the Timna mines in southern Palestine

The long and complex history of copper mining and production at the Timna Valley in the Naqab continued from the late Neolithic Age to the Middle Ages under Islam (Lepinski n.d.). In the 1970s, archaeologists recovered camel and equid (related to the horse family) remains from copper smelting sites at Timna and more recently these remains were re-dated to the Iron Age (I and II), and the remains were linked to the domestication of the Arabian camel. These archaeologists came to the conclusion that camels and donkeys were employed in the transportation and distribution of copper from the Timna valley and from mines in the eastern Arabah, prior to the large-scale growth in use of camels in the Trans-Arabian incense trade between Yemen and the port cities of Palestine in Iron II (Grigson 2013: 82-100).

The Timna valley is located in southern Palestine in the south-western Arabah, approximately thirty kilometres north of the Gulf of Aqaba. The area is rich in copper ore and has been mined since the fifth millennium BCE. A large section of the valley contains ancient remnants of copper mining. Archaeological excavation shows that the copper mining and smelting in the Timna valley occurred since the sixth or fifth millennium BCE and later in the Iron Age by the Edomite Arabs (Shaw 2002: 583).

Archaeological excavations at Timna valley indicate that the copper mines were also part of the Arabian kingdom of the Edomites, which appears in written sources relating to the late Bronze Age and to the Iron Age in the ancient Near East and appears in the chronicle of a campaign by Ramesses II (*r.* 1186–1155 BCE) (Negev and Gibson 2001: 149-150).

Mining in the Naqab continued by the Nabateans through to the first and second centuries CE during the Roman period, and then, after the seventh-century Arab conquest, by the Umayyads until the copper ore became scarce (Beit-Arieh 1996: 28–36). Recent excavations of copper mining sites in the Naqab also discovered camel bones with signs of the earliest camel domestication and breeding found in Palestine, dating to Iron Age II. Mining also continued in the Naqab area by the Nabataean Arabs throughout the first and second centuries CE and later during the Roman and Byzantine times and subsequently the Umayyad Arab rule. By 1990 during extensive excavations at the Timna valley archaeologists had discovered 10,000 copper mines and smelting camps with furnaces, rock drawings, geological features, an ancient Egyptian mining sanctuary, jewellery, and other artefacts (Levin 2020: 487).

The Palestine copper mining industry and shared religion in ancient Egypt and Palestine

Often long-distance trade and ancient trade caravans were keys factor in the spread of religious traditions and religious practices and the construction of shared deities in the ancient Near East – and in the Bronze Age religious traditions began to spread with the international trade in copper and semi-precious mineral as well as the rising incense trade from south Arabia and the Horn of Africa. Being a 'cross-road country' for transit trade routes Palestine came under the influence of multiple religious traditions from Mesopotamia and Persia in the East to Phoenicia in the north, to ancient Egypt in the south. As we have already discussed in the Introduction, the copper industry and copper trade via the transit routes of Palestine accelerated the rise of the Palestinian city-states in the Bronze Age.

Archaeological excavations at the mining industry and copper trade of Timna uncovered traces of the early evolution of *shared* religious traditions between ancient Egypt and Palestine. Archaeologists uncovered at Timna an Egyptian temple dedicated to the Egyptian goddess of mining, Hathor, which was built during the reign of Pharaoh Seti I at the end of the fourteenth century BCE. Egyptian temples were often not just places of worships but (like the great medieval mosques of Islam) included schools and libraries. Hathor, a major goddess in ancient Egypt took many forms and was associated with a wide variety of roles in ancient Egypt across millennia. Local Palestinian and Egyptian miners – rather than slave workers – were employed in the mining industry of Timna and the transportation of the copper to Egypt. For the ancient Egyptians, Hathor was at the heart of the mining industry and the copper trade.

As we saw in Chapter 1, the *Way of Horus* was a key international highway connecting trading caravans between Syria, Palestine and Lower Egypt. The deity of Hathor (lit. the 'House of Horus') was connected by the Egyptians' foreign trade with countries such Palestine in the north and Nubia in the south; Hathor was also connected with the Sinai Peninsula, which was not considered part of Egypt proper but was the site of Egyptian mines for copper and turquoise during the Middle and New Kingdoms in the Bronze Age. Crucially Hathor was also connected with the import to Egypt of valuable material such as copper and precious commodities such as incense, perfume and semi-precious stones and as she had multiple roles, including roles in Egyptian religious festivals and love poetry, Hathor was celebrated in connection with the sensory pleasures of life – pleasures believed to be among the gods' gifts to humanity. These religious festivals' pleasures included eating, drinking wine, dancing and the use of incense, perfume, myrrh and precious commodities much of which were imported by the Egyptians from south Arabia, Palestine and Nubia (Hart 2005: 61–5, 132; Pinch 2003a: 49–50, 52; Wilkinson 2003: 143). Being *Goddess of the Sky* – and because Hathor was believed to protect ships on the Nile and in the seas beyond Egypt – her connection with international trade from foreign lands linked her with the international copper trade with travel and navigation and knowledge of the stars (Hollis 2019: 53).

Egypt maintained strong trading relations with neighbouring countries and with the coastal cities of Palestine, particularly Gaza and Ascalon, and Phoenicia, Byblos and Syria. This placed Egyptian religious traditions in direct contact with other religions in the ancient Near East and influenced the creation of shared religious traditions and even *shared deities* in the region. In the case of the shared religious traditions of Palestine and Egypt, the Egyptians sometimes equated the Canaanite goddess Anatu (Anat) – a major Palestinian deity who came to be worshipped in Egypt during the New Kingdom, with Hathor (Wilkinson 2003: 137). A warrior goddess, who, like

Hathor, was also called 'the mistress of heaven' Anatu – who was closely related to Baal, of the Levantine and Palestinian pantheon – at the height of the copper trade in the Bronze Age was introduced to Egypt and achieved a degree of prominence during the reign of Ramesses II who was particularly devoted to Anatu (Cornelius 2008: 35).

Evidence for the shared Palestinian and Egyptian worship of Anatu (and of the worship of Hathor found in Canaanite artworks of Hathor's iconography excavated in Palestine) is available from various sites in Palestine, especially on sites which came under the influence of the Egyptians in the Bronze Age. Temples dedicated to Anatu have been identified in Egypt and a festival of Anatu celebrated in Gaza alongside the attestations connected to the Egyptian devotion to this goddess (Cornelius 2008: 92: Wilkinson 2003: 137). Anatu would remain a part of the Egyptian pantheon as late as in the Roman period.

Copper mining in southern Palestine and the birth of the proto-Canaanite Alphabet: The shared history of early writing of ancient Egypt and Palestine

According to recent theories the early pro-Canaanite alphabet was a modified version of the Egyptian hieroglyphic writing. The Bronze Age copper industry and the ancient Egyptian mining operations in Sinai and Palestine are significant in revealing the early history of the alphabet. These copper and turquoise mining sites in the south of Sinai and southern Palestine were also linked to the early evolution of the alphabet in the Bronze Age. An early trace of alphabetic writing was uncovered by archaeologists at Serabital-Khadim in the south of Sinai at temple of Hathor: four-thousand-year-old inscriptions uncovered in the form of proto-Canaanite (also known as proto-Sinaitic script), the ancestor to the Phoenician, Greek and Arabic alphabet, and all modern alphabets.[3] The nearby site of Wadi al-Nasb served as the base of operations for much of Egypt's mining activities in the Sinai. Both copper and turquoise mines were located within a few miles of the site. The modern border between southern Sinai and southern Palestine is not something the ancient Egyptians would have recognized, and Wadi al-Nasb was not only the centre for one of the largest ancient Egyptian copper smelting facilities in southern Sinai, but also the administrative centre for the main Egyptian mines and copper smelting sites in southern Palestine. Also, these proto-Sinaitic inscriptions uncovered recently, generally dated to the nineteenth century BCE, are believed to have been written by 'Canaanite/Palestinian labourers' who worked in these mines – labourers who contributed to the modification of the *pictorial* Egyptian hieroglyphic to the *phonetic* writing form known later as the 'proto-Canaanite alphabet' (Masalha 2022). Although many questions remain unanswered about the origins of the proto-Canaanite alphabet, these new discoveries in southern Sinai provide new evidence and context relating to the early proto-Canaanite alphabet that evolved in the mines of Sinai and southern Palestine and became part of the shared heritage of both countries.

3

The Nabataean Arab Cities of Spice and Aromatics

The Trans-Arabian Global Incense Trade and the Transformation of the Palestinian Cities of the Naqab (Classical and Late Antiquity)

From Petra to Gaza: The historic cities of southern Palestine and UNESCO's World Heritage Sites along Naqab's incense routes

In the late Roman and Byzantine periods there were twenty-five cities in Palestine, six of which existed along the historic *Incense/Spice Routes* (and sub-ways) of Petra-Gaza in the Naqab (southern Palestine). These six Naqab cities were strategically situated on ancient commercial routes in southern Palestine, which facilitated the highly lucrative trade of the time, of both incense and spices. Despite the dry and arid climate of the region, the Naqab's 'spice cities' flourished for centuries, together with several hamlets and trade stations, forts and caravanserais created along the main routes and sub-ways of the Naqab trade stations located every fifteen kilometres.

More than a millennia before the rise of Islam and centuries before the Roman conquest of Palestine the Nabataean Arab traders, who controlled a vast arid region between Yemen and Gaza in Palestine, and created spectacular trading cities such as Petra, Madain Saleh (in modern Saudi Arabia) and Oboda (in Palestine). Nabataean Arab trade routes, flourishing urban civilization and Nabataean Aramaic script were also instrumental in the emergence of the earliest Arabic script and cultural Arabic activity of Antiquity. Harvesting rainwater and ground water, the collection and storage of rain, rather than allowing it to run off, and its redirection to cistern, well, shaft or aquifer has been used in Palestine for many thousands of years. The Nabataean engineers of southern Palestine and northern Arabia were particularly skilful in harvesting rainwater. Most Nabataean cities were usually surrounded by large agricultural fields, and their trade stations were supplied with water from cisterns, dams and streams that could provide the travelling merchants nomads and their animals (camels and donkeys), as well as the needs of surrounding agriculture. Agricultural developments in this arid region were also essential as pastoralists and nomads were dependent on livestock of goats, sheep, camels and cattle.

In the post-Nabataean period, during the late Roman and Byzantine periods these cities of southern Palestine developed significant agriculture and the cultivation of vineyards, which supported the then internationally famous Palestinian wine-making industry. A couple of these cities in the Naqab, Elusa and Kurnub (Memphis) also enjoyed the formal municipal status of *polis*. At the height of the Byzantine period, one estimate put the mostly urban population of the Naqab as high as 80,000 (Broshi 2001: 94).

Historians continue to argue whether the introduction of large-scale 'agriculture' in the Naqab began with the Nabataean Arab period of classical Antiquity or was more related to the Christian Byzantine period of late Antiquity. However, there is archaeological evidence to suggest that from the fourth century BCE onwards the Nabataean Arabs began to construct dams and develop some form of sophisticated irrigation and water drinking systems that supported significant urban centres, caravanserai and hamlets located along the Incense Road (Shahin 2005).

However, in the fourth century CE Saint Jerome (*c*.347–*c*.420) – who lived and carried out research in the libraries of Palestinian city of Caesarea Maritima and the monastery of Bethlehem – commented on the practices of growing vines up elaborate terraces in the ancient Nabataean towns and cities of the Naqab; these vineyards were geared towards wine export what became known in late Antiquity as Gaza wine (Unwin 2005: 149).

In fact Gaza wine was produced in, and originated from, multiple regions in Palestine, including the region of Ascalon and even in towns such as Yubna ابني in central Palestine. However, the scale of the wine industries of the Naqab was such that some European authors began to conflating the wine of Gaza with the wine produced by the vineyards of the Naqab:

> During the fifth and sixth centuries the wines of Gaza, in the Negev in Palestine, became particularly famous ... with Gregory of Tours (*History of Franks*, Vol. VII, 29) noted that they were stronger than the wines of Gaul. The development of vineyards in this region seems to have been closely related to the rise of monasticism there during the fourth century, and to the activities of the proto-monk Hilarion. If Jerom's life of Hilarion (*Vita Hilarionis*), were to be believed, it would appear that one of the main activities of the monks and monastery that he established was the cultivation and production and marketing of wine. The expansion of these vineyards, evident also by the discovery of remains of numerous wine presses in the vicinity of Gaza and Elusa, was further enhanced by the pilgrimages to the Holy Land undertake by people from France, Italy and Spain during the fifth and sixth centuries.
>
> (Unwin 2005: 149-50)

The entire Roman province of *Arabia Petraea* (including Petra), the Naqab and the Sinai Peninsula were subsequently annexed into the Byzantine province of *Palaestina Salutaris* (*Palaestina* Tertia; 'third Palestine'). Petra can also be seen on the Madaba Map of the sixth century. Below we will see how the wine industries of the Naqab affected different cities in southern Palestine (and the Byzantine province of *Palaestina*

Tertia) and generally the growth of the urban environment of the country in late Antiquity. However, the combination of the traditional incense trade, and the new agriculture-based cities in the Naqab under the Byzantines ensured that the urban population of the Naqab grew exponentially.

Sedentarization and urbanization in the Naqab desert was never static; urbanization, in particular, rose and declined depending on the wider regional and international trade systems. Urbanization and the prosperity of the cities of the Palestine Naqab desert depended largely on the historic *perfume/incense roads* from Petra and to the port city of Gaza, a road which stretched across some 150 kilometres. This Palestinian section in the Naqab was part of the 2,400 kilometres of Incense Routes and the Nabataean Arab caravan trails of classical Antiquity that ran all the way from Yemen to the Palestinian port cities on the shore of the Mediterranean Sea. Energizing as key urban centres in southern Palestine and culturally *melting pot cities* along the spice route, the Palestinian cities, hamlets, trade stations, forts and caravanserais which sprung up along this key international trade route flourished for more than a millennium and a half initially as *spice cities* and *incense market towns*; but they subsequently developed their own perfume industry and perfume factories; these cities also had to accommodate changing historical circumstances transforming themselves economically and commercially.

The Nabataean Arab kingdom of classical Antiquity ushered in more than a millennium of Arab political, cultural, commercial and architectural urban presence in southern Palestine (and the Naqab) long before the arrival of Islam in Palestine from Arabia in the 630s CE. However, the changing historical circumstances of southern Palestine belong to four distinct periods:

- the Nabataean Arab kingdom of classical Antiquity;
- the Roman period of *Arabia Petraea* and *Provencea Arabia;*
- the Byzantine Christian province of *Palaestina Tertia* and the Gassanid Arabs of southern Palestine during this period;
- the early Islamic period of *Jund Filastin* (the Arab province of Palestine).

Furthermore, in reality the Nabataean *Incense Route* was not a single road but consisted of a network of trade routes roads and trails with multiple branches that encompassed villages, towns, cities trade stations and caravanserais. This network included some key routes and minor byways:

- The two key routes were: *Petra-Oboda-Elusa-Gaza* and *Petra-Philadelphia (Amman)-Bosra-Damascus;*
- The minor branches passed through the Naqab city and caravan station of Nessana, an ancient Nabataean city located in the southwest Naqab close to the modern Sinai border with Palestine; this route followed a western branch of the road that allowed access to central Sinai and then Egypt (Negev 2001: 367–8).

Another minor branch of the same Naqab *Incense Road* continued northwards from Elusa to Beersheba, Al-Khalil (Hebron) and Jerusalem.

The *Incense/Spice Roads* in the Naqab became known to the Arabs as the *Sultan Road* (*Darb al-Sultan*). With its formidable forts and caravanserais, the road served Nabataean Arab merchants, the army of the Nabataean kingdom of classical Antiquity and the armies of the Romans, Byzantines and Muslim Arabs as a key route between northern Arabia, southern Palestine and the Mediterranean; the *Incense Routes* continued to function as a major artery between Yemen, Petra and Gaza in Palestine for over one and a half millennia. During the Roman empire, with its superior military power and massive economic and commercial empire, milestones were constructed for speedy troop movement and as part of the travel of merchants on the *Incense Roads* and strategic movement of armies; also the section of the road from the city of Petra to the city Oboda in the central highlands of the Naqab was paved (Ben David 2005: 31–48; Cohen 1982: 240–7). It was once an outpost on the Nabataean caravan routes that ran all the way from Yemen, through Petra, into the Negev, finally ending at the port of Gaza.

Relying primarily on an international trade system and caravan trade, the capital city of the Nabataeans Petra and their other cities in southern Palestine became very wealthy and socially, culturally and linguistically diverse. Being trading cities, the urban centres of the Nabataeans became multilingual, with Arabic, Aramaic and Greek all being used. The Nabataeans wrote mainly in Aramaic; a language closely related to their spoken Arabic. Their capital city Petra (Greek *Πέτρα*, 'Rock') was originally known by its Aramaic name: Raqmu (Schmid and Mouton 2013; Shaddel 2017: 303-18).

A historic and archaeological city in modern-day southern Jordan, Nabataean Arabs might have settled in what would become the capital city of their kingdom as early as the fourth century BCE (Elliott 1996: 47-60; Taylor 2001: 30-1). Raqmu's population peaked at an estimated 20,000 inhabitants.[1] The first-century Roman-Jewish historian Josephus describes the splendour of Petra and says the city 'ranks highest in the land of the Arabs' and was still called Raqmu by all the Arabs of his time (Josephus 1930, 7, 1; 4, 7). Modern excavations of the Byzantine period in Petra discovered in one Byzantine Church 140 papyri documents that contained mainly commercial contracts dated from 530s to 590s, establishing that the city and its Trans-Arabian spice trade was still ongoing in the sixth century CE, at a time when Petra was still a major centre for Palestinian Arab Christianity and the metropolis of *Palaestina Salutaris* (Ward 2008: 93).

A major regional trading hub, the city of Petra boasted shops, merchant caravanserais and large markets for a diverse community of money-changers and traders and their luxury goods. Aramaic had been the language of trade and international commerce in western Asia from the beginning of the first millennium BCE, and became the language that many northern Arabians used to trade as well the language of the court of the Achaemenid (Persian) empire. Both Greek and Aramaic were also the languages of trade in Palestine under the Ptolemians in classical Antiquity. The Nabataeans spoke Arabic among themselves and their spoken Arabic language subsequently influenced the written Aramaic language used by the northern Arabians. Also, not surprisingly, for practical reasons the earliest form of Arabic script (also known as the Kufi script) – which evolved from the Nabataean Aramaic and proto-Arabic scripts, which, in turn, can be traced to the Phoenician alphabet – evolved under the impact of these important trade routes of Palestine and Arabia and the growing urbanization of the Arab Near East.

Practically all the Palestinian Naqab cities, which included Elusa, Oboda, Sbeita, Kurnub (Mempis), Oboda and Nessana, were founded by the Nabataean Arabs in classical Antiquity, in around the late fourth and third centuries BCE. The Nabataean Arab kingdom of classical Antiquity controlled the Trans-Arabian trade of the spice/incense routes between their capital Petra and the seaport of Gaza on the Mediterranean. The Nabataean kings are often cited in Western literature by their Hellenized sounding names; however, their original Arabic names are clearly discernible. These Arab kings also adapted the Arabian camels, which they used extensively in caravans on the incense route. They also minted internationally recognized and traded currency and the remains of their civilization, and of red and orange potsherds identified as a trademark of their material culture, have been discovered along the spice routes of the Naqab (Shahin 2005).

The Nabataean global incense trade, religion and temple construction encompassed a vast region from Arabia and through southern Palestine to the Italian cities of the Mediterranean in the north and all these went hand in hand. The Nabataean religion itself evolved as a religion of a trading nation subjected to multiple religious and cultural traditions; the religion was an earlier form of Arab polytheism (and pantheism) and the main deity of the Nabataean Arab state was called Bushara (also known 'God of the mountains'). The Nabataeans shared other deities with other polytheistic Arabians including *Alaat* and *Uza,* deities that were worshipped in pre-Islamic Mecca. However, under the impact of Hellenization, by the end of the first century BCE a Greek-style temple (an acropolis) can be found in the key Nabataean city of Oboda, along the western edge of the city. The Nabataean Arabs were polytheistic and they worshipped a wide variety of Levantine and Egyptian deities such as Baal and Isis – in ancient Egypt the divine mother of Horus, 'protector of trade route' – as well as such as the eastern/Palestinian deity of Dionysus; however, many of them later embraced monotheistic Christianity during the Byzantine rule in Palestine. The Nabataean Arab merchants in Gaza also linked up with Mediterranean mariners and shippers who received incense from colleagues based at Gaza and Alexandria. Aramaic inscription from Puteoli (Pozzuoli), a city in the metropolitan area of Napes, indicates the presence of a Nabataean temple and trade station at this important Italian harbour city (McLaughlin 2014: 103).

The Nabataean incense and spice routes of the Naqab were also served by an elaborate system of trade stations, forts and caravanserais with bathhouses. These included the *Moa Fort* and caravanserai, which is located at the eastern end of the Naqab Incense Road close to the modern border of Jordan. The archaeology of Moa Fort shows the site was constructed of limestone, its caravanserai for travellers and merchants were served by a bath house and a water cistern and a laid-out water system sourced from underground springs; the water system fed the caravanserai and bathhouse through a canal; also, evidence of agricultural tools was uncovered on the site.

Palestine as a key route for the south Arabian frankincense trade

Used for multiple purposes, from medicinal treatment to the purification of crowded sacred temples throughput the Mediterranean region and the mumification of Pharaohs in ancient Erupt, frankincense became an elite commodity par excellence and the most precious globally traded commodity of the ancient world. Throughout ancient history, the frankincense route, or the Trans-Arabian-Gaza route was perhaps the most important trade route at the time. Through the Red Sea-Gaza trade route came caravans loaded with wine amphorae and this international route became an important aspect of the Palestinian's and Mediterranean region trade. The Nabataean Arabs from the Naqab in Palestine and Petra and Mediterranean traders shipped incense to Europe through colleagues based at Gaza and Alexandria. Aramaic inscription from Puteoli (Pozzuoli) indicates the presence of a trade station at this important Italian harbour and there was a large increase in the Mediterranean and Eastern trade during the Roman era (McLaughlin 2014: 103)

The practices associated with incense, perfumes and frankincense were widely used in Roman Palestine. Frankincense, the English word derives from *franc encens* ('high-quality' or 'pure' incense - also known as olibanum), is an aromatic resin used in incense and perfumes obtained from trees of the genus *Boswellia*. The name of frankincense is found in the koinē Greek of the New Testament. λίβανος, *líbanos* (or λιβανωτός, *libanōtós*), is cognate with the name Lebanon (Greek: Λίβανος); cheap resin is produced in south Arabia, India and the Horn of Africa, which are the Roman Catholic Church's main sources (Howell 2010). Frankincense has been traded on the Arabian Peninsula for more than 5,000 years (Simla 2005). Frankincense was also traded from the Horn of Africa (Killion 2006: 66). The historian Herodotus wrote in *The History* that frankincense was harvested from trees in south Arabia (Herodotus 1904). The frankincense kingdom is described further east along the southern coast of the Arabian Peninsula, with the harbour of Cana (South Arabic *Qana*, modern Bir Ali in Hadramaut).

> After Eudaemon Arabia there is a continuous length of coast, and a bay extending two thousand stadia or more, along which there are Nomads and Fish-Eaters living in villages; just beyond the cape projecting from this bay there is another market-town by the shore, Cana, of the Kingdom of Eleazus, the 'frankincense country'; and facing it there are two desert islands, one called Island of Birds, the other Dome Island, one hundred and twenty stadia from Cana. Inland from this place lies the metropolis Sabbatha, in which the King lives. All the frankincense produced in south Arabia is brought by camel caravans to that place to be stored, and to Cana on rafts held up by inflated skins after the manner of the country, and in boats. And this place has a trade also with the far-side ports, with Barygaza and Scythia and Ommana and the neighbouring coast of Persia.
>
> (Schoff et al. 2021)

Frankincense was used in the Christian Byzantine empire where it was commonly used in church services. Southern Arabia (including Yemen and Oman) remained an exporter of frankincense through Palestine to the Mediterranean world in Antiquity, with some south Arabian frankincense was being traded as far as China. It was used by makers of perfumes, natural medicines and essential oils. It can be inhaled or applied to the skin for its supposed health benefits. The use of *Boswellia* resin for spiritual and medicinal purposes dates back to ancient civilizations. Numerous compounds of different chemical categories are identified in the resin; the pharmacological actions of *Boswellia* resin are attributed to the complementary effects exerted by these compounds. Modern clinical studies have demonstrated some effectiveness of frankincense resin in some disease conditions like asthma, rheumatoid arthritis, irritable bowel diseases and osteoarthritis. The essential oil obtained from the oleogum resin of *Boswellia serrata* showed antimicrobial activities. Also, in vivo studies on animals revealed that frankincense oleogum resin exhibits neuroprotective activity. The Egyptians cleansed body cavities in the mummification process with frankincense. Generally, the oil was also used in ancient religions of the Near East to cleanse the house or building of bad or evil energy. The incense offering occupied an important position in the ancient religions of the Near East. In traditional ancient medicine frankincense along with myrrh have anti-bacterial properties as well as blood-moving uses. It can be used topically or orally, also used in surgical and internal medicine of traditional Chinese medicine. It is used to relieve pain, remove blood stasis, promote blood circulation.[2]

Before the Christianization of Gaza in the early fifth century, the pagan fertility cult of Aphrodite – which in Antiquity had its own particular Palestinian version: *Palaistine Aphrodite Urania,* and was often associated with ancient Near Eastern fertility goddess of Ishtar – stood at both the centre of the city of Gaza and at the gate of the neighbouring city of Maiumas Gaza, the port city of Gaza. Local women attached lamps and burned incense in front of it, to get help with pregnancy and marriages (Trombley 1995, Vol. 1: 191).

The prices of frankincense and pepper: Taxing trade during the Roman and Byzantine periods

By the first millennium BCE, with the domestication of the camel, overload trade routes became established between southern Arabia and Palestine. Frankincense, a product of southern Arabia and north-eastern Africa, along with other items of trade, was traded from southern Arabia, Eritrea and Somalia, to Palestine and Jordan. Frankincense was highly regarded by ancient Roman and was in great demand. The earliest recorded account for the use of frankincense and myrrh from Arabia from ancient Greeks comes from Herodotus (Groom 1981), suggesting that by 500 BCE a well-established trade existed between southern Arabia and the Mediterranean world via Palestine. The incense trade expanded considerably during the first two centuries CE. By the fourth century with the decline of the Roman Empire and spread of Christianity, the south Arabian frankincense and myrrh trade declined (Singh and Jauhar 2011), although the market prices of frankincense and perfumes in Mediterranean Europe are unknown and may have fluctuated and amounts bought are rarely recorded. Some of the later prices for frankincense recorded in the Greek island of Delos without amount of purchase fit this pattern too.

In particular, the outlay in 194 BCE of 1.667 drachma conforms perfectly to a purchase of one-quarter of a mna at 6.668 drachma/mna. The price of frankincense was governed by the amount of purchase: five drachma for mna in the period 250–169 BCE (Scheidel 2019: 140). The mna, a unit of currency, was, in ancient Greece, originally equal to seventy drachmae and was later increased to 100 drachmae.

The Greek term μνᾶ, *mna* or *mina*, refers to an ancient Near Eastern unit of weight and later a unit of currency. The Greek term was borrowed from the Akkadian *manu*, meaning to 'count' or a 'unit of account'.

However, before it was used as currency, a mina was a unit of measurement, equal to 1.25 pounds (0.57 kg). From earliest Sumerian times, a mina was a unit of weight.

The Romans imposed 25 per cent in tax on all goods imported into Roman controlled territories (source: the Muziris Papyris).

Town planning, trade and urban life in southern Palestine under the Romans and Byzantines

From the extensive archaeological excavations undertaken in the modern period and available classical literary sources, we know that most of the sophisticated of urban life and cultural institutions of classical Antiquity were present in these Naqab cities: military fortifications and city walls, trading markets and wine presses, hostels for merchants, large courtyards with mosaic floors with colourful geometric patterns, pagan temples and Christian churches, schools, sport facilities, amphitheatres and racecourses for entertainments, dam constructions for regular water supplies and bathhouses (Broshi 2001: 100).

Paradoxically the desert conditions of the Naqab preserved much of the evidence for the flourishing of urban life in southern Palestine in Antiquity. Partly due to the desert conditions, the archaeological and historic remains of some of these Naqab cities are far better preserved than many of the towns and cities of the northern parts of Palestine of Antiquity. Much of the building materials for these urban centres was sourced locally from local stone quarries, and the Nabataean architecture of classical Antiquity and Roman period stimulated the growth of marble mining in southern Palestine. During the Roman and Byzantine periods the large investment in urban infrastructure and public buildings, such as the construction of the large theatre of Elusa, was most likely undertaken with the support of the local merchant communities, while imperial support was confined to the maintenance of military fortifications and the construction of roads and water supply systems.

Being on the historic *Incense Roads* and among some of the best preserved cities in the country, in 2005 four of the sites of the historic cities of the Nabataeans, Oboda, Elusa, Kurnub (Memphis) and Sbeita, were declared UNESCO World Heritage Sites 'in Israel' – but with no references to their centrality to the material culture of

Palestine or the millennia-old Arab heritage of the country and the Palestinian Arab transit trade routes of Antiquity. The Naqab cities in question had been established by the Nabataean Arab kingdom in classical Antiquity; they subsequently became part of the Roman Arab province of *Arabia Petrea* and later part of the Byzantine province of *Palaestina Tertia;* under early Islam they became part of the Arab province of *Palestine* (*Jund Filastin*). Endorsing the new Israeli toponyms in the Naqab and Israel's retrospective colonization of Palestinian history, UNESCO uses the Israeli Hebrewized place names of the sites of the cities – placenames Hebrewized after the Palestinian Nakba of 1948 (Masalha 1992, 2012) – rather than the original historic Arabic names or the Greek names of Byzantine Palestine. The UNESCO website reads:

> The four Nabatean towns of Haluza [Elusa, al-Khalus], Mamshit [Kurnub] Avdat [Oboda] and Shivta [Sbeita], along with associated fortresses and agricultural landscapes in the Ṅegev Desert, are spread along routes linking them to the Mediterranean end of the incense and spice route. Together they reflect the hugely profitable trade in frankincense and myrrh from south Arabia to the Mediterranean, which flourished from the 3rd century BC until the 2nd century AD. With the vestiges of their sophisticated irrigation systems, urban constructions, forts and caravanserai, they bear witness to the way in which the harsh desert was settled for trade and agriculture.[3]

As we have already mentioned in Chapter 1, Apollodorus of Damascus was the chief architect and engineer of the Roman Empire during the time of emperor Trajan and Hadrian.

Trajan had served as the governor of Syria and the famous building programme Apollodorus of Damascus included the rectangular *Roman Forum* (a plaza which had everything) and *Trajan's Market* (*Mercatus Traiani*), now known as the world's oldest shopping mall, with shops that sold perfumes, frankincense, spices, ivory and luxury goods transported through the long-distance spice trade from the East. The Forum marketplace was one of the most distinctive features of the urban landscape of Palestine and Syria during classical Antiquity.

Western historians often view Roman urban planning through Western imperial prisms with little attention to the monumental contribution made by indigenous eastern architects such as Apollodorus. Apollodorus's original approach to urban planning and urban centres also echoes the construction of the commercial heart of urban Petra of the Nabataean Arabs, a melting pot trading city at the centre of the Trans-Arabian spice trade with Hellenistic and Arabian building traditions. The commercial centre of Petra included monumental temples as well as a colonnaded 'Upper Market' – built at the height of Apollodorus's career and modelled on Apollodorus's *Trajan's Market* in Rome – a market with a honorific inscription to emperor Trajan created in Petra in 114 CE (Peaccock 2013: 169–93). Later we can see the colonnaded streets and standarization of these large commercial markets in other cities of Roman and Byzantine Palestine. This approach of Apollodorus's to urban planning in the Roman empire also reflects the approaches of modern city planners of big urban shopping centres, including department stores, specialist shops and restaurants (Toussaint-Samat: 2009: 266).

Apollodorus was also credited with introducing several eastern innovations to the Roman style, such as making the dome a standard, and his urban building programmes, bridge constructions and road engineering works gained him immense popularity and as Trajan's chief military engineer he may have been involved in the construction of the *New Road of Emperor Tranjan* through southern Palestine and the former Nabataean Arab kingdom. Fiorella Festa Farina, Director of the Italian Institute of Culture in Damascus, described the engineering skills of Apollodorus as stemming from his mixed cultural roots and the architectural tradition of Syria, owing his mastery to 'Nabataean culture' of southern Palestine, culture 'filtered through Greek modes of thought'.

Spices, aromatics and trade wars: The Nabataean-Hasmonaean conflict

In my 2018 book *Palestine: A Four Thousand Year History* I argue that the archaeology of ancient Palestine has demonstrated that the biblical stories about the kingdom of David and Solomon are fiction – not facts; these legends were products of fertile imagination and were put together, partly for entertainment, many centuries after the event they meant to describe. But the Nabataean Trans-Arabian trade in frankincense, aromatics and gold with the kingdoms of Yemen in Antiquity produced fertile ground for story-telling and the creation of legends and give us some clues as to the historical origins of these fictional stories of the Old Testament. The Old Testament tells us the legend of the Queen of Sheba (*Bilqis* of Yemen, in medieval Arabic story-telling and legends) visiting Jerusalem and bringing a caravan of valuable gifts to King Solomon, including frankincense and myrrh (1 Kings 10:1–13 and 2 Chronicles 9: 1–12). Immediately following these verses, the Old Testament tells us that King Solomon gained tremendous wealth from the visit of the Queen of Sheba. Yet in the archaeology of both Palestine and Yemen yet no trace of King Solomon and the Queen of Sheba herself have been found (Finkelstein 2007: 167).

During classical Antiquity the Hellenized kingdoms of Palestine included the independent Nabataean Arab kingdom of southern Palestine, which for centuries dominated the Trans-Arabian spices and perfume trade, and the Jewish Hasmonean kingdom (Greek Ασμοναϊκή δυναστεία) of Judaea which flourished in Palestine from *c*.140 BCE to 37 BCE. The latter was a client kingdom of the Seleucid and Roman Empires. The Hellenized Hasmonean kings of Judaea took the Greek title *basileus* ('king'). Among the most important of the Hasmonean kings was Alexander Jannaeus (Greek: Ἀλέξανδρος Ἰανναῖος *Aléxandros Iannaîos*); as the Seleucid empire began to weaken, Alexander Jannaeus sought to assert his rule and expand his kingdom from Judaea to the rest of Palestine. He also sought to control the lucrative Nabataean spice routes from Petra to Gaza and from Petra to Damascus. The Hasmoneans could not occupy Petra or the powerful Nabataean Arab kingdom directly, so they chose to occupy the city of Gaza at the Palestinian end of the spice route at around 99 BCE. This gained the Hasmonean control over the Mediterranean outlet of the main Nabataean trade route but also effectively interrupted the spice trade for a short while (Atkinson 2012: 136; Schäfer 2003: 74–5).

The Arabian camel was not only central to the success of the Nabataean long-distance trade system, it was also at the heart of the Nabataean fighting forces and the defence of this kingdom and its trading routes. Camel-mounted forces were widely known in the history of the Middle East, and this history began with the Nabataean camel corps as an effective fighting force. The British 'Camel Corps Brigade' was a camel-mounted brigade that the British raised during the First World War to fight in the Middle East and Palestine and 'Battle of the Camel' (656 CE) is a well-known battle fought outside Basra between different fractions in early Islam. After the Nabataean kingdom was annexed by the Romans the Nabataean fighting forces were integrated into the Roman regiments in southern Palestine and the province of Arabia Petraea and the Emperor Trajan established a Roman legion to protect trade routes and border regions in these areas, a legion which consisted of a mounted-camel corps of 1,000–2,500 camels.

The trade conflict between Nabataeans and Hasmoneans was largely decided by the strong camel-mounted forces of the Nabataeans. With the interruption of his direct access to Gaza, the Nabataean King Oboda mobilized his camel-mounted army and managed to defeat the Hasmonean army at a battle east of the Sea of Galilee on the Golan Heights at around 93 BCE. Alexander Jannaeus barely managed to escape from the battle ground of Umm Gais and to Jerusalem only to be confronted by a civil war in his kingdom (Eshel 2008). The Hasmoneans soon lost control of Gaza which resumed its Nabataean spice trade to the Mediterranean world and King Oboda went down in history as the leader who both saved the Nabataean trade routes and helped to revive the economic fortunes of his kingdom. His military and political successes resulted in the naming of the city of Oboda after him.

The ancient Nabataean cities of southern Palestine: The city of the Nabataean King Oboda

The following briefly examines the history of five major *spice cities* founded by the Nabataean Arabs in classical Antiquity – cities that rose along the incense and spice routes of southern Palestine; their archaeological remains today provide evidence for vanishing wealth and splendour. The cities are Oboda, Elusa, Sbeita, Kurnub and Nessana.

Because of its spectacular beauty and its rock-cut-architecture, and because of the colour of the sandstone from which it is carved, Petra, the 'Rose City', is often treated by historians as a uniquely iconic Nabataean city. However other Nabataean cities in Palestine, constructed from red sandstone and with the help with workers and artisans from Petra, were no less spectacular.

Located in the central Naqab highlands, Oboda was founded in the third century BCE and flourished at the height of the Nabataean kingdom in classical Antiquity. Beginning as a major trade station for camel caravans, the city developed into one of the most important Palestinian cities on the Petra-Gaza incense route. Damaged from time to time by local earthquakes, Oboda kept recovering from natural disasters and continued to prosper for more than a millennium; it continued to be inhabited under early Islam after its partial destruction by an earthquake in the early seventh century CE (Fabian 1996: 25; Korjenkov et al. 1996: 52). Established on a mountain top protecting the perfume route and prospering primarily on the 'transit trade' of spices and aromatics, the archaeology of Oboda shows the city developed into a multicultural melting pot city in southern Palestine, a city of cultural hybridization of Arab and Hellenistic cultures and a city inhabited by Nabataean Arab merchants, Ghassanid Christian Arabs, Greek and Roman merchants, Greek Orthodox clergy and later Muslim Arabs; the urban cemeteries of Obada reveals polytheistic pagans and Christians lived side by side during the Byzantine period (Bucking et al. 2022: 754–61).

Apparently the city's original Nabataean name was changed to 'Oboda' in the first century BCE in honour of the formidable Nabataean Arab King Oboda I (Nabataean Aramaic: *ʿŌbada;* Greek: Ὀβόδας, Obodas) who had succeeded the Nabataean King *al-Haritha al-Thani* (Greek: Aretas II), and created a formidable army that defeated the regional enemies of the Nabataeans; archaeological discoveries show Oboda was revered by his people for defeating the Seleucid ruler Antiochus XII Dionysus in 86 BCE and the Hasmonean King Alexander Jannaeus of Judaea at around 93 BCE that Obada was revered by his people as a deity after his death; he was also buried at his request in the city and a temple was built and named after him. Remains of Nabataean temple at Oboda can still be seen today (Eshel 2008: 117–18; Neuwirth et al. 2009: 233).

Oboda continued to prosper as a major trade station along the Incense/Perfume Road from Petra to Gaza after the Roman annexation of Nabataean kingdom and the creation of the new Roman province of *Arabia Petraea* in 106 CE. Forts and towers on the site were excavated by archaeologists and a bathhouse was constructed on the plain below the site. The bathhouse was supplied with water by way of a well, tunnelled seventy metres through bedrock. At a later stage a wall was built around the city. Evidently some of the builders who worked on the buildings and structures in the town hailed from Petra, the capital of the old Nabataean kingdom.

Under the Byzantines, in fifth and sixth century CE, the city was transformed once again by Christianity and its powerful monastery with two churches were built on the site of the pagan temple of Oboda (named after the Nabataean King Oboda); the Hellenistic style acropolis of the city was Christianized. Furthermore, the rise of Christianity in Palestine and the Near East as a whole brought about the transformation of the economy – with the rise of wine industry in the Naqab – and urban environment of the city. Archaeologists uncovered a continuity of urban activity on the site during the early Islamic period, between 650 and 900 CE – evidence of continuation of life from Christian rule to Islamic rule (Bucking et al. 2022: 754–61; Negev 1991: 62–80).

Crucially from the mid-third century CE onwards, with the decline of the incense/spice trade routes in the Naqab and dramatic rise of the Palestine wine industry – what became known internationally famous as *Gaza wine* (see Chapter 6) – the merchants of Oboda began to diversify their sources of revenue by utilizing and developing further old Nabataean water-storing technologies in a semi-arid desert region. Local farming and agriculture were encouraged, particularly the cultivation of vineyards and production of wine for export via the port city of Gaza to countries overseas. Archaeologists uncovered water systems and Roman bathhouses, and pottery houses and wineries from the Byzantine period. Numerous terraced vine farms and water channels were built throughout the region in order to collect enough runoff from winter rains to support agriculture in the region of Oboda. At least five wine presses, dating to the Byzantine period (fourth to early seventh centuries CE) and the height of the Palestine wine-making industry, were uncovered by archaeologists at Oboda.

The evolution of Elusa (Al-Khalasa): From a Nabataean spice city to a wine city and the Christian metropolis of *Palaestina Tertia*

The ancient city of Elusa (Greek: Χελλοὺς, Chellous; Arabic: Al-Khalasa) was located in the north-western part of the central Naqab: its ruins are located in a large plain twenty kilometres south-west of Beersheba. Elusa was founded by the Nabataean Arabs in the late fourth or early third century as a key station on the Petra-Gaza incense routes. The modern Arabic name of the site, Al-Khalisa, has preserved its ancient Arabic form. The city was also known to us from the Nessana papyri as *al-Khalus*, a form close to the modern Arabic version. Belonging to a group of early Nabataean towns and cities Elusa became the principal 'spice city' of the central Naqab, and was mentioned in many ancient sources. Elusa was mentioned in the second century CE by the Roman-Greek historian Ptolemy (died *c.*150 CE) in his *Geography* as among the towns of Idumea. In the Christian Mdaba Mosaic Map of Byzantine Palestine the city appears as a large city, with an officially recognized municipal status. Archaeological evidence for Elusa is provided by many inscriptions and Nabataean-Hellenistic style pottery found on the site and by a Nabataean inscription of the first half of the second century BCE in which king of the Nabataeans al-Haritha (Aretas) is mentioned. At that time Elusa and Oboda were the most important stations on the main trade route running from Petra to the emporium of Gaza.[4] Also Nabataean streets have been excavated, along with two Byzantine period churches, a Roman period theatre, wine presses and a tower. While Oboda was the principal city and trading centre in the Naqab during the Nabataean kingdom of classical Antiquity, Elusa was transformed to became the principal city and capital of the Byzantine Naqab (in *Palaestina Tertia*) and a Bishop's See in late Antiquity. By this time Elusa appears to have reached its greatest eminence, when it became the most important city in the central Negev and the Naqab as a whole, first, part of the *Provincia Arabia* (*Arabia Petraea*) and later part of the Byzantine province of *Palaestina Tertia*.

A key business and wide-production centre in the Naqab, Elusa, at its economic and cultural heights, was the birth place of Zenobius, a prominent fourth-century philosopher and rhetorician in Antioch. Elusa was also the birth place of Libanius, a prominent pagan sophist and a professor of rhetoric who went to teach in Antioch and mentioned Elusa in his letters between 356 and 359 CE.[5] Libanius was also a rich businessman, although his private business affairs were not a proper subject for a literary letter. In his correspondence Libanius the businessman is completely eclipsed by Labanius the Sophist (Kingsley and Decker 2015: 12). In the fourth century CE Saint Jerome mentions in his work *Life of Saint Hilarion*, a great temple of Aphrodite in Elusa. This was possibly the '*Palaistine Aphrodite Urania*' goddess. According to Herodotus, the Arabs called this goddess *Alitta* (*Ἀλίττα*) or 'Allat' (Schmitz, 1870: 132). Recent scholarship sheds more light on the cultic veneration to goddesses of ancient Arabia and Palestine (El-Badawi 2024).

Like Oboda, for many centuries Elusa maintained its social character as a socially and religious diverse trading centre and a melting pot city in southern Palestine throughout classical and late Antiquity a large Christian (monotheistic) Arab population continued to live side by side with Arab and Greek (polytheistic) pagan population. Also at its height Christianity impacted on Elusa earlier and more profoundly than the other cities of the Naqab, and there is literary evidence of pagan and Christian communities living side by side during the late Roman and Byzantine periods; tomb-stones found in the local cemetery indicate that there were pagans at Elusa as late as the early fifth century. The Christian Bishops of Elusa participated in the ecumenical councils of the Orthodox Church in 431 and 451. During this period Elusa became a key city in the Byzantine province of *Palaestina Tertia* and the city was frequently mentioned in the papyri of Nessana, in which it is referred to as a *polis*.[6] According to the same sources Elusa was still an administrative centre in the Naqab during the early Arab period, at least up to the end of the seventh century AD.[7] Today the bishopric of Elusa in *Palsestina Tertia* is still included in the Catholic Church's list of titular sees.[8] As we shall below, the city of Elusa, in addition to developing an extensive wine industry during the Christian Byzantine period, continued to flourished as a key station for the rising of a new maritime trade route in southern Palestine: the Red Sea maritime Trade Route of *Iotabe-Aylah-Elusa-Gaza*, a new spice route that effectively replaced the older Incense Route of Petra-Gaza as the main Palestinians spice route from India and south Arabia to Europe.

Gaza wine and the transformation of Sbeita[9] from a Nabataean spice city to a Christian wine-producing city

Located forty-three kilometres southwest of Bersheba, Sbeita (Greek: Σόβατα)[10] was a key Nabataean city and an important station on the Incense Road of southern Palestine. Regarded as a classical Nabataean Arab 'spice city', today Sbeita, like Memphis (Kurnub), is one of the better preserved of the historic cities of the Palestine Naqab and most of its excavated buildings are from the Byzantine period (Röhl 2010: 18). Both the Arabic and Greek names of Sobata were mentioned in the Messana papyri archives (see below).

Like Elusa, under the Christian Byzantines the economy of the city was transformed and Sbeita became an agricultural city with a wine producing industry as well as a key station for Christian pilgrims en route to St Catherine's Monastery in Sinai; most of the archaeological findings from the site of Sbeita date to the Byzantine period. This combination of the rise of Christianity with wine production industry in Sbeita is attested by the archaeology of the city: a mosque dated to the early Islamic period and three churches dated to the earlier Byzantine period (a main church and two smaller ones; the third church was built when the city expanded in the fifth to sixth centuries) and two wine presses were excavated. Also urban residential areas and administrative buildings were uncovered. Water supply to the city and its agriculture was largely based on surface runoff collected in large reservoirs.[11] The city's large farms also used ancient Nabataean agricultural techniques of irrigation, sowing and reaping (Benzaquen 2012). The wine presses at Sbeita give us an insight into the scale of wine production during the Byzantine period.[12] According to some calculations of archaeologists, the city of Shivta produced about two million litres of wine annually.[13]

By the early sixth century cultivation of vineyards in the Naqab and the production wine as part of overseas export what became known in Latin Europe *vinum Gazentum* (Gaza wine) experienced a major boom in Sbeita, mainly due to the high demand for the luxury good of Gaza wine throughout Europe and in many parts of the Byzantine Middle East (David 2020).

Agricultural development using innovative irrigation practices, and the scale of wine production at Sbeita and other former cities of the Nabataeans under the Byzantine, has been documented by studying ancient trash mounds at Sbeita, Elusa and Nessana. In the sixth century CE these mounds showed a sharp peak in the presence of grape pips and broken 'Gaza Jars' – a type of amphorae used in this period to export Palestinian wine from the port of Gaza to Europe and the Mediterranean world – following a slower rise during the fourth and fifth centuries CE (David 2020).

While grape cultivation and wine for export was the key industry in the Naqab under the Byzantine, there is also evidence for the existence of subsistence farming and the cultivation of barley and wheat in this region. The previously widely accepted theory that the Muslim conquest in the 630s CE and the Muslim ban on alcoholic beverages were the cause for the decline of the wine industry in the Naqab has now been challenged and that the decline of the Naqab wine industry was caused by climate changes and plagues in the second half of the sixth century CE.[14] For instance, in nearby Nessana, the number of grape pips is on the rise during the early Islamic period, probably due to the needs of a local Christian monastery in the city. This seems to indicate that the wine industry of the Naqab could well have been sustained over centuries through appropriate agricultural techniques and in spite of the arid climate, but that the grape monoculture was economically unsustainable in the long run.[15]

Sbeita continued to prosper under early Islam, but was finally abandoned in the ninth or tenth century CE. Archaeological discoveries of artefacts, consisting of items like jewellery, pieces of glass, objects made from bone, ivory and wood, and shards of pottery inscribed with Arabic and Greek writing, are now on display at the Hecht Museum at the University of Haifa.[16]

Kurnub (Memphis): From a garrison town in *Limes Palaestinae* to a city of hospitality, services and finance

The ancient Nabataean city of Kurnub (Memphis) – located forty kilometres east of modern Beerdheva – was founded in the first century BCE as a Naqab trade post between Petra and Gaza, through which the traded merchandise continued travelling to the Mediterranean cities, Rome included. While its Arabic name, Kurnub, describes a drink made from milk, honey and dates, the subsequent city's Greek name was Memphis. The city of Memphis appears in the Madaba Map, which describes the major cities of Palestine in the Byzantine period – an indication that Memphis was a significant city in southern Palestine in the mid-sixth century CE. Under the Late Romans and Byzantines, the Nabataean city of Memphis reached its zenith and most developed social urban and commercial space. It served as a major trade station on a secondary road of the Incense Route and in the fourth century CE Memphis became the only fully walled (fortified) Nabataean city in the Negev. Also after the Nabataean kingdom was annexed to the Roman empire, a Roman garrison was stationed in the city.

The Romans stationed this garrison in the city and fortified the city as part of a system they called *Limes Palaestinae* (the 'Borders of Palestine'), a system designed to protect the eastern trade routes of the Roman empire in Palestine and the Roman strategic routes in southern and eastern Palestine. The *Limes Palaestinae* – a chain of forts, fortifications with watchtowers (equipped with rooms and caravanserais, cisterns and watering stations, and watch towers) along the southern and eastern frontier regions of Palestine and along the trade routes from Petra to Gaza and from Aelas to Gaza. Under the Byzantines the *Limes Palaestinae* in the province of *Palaestinae Tertia* and *Palaestina Secunda* were an integral part of what was known as *Limes Arabiaea* series of forts that stretched from Aelas (Aylah) *in Palaestnae Tertia* to the Byzantine eastern frontiers in modern Jordan and Syria and demarcated the eastern borders of the Roman empire. Later, in the sixth century, under the Byzantines the Christian Arab *phylarchs* and Ghassanid Arab *federate* moved into these forts and contributed into the fortifications that helped secure the border regions and some of the old trade routes of southern Palestine (Shahid 1995).

During the Byzantine period, the Ghassanid Arab kings of southern Palestine became closely associated with the military fortifications and border tax collection posts of the *Limes Palaestinae*. The first appearance of the Ghassanid Arab kings in connection with southern Palestine is found in a tomb inscription written in Arabic in Nabataean script dating to the fourth century CE. Nabataean Aramaic had been spoken for several centuries before Islam (Fiema et al. 2015: 396–497). The tomb inscription refers to the Ghassanid King Imru al-Qais, 'king of all the Arabs', who died in Byzantine service in 328 (Sartre 2005: 519). Known in Greek sources as Amorkesos (Αμορκέσος), Imru al-Qais signed a treaty with the Byzantine empire acknowledging his status as *foederati* and as controlling major parts of *Provincia Palaestina* and its trade taxation system. Amorkesos was appointed by the Byzantine Emperor as supreme *phylarch* in what soon to become the Byzantine province of *Palaestina Salutaris*. By the late fifth century the Ghassanid kings had dramatically risen to become the powerful supreme phylarchs of *Palaestina Tertia*, effectively transforming major parts of two Palestines into two Palestinian Arab vassal kingdoms. Nominally the 'two Palestine' provinces were still imperial provinces, but in reality, under Ghassanid military and political control, they functioned as client monarchical states, having and commanding their own Arab armies, enforcing law and order within their jurisdiction, raising revenue and taxes from the lucrative Trans-Arabian trade passing through their territories. Monumental epigraphic evidence from Yemen shows that the Ghassanid Arab kings and *phylarchs* of *Palaestina Salutaris*, Abu Karib and Arithas, pursued independent foreign policies towards Arabia (Shahid 2009, Vol. 2, Part 2: 44).

Roman and Byzantine Memphis was not among the largest Nabataean cities of the Naqab. Its urban size was about forty dunum in size. Although it was the smallest of all urban centres in the Naqab, modern archaeology has shown the city was among the most sophisticated cities in Palestine. It is also best preserved historic city in the region, with whole streets having survived intact and with luxurious urban houses; two-floor grand houses with supportive arches, courtyards, terraces and patios and beautiful Roman and Byzantine architecture; massive buildings were constructed in Memphis from locally chiselled limestone. The gate of the city, its watch towers, water dams, bathhouses, market stores and private horse stables for horses have been excavated. Two churches, serving both local Arab Christians and Greek Orthodox Christians, one church with courtyards and large mosaic floors, and colourful geometric patterns, birds including peacocks, and the other with marble pillars, were found.

There is a debate among historians as to whether the Palestine Nabataeans (before the Roman annexation of the Nabatean kingdom) had bred Arabian horses themselves or simply imported these horses from Arabia;

> When discussing the Nabataeans ... Strabo [64 BC– *c*.24 AD] tells us that "they were well supplied with pastorage" and that there was a plain "which is well supplied with trees and water and is full of all kinds of domestic animals – mules among others". Since the Nabataeans possessed mules, which are the offspring of donkeys and horses, it seems probable that they also possessed some horses. The Nabataeans had extensive trading links with Palestine and so it seems likely that such mules and horses as they possessed were obtained by trade since Palestine was a central point in the trading route between Egypt and the Near East along which numerous horses travelled.
>
> (Donaghy 2014: 198–9)

However, there is some evidence to suggest that Memphis, beginning with the Roman period, began local breeding of Arabian horses (Negev 1988: 8).

While camel breeding was introduced by the Nabataean Arab kingdom in the Iron Age, and the camel became central to the desert trade and incense routes, and the cavalry force of King Oboda I was still based on camels, the Roman period, and probably the Roman garrison in the city, ushered in the breeding of the Arabian horses and stabling for horses in the Palestine Naqab, especially by the wealthy classes of the urban centres. After the Roman conquest of the Nabataean kingdom, the inhabitants of Memphis began breeding and marketing horses and the city became known for its breeding of the renowned Arabian horses used in Roman chariot races throughout this period. Thus large mansions inside the city contained the remains of horse stables that once housed the famous Arab horses that made fortunes for their wealthy city owners. These Arabian horses were prized for their stamina, and their acclimation to the harsh conditions of the Arabian deserts made them eminently suited for the desert conditions of southern Palestine (Culbertson 2014).

During the late Roman and Byzantine periods, Memphis seems to specialize in providing hospitality for merchants, travellers and pilgrims as well as financial services and trade in luxurious goods such as spices and aromatics: remains of fresco wall paintings that include a depiction of the Greek myth on *Eros* and *Psyche*, dating to between the end of the second century and the early third century CE, and a fresco found in a structure with arches, possibly a Roman brothel, usually found in other Roman cities offering services to passing merchants and soldiers stationed in the local garrison, can be seen. During the Nabataean Arab kingdom of classical Antiquity, the city of Oboda appears to be the financial capital of the Naqab.

However, the economy and the urban environment of the Naqab change under the Byzantines, and judging by the size of the marketplace in Memphis, its massive building structures and affluence, the luxurious urban space, and crucially, the large gold coin treasures that were excavated on the site of this city, Memphis seems to have emerged as an important centre for services and a key financial trading centre for the Byzantine Naqab.

Nessana (Auja al-Hafir): Papyri discoveries and commercial life in late Byzantine and the early Islamic Palestine

Nessana is an ancient Nabataean Arab city located in the southwest Naqab, close to the modern Sinai border with Palestine, on a branch of the ancient *Incene Routes*. The city started as a caravan station on the ancient incense routes, protecting a western branch of the road that allowed access to Sinai and Egypt (Negev and Gibson 2001: 367–8). One of the earlier Nabataean Arab cities of the Naqab established as a caravan station for merchants in the late the fourth or the early third century BCE, in Byzantine times it became a key route Christian pilgrims to the Holy Land (Negev and Gibson 2001: 367–8). After the annexation of the Nabataean kingdom to Rome in 106 CE, Roman soldiers garrisoned the city, which was inhabited by Christian Arabs from the fourth century at the latest, until after the Arab Muslim conquest of the early seventh century.

During archaeological excavations in British Mandatory Palestine in 1935–37, a major trove of sixth- and seventh-century papyri documents in Arabic, Greek, Latin and Syriac were unearthed on the site, revealing an extraordinary wealth of social and economical information about the economic and day-to-day life in the Nabataean Arab society of the Naqab between in the period between 505 and 689 CE, the last phase of Byzantine administration in Palestine and the earliest period of Arab Islam in Palestine (Stroumsa 2014: 143–57). The papyri archives of Nessana, including personal documents, private wills, land ownership and trade contracts, make the social life in this city the best-documented of all the old Nabataean in the Naqab of late Antiquity and early Islam (Shahid 1989: 143). Early in the fourth century Onomastics of Eusebius of Caesarea-Palestinia shows that the largely Nabataean Arab inhabitants of the city had become Christianized and as well as documenting the arrival of the Ghassanid Arab inhabitants in the city (Shahid 1989). By this stage the Christian Ghassanid Arabs also inhabited other cities of the Nakba that belonged to the Byzantine province of *Palaestina Tertia* (see Masalha 2018).

Many names of the ancient towns and cities in the Naqab come to us from Eusebius' *Onomasticon* (Greek: *Ὀνομαστικόν*; place names in Palestine) and the papyri documents of Nessana. Some of the papyri documents of Nessana describe the coinage struck by the Caliph 'Abd Al-Malik Ibn Marwan, during his famous administrative and financial reforms, replacing the Byzantine coinage and institutions with a new Umayyad financial and political structure (Bowersock 2007: 91; Magness 2003; Shahid 1989: 143). Pointing the wealth of the city of Nessana, the Nessana papyri also mention loans in Byzantine *solidi* gold coins 'according to the Nessana standard' ('Gaza' in Ameling et al. 2014, Vol. III).

Continuities in the currency of Palestine across the Byzantine-Islamic eras can be seen in the minting of the *solidus* coins and their wide use of regional trade. The *solidus* was originally a very pure gold coin issued in the Byzantine empire, under emperor Constantine I in the fourth century; Constantine introduced it on a wide scale, it had a weight of about 4.5 grams. The Byzantine *solidus* also inspired the subsequent gold *Solidi-dinar* issued by the Arabs and Muslim Umayyad Caliphate through the end of the seventh century which was also minted in the cities of the Arab province of Palestine (*Jund Filastin*).

4

The Myth of the Single 'Silk Road' and the Palestine Red Sea Silk Route from China

The Rise of the Maritime Trade Route of Iotabe-Aylah-Elusa-Gaza and the Ghassanid Arabs of *Palaestina Tertia*

The Red Sea was one of the most important and busiest global trade routes of Antiquity. While the land desert route and the Nabataean Arab city of Oboda, in the eastern-central Naqab (in tandem with Petra) was the premier city of spice/incense trade in southern Palestine during the Nabataean Arab kingdom of classical Antiquity and the early Roman period, the cities of Aylah (modern Aqaba) and Elusa, in the southern and western-central Naqab respectively, became the premier trading cities of the Naqab and of the province of *Palaestina Tertia* during the Christian Byzantine period of late Antiquity. Most of the historical works on the rise of Elusa as the most important city in the Naqab under the Byzantines focused on the transformation of the economy of Elusa into farming vineyards and the wine industry of Christian Palestine. But the rise of the Palestine wine industry in the fourth- to sixth-centuries CE provides only part of the explanation. In fact, the Palestine spice/incense trade shifted from Trans-Arabian spice trade through Petra to the Red Sea maritime trade through the island-town of Iotabe and then via the route of *Aelas-Elusa-Gaza*. During this period, Arab Christianity flourished for at several centuries in the towns and cities of southern and eastern Palestine before the arrival of Islam in the 630s CE.

The Red Sea global maritime trade route through Palestine: Iotabe-Aylah-Elusa-Gaza-Europe

In Antiquity silk and silk products were traded at great profit and the global silk trade originated in China linking China, with Palestine and the Middle East and Europe. Like all other luxury goods, silk was associated with power, money and social privilege. A key route of the global silk trade under the Romans and Byzantines, the Red Sea was called by Arab merchants and geographers in the Middle Ages as the 'Sea of China' (Le Strange 1886: 3; Ramadan 2010a, 2010b; Wa'ari 2023, Vol. 1: 51), partly because of the huge volume of trade passing through from China and south-east Asia, silk included. However much of modern Western writings and Orientalism on the Chinese global silk trade system of Antiquity and Middle Ages centred on the legendary central Asian 'Silk Road' from China to Europe. But as a recently published book by the British Museum, entitled *Silk Roads*, show, there was no single 'Silk Road' from China in Antiquity and the Midde Ages; there were a variety of maritime and land silk routes imported from China to the Middle East and Europe, including an important silk route via the Red Sea (Brunning and Yu-ping et al. 2024). The centrality of the Red Sea to the global trade in silk and many goods in Antiquity can be seen in *The Periplus of the Erythraean Sea* (Greek: *Περίπλους τῆς Ἐρυθρᾶς Θαλάσσης*, Períplous tês Erythrâs *Thalássēs*), a famous mid-first-century Greco-Roman traveller's handbook that describes navigation and trading opportunities from Roman Empire through the Red Sea to south Arabia, the Horn of Africa and Indian Ocean cities; among the many trade goods mentioned were silver, gold, iron, drinking cups, myrrh, cinnamon, cloves and other spices, slaves, ivory, exotic animal skins, frankincense, aromatics and silks. Providing an insight into the silk import from China and describing the extensive silk trade exchange and route through the Indian Ocean and Red Sea and between Rome and China in Antiquity, the handbook mentions the Ganges and China as a great inland city called *Thina* (*Θῖνα*), an ancient Greek name of China that is a source of raw silk imported through the Red Sea (Brunning and Yu-ping et al. 2024; Casson 1989; Hildebrandt 2017: 242). Under the Byzantines the goods passing through the Red Sea were taxed at the island of *Iotabe* (within the jurisdiction of *Palestina Tertia)* before being shipped to the city of Aelas and then on land by camel caravans to Gaza (see below). Also, often these goods were exchanged with Gaza wine and olive oil produced in Palestine and the Eastern Mediterranean and exported to south Arabia and Indian Ocean countries (see Chapter 6). While silk, spices, aromatics and exotics from China, India, Indonesia, south Arabia and the Horn of Africa went westward, Mediterranean olive oil, wines, wools, gold and silver went east. Like goods, intellectual and religious ideas and people also moved in both directions.

In the sixth century Procopius of Caesarea Palaestina, then the capital of Byzantine Palestine and a major centre for the silk textile industry in the country (see Chapter 5) wrote that Emperor Justinian (527-565 CE) was seeking in the year 552 to introduce local breeding of silkworms, which had recently been smuggled from China, and develop local silk industry in the Byzantine Empire (Dignas and Winter 2007: 207). In previous centuries raw silk had been arriving in Palestine and Syria through multiple routes including from Iraq, the Sassania empire and the Red Sea route. However, discussing the importance of the maritime port cities of Palestine and the Red Sea silk route within the context of the global trade systems and global silk trade and textiles industries of Antiquity, *The Periplus of the Erythraean Sea* should be read with another famous Greek-language trade handbook of Antiquity: *Expositio Totius Mundi et Gentium*: *A Commercial-Geographical Description of the World and Its People.*[1] Compiled in the mid-fourth century CE at the height of the global raw silk import from China by a textile merchant, who was a native of Palestine/Syria (Grüll 2014: 629-42). According to Jean Rougé, the author of *Expositio Totius Mundi et Gentium* first lived in the Palestinian city of Nablus (Neapolis); afterwards he moved to port city of

Tyre (Rougé 1966: 27–38). *Expositio Totius Mundi et Gentium* gives a description of all territories of the ancient world and their goods, with emphasis on the textile industries of the cities of Palestine and Syria.

The Gaza-Aelas-Red Sea trade with India and East Asia and the importation of exotic animals from Asia can also be seen the story of the elephant arriving from India through the Red Sea port of Aelas and then in Gaza in the sixth century, a story told in zoological treasures by Timotheus of Gaza (491–518 CE). A Palestinian scholar active during the reign of Emperor Anastasius, Timotheus reported on diverse communities of merchants in Aelas and Gaza shipping Indian goods via the Red Sea (Timotheus 1949). These communities of merchants in Gaza and Aelas included local Palestinians, Ghassanid Arabs, Greeks, south Arabians, Indians and Egyptians, who also exported locally produced olive oil, wine and linen and garments to Egypt south Arabia and beyond (see Chapters 5 and 6).

This important maritime silk route evolved the international trading links of Palestine with south Asia and East Africa expanded considerably during the Roman and Byzantine periods. Huge amounts of commodities and customs were generated and levied on trade passing through 'transit routes' of Palestine; the 'transit customs' were collected through the collection posts dotted along the eastern and southern frontiers of Palestine and from the maritime shipping through the Red Sea to the Palestinian city of Aylah (Aelas) on the Gulf of Aqaba. As we shall see below, this Christian Byzantine period of late Antiquity was also characterized by the rise of the Christian Ghassanid Arab communities and kingdoms of southern Palestine in late Antiquity, monotheism Arab communities that embraced Christianity and allied themselves with the Byzantine and replaced the polytheistic and pagan Nabataea Arab kingdom of classical Antiquity as a major organized force (and formed new frontier kingdoms) in both eastern Palestine (*Palestainia Seconda*) and southern Palestine (*Palaestina Tertia* and the Naqab) in late Antiquity. During this period the Ghassanid Arabs controlled and taxed the southern trade routes of Palestine. The paramilitary Ghassanids of *Palaestina Tertia* were also involved in trade and taxation station of the Red Sea island of *Iotabe* during the Byzantine period and for periods (457–474 and 491–518 CE) their kings controlled the island and its 'considerable tax revenues' (see also below) (Shahid 1995: 29–30). The Ghassanid paramilitaries also had extensive presence in and around the port city of Aylah and one of the Arab poets speaks of the '*glittering dananirs (*dinars*)* of Aylah' which he presumably observed or received while transacting some business with the Ghassanids there (Shahid 1995: 31).

Maritime shipping arriving through the Red Sea to Aylah (Aelas) was hugely profitable. Maritime shipping of goods was five times cheaper than land transportation of the same goods, hence the popularity of the long-distance international maritime routes of Palestine via both the Red Sea and Mediterranean Sea and the growing long-distance trade with the Ocean trade via the Red Sea and Palestine to the Mediterranean world in classical and, mostly, late Antiquity. Often this Indian Ocean trade in spices, cotton and Chinese silk via the Red Sea and Aelas and then on land to Gaza is portrayed as a one-way (spices, incense and silk) trade from Asia and south Arabia to Mediterranean world via Gaza. But, in fact, the trade was in both directions, and as we shall see in Chapter 6, the famous Gaza wine was also exported to Yemen and southern

Arabia in large quantities via the Aelas and the Red Sea. However the balance of this trade in Antiquity was often in favour of southeast Asia and south Arabia. Also due to the huge volume of this lucrative maritime Red Sea-India trade, the struggle for the control of this trade routes passing through the Byzantine province of *Palaestinia Tertia* (*Palaestina Salutaris*) reached new heights in the fourth to sixth centuries CE.

The custom stations and navy of *Iotabe* in *Palaestina Tertia*

Of primary importance was the fact that southern and eastern Palestine had taxation posts for both the Roman and Byzantine Empires: there was a high custom barrier along the eastern frontier of the Roman Empire. In the first century the Roman duty of 25 per cent at this frontier was charged on incoming goods and probably also on exports. There were also local tolls. Under the Byzantine from the fourth century, the rate dropped to 12 and half per cent (Jones 1970: 1-10).

A key trading post on the Red Sea-Indian trade route of Palestine was the island of Iotabe (Greek Ἰωτάβη), located to the south of the city of Aelas and controlling the Straits of Iotabe – currently known Straits of Tiran – and the access to Red Sea. Under the Byzantines both Iotabe and Aelas were within the jurisdiction of the province of *Palaestinia Tertia*. Located at the Palestine end of Indian Ocean trade route with Europe, the port city of Gaza was within the Byzantine province of *Palaestina Prima*. But the merchants of Gaza, Aylah and Iotabe were closely connected. Widely cited in documentary evidence of late Antiquity as *Iotabe in Palaestina*, today Iotabe is known in Latin Church sources as Iotabe *in Palaestina*, and is listed by the Roman Catholic Church as the Titular See of *Iotabe in Palaestina* (or *Iotapensis in Palaestina*). Iotabe is thought to be what is now known as Tiran Island, located at the entrance of the Straits of Tiran, and connecting the Red Sea with the Gulf of Aqaba. Iotabe was until 2017 administered by Egypt but is now a Saudi Arabian island. In late Antiquity merchants of *Iotabe in Palaestina* played a key role in collecting transit tax revenues from the Indian trade shipping to the port city of Aelas and then the same goods were transported on land via camel caravans to Gaza, and then shipped again to the Mediterranean world.

Much of the Red Sea-Indian trade naval route to Iotabe and then Aelas and on land to Gaza came from Muziris, an ancient harbour port on the Malabar coast in India that dates from at least the first century BCE and a key to the international trade between South India and Persia, the Middle East, North Africa and the Roman Mediterranean region. As the travel handbook of traded goods, *The Periplus of the Erythraean Sea* – Red Sea – (first century CE) on navigation and trading opportunities from Roman Egyptian ports along the coast of the Red Sea – and the frankincense kingdom of south Arabia, the African kingdom of Aksum and the spices of southwestern India – shows the important known commodities exported from Muziris were spices, including black pepper, pearls, diamonds, ivory and Chinese silk. Though the Roman trade declined from the fifth century CE, the former Muziris attracted the attention of other nationalities, particularly the Arab, Greek, Egyptian, Persian and Chinese merchants and seamen (Casson 1989). Other papyrus records show a strong base to ancient international trade cargoes from India through the Red Sea and ancient trade laws governing this international maritime trade (McLaughlin 2010).

A strategic island and a frontier custom station, *Iotabe in Palaestina* was an important toll station in Palestine in Antiquity for the collection of the considerable customs taxes on cargoes transported from the Indian Ocean by ships passing through the Gulf of Aqaba and on their way to cities of Aelas and Gaza in Palestine The importance of Iotape as a toll station within *Palaestina Satutaris* grows considerably during the Byzantine era (La gerarchia cattolica 2013: 911).

Iotapa in Palaestina served both as a port town and a major customs post for cargoes of the Indian Ocean produce to Aelas and from Aelas; it also collected taxes from ships in both directions. The considerable revenues from these taxes collected in both directions often resulted in a fierce struggle for the control of the island and its lucrative revenues. Both Iotapa and Aelas also became an integral part of the Byzantine administration of Palestine and an important source of revenues for the military, fiscal and civil administrative of Palestine.

Equally important is the fact that Islam inherited these trading and administrative traditions of Byzantine Palestine and for several centuries throughout early Islam both Aelas and Iotapa became part of *Jund Filastin* (the Arab 'province of Palestine') and continued to play an important part of the two-way Indian-Red Sea-Mediterranean trade through the port city Gaza. This also explains why Islamic Aylah (Byzantine Aelas) minted its 'Filastin currency' throughout early Islam, a currency used in long-distance trade routes.

In Antiquity *telōnēs* (τελώνης from Greek: *télos*, 'tax') were tax collectors of the tolls, customs and various taxes of the state. In Roman times they became known as *publicani* (plural). They were public contractors who served as tax collectors of various taxes and in whose official capacity they often supplied the Roman legions in the provinces with equipment. They also managed the collection of port duties, a highly lucrative source of income, and oversaw public building projects and road constructions. *Publicani* officers were stationed along the frontiers of the Roman Empire in Syria and Palestine and levied a uniform tax of 25 per cent on all merchandise crossing in either direction, and archaeologists have excavated a great many currencies from sites at the frontiers' customs collection posts of Syria and Palestine and the sites connected to the Trans-Arabian spice and incense trade to the Mediterranean region (Sartre 2005: 256–7).

The Greek-speaking ruling elites of Byzantine Palestine (fourth to early seventh century) maintained the frontiers' custom post stations and port duties collections. However, the Byzantine imperial policies in Palestine were formulated to minimize imperial expenditure and maximize tax revenues levied on imported produce and collected from the transit routes trade and custom posts of Palestine. To 'rationalize' their economic and defence policies, the eastern and southern frontiers of Palestine and its revenue custom stations were entrusted to their Ghassanid Arab allies of the Palestine provinces of *Psalestina Tertia* and *Palaestina Seconda* (Power 2012).

During this period the allies of the Byzantines, the Ghassanid Arabs of *Palaestina Tertia*, during various periods in the late fifth and early sixth centuries, controlled the custom post island-town of Iotabe (in Palaestina). But the island was also inhabited by diverse communities of powerful traders and maritime merchants (Greek, Ghassanid Christian Arab and Jewish population) who often sought to assert their autonomy from the central authorities in Byzantine Palestine. As a powerful and wealthy community, they sought to assert their 'autonomy' and the local laws of their trading town (Mayerson 1992a: 1–4; Power 2012).

Often Western historians refer to the island of Iotabe as a backwater and a remote custom collection station inhabited by Arab tribesmen who manned this tax collection post for the Byzantine state. In fact, the powerful and wealthy merchants of Iotabe *in Palaestina* manned the tax stations. In Antiquity tribes did not develop navies – wealthy merchants, especially maritime merchants, did construct navies as we have seen in the case of the merchant classes of the Phoenician and Palestinian coastal cities of Antiquity. By the early sixth century, the powerful and self-confident merchant community of Iotabe – who had their own Palestinian bishops – developed their prosperous town and owned their own navy and mercantile fleet and developed their international trade links backed by their maritime trading ships. The Christian Arab *Martyrium Arethae al-Ḥarith bin-Ka'ab*, a leader of the Christian community of Najran – then a major centre of the textile industry in Yemen and an important stopping place on the incense routes – who was executed by the Arab-Jewish Himyarite king Yusuf Dhu Nuwas in 523 recorded that the merchants of Iotabe contributed, with the approval of the Byzantines, seven ships to the Ethiopian Aksumite invasion of Yemen in 525. This indicates that the merchants of Iotabe not only levied taxes on ships sailing to and from Aelas in *Palaestina Tertia*, but also were involved in the southern Red Sea and the Indian Ocean produce themselves (Power 2012). This shows that powerful merchants of Iotabe also used their navel power to compete and cooperate with other regional trading powers such as the Himyarite kingdom of Yemen, the Aksumie Kingdom of Ethiopia and the Byzantine authorities in Palestine for the control the vast revenues from the Indian Ocean trade through the Red Sea.

As the island Iotabe flourished within the framework of the administration and the international trade routes of Byzantine Palestine, under the Byzantines the church hierarchy in southern Palestine seems to have expanded along the historic Red Sea trade route to the Palestinian Mediterranean coast. Officially the island/city Iotabe was represented in the Orthodox Church councils by a bishop; its bishop Macarius participated along other Palestinian bishops, in the ecumenical Council of Chalcedon in 451. Other bishops of the island attended the synod of the All Palestine Church of Jerusalem in Jerusalem in 536. Orthodox ecclesial sources always listed the diocese of Iotabe as an integral part of the church hierarchy of *Palaestina Tertia* (Ward 2008: 162–8).

Palestinian trade routes and the urban church hierarchy in the south of the country also went hand in hand. Under the Byzantines the bishop system and bishop hierarchy of Palestine corresponded to the importance of key urban centres in the country. All the Christian bishops of *Palaestina Prima*, of the city/island of Iotabe, Aelas (modern

Aqaba), Elusa (in the Naqab), Zoara (east of the Dead Sea in Transjordan, famous for its sweet dates) and Petra, were listed as belonging to this diocese of southern Palestine, while Gaza was part of the diocese of *Palaestina Prima*. However, both the bishops of Iotabe, Aelas and Pharan – an early Christian city in the southern Sinai Peninsula – were subordinate to the Palestinian bishop of Elusa in the Naqab (Palestine) (Grillmeie 1975: 24; Shahid 1984: 103).

The mistake almost all Western historians of Byzantine Palestine make is to assume that Greek sounding names referred to ethnically Greek individuals in Palestine. In fact, many Greek sounding names in the church hierarchy were Christian Arabs. For instance, the Arab bishop of the Arab *federate* Christians on Iotabe in the mid-fifth century was called Petrus (Peter) (Shahid 1989: 72–3). Also in the famous excavated Nessana Papyri at *Nessana,* which revealed the intimate life of its inhabitants and have made it the best documented of all the old Nabataean Arab sites of the Naqab after 106 CE, shows that Flavius Sergius the Romanized name was an Arab inhabitant of the town of Nessana (Shahid 1989: 143–4). Moreover, the All Palestine Orthodox Church of Jerusalem was headed by both Greek-speaking and Arab bishops (Shahid 2006a: 46–8, 193–4, 523) and several Arab bishops of Palestine – including the bishops Elusa, in *Palaestina Tertia*, Abdelas (Arabic 'Abdallah; Greek *odulos,* which was a translation of his Arabic name: 'Servant of God') and *Aretas* (al-Harith) – participated in the crucial ecumenical councils of Ephesus and Chalcedon in 431 and 451 respectively (Shahid 2006a: 523; Sharon 2013, Vol. 5: 75).

The enormous volume of the international transit trade passing through southern Palestine brought about unprecedented urban development in the Naqab. The key Palestinian trading city of Elusa in the Naqab had several Arab bishops during the Byzantine era and the bishops of Iotabe and Aelas were subordinate to these Arab bishops of Elusa. 'Elusa' was also preserved in the modern Arabic name of the site. The ancient city of Eluas had developed into a major urban and administrative centre in southern Palestine, primary due to location at the heart of the international transit trade routes in the Naqab. At its height during the Byzantine period Elusa became the home of one of three classical schools of rhetoric in Byzantine *Palaestina*. Under Arab Islam the city continued to function as a major urban centre and a major trading hub and became known by its modern Arabic name Al-Khalisa, but was abandoned sometime during the late Mamluk period in the fifteenth century CE. Modern Elusa, or Al-Khalisa, was repopulated by Palestinian sedentary Bedouins in the early twentieth century. After the destruction of the Arab village of Al-Khalisa in 1948 the Israelis renamed it 'Haluza' (Hebrew: 'pioneer'), a Hebrew-sounding name based on the Arabic toponym 'al-Khalus' (also Masalha 2023: 37–71); and more recently (in 2005) UNESCO declared the archaeological site a World Heritage Site, ironically due to its historic commercial importance but, in fact, without acknowledging the centrality of the site to the twenty-four centuries of Arab history and heritage in Palestine.

In modern times Eusa was preserved in the name Arabic name 'Al-Khalasa', a Palestinian Muslim village located twenty-three kilometres south-west of the modern city of Beersheba and depopulated by Israel in 1948. The city had been founded by the Nabataean Arabs in the early fourth century using the Arabic name 'al-Khalus', and the town became a major centre for the Trans-Arabian spice caravans and the Nabataean Palestine Arab incense route. The Greco-Roman historian and geographer Ptolemy identifies it as a town in Idumaea. In the late Roman period, it grew to become the principal city of the western Roman *Arabia Petraea* province and later under the Byzantine it became the first capital of *Palaestina Salutaris* and a flourishing urban centre in Palestine, influenced by many of the features of classical urban planning and classical building programmes financed by being a commercial hub at the intersection of two international transit trade routes through the Naqab: the (Red Sea) Iotabe-Aelas-Nessana-Elusa-Gaza route and the Trans-Arabian Petra-Oboda-Elusa-Gaza route.

The economic and commercial importance of Elusa may partly explain the subordination of the bishops of Iotabe and Aelas to the bishops of Elusa.

Back in 473 CE an Arab army commanded by Imru al-Qays, known in Hellenized Byzantine sources as Amorkesos, sought to take over the trading island of Iotabe; he occupied the island/city and got rid of the Byzantine customs officers stationed on the island and diverted considerable revenues from the Byzantine treasury and the treasury of Byzantine administration of Palestine (Fisher 2015: 87; Mayerson 1992a: 1-4; Shahid 1989: 61, 126). Only a generation later the military governor of Palestine, *Dux of Palsestina*, would muster enough forces to recover Iotabe, and this was with the support of the Ghassanid Arab Christians of Palestine allied with the Byzantine Empire.

During the fifth and sixth centuries the Ghassanid Christian Arab kingdoms of *Palaestina Tertia* in southern Palestine and *Palaestina Seconda* in eastern Palestine were known as *foderati*, formally allied with the Byzantine Empire, and controlled many of the transit trade routes, with their lucrative border custom revenues, into Palestine. In the south they controlled many of the toll stations of the Trans-Arabian trade passing through *Palaestina Tertia* and also sought to control the important toll station of Iotabe. This control of Iotabe passed to another Ghassanid Arab king, Jabala. But the Ghassanid rulers' grip on Iotabe was not always strong and the wealthy local trading merchants were often powerful enough to assert their autonomy from the far-away central administration in Palestine. In 500 CE, during the reign of Emperor Anastasius, the *dux of Palaestinae,* the military governor of Palestine, Romanus, commanded a military expedition to wrest control from the merchants of the island and re-assert central control over Iotable and its lucrative custom revenues (Sivan 2008: 43).

Romanus may have also been motivated by personal financial gains and the desire for direct control of the tax revenues of the island (Shahid 1989: 125-6). However, when *dux of Palaestinae* re-took the island he granted its merchants autonomy subject to the payment of taxes on goods levied. But around 534, the Byzantine army commanded by *dux of Palaestinae* had to occupy Iotabe again after a group of inhabitants refused to pay taxes to the central Byzantine administration of Palestine based at its capital Caesarea Palaestinae (Prokopios (Procopius)) 2005; Shahid 1995: 184; Ward 2008: 162-8).

The Red Sea trade and the rise of Aelas (Aylah) as a port city in the province of *Palaestina Salutaris* and *Jund Filastin*: The Islamic coins of '*Aylah in Filastin*'

In the Middle Ages the Red Sea was known to Arab geographers and mariners as the Sea of China and Aylah was often described as a famous town on the Hajj road to Mecca, with a caravanserai for pilgrims and merchants and large markets for goods and fruits (Wa'ari 2023, Vol. 1: 60). Aylah was also often described as a port city on the edge of the Sea of China (Le Strange 1886: 3; Wa'ari 2023, Vol. 1: 51). This was partly the outcome of the extensive international maritime trade with Asia and China. When the Byzantine province of *Palaestina Salutaris* was taken over by the Muslim Arabs in the 630s CE, the port city of Aylah (present-day Aqaba) was the first major city in Palestine to be taken over by Muslim forces under the leadership of Prophet Muhammad in 630 CE (9 AH). This is hardly surprising: in his teens, Prophet Muhammad had joined his uncle on Syrian-Palestinian trading caravans and had gained experience in international trade and regional geography. Later in adult life, the Prophet acquired the reputation of being a trustworthy and very successful trader, and he was involved in international trade between the Red Sea and Mediterranean Sea; the Prophet must have also been closely familiar with port cities such as Aylah and Gaza, which, at the time, linked the international trade networks of *Palaestina Salutaris* and *Palaestina Prima*. Indeed, throughout early Islam Aylah became the major trading port of *Filastin* to Asia and China (Ramadan 2010a).

In the eleventh century Andalusian Muslim geographer Abu ʿUbayd al-Bakri (died 1094), who travelled extensively in the Levant, mentions the port city of Aylah and says:

> Aylah is a large village with markets and mosques in which there are many Jews, and they claim that they have the Prophet's garment, may God bless him and grant him peace. [They say]. He sent it to them as a safe haven for them, and they showed him [al-Bakri] a golden garment wrapped in clothes, some of which had protruded from it.
>
> (cited in Wa'ari 2023, Vol. 1: 51)

For several centuries the city of Aylah, the present-day Jordanian port city of al-Aqaba on the Red Sea, was part of the Islamic administrative province of Palestine. The Arab province of *Jund Filastin*, whose governors (*walis*) were also in charge of looking after the safety of the caravans of Muslim pilgrims from Mecca through Aylah and al-Ramla to Damascus and beyond. Umayyad numismatic and epigraphic evidence shows that Aylah was an early Islamic town in the province of Jund Filastin. Originally a Roman and Byzantine town called Aelas, now the ruins of Aylah lie within the present-day port city of al-Aqaba (Ramadan 2010b). '*Aylah in Filastin*' ('Aelas in Byzantine Palaestina') was also the reason, within the Israeli settler toponymic project post-1948, for calling the nearby new Israeli settlement Eilat.

Under Islam, for hundreds of years the city of Aylah (in Palestine) functioned as a key Palestinian tax collection station and a famous pilgrim station on the Palestine-Hijaz road; Muslim historians and geographer repeatedly mention the large market Aylah that was regular frequently by the merchants and 'people of Gaza' (*ahl Ghazza*) (Wa'ari 2023, Vol. 1: 66). A glimpse into the continuing commercial significance of Aylah throughout early Islam also gives us insight into the commercial importance of Byzantine Aylah to the Red Sea-Gaza maritime trade: Muslim historian 'Abdel-Qader al-Juzairi wrote during the late Mamluk period:

> When pilgrims and merchants return to it [Aylah from the Hijaz], it is customary that the person in charge of tax collection of money [*multazim*] to arrive himself and send someone he relies on to come, along with the [trade] inspector and his assistants to inspect[imported] clothes and spices ... and they inspect and identify everything brought in by the pilgrims and they register these goods in their notebooks when [merchant and pilgrim] caravans arrive ... they collect the [Islamic tax] of tenth of every type of goods if they were acting justly .... A large open market will be set up in Al-Manakh, containing goods and fruits that are not found elsewhere. It sometimes contains an abundance of fruits, raisins, prunes, and almonds. Walnuts brought from Gaza, Karak and Shobak [in Transjordan], pomegranates, grapes, apples and pears and from Jerusalem and Al-Tur, which is not found anywhere else except for the highest price, and brings to it the company of the Gazan caravans. Among those sold are: molasses, flour, barley, oil, and ash, as well as sheep and milk. Grass [*hashish*] is for the fodder of camels, genuine dates are sweet and good for vision, and honey is sold. It contains rubrics taken from the salt sea, and in it I saw pure white salt in the form of sugar blocks. It is sold in its market during the seasons, and anyone who saw it would not doubt that it was Tabarzad sugar. She asked about its manufacture and was told. The pottery moulds are placed on the roofs of the inn at night, and they become filled and solid. It is sold, and this is a strange thing to say, and there are horses, mules, donkeys, camels, and axes, sheds and other things needed by the riders and serving men.
>
> (cited in Wa'ari 2023, Vol. 1: 60)

The port city of Aylah became a centre of economic activity in southern Filastin and also served as a major stop-over for Muslim pilgrims en route to Mecca (Ramadan 2010a; 2010b). As for the Bilad al-Sharat region, its principal city is al-Karak, known today for its Crusader castle, located 140 kilometres to the south of Amman and then a site on the ancient King's Highway. Earlier during the Byzantine period the economic, commercial and urban rise of the port city of Aylah as an urban centre in *Palaestina* depended on two things: (1) the Red Sea maritime trade from south Arabia, India and the Horn of Africa; (2) the economic and trading fortunes of the island of Iotabe, which had also flourished within the framework of the administration and the maritime international trade routes of Byzantine Palestine. In his multi-volume work, *The Wars of Justinian* (*c.*560), Palestinian historian Prokopios, of Caesarea Maritima, wrote: The boundaries of Palestine extend towards the east to the sea which is called the Red Sea. Now this sea, beginning at India, comes to an end at this point in the Roman domain.

And there is a city called Aelas [present-day Aqaba] on its shore, where the sea comes to an end, as I have said, and becomes a very narrow gulf (Prokopios 2014).

For several centuries Aylah, the present-day Jordanian port city of al-ʿAqaba on the Red Sea, was part of the Islamic administrative province. The Arab province of *Jund Filastin*, whose governors (*walis*) were also in charge of looking after the safety of the caravans of Muslim pilgrims from Mecca through Aylah and al-Ramla to Damascus and beyond. Umayyad numismatic and epigraphic evidence shows that Aylah was an early Islamic town in the province of Jund Filastin.

'Aelas' in Byzantine *Palaestina*, which became 'Aylah' in the Muslim province of Palestine (*Jund Filastin*), should be clearly distinguished from the northern 'Ilya-Filastin' (Jerusalem) under Islam (Aelia Capitolina under the Romans and Byzantine). Aylah (Aelas) was a vibrant Palestinian port town under both the Byzantines and Muslims and at the centre of the Indian and South Arabian spice trade. Rising to prominence after the Islamic conquests, *Aylah-Filastin*, located strategically on the Red Sea – also known to medieval European geographers as Mare Mecca, or the Sea of Mecca, and Sinus Arabicus, or the Gulf of Arabia – developed into a major trading port town and benefited hugely from the annual caravans of Muslim pilgrims to and from Mecca (Lev 2006: 591) and from the linking of the al-Sham region with the Arabian Peninsula and Indian Ocean. Apparently, Umayyad 'Aylah in Filastin' coins were also minted in Iliya-Filastin for the use in the Red Sea town and beyond (Ramadan 2010a, 2010b) and tenth-century Palestinian geographer al-Maqdisi, after visiting Aylah-Filastin, described it as 'a port of Palestine on China Sea' (Ramadan 2010a, 2010b).

The combination of Arabic written sources, Umayyad numismatic and epigraphic evidence and Byzantine sources gives us a good idea about the way the large Arab province of Jund Filastin emerged out of the combination of two provinces of *Palaestina Prima* and *Palaestina Tertia*. In this regard, it is worth noting that Palestinian historian Prokopios of Caesarea Maritima had already written in 560 CE: The boundaries of Palestine extend towards the east to the sea which is called the Red Sea. Now this sea, beginning at India, comes to a Palestine end at this point in the Roman domain. And there is a city called Aelas on its shore, where the sea comes to an end, as I have said, becomes a very narrow gulf. And as one sails into the sea from there, the Egyptian mountains lie on the right, extending towards the south; on the other side a country deserted by men extends northward to an indefinite distance; and the land on both sides is visible as one sails in as far as the island called Iotabe, not less than 1,000 *stades* (100 miles) distant from the city of Aelas (Prokopios 2005).

The Red Sea trade route to the port city of Aylah brought caravans-loaded spices and other precious good to Gaza and in return, at the height of the Palestine wine industry in Antiquity, Palestinian wine, with Gaza wine amphorae, were exported to south Arabia and Yemen by sea. A 200 tons cargo of black pepper imported from India through the Red Sea and via camel caravans via southern Palestine was valued in Roman markets at over 6 million sesterces or 1,000 Greek talents and the sum could have paid the annual wages of 6,000 legionaries. The huge profits from this international trade gave Roman merchants a huge sum of disposable wealth.

Ancient economies thrive through the efforts of international merchants and the eastern trade and Red Sea trade and Red Sea ports like 'Aylah in Palestine'. These profits helped finance the academies of Athens and Alexandria (McLaughlin 2014: 104–5) and subsequently contributed to the financing of the Rhetorical School of Gaza during Byzantine era. A papyrus in Egypt records how a Roman banker loaned money to four shippers from Ascalan in Palestine to finance a Mediterranean trade run (McLaughlin 2014: 105). Trade through the Red Sea involved merchants from many Arab regions and pottery shards scratched with Himyarite and Sabaean writing have been found Myos Hormos, which show Arab merchant trading in Roman territory of the Mediterranean and graffiti from Arab merchants have been found on the road leading from Myos Hormos to Koptos (McLaughlin 2014: 106). Myos Hormos was a Red Sea port constructed by the Ptolemies around the third century BCE, the site located eight kilometres north of the modern town of El Qoseir in Egypt. Koptos was a town in Upper Egypt.

Other silk routes: The Red Sea as 'Sea of China' and the maritime silk route to Palestine and Egypt

Being known as the 'Sea of China' by Arab mariners and geographers, for centuries much of the imported silk form China arrived through the Red Sea. Silk as a fabric was first produced in ancient China from the filaments of the cocoon of the silkworm. As China's most important export, the reputation of the Chinese silk as a luxurious elite product began to spread in classical Antiquity across the ancient world, leading to the creation of global trading networks and silk routes that connected China, India, the Middle East, Africa and Europe. With this global land and maritime trade in Chinese silk, sericulture – that is the cultivation of mulberry leaves, the tending of silkworms – also began to spread. However, the 'Silk Road' is a modern European construct. In fact there was never a single Silk Road; there was, however, networks of silk trade routes from China and South Asia (including both land and maritime trade routes to the ancient Middle East) dating from the second century BCE until the mid-fifteenth century. However, much of the writings on the Eurasian 'Silk Road' (a term coined in the nineteenth century) is still dominated by Western romantic Orientalism and modern ideological construct such as 'East' and 'West' (Billé et al. 2022) – a construct that has been thoroughly critiqued by Edward Said.

Around the beginning of the first century CE, a great expansion of international trade took place, partly driven by the strong demand for Chinese silk and Asian spices by the Roman Empire. However, in classical Antiquity and throughout the Middle Ages these land and maritime silk routes – combined with the highly lucrative trade of raw silk textile that was produced initially almost exclusively in China – played an important role in facilitating commercial, intellectual, cultural, political and religious interactions between a wide range of countries in Asia, the Middle East and Europe. Also many regions of south and southeast Asia were directly involved with, and connected by, the maritime silk routes at various points in history.

While much of the focus in writing is still on the Eurasian land caravans of silk, which spanned over 6,400 kilometres, the maritime silk routes and the Red Sea silk route have been given less attention. The central Asian land caravans, which carried Chinese silk along long distances and mountainous routes, were very arduous and slow. By contrast, the maritime transport of silk and other precious goods was much cheaper and ships travelled more rapidly from ports on the Indian sub-continent to the Arabian Sea and then through the Red Sea to the port cities of Egypt and Palestine. This far more lucrative maritime route transported silk as well as a wide range of luxurious goods, including spices, gems and precious stones. Since Antiquity between the ancient Palestine Red Sea port city of 'Aylah in Palestine', south Arabia and India and into southeast Asia and China, shipping trade has existed. Thus pepper, sugar, cinnamon, wood, silk and other valuable goods were traded regularly. This maritime route was more than substitute for the silk routes of the north; it was a vital trade route in its own right (Barisitz 2017: 43).

In the *Silk Road Encyclopedia*, we find the following entry for 'Gaza':

> An ancient city located on the Mediterranean coast at the junction of Egypt and Palestine. It has been a hub connecting the Mediterranean and Red Seas and the regions of Egypt and Syria ... Its position at the intersection of a Silk Road oasis course and matriline route allowed for large number of transactions in incense and other goods, and frequent meetings occurred there among merchants, religious figures, migrants, and travellers.
>
> ('Gaza', in Su-il 2016)

Silk making was widely known in Palestine in late Antiquity and the Middle Ages. Visiting Gaza in 1326, during the Mamluk period, the great Arab traveller Ibn Battuta recorded:

> The city is orderly in its division, with many buildings and excellent market streets ... it also has many mosques and is surrounded by ramparts'
>
> ('Gaza', cited in Su-il 2016)

In Antiquity raw Chinese silk arrived in Palestine via multiple routes and from multiple sources including the Eurasian silk routes and via Iraq and Iran as well as the speedy Red Sea maritime route leading to the city of Aylah in Palestine:

> The Red Sea became a significant maritime route for the Ptolemies ... in the first century BC, enabling them to be harnessed by mariners; hence the Red Sea became the gateway to commercial relations with the world of the India Ocean, as spices, aromatics, precious stones, ivory, Chinese silk, and other products were imported were imported from its African and Indian shores. The route continued to be travelled in the Roman period, though its importance declined in certain periods (for example, the latter part of the fifth century). But it revived in the sixth, especially in the 520s, when during the long reign of Justinian south Arabia became Christianized after the Ethiopian military intervention supported by Byzantium .... Bringing to light the Arab connection to this maritime trade route, and to the overland trade route, imparts a new paramilitary dimension to [the Ghassanid

> Arab phylarch of *Palaestina Tertia*] Abu Karib's role in the Byzantine economy" [and involvement in the Red Sea trade of Itotabe].
>
> (Shahid 1995: 29)

During late Antiquity under the Byzantine, the Emperor Justinian's imposed monopoly on silk making and several different types of merchandise (Conor 2016: 42).

By the fourth century, the Palestinian city of Caesarea Maritima was known for exporting purple dye and locally produced flax growing and Linin weaving and for silk textiles from raw silk imported from China (Patrich 2011: 117). This raw silk was obtained in Palestine from multiple sources and multiple routes, including the Red Sea maritime route leading to the port city of Aylah and through the wealthy and 'autonomous' maritime merchants of the island-town of Iotabe in the Red Sea, some of whom were Ghassanid Arab and Jewish merchants (Mayerson 1992a: 1-4; Shahid 1995). In the third century, some Palestinian Jewish rabbis were silk merchants who had business in Tyre and contacts with Babylonian Jewry and imported raw silk from the Far East through the territories of the Sassanian Persia (Patrich 2011: 119) as well as raw silk imported from China via the key maritime route of the Red Sea. There was a massive increase in the Mediterranean and Red Sea-Indian trade in a variety of luxury goods including raw silk during the Roman and early Byzantine era. The ancient economies of Palestine and Egypt thrived through the efforts of international merchants and the eastern trade and Red Sea trade and Red Sea ports like Aylah-Gaza (McLaughlin 2014: 103-6). The lucrative Red Sea involved merchants from many Arab regions and pottery shards scratched with Himyarite and Sabaean writing shows Arab merchant trading in Roman territory of the Mediterranean, and graffiti from Arab merchants has been found in Egypt (McLaughlin 2014: 106).

The huge profits from this international trade gave local and Roman merchants a huge sum of disposable of disposable wealth, some of which was invested in local economies. These profits helped finance the academies of the ancient Mediterranean world from Athens to Alexandria (McLaughlin 2014: 105) and almost certainly contributing to the financing of the rhetorical college of Gaza in Byzantine era.

The Indian Ocean and Red Sea trade with Palestine: Ancient Palestinian accounts

In the sixth century the historians and writers of *Palaestina* gave us various accounts of the commercial, strategic and military struggles for the control of this key tax station on the India-Palestinian Red Sea Trade route. Procopius of Caesarea Maritima (*c*.500–565 CE), the premier historian of sixth-century Palestine and one of the most important historians of late Antiquity (Cameron 1985), often distinguished between what he called the 'Saracens of Palestine' and the 'Saracens of Arabia'. Derived from the Arabic word for *sharqi* or *eastern* the term *saracen* was used in late Antiquity in both in Greek and Latin writings to refer to the Ghassanid Arabs who lived in Byzantine Palestine or Arabia (Retsö 2003: 505-6). The Ghassanid Christian Arabs of Palestine were allied with the Byzantine Empire and controlled the much of the transit trade of *Palaestina Tertia* (Shahid 1995: 183).

Procopius of Caesarea Maritima ('*Metropolis Palaestina*') – who was intimately familiar with the geography of Palestine, and with the Greek and classical literature about Palestine and the Ptolemaic map of Palestine and with the Latin literature about *Limes Palaestinae* (the 'Borders of Palestine') – wrote:

> The boundaries of Palestine extend eastwards to the sea called Red. This sea had its starting point in India and end here, in the Roman Empire. A city called Aela is situated on the coast of the empire here, where the sea, as I mentioned, comes to an end, forming an extremely narrow strait. As one sails from there into the strait, the mountains of Egypt stretch out southwards on the right; ... The land on either side is visible to one sailing into the sea, as far as the island called Iotabe, which lies less than a thousand *stades*[2] [100 miles] from Aela ....From this point a great open sea takes over. Those who sail [from Aila] into it no longer see the land on their right, but when night falls they always moor on the left bank. For it is impossible to sail in this sea in the dark because it happens to be filled with shoals over a wide area, But there are many [Arabian] harbours there formed not by the hands of men, but by the nature of the terrain, and consequently it is not hard for sailor to find mooring wherever they happened to be.
>
> Saracens [Ghassanid Arabs] occupy the coastline immediately beyond the frontier as one crosses over from Palestine .... Abu Karib, the ruler of the Saracens there presented ... Palm Tree as a gift to the Emperor Justinian and the emperor appointed him as a phylarch [tribal chief, or king]over the Saracens [Ghassanid Arabs] in Palestine, and Abu Karib kept the land consistently free from raiding since he appeared fearsome and remarkably energetic to the barbarians over whom he ruled and no less to his enemies.
>
> (Procopius 2022. 88-90)

Another account of the lucrative Red Sea trade route to Palestine and the struggle to control the lucrative taxes levied by Iolabe was given by Choricius of Gaza, the chief rhetorician of the School of Gaza. Not a historian by profession, Choricius commented in his rhetorical speeches, or *encomia*, of the mid-530s, praising *dux of Palaestina*, general (*strategos*) Aratius and the military commanders and governors of Palestine who sent troops (probably aided by the Ghassanid Arabs of *Palaestina Tertia*) to re-assert control over the island and recover its customer venues. Sections of 67-78 of Choricius's *encomia* describe restoring direct Byzantine control of the island after it had been taken over an unidentified hostile (presumably Arabians) group that had lived on the island and also possessed what was then considered an impregnable fortress on the nearby Arabian mainland:

Choricius describes Iotabe as an important station for cargoes coming from India and for collecting taxes on ships that put in there. 'The unidentified people [on the island who had a fortress on the mainland] attacked the island, destroying the Church of the Mother of God, and thus usurp the taxes belong to the emperor. Choricius then describes how Aratius [*Dux of Palaestina* in 535-6] stormed the fortress, captured it, enslaved those of the defenders who survived the assault, and then left the fortress in the hands of the 'trustworthy men' [presumably the Gassanid Arabs of *Palaestina Tertia*] ... In this way the island revenues returned to the emperor (Shahid 1995: 182-5).

Earlier in the sixth century Timotheus of Gaza (491–518), a Palestinian scholar active during the reign of Emperor Anastasius reported on merchants in Aelas and Gaza shipping Indian goods via the Red Sea. Timotheus also authored a zoological book, written in Greek (with some sections survived in Syriac and Arabic), *On Animals* written within the revival of secular Greek classical education of late Antiquity Palestine (Timotheus 1949). This work may have been one of the sources of the Arabic Nu'ut al-Hayawan (Kopf 1956: 390–466). Timotheus also wrote a work in four volumes titled *Indian Animals or Quadrupeds and Their Innately Wonderful Qualities or Stories about Animals* that survives only in an eleventh-century prose summary. This prose summary was a very popular school text, and includes accounts of the giraffe, tiger, and other animals (Scarborough 2005). Timotheus of Gaza also wrote about the Arab horse and other four-footed beasts among the Arabs, Indians, Egyptians and Libyans. He describes the Arab horse as follows: he says the Arab horses 'near to the mountain of the land of India' are of a good size, generally red bay, carrying their necks high, with well proportionate face carrying their heads close to their rider's faces, haughty and spirited, very keen, swift with supple limbs, with compact flanks and lean bodies, such a shores far more comfortable to rise horseback. The Arab horse is unwearied in the heat, rather rejoicing in the sun. His coat is beautiful, his diet is simple, his bearing dignified. He crosses obstacles without being forced (Anderson 1961: 26; Terpstra 2019: 180).

Timotheus's exceptional work was composed in a sophisticated prose and with accurate factual scholarly description, and without touching on theological perspectives, around 512 CE. The work was also quoted by Muslim 'natural scientists' such as physician al-Marwazi (1056–1124) – the author of the Arabic *Book on the Nature of Animals* – who describes vividly two giraffes passing through Gaza and brought via the spice route through the Palestinian Red Sea port city of Aelas from India (together with an elephant) as gifts for the Byzantine emperor:

> There came to us a man from India [or, according to some versions, the man was a merchant hailing from Aelas and dealing in Indian products], a messenger of the king of India, with two giraffes, covered with cloths and harnessed with many bridles and nose straps, that he wanted to bring to the king of Constantinople. He came to our house and I was full of amazement about what I saw of their nature and shape. They had the stature of a camel in height, a skin like that of a panther, long forelegs, a prominent breast and a slender neck. Their head was like that of a camel and so was their mouth. Their teeth were like those of a cow, and their

> tales were the size of a gazelle's. A rider (*Sawwad*) sat upon them, and they walked forward by pushing forward their right foreleg and then their left foreleg and then their left hind leg.
>
> (Kruk 2008: 575; also Alda 2014: 191-200)

Further discussion of the indigenous Palestine silk and linen industries will be found in the next chapter.

5

Elite Fashion, Linen, Silk and Purple Dye

The Palestine Clothing Industry and a Tale of Five Textile Cities in Antiquity

Palestinian traditional textile crafts were handmade techniques—including dying, weaving, and embroidery—passed down through generations. Often using local materials to create functional and economically significant clothing industry, they also represented deep-rooted cultural identity. This chapter will focus on the rise of the textile industry of Palestine in Antiquity and the five Palestinian cities that were at the centre of this textile revolution in Roman and Byzantine Palestine: Beisan (Schythopolis), Sepphoris (Safuriyya), Nablus (Neapolis), Lydda and Caesarea Maritima - the latter being the overall administrative capital of Palestine (*Metropolis Palaestinea*) and the capital of the province of *Palaestina Prima*. The chapter will begin with Beisan, a metropolitan city in Antiquity and the capital of the Palestine linen industry for several centuries under the Romans and Byzantines and the capital of the province of *Palaestina Secunda* under the Byzantines. It will also explore how the sprawling urban cemetery of Beisan in Antiquity can teach us a lot about urban life in ancient Palestine.

Ancient urban cemeteries as markers of wealth and urban life

The ancient Palestinian city of Beisan (Schythopolis; *Σκυθόπολις*) was one of the oldest wealthiest cities in ancient Palestine whose origins are in the Chalcolithic Age. The excavation of its ancient cemetery revealed one of the largest ancient cemeteries in Palestine. As we shall see in Chapter 6, the Christian revolution of Byzantine Palestine brought about global fame for the locally produced Palestinian wine. The pre-Christian wine traditions and wine industry of Palestine were already associated with the Palestinian deity of Dionysus, the God of wine and fertility and the patron deity of the ancient Palestinian city of Scythopolis (Beisan). A multi-cultural and multi-religious metropolis under the Romans and Byzantines, the golden age of the city of Scythopolis was during this period with the city developing into one of the largest industrial urban centres in Palestine and serving as the capital of the Byzantine province of *Palaestina Secunda*. Under both the late Roman Empire and the

Byzantine Empire, the city benefited from high levels of urban planning and extensive construction of public and civic buildings and the city boasted one of the best-preserved theatres of ancient Palestine. The demographic size of Schythopolis during late Antiquity can be gauged from the scale of its necropolis; excavations carried out at the site during the British Mandatory period show that the urban cemeteries of ancient and medieval Palestine teach us a lot about the prosperity and wealth of urban life in the country. Many of the necropolises (*Νεκρόπολις*) ('cities of the dead') of urban Palestine in Antiquity and the Middle Ages were large with elaborate and decorated tomb monuments, reflecting the wealth and sophistication of urban life in Palestine. Other aspects of urban life can be revealed from excavating ancient cemeteries. For instance, the large cemeteries of the ancient cities of Elusa and Oboda in the Naqab (Negev) show that pagans and Christians lived side by side in Palestinian cities until the fifth century CE. The colossal necropolis of the ancient city of Beisan reveals the industrial wealth and power of this city in Antiquity, while the large Mamilia cemetery in Jerusalem, a 1,000-year-old Muslim cemetery (which was mostly demolished by Israel in recent decades partly in the name of building a 'Museum of Tolerance' on its site), housed highly elaborate and decorated tomb monument reflecting the wealth of urban social and artistic life in medieval Jerusalem under Islam.

The great cemetery of the ancient metropolis city of Beisan is also a case in point: this is 'one of the largest, if not quite the largest, of all the ancient cemeteries of Palestine' in Antiquity (Avi-Yonah 1936: 11). And the archaeological evidence from this period shows the markets of Beisan sold various kinds of fruits such as figs, apples, pomegranates, pears, grapes, melons, lemons, dates and the city had a number of wine presses (Avi-Yohah 1935: 16–17). Economically the city played an important role in the international trade of the country due to its geographical location at the junction of two important valleys: Marj Ibn Amer (Plain of Esdraelon) and the Jordan River Valley. Its geographic location also allowed it to develop into the textile capital of Palestine and one of the most important textile centres in the ancient world. As we shall see below, Beisan was one of several industrial cities and great, prosperous centres of textile industries in Palestine. The development of the textile industry, clothing and fashion and the trade in fabrics and finished garments began in Antiquity and this trade became an important feature of urban social and economic life, reflecting social status in society in the Near East. The ancient textile industry used in the Near East, combined with jewellery, cosmetics and aromatics (discussed in Chapter 3), reflected the technologies used by people in the Near East at the time. In many ways, the urban attire, more than anything else, reflected the taste, fashion and social status of various social classes in urban society.

Already in ancient Egypt, the material quality of garments differed between the classes, where those of the upper class used finer linens depicted in statues and paintings by their translucency (Vivian 2008: 321). As we shall see below, purple dye articles, fine linen and silk garments were elite attire in Palestine in Antiquity. Also, we know in Ancient Egypt and Palestine fine linen garments were expensive and the wearer of fine linen showed greater social and urban status. On the other hand, cheaper and thicker linen was used within the lower middle and working classes, and shorter garments were worn by the working class for better mobility in the fields (Vivian 2008: 321). The textile industries became the most important export-oriented industries of the Roman province of *Syria–Palaestina* under the Romans and one of the most biggest and finest textile industries of the Roman world (Safrai 1994: 107–14, 2003: 134).

The remarkable rise of the Palestine textile industries in Antiquity took place against the back of major social, economic and urban developments in the country. Six centuries of Hellenistic/Ptolomaic and Roman rule in Palestine created a dense network of roads and trade routes (discussed in Chapter 1) and planned cities and towns supported by a strong rural agricultural economy. Cities and towns governed by local social elites functioned as administrative centres for the government by minting coins, collecting taxes, keeping registers and organizing civic service projects and as cultural, religious and focal points of the community (Walmsley 1996: 126).

The textile industries of urban Palestine flourished locally and gained an international reputation for excellence against the background of the urban density and commercial and cultural sophistication of late Roman and Byzantine Palestine as shown by the fact that there were some twenty-five cities in Palestine enjoying a municipal status – including one major wine producing city in the Naqab, Elusa (see also Chapters 3 and 6).

> This is a relatively high density, considering that in an area of about 15,000 sq. km there was a city to an average of every 600 sq km … These were generally true cities in the full sense of the term *polis*. These settlements had most of the typical features of the ancient city. From the archaeological remains and from the ancient literary sources we know that most of the essential urban institutions were present: fortifications, cults (temples, synagogues and churches), education and culture (schools), entertainments and sports (theatres, stadiums and racecourses) and public amenities (regular water supplies, bath houses.) Almost all these cities issues coins at one time of another in this period, an indication of a degree of autonomy.
>
> (Broshe 2001: 99-100)

Using local raw materials such as high-quality flax and cotton from Galilee and wool from Judaea and central Palestine and silk imported from China, the scale of the textile industries of Palestine during the Roman and Byzantine periods can be seen from the fact many Palestinian cities and towns and dozens of villages were involved in this textile industry (with its multiple branches: flax cultivation, linen weaving, silk clothing and dye works and tenancies) including the cities of Schythpolis, Caesarea Maritima, Neapolis (Nablus), Lydda (Diospolis), Sepphoris/Safuryya (Diocaesarea/ Eirenopolis), Ascalon, Gaza and the coastal town of Dora (Tantura). A large number of local women, in particular, were involved in the various stages of the production of the Palestine flax, which was one of the most important raw and pricy materials for clothing in the Roman Empire (Peskowitz 2004: 129-45; Safrai 2003: 88, 113). Due to this extensive involvement of women in the various stages of production on the clothing industries of the ancient Palestine and the Middle East, industries geared towards foreign export, and consequently in the long-distance trade has been often overlooked by historians.

The master tanner of Ascalon in Al-Khalil (Hebron)

Generally tanners and textile workers in Palestine in Antiquity were professional and, to protect their profession and rights workers organized themselves in the cities in guilds. But there were also many family owned private tanneries. An inscription engraved on a tabula ansata ('tablet with handles') from Khirbet Dah in the countryside of the al-Khalil city (Hebron) dated to 527 CE refers to a private workshop: '*This is the shed of Master Zenonos the tanner from Ascalon*' – a profession Zenonos probably learned in his hometown of Ascalon (Di Segni 2022: 128; Kingsley 2003: 113–38; 2004: 83). A coin of Justin I was also found in the excavation which corroborates the date and the use of the currency of Ascalon. Enclosed in a shed, and because of the odour, the location of this private tannery was most generally, the tanners' workshops in Palestine, because of the odour, were often kept out of the residential parts of the cities (Di Segni 2022: 128).

This out of town location is akin the modern industrial zones such as the city of al-Khalil in which family owned leather tanneries, with their unpleasant odour and emission, are kept out of sight. However, the modern family-owned leather manufacturing and tanneries of al-Khalil – leather supplied to the family owned shoe factories of the city (unlike the ancient tanning industry of ancient Palestine) – use a range of chemicals with problematic conditions; in addition, these Palestinian tanneries faced an assortment of restrictions from the Israeli occupation.

The Palestine tannery industry in Antiquity continued into the modern period and in modern times, the name, *al-Dabaagh, the tanner*, has survived in the family name of Palestinian Arab family of Jaffa, and the name of Mustafa al-Dabbagh (1897–1989), one of the most prominent Palestinian historians and educators and the author of an encyclopaedic work, *Our Country Palestine* (*Biladuna Filastin*) (Al-Dabbagh 1965 and 1972–86).

The impact of neighbouring Phoenician cities: The Tyre purple and Palestine's textile industries in Antiquity

As a millennia-old industry, the historical roots of the tannery workshops and textile industries of Palestine in Antiquity were closely related to the early production of purple dye as a fabric dye by the Phoenicians. Purple-dyed garment production was centred in the Phoenician cities of Tyre and Sidon on the Mediterranean coast. The term *Phoenicians* itself is an ancient Greek term for the 'people of purple' – a term closely associated with the Phoenician maritime trade in purple dye-works and with their seafaring and commercial empire across classical Antiquity, which lasted over a millennium. Beginning as early as 1200 BCE, the reddish-purple, which became internationally famous as *Tyrian purple* (Greek: πορφύρα *porphúra*; Latin *purpura*), became known as the Phoenician red and royal dye. Produced initially in the port cities of Tyre and Sidon, the *Tyrian purple* was a naturally created dye secreted by several species of sea snails and rock snails originally known by the name 'Murex snails'. In modern times mountains of empty shells were uncovered at the ancient sites of the cities of Tyre and Sidon showing that the merchants of the cities were producing and marketing purple dye. During the Roman period the cities of Tyre, Sidon (modern Lebanon) and other coastal cities in Palestine were key provider of dyed material for the imperial court in Rome (Sartre 2005: 247).

Furthermore the mention of the colour purple, the colour of royalty and of important people, in the Roman Empire in the New Testament was significant in the way the Roman authorities in Palestine used the colour to dress Jesus of Nazareth in a purple robe to mock and torment him. This mention occurs in two of the Gospels, Mark and John.

- Mark 15:17: They put a purple robe on him, then twisted together a crown of thorns and set it on him.
- Mark 15:20: And when they had mocked him, they took off the purple robe and put his own clothes on him. Then they led him out to crucify him.
- John 19:2: The soldiers twisted together a crown of thorns and put it on his head. They clothed him in a purple robe.
- John 19:5: When Jesus came out wearing the crown of thorns and the purple robe, Pilate said to them, 'Here is the man!'

In Antiquity, extracting this natural dye involved tens of thousands of snails and intensive labour, and, as a result, the dye works became very expensive and highly valuable. The Tyrian purple combined with Phoenicians' purple garments was spread widely by the Phoenician merchant-mariners first to neighbouring Palestinian cities such as Caesarea Maritima, Lydda and Neapolis and then further afield to other Mediterranean port cities, following the expansion of the Phoenician maritime and trading empire and settlements across the Mediterranean. Together with the trade of Tyrian purple, the proto-Canaanite alphabet was also spread by the Phoenician and Canaanite merchant-mariners from the Near East to the Greeks and all Mediterranean cultures (Kassinge 2003).

Greatly prized in Antiquity because the colour did not easily fade, the Tyrian purple dye-works were taken up by Greek and Roman merchants and later worn by Roman and Byzantine emperors and senior Roman officials of these empires of Antiquity – hence the elite designation of the Tyrian purple, as *the royal purple*. This idea of *purple* being an elite colour contributed to the modern-day belief that purple is a 'royal colour'. Because Tyrian purple was extremely difficult to make, Tyrian purple was expensive, Greek historian Theopompus noted in the fourth century BCE 'Purple for dyes fetched its weight in silver at the ancient city of Colophon in Asia Minor' (Athenaeus 1941). Under the Romans the purple dye became symbol of power, nobility and riches. During the early years of Rome, wearing purple garments was reserved for kings and priests. Under the Roman republic its use was extended to higher magistrates who wore a toga decorated with purple ribbons, which signified that they held political power. Later with Roman military conquests, the consumption of luxury goods increased and purple became used more widely across upper classes and functioned as an outward sign of the possession power and of riches. In consequences the art of dyeing developed in workshops and factories across the Roman Empire and in a number of cities in Palestine dyeing factories and workshops combined purple dye with the production of silk garments. Also new shops were erected in various city markets and various localities across the Mediterranean for marketing these luxury products (Brunello 1973: 105–6).

The difficulty in producing the dye and huge expense meant that Tyre purple-dyed textiles became status symbols and the colour of royals, aristocrats, priests, generals and magistrates, especially as ceremonial robes, all around the Roman Mediterranean world; the most senior Roman magistrates wore a purple-bordered toga (*toga praetexta*). The use of this colour in clothing was restricted by *Sumptuary laws* (Latin: *sumptuariae leges*). These laws tried to regulate consumption of luxury items through clothing and were intended to regulate and reinforce social hierarchies and class privileges. The laws were also used to try to regulate the balance of trade by limiting the market for expensive imported goods. The colour of these expensive textiles from this ancient period also provides insight into socio-cultural relationships within ancient societies, in addition to providing insight to ancient and modern technological achievements, fashion designs, social stratification and trade connections across countries (Sukenik et al. 2021).

Accounts of the early introduction of purple dye in Palestine are rare. However in the coastal cities of Phenicia, Syria and Palestine, there existed many purple dye workshops early on. According to *The Art of Dyeing in the History of Mankind*, the dyeing workshops 'had been founded chiefly by the Phoenicians [themselves] at Sarepha [Sarepta] Caesarea [-Maritima], Neapolis [Nablus], Lydda and Tyre' (Brunello 1973: 106). Also impressive dyeworks and tanneries have been excavated at the Palestinian Mediterranean coastal cities of Ascalon, Gaza and the town of Tantur (Dora; modern Tantura) (Kingsley and Decker. 2015a 44–68; Mommsen and Dickson 1886: 137).

To facilitate trade and the movement of goods and soldiers between key Palestinian cities, well-maintained *Neapolis-Schythopolis road* (Nablus-Beisan road) and *Neapolis-Caesarea Maritima road*, with milestones as road marks, were constructed. The sources about the importance of the global trade under the Romans and the dye workshops as well as the textile factories of Palestine in Antiquity are extensive and wide-ranging:

> Textual sources provide us with a useful idea of the minimum extent of cloth production and dying. In Palestine, Talmudic literature refers to purple dye production in Diospolis [Lydda]; Caesarea and Neapolis [Nablus] are also listed as exporters of purple-dyed cloth in the *Expositio Totius Mundi et Gentium* thought to date to A.D. 359. The same source suggests that cloth manufacture at Scythopolis was most renowned in Palestine; it refers to abundant cloth production in this city and its export throughout the world. To this list of sites we may add Ascalon: an inscription found on a *tabula ansata* from Khirbet Dah-Dah in North Hebron, dated A.D, 527 refers to shed of Zenonos the tanner from Ascalon, who presumably learned the trade inn his city of birth .... At Dor [Tantura] complex rock-cut basins, water channels and courtyards of the 4th and

> 6th c. date sheltered along the north harbour are plausibly associated with the city's long tradition of purple-dye production, which dates back to the 5th c. B.C ....More substantial remains of the 5th c. A.D. have been excavated next to the synagogue at Constantia [Gaza Mauimas], the maritime city of Gaza. The size of the industrial area there suggest it saw high capita investment, by either the state or private investors, with the manufactory processing pigment procured from the Negev, Sinai, Italy and Greece.
>
> Historical texts also give us important information on the organisation of production. They suggest that at least urban operations were initially state-controlled (although challenged by private enterprise). Thus, an edict of A.D. 374 in the Theodosian Code that anyone illegally sheltering linen workers at Scythopolis would be liable to a fine of 5 lbs of gold. The underlying assumption was the dye-works were staffed by state employees whose employment rights were tightly regulated. Another law from the same source, issued in 385, ordained that "if any person should dare to usurp the use of a boat that is assigned to the compulsory public service of purple dye collection and to the collection of shellfish, he shall be liable to the payment of two pounds of gold". But the first half of the 5th c. the State's attempt to monopolise may well have become unenforceable.
>
> (Kingsley: 2003: 123)

The textile industry of Neapolis (Nablus) in historical perspective

As we have already seen, the ancient Palestinian city of Neapolis (Nablus) was a key centre for the textile industries of Palestine in Antiquity. In fact Nablus has always been, since its foundation in the first century, on an older Palestinian urban centre which dates back to the Bronze Age – one of the greatest urban centres in Palestine and among the most industrious cities in the country. Today Nablus is one of the largest cities in Palestine with a population of 160,000 and is a major commercial and cultural centre in the West Bank. Its modern Arabic name can be traced back to the Roman period, when it was named *Flavia Neapolis* by Roman Emperor Vespasian in 72 CE, named *Flavia Neapolis* ('new city of the emperor Flavius'). In classical Antiquity local currency and coins minted in Nablus (Neapolis) had the names of various Roman emperors. Roman Neapolis was about 900 acres in size, making it one of the largest urban centres in Roman Palestine with a population around 20,000 people. Neapolis also flourished during this period as an intellectual and learning centre for Platonic and neo-Platonic philosophies.

The urban economic, social and cultural life of ancient Neapolis was shaped by the fact the city became important to the Samaritan religion in Palestine and during the early Byzantine period, the Samaritans used Neapolis as their seat and dominated the town life; they were also involved in competition and even clashes with the growing Christian community in the city (Pappe and Mansour 2022: 313). Administratively during the Christian Byzantine period Neapolis was within the province of *Palaestina Prima*, whose capital and key Mediterranean port city was the city of Caesarea Maritima, and the economics and textile industries of these two great cities of ancient Palestine were intertwined.

Islamic Nablus: Urban continuities and innovations

Originally constructed as a long (Roman-style) stone city between two mountains with colonnaded public buildings, early Islamic Nablus preserved many of its original planned architectural heritage and its ancient urban life. But Islamic Nablus also introduced urban innovations that linked the mosque, urban market (and shops) and the merchants' caravanserai as mutually supporting key features of urban life in Palestine.

Also, under the impact of the expanding commercial life and regional trade of the city, the urban space of Islamic Nablus expanded and the city developed several industries during the early Muslim period – a tenth-century mosque is still intact. There is also some evidence of the mass conversion by Samaritans to Islam in Palestine in general and in Nablus in particular during the course of the early Muslim period (see Levy-Rubin 2000). Throughout the Islamic period the rich urban fabric of Nablus was socially and religiously diverse; in the ninth century Muslim geographer al-Yaqubi (*d.* 897/8) reported that Nablus had a mixed population of Arabs and non-Arabs (*ajams*) and Muslims, Samaritans and Christians (Levy-Rubin 2000: 257–76). Al-Yaqubi wrote:

> Nablus lies between two mountains, has plenty of olive groves, it is called a Small Damascus, its markets from the gate to the gate, while the other reaches to the town centre, where there is the Great Mosque, it is clean and finely tiled, there is a river in it, and it is built from stone with strange Dawamis.
>
> (Abujidi 2014: 90)

A century later, in the tenth century, the Palestinian geographer al-Maqdisi described Nablus as abundant of olive trees, with a large marketplace, houses built of stone, a fine Great Mosque, a stream running through the centre of the city, and many industrial mills (Muqaddasi 1886: 55).

Developing multiple industries under Islam in the Middle Ages, including paper, pottery, soap and olive oil industries, and becoming a great trading city, in the tenth century al-Maqdisi also noted that Nablus was nicknamed 'Little Damascus' (Muqaddasi 1886: 55l; Pappe and Mansour 2022: 313). This nickname was given to Nablus in view of its strong trading relations with the great Syrian city, trading relations which date back to the shared textile industries and foreign export of Palestine and Syria in classical Antiquity and in view of the fact that Nablus developed and sustained a sophisticated culture and a 'high cuisine' culture comparable to the culture of the great city of Damascus. Even in the Middle Ages the textile industry and linen produced in Nablus was well known throughout the old world (Runciman 1987: 353). As we shall see below, across millennia, in Antiquity, the Middle Ages and the modern period, Nablus developed many successful traditional industries in Palestine. Throughput the Ottoman period (1171-1918) Nablus and its environs served as the administrative and commercial centre for the surrounding area corresponding to the modern-day northern West Bank as well as parts of Transjordan, and from the late Ottoman period until 1948, its most successful industry was the soap factories.

The high-quality of the linen and textile of Beisan: Diocletian's *Price Edict*

Throughout classical and late Antiquity the high-quality textile and linen clothes produced by the weavers of the Palestinian city of Scythopolis (Beisan) and in four other Syrian cities were 'exported to the whole world' (Sperber 1976: 133–6). Fine Syrian and Palestinian manufactured textile and clothes were widely exported to all parts of Europe including – as was discovered in 1938 in the Sutton Hoo burial treasures in England – to the Anglo-Saxon kingdom of the sixth and early seventh century (Karkov 2013: 451; Owen-Crocker 2004: 295). High praise for the linen of Schythopolis is found in several Jewish rabbinic sources before and after the fourth century CE (Mango 2016).

The Palestine textile industry was one of the most important industries in the Roman world, while linen industry seems to have played a larger role in the Levant (with *Syria–Palaestina* being a leading centre in weaving and dyeing of cloths) than in the Western parts of the Roman Empire. During the Roman and Byzantine periods, the high-quality of the textile industries of Palestine, and especially the *Linen of Scythopolis*, is widely documented. In Palestine high-quality flax was grown for the weaving of linen and manufacturing of textiles, which was considered among the best (if not the best) in the Roman Empire. This high reputation of the linen of Scythoplis and the economic-industrial importance of the city throughout the Roman Empire may have contributed to the fact that Scythopolis would become in the subsequent Byzantine period a regional capital in Palestine and the capital of the province of Palestina Secunda. However, it is important to make it clear that the rise of the linen and textile industries of Scythopolis – as in the case of other cities in Palestine – was confined to the city.

The success of the linen and textile industries of Scythopolis should be seen in the wider context of the collaboration of merchants/industrialists and peasants, with the basic raw materials for linen weaving in Scythopolis being flax cultivated by peasants in the Galilee. In the case of the linen of Scythopolis, the wider Galilee region, Marj Ibn Amer (Jizreel valley) as well as the countryside of the city of Tiberias all played an important part in the flax of Scythopolis during this period.

In terms of production, textile manufacturing was probably more important than purple dye. Ancient sources give Syria little credit for fine textile, except for its silk, but this is somewhat misleading. It was actually not until the sixth century CE, when silkworms were imported clandestinely from China, that [the province of] Phoenicia produced true silk. Procopios who would have known about this innovation in his day attributed to Phoenicia a long tradition of silk fabric production and trade; his claim can be accounted for in several ways. First, there seems to have some silk manufacturing in Galilee (in Gischala) [modern Arab village of Jish] during the Hellenistic period, using species other than the ordinary silkworms (*Bombyx*) … the silk fabric had been woven in China and dyed purple in Sidon … linen production in Galilee seems to have been more significant [than the wools produced in Judaea]. In a reference to flax from Palestine, Pausanias (110–180 CE) an ancient Greek geographer and travel writer implied that it represented the highest standard of quality. Flax from Scythopolis was right at the top of Diocletian's Price Edict[1] in terms of cost, but the term *Scythopolitan* should not mislead us: the flax sold in Scythopolis came from throughout the Galilee and even beyond, for some linen was made in the Damascus region … Workshop for treating flax dating from the beginning of the third century have been excavated at Gaza … [were] too extensive to have been own by a single producer, the complex must have belonged to a trade union association. Although the association with Scythopolis has reduced, flax has also been found around Tiberias … and in the Jisreel valley [Marj Ibn Amer], were dozens of similar workshops have been recovered, the oldest clearly date from the third century (Sartre 2005: 242; also Sperber 1976: 113–47).

The clothing price in Diocletian's Edict is an important indication highlighting the world-famous linen and textile industries of Scythopolis and elevating these industries above the contemporary linen and textile manufacturing of the four other Palestinian cities of the period: Lydda, Caesarea Maritima, Neapolis (Nablus) and Diocaesarea/Eirenopolis (Sepphoris/Safuriyya in Galilee). Here, the clothing-makers of Scythopolis are authorized to ask for the highest price for tunics and other clothes made of linen. The edict mentions more than a dozen different kinds of garments, for men and for women, each of them is rated according to three quality grades (*formaea*). The reason for such a high reputation of the linen from Scythopolis is unknown; perhaps it was the soil, the climate or a special production technique of processing the materials. The fact that at least some of the workshops belong to the state undoubtedly encouraged the high rating of the linen of Schythopolis … many pools and water conduits discovered [by archaeologists] in and around the city that might be connected with this industry. In addition to the highest price set by Diocletian's *Price Edict* for the linen of Scythopolis, a maximum price limit was set on one pound of purple-dyed silk which was 150,000 denarii, although in the neo-liberal economics of the Roman Empire these maximum price limits were often ignored by the merchants.

Sepphoris/Saffuriyya: *The City's* weaving industry and organized guilds and workers

In Galilee, the town of Sepphoris (the modern Palestinian Arab town of Saffuriyya until 1948) was one of the important ancient towns in Palestine. Located about five kilometres west of the ancient town of Nazareth – which is traditionally associated with Jesus of Nazareth – the ancient city of Sepphoris – which is also associated with Mary, the mother of Jesus – became a major centre of textile and weaving industry in Roman and Byzantine Palestine. Under the Romans, Sepphoris, with a population 15,000–20,000 inhabitants, was one of the largest and most industrialized cities in Galilee, a city which was officially granted a municipal status of a Roman *polis* (city) and boasted many governmental institutions and public buildings: Roman forum/marketplace, a pagan temple, bathhouses, a theatre and a large water reservoir. A Palestinian city steeped in Roman culture, initially Roman Emperor Hadrian changed Sepphoris' name to Diocaesarea ('city of Zeus and Caesar'). The city retained its urban plans, large market and commercial centrality in Antiquity-mixed population and hybridized culture prospered and meant that (like other religiously mixed cities of Palestine in Antiquity) pagans, Samaritans, Hellenistic-Jews, and Christians lived side by side in Antiquity (Crown 1989: 67) – and many of the Samaritans subsequently converted to Islam.

Financially, the city began minting coins bearing another new Roman name: *Eirenopolis*, 'City of Peace', in honour of Roman Emperor Vespasian. Across more than two millennia the city had rich and diverse historical urban, architectural and cultural legacies that included Hellenistic, Roman, Byzantine-Christian, Jewish, Samaritan and Arab-Islamic traditions. In late Antiquity major public buildings existed in the town include a Roman theatre, a Roman temple, a number of synagogues for Samaritans and Jews, and several Christian churches. In the modern period Crusader fortress was rebuilt by the Palestinian leader Dhahir al-'Umar, the ruler of the Galilee, in the eighteenth century.

Inevitably the large scale of the textile industries of the cities of Roman and Byzantine Palestine began to produce organized labour: guilds of textile merchants and workers and linen weavers. There are references to 'guilds' of textile workers in a number of Palestinian cities: a guild of linen weavers in Diocaesarea/Sepphoris and inscriptions mentioning guilds of weavers have been found in Tiberias (Safrai 2003).

Metropolis Palaestina: The textile and silk industries of Caesarea Maritima

In Palestine, agricultural settlements evolved from *hamlets* and *villages* during the Neolithic Age to market *towns* and trading *cities* in the Bronze Age. By the time we get to late Antiquity, in the Roman/Byzantine period, we see the industrial port city of Caesarea Maritima becoming one of the largest cities in the eastern Mediterranean – an industrial urban sprawl inhabited (together with its satellite villages) by over 100,000 people. By compassion Roman London (Londinium), the largest city and capital of Roman Britain, was about 40,000. Caesarea also the largest port in Byzantine Palestine and one of the largest in the eastern Mediterranean. Being the capital of the province of *Palaestina Prima,* Caesarea became also widely known as *Metropolis Palaestina*, had one the largest and busiest ports in the Mediterranean region and possessed one of the biggest marketplaces in Palestine; it also functioned as an industrial hub in Byzantine Palestine and the capital of the province of *Palaestina Prima* as well as the administrative, commercial, political, financial and military capital of the three provinces of Byzantine Palestine: *Palaestina Prima, Palaestina Secunda* and *Palaestina Tertia.* Caesarea also became a major hub of the Palestine textile and silk industries in Antiquity.

In the mid-fourth century, in that unique commercial treatise *Espositio*, the textile industries of Palestine (and Syria) are described: the export commodities of the country (twenty-two mentions, 20 per cent); the second most often cited export products are an equal share of wine (nineteen mentions, 17 per cent) and olive oil (nineteen mentions, 17 per cent); the third most often mentioned export goods are grain/wheat with eleven mentions (10 per cent). However, as we shall see in Chapter 6, by the time we get to the fifth to sixth centuries, the top export commodity of Palestine is *Gaza wine.* Among the other export goods mentioned in *Espositio* are livestock (seven mentions), fish (and *garum:* fermented fish sauce) (four mentions), rice, fruits, bacon, cheese, dates, spices, honey, stone, lead, iron, wood, asphalt, papyrus, ropes, sails, ships and slaves (one or two mentions). Chapter 5 will show that the textile and linen products of late Roman and Byzantine Palestine, and the Palestinian city of Beisan, in particular, are not only among the most popular export goods, but they are also among the most specialized and highly prized goods of the Mediterranean world.

Often traditional industries such as the flax, linen clothes and textile industries of Palestine flourished in combination with other related industries. During the Roman and Byzantine periods, a series of closely related industries developed in the cities of Palestine and Syria, which came into account for export in the vast markets of the Mediterranean world. Under the Romans, royal purple was used extensively as a dye in the Palestinian city of Caesarea Maritima for silk textiles imported from China and this combination of two expensive items, royal purple and silk from China (at this time), enhanced the elite reputation of the manufactured textile of Caesarea Maritima. According to the *Expositio*, Caesarea Maritima – then premier port city of Palestine and one of the largest cities in the country – was a 'pleasant city and rich in everything' including wine, olive oil and corn and distinguished in exporting purple dye to the Mediterranean world. Its large harbour served the maritime trade of the city across the Mediterranean. The city also had five land trade routes radiating in all directions, and with a highly developed infrastructure for inland commence (Patrich 2011: 117).

By the third century CE, Byzantine Palestine was centred on its wealthy, largely well-educated and highly developed Mediterranean capital city, Caesarea Maritima was also treated as a distinct metropolitan city in Palestine in the writings of its educated urban elites. With a major Mediterranean harbour – bigger than the harbour of Piraeus in Greece – the city of Caesarea Maritima was also an important city in the spread of Christianity in Palestine and throughout the Mediterranean world. From this capital of Palestine, the leading Christian intellectual of his age, Origen (*c.*185–*c.* 253), who had migrated from Alexandria to the rising city of Caesarea Maritima and set up an influential school of Christian philosophy in the city, corresponded with the Roman Emperor Philip (Marcus Julius Philippus, who reigned from 244 to 249 CE), also known by his Latin nickname 'Philippus Arabs'. A native of Provincia Arabia, the Roman province of Arabia Petraea (Bowersock 1994: 122), 'Philip the Arab' was a religious tolerant Roman emperor with evidently sympathetic attitudes towards Christians (Eusebius 2011: VI. xxxiv; Shahid 1984: 76–7).

In the history of Palestine and its people, the importance of the port city Caesarea Maritima for Christianity in its formative period was great; the city helped in the spread and consolidation of the new religion in Palestine, and created many iconic cultural texts and objects and making Palestine probably the best-known country in the world at the time, due to the many descriptions, artefacts, literary, religious and historical works that made it a household name within Christianity and beyond. Some of the iconic texts about the country were produced by the 'Father of Church History', Eusebius of Caesarea, who took pride in his native country of *Palaestina*; he repeatedly used the name Palaestina in his works, which later influenced generations of Christian writers worldwide. *De Martyribus Palaestinae* by Eusebius (1861) gives us a clear indication of the consolidation of the concept of *Palaestina* as a country during the early Byzantine period. The Martyrs of Palestine relates to the persecution of early Christians in the capital of the country, *Caesarea Palaestina*, and the country at large in the early fourth century CE. This account may have originally been composed in Palestinian Aramaic, the language of Jesus of Nazareth. Hebrew at the time of Jesus was largely an extinct language, with the Jews of Palestine speaking Aramaic, and Hebrew being confined to liturgical uses. Closely related to Arabic, Palestinian Aramaic was a language with which Eusebius was well acquainted. At the time, Aramaic was the main vernacular speech of the country and was spoken in the capital, *Caesarea Palaestina*. Aramaic would also influence the evolution of Palestinian vernacular Arabic. Byzantine Palestine also gave birth to the sixth-century world's most important historian, Prokopios of Caesarea Maritima, an illustrious scholar from *Palaestina Prima*, the principal historian of the sixth-century Byzantine Empire.

Prokopios travelled extensively throughout the Mediterranean region and the Near East, accompanied the Byzantine general Belisarius as secretary in the wars of Justinian and commented extensively on the Ghassanid tribal Arab kings (top *phylarchs*) of *Palaestina Secunda*, *Palaestina Prima* and *Palaestina Salutaris*. In his multi volume work, *The Wars of Justinian* (*c*.560), Procopios wrote:

> The boundaries of Palestine extend toward the east to the sea which is called the Red Sea. Now this sea, beginning at India, comes to an end at this point in the Roman domain. And there is a city called Aelas [present-day Aqaba] on its shore, where the sea comes to an end, as I have said, and becomes a very narrow gulf.
>
> (Prokopios 2014)

During the early Christian period, particularly from the fourth century onwards, the Holy Land – a nebulous, abstract and semi-mythical location – was transformed into a real country called *Palaestina*, with thriving cities, ports, beautiful churches and numerous monasteries, famous philosophical schools and libraries, an extensive road system, villages and a large, commercially and culturally active population, which added to the interest shown by (Latin-speaking) Europeans. It was in the course of this early Christian period that the Latin term Terrae Sanctae became synonymous in Christian texts with the extensive use of the term Palaestina by Christian pilgrims and local historians. *On the Martyrs of Palestine* (311 CE) was written by the church historian and Bishop of Caesarea Palaestina, Eusebius (263–339 CE), 'Father of Church History', who composed his monumental work *Historia Ecclesiastica* and his *Onomasticon* (On the Place Names in the Holy Scripture) (1971), a comprehensive geographical-historical study of Palestine, in the city: 'Eusebius states that he compiled On the Place Names in the Holy Scripture by working through the Bible piecemeal' (Barnes 1981: 109). This major biblical enterprise has been described by British classicist Timothy David Barnes (1981: 106) as a 'biblical gazetteer', which is still the main literary source for the historic geography of Palestine both in biblical times and under the Roman Empire.

During the late Roman and Byzantine periods the local manufacturing and international maritime trade of Caesarea Maritima continued to grow, and together with port cities in Palestine such as Gaza and the hinterland industrial cities of Scythopolis, Neapolis and Lydda, Caesarea Maritima became perhaps the largest and among most developed urban centres in Palestine; the city also became among the most important cities of learning in the country attracting many students, researchers, intellectuals and travellers from the eastern Mediterranean world and beyond and consequently bringing more revenues to the city (Masalha 2022).

During this period the proliferation of the industries of Caesarea Maritima included purple dye, glass, flax growing for textile and fine linen weaving and of lucrative silk textile imported from China. The 'presence of amorphous glass ingots in shops' was also found in the markets of Palestinian cities such as Scythopolis and Jerusalem, were the semi-finished glass ingots blown and cast into refined glass vessels and then exported to cities around the Mediterranean; also exported 'Palestinian glass-wares' may have turned up in the harbour of Apollonia, an ancient Greek trading town and later a major Roman city on the Adriatic, in modern-day Albania (Kingsley and Decker 2015a: 1–27, 2015b: 44–68). This Adriatic city Apollonia (Ἀπολλωνία) should be distinguished from the ancient Palestinian Mediterranean port city of Apollonia, known in the early Islamic period as *Arsuf*, situated about thirty-four kilometres south of Caesarea; Arsuf was a major walled city in Islamic Palestine with a large market (Wa'ari 2023, Vol. 1: 27).

In the free market economy and urban growth of Roman Palestine, the multiple industries of Caesarea Maritima and urban development went hand in hand. For over six centuries, from the first to the early seventh century, the city (also known as *Metropolis Palaestinea*) was the administrative and commercial capital of Roman and Byzantine Palestine and the largest city in the country. Since Hadrian in the second century CE, the city had a steady supply of water by several aqueducts. In the mid-fourth century, the *Expositio Totius Mundi et Gentium*, a commercial-geographical description of the world and its people, thought to date to 359 CE tells us Caesarea Maritima in Palestine has a newly-built *tetrapylon*. The *tetrapylon* (Greek: *τετράπυλον*, 'four gates', plural *tetrapyla*, known in Latin as a *quadrifrons*: 'four fronts') was a type of classical architecture and ancient Roman monument of cubic shape, with a gate on each of the four sides, generally built on a crossroad and they were built as landmarks at significant geographical crossroads. And subsequently during the Byzantine era the city had five trade roads radiating in all directions established the infrastructure for inland commerce to all major cities in Palestine. Furthermore;

> Some Palestinian rabbinical sages of the third century were silk merchants who had business in Tyre. Contacts with Babylonian Jewry made easier the import of raw silk from the Far East through the territories of the Sassanian Persia under the protection of which the Babylonian Jewry lived (Patrich 2011: 118–19);
>
> Flax-growing and linen-weaving also figured prominently in the economy of Syria and Palestine, although meagre, there is evidence of this industry in Caesarea. An inscription dating for the later Empire reveals the presence on Caesarea of a weaver who produced textiles according to Babylonia styles.
>
> (Levine 1975: 52)

Often quality sells and often great traditional industries flourished in Palestine in connection with other related industries. A series of closely related high-quality industries developed in the cities of Palestine and Syria, which came into account for export, in classical and late Antiquity. In Palestine these industries, silk manufacturing, tanneries and linen production, centred on four major cities in Palestine: Caesarea Maritima, Lydda/Diospolis, Neapolis/Nablus and Scythopolis (Beisan) (Mommsen and Dickson 1886: 137).

Also glass was produced in these cities. All these four industrial cities played an important part in the economy of Palestine and its foreign trade; as Chapters 3 to 6 show, other key cities such as Gaza and Ascalon (and a number of cities in the Naqab) played an important role in the wine export economy of Palestine during this period.

The particular association of dyeing industry with the Syria-Palestine coast is due to the large quantities of its native murex, from which purple dye was extracted. While the industry cantered in Tyre and Sidon, Caesarea, along with Lydda and Neapolis, is also mentioned by the *Expositio* as producers of various kinds of dye. The Caesarean Talmud preserves an account concerning wool being dyed the wrong colour.

At some stage prior to actual dyeing, textiles must be washed and bleached, since dye will not adhere to fibre improperly prepared. The fullers and washers were thus closely associated with weaving and dyeing industries. Special pools for the preparation process existed in Caesarea, and regulations were enforced to keep them sufficient removed from other buildings because of their stench and corrosive effects.

Talmudic references imply that silk manufacturing, another major industry of the Syrian coastal cities, played a role in the economy of Caesarea as well.

All these industries – dyeing, washing, and manufacturing of silk – were all interrelated is evident from the *Theodosesian Code*:

> We command hereafter the supplies of dyed silken stuff and of raw silk shall be delivered washed'.
>
> (Levine 1975: 53)

Purple clothes of good quality (*purpura bona*) were produced in Caesarea Maritima. *Expositio,* that fourth-century 'description of the earth', mentions a fourth Palestinian city (together with four Syria/Phenicia cities) involved in the textile industry and the export of fine linen; the Palestinian city of Scythopolis [and these cities] 'send out their linen into all the world' (Mommsen and Dickson 1886: 137).

All five ancient cities at the heart of the considerable Palestinian textile industry: dyeing workshops, linen manufacturing, silk trade and textile manufacturing industries, much of which was geared towards foreign export: Beisan, Caesarea Maritima, Lydda, Nablus and Saffuriyya acquired official *municipal* status of a *polis* (city) during the Roman period. Lydda (ancient Greek: *Λύδδα*) is a city fifteen kilometres southeast of the coastal city Jaffa. During the Greek, Roman and Byzantine periods, the city was a major centre for trade and industries. Around 200 CE, the city acquired a formal municipal status and was renamed *Diospolis* (Greek: *Διόσπολις*, 'city of Zeus'). Also, Palestinian tradition identified Lydda as the early fourth-century Christian martyrdom site of Saint George ('*Geṓrgios* of Lydda'; died in 303 CE) – known as al-Khadr according to local Palestinian traditions. Both the Orthodox Church of Sain George and the neighbouring Mosque of Khadr in the city located are believed to have housed his remains (Walter 1995: 295–326).

Because of the historic urban, commercial and industrial importance of Lydda during the Roman and Byzantine periods, the city served as the first capital of the 'province of Palestine' (*Jund Filastin*) under Islam from the 630s onwards. However, several decades later, Lydda was replaced by the new Arab city of al-Ramla as the administrative, commercial and financial capital of Palestine – a status that Ramla retained for over four centuries. Al-Ramla was built by the Arabs at the heart of the strategic and trade routes linking Damascus and medieval Cairo. But in effect the commercial, financial and industrial rise of major city in Palestine under Islam: al-Ramla, also signalled the relative decline of its neighbouring twin city: Lydda, until the revival of Lydda in the modern period.

Unlike the largely free market economy of the Roman period, the production of both Tyrian purple and silk textiles became tightly regulated during the Byzantine period, especially at the time of Emperor Justinian, and the industry was subsidized by the imperial court in Istanbul, which restricted their use for the colouring of imperial silk (Jacoby 1992: 452-500; 1997). Hence the concept of the 'royal purple' – the idea that because of its expensive value, the colour was to be worn only by royalty, although throughout much of Antiquity and the Middle Ages the colour was often restricted to social elites and privileges groups in society. Justinian did not live to see the expansion of this trade in silk and purple colour across the Mediterranean. Garments of silk and linen from the factories of Tyre and Berytus (Beirut), purple dye from Caesarea Maritima and Neapolis (Nablus) in Palestine and the strong Palestinian wine, wines of Gaza and Ascalon were soon to be traded across the Mediterranean. During this Byzantine period, trade in the Mediterranean was almost entirely in the hands of Syrian, Palestinian and Greek merchants. The scale and quality of the textile industries of Syria and Palestine meant that in Constantinople, Rome, Naples, Carthage, Marseilles and Bordeaux we find settlements of oriental merchants. Their ships conveyed to the West garments of silk and wrought linen from the factories of Tyre and Berytus, purple from Caesarea and Neapolis [Nablus], pistachios from Damascus, the strong wines of Gaza and Ascalon, papyrus from Egypt and fur from Cappadocia. There was a large demand for embroidered goods, especially for ecclesiastical use, cloths for altars, curtains for churches ... The Empire's trade with the East had always been mainly a trade in import. The East supplied the Mediterranean peoples with many products that they could not do without, while they had themselves less to offer that was greatly desired by the orientals. There had, from of old, been a certain market in China for glass, enamelled work, and fine stuffs from Syria [and Palestine], but whatever exports found their way thither or to India or Arabia were far from being a set-off by the supplies of silk, not to speak of spice, precious stones and other things that the East sent to the West. The balance of trade was therefore decidedly against the Empire, and there was a constant drain of gold to the East.

While China continued to export large quantities of silk to all countries of late Antiquity and the early medieval world, another international centre of silk production and silk trade arose in the eastern Mediterranean after the smuggling of silkworms from China into the Byzantine Empire in the sixth century CE and the Byzantines developed their own sericulture under the reign of Justinian I (527-565). This big volume of silk manufacturing of the Byzantine Empire, especially in the provinces of Syria and Palestine, was established after Christianity became the state religion, and with new fashions in clothing, and the use of the colour purple on silk textiles as the highest emblem of social status. Silk textiles increasingly became used as an emblem of status (Liu 1998: 73).

Byzantium's use of various shades of purple colour and weaving-embroidery technology served to designate an increasing complicated state control of the silk industry and increased bureaucratic and religious hierarchies. Also, crucially, in the sixth century the Byzantine state maintained a monopoly over the supply of silk and fixed the prices (Liu 1998: 74-6). Prominent Palestinian historian Procopius of Caesarea Maritima reports that Justinian fixed the highest sale price on silk at eight old pieces per pound (cited in Liu 1998: 74-6). Under the government tight control and monopoly, the manufactured silk was dyed with purple or embroidered with gold thread.

With the Islamic conquests of the Levant in the 630s the silk industry of Syria and Palestine continued to flourish and the great port cities of the Eastern Mediterranean, Alexandria, Gaza, Beirut and Antioch, were used to export locally manufactured textile and silk, including what became known in Europe as *Damask* – a patterned fabric of silk and linen and cotton, named after the Syrian city of Damascus – to the rest of the Mediterranean region and the Italian cities in Europe (Liu 1998: 77).

The *City of Man* versus the *City of God:* The impact of the new Christian ideals

In Antiquity all these products were highly lucrative luxury goods produced by the merchants of the city but bought primarily by the social elites of Palestine and the rich classes of the Mediterranean region; this international trade in luxury goods produced huge profits for the merchant classes of Palestine, but also deepened social inequalities between *urban rich* and the *urban poor*. This commerce without morality pursued by these wealthy merchant classes involved in these elite products of the Roman Empire would subsequently single out the merchants of Tyre and Babylon for criticism by early Christians in Palestine and the New Testament authors in the first century CE. In the early fifth century Saint Augustine of Hippo (in modern-day-Algeria), one of the most important founding father of the Christian church and a leading figure in the Christian revolution would harness these early Christian criticisms of the wealthy merchants and big business and unfair economic and wealth distribution in society to argue against the *city of man* and in favour of the ideals of *The City of God* (Augustine 2017). However, as we shall see in Chapter 6, the Christian church establishment in Palestine itself, after becoming a state religion in the country, would become big business and the largest land owner in the country in control of taxes and the highly lucrative wine-making industries and international wine export of Palestine in the fifth and sixth centuries. During this period Christianity would also preside over the greatest building programme and the economic and urban boom of the '*city of man*' in Palestine in late Antiquity. The challenge of the unequal and phenomenal wealth generated by global trade and local markets and the idea of *moral economy* combining commercial activity with ethical behaviour was instituted under Islam in the post of market inspector, *muhtasib*, who would ensure that correct weights and measures were used and maintain the quality of products sold in urban markets. But the role of the *muhtasib* institution was wide-ranging, from regulating the quality of products and corrects weights to enforcing market prices and collection of correct taxes, to emphasizing the common good and greater good of society.

Indigenous silk industry

Before the sixth century, the Palestine silk industry relied on raw silk imported from China. Indigenous silkworms for producing local would not be available until the sixth century CE after these silkworms were smuggled from China. Christian monks and Christian missionaries smuggled silkworms from China to Byzantine Palestine and Syria in the late fifth or sixth centuries, thus contributing the rise of the Palestinian *sericulture* and indigenous silk industry of the Middle Ages.

Islam developed extensive cotton, wool and silk industries in the Middle Ages and in the tenth and eleventh centuries the towns and cities of Syria and Palestine developed highly skilled specialisms in the cotton and silk industries with silk products being the most valuable and profitable of the textile industries. Four cities in the Levant: Damascus, Hims, Aleppo and Tyre in Syria, and four cities in Palestine: al-Ramla, Tiberias, 'Asqalan and Gaza became the most important centres for silk and textile production and textile export (Yusuf 1985: 127). The cultivation of the mulberry tree, which was essential for breeding silkworms, flourished in southern Palestine in the Middle Ages. In the tenth century Palestinian historian al-Maqdisi speaks of the silkworms of Asqalan (Ascalon) as renowned (Conder 2018: 136). Under Islam 'Asqalan became the most important centre for the Palestinian textile and linen industries in the Middle Ages and the city exported fine textiles and locally manufactured silk to Egypt and beyond.

As we shall see in Chapter 6, the monks and monasteries of Palestine also played a major part in the spectacular rise of the Palestinian *viticulture* and wine industries in fourth to seventh centuries CE. However, key industries in ancient and modern Palestine (*Gaza wine* and *Nablus soap* in particular) were capital intensive, whereas the silk industries of the Levant were labour-intensive industries. The silk industry of Palestine and the city of ʿAsqalan under Islam occupied an important place in the Palestinian economy in the Middle Ages, although Palestine did not rise to the scale of the textile levels of Syria and the high-quality of the silk industry of Syria under Islam. A highly successful cultivation of mulberry trees and silk manufacture in Syria and Lebanon contained to flourish into the modern period (Gilbar 1998: 281-92), while Palestine excelled in other industries such as soap production and orange growing in the modern era. Named after the Syrian capital Damascus, a large Syrian metropolis and a trading centre on the silk routes in the Middle Ages *Damask* became an international famous woven, reversible-patterned fabric. Yarns used to create *damasks* include silk, linen and cotton. *Damask* silk was widely exported to Europe and Asia and was also produced in China.

6

The Christian Revolution and Palestinian Wines on Western Tables

Monasteries, Urban Boom and the Golden Age of the Wine Industry of Byzantine Palestine (Fourth to Early Seventh Centuries)

For over three centuries, in the fourth to early seventh centuries, under the Byzantines the city of Gaza shot to international fame and became closely associated with some of the most spectacular social, economic, industrial and intellectual developments in Palestine and the eastern Mediterranean. These developments include:

1. The global rise of the Palestine wine industry and what became internationally branded as *Gaza wine*, evidently one of the best produced wines in the world in late Antiquity.
2. The international rise of Palestinian monasticism and what became known as the *Monastic School of Gaza*. Accompanying the Christian revolution, which saw the overthrow of the Roman Empire and the Christianization of the Byzantine state and Palestine, these developments included the rise of the Holy Land pilgrimage industry and emergence of the port city of Gaza (Maiumas Gaza) as the main port of entry into Palestine for European pilgrims on their way to the holy city of Jerusalem and other Christian holy sites in the ancient towns of Bethlem and Nazareth.
3. Like the earlier temples of Antiquity in previous centuries, the monasteries of Palestine under the Byzantines became economic powerhouses and manufacturing hubs, leading to the influx of pilgrims and the growth of local markets and the economic, urban and cultural development of surrounding areas.
4. The rise of the internationally famous classical *Rhetorical School of Gaza* transformed Gaza into a leading 'city of learning' and a self-governing community of citizens in Palestine; the rise of Gaza into a classical city of learning attracted students from far and wide and gave the city the name: 'Athens of Asia' (Masalha 2022).

5. The emergence of a distinctive *Mosaic School of Gaza*, with its wide ranging impact mosaic floors in churches across Palestine and in Transjordan.
6. Technological developments connected with the invention of the *Water clock of Gaza*, with its lasting technological impacts on clocks and time-keeping in the urban centres of Palestine and Syria under both the Byzantines and Muslim Arabs.
7. In addition to the historic silver standard and silver coins that were in common use in Palestine, an additional monetary and currency developments took place in Palestine and these developments were connected with the creation of the *Gold Standard of Gaza* and its impact on trade, across urban centres in Palestine.

The rise of the Palestinian wine industry in Antiquity: Monks, viticulture, building boom and urban transformation

If grapes were a major contributor to prosperity in ancient Palestine, the export-oriented wine industries of late Antiquity were a top earner for the country. Late Antiquity is widely perceived to be a 'Golden Age' in both the ancient history of Palestine and the history of the Palestine wine-making industries. With the rise of Christianity from its persecution and humble origins to the dominant state religion in Palestine, between the fourth and seventh centuries hundreds of new towns and villages were established in response to the pressure exerted by regional population growth. Swamps were drained and replaced by fertile fields, pools of fresh water dammed, and choice crops cultivated within an extensively terraced landscape (Kingsley and Decker 2015b: 44).

The rise of *modern capitalism* is often ascribed either to the *Protestant work ethic* thesis (Max Weber) or to pre-Reformation Catholic communities (Fernand Braudel), yet *Orthodox Palestine* of late Antiquity exhibited many of the features of the fusion of religious diligence with business and industrial enterprise. Byzantine Palestine fused Christianity with power, industrial manufacturing and commercial enterprise combined with urban transformation and building booms. During this period the urban transformation of Palestine (and Syria) was staggering. Under the Byzantines, the fields of geography, cartography and the urban environment were considered an essential knowledge for locating the cities of the Holy Land/Palestine. Not surprisingly in the fifth and sixth centuries among the best-known authors in these fields were the Palestinian historians, geographers and town planners who were natives of some of the wealthiest and most developed Palestinian cities of this period: Ascalon, Caesarea Maritima and Gaza. These include Julian of Ascalon (see below), Procopius of Caesarea Maritima (Masalha 2022) – with his work *Of the Buildings of Justinian* (*Περὶ Κτισμάτων*: Latin: *De Aedificiis*) (Procopius 1999) on Justinian's public works projects, with particular concern for the water supply, the building new aqueducts to transport clean water to the cities and the restoration of old buildings – and John of Gaza (*Ioannis Gazaios*), a renowned Palestinian scholar and teacher at the Rhetorical School of Gaza, a native of Gaza who lived in the second half of the fifth century and early sixth century, and the author of what is known as *Tabula Mundi* ('A painted map of the World' located in the public baths of Gaza), with a mixture of Christian and pagan elements, which depicts a cosmological mural in the winter baths of Gaza (Hanfmann 1939: 111–18).

The holy city of Jerusalem expanded massively during the Byzantine period and experienced three centuries of building activities between the fourth and sixth centuries, with women playing a major part in the transformation of the city into one of the most important cities of Christendom; the first stage began in the fourth century after the visit to Jerusalem of Constantine's mother, Helena, in 326; Helena contributed to the establishment in the fourth century of the most important monument in Jerusalem: the Church of the Holy Sepulchre; also in the fourth century the All-Palestine Church, the Church of Jerusalem, became one of the five autonomous international churches of Christianity (Masalha 2018). The second stage of Byzantine building expansion in Jerusalem was also associated with another leading woman – the Empress Eudocia, wife of Emperor Theodosius II. After separating from her husband in 443–44, Eudocia lived in Jerusalem until her death in 460. Among her many activities in the city, Eudocia repaired and enlarged the city walls and established a home for the aged and a church dedicated to Saint Stephen (5–*c*.34 CE) a deacon of the early Church of Jerusalem and the first martyr of Christianity (Ben-Dov 1977). The third stage of building expansion in the city is associated with Emperor Justinian in the sixth century.

> After Constantine decided to make Jerusalem the Holy City of Christendom, gifts and pilgrims followed. Gradually Jerusalem was transformed into a city of churches and monasteries, hospices and asylums for pilgrims—as depicted on the mid-6th century Madaba map.
>
> (Ben-Dov 1977)

> The Byzantine period was a prosperous one, and Jerusalem shared in this prosperity. Marked by intensive building activity, this period saw almost every inch of the city covered with construction of one kind or another.
>
> (Ben-Dov 1977)

The representation of this massive building programme in Jerusalem was one of the most spectacular buildings of urban Palestine on the Madaba Mosaic Map, the new Basilica of the 'Mother of God', or *Nea Church* (*Νέα Ἐκκλησία*) in Jerusalem, built by Justinian and consecrated on 20 November 542; a detailed account of the church and its construction comes from Procopius's *De Aedificiis*. The church – at the time, one of the largest churches in the Christian world – was linked to the Church of the Holy Sepulchre by the Cardo. The church, which can be seen on the Madaba Map, was severely damaged or destroyed during the Persian conquest of Jerusalem in 614. In *De Aedificiis*, Procopius of Caesarea wrote: 'It becomes … important to have a clear record as to what Justinian did, not only in Palestine but in other countries' (Procopius 1999; also Ben-Dov 1977).

Often 'classical civilization' is equated with monumental and enduring 'classical' urban structures, fine urban architecture and sophisticated urban public institutions and amenities, and the Madaba Floor Map shows that the cities of Palestine had some of the most impressive collections of 'classical' buildings and 'classical' architectural gems in the Mediterranean in the sixth century. In the debate about 'classical civilization' and the 'city' versus barbarism, often Western writers view the Arabo-Islamic conquest of the Byzantine-ruled Palestine and the Levant in the 630s as 'barbarian' invasion of the 'classical cities' of the Levant, while the same authors see the 'Persian civilization' of Antiquity far superior to Islamic civilization of the Middle Ages. But, when the Persians occupied Palestine two decades before the rise of Islam, they destroyed not only one of the greatest churches of Antiquity (the Nea Church in Jerusalem), but also one of the greatest libraries of Antiquity, the classical library of Caesarea Maritima (Masalha 2022) and much of the cultural and intellectual institutions of Gaza. In contrast, the Islamic peaceful occupation of Palestine in the 630s not only preserved the cities of Palestine intact, but began developing spectacular cultural, artistic and architectural civilization in the country which preserved and enhanced further the classical heritage of Palestine.

Other historians and cartographers of Byzantine Palestine followed various itineraries and travelogues with much geographical information, especially about urban Palestine and the Holy Land, since they were of practical use for the pilgrims and merchants (Manimanis et al. 2012: 23–40).

The Madaba Map, created towards the end of the life of Procopius of Caesarea Maritima, listed twenty-five cities with fully recognized municipalities in Palestine give us a good illustration of the building boom of urban Palestine during this period. The urban sophistication of the cities of Palestine under Christianity in late Antiquity can be seen in the phenomenal rise to fame of a large number of authors, intellectuals, poets, theologians, historians, architects and town planners and scientists (Masalha 2018, 2022) as well as international bankers and merchants, including wine merchants.

Urban planning in late Antiquity Palestine: Julian of Ascalon

The city of Ascalon, twenty kilometres to the north of Gaza – also a major wine-producing city during the Byzantine era – gave birth to several distinguished Palestinian merchants, intellectuals and scientists including Julian of Ascalon, a sixth century architect, author and town planner whose work was devoted to urban building laws, architectural designs and local civic regulations for the maintenance of public areas, and who wrote on *metrology*, the scientific study of units of measurements, with reference to technical, economic industrial metrology, with generally accepted measurement standards and architecture based on distinct systems of measurement. Julian's work on building laws, concerning public and private buildings, and as a guide between good neighbours, is of fundamental importance to the study of developed urban environment in Palestine and in the entire Near East in late Antiquity (Geiger 1992: 112: 31–43; Hakim 2001: 4–25; Isaac 2003: 437–60; Lieberman 1970–1971: 409; Masalha 2022; Robertson and Swanepoel 2015).

The treatise on the built environment, town planning and building regulations by Julian of Ascalon was designed for his native city of Ascalon and other Palestinian cities of the period. The treatise explored the climate, topography and traditions of building in Antiquity by ensuring minimum damage to existing structures and ensuring rights and responsibilities among various groups during a process of urban growth and change in Palestine (Hakim 2001: 4–25). In both Palestine and Syria, Besim Hakim, a scholar of Mediterranean and Islamic urbanism, comments on the contribution of agricultural industries to phenomenal economic growth and urbanism in Palestine and Syria in late Antiquity: from the fourth to six centuries building activities flourished in Palestine and Syria and economic growth was robust in the fifth century; economic growth was constant and rising between 270 and 550 (Hakim 2001: 4–5). In both Syria and Palestine, the export of wine and olive products produced economic wealth for landowners.

In the case of Ascalon and nearby Gaza, the export of wine was also a chief economic activity. Landowners lived in the cities and took part in social and political activities, and their presence was an important component of city life. According to A. H. M. Jones,

> The city [of Ascalon] was a social phenomenon, the result of the predilection of the wealthiest classes for the amenities of urban life.'
>
> In Ascalon, however, there was a tendency by the elites, notably the landowners, to move to newly built provincial estates nearby. In order to discourage the flight of the urban aristocracy, the local government authority enacted laws designed to maintain and enhance aesthetic beauty of the city, and for controlling change that could be detrimental.' ...
>
> Ascalon was well known for its fine buildings and urban order, and this reputation continued well into the seventh century. In A.D. 636, Ascalon's city father accepted in peace the hegemony of the Arab Muslims, and there is evidence that the Arabs fully admired the city's beauty and architecture ... Many of the buildings comprising housing stock were three or four stories high, as demonstrated by prescriptions for such buildings in Julian's treaties, and evidence from contemporary descriptions. I have calculated an estimated area of 57 hectares (140 acres) for the city within its walls, with a gross density of approximately 270 persons/hectare (107 persons/acre).
>
> (Hakim 2001: 4–25)

Furthermore archaeologists have uncovered a large number of impressive public buildings in Ascalon dating to the Greco-Roman-Byzantine periods and a multipurpose *forum* (*agora*; and marketplace) from the third century CE. A Christian Basilica, located just north of the forum, and dating to the same period, was also uncovered, together with many private villas, which show a wealthy and prosperous city.

Between the fourth and seventh centuries public buildings and Christian houses of worships and churches were erected by the thousands in the Levant, and labourers benefited from what can only be described as a building boom that included many new urban dwellings, bridges, and many urban bathhouses and porticos. The economic and industrial activities of the 'new religion' were not restricted to Holy Land pilgrimage, tourism, trade and building programmes, but also involved estate ownership and large-scale agricultural production (Kingsley and Decker 2015: 10–11). From the time of Emperor Justinian I (emperor from 527 to 565) onwards, the Christian church was a landowner on a vast scale. Also the ecclesiastical establishment, monasteries and *monk-merchants* in Palestine were a key 'motivator of trade and industry', 'we find monks in Palestine weaving baskets for their livelihood' (Kingsley and Decker 2015: 10).

However, the remarkable transformation of the Christian church establishment in Palestine within a century from an oppositional organization which denounced the wealthy merchants, big business and politics of *Earthly City* (often colloquially referred to as the *City of Man* in the work of Saint Augustine,[1] one of the most influential of the Church Fathers who was in favour of the ultimate triumph of the *heavenly/spiritual* '*City of God*' or the 'New Jerusalem') into becoming a big business and the largest land owner in the country and the main driver of the highly profitable wine-making industries of Palestine is astonishing:

> the pilgrims who came to visit the Holy Land, who often returned home with physical reminders splendid products of the *terra sancta*. Many travellers remained in the Holy Land ... such movement of people provided unprecedented marketing of Palestine's holy wines. While the impact of the pilgrim trade on the macro economy of Syria-Palestine still debated, we can comfortably admit one firm fact: ecclesiastical building was big business
>
> (Kingsley and Decker 2015: 10)

In Christianity, wine early on became a necessity for the celebration of mass. The first miracle of Jesus of Nazareth was the conversion of water into wine at Cana, in Roman Palestine, and wine figured prominently in the Last Supper. Crucially wine became a crucial element in the celebration of the Eucharist, which involves the transubstantiation at consecration the body and blood of Jesus. Thus, the vine, the 'mother of the grape' and the vineyard have also strong sacred Christian association (Shahid 1995: 141).

The vine is also used as symbol of Jesus of Nazareth based on his own statement, 'I am the true vine' (John 15:1). This New Testament narrative about the miracles of Jesus of Nazareth, and of 'wine and bread' were spiritualized and ritualized. Thus the history of the close relationship between Christianity and wine in Palestine and the relationship between monks, monasteries and wine-making and how monks cultivated and developed viticulture and the art of vine-growing and wine-making, improving both quality and yields, and then exporting wine of excellent quality (*yinum optimum*) across Europe in late Antiquity is extensively documented (Kimberling 2021).

But this long history of monks, monasteries and wine-making began in Palestine/the Holy Land (and in other countries such as Armenia) in Antiquity. The rise of the *monk-wine-grower and wine merchants* in Byzantine Palestine was also accompanies the complete transformation of the religious status of Palestine/the Holy Land under

Emperor Constantine I (307–337). The official acceptance of Christianity transformed urban life in Palestine and the country became the most hallowed spot on earth frequented by masses of travellers, pilgrims and adventurers: the *Holy Land* in which the momentous events in the life of Jesus of Nazareth had occurred. Therefore, the many holy places located in the urban centres of Palestine received the attention of the imperial court in Istanbul with the construction of magnificent churches and many monasteries across the countries (Walmsley 1996: 126). Urban expansion and prosperity peaked in Palestine in the fifth and six centuries and the country was characterized by a high level of building activity and the expansion of the existing civil infrastructure (Walmsley 1996: 126). The economy also expanded phenomenally due to agricultural and industrial advances and innovations, and the revival of regional trade and the influx of pilgrims and religious endowments. Most towns and cities outgrew their early Roman predecessors (Walmsley 1996: 126).

The monks, monasteries and the ecclesiastical leadership provided much of the stimuli and became key motivators of the trade and industry that transformed Palestine into a vibrant economical, industrial and agricultural country in the three-in-one provinces, *Paelestina Prima*, *Paelestina Secunda* and *Paelestina Tertia*, within the Byzantine Empire. This agricultural-industrial revolution and urban transformation of Palestine also gave rise to *Gaza wine* (Latin: *Vinum Gazetum*) in the fifth and sixth centuries CE. Gaza around 500 CE was a very prosperous city. The city was situated close to Egypt and on the nexus of a number of international trade routes. The climate was pleasant and *Gaza wine* became a global brand. The Gaza region was also an early major centre for monasticism in Palestine and monasteries were involved in the industrial expansion of the Palestine wine-making industries (Westberg 2017: 394–417).

The fame of Gaza wine as a top wine brand in Europe in late Antiquity was matched only by the high reputation of the *linen and textiles of* Beisan during the late Roman period and Byzantine period (Chapters 5 and 6) and the international fame of *Jaffa oranges* in the modern period (see Chapter 17). Although the traditional industries of Palestine produced other quality goods for export, from an international perspective, these three top brands: *Gaza wine*, the *linen of Scythopolis* and *Jaffa Orange* attracted international high praise and enhanced the reputation of Palestine international consciousness not only as a *holy land* but also as a manufacturing country and producer of top international brands.

Under Christianity, wine production and olive oil production in Palestine grew phenomenally during the Byzantine period and became pivotal to the Palestinian economy and a staggering numbers of wine presses and oil presses have been uncovered in Palestine from the Byzantine period (Kingsley and Decker. 2015b: 44–68). Between the fourth and seventh centuries under Christianity, the scale of the Palestinian wine industry at its height can be seen from the following examples:

1. Wine presses excavated in many sites in Palestine reveal complex installations designed for speedy processes, some of these gargantuan wine presses from the sixth century CE held as much as 60,000 litres of wine (Decker 2009: 5–7).

2. Excavations and the discovery in 2021 by Israeli archaeologists of a historical site in Byzantine Palestine – at *Tell Yubna* (archaeological mound of Yubna) – uncovered a mega wine factory, and perhaps the largest wine-making facility in the entire Byzantine world. This major archaeological discovery of a large making facility is closely related to the internationally famous Palestinian white wine of the Byzantine era, internationally known as 'Gaza Wine'. Excavations at *Tell Yubna* also uncovered a kiln, a type of furnace, used to turn objects made from clay into pottery, for the purpose of firing ceramics and pottery. Known in Byzantine Palestine as Jamnia (Greek: *Ἰαμνία Iamnía*) the town of Yubna (Hebrew: Yavne) was one of the major towns of the ancient Philistines. Situated fifteen kilometres north of the Mediterranean town of Azotos (Isdud; Ashdod) and seven kilometres east of the Mediterranean Sea, Yubna was at the heart of the wine-making industry of southern Palestine. And like many cities and towns in Byzantine Palestine that were involved in the wine-making industry during the Christian Byzantine era, with the expansion of the Palestine wine-making industry, Yubna expanded considerably to cover part of the plain and hills surrounding *Tell Yubna* (Fischer et al. 2008: 7–35. Kletter et al. 2010: 2, 13).
3. Many monasteries and ecclesiastical buildings in Palestine – in the Gaza region, the Galilee and Jerusalem areas – were equipped with wine presses and other agricultural installations and an army of monks guarded these wine presses and wine installations in Palestine. Wine presses attached to monasteries were built with mass production in mind: the [wine] vat [barrels] at Caparbaricha [the modern Palestinian village of Bani Na'im] in the Jerusalem region, for examples, held more than 6,800 litres (Kingsley and Decker 2015: 10–11).

One of the best-known monasteries of Byzantine Palestine, Mar Saba, east of Jerusalem, founded 483, which provided worldwide model of monastic life and became an international centre for cultural, intellectual and translation activities (Masalha 2022), was also involved in trade, including the wine trade, and this trade activity facilitated the symbiotic relations between monks and the local communities (Kingsley and Decker 2015: 11). Also, as we have already seen in Chapter 3, key contributors to the large Palestine wine-making industry in late Antiquity were the wine-making towns and cities of the semi-arid region of the Naqab in southern Palestine; for three centuries under Christianity, this southern region became a major producer of wine.

The expansion of the wine industries of Palestine and its consequent economic prosperity involved a large number of towns of the Naqab. This economic prosperity of the Naqab towns depended on the international reputation of, and revenues obtained from, Gaza wine; reinvestment of the wine revenues from this international trade in wine brought about urban renewal in the Nabab and the establishment of schools in the Christianized cities of Nessana and Elusa; the schools of these cities appointed official teachers of rhetoric (Colt 1962; Hidary 2017: 6; Hoyland 2015: 65–6; Magness 2003; Shahid 1984a: 275; 1989: 143) – teachers who were trained at the Rhetorical School of Gaza.

A complex urban society continued to flourish in the Naqab desert for at least four centuries (fourth–eighth centuries). This society was able to establish a sustainable routine of sophisticated agricultural infrastructure, which provided, among other things, the foundation for intensive viticulture and wine production; the Naqab wineries became among the largest producers of Gaza wine in Palestine.

Although bordering the arid deserts of Arabia, overall the Mediterranean coastal regions of Palestine are highly fertile. Both ancient Palestine and Syria were rich in wheat and olive oil and producers and exporters of several varieties of dates and other fruits and a source of aromatics and medical plants:

> Among these were storax [known in Palestine as *'Abhar*], galbanum [an aromatic gum resin] and BALSAM; the latter came from plantations in Palestine, at the southern extremity of Syria .... Ascalon in Palestine was noted as the origin of a species or variety of ONION; in late Roman and Byzantine times Ascalon and Gaza were major producers of wine.
>
> (Dalby 2003: 321)

The international Gaza wine *amphorae*

Despite its ancient Greek name an *amphora* (Greek: ἀμφορεύς, *amphoreús*; pl. *amphorae*) is a type of large ceramic vessel that was first developed during the Bronze Age, approximately 3500 BCE, by the ancient trading city-states of the Phoenician coast of the eastern Mediterranean. The *amphorae* of the Phoenicians, who were the archetypical mariner-merchants of the Mediterranean world in the late Bronze Age and Iron Age, were inherited by the Greek and Roman Empires of classical Antiquity. Commercial amphorae became highly popular in classical Antiquity throughout the Mediterranean and played a major part in the history of the Palestinian maritime trade, especially in the long-distance transport of Palestinian wine, olives and olive oil to markets overseas. Amphorae remained in use to ship *Gaza wine* and other Palestinian products throughout the Mediterranean and to Europe until the seventh century CE. Amphorae also supplied the ancient Greek and Roman Empires and early Byzantine Empire with a range of commodities and as the principal means for transporting and storing grapes, olives and olive oil, wine, grain, fish and other commodities (Adkins and Adkins 1994: 196; Twede 2002: 98–108).

Relatively cheap to produce, commercial amphorae, Gaza amphorae of late Antiquity included, were vessels with a pointed bottom and characteristic shape and size that fit tightly (and therefore safely) against each other in storage rooms and packages, tied together with rope and delivered by land or sea. Their shape and design were clearly the result of the same reasoning that we use to design commercial and transport packaging today, although their unusual physical shape, especially the pointed base, facilitated logistical and marketing advantages and handling, storage, maritime transport, and use in marketing methods that were very differently shaped from those that are used today (Twede 2002: 98–108). In classical Antiquity amphorae were used in vast numbers for the transport and storage of various products, both liquid and dry, but mostly for wine and olive oil. The necks of amphorae are narrow for pouring by a person holding it by the bottom and a handle. Most Amphorae were produced with a pointed base to allow upright storage by embedding in soft ground, such as sand. The base facilitated transport by ship, where the amphorae were packed upright or on their sides in as many as five staggered layers. Amphorae were cheap and plentiful and so, when empty, they were broken up at their destination. Amphorae are of great use to maritime archaeologists as they often indicate the age of a shipwreck and the geographic origin of the cargo. They are occasionally so well preserved that the original content is still present, Not surprisingly, studies of modern amphorae production and usages in Antiquity focused primarily on areas of the eastern Mediterranean (Peacock 1975: 30; Peacock and Williams 1986: 45; Piéri 2005). These studies enabled archaeologists and historians to track the routes of ancient trade networks. These studies also show the *Gaza amphorae* became one of the most popular amphorae, if not the most popular amphora in late Antiquity between the fourth and the seventh century CE throughout the Mediterranean world and this popularly accompanied the global rise of the Palestine wine (*Gaza wine*) and olive oil industries during the Byzantine period (Mayerson 1985: 75–80; 1992: 76–80; Reynolds 2005: 563-612; Vroom 2018: 648).

The largest Palestinian wine factory in the Byzantine world: The town of Yubna

In late Antiquity, Palestine produced a variety of high-quality wines; for instance, *Gaza Wine* and *Ascalon Wine* were distinct; *Gaza White Wine* was rich and heavy, while the Ascalan region produced a variety of *light wines*. The archaeological evidence shows that Ascalon explored its variety of light wines in the 'Gaza style jars' which were actually manufactured at numerus sites in southern Palestine, including at the coastal cities Azotus (Ashdod, Isdud) and Ascalon. Gaza jars have been found throughout the Mediterranean region and in Europe as far west as London, and in the east as far as the Crimea.

Moreover, throughout the Byzantine era, wines produced in other regions in southern Palestine, including the town of Yubna (Yavneh), became generally and internationally labelled as *Gaza Wine*. This particular brand of *Gaza White Wine* attracted most attention and was exported in large quantities to all Mediterranean countries and as far as Gaul, southern Germany, Spain and even England in what also became internationally known *Gaza amphorae*. This style of *amphora* also became famous throughout the Mediterranean world.

The distinct style of *Gaza amphorae* was the cylindrical, dull-brown amphora, a wine jar of 70–85 centimetres in height, produced for international wine export, with its distinctive Palestinian 'bag-shaped' form it became known as a 'classical' jar around the Mediterranean region. The enormous variety of styles of Palestinian amphorae excavated is a result of their production throughout Palestine and the evolving styles across several Roman and Byzantine centuries. This variety included: (1) the classic Palestinian 'cigar-shaped' amphora from the early second to third century CE, examples of which were wide-bodied and thick-walled, with a broad sagging base, while later in the fifth to the early seventh century CE the amphorae were longer and narrow-bodied, with corresponding smaller, more cone-shaped bases and steeper shoulders. All had a short vertical band rim. Early examples being tall and triangular, fourth-century examples were more slanted and shorter, fifth-century examples small and square, and those of the late sixth and seventh centuries more rounded. Loop handles were attached to the shoulders and there was a wide band of heavy ridging on the shoulder, where the handles are attached near the base. The same method was used to produce the other 'classic' Palestinian form, the 'bag-shaped'. This classic form was produced in coastal southern Palestine, the Gaza district and the region between Gaza and Asqalan (Mayerson 1985: 75–80; 1992: 76–80; Vroom 2018: 648). (2) A slender tapering cone-shaped amphora form covered by riling and ending with a small flat base. This form had a high neck and a simple flanged rim. Its handles were ridged and stretched from the rim to the shoulder; it was produced in northern Palestine. (3) A small vessel-shaped amphora with a pointed bottom and close-set riling covering the body. The amphora had a wide mouth with a small lip, small semi-circular handles and a small hollow point at the base (Archaeological Data Service 2005; Mayerson 1985: 75–80; 1992: 76–80; Vroom 2018: 648).

Furthermore from the third century to the early seventh century CE, many Egyptian wine merchants arrived in Maiumas Gaza and began importing Gaza wine into Egypt – wine consumed in large quantities by the upper classes of Egypt. *Gaza amphorae* have been excavated by modern archaeologists in Egypt, other parts of North Africa and even in south Arabia. Moreover in classical Antiquity (as discussed in Chapters 3 and 4), the spice and aromatics goods arrived in Gaza, on their way to the Mediterranean region in large quantities, in the golden age of the Palestine wine industries (late Antiquity). Gaza wine was exported to south Arabia in large quantities via the southern Palestinian city of Aelas (Aylah, Aqaba) and the Red Sea:

> *Amphorae material* from [Qana, in Hadramout in south Arabia] ... show very strong trade links between "Late Qana" and the regions of southern Palestine or south-west Jordan. The principal content of amphorae produced in the Aqaba kilns is unknown, but most likely it was wine or oil as it was assumed for the similar type of [Gaza] amphorae om Berenice and Carthage ... It is thought that amphorae from Gaza carried the famous white wine from the region. However, there is evidence that olive and sesame oil was carried in such vessels ....the storage jars with inner coating which probably carried wine as well as continued to arrive in Qana' from somewhere in Palestine ...
>
> The evidence of intensive trade contacts with Palestine. i.e. with the regions of Byzantine Empire, fits very well with the political situation of south Arabia at that time, when Christian Aksumite Kingdom [of Ethiopia] dominated the area [and its sea trade]'
>
> (Ray1996: 28)

Archaeologists have also discovered Gaza amphorae in the royal cemeteries in Egypt, and written documents show that a large number of Egyptian wine merchants resided in Maiumas Gaza during the Byzantine era – it is evident that the upper classes and social elites of Egypt drank a lot of Palestinian wine during this period (Ring et al. 1996: 287). Archaeological evidence of Gaza amphorae also show that wine from Gaza (and Ascalon) was also exported widely and globally from the mid-fourth century onward – a period that coincided with the official Christianization of the Roman Empire and globalization of Christianity – and particularly in the fifth and sixth centuries as indicated by references on papyri and numerous jars, manufactured in Palestine and discovered on sites as far as London, Trier, a city on the banks of the river Moselle (a tributary of the Rhine) in Germany and Germany's oldest city as well as in the Crimea (Ameling et al. 2014, Vol. III, 421).

The Cambridge Ancient History: Late Antiquity comments:

> For the fifth and sixth centuries, it is striking that Gaza wine amphorae appeared in quantity on eastern and even western sites [of the Mediterranean] at the very period that the small towns and villages of Gaza's desert hinterland, the Negev, reached their greatest size and displayed their most evident signs of prosperity. It is equally striking that the period of extensive and large-scale export of amphorae known prosaically as Late Roman … concedes with the period of the best evidence for settlement and prosperity in the nearby Syrian limestone massif.[2] Neither the Negev [in Palestine] not the limestone massif [of Syria] ever again sustained a large population, and yet in the late Roman period both were excessively settled by people who seem to have been well-off. Furthermore, in fifth- and sixth-century western texts Syrians are often referred to as traders, to the point that the very word 'Syrus' appears to have acquired the partial meaning of 'merchant': so that Sidonius Apollinaris,[3] describing a topsy turvy world in Ravenna in 486, could write 'the clergy lend money, while the Syrians sing Psalms', confident that his audience could understand the paradox.
>
> (Ward-Perkins 2008: 374)

Evidence for the extraordinary levels of prosperity in Byzantine Gaza and its hinterland we find in the following:

> Like elsewhere in Palestine in the late fifth and early sixth centuries Gaza and its hinterland enjoyed an extraordinary level of prosperity, stemming primarily from the city's reputation as a producer and exporter of top-quality wine. One contributing factor to Gaza's outstanding viticulture was monastic demographics. In ever-increasing numbers of monks of the Gaza region combined fierce missionary zeal with agricultural pursuits.
>
> Already in the middle of the fourth century the calendar of monastic visits kept by Hilarion [monastery] largely revolved around the dates of the vintage. A century later Peter the Iberian was asked to pray over the vineyards of the villages surrounding Gaza … Beyond the Gazan hinterland, the wine industry spread as far south as the Negev townlets. Wine produced in the Negev was shipped in Gazan

> ware all the way to Gaul, Italy, and Spain to appreciative palates such as those of Sidonius Apollinaris of Clermont, Gregory in Tours, Cassiodorus of Ravenna, and Isidore in Seville.
>
> (cited in Sivan 2008: 346; and 342–3)

We can also see the celebration of Gaza wine in Holy Land pilgrims' travelogues. (Canar et al. 2010).

Also the evidence from Gaza amphorae finds around the Mediterranean and from rural surveys show that the prosperity of Palestine and Syria in the fifth to sixth centuries was based in large measure on their maritime trade and their ability to sell their products overseas. Overseas demand seems to have put cash and spending power and reinvestment into this region (Ward-Perkins 2008: 374).

The peasants, landlords and potters and marble workers of Italy seem to have lost out in the fifth and sixth centuries to those peasants, industrial workers and wine merchants of Palestine and Syria (Ward-Perkins 2008: 374).

Generally Palestine and Syria were widely open to the Mediterranean network in Antiquity and became the barometer for maritime trade trends and foreign export to Europe:

> We can conclude that it was above all that the maritime strip of Palestine that was focused on expert; the inland wine producers of the sub-region; numerous around Jerusalem, as the distribution of presses shows, were producing for local customers, in the city network of the interior. They still did so on a large scale, but their exchange networks in that respect were restricted. Indeed, inland Palestine did not buy much Gaza wine either, although its restage and/or quality at least meant that a little went inland to Jerusalem, Pella, even Rusafa in northern Syria.
>
> ... This separation, between a coast focused on (large-scale, export-oriented production and) demitarian export and an inland with more localized distribution networks, has parallels elsewhere; Spain is one example, Anatolia another ... [However] inland areas of Syria and Palestine were more open to the Mediterranean than inland areas anywhere else. But the separation in wine and oil production would at least make one conclude that the end of the Mediterranean world-system would have different effects in different areas of the region.
>
> (Wickham 2005: 772)

Even in the eighth century, when the Palestinian wine industry hit a crisis – a crisis that badly affected the Palestinian 'wine cities' of the Naqab – the coastal cities of Palestine showed resilience: Caesarea Maritima and Apollonia (Arsuf) seemed to have maintained themselves as Mediterranean trading cities in the Umayyad period and even later (Wickham 2005: 774–6). The Palestinian port city of Acre in Abbasid Palestine was described by al-Baladhuri, a ninth-century Muslim historian and one of the eminent Middle Eastern historian of his age, as the first naval centre of the Arabs (Wickham 2005: 774–6). New Arab naval bases and shipyards were established in other port cities in Palestine (Nicolle 1996: 47).

The extraordinary industrial scale of the export-oriented Palestine wine industries during the Byzantine period was confirmed by recent archaeological discoveries. In 2021 Israeli archaeologists uncovered what may have been 'largest wine-making facility' in Byzantine world at *Tell Yubna*. Yubna was an important town in ancient and medieval Palestine located fifteen kilometres north of the coastal city of Azotos (Isdud; Ashdod) and forty-eight kilometres from the city of Gaza. Known in classical Antiquity as *Jamnia*, Yubna, like Gaza and Ascalon, was at the heart of the wine-making industry of the Byzantine era. The archaeological discoveries at Yubna show this was a vast industrial complex (with pottery kilns producing Gaza *amphorae*), situated by the Sorek stream, providing a reliable source of water for the people of the town and for wine industry – industry that was exporting 'Gaza wine' to Mediterranean countries and Europe. The complex, which employed about 300 people and included five large wine press ones – as well as small wine presses – in one place is 'unique'; each of the five large wine presses was about 225 square metres (2,422 square feet) in area. 'These large wine presses were thoroughly planned'; 'All were symmetrical, and their features are all the same. They were built as one complex down to the very last detail. It seems to show that they were all designed as part of one industrial move. There was one decision-maker who made the decision to build a complete wine estate with streets, storerooms [where the fermented wine would age in amphorae], winepresses and kilns to make the vessels.' The wine-making complex at *Tell Yubna* may have been capable of producing two million litres of wine a year – something which, if true, would be akin to wine production on a modern industrial scale (Schuster 2021).

Also between the fourth and seventh centuries European medical writers were highly complementary of the wine made in Palestine (Mayerson 1993: 169–73). Both the wines of Gaza and Ascalon were commended by Alexander Trallianus (Ἀλέξανδρος ὁ Τραλλιανός), (525–605 CE). 'Alexander the Physician' was one of the most eminent physicians in the Byzantine Empire (Kudlien 1970: 121; Langslow 2006: 10). Trallianus also though wine from Tyre was good for medical purpose, especially when it was old (Komar 2021: 109). In Gaul as well as in Italy, medical authors expressed their admiration for the wine of Ascalon, which he used as his principal component of the treatment of bacteria (Mayerson 1993: 169–73).

The international importance of both the rich *Gaza White Wine* – as well as the lighter variety from the vineyards of Ascalon nineteen kilometres further north – was exemplified by the use of Gaza wine by the Byzantine Emperor Justin II in Constantinople 566 at his table during his coronation festivities. On this occasion Justin's encomiast and wandering epic poet, Flavius Cresconius Corippus, a north African schoolteacher (*grammaticus*) from Carthage (modern Tunisia), then based in Constantinople, writes in his epic poem *In praise of the younger Justin* (*In laudem Iustini Augustiminoris*), of a descriptive list of Palestinian wines from Gaza and Ascalon served at the coronation banquet for the emperor and his wife:

> Meanwhile the happy emperor with his holy wife [Justin II and the empress Sophia] had begun to partake of the blessed joys of the imperial table, the royal banquet and the sweet gifts of Bacchus [the grape-harvest and wine-making], which wild Sarepta and Gaza had created, and which lovely Ascalon had given

her happy colonists ... The ancient gifts of the Palestinian Lyaeus [Bacchus[4]] were mingled in, white with the colour of snow and light with a bland taste.

(Corippus, *In Praise of Emperor Justin* in Cameron 1976; Shahid. 1995: 139-40)

The rise of the Palestinian wine industries during the Byzantine period was not confined to Gaza or its adjacent regions. In fact the entire region in southern Palestine provided modern historians and archaeologists with an opportunity to explore several themes in the history of Antique Palestine, from the fourth to the seventh centuries.

1. The rise of Christianity in Gaza and Palestine from the fourth century onwards (Masalha 2022; Sivan 2008: 329).
2. The equal rise to international fame and trade of the iconic Gaza wine.
3. The parallel prosperity of Palestinian monasteries and monasticism (Masalha 2022; Sivan 2008: 329).
4. The growth of Palestinian literature devoted to urban planning laws and the urban environment in Palestine in late Antiquity.
5. The intellectual flourishing of the rhetorical and philosophical school of Gaza (Masalha 2018, 2022).
6. The arts and crafts of Palestine – as seen in two case studies of technological developments, design and measurements: the sophisticated Gaza water clock, urban town planning and the scientific study of units and measures (*metrology*) of Julian of Ascalon. These scientific achievements, the water clocks of urban Palestine and *metrology*, with its application to economic and industrial metrology, were clear markers of the technological progress of urban Palestine in late Antiquity.

Liquors Palaestini and the Palestinian Dionysus: *Dionysus* as patron deity of the city of Beisan (Scythopolis)

The historical connection between the social pleasure wines offered, social interaction and hedonism are easy to understand. But the connection between wine and pagan (pre-Christian) religions is complex. The sanctification of wine by Jesus of Nazareth in Roman Palestine is universally known. But less well-known is the fact that *Dionysus* (Bachus), the Roman god of wine, was known in Roman sources as *Palestinian Dionysus*. Dionysus also served as patron god of the Palestinian city of Scythopolis, located thirty-five kilometres to the south-east of Nazareth.

The close connection between wine and religion was not invented by early Christians; in fact the historical roots of the Christian rituals of wine and bread are located in the pre-Christian traditions and rituals of nourishment, harvest, fertility and the agricultural societies of ancient Palestine and the Fertile Crescent. In fact, the growing and fermenting of grapes began as early 7000 BCE in the ancient Near East and Palestine. In 2013-14 a joint Israeli-US archaeological team excavating at the site of a middle Bronze Age Palestinian city-state at *Tell Kabri*, in upper western Galilee, uncovered a large Canaanite palace and the oldest and largest-known palatial wine cellar in the ancient Near East; at Tell Kabri's palace, a 3,700-year-old storeroom complex that held 2,000 litres of strong, sweet wine was uncovered.[5]

Wine has been an important part of the religious rituals and cultures of Near Eastern and Mediterranean civilizations for thousands of years. Some ancient Middle Eastern and Egyptian deities were associated with the idea of *nature god*, and of rural life, agriculture, harvest and 'grape-vine' (Black and Green 1992: 88; Flusser and Amorai-Stark 1993: 217–33; Pinch 2003).

Moreover modern wine-making owes much to the ancient Mediterranean world, where wine first achieved its place as a dietary staple. In Antiquity, the ability of vines to flourish over a wide range of conditions and the pleasure wine offered, made the manufacturing of wine central to religious functions and private social gatherings, a legacy bequeathed by the Roman and Byzantine worlds to Christian church and then passed on to medieval and modern Europe. Armenians, Palestinians, Syrians, Phoenicians, Greeks, Roman and Christian Byzantines added to a rich wine matrix that still influences tastes and expression today (Decker 2008: 63-92).

During the Roman period Palestinian wine, known as *liquors Palaestini*, was well-known around the Mediterranean region, and Publius Papinius Statius, a classical Roman poet of the first century CE, refers in the Silvae to *liquors Palaestini* (Palestinian wine) (Feldman 1996: 565; Zeiner 2005: 104), which was of fine quality and exported throughout the Mediterranean region. The fame of *liquors Palaestini* was partly derived from the application of south Arabian spices and local herbs and the Palestinian aromatic balsam to wine-making in Palestine and the Arab region as a whole, something which Statius called *liquors Arabes* ('Arab Wine') of Antiquity (Zeiner 2005: 104). Palestinian balsam, dates and a variety of fruits were also widely exported throughout the Roman Empire (Lapin 2001: 124). At the height of the Roman Empire the capital city Rome consumed as much as 75 million litres (the equivalent of 8 million cases) wine per year (Decker 2008: 63-92). The Christian Byzantine state imported vast quantities of Palestinian wine (Gaza wine) to its capital city, Constantinople, which had a population of 300,000 in the fourth century. It is easy to see why Italian, Palestinian, Syrian and Armenian viticulture flourished during the Roman Byzantine empires.

Like in other countries around the Mediterranean region, in Palestine the Byzantine clergy inherited many of the consumer habits and religious sites and spiritual and physical wealth as well the wine-making traditions of the Roman pagan past (Kingsley and Decker 2015: 9).

The Roman god of viticulture, grape-harvest and wine-making, Bacchus, was mentioned in the panegyric of Corippus, the Christian poet of the sixth century who flourished under Byzantine Emperors Justinian I and Justin II, was originally a member of the pantheon of Greek gods. Known as the 'deliverer from care', an epithet of Dionysus as the god of wine and pleasure who freed people from anxiety, Dionysus was often referred to in Roman sources as *Palestinian*. Bacchus/Dionysus was also the patron of the Palestinian city of Scythopolis, a key centre of the Palestine text tile industry during the Roman and Byzantine period and the capital of the province of *Palaestin Secunda* under the Byzantines (Shahid 1995: 139-40).

The cult of Bacchus in Roman Palestine – which was equivalent to cult of Dionysus in Hellenistic Palestine – and which looked over the harvest of grapes and the production of fermented grapes and wine – had the power to stimulate, liberate and inspire. This cult flourished for centuries in Roman Palestine and early Byzantine Palestine, But both the cults of Bacchus and Dionysus (like wine) had a dual contrasting nature: they can delight, liberate and inspire, but excessive use can also lead to religious ecstasy and inebriation, destruction and personal addiction to alcoholism, and great suffering and ruin. However, it would be wrong to view Bacchus/Dionysus as 'a god of drunkenness', as he was often stereotyped in Europe in the Middle Ages. The religion of Bacchus/Dionysus in Roman Palestine centred on the correct and moderate consumption of wine, something that the leaders of the Palestinian monastic schools sought to regulate to discourage excess and encourage moderate consumption by the monks and monasteries during the Byzantine era.

Bacchus, the 'god of wine and viticulture' and festivities, was widely worshipped throughout the country during the Roman period and became the patron saint of the Palestinian city of Scythopolis, the city being also a major centre for the Palestinian textile industries during this period (Chapter 5). After the Romans conquered Palestine they encouraged the spread of viticulture in effect making Palestine, with its grape varieties, a major wine-producing country.

Performance art and drama at festivals were also central to the religion of Bacchus (Dionysus) and these traditions were the initial driving force behind the development of theatres in the urban centres of Palestine; these theatres and amphitheatres were a major feature of the urban environment of Palestinian cities in Antiquities – amphitheatres for chariot races and gladiators for cheap mass entertainment under the Romans and high-quality urban theatres for the social elite cultures at which major classical Greek tragedies were preformed (Masalha 2022).

The cult of Bacchus (Dionysus) continued to be celebrated in Palestine under Christian Byzantine rule. According to sixth-century Byzantine Syrian (and Syriac) Chronicler John Malalas (Ioánnes Malalas), 'the Mysteries of Dionysus and Aphrodite ... is known as the Maiumas [Gaza] because it is celebrated in the month of May-Artemisios'. The port city of Gaza, known as *Maiumas Gaza* (Gaza 'harbour place'), was an early centre of the spread of Christianity, which may explain the treatment of its status by Constantine. As the city regained its independence from Gaza, for a certain period of time it had its own bishop, due to Gaza's relatively long resistance to introduction of Christianity. The first-known bishop of the city was a certain Zenon in the late fourth or early fifth century, mentioned by Sozomenos. Peter the Iberian was elected by the citizens in 452 as Bishop of Maiumas is identified with *al-Mina*, about four kilometres from the city of Gaza towards the sea.

However, other evidence show that Gaza in the sixth century (under the Christian Byzantines) celebrated the *Brumalia*, an ancient Roman pagan winter solstice festival that had originally honoured Dionysus/Bromios, god of Seeds and Wine, and Bacchus (in some cases) (Bitton-Ashkelony and Kofsky 2004: 14; Sivan 2008: 332). We know of it through a speech given on this occasion by the famous Christian rhetorician Choricius, head of the School of Gaza, whose comments were replete with classical references, in the fashion of the school of Gaza (Bitton-Ashkelony and Kofsky 2004: 14).

The *Brumalia* festivals included night-time feasting, drinking and merriment. They were associated not only with wine but also with crops of which seeds are sown in the ground before sprouting. Vine growers would sacrifice goats in honour of Bacchus – for the goat was seen as an enemy of the vine. Civic officials would bring offerings of first fruits (including wine, olive oil, grain, and honey) to the priests of Ceres. Although *Brumalia* was still celebrated as late as the sixth century, it was uncommon and celebrants began to be ostracized by the Christian church. However, some pagan practices did persist as November and December time customs (Bitton-Ashkelony and Kofsky 2004: 16).

Agricultural and technological developments: Impact on the wine and olive oil industries of Byzantine Palestine

Wine production in late Antiquity in Palestine and the Levant depended on the existence of large internal and overseas markets. The Palestine monasteries and estate owners and farmers reacted to the flourishing overseas markets by investing heavily in the land and vine cultivation. This included the adoption of hitherto underutilized and more efficient wine presses. Accompanying the use of the 'screw press' in wine production was the simultaneous spread of the *saqiya*, a highly effective mechanical water lifting device used mainly for irrigation, with *saqiya* wheels range in diameter from two to five metres. Archaeological evidence and the written sources show the widespread use of new technology of the *saqiya* within wine production; large-scale production and shipment of wine were also recorded. This new technology required significant capital outlay and a deep pool of technologically skilled craftsmen. The pace of the agricultural-technological developments in Palestine was partly driven by market conditions and the spread of technology in the countryside (Decker 2008: 65).

> The *saqiya* was a major component of the period of agrarian expansion that occurred in the fifth-sixth centuries … A complex machine with over several hundred different parts, these machines represent a capital investment. In the *saqiya*, an animal is connected to the drive shaft via harnessing. The drive shaft turns a wheel on the horizontal that meshes with the vertical gear, thus converting the horizontal treading of the driving animal to vertical power. The vertical weal then turns on its axis and to this axis is affixed a loop of rope, to the outside of which is attached a series of vessels, most often pointed clay jars. The entire machine is placed over a well or cistern, and as the animal circumnutates, the empty jars plunge into the water source, then rise to the other side and discharge on their way down once again. *Saqiyas* were not cheap. In Late Antiquity they are found most often on Egyptian estates belonging to wealthy landowners engaged in cash cropping … In early Byzantine Palestine numerous finds of early Byzantine *saqiya* jars point to the importance of the machine there, probably in connection with vineyard irrigation where the cash generated from increase viticultural output could justify the expense of the machine'.

The *saqiya* was a flexible and efficient irrigation device and enabled the irrigation of large amount of land (Decker 2006: 400–5).

The agrarian expansion not only in Palestine but the whole Levant in the fourth to sixth centuries underpinned the vibrant urban life in late Antiquity. A vast and growing archaeological corpus that hypotheses that the Levant as a whole witnessed rural settlement peaks accompanied by economic prosperity and urban growth. The economic and building boom period was from to the fifth into the seventh century. Technology played an important part in this economic boom and trade in wine and other agricultural commodities was part of this economic expansion in Palestine and Syria (Decker 2008: 66).

The large wine press devices, used on an industrial scale to extract juice from the crushes grapes during wine-making, also underwent significant developments. The pressure controlled by these large presses, especially with grapes, in order to avoid crushing the seeds and releasing a great deal of undesirable tannins into the wine, became more elaborate. In the middle Byzantine period most wine and oil presses employed 'screw technology' in one form or another. Together with the spread and application of the *saqiya*, the development of 'direct screw presses' and wine and oil press technology in Palestine was impressive (Decker 2006: 400–1). This technological and agricultural revolution of Byzantine Palestine also demolishes many myths about Palestinian farming, especially the often-repeated myth that Palestinian agricultural technology centres on the ploughing technology that has changed little since Antiquity and that the modern Palestinian peasant still used a primitive ancient ploughing and irrigation technology unchanged since time immemorial.

Time-keeping in Byzantine Palestine: The water clocks of urban Palestine

In late Antiquity Gaza was an intellectual, cultural, economic and industrial-technological urban centre. Internationally known for bustling marketplaces, lavish theatre and baths and repleaded churches, adorned with the locally produced mosaic industry, Gaza had all the amenities of a prosperous and dynamic urban centre in Antiquity. Local products such as wine, dried fruit and flax were exported from Gaza Miaumas to the rest of the Roman and Byzantine world (Hevelone-Harper 2005: 3).

Gaza was also at the centre of important technological developments that were taking place in urban Palestine at the time. One of the most important technological innovations of Byzantine Palestine was the *Water Clock of Gaza*. *Ekphrasis* was a rhetorical essay written to vividly describe an experience of a visual work of art in late Antiquity Palestine and became important evidence for art historians working on ancient Palestine. The features of this water clock were described in the *ekphrasis* of sixth century leading intellectual of Gaza, Procopius of Gaza, the head of the famous *Rhetorical School of Gaza*. According to his detailed description, an elaborate water clock stood in the centre of Gaza, forming the centre of a public clock in the city's marketplace, marking the hours both by a bell and by moving bronze figures, representing a sol-Helios twelve eagles (in ancient Greek mythology the god who personified the sun; also a guardian of oaths and the god of sight) appearing in each of the twelve doors in turn, and the twelve labours of Hercules (Stark 1852). The Gaza water clock contained a Gorgon whose eyes rolled at the end of each hour, and a double row of twelve doors from which Hercules emerged in each of his labours hours passed. The inauguration of this landmark urban feature for *measuring time* was celebrated by a speech delivered by Procopius of Gaza (*c*.500), whose Christian piety despite his lavish used of classical pagan imagery and metaphors[6] should not to be doubted (Romeny 2007: 173-90; Sivan 2008: 323; Talgamm 2004: 209-34; Westberg 2009: 187-211). Celebrating the wonder and craftsmanship of his native city Procopius wrote:

> The clock was contained in a small temple like building in the marketplace. A Meduza head[7] decorated the tympanum[8] of the façade. Beneath the cornice were two rows of doors-twelve plain doors for the hours of the night and twelve decorated double doors for the hours of the day. In front of the doors for the hours of the day stood a figure of the sun god which moved from left to right to mark the passing of time. On the level of the temple floor stood three figures of Hercules in decorative settings. At each hour of the day one of the doors of the hour opened and one [out of twelve] of the labours of Hercules[9] was displayed by figures. The eyes of Meduza moved. One of the figures of Hercules below struck the numbers of the hours, counting from one to six for the morning and again from one of six for the afternoon. The hours of the night were indicated by the opening of the appropriate doors, which were illuminated by lamps ... the monumental clock represents a combination of the water clock in its simplest forms with and the puppet theatre as described by Hero. This combination of mechanical effects remained popular throughout the history of the water clocks and one of the chief legacies of the older to the newer instrument was this combination of the clock and the mechanical puppet show.
>
> (Usher 2003: 189-90)

Other outstanding scholars of the Rhetorical/Philosophical School of Gaza celebrated the economic and cultural achievements of the city by composing speeches (*apologia memorum*), defending the stunningly popular forms of entertainment and cultures in the city (Sivan 2008: 346). Overall the intellectuals of the Rhetorical School of Gaza celebrated the arts and crafts of the city and the fusion of cultures and a mixed culture with classical fables and pagan narratives and new Christian ideas and the city wealth and cultural diversity (Masalha 2018; 2022).

Since Antiquity *time-keeping* was always a signal of social and technological progress and essential for trade and public life. The public celebration of the Water Clock at the centre of Byzantine Gaza chaired by Procopius of Gaza meant signal urban confidence and social and technological progress combined with a political message about the triumph of Christianity in Gaza, similar to the way the seven clock towers were built – with stones quarried in Palestine by the famous Palestine stone industry (see Chapter 11) and by local financial resources and local labour – in late Ottoman urban Palestine (in Jaffa, Acre, Haifa, Nablus, Safad, Nazareth, and Jerusalem) and was meant to a signal the arrival of progress and modernity and monumentalization by the Ottoman state. However, in contrast with the modern period, water clocks were unknown in Europe in the fifth and sixth centuries and technological knowledge and progress often flowed from the East to the West. Monumental water clocks, like the Gaza water clock, became part of the urban landscape of Palestine, Syria and Iraq in the golden age of Islam. The Byzantine water clocks of the urban public spaces in Palestine and Syria survived into the Umayyad era, influenced the mechanical evolution of the Islamic clocks and clocks in Damascus, such as *Bab al-Sa'a* (the Gate of the Clock) and *Bab al-Jarum* (Flood 2001: 129–30) and the water clock of Iraq under Islam. These urban water clocks not only became an important symbol of the technological progress of Byzantine Palestine, but they became a common feature in the major cities of classical Islam in the Middle Ages. The development of this water clock of Gaza during the Byzantine period was one of the most likely sources for the development of Islamic water clock technologies during the Abbasid period, a development which can be seen in the story of the brass water clock that the Baghdad-based Abbasid Caliph Harun al-Rashid (*d.* 809) gifted in 807 to Charlemagne, the Holy Roman Emperor (*d.* 814 CE) (Hodges 1983: 121). Apparently, the Abbasid delegation to visit Charlemagne that brought with them the water clock included three Palestinian Christians from Jerusalem: Thomas, the Patriarch of Jerusalem, Palestine, and two monks by the name of George and Felix.

Furthermore, the monumental water clock of Gaza found later echoes in the golden age of Islamic craftsmanship and practical mechanical engineering and the water clocks of Ismail al-Jazri (1136–1206), a Muslim polymath, mathematician and mechanical engineer in Iraq who is known for authoring *The Book of Knowledge of Ingenious Mechanical Devices* (*Kitab fi Ma'rifat al-hiyal al-Handasiya*; or *Book in Knowledge of Engineering Tricks*) in 1206, where he described fifty mechanical devices, along with instructions on how to construct them; al-Jazri was also credited for the invention of the *elephant clock*, whose general features echoed the water clock of Gaza. Constructing a variety of innovative monumental urban water clocks and citing Byzantine sources al-Jazri's innovative monumental clock known as the 'castle water clock' was a complex device with a façade of 12 feet (3.5 m) and included a display of an arch at the top of the figure contains a movable strip bearing the *twelve signs of the zodiac* (al-Jazri 1206; 1700/1799), reflecting at the time a geocentric model of the cosmos, but also constructing a model of time-keeping based on the observation of changes in the Sun and Moon and the development of a calendar to help advance agriculture and urban time-keeping.

Arabian gold, Byzantine *Gold Solidi* and Gaza gold standard: *Zygos ton Gazeon*

Historically, the pre-modern *silver standard* (and silver currency) was far more common than the pre-modern *gold standard* throughout the ancient Near East. For millennia throughout Antiquity the *silver standard* was the main basis of domestic and retail economies and regional trade and for the payment of urban wages and salaries and generally for the monetary systems of the ancient Near East. The *solidi gold standard* was an additional standard to the dominant silver standard; it was introduced by the Byzantines in late in Antiquity and was based on a fixed quality of the Byzantine solidi coins.

Gold and silver were mined in western Arabia before Islam and the gold of western Arabia and the Hijaz – regions being bordering the province of *Palaestina Tertia* – came under the influence of the Byzantine Empire (Shahid 1995: 47–8) were important in the production of Byzantine solidi gold coins in late Antiquity before the rise of Islam. With the rise of Islam in the seventh century, 'The Arabs, as heirs to the Sassanid Empire, effectively engrossed the greater part of the world's gold production' (Blanchard, Vol.1, 2001: 205).

Gold from the Horn of Africa, mined and exported by the Ethiopian Kingdom of Aksum, and western Arabian gold were important to the Emperor Constantine I, who had confiscated pagan temples in Palestine and the region and used their gold for minting his *gold solidus* coins (Achi 2023; Shahid 1995: 48). As we saw in Chapter 3, Gaza had traded with western and southern Arabia for centuries in classical Antiquity and was at the centre of the Nabataean Arab and trans-Arabian trade with the Mediterranean world in spices, aromatics, gold, silver and other precious metals throughout the Nabataean and Roman eras. In the context of the close connection of the western Arabia gold and Palestine at the height of Byzantine Gaza and its famous Rhetorical School of Gaza,

> Especially relevance and important is the explicit reference of Choricius of Gaza [Chair of the Rhetorical School of Gaza], unique in the Byzantine sources, to a Byzantine encounter with Arabian gold. In his *encomium* on Aratius, the *dux* [military governor] of Palestine in the 530s, Choricius mentions an operation that the *dux* conducted against the Saracens [Arabs] of northern Hijaz and his capture of their fortress, which the rhetorician describes [in a way that] ... there is no doubt that gold is involved.
>
> (Shahid 1995: 48)

Under the Byzantines western Arabian gold and the spectacular economic rise of the city of Gaza under the Byzantines, and the wealth produced by the international scale of the Palestine wine industry, and what became globally known as *Gaza wine*, all contributed to the monetary developments in Palestine. For nearly three centuries during the Byzantine era the global trade in Gaza wine was backed by an additional strong local Palestinian currency, currency known as the *Gaza Gold Standard*, a global currency that made the city of Gaza a regional financial centre in late Antiquity, with an impact on trade and payments in other cities in Palestine and beyond. Minted in Gaza, the international trade *Gaza Gold Standard* was based on Byzantine *gold solidi* or *nomisma* (currency) which became an additional standard of international trade and payments for hundreds of years in late Antiquity and the early Middle Ages. In late Antiquity and early Middle Ages minting local *gold solidi* and standard of the gold coinage gave the minting city a high degree of local monetary autonomy. The standard of the gold coinage of different cities and different countries under the Byzantines is also an important way of studying the monetary system of a country through the coins themselves (Achi 2023). In the case of Byzantine Gaza the powerful economy of the city and its pivotal role in the wine industry of Palestine as well as the global trade of Palestine during the Byzantine era can also be seen in the fact that the city possessed its own locally minted *gold standard for the solidi.* This *Gaza Gold Standard*: *zygos ton Gazeon*, or *Gazes,* also applied to trade and payments far beyond Palestine. The *Gaza Gold Standard* in Palestine was also distinct from the *Alexandrian Gold Standard* of neighbouring Egypt (Hendy 2008: 350). In late Antiquity the differing Gazan and Alexandrian standards allowed these cities exercise a great monetary and economic power over their respective countries:

> The imposition of a general discount upon the [*solidus gold*] coinage was not a phenomenon that was confined to Egypt [Alexandria] ... Nearby Gaza seems to have possessed its own [gold] standard, the *zygos ton Gazeon*, or *Gazes, payment in it being made.* These payments seem invariably to involve a number of numismatic minus an equal number of keratia.
>
> (Hendy 2008: 350)

The Palestinian wines of Gaza, Ascalon and the Naqab: Modern archaeology and *Gaza amphorae*

In the fifth and sixth centuries, Gaza wine rose to become a top international brand, attracting an unprecedented international fame and reputation and competing successfully with some of the best-known wines of Antiquity. Although becoming a common trade name on international markets, the label *Gaza Wine* encapsulated the entire wine-making industries of southern Palestine in Antiquity – this included the regions of Gaza and Ascalon as well as the wine-making industries of the Palestinian towns and cities of the Naqab: Oboda, Elusa, Sbeita, Kurnub and Nessana. Administratively southern Palestine was located in the Byzantine provinces of *Palaestina Prima* (*ἐπαρχία Πρώτη Παλαιστίνης*) and *Paelestina Tertia.* For several centuries the wine-making industry of southern Palestine was probably the most developed wine-making industry in the Mediterranean world.

Economically, socially and financially for millennia southern Palestine had been one of the integrated parts of Palestine. Geography, international trade routes, Christian monks and early Palestinian monasticism, which began in southern Palestine and the Gaza region and was influenced by *Egyptian desert monasticism*, all played a role in the phenomenal rise of Gaza wine in Byzantine Palestine. The earliest Palestinian wine-making monastery, dating to the early fourth century, is attributed to Saint Hilarion (291–371 CE), a native of the Gaza region and the father of Palestinian monasticism. Introducing monasticism into southern Palestine Saint Hilarion built the first monastery about seven kilometres south of the city of Gaza:

> Gaza around 500 [AD] was a prosperous city. Kilian Seitz, among others, speaks of its glücklichegeographische Lage' [fortunate geographic location]. The city was

> situated close to Egypt, on the nexus of a number of important trade routes and on the border of the desert, which allowed for trade with the Arab nomads. The climate was pleasant, and Gaza was famous for its wine production.
>
> Along with trade, intellectual life also thrived in Gaza during the late fifth and early sixth centuries, and the 'rhetorical school of Gaza' is the immediate context of Procopius. There is mention of a sophist from Gaza already in the late fourth century in an oration in Libanius. but the extant Gazan material dates from around 500, when rhetorical and philosophical activities seem to have peaked in the city. The 'rhetorical school of Gaza' … often used in a broad sense, encompassing various intellectuals, either active in the city or born there, such as Procopius, Aeneas, Zacharias, Choricius, Timotheus, John, and others …
>
> The region was also an early centre of monasticism.
>
> (Sono et al. 2019: 398)

Furthermore archaeologists throughout the Mediterranean counties have discovered pottery related to Gaza wine across the Mediterranean world of late Antiquity. The famous *Gaza amphorae* were exported from Maiumas Gaza, the port city of Gaza, then one of the most port in Byzantine Palestine. At the time Byzantine Palestine had busy ancient Palestinian ports, including Gaza, Ascalon, Caesarea Maritima, Jaffa, Apollonia (Arsuf), Dora (Tantura) and Ptolemais (Acre), which exported commercial cargoes to the rest of the Mediterranean region (Kingsley and Decker 2015a: 44). So why did the most famous wine in the world in late Antiquity become known in Europe as *Vinum Gazetum*?

One plausible answer advanced for this question is that in late Antiquity Gaza wine, becoming at the centre of Palestinian international export trade, was transformed into a top international brand because it was exported for several centuries primarily through the port of Gaza (*Maiumas Gaza*) – in the same way that the modern Palestinian *citrus industry* became internationally known in modern Europe and beyond from the second half of the nineteenth onwards as *Jaffa Orange*, because the oranges were exported from the Palestinian port city of Jaffa; i.e. both *Gaza Wine* and *Jaffa Orange* became top brand and common names *named after the port cities of export*. Also the appearance of a steady stream of *Gaza amphorae*, dated from the second quarter of the fourth century onwards, at archaeological sites across the Mediterranean region, confirmed the international fame of Gaza wine as a top Palestinian brand.

Historically grapes were central to the polyculture and horticulture of Palestine and as a major source of prosperity in the country since Antiquity. The hillsides and slopes (or *hawakeer*) of Palestine were preferred over flatter terrain (which were preserved for *basateens* in Palestine): vines growing on the slopes can receive a greater intensity of the sun's rays. Wine ('the daughter of grape') and *viticulture*, the cultivation and production of grapes, was intended for wine-making. But the Palestinian wine-making industries became central to the Palestinian economy and Palestinians international trade, which in turn contributed to the reinvestment of profit into the expanding urban environment in the country, during the Byzantine era (fourth to sixth centuries CE). The Palestinian international trade and export to the Mediterranean world and Europe, in Antiquity, the Middle Ages and modern times is often misunderstood, if we consider the common trade names conventionally assigned to two types of products: the ancient *Vinum Gazetum*, or Gaza wine, and *Jaffa Orange* in modern times. These titles often refer to seaports in Palestine from which such goods were shipped, rather than their actual places of manufacture. While focusing in this chapter on the international rise of Gaza wine, and what, in effect, became in major brand in late Antiquity, modern brand name products often associated with manicured products following mass manufacturing and industrialization; pre-modern industrial brand names are quite rare in pre-industrial societies, with predominantly rural and agricultural cultures. However, common name products did emerge in trading societies of Antiquity.

The wines produced in southern Palestine (which includes Gaza and its town city Ascalon regions and parts of the northern Naqab in late Antiquity in general) was referred to as 'Gazan', or *Vinum Gazetum* because it was exported through Maiumas Gaza, the port city of Gaza, in the same way Palestinian silk and textile products were exported in the Middle Ages through the port of Gaza and Palestinian citrus exported to Europe in the modern age became known as *Jaffa Orange* because it was exported through the port of Jaffa. Gazan wine was very highly considered abroad. Like Gaza wine – whose production was not confined to Gaza as it was produced throughout southern Palestine – 'Gauze' and the Palestine silkworm industry flourished in the Ascalon and Gaza regions.

Egypt as a key destination for Palestinian wine in Antiquity

A large number of ancient *Gaza wine amphorae* have been excavated in Egypt. The ancient Egyptians were heavily into wine and they packed their pyramids with amphorae of wine, and labelled these amphorae with a variety vintage and wine types. In late Antiquity Egypt was among the biggest importers of high-quality Palestinian vintage and a large community of Egyptian wine merchants resided in the port city of Gaza. A large number of Egyptian sources mention Gaza wine in Egyptian markets (Johnson and West 1949: 148; Mayerson 1985: 75–80, 1992: 76–80, Sperber 1976).

Evidently, for millennia, there was a steady trade between Egypt and Palestine and the Egyptians imported Palestinian products such as wine, olive oil, dates, wood and copper. Wine and olive oil originating in Syria and Anatolia also arrived in Egypt via the international trade routes of Palestine (Smith 2008: 40). Palestinians also imported some of the produce of Egypt; for instance, Egyptian dried fish was exported into Palaestine in bulk, and it was approved as *kosher* by the Jewish rabbis of the second to fourth centuries CE (Sperber 1976: 119–23). In fact, large quantities of Palestinian pottery from the Bronze Age were discovered in northern Egypt – and pots manufactured in Palestine and transported to Egypt were presumably used as containers of Gaza wine and olive oil (Grainger 2016: 27). Moreover, for several centuries in late Antiquity Egypt became a key destination for *Gaza White Wine*. The social elites of Egypt and the Mediterranean regions were key consumers of wine and olive oil which were sold as semi-luxury produce for their 'exotic' value (Kingsley and Decker 2015: 13).

Holy Land pilgrims and Palestinian monasteries: The hospitality industry under the Byzantines

The Christian pilgrimage and hospitality industry of Palestine, which expanded massively during the Byzantine era, and centred on major towns and cities in Palestine connected with the life of Jesus (Jerusalem, Bethlehem and Nazareth included), was a major source of income for many Palestinians both in Antiquity and the modern period; local Palestinians provided services to tens of thousands of international pilgrims and sold these pilgrims local produce of Palestine, including arts and crafts and Holy Land wine, which the pilgrims took with them back home.

These pilgrims contributed to the spread of the international fame of Gaza wine during the Byzantine era, particularly during the fifth and sixth centuries CE, when pilgrimage to the Holy Land reached its peak. This made the name of the city of Gaza, as well as the names of the towns and cities of Jerusalem, Bethlehem and Nazareth, synonymous with wines and emporia of the Holy Land pilgrimage. But the vineyards and grapes were grown mostly far in the hinterland of southern Palestine and crushed by large complex presses close to the vineyards (Mayerson 1992: 76–80). Besides the ordinary communities in the towns and villages of the Gaza district, who converted to Christianity in the fourth and early fifth centuries, Marcus the Deacon reports about local communities of hermits and monasteries emerging all around the Gaza region. These monasteries first sprung up in Palestine – many of which along the country's main pilgrimage routes – under the high influence of Saint Hilarion, and his namesake monastery. A native of the village of Thabatha, a few miles south of Gaza city, Saint Hilarion founded the populist *Gaza School of Monastism* and set up as a hermit about eleven kilometres from Maiumas Gaza. With thousands of followers, Saint Hilarion became a chief figure in the rise of Christian monasteries and proliferation of monastic communities first in the Gaza region and subsequently throughout Palestine – monasteries which played a major role in the rise of the Palestinian wine-making industries from the middle of the fourth century onwards (Marcus Miaconus 1913; Masalha 2022).

European pilgrims who arrived in Palestine by sea from the fourth century onwards came through the port cities of Maimuas Gaza and Ascalon. The port city of Ascalon itself became a pilgrimage centre in Palestine; this could also explain why in the fourth century the Bishop of Caesarea Maritima, Eusebius, described Ascalon as the most famous city in Palestine. Pilgrims arriving in Ascalon were supported by the local church and purchased locally sold *eucharistic wines* which, on their return, they took to their home churches in Europe, something which boosted demand for Holy Land wine in Europe (Mayerson 1985: 75–80). In the fourth century, Saint Jerome, in his Life of Hilarion, described monks cultivating wine near their monasteries in the Gaza region (Ameling et al. 2014, Vol. III: 421). By the time Saint Hilarion was sixty-three, his monastery was large and attracted many visitors and Holy Land pilgrims (Hirschfeld 2004: 67–9) and provided lodging and essential hospitality services (food and wine included) for travellers, pilgrims and rulers. The monastery functioned for more than four centuries, from 340 to the Umayyad period. Archaeological excavation of the site on the monastery revealed a large complex consisting of five extensive church buildings, bath and sanctuary rooms, high-quality geometric mosaics, and an expansive crypt of large cellars found underneath church buildings which served for storing important items, including sacred ones.[10] A proportion of the crypt may have also been used as a wine cellar.

Holy Land pilgrimage and the hospitality services industry became central to the successes of early Palestinian monasteries. The crypt of the monastery of Saint Hilarion included a mosaic pavement in the monastery. The monastery was also associated with Roman style thermal bath system or thermae (from Greek *θερμόςthermos*, 'hot'). These bath houses were built around three main bath chambers namely *frigidarium* (cold room), *tepidarium* (warm room), and *caldarium* (a hot room, with underfloor heating). The wide space of these halls ensured that the baths could adequately serve the Christian pilgrims and wine and olive merchants crossing the Holy Land from Egypt to Palestine and to Syria through the main Palestine travel route of *via maris* (Sadeq 2015: 47). Many of these hospitality services provided by the monasteries of Palestine for pilgrims, merchants and travellers during the Byzantine were gradually taken over by the great khans and caravanserais of Palestine during the subsequent Islamic period.

During the Roman and Byzantine periods the *thermae*-style bathhouses were a common feature of urban *Syria-Palaestina* and *Provincia Arabia* (Kowalewska 2021), which under the Byzantines was renamed *Palestinian Salutaris* and included the Naqab, part of Sinai and the former Nabataean capital city of Petra. Private baths were rare in Antiquity and confined to the super rich. By contrast, ancient communal Roman bath houses were a common feature of every city in Palestine (while big cities had several public baths); these baths played a major part in the ancient culture and urban social life in Palestine; ordinary people met, bathed, socialized and even read literature and poetry.

The Islamic conquest of the Gaza area in the 630s was swift and peaceful starting a new era in the history of the city and Palestine as a whole. Saint Hilarion Monastery itself, which interacted closely with its urban surrounding, and surrounded by agricultural and wine estates, survived into the Umayyad period, located the heart of the Umayyad state, saw some of the first Islamic urban bath houses (*hammams*) and these *hammam* evolved from their Roman/Byzantine prototypes in Palestine and Syria (Dow 1996). Interestingly the Arabic *hammam* is also derived from the word hot and is closely related to the term *thermae* (from Greek *θερμόςthermos*, 'hot'). Greek was the lingua franca of the Byzantine Empire in Palestine.

Today the 700 year old Mamluk bath house of Jerusalem, '*Hammam al-Ayn*', built around 1336, is considered part of the golden age of Islamic architecture in Palestine. It is one of two *hammams* of the period, located near the caravanserai *Khan Tankaz*, the other being the nearby al-Shifa Hammam, located in the central part of the Cotton Merchants' (*Qattanin*) market, which is one of the great jewels of historical urban landscape of Palestine – an urban landscape that had one of its zeniths in Byzantine Palestine. After years of restoration this Mamluk style Islamic *Hammam* was opened in 2019 offering steam baths and spa treatments; the spa is operated by the Palestinian al-Quds University and its Centre for Jerusalem Studies.

In the Byzantine era the entire region of Gaza became renowned for its distinctive agricultural and commercial and intellectual monastic traditions. Indeed, one of the most spectacular chapters in the history of late Antiquity Palestine was the monastic culture and monastic legacy of the Gaza region. An intellectual monastic community flourished in the region of Gaza, in the province of *Palaestina Prima*, from the fourth to the seventh century, creating a distinct Palestinian monastic tradition, shaped by the Christological intellectual battles of the fifth and sixth centuries, and producing a wealth of literary works that might be termed the *Monastic School of Gaza* (Bitton-Ashkelony and Kofsky 2006; Hevelone-Harper 2005: ix). Subsequently another world-famous monastic school emerged in the desert region east of Jerusalem: *the Monastic School of Mar Saba*, in a region which witnessed the proliferation of more than 100 monasteries and monastic communities (Masalha 2022).

By the end of the fourth century there were dozens of monasteries and monastic communities, with thousands of monks and nuns, in Palestine. The leaders of the early monasteries in the Gaza region advocated self-sufficient community and most of these monasteries were land-based and engaged in agriculture and viticulture. This type of agricultural monasticism in Palestine evolved radically from the original 'desert monasticism' of Egypt, with its 'detachment' from the world – to advocate social engagement with the key urban centres in the country (and hospitals and schools) and strive for economic and agricultural and industrial production; this new philosophy became central to the phenomenal growth of monasteries owning land, wine presses, pottery workshops, olive oil factories and mills and a large number of wine factories and vineyards – which planted hundreds of thousands of vine trees – of Palestine in the fifth to sixth centuries.

These socially active and economically productive monasteries of Palestine were a centre for knowledge preservation and knowledge production, from the preservation of the ancient technology of wine-making (of *Gaza Wine* and *Palaestini liquors*) to the copying and archiving of ancient manuscripts (Masalha 2022). The monitories of Palestine also cared for the holy sites and provided lodgings, food and wine for pilgrims and travellers and this influx of pilgrims who purchased wine and in time helped to spread the international reputation of wines of the Holy Land, and especially of Gaza wine as a top brand. In around 540 CE, the city of Gaza became important in the wider Christian world and served (together with Mainumas) as a main station for pilgrimages between the holy sites in Palestine and Saint Catherine's Monastery in the Sinai Peninsula (Sadeq 2015: 47).

Intellectually, the libraries of the monastic communities of Gaza were likely to include a major portion of the classics as well as 'best sellers' of the monastic literature of the age (Bitton-Ashkelony and Kofsky 2006: 183). Also the flourishing Palestinian port cities of Gaza, Ascalon and Caesarea Maritima, with their renowned scholars and libraries, intellectuals, architects and town planners rose spectacularly during the Byzantine period and became 'cities of learning' with an international reputation throughout the Mediterranean world (Masalha 2022). But perhaps the most important academic, intellectual and literary development in Byzantine Palestine was the rise of the city of Gaza as the premier *learning city* in Palestine in the fifth and sixth centuries.

Jennifer Hevelone-Harper, in *Disciples of the Desert: Monks, Laity, and Spiritual Authority in Sixth-Century Gaza* (2005), describes sixth-century Gaza as a major economic, intellectual and cultural centre not only for Palestine but for the whole eastern Mediterranean region:

> late antique Gaza was a commanding cultural and economic centre … the sixth-century city was known for its bustling market-places, its lavish theatre and baths, its resplendent churches adorned with mosaics and all the other amenities of a prosperous urban centre. With its port, Maiuma Gaza, a couple of miles away on the coast, Gaza served as a key commercial centre, not only for its own province, Palestine I [*Palaestina Prima*], but for the entire eastern Mediterranean. The city was a major destination for spices, silk and luxury goods coming overland by caravan from the East; these items would then be dispersed by sea to all parts of the western empire.
>
> (Hevelone-Harper 2005: 3)

Local products such as wine, dried fruit and flax were exported from Gaza to the rest of the Roman world, while wheat was imported from Egypt to feed the crowded city (Hevelone-Harper 2005: 3). Moreover, a road to the northeast led from Gaza to Jerusalem, the chief centre for Christian pilgrimage, only forty miles away. Visitors to the Holy Land from all over the Mediterranean world made sure to include a trip to Gaza in their itinerary to see, according to the biblical story, the 'ancient city of Samson and Delilah'. In addition to boasting local amenities, the mass pilgrimage and the economic prosperity of late antique Gaza nurtured remarkable intellectual and cultural developments in the city. The Rhetorical School of Gaza was famous throughout the Mediterranean world. Its distinguished orators and professors were instrumental in bringing about a revival of rhetoric and classical studies in the Mediterranean world in the sixth century (Hevelone-Harper 2005: 3).

Gaza city became a famous classical 'city of learning' in late Antiquity and was often referred to as the 'Athens of Asia', with a considerable number of intellectuals who contributed to the spectacular revival of classical literature in the fifth to sixth centuries and intellectual revolutions throughout the Mediterranean region. Commenting on the highly developed civic culture and institutions of Gaza, the city was often referred in European Latin sources of late Antiquity *civitas splendida deliciosa* – bright delightful city. In the fifth to sixth centuries the city was the home of a famous philosophical school of rhetoric in which Procopius of Gaza and Choricius of Gaza are the most celebrated scholars (Romeny 2007: 173–90; Talgamm 2004: 209–34; Westberg 2009: 187–211). Among the earliest in the world, the Egyptian and Palestinian monasteries, together with the port cities of Palestine and Egypt (including Gaza, Alexandria, Caesarea Maritima), played an important role in the rise and spread of Christianity in the eastern Mediterranean (Masalha 2022). The Christian Rhetorical School of Gaza, with its classicizing orientations, became one of the most important centres for the study of philosophy, rhetoric, drama and law in late Antiquity (Masalha 2022).

Highly developed classical Gaza in late Antiquity also combined academic excellence with Hellenistic traditions of education under both the Greeks and Romans, and always combined academic study with physical education (*gymnastics*), especially for males; athletics and sports were an essential component of a person's education. Elite and professional sports were evident in Gaza's schools and public arenas. The *Expositio Totius Mundi* details the varieties of sports and contests in which the most important Palestinian (and Syrian) cities distinguished themselves (Masalha 2022; Remiisen 2015: 110; Schurer 2014: 45).

The *Asceticon*: Palestinian monasteries and regulating wine consumption

The alcoholic content of wine varied from the ancient to the modern period and depended on the fermentation period and distillation methods. However, throughout the early centuries of Palestinian monasticism, and especially during the Byzantine period, local priests generally consumed wine as a common part of everyday life and used 'the fruit of the vine', as a gift from God that makes life enjoyable, and in one of their most important rituals – the *Eucharist* (Greek: *εὐχαριστία*; thanksgiving), also known as the Lord's Supper. But the implication of widely available cheap local wine and the direct involvement of the local monasteries in the production of vast qualities of wine did concern the leaders of the monastic communities who were concerned that over-indulgence would lead to drunkenness and sinfulness. At the same time the leaders of Palestinian monasticism also needed to separate the *new wine rites* derived from the stories of the New Testament from the *old deeply ingrained wine rituals* which were associated with the Palestine god of wine, Dionysus. Furthermore the wide availability of cheap wine in Palestine prompted some monasteries in Byzantine Palestine to regulate wine-drinking customs among clergy and develop regimes of moderate wine consumption by the monks, as seen in wine and *Asceticon* by Abba Isaiah of Gaza (died 11 August 491), who was a Christian ascetic and monastic writer known from the *Sayings of the Desert Fathers* and various Palestinian Monophysite sources (Harmless 2004: 265–67; Houdaille 2018).

The *Asceticon* ('ascetic discourses') was a collection of about thirty essays by Abba Isaiah of Gaza on a range of subjects including advice for novice monks, and it became especially popular among Palestinian monasticism and in the Eastern Orthodox monastic traditions. Essay No. 11 focused on the grain of mustard seed. And No. 12 focused on temperance in food and wine consumption (Harmless 2004: 265–67).

> Abba Isaiah [in his *Asceticon*] recommended eating one meal a day. The golden rule was to stop eating while still hungry. The quantity of wine recommended by Abba Isaiah was up to three glasses daily. The inclusion of wine in the regular ascetic diet seems to represent departure for the common practice and at the

> Pachomian monasteries [Pachomian of Ancient Egypt], Evagrius,[11] Basil,[12] and Shenoute[13] advised against the regular drinking of wine advised against the regular drinking of wine recommended it only for the sick. The *Rules of Rabbula*[14] strictly prohibited wine drinking, whereas the so-called *Canons Maruta*[15] permitted wine drinking only on holidays. In the Judean desert monasteries, however, wine seem to have been readily available and abstinence from wine regarded as a mark of extreme ascetism.
>
> (Bitton-Ashkelony and Kofsky 2006: 183-4)

The general emphasis was on moderation and avoiding extremes. Also, according to Barsanuphius of Palestine (Barsanuphius of Gaza) the difference between summer and winter should be taken into account prescribing the appropriate quantity of food and drink, although in terms of the actual quantity he was stricter than Abba Isiah, recommending one glass of wine a day (Bitton-Ashkelony and Kofsky 2006: 185).

Palestinian wines on European tables: Singing the praises of Gaza white wine

In Eastern Wines on Western Tables (2020), Paulina Komar describes the consumption of the wines of Gaza and Ascalon in ancient Italy as follows:

> According to Corippus, the 6th c. AD poet, the area of Palestine produced white, sweet and light wines, which became popular during late antiquity. A number of wine presses [excavated], as well as Christian sources, confirm the production of wine in Palestine, especially around Gaza. Thanks to Gregory of Tours, we know that Gazan wine was strong. This wine was also mentioned around 460 AD by Sidonius Apollinaris, together with Chian and Falernian, which were the best *crus* of the Hellenistic and early Roman period. This, as well as the fact that it was served on the funerary banquet of Justinian organised by Justin II, suggests that it was a high-quality drink. Alexander of Tralles provides us with information regarding wine from Ascalon. It was watery (υδα τ ωδης), when matured for a considerable time. Literary evidence also suggests that Gaza and Ascalon '*export an excellent wine all over Syria and Egypt*'.
>
> (Komar 2021: 109)

It seems that the majority of vineyards cultivated in Palestine during the Byzantine period were with foreign export in mind. The accolades given to Gaza wine for its fine quality by European writers, poets and senior clergy of the fifth and six centuries made it super-famous throughout the Byzantine world and in Europe. The boom in the Palestine wine industries and the export-oriented Palestinian wines under Christianity in late Antiquity was driven by seven major factors:

1. quality sells: the high-quality of the wines of Palestine in Antiquity;

2. the spectacularly 'good press' given to Gaza wine in Europe by authors, poets and senior church leaders;
3. the greater profits achieved for fine wine in Europe compared with the foreign export of olive oil or grain;
4. the large number of Palestinian monasteries, backed by the state, involved in the wine industries. The monasteries were not only the biggest land holder in the country, but also the only institutions in Palestine with sufficient resources to invest in the viticulture and the manufacturing and maintenance of large-scale production;
5. the agricultural-technological revolution that enabled great expansion of agriculture and land cultivation, especially the agro-industries of wine and olive oil in Byzantine Palestine;
6. traditionally in Europe of late Antiquity and the Middle Ages, while beer was the drink of ordinary people, the Christian wealthy social elites of late Europe drank wine and a great deal of this wine, dubbed as Gaza wine, was imported in the fourth to sixth centuries from the Holy Land;
7. the northern European barbarian invasion of Italy in 405 disrupted the Italian wine industry and indirectly contributed to the international rise of the Palestinian wine from the mid-fourth century and throughout the fifth and sixth century, this time within the context of the rise of the Christian Byzantine Empire:

> By then, upper-class tastes had changed to favour those wines then in fashion in the imperial court of Constantinople-primarily strong white wines from Gaza and Ascalon on the southern Palestinian coast. The arrival of Islam ended this golden age of Palestinian wines, and the West took centuries to recover its pre-eminent skills in wine-making.
>
> (Decker 2009: 5–7)

In time even the north European upper classes came to appreciate Palestinian wine, as shown when Gaza wine amphorae were uncovered in modern Germany.

As we have already seen, by the mid-fourth century, in *A Description of the World and Its Peoples* (*Expositio Totius Mundi et Gentium*), the wines of Gaza and Ascalon were highly celebrated and the author of the *Expositio* remarks: 'Ascalon and Gaza are distinguished cities full of commercial activity and having everything in abundance. They export an excellent wine all over Syria and Egypt' – and a large number of Egyptian wine merchants were residents in the port town of Maiumas Gaza. The *Expositio* states that the second most often quoted export product of Palestine is wine. However, the wines of Gaza and Ascalon were distinct; Gaza wine – white wine – was rich and heavy, while Ascalan produced a variety of light wines. However, archaeological evidence shows that high-quality *white wines* from the regions of Gaza and Palestine as a whole began to be exported widely to the whole Mediterranean world from the mid-fourth century onwards – a period that also coincided with the official Christianization of the Roman Empire and the rise of the Constantinople-based Byzantine Empire – and we have a sharp rise in the fifth and sixth centuries as indicated by references in papyri documents and numerous Gaza jars, manufactured in Palestine and discovered in sites as far as London, Trier, in Germany and the Crimea (Ameling et al. 2014, Vol. III: 421).

Moreover, the Palestinian wine export to Europe benefited from the fact that during late Antiquity much of international trade in the Mediterranean region was in the hands of Syrian, Palestinian and Greek merchants; many of these merchants resided in Constantinople, Rome, Naples, Carthage, Marseilles, Bordeaux and several Italian cities. Commenting on the extraordinary presence of large number of 'Oriental merchants' in the Mediterranean cities of Europe:

> we find settlements of oriental merchants. Their ships conveyed to the west garments of silk and wrought linen from the factories of Tyre and Berytus [Beirut], purple from Caesarea and Neapolis [Nablus], pistachios from Damascus, the strong wines of Gaza and Ascalon, papyrus from Egypt and fur from Cappadocia. There was a large demand for embordered stuffs, especially for ecclesiastical use, cloths for altars, curtains for churches ... The Empire trade with the East had always been mainly a trade in import. The East supplied the Mediterranean peoples with many products which they could not do without, while they had themselves less to offer that was greatly desired by the orientals. There had, from of old, been a certain market in China for glass, enamelled work, and fine stuffs from Syria [and Palestine], but whatever exports found their way thither or to India or Arabia were far from being a set-off to the supplies of silk, not to peak of spice, precious stones and other things which the East sent to the West. The balance of trade was, therefore decidedly against the Empire, and there was a constantly drain of gold to the East.
>
> (Bury 2019)

In Europe in late Antiquity, Gaza wine was held as the benchmark among the best wines in the world. Produced in the region of the city of Gaza as well as in nearby towns and cities in southern Palestine – and especially in the city of Elusa (al-Khalus) in the Naqab in which archaeologists have uncovered huge quantities of jars with grape seeds dating to the Byzantine period Gaza wine was exported out of Maiumas Gaza and found its way to many markets overseas from Spain in the west to the Crimea in the east (see Mayerson 1985: 75–80). It was exported as far as Gaul, a vast region of Western Europe that covered an area of 494,000 km and then encompassed present-day France, Belgium, Luxembourg and parts of Switzerland, the Netherlands, and Germany, in addition to northern Italy. Immensely popular among the social elites of Europe and the Byzantine world, as attested by multiple contemporary sources, Gaza wine became a world brand and Palestine's top export commodity – a phenomenon which we would see repeated in the case of the export of Jaffa Orange to Europe in the early twentieth century.

Sidonius Apollinaris (Gaius Sollius Modestus Apollinaris) (*c*.430–481/490 CE) was a poet, diplomat and bishop. Born in today's Lyon, 'the single most important surviving author from fifth century Gaul' praises Gaza wine and says:

> As for wines, I have none of Gaza, no Chian [from Chios] or Falernian, none sent by the vines of Sarepta for you to drink [...] Nevertheless, we beg you to come; Christ will provide all things, by whose grace this has been made a real homeland for me through your love.'
>
> (Sidonius Apollinaris 1936; Ameling et al. 2014, Vol. III: 421)

Cassiodorus (Magnus Aurelius Cassiodorus Senator) (*c*.485–*c*.585), commonly known as Cassiodorus, a Roman statesman, renowned scholar and educationist of Antiquity, who also founded a monastery Vivarium, where he spent the last years of his life (Chisholm 1911c: 459-60), is another western source, and he notes in the sixth century:

> The wine, to which Antiquity gave the name of praise, Palmatiana, must be selected not of a rough but sweet kind. Though last [in geographical position] among the wines of Bruttii it is by general accounted the best, equal to that of Gaza.
>
> (Ameling et al. 2014, Vol. III: 421)

In the sixth century Venantius (Venantius Honorius Clementianus Fortunatus *c*.530–*c*.600/609 CE) was a Latin poet and hymnographer in the Merovingian court and a bishop of the early church from Veneto praises Gaza wine (Ameling et al. 2014, Vol. III.42).

Gregory of Tours (538–594 CE), a Gallo-Roman historian and Bishop of Tours praises Gaza wine imported into France and singles it out for its strength: (Ameling et al. 2014, Vol. III: 421).

Gregory of Tours also tells a story about a dishonest subdeacon at Lyons who substituted vinegar for the precious Gaza wine offered at the Eucharist by a widow for the repose of her husband's soul (Nicholson 2018: 648).

Corippus (Flavius Cresconius Corippus), a late Roman epic poet of the sixth century, who flourished under Byzantine Emperors Justinian I and Justin II, says in references to Gaza wine: 'Meanwhile the happy emperor with his holy wine' (Ameling et al. 2014, Vol. III: 421).

In the seventh century, Isidor of Seville (*c*.560–636), a Spanish scholar and cleric who for three decades was Archbishop of Seville, writes: 'wine from Gaza refers to the region from where it is imported, for Gaza is a city of Palestine' (Ameling et al. 2014, Vol. III: 421).

Arab wine poetry before and throughout early Islam: The Ghassanid Christian Arabs of Palestine and Syria under the Byzantines and Umayyads

Wine poetry and the social etiquette of wine drinking are found in all periods of Arabic literature, though with fluctuating frequency, and variation between incidental references and pieces devoted wholly to wine; in some periods, the theme of wine dominated poetic production in the pre-Islamic period. In the pre-Islamic period famous Roman, Byzantine and Arab poets were singing in praise of 'Palestine wine'. Also from pre-Islamic poetry it is evident that Arab merchants sold wine to various regions of Arabia and Arab poets sang of wine (Kingsley and Decker 2015: 9). Wine was an important beverage for the Arabs of the Arabian Peninsula and the Levant before Islam. The grape was not native to Arabia and wine was largely exported into Arabia and Yemen from Palestine and Syria, then known as *Oriens* to the Byzantines, and Bilad al-Sham to the Arabs (Shahid 1995: 139).

Under the Byzantines the wines of Palestine and Syria were the most celebrated wines, and wine had a great deal of appeal to the Arabs of the *federate of Oriens*, especially the Christian Ghassanid Arabs of Palestine and Syria allied with the Byzantines and sources that refer to Ghassanid social life indicate that wine became a principal beverage. The paramountcy of *Oriens* as a wine-producing region is emphasized in both Byzantine poetry and in the pre-Islamic and early Islamic Arabic poetry (Shahid 1995: 139–40). Also the importance of Palestinian wine, especially the wine production associated with two cities Gaza and Ascalan, was also highlighted (Shahid 1995: 139–40). As we have already seen, the Roman 'god of wine and viticulture', Bacchus was referred to as a *Palestinian deity* and the patron of the Palestinian city of Beisan, which became the capital of the province of *Palaestina Secunda* under the Byzantines. The Arabic sources on the Ghassanid Arabs provide a few additional names to that of Bilad al-Sham that were famous for their wine production (Shahid 1995: 139–40).

The capital city of Constantinople itself, with its imperial banquets, was another important influence in promoting wine drinking among the Ghassanid Arabs of Palestine and Syria. Through their long tenure as *federate* allied with the Byzantines, the Ghassanid Arabs assimilated much of the Byzantine way of life. Palestinian wine was an important component of the imperial banquet, which the kings of Ghassan as *patricci* attended when they visited Constantinople. Byzantine connoisseurship of wine was known among the Arabs and was recorded in their own sources on wine. Following Jesus's first miracle, the Christianization of the Byzantine Empire in the fourth century gave a new impetus to the importance of wine in the cosiness of the newly Christianized Arab *federate*, and bread and wine came to be spiritualized and sanctified among the Christian Arabs (Shahid 1995: 140).

Furthermore the pre-Islamic Arabs themselves contributed to the refinement of the distillation of the ancient wine industry of the Near East:

> The Arab method—the custom of abstinence had not yet been adopted by Islam—spread to Europe, and distillation of wine to produce spirits commenced on the Continent in about A.D. 1100. The venue was the medical school at Salerno, Italy,

> an important center for the transfer of medical and chemical theory and methods from Asia Minor to the West. Joining the traditional alcoholic drinks of beer and wine, which had low alcohol concentration and positive nutritional benefit, were beverages with sufficient alcohol levels to cause the widespread problems still with us today. The era of distilled spirits had begun.

Wine is important in the *Diwan* of Hassan ibn Thabit, a Christian Arab who later converted to Islam, and who is the principal Arab poet who frequented the court of the Ghassanid Arabs in Palestine and Bilad al-Sham, and was in effect their poet laurate and he may have composed poems devoted exclusively to wine (Bacchic poetry) (Shahid 1995: 141).

Hassan ibn Thabit later became the virtual poet laureate of the Prophet Muhammad, and the later Muslim tradition was more interested preserving his poems on Islam and the Prophet.

However in his pre-Islamic life wine meant much to Hassan ibn Thabit; it released his inhibitions and fired his poetic imagination and his wine lyrics give us an intimate glimpse into the social and cultural life of the Ghassanid Arabs in Palestine. Hassan's verse reveals a wide range of references to the varieties of wine and its consumption among the Arabs and about wine in Byzantine icon arts, vats and casks, vineyards; the tavern; the *saqi*, the server of wine; the praise of wine (Shahid 1995: 142).

Another famous piece of Arab wine poetry is by the Arab king and poet Imru' al-Qais, the king of the Ghassanid kingdom of northern Arabia and southern Palestine during the Byzantine. Imru' al-Qais is considered the father of pre-Islamic Arab poetry and whose long poem, 'Let us stop and weep', was one of the seven long *Mu'allaqat* poems, hung in the Ka'aba in Mecca, prized as the most sophisticated poetic production in the history of Arabic letters. Another source of friction with his father, the king of Kinda tribe, was Imru 'al-Qais's excessive dedication to wine drinking parties and his scandalous pursuit of women. In his exile Imru' al-Qais wandered with his group of rebellious friends from oasis to oasis, stopping to drink wine, and recite poetry and enjoy the performance of the singing-girls. His last journey was to Constantinople to seek support from Emperor Justinian I.

By the seventh century the gradual sophistication by which economic sophistication had moved southwards and then eastward was complete. In around 700 CE only the provinces of the Arab-held Near East had an economy similar in its complexity and sophistication to that of the Roman and Byzantine periods (Ward-Perkins 2008: 360).

Furthermore Arab wine poetry continued throughout early Islam, especially during the Damascus-based Umayyad state. Archaeological discoveries show that the extensive wine and olive industries of Byzantine Palestine, which produced a wide range of Palestinian amphorae styles, including *Gaza amphorae*, continued into early Islam and Umayyad Palestine. For several centuries these Gaza amphorae were used to transport and export the famous Gaza as well as dried fruits. Other commodities possibly traded in the same *Gaza amphorae* included pickled fish and honey (Sperber 1976: 113–47).

Despite the discouragement wine drinking during the Abbasid period, Arab wine poetry and the social etiquette of wine drinking continued to flourish at the height of classical Islam. Abu Nuwas (757–814) was the most famous and infamous poet who composed in extravagant Arabic style during the Abbasid era and attended the court in Baghdad of one of the greatest Arab caliphs of Islam: Harun al-Rashid. His most famous, most loved poems were his wine poems, known as *khamriyyat*, that influenced many Arab and Muslim poets to come including Obeyd Zakani and the great Hafiz and other Sufi Muslim poets (Smith 2010).

However, the social response to Abu Nuwas *khamriyyat* poetry encapsulated the ambivalence of the society of his time towards open wine drinking and public pleasure: predictably for most of that Abbasid period, major parts of his openly and publicly pleasure-seeking poetry, with its engaging wine-server: *saqi*, with its subversive message, religiously and socially, were censored by state and mosque (Caswell 2015).

Moreover, the urban sophistication of Umayyad and Abbasid Palestine inherited many of the cultural, social, administrative, architectural and artistic traditions and material culture of urban Byzantine Palestine. For instance, around the city of Jerusalem fine Palestinian Byzantine ware not only continued into the eighth and ninth centuries under Islam but the luxurious glazed ceramics of Palestine achieved more sophistication and exquisiteness in Abbasid Palestine (Wickham 2005: 772). Also, archaeological evidence indicates that Gaza wine continued to be produced in large quantities during the Islamic Umayyad period in Palestine, despite the official ban on wine in Islam – but wine-making declined during the Abbasid period. Hassan ibn Thabit was a great spiritual ancestor of the great Umayyad wine poet al-Akhtal and, like Hassan, al-Akhtal was Christian and inspired by the wines and vineyards of Palestine and Syria (Shahid 1995: 142).

Under stricter interpretation of Islam, wine was associated with intoxication and was officially banned and many of the large wine presses in Palestine were converted into oil presses during the Abbasid period. Islam effectively separated the viticulture of Palestine, which continued under Islam to be a major source of prosperity in Palestine, from wine-making and wine production, which became marginal to the economy of Palestine even after its revival by some Palestinian monasteries in the modern period.

In modern time attempts to revive the ancient wine-making production by the monasteries of Palestine began during the late Ottoman period. Latrun monastery, located near the Jerusalem–Jaffa Road and close to the historic Palestinian village of Emmaus, a site mentioned in the New Testament, was built in 1890 by the French order of the Trapists, who embraced the monastic tradition of silence, set about to cultivate the land and producing wine. Today the monastery sells a range of the monks' produce, including a range of French-inspired wine (Merlot, Pinot noir, Cabernet sauvignon, Chardonnay and Semillon), as well as olive oil and olive oil soaps – the latter being a tradition the monks learned from the Palestine soap industry of Nablus.

Another wine-producing monastery in modern Palestine is Cremisan Monastery. Just five kilometres from Bethlehem, and located along the Cremisan Valley, the Cremisan Monastery belongs to the Salesian priests who came from Italy at the end of the nineteenth century. They bought the land, and in 1882, the monastery was built in the middle of the beautiful landscape. The monastery contains one of the few wineries in Palestine that specializes in producing various types of red and white wine, and only local Palestinian grapes are used in the process.

7

A Tale of Two Cities

Seamen, Merchants and Clergymen and the Port City of *Maiumas Gaza*

In Antiquity the merchant communities of several powerful Palestinian Mediterranean cities developed *port cities* – effectively autonomous port cities, or 'cities within cities'; they were called *Maiumas Gaza, Maiumas Ascalon and Maiumas Asdod (Isdud).* The most famous of the three *Maiumas* was Maiumus Gaza, which became an autonomous city during the early Byzantine period and remained as a separate city from Gaza for nearly four centuries. Even in the tenth century under Islam, Palestinian historian al-Maqdisi mentioned Maiumas as a separate city in Palestine, together with the other key Palestinian cities, governed from the capital city of *Jund Filastin,* al-Ramla (cited in Wa'ari 2023, Vol. 1: 26).

The *maiumas* (port cities) of Gaza and Ascalon, in particular, would grow into perhaps the most important trading posts in ancient Palestine and the whole Levant. Gaza, in particular, strategically linking three continents (Asia and Africa and Europe) was at the centre of the Trans-Arabian/Indian spice trade to Europe. The Trans-Arabian spice trade was placed on at the cross-road of three international trading axes: (1) a north-south axis from Syria to Egypt; (2) an east-west axis connecting the south Arabian Peninsula to the Mediterranean region; (3); a north-south axis linking Gaza with the port city of Aelas, or Arabic: Aylah (modern Aqaba) and the Indian trade via the Red Sea (Terpstra 2019: 170).

In Antiquity, Gaza harbour was the principal port on the Mediterranean serving the Nabataean *incense trade* arriving on the backs of camels from southern Arabia through Petra and for many centuries Gaza port had been central to the long-distance spice trade route from India and Indonesia to be dispatched to the European markets. Its port and its geographic location gave the city of Gaza unrivalled economic, social and commercial prosperity, being at the centre of the traditional King's Highway from Egypt, with routes running through Naqab and Transjordan – a highway that confirmed its status as a major port city. Its port was not only the gateway to the towns and villages of southern Palestine but also for merchandise arriving from southern Arabia and India to the Mediterranean region (Hirschfeld 2004: 63).

The port city of Gaza, Maiumas Gaza, expanded phenomenally during the Roman and Byzantine Empires under the impact of global trade passing through Palestine during the *Pax Romana* of the Roman Empire and the subsequent period under Christian Palestine, which gave rise to Gaza wine and global export of this wine in the fifth and six centuries via the port city of Gaza. The Roman and Byzantine ages brought about six centuries of continuing peace and unprecedented economic prosperity to the city of Gaza and the port city of Maiumas. The twin cities, which depended on each other, became large flourishing urban centres in Palestine, both served by two busy harbour towns, and the locus of east-west international trade and north-south commerce from Syria to Egypt. The high levels of urbanization not only in Gaza and Maimuas Gaza but also in the whole Gaza region under the Byzantines can be seen in the series of other Christian urban centres associated with the city of Gaza, which were identified along the *Via Maris* highway leading from Gaza to Egypt (Sadeq 2015: 47–54).

The extent of the development of the city of Gaza during this period was depicted in the Madaba Map of the mid-sixth century, showing it as the second largest city in Palestine after Jerusalem; a wealthy and prosperous *walled city*. Many (if not all) of the twenty-five cities of ancient Palestine were also walled cities. Eleutheropolis (Beit Jibrin), for instance, was also shown as a walled city with three towers; a curving street with a colonnade in the central part and a large Christian Basilica. A major city in Byzantine Palestine, Eleutheropolis, in the fourth century CE had a Christian bishop with the largest territory in the Byzantine province of *Palaestina Prima* under his jurisdiction.

The Byzantine city of Gaza was characterized by high levels of urban planning and cultural and technological developments; the agri-industrial and technological development of its hinterland was connected with new irrigation technology and with the wine and olive oil industries of its surrounding regions. The urban landscape of Gaza is depicted on the Madaba Map as a carefully planned space: the city is laid out on an orthogonal grid street plan, with seven gates, a theatre in the south-eastern quarter and a colonnaded cardo (a north-south street) intersecting with the decumanus (an east-west-oriented road in a Roman city) at a rectangular Roman-style *forum*, a public space and the centre of day-to-day life in the city. The colonnaded streets intersected in the centre of the city. Each street is lined with *stoas* – covered walkways or porticos lining the side of the building; they created a safe, enveloping, protective atmosphere – represented by white columns supporting red roofs. The streets apparently lead to the city gates. The streets were running north-south and east-west crossing the centre of the city. Gaza also had a big theatre, whose front was lined with pillars, represented on the Madaba Map by a massive semi-circular structure in the south-eastern corner of the city, i.e. in the south-eastern part of the present al-Zeitun quarter of the old city of Gaza. In the same street leading to the theatre the Madaba Map depicts a large central *forum* (*agora* combined with a marketplace), which for centuries was the centre of day-to-day life in the city: this was also the site of festivals and triumphal processions, public speeches, elections and civic life.

While each of the major (inland located) coastal walled cities in ancient Palestine were served by one of the fourteen ports on the Mediterranean shore, the (inland) city of Gaza was served by two ports (and port towns) in Antiquity: *Maiumas Gaza* and *Anthedon*. The volume of the international maritime commerce of Gaza city in Antiquity can be seen in the fact the city was served by a second Mediterranean harbour (and port town), known in Greek as Anthedon (Ἀνθηδών, 'Flower City'), located near modern Beit Lahiya. Anthedon had a mixture of pagan temples and *agora* (the combination of market and public space) and, like *Maiumas Gaza*, the lives of its inhabitants were dominated by fishing, shipbuilding and seafaring and maritime commerce. But the town of *Anthedon* had a small harbour (Safrain 2003) which perhaps could not compete with the bigger harbour of Maiumas *Gaza*. However, what made *Maiumas Gaza* far more important (and internationally famous) was both the large scale of its maritime commercial activities and its close links with the rise of Christianity in the Gaza region and Palestine as a whole and the fact that for centuries under the Byzantine Empire and Islam *Maiumas Gaza* was an important centre for Christian bishops and intellectuals (Masalha 2022).

Much of the Palestinian works on the *Mountain* and *Sea* focus on the centrality of religion in the culture of the cities of mountainous region of Palestine, while the more relaxed and hedonistic culture traditions centre on the Mediterranean coastal and port cities of Palestine (see, for instance, Salim 2008). However, in the ancient history of Palestine the term *maiumas*, or *naiuma*, meant 'a place on the sea' or a 'harbour place', does not appear until Christian times.

Mediterranean port cities are widely known to have played an important role in the spread of early Christianity around the Mediterranean world. This was also the case in Gaza. Of all the parts of Gaza, its port city, *Maiumas Gaza*, was the most assertive in the activities of early Christian missionaries and intellectuals. Porphyry's deacon and chronicle, Marcus the Deacon (Μάρκος ὁ Διάκονος; *c*.347–420), Deacon of the church in Gaza, in *Life of Saint Porphyry*, writes: 'Gaza is a city of Palestine that is on the borders of Egypt; and it is of no small account, being a populous city and notable' (Marcus Miaconus 1913). The intersection of religion and class was central to the Christianization of, and subsequent rise of Christianity in Gaza and Palestine as a whole. Marcus the Deacon goes on to say that the populations of the Palestinian ports, *Maiumas Gaza* in particular, were 'nautical rabble', a term associated with seamen, navigation and ships, and notoriously susceptible to new influences, especially the new radical ideas of Christian missionaries and preachers (Marcus Diaconus 1913). In the late Roman and Byzantine periods, trade was dominated by the middle classes in Palestine and using trade as a primary source of income was still frowned on by land-owning elites. Furthermore *Maiumas Gaza*, like other Mediterranean port cities, with its working-class populations and sailors-mariners, played a major part in the rise of early Christianity in Palestine and beyond. Early Christianizing influences on Maiumas Gaza come from both directions: from the port city of Alexandria in Egypt and from the port city of Caesarea Maritima, also known as *Caesarea Palaestina*, as well as from other port cities in Palestine. By contrast, the pagan, old-fashioned upper class and conservative landed gentry of (the inland) Gaza city was known to be hostile to early Christians. Deeply wedded to polytheistic traditions, the city had eight pagan temples at the time of emperor Hadrian, and the city was still largely pagan, with the admixture of cults, at the beginning of the fifth century CE (Trombley

1995, Vol.1: 189-91). At the centre of the city stood the temple of the goddess of Aphrodite (Venus) in the shape of a square structure; a platform (intended as the altar) served as a base for a prominent marble pillar surmounted by the statue of Aphrodite in the shape of an elegant naked woman (Marcus Miaconus 1913; Sadeqi 2015: 47-54) – the marble bases and pillars may have been imported from Corinth. In ancient Palestine, the cult of Aphrodite was closely associated the multifaceted goddess Ishtar, the Near Eastern goddess of love and fertility, marriage and pregnancy. Local women in Gaza attached lamps and burned incense in front of the statue of Aphrodite (synonymous with Palestinian deity *Astarte*, Ἀστάρτη) to get help with pregnancy and marriages (Trombley 1995: 191). Other originally pagan traditions were also found in sixth century Christian Gaza: a 'Day of Roses' was held in Gaza as a spring festival that may have been a Christianized continuation of the Roman Rosalia (Belayche 2004: 17; Masalha 2022; Talgam 2004: 223-4). Also the powerful aristocratic elites of landed gentry of Gaza city looked down with contempt on the seamen and working classes and middle class wine merchants of Maiumas Gaza, some of whom were Egyptian wine merchants – although, according to Marcus the Deacon, these foreign Egyptian wine merchants resident in Maiumas Gaza were pagan (Marcus Diaconus, 1913). However, overall, the residents of Maiumas Gaza and those of the port city of Caesarea Maritima, the port city of Ascalon (*Maiumas Ascalonis*) and the port city of Isdud (known in Greek: *Azotos Paralios, or* 'Asdod by the Sea') became early converts to Christianity. The now vanished port of *Maiumas Gaza*, the port city of Gaza – its remains are situated at present-day Rimal Neighbourhood which is part the modern city of Gaza – was repaired and expanded, and the overland trade route brought wine merchants from Egypt and all parts of Arabia and the Middle East to the port city of Gaza (Ring et al. 2014: 287).

*Gaza Maiuma*s, which for several centuries was distinct from the ancient city of Gaza was situated on *Tell Harube*, the highest point of the modern city, in the north-eastern part of it, five kilometres from the sea shore and separated from it by high sand dunes. The city of Gaza, like other ancient cities of the Philistines, Ascalon and Isdud, was not built on the sea; and like Athens (whose port city was Piraeus), they were built at a distance inland, perhaps from fear of the raids of pirates. But they all had port towns connected with them by road. A road linked the ancient city of Gaza with the ancient port town of Gaza, which developed into an important urban centre in its own right known in the Byzantine period as *Maiumas Gaza* (Ameling et al. 2014, Vol. III: 409). Paganism was firmly entrenched in Gaza city – located at a distance from the harbour town of Mainumas Gaza – until the beginning of the fifth century CE until the activist bishop of Maiumas Gaza, Porphyry of Gaza (Porphyrios *c.* 347–420),[1] took the risk of ordering the destruction of eight major pagan temples of the city (Marcus Diaconus 1913; Ring et al. 2014: 287).

Today the Orthodox Church of Saint Porphyrios is the oldest active church in the city of Gaza. Located in the Zaytun quarter of the old city of Gaza, and it houses the tomb of Porphyrios, and is one of the oldest continuously functioning churches in the world and a reminder of the spectacular rise of Christianity in Byzantine Palestine. On 19 October 2023 the church's exterior was damaged (and adjacent buildings belonging to the church complex collapsed) by an Israeli air strike which killed between

16 and 18 Palestinian civilians sheltering in the church (*Caritas Internationalis* 2023). There is some evidence that inhabitants of Maiumas Gaza converted to Christianity en masse in 331 (Meyer 1907). For this early embarking of Christianity and its major contribution to the rise of Christianity in Gaza, the Great *Maiumas Gaza* (or Maiumas Gazae) was granted an independent urban city status with a separate official municipality after the rise of Christianity in Palestine (Sadeq 2015: 47–54).

The Madaba Floor Map depicts Gaza Maiumas as a town with a non-colonnaded main street leading to the western gate of the city of Gaza. The buildings of the town lining the main street were roofed by red clay (baked) tiles resembling those building roofs of the city of Gaza. The Gaza region developed its own mosaic industry during the Byzantine era with its own techniques, high-quality coloured mosaic pavements and decorative elements depicting series of images such as hunt scenes, human figures, animals, birds, floral and geometrical elements, mounds and rivers (Humbert 2000). These high-quality coloured mosaic pavements of Byzantine churches found in the Gaza region, and a Byzantine style mosaic pavement of a basilica were uncovered by archaeologists at Maiumas. Also the Greek name *Neapolis* ('the new city'), or *Constantia Maiumas Neapolis*, was used in reference to *Gaza Maiumas* – and for a period two cities in Byzantine Palestine, with two officially recognized autonomous municipalities, were referred to as 'Neapolis': Nablus and *Constantia Maiumas Neapolis*. This port city (Maiumas), located at a distance from the main Gaza city, became a large town, very famous and important enough to have, in Christian times (and even later under Islam), an autonomous bishop of its own; in fact for many centuries under both Christianity and Islam *Gaza Maiumas* had its own autonomous Palestinian bishop and clergy so for a while during the Byzantine period there were two officially recognized cities of Gaza: the old city of Gaza and Gaza Maiumas. While Gaza Maiumas, with its working classes of sailors and mariners, was an early centre of the spread of Christianity in southern Palestine and had converted to Christianity early on, many social historians have attributed the late acceptance of Christianity by the (pagan) city of Gaza to its relative wealthy merchants and conservative land-owning urban aristocracy (Shahin 2005: 418).

Overall, there is much evidence about the mix urban population of Maiumas Gaza under the Byzantines and for its working-class and seamen communities and the foreign and Egyptian wine *merchants* resident in Maiumas as well as Ghassanid Christian Arabs and Nabataean Arab merchants resident in the port city (Masalha 2018; Shahid 2009, Vol. II, part II: 63–4). There is also evidence for Syriac-speaking Samaritan and Jewish communities in the villages around both the port city and the inland city of Gaza (Glucker 1987: 102).

However, the particular story of the predominantly Christian Gaza Maiumas was probably the only case in the ancient history of Palestine in which one city evolved into two autonomous and officially recognized separate cities. Another Palestinian harbour, Isdud – its name means stronghold or fortress, or in Greek: *Azotos Paralios* ('Asdod by the sea') – appears as a major town on the Madaba Map of the sixth century, featuring large buildings and major civic infrastructure, but, unlike *Gaza Maiumas*, the port city of Isdud was never recognized an autonomous city independent from the main inland city of Isdud. Another major port city in southern Palestine, *Maiumas*

Ascalonis (Maiumas of Ascalon), became a large town during the Byzantine era, under the impact of international commerce and the building boom of Byzantine Palestine, and merited an autonomous Bishop of Maiumas of Ascalon, although the port town was never recognized as an autonomous municipality independent from the inland city of Ascalon; *Maiumas Ascalonis* also remained less well known than *Gaza Maiumas*, the latter with famous Christian bishops and the internationally famous maritime port as well as an internationally famous emporium. The Byzantine name *Maiumas Gaza* not only survived into the Muslim period; in fact, according to the Palestinian historian al-Maqdisi of the tenth century Maiumas was still a separate city in Palestine, and together with the other key Palestinian cities, it was governed from the capital city of Palestine at the time (*Jund Finlastin*) *m*al-Ramla (cited in Wa'ari 2023, Vol. 1: 26). Throughout the Byzantine period and for 400 years under Islam Maiumas Gaza effectively retained its distinct name (*maiumas*) and its character as the a separate city and 'seaside town of Gaza'. Also for many centuries under both the Byzantine and Islam, Maiumas (Gaza) as the older of the two places in the Christian faith remained ecclesiastically independent and was represented by an independent bishop.

8

The Founding of a New Capital City in Palestine in Early Islam

Al-Ramla, the Administrative and Commercial Centre of the Arab Province of Palestine (Seventh to Eleventh Centuries)

The cities of Palestine are beautiful, and are the smartest of al-Sham [Levant]. The two [top] cities of Al-Sham are Ramla and Bayt al-Maqdis [Jerusalem].
Arab geographer Muhammad al-Idrisi (1100–65).

(citied in Wa'ari 2023, Vol. 1)

Spaces of proximity and overlapping: the great mosques and urban bazaars

Conceptually distinct, *empirically* the *Great Urban Mosques* (sacred spaces) and the *Great Urban Markets* (secular spaces) of Palestine were deeply interconnected and this can be seen in the founding and urban planning of a new Arab-Islamic metropolis in Palestine: the city of al-Ramla. The city al-Ramla was founded by the Umayyad caliphs at the start of the eighth century, within the first century of Muslim rule in Palestine, as the new capital of the Arab province of Palestine. Soon the city evolved to become the financial and commercial centre of the country and the largest city in Palestine. The urban planning of a newly founded multicultural capital city in Palestine exhibited both a new Islamic beginning as well as continuities and an exquisite melange of Islamic and Roman/Byzantine styles and modes of organization. With a majority Muslim population, al-Ramla had a *Great Mosque* at the centre of the city (the White Mosque), and its urban layout was characteristic of early Islamic Palestine, a layer which emerges from archaeological excavations shows a well-planned city, with clearly defined quarters with grid-patterned streets (Avni 2014: 177–8).

The great mosques and great urban markets were 'prerequisite' for an Islamic city and central to urban life of Palestine under Islam; the city of al-Ramla was a planned

Islamic city from its start in which commerce and markets went hand in hand with the construction of a great mosque supported by these markets and shops. Prophet Muhammd's profession as a merchant meant that markets and commerce have played a big role in Muslim life and the urban life of the Islamic cities and this was also the case in the way the urban life of new city of al-Ramla evolved:

> The link between religion and currency can be seen in the plan of many traditional Islamic cities; the markets are located around the man Friday mosque, with markets selling more valuable goods (e.g., gold) located closer to the mosque or stalls selling less pure or more polluting goods (e.g., pottery) located further way. The division of market into different commodities is not unique to the Islamic world ... in many case markets were incorporated into the fabric of the mosque and were used to subsidize the functioning of the mosque. Famous examples include the White Mosque in Ramla (720 CE).
>
> (Petersons 2006: 479–80)

Yet, it would be wrong to assume that the Great White Mosque of al-Ramla (like other great mosques of Jerusalem, Nablus, Acre, Jaffa and Gaza) was simply an annex to the urban bazaars. In fact despite its proximity to the urban market, this great mosque, like other great mosques of urban Palestine, which were often designed as tranquil places and 'cities within cities' surrounded by inner walls, was a tranquil places and which provided peace and reflection and a respite away from the hassle and bustle of the crowded urban bazaars and the business of selling and buying.

Archaeological discovery of Byzantine-style mosaics and motifs in the city shows elements of continuity in material culture between Byzantine Palestine and Islamic Palestine. Also the urban architecture of al-Ramla under the Umayyads, like the architectural forms of early urban Islamic Palestine, in Jerusalem, Jericho Hisham Palace (Khirbat al-Mafjar), al-Ramla and Khirbet al-Minyar, near Tiberias, all exhibit continuities and an exquisite melange of Islamic and Roman/Byzantine styles and modes of organization. The adaption of ideas and art forms from Late Antiquity *Palaestina* continued under Islam throughout the Middle Ages and this was combined with new Islamic architectural forms, thus creating a mix of Islamic and Roman/Byzantine styles.

However some changes to the monumental architecture of urban Palestine during the Byzantine followed the Islamic conquest of the region in 637 CE. The Byzantine churches, predominant features in many towns and cities in Palestine over the previous centuries, were quickly joined by the 'great mosques' and much of the construction of the Umayyad period was centred on Jerusalem and al-Ramla. One of the most famous early monuments expressing the new role of Islam in urban Palestine was the Dome of the Rock (*Qobbat al-Sakhra*). Dedicated in 692 CE, today the Dome of the Rock is one of the most famous building in the world and a key symbol of the monumental architecture of urban Palestine. The great mosques of urban Palestine under the Umayyads included the Al-Aqsa Mosque of Jerusalem and the White Mosque of al-Ramla, which was built in that city by the Caliph Sulieman ibn 'Abd al-Malik in 715–717. Other major towns and cities of Byzantine Palestine, Beisan, Gaza,

Tiberias, Lydda, Nablus, Acre, Caesarea, Asqalan (Ascalon), Aylah (al-Aqaba), Arsuf (Apollonia) and Yubna, continued to occupy a central role in the economy, trade and urban life of Islamic Palestine.

While, in the Middle Ages Islam inherited the vast Roman and Byzantine road and trade systems of the Middle East, it further developed this road system for both military purposes and for the sake of long-distance trade; it also added the new postal service (*barid*) to this vast empire. Also, under Islam international and regional trade remained central to the prosperity of Palestine, being a transit country a hub of international trade routes. Becoming Caliph in 715-717, Suleiman ibn ‘Abd al-Malik ibn Marwan, the governor of the Arab province of Palestine (*Jund Filastin*) founded al-Ramla, and permanently transferred the capital of Palestine to that city. The new city was also capital of the Islamic caliphate of Suleiman and for a short period a Palestinian city functioned as the capital of a vast Islamic empire from central Asia to Islamic Spain. The province of Palestine under Islam (*Jund Filastin*) was described by the tenth century Muslim geographer al-Istakhri, who visited Palestine during the golden age of Islam under the Abbasids, as follows: the *Jund Filastin*, ‘which is the first province of al-Sham [Levant]’, extends from Rafah [in the south] to the border of Lajjun [in marj Ibn Amer] in the north, and from the city of Jaffa in the West to the city Jericho in the east (citied in Wa’ari 2023, Vol. 1: 30; Masalha 2018).

Under Islam the newest city of Palestine, al-Ramla, became the governing capital of the oldest city of Palestine, Jericho, an agricultural town known for cultivating high-quality dates, banana and sugar cane, and one of the oldest cities in the world. While al-Ramla became the administrative and political capital of Palestine, Ilya (al-Quds, Jerusalem), remained the religious capital of Palestine and the third holiest city in Islam. When talking about the economy, trade and industries of Palestine, al-Maqdisi describes the economy of the ancient city of Jericho as follows:

> Jericho is the city of the mighty … its livelihood is in the valley, and its crops are watered by springs. Extremely hot, a habitat of snakes and scorpions, native to dark skinned people … Its water is the lightest water in [the] Islam[ic world], and it is abundant in bananas, dates, and basil ….And in the valleys there are minerals, sulfur and other things, and it rises. From the upturned lake there is scattered salt, and the best honey is what grazed on the *Sa'atar* [Za’atar] in Ilya (Jerusalem) (cited in Wa’ari 2023, Vol. 1: 5and 174–5).

Popularly used in Palestine as a spice since Antiquity, today the indigenous Za’atar, known for its strong aroma and distinctive taste, is a popular staple spread that is a key item in the Palestinian kitchen and used together with olive and bread as well as with many other foods, especially with the popular dish *manaqeesh*.

The new city of al-Ramla, approximately twenty kilometres south-east of Jaffa, was established on the intersection of two major trade routes: the important strategic location along the historic trade route of the *Via Maris* (‘way of the sea’ or ‘way of the Philistines’) and the international highway of Damascus-old Cairo (al-Sham-al-Fustat), the latter being the first capital of Egypt under Muslim rule and on the Jaffa-Jerusalem road. Al-Ramla remained the administrative and financial capital of the

Arab Muslim province of *Jund Filastin* and an economic hub for the country for nearly four centuries until the late eleventh century.

While geographically the religious capital of Palestine, Jerusalem was isolated in a mountainous region, whereas the new city of al-Ramal, the secular administrative and commercial capital of the Arab province of Palestine under Islam, which was founded by the Umayyads within the first century of Muslim rule, was commercially and strategically located close to the historic coastal highway leading to the two great capital cities of Islam, al-Sham (Damascus) and Misr al-Fustat and Fustat-Misr (Fustat-Egypt). This greatly enhanced the prosperity and international reputation of al-Ramla. Also for many medieval Arab historians and geographers, the name Palestine: *filastin*, also became synonymous with the capital city of al-Ramla. Commercially and geo-politically located at the centre of the country and linking the holy city of Jerusalem with Jaffa, the main Mediterranean port of Palestine at the time, al-Ramla flourished as the administrative, military and trading hub of the country for centuries throughout early Islam (Masalha 2018). Under Islam for several centuries the Damascus-Cairo trade caravans and caravanserais of the country made al-Ramla the political, economic, commercial and banking hub of Palestine and the Damascus-Cairo trade system made al-Ramla largest, richest and most powerful trading city in the country; al-Ramla remained the capital of Palestine through the Fatimid period (tenth–eleventh centuries), in which the Fatimid 'Military Governor of Palestine' (*Mutawalli Harb Filastin*) resided (Masalha 2018). Al-Ramla remained the administrative and political capital city of Palestine until the eleventh century, while the city of Jerusalem maintained its historic status under Islam as the religious capital of Palestine.

Al-Ramla was also at the centre of the north-south and west-east trade routes and the large number of caravanserais (*khans*) that dotted the country under Islam, with a distance of approximately twenty to thirty kilometres between them, allowed merchants and pilgrims to rest overnight. These merchant khans were also intended to facilitate the postal service (*barid*), which had been introduced to Palestine by the Umayyads (Rosen-Ayalon 1998: 515) and developed further under successive Muslim dynasties. The other historic cities of the Arab province of Palestine (*Jund Filastin*) in early Islam were al-Quds, 'Asqalan, Gaza, Lydda, Arsuf (Greek: Apollonia), Jaffa, Beit Jibrin, Nablus, Jericho and Qaysariah (Caesarea Maritima), with Amman east of the river Jordan. Throughout early Islam the decline of the textile industry of Lydda and its replacement by new industries of al-Ramla heralds other changes in urban Palestine under Islam. For instance, the economic prosperity of Qaysariah (Caesarea Maritima), the great maritime and capital city of Byzantine Palestine depended on its being a regional services centre rather than on its formerly being a maritime city with a major Mediterranean harbour, while the economy of the city of Jaffa, because of its proxy to the capital city of Jund Filastin, functioned as a port for al-Ramla and for trade exchanges with the Greeks (Wheatley 2001: 124).

During this period, we can observe both continuities and transformation in the international trade of Palestine and the social, economic, administrative and geo-political identities of Palestine. Throughout the Middle Ages Muslim merchants, pilgrims and travel writers reported that the name Palestine (*Filastin*) was equated throughout the Muslim world with the capital city of the country: al-Ramla (Ibn Battuta 2005: 57; Khusrau 1888). Indeed, for centuries throughout early Islam the name of the capital city of Palestine, al-Ramla, became synonymous with the name of the country as a whole, *Filastin* (Palestine), and the capital city was often called by *al-Ramla-Filastin* by medieval Arab merchants, travellers, geographers and historians. For four centuries throughout early Islam international and regional trade made al-Ramla the largest metropolitan city in the country. Al-Ramla was described in the late tenth century by the Jerusalem-born Palestinian historian and geographer al-Maqdisi as one of the 'best' and most prosperous cities in the whole Muslim region (al-Maqdisi 2002: 35). As the capital city (*Qasabah*) of Palestine, Al-Maqdisi also mentioned the other key Palestinian cities governed from al-Ramla: Jerusalem, Bayt Jibril [Beir Jibrin], Gaza, Ascalon, Jaffa, Arsuf, Maiumas[-Gaza], Caesarea, Nablus, Jericho, Amman (cited in Wa'ari 2023, Vol. 1: 31).

Other important trading cities in historic Palestine included the port city of Acre. An important shipyard was established in Acre by the Umayyad Caliph Mu'awiya in mid-seventh century and the early Umayyad caliphs (who ruled a vast empire from Damascus) established a large Islamic arsenal in the port of Acre that became central to their Mediterranean sea power (Bessard 2020: 159; Pryor 2016: 114); later Caliph Hisham Ibn Abd al-Malik (724–743) later decided to move the Islamic arsenal from Acre to the port of Tyre. However, for hundreds of years under Islam the port of Acre served the main trading port of Palestine throughout the Umayyad and Abbasid periods and extensive work was done in expanding this port, together with the port of Sidon, especially under the Umayyads. Writing at the time of the Ayyubids in Palestine, the Andalusian Arab geographer and traveller Ibn Jubayr described the port of Acre in late twelfth century as been created by a sea wall and closed by an iron chain running from a tower at the eastern edge of the northern mole to another on land. A large arsenal had existed there from Umayyad times (Pryor 2016: 114). Expanded as an important stronghold of the second Crusader kingdom of Jerusalem, the port of Acre was reduced after its occupation by the Mamluks in 1291, marking the end of the European Crusades in the eastern Mediterranean.

The monetary system of Islamic Palestine: Minting gold and silver coins in *al-Ramla-Palestine*

In Antiquity and the Middle Ages international trade required the development of financial systems and trading currencies. Under classical Islam, global international trade systems linking Asia, the Mediterranean world and Europe combined with the minting of local silver and gold currencies became highly sophisticated. Since Antiquity international trade, financial system and the minting of gold and silver often went hand in hand with gaining a substantial degree of independence. We know that large quantities of Hellenistic style silver coins were minted at the city of Ascalon during the Ptolemaic/Hellenistic/Seleucids periods. In the second century BCE Ascalon became a financial centre in Palestine from the Seleucids after receiving financial autonomy from them to mint silver coins and the city continued to be a financial centre and produce silver coins under both the Romans and Byzantines – which was also the basis for the city's claims to great degree of independence ('free city'), a special status obtained from imperial authorities (Ameling et al. 2014, Vol. III, 242).

In the Middle Ages the geo-political and commercial importance of al-Ramla enabled it to develop a large number of successful industries, including oil and soap industries (industries that the city shares with the cities of Jerusalem and Nablus); al-Ramla also boasted an extensive textile industry. At least one of these industries of the city, the linen industry, was linked the neighbouring city of Lydda in Roman and Byzantine Palestine (see Chapter 5), an ancient city that was the first capital of *Jund Filastin* and the first residence of its governor Suleiman, the founder of al-Ramla. But soon Lydda experienced a sharp industrial decline after the foundation of al-Ramla in the early eighth century and the forcible relocation of Lydda's textile industry to the new capital of Palestine. But Suleiman clearly employed skilled Christian craftsmen from Lydda and some of his senior officials were senior clergymen from Lydda. Also the archaeological findings from al-Ramla seem to confirm many of the Islamic writings about some of the early industries of the new city, especially the tannery and textile industries. The tenth century Muslim historian and geographer ibn al-Faqih writes about the construction the water canal of al-Ramla, known as Barda, a remarkable name for Suleiman's new canal for his Palestine capital and a name identical to the name of Barada, the main river of Damascus, the original Umayyad capital. Ibn al-Faqih writes:

> Barada: A water canal in the city of Ramla, built by Suleiman bin Abdel Malik'. 'Suleiman ibn Abd al-Malik was … the first to build his palace there and the house known as the Dyers House, and he made a medium cistern in the house. Then he planned the mosque [White Mosque] and built it, and gave people permission to build, so they built, and he dug a canal for the people of Ramla. Which is called Barada. He also dug fresh wells and paid for the construction and for the mosque. [Sulaiman] chose his official registrar [*katib*] a Christian from Lydda called the Patriarch [*Al-Batriq*] bin Baka. The city of Ramla did not exist before Suleiman. Its location was sandy, and it became [the site of] the Dyers' House. To the heirs of Saleh bin Ali bin Abdullah bin Abbas because it [the Dyers' House] was [later] seized from the Umayyads.
>
> (cited in Wa'ari 2023, Vol. 1: 104)

Also the founding of a new capital in Palestine, in some ways like the founding of other new capital cities, from Baghdad by the Abbasid Caliph al-Mansour in 762 CE to Saint Petersburg by Peter the Great in 1703, was always the hallmark of an ambitious leader and a radical reforming ruler. Apparently Lydda, a predominantly Christian city in the first century of the Islamic rule in Palestine with vast church properties accumulated during the Byzantine period had properties which Suleiman was reluctant to confiscate. Lacking the large urban space and sufficient lands for the large wide-scale ambitious economic and industrial developments that the governor of

Palestine, Suleiman ibn 'Abd al-Malik, was seeking to implement, especially following the far-reaching administrative, financial, currency, linguistic (Arabization) reforms his father, Caliph 'Abd al-Malik Ibn Marwan, had successfully implemented (Luz 1997: 52-3; Masalha 2018).

The most consequential reforms of 'Abd al-Malik ibn Marwan (ruling from 685 until his death in 705) were the introduction of a single Islamic currency in place of the Byzantine currency and Sasanian coinage and the establishment of Arabic as the language of the bureaucracy in place of Greek in Palestine and Syria. These new financial and linguistic reforms were soon implemented in the new capital city of Palestine, al-Ramla. The establishment of Arabic as the official language of the Islamic caliphate (Ochsenwald and Fisher 2004: 57) also had far-reaching consequences for the administration and economy of Palestine. For the first six decades of Islam in Palestine, prior to 'Abd al-Malik's linguistic and administrative reforms, much of the local government's work in Palestine was recorded in koinē Greek and many prominent positions in the country were held by Christians, some of whom belonged to families that had served in Byzantine administrations. The linguistic revolution that began with 'Abd al-Malik ibn Marwan and was maintained by subsequent Marwanid Caliphs meant that Arabic became the lingua franca not only of Palestine but the Islamic empire, which, at the time, included more than 30 per cent of the world's population. The linguistic revolution, and having Arabic as the single lingua franca for tens of millions of people from Spain to central Asia, was also central to the expansion of global trade under Muslim rule. Throughout the Middle Ages, as in ancient times, regional and distant trade remained a key source for the prosperity of a strategically located Palestine.

The founding of al-Rama suited Suleiman's ambitious schemes and al-Ramla served as a capital city not only for Palestine for Suleiman during his caliphate of the vast Islamic empire. Under Suleiman ibn 'Abd al-Malik and his Umayyad successors Arabic and the Arabization of Palestine were in the financial and administrative new capital city of Palestine, al-Ramla. These reforms added more cultural layers to Palestine's already rich and complex identity. The Arabization of Palestine benefited from the fact that the predominantly Palestinian Christian peasantry spoke a Palestinian dialect of Aramaic, a Semitic language closely related to Arabic. However, if under the Romans and Byzantines koinē Greek was the elite language of Palestine and the Levant and Hellenization was closely associated with cosmopolitanism and high culture, under Islam Arabic and Arabization became a vehicle for globalization. Literary Arabic and translation into Arabic became closely associated with scientific inquiry and cultural innovation, expanding international trade and cosmopolitanism. Furthermore, Byzantine Palestine had been bedevilled by deep class divides reflected in linguistic divisions. If speaking Greek was a key marker of metropolitan and urban elite identity and speaking Aramaic was a key marker of identity for ordinary people and Palestinian peasantry in Christian-majority Byzantine *Palaestina*, Arabic and Arabization encouraged egalitarianism in Palestine and became key markers of identity for both urban elites and the increasingly Arabized Palestinian peasantry. Under Islam, the metropolises of Damascus, Baghdad and Cairo stood out as imperial centres, but their trade and strategic linkages through overland and sea routes tied them to an archipelago of hinterland cities in Palestine: the two Arab provinces of Palestine (*Jund Filastin* and *Jund al-Urdun*) included the cities of al-Ramla, Gaza, 'Asqalan, al-Lajjun, al-Quds, Jericho, Nablus, al-Khalil, Acre, Jaffa, Safad and Tiberias. The profound religious, social, cultural and linguistic transformation of the country under early Islam is evident throughout the land. The powerful Arab Muslim impact on Palestine has continued for nearly 1,400 years, to the present day.

The archaeological evidence on the early history of Islam in Palestine and its capital city al-Ramla also debunks the common perception and insidious myth that the Muslim conquest of Palestine in the seventh century caused a decline in the number of localities and the overall prosperity of the country (Magness 2003: 1-3). On the contrary, the Muslim Arabs ushered in a period of prosperity and religious toleration and religious and cultural autonomy for Christian and Jewish religious communities (Arabic: *millah*) in Palestine and permitted the previous administrative organization to continue (*The Encyclopaedia of Islam* 1965, Vol. II: 911). The Islamic states, like the Roman and Byzantine Empires, also applied a patron-client system in Palestine and this patronage system allowed the emergence of a degree of local autonomy and powerful urban elites.

Secular versus religious capitals in Palestine: *Caesarea Palaestina*, *al-Ramla-Filastin* and Ilya/Bayt al-Maqdis (Jerusalem)

> *During the season of pilgrimage [Muslim Haj], thousands who cannot travel to Mecca, come to Jerusalem. They approach the sanctuary [al-Haram] and offer sacrifices as is customary. In some years, over 20,000 [Muslim] people fulfil the [Haj] law here ... Christians and Jews come here too, from the land of the Christians.*
>
> (Nasir Khusro 1050 CE, cited in Matar 2013: 913)

The Arab-Islamic province of *Jund Filastin* was one of the military administrative provinces of the Umayyad and Abbasid region of al-Sham, provinces organized soon after the Muslim conquest of the Levant in the late 630s. The official name, *Jund Filastin*, was universally adopted from early Islam onwards by Muslim rulers and Arab governors (*walis*) of the province of Palestine (*Filastin*), Arab and Muslim geographers, cartographers, historians, translators, engravers, coiners, pilgrims and merchants. They all relied on the Palestine classical heritage of Palestine and the Near East. Arab administrators, historians and geographers also translated and preserved many of the ancient place names of Palestine and much of the classical heritage of Greece and Antiquity in the Levant.

Islamic pilgrimage to Jerusalem began very early and this was enhanced by the grandeur and centrality of the holy city and Umayyad Filastin (661-749), which can hardly be overstated. The Dome of the Rock was the first monumental sanctuary erected by Umayyad Islam between 688 and 691 (Murphy-O'Connor 2008; 2010: 27). The Umayyads, like the Romans and Byzantines, promoted urbanization in

Palestine. They also respected the multifaith and shared heritage of the country and continued many of the Byzantines' administrative traditions and architectural styles. For the Muslim Arabs, as for the Byzantine Christians, Palestine (Holy Land: Arabic: al-Ard al-Muqaddasah (al-Maqdisi 2002: 135); Hebrew: Eretz HaKodesh) and Jerusalem were a special, sacred space. The sanctity of Jerusalem is enshrined in its very Arabic name: Bayt al-Maqdis (the 'house of the holy') or al-Quds (the 'holy'). According to the traditional Muslim view, the Qibla (Arabic: 'direction'), in which the first Muslims had prayed, originally faced the Noble Sanctuary in Jerusalem. The sacred city was always a focus of intense Islamic devotion and pilgrimage. The governors of the province of Jund Filastin were appointed by the Caliph. They were in charge of the army commanders, Muslim clergy, religious officials, tax collectors, police and civil administrators of the province. But the Umayyad rulers, especially the Marwani Caliphs, took a personal interest in Palestine. The Umayyad caliphs, like the Byzantine Christian rulers, made a clear distinction between the 'secular' (political, worldly) and 'sacred' spheres and between the political (secular/administrative/military) and sacred capitals of Palestine. For the Byzantine Christians that distinction, formalized at the Nicaea Council in 325, produced a rather complicated and confused ecclesiastical arrangement between the Archiepiscopal See of *Caesarea Palaestina* and the Archbishopric of Aelia Capitolina. However, for the Umayyad rulers the distinction between political/secular/administrative and sacred capitals of Jund Filastin was simpler and more straightforward. Also, subsequent accounts by Arab geographers from the tenth century lends some insight to the concept of the Arab province of *Jund Filastin* and to the secular/administrative versus religious capital ('double capitals') concept in Palestine suggested in this work. Aelia Capitolina remained the official name of Jerusalem until 638 CE when the Arabs conquered the city and kept the first part of it as Iliya. Iliya (later Bayt al-Maqdis and al-Quds) was the sacred/religious capital of the Umayyad state and of Palestine. The Umayyad caliphs loved and honoured Jerusalem, and Mu'awiyah (602–680 CE), founder of the Umayyad dynasty, was reported to have had himself proclaimed Caliph in Jerusalem (*The Encyclopaedia of Islam* 1965, Vol. II: 911). The Umayyads devoted a great deal of effort and resources to its expansion and the prosperity of Jerusalem and other Palestinian cities. Interestingly, the Umayyad Marwanid Caliphs considered relocating their capital from the secular capital Damascus to the holy city of Jerusalem. Although the move was abandoned for strategic reasons, in preparation they symbolically built their large 'palaces' adjacent to the al-Aqsa Mosque. In excavations carried out by Hebrew University archaeologist Benyamin Mazar in the 1970s, south and south-west of the al-Haram al-Sharif (the Noble Sanctuary) the remains of six massive buildings were uncovered; these buildings were not mentioned in any of the Arabic written sources describing the period. The buildings were labelled 'palaces' as they were probably part of the government complex and the administrative centre of the Umayyad government in Jerusalem. Nothing similar or comparable to this government complex in Umayyad Jerusalem was found in the secular capital of Jund Filastin, al-Ramla. The Marwanid Caliphs also renewed and enhanced the centrality of Jerusalem in the Muslim Empire. If al-Ramla became the administrative head of Muslim Palestine, Jerusalem became the religious heart of Muslim Palestine, but also of the rest of the Umayyad Empire. Now, added to the Christian pilgrims who continued to arrive, were the convoys of Muslim pilgrims who came to Jerusalem in their thousands from the Maghreb, Iran and even central Asia. The largest and most impressive palace at the centre of the magnificent secular Umayyad architecture in Ilya (Bayt al-Maqdis) was near the southwest corner of the al-Haram and was the seat of the Umayyad caliphs who visited the holy city on a regular basis. The palace was apparently constructed during the reign of al-Walid ibn Abd al-Malik (who ruled from 705 to 715) and is similar to other fortified Umayyad palaces in Palestine (near Jericho and near Tiberias) and Syria. The palace measured 96 by 84 metres and was surrounded by a three-metre protective wall, constructed of large, trimmed stones. Two main gates, one facing east and one facing west, gave access to the palace. A broad, stone-paved courtyard in the centre of the building was surrounded by rows of columns supporting the roofing of the porticoes. Many of the columns came from Byzantine churches and buildings in Palestine, as evidenced by traces of engraved crosses on them. The rooms around the central courtyard were paved with small stone slabs and mosaic. Plaster, decorated with geometric designs and floral motifs, covered the thick walls. A bridge was built from the roof of the palace to the al-Haram al-Sharif (Noble Sanctuary compound), providing direct access to the al-Aqsa Mosque. The magnificent complex of Muslim buildings was destroyed by the earthquake of 749; evidence of this is the fallen columns and collapsed walls. The Umayyad undertook monumental building programmes in Jerusalem, the centre of which were the Dome of the Rock (completed in 691 AD) and the al-Aqsa Mosque (completed in 705 AD), both still standing, and both remaining the most potent religious and cultural symbols of Palestine. The al-Aqsa Mosque itself was constructed on the basis of an earlier Islamic mosque built within the Haram al-Sharif compound and with reference to a key Islamic tradition, the Isra and Mi'raj. This tradition, according to Islam, involved Prophet Muhammad's night-time journey to Jerusalem, which took place around the year 621 AD. The Umayyads magnificent public (secular and religious) rebuilding programmes in Jerusalem and al-Ramla and their large palaces in Jerusalem and near Jericho and Tiberias show the extent to which Palestine had become central to the Umayyad state and early Islam. But the founding of a completely new metropolitan city for Palestine also represented a break from the Byzantine past and a reorientation of Palestine under the Marwanid rulers. This resulted in the creation of a new capital city for the province of Filastin, al-Ramla. But in the end, during the Umayyad, Fatimid and Ottoman periods, the new city of government built at al-Ramla could never rival the sacredness and splendour of the Dome of the Rock and al-Aqsa Mosque and other new monumental Arab-Islamic architecture in Jerusalem, the religious capital of the country – the city that continued to flourish as the religious centre of the whole country as well as a holy city for Jews and Christians – or its religiously rich history, and a city which, would, once Salah-al Din had recovered from the Latin Crusaders in the twelfth century, become the centre of the administration of Muslim-majority Palestine.

However in early Islam, al-Ramla developed quickly into the new economic, industrial and financial hub of Palestine, the vast industries of the new capital city of Islamic Palestine began to encroach on the residential areas of a large crowded city; and Suleiman was 'credited with the construction of a palace, a mosque, an extensive water supply and storage system and the House of the Dyers'; subsequently, and for several centuries, al-Ramla flourished as a fortified city with many cisterns and a highly developed system of rainwater collection and storage (Lev 2006: 590-1). Moreover, throughout early Islam the two political/secular and sacred cities of al-Ramla and Jerusalem were at the heart of a distinct Palestinian Arab province - a province that combined the Byzantine provinces of *Palaestina Prima* and *Palaestina Tertia*. This Arab province of *Jund Filastin* included most major Palestinian cities and more than two-thirds of the territory of British Mandatory Palestine (1918-1948). Throughout early Islam al-Ramla was central to Palestine.

> A major urban component of ancient Ramla was the numerous industrial installations incorporated into the residential areas of the city, pointing to a high degree of industrial activity, the nature of which has not been entirely ascertained. The large number of water installations (plaster pools, cisterns and clay pipes) indicates that these industries involved the use of large amounts of liquids. The installations, particularly the plastered pools, some of them contains remains of red paint, could be linked to the linen dyeing industry. This was a well-known industry in [neighbouring] Lod-Diospolis [Ludda] during the Byzantine period. A different interpretation connects the industrial installations in Ramla to the processing of flax into textile fibre ... the cultivation of flax in the hinterland of Ramla, which provided its [exported textile] products to Egypt, and on the wide distribution of flax as one of the main agricultural crops of the region until the modern period. Other main crops included cotton and linen, olives, and fruit for local consumption. Olive oil was used for the local soap industry and the products were exported from Palestine.
>
> (Avni 2014: 177)

Under Islam, and for several centuries between the early eighth and late eleventh centuries, al-Ramla was the economic and political hub of the province of Filastin and the largest, richest and most powerful trading city in the country. Being the political, administrative and commercial capital of Palestine throughout the early four centuries of Islamic rule in Palestine, al-Ramla became also the key centre for minting gold and silver coins - coins which also contributed to cementing the indigenous collective memory of Palestine as a distinct geo-political entity in the Middle Ages. In Antiquity the Mediterranean city of Ascalon was a major trading and banking city and a 'free city' that minted its own coins and achieved a degree of financial autonomy that allowed the city to trade with the maritime nations of the Ptolomaic, Hellenistic and Mediterranean worlds. Under Islam, al-Ramla, being the capital and key financial centre in Palestine allowed the city to mint a Palestinian currency with words: '*minted in Palestine*'. Like the location of Ascalon on the Mediterranean coast in Antiquity and the geo-political location of the city Memphis in the Naqab as a regional financial centre for the Arab spice, the economic and monetary prosperity of Palestine throughout early Islam depended significantly on the stability of the currency and the quality of gold and silver coins minted locally in the province of Jund Filastin, especially in the administrative and financial capital al-Ramla.

Currency is about monetary power and the currency minted locally in Palestine (and its capital al-Ramla) gives us a sense of the extent of the local autonomy exercised in the province of Palestine (Filastin) under Islam. The earliest numismatic evidence for the official designation of the country as *Palaestina* on Roman coins comes from the period of Vespasian (69 to 79 CE) and subsequently for the name '*Syria Palaestina*' from the period of Marcus Aurelius, who was Roman Emperor from 161 to 180 CE. In the first century CE, the Roman Empire also granted many Palestinian cities the right to mint bronze coins. Sir George Francis Hill, the Director and Principal Librarian of the British Museum (1931–36), produced the British Museum Catalogue of Palestine coins showing sixteen Palestinian cities minting their own coins (Hill 1914). This tradition of economic autonomy and Palestine city-coins came to an end in the third century CE when the (western) Roman Empire disintegrated, but it was renewed and expanded in Muslim-ruled Palestine in the Middle Ages to include the minting of coins in silver and gold in the Palestine cities of Ilya (Bayt al-Maqdis, al-Quds, Jerusalem), al-Ramla, Tiberias (*Tabariyyah*), 'Asqalan and others. This autonomous bronze coinage of Palestine cities under the Romans and Byzantines and silver and gold under Islam suggests the development of a considerable degree of regional Palestinian autonomy and of distinct local traditions, away from rigid imperial control. Under Islam, especially from the early eighth century onwards, Palestine began to develop its own distinct Arab-Islamic traditions of coinage, weights and measures; crucially coins were produced in several Palestinian cities with the mint formula 'struck in Filastin' (Gil 1997: 257) and circulated locally, regionally and globally. Not surprisingly, in view of the hoard of coins uncovered in near Jericho and the centrality of the province of Palestine and its capital in the Umayyad period, the provinces of Jund Filastin and Jund Dimashq 'provided an almost equal number of coins' excavated from the Jericho site (Walmsley 2000: 338). Originating from a range of mints in Bilad al-Sham, the percentage of these coins was as follows:

- 32 per cent minted in the province of Jund Filastin;
- 35 per cent from the province of Jund Dimashq;
- 20 per cent minted in Jund Hims;
- 6 per cent from Jund al-Urdun;
- 5 per cent from al-Jazirah;
- 1 per cent from Jund Qinnasrin;
- 1 per cent from Egypt (Walmsley 2000: 336–7).
- These coins were from the following mints:
- twenty-seven Jund Filastin (twenty-three from the mint of the capital al-Ramla; three Lydda; one Iliya [Jerusalem]);
- twenty-nine Jund Dimashq (all from the mint of the capital Dimashq);
- five Jund al-Urdin (four Tiberias; one al-Urdun);
- seventeen Jund Hims (all from Hims mint);
- one Jund Qinnasrin (Aleppo mint);

- four al-Jazirah (al-Ruha mint);
- one Egypt (Alexandria mint) (Walmsley 2000: 338).

Its coins were minted in al-Ramla and several Palestinian cities with the inscription 'in Palestine', in the same way as the country of manufacture or production is stated on goods today. Al-Maqdisi devotes an entire section of his work to these distinct traditions, measures and coins of his native country (Gil 1997: 257). The minting of Islamic coins (*dinar* in gold and *dirham* in silver) in Filastin began under the Umayyads and continued under the Abbasids, Fatimids and other Islamic ruling dynasties:

> [in the 9th century Palestinian] coins began to appear with the inscription *bi-filastin* ['بفلسطين', 'in-Palestine']. The first of these were produced in the days of Khumarawayh and his son, Harun, from 890 until 904, and these were gold dinars with the unusual weight of 3.2 grams. These practices continued during the period when the Abbasids reconquered Egypt and Palestine ... The Ikhshidids continued to mint coins in Ramla, as previously, but unlike the inferior quality of the Palestinian coins produced under the Tulunids, Muhammad ibn Tughj, the Ikhshid, ordered the minting of dinars of a finer quality ... The mint in Ramla continued working during Fatimid times as well.
>
> (Gil 1997: 258; see also Album 1998)

Al-Ramla was at the centre of the north-south and west-east trade routes and the large number of caravanserais (*khans*) which dotted the country. These khans were also intended to facilitate the postal service (*barid*) which had been introduced to Palestine by the Umayyads (Rosen-Ayalon 1998: 515).

Throughout the Middle Ages Muslim pilgrims and travel writers reported that Filastin was equated throughout the Muslim world with the capital city of the country: al-Ramla (Ibn Battuta 2005: 57; Khusrau 1888). Indeed, for centuries throughout early Islam the name of the capital city of Palestine, al-Ramla, became synonymous with the name of the country as a whole, *Filastin* (Palestine), and the capital city was often called by *al-Ramla-Filastin* by medieval Arab travellers, geographers and historians, in the same way as the former capital city of Byzantine Palestine, Caesarea Maritima, had become synonymous with the name of the country as a whole, *Palaestina*, and had often been called Caesarea Palaestina. Once again, we see urban Islam continuing and pragmatically adapting Palestine traditions and the Byzantine administrative and geo-political traditions of Palestine rather than replacing them completely. This adaption and transformation of Byzantine administrative and geo-political traditions was also influenced by the tendency in Palestine and the Near East as a whole (the Arab Muslim Near East included) to equate countries with capital cities. For international and regional trade was always central to the prosperity of Palestine, being a transit country. While geographically Jerusalem of the period was isolated in a mountainous region, the fact that the secular capital of the province of *Filastin*, al-Ramla, was strategically and commercially located on the highway leading to the two great capital cities of Islam, al-Sham (Damascus) and Misr al-Fustat and Fustat-Misr (Fustat-Egypt) greatly enhanced the prosperity and international reputation of al-Ramla. Thus Filastin was not only the official name of the province/country but, for some medieval Arab historians, the name also became synonymous with the capital city of al-Ramla. Strategically, geo-politically and in trade terms located at the centre of the country and linking the holy city of Jerusalem with Jaffa, the main Mediterranean port of *Jund Filastin*, al-Ramla, flourished as the administrative, military and trading hub of the country for more than three centuries (Foster 2016).

Al-Ramla was described in the late tenth century by the Jerusalem-born historian and geographer al-Maqdisi as one of the 'best' cities in the whole Muslim regions (al-Maqdisi 2002: 35). He had this to say:

> Ar-Ramlah is the capital of Palestine [Arabic: *Qasbat Filastin*]. It is a beautiful and well-built city. Its water is light and plentiful, its fruits are abundant. It encompasses manifold advantages ... situated as itis in the midst of virtuous landscape, of pleasant villages and lordly towns and near to holy places. Commerce in it is prosperous and the markets are excellent. There is no finer mosque in Islam than the one in the city ... there are no fruits in Islam tastier than in the city and its surrounding towns ... its hostels are pleasant and its *hammams* [public baths] are elegant ... its houses are large ... its mosques are good, its streets are wide ... its roads lead ... to Bayt al-Maqdis [Jerusalem] road ... Lydda road, Jaffa road, Egypt road, Dajon toad ... The chief mosque in the capital [Ar-Ramlah], located in the markets, is even more beautiful and graceful than that of [the Great Mosque] of Damascus. It is called Al Abyad [the White Mosque]. In all Islam there is found no bigger *mihrab* [prayer niche] than the one here [in Ar-Ramlah] and its pulpit is the most splendid to be seen after that of Bayt al-Maqdis; also it possesses a beautiful minaret built by Hisham ibn 'Abdel-Malik.
>
> (Al-Maqdisi 2002: 143-4; also cited in Le Strange 1890: 304-5)

Throughout early Islam the administrative capital of Palestine, al-Ramla and Palestine the *Filastin* as a whole maintained its economic prosperity partly by being strategically located at the centre of regional and distant and global trade and partly by developing its own distinct monetary system, within the wider monetary zone of Islam. Under Islam, *dinar* coins were minted in gold, *dirham* coins in silver, while *fals* (plural *fulus*) was a copper coin first produced by the Umayyads in the late seventh century. The name *fals* derives from *follis*, a Roman/Byzantine copper coin. Various Islamic copper *fals* were in production until the nineteenth century. Today the word *fulus* (or *flus*) is still used in Palestinian Arabic vernacular as a generic term for money and the term has also given rise to the modern Arabic terms *iflas* (financial bankruptcy) and *muflis* (bankrupt). In the Middle Ages, the monetary system of the province of Palestine included *dinars*, *dirhams* and *fals*, which were minted in several Palestinian cities. Also, governed from the industrial city of al-Ramla, Filastin is accounted by tax figures given in certain sources, to have been the richest province of al-Sham throughout the late Umayyad period (Blankinship 1994: 48). The industrial economy of Islamic Palestine was boosted by the country's strategic location and its global trade, including its global trade with India, China and Europe. An extensive global silk trade from China to the Near East existed from Antiquity. Silk fabric, a natural fibre produced by silkworms, was first developed in ancient China and, because of its texture and lustre, silk rapidly became a popular luxury fabric in the Near East. It was made accessible by both Chinese and Arab traders in Antiquity and the Middle Ages. In 985 CE al-Maqdisi, in his work *The Best Divisions for Knowledge of the Regions* (*Ahsan al-Taqasim Fi Ma'rifat al-Aqalim*), gives us a detailed account of all the place names, cities and towns he had visited in Palestine (al-Maqdisi 1994, 2002). Describing in detail his native country and the fertility of its land, al-Maqdisi comments in the tenth century on the agricultural produce and manufactured goods of Palestine:

> within the province of Palestine may be found gathered together 36 products that are not found thus united in any other land ... From Palestine come olives, dried figs, raisins, the carob-fruit, stuffs of mixed silk and cotton, soap and kerchiefs. From Jerusalem come cheeses, cotton, the celebrated species of raisins known as 'Ainuni and Duri, excellent apples, bananas – which same is a fruit in the form of a cucumber, but when the skin is peeled off, the interior is not unlike the watermelon, only finer flavoured and more luscious – also pine-nuts known as 'Kuraish-bite,' and their equal is not found elsewhere; further, mirrors, lamp-jars and needles. From Jericho is brought excellent indigo. From Sughar and Baisan came indigo and dates [and rice], also the treacle called *Dibs*. From 'Amman –grain, lambs and honey. From Tiberias – carpet stuffs, paper, and cloth. From Kadas – clothes of the stuff called *Munayyir* and *Bal'isiyyah*, also ropes.
>
> (Cited in Le Strange 2014: 18–19; also Le Strange 1890: 16–19; al-Maqdisi 1994)

Although the export of Palestinian wine stopped under Islam, exports continued throughout the Middle Ages and camel caravans transported olive oil from Palestine to the city of Medina in Arabia (Gil 1997: 236). Also, various woven items and textiles and types of *qazz* silk mixed with rabbit wool made in Palestine were loaded onto ships and exported to Mediterranean markets, including Egypt (Gil 1997: 238). Interestingly, many of these key manufactured and exported products, such as cotton, oil, soap, glassware, woven, embroidered and silk items, would still play a role in the Palestinian economy of the modern era. As we shall see in Chapter 10, products of global export of Palestine in the Middle Ages such glassware, glass-making and exquisite produced in the city of al-Khalil reached Germany in Europe and China in the Far East (Gil 1997: 238).

Earthquakes badly affected urban Palestine in the Middle Ages and the modern period, with the urban infrastructure and urban markets of key cities such as Gaza, al-Ramla, Jerusalem and Nablus had been badly hit by these earthquakes. A devastating earthquake in 1927 destroyed a big part of the Old City of Nablus. Many centuries earlier, in 1294, a major earthquake devastated Gaza, and five years later the Mongol invasion again destroyed many buildings in the city (Ring et al., 1994: 289). Also global trade routes and the movement of large number of people and goods allowed the bubonic plague to spread globally and in the city of Gaza in 1348 (Ring et al., 1994: 290). However the strong networks of families and mutual social support in these urban centres also enabled these affected cities to recover socially and economically fairly quickly; for instance, Syrian geographer al-Dimashqi described Gaza in 1300 as a 'city so rich in trees it looks like a cloth of brocade spread out upon the land' (cited in Doughty 2006). Furthermore under the impact of its location on the regional trade routes and during the governorship of Emir Sanjar al-Jawli, Gaza was transformed once again into a flourishing city with a spectacular Islamic architecture of the Maluku period (Meyer 1907: 83). The famous Arab traveller Ibn Battuta who visited the city in 1355 noted that Gaza was 'large and populous, and has many mosques' (cited in le Strange 1890: 442). Gaza's exquisite Islamic architecture impacted on local mosques, Islamic madrasas, hospitals, merchant caravanserais, covered urban markets and public baths (Filfil and Louton 2008).

Earlier in the middle of the eleventh century, Muslim traveller Nasir Khusro (Khusrau), who visited Fatimid Palestine in 1047, commented on the devastation of al-Ramla by an earthquake. Khusro produced an account of his seven-year journey (*Safarnama*) through the Muslim world of the eleventh century (*Diary of a Journey through Syria and Palestine*). He wrote about the cityscape and urban life of the city of al-Ramla whose name was synonymous with the name Palestine (*Filastin*):

> Sunday, the day of the new moon of the month of Ramadan (the 1st of March), we came to Ramlah. From Caesarea to Ramlah is eight leagues. Ramlah is a great city, with strong walls built of stone, mortared, of great height and thickness, with iron gates opening therein. From the town to the sea-coast is a distance of three leagues. The inhabitants get their water from the rainfall, and in each house is a tank for storing the same, in order that there may always be a supply. In the middle of the Friday Mosque, also, is a large tank; and from it, when it is filled with water, anyone who wishes may take. The area of the mosque measures two hundred paces (*Gam*) by three hundred. Over one of its porches (*suffah*) is an inscription stating that on the15th of Muharram, of the year 425 (10th of December, 1033 A.D.), there came an earthquake of great violence, which threw down a large number of buildings, but that no single person sustained an injury. In the city of Ramlah there is marble in plenty, and most of the buildings and private houses are of this material; and, further, ... they do most beautifully sculpture and ornament. They cut the marble here with a toothless saw, which is worked with 'Mekkah sand'. They saw the marble in the length, as is the case with wood, to form the columns; not in the cross; also they cut it into slabs. The marbles that I saw here were of all colours, some variegated, some green, red, black, and white. There is, too, at Ramlah, a particular kind of fig, that which no better exists anywhere, and this they export to all the countries round. This city of Ramlah, throughout [al-Sham] and the West [al-Maghreb], is known under the name of Filastin.
>
> (Khusrau 1888: 21-2)

9

Regulating Trade and Inspecting Urban Markets in Byzantine and Islamic Palestine

The *Agoranomos* and *Muhtasibs* in Historical and Comparative Perspectives

For hundreds of years throughout the Middle Ages and the modern period, the *hisba* (market) and *muhtasib* (market supervisor) were a key feature of urban Palestine under Islam. The *muhtasib* institution developed in the great urban centres and great cities of Islam beginning with the Abbasid revolution of the mid-eighth century onwards; the institution had its roots in the social, economic, intellectual and scientific revolution of classical Islam. This key institution of regulating trade, prices and generally the overall environment of urban markets was also facilitated by the Abbasid *papermaking revolution*, which began in the mid-eighth century and spread from the capital Baghdad throughout the vast Islamic empire. Ushering in one of the most important golden ages of Islam, the great cities of Islam became not only flourishing centres of global commence, but also centres of science and learning, of the study of mathematics and accounting (*hisab*) and generally centres of invention and manuscript and book production (Masalha 2022).

In Arabic the term *muhtasib* literally means 'arithmeticians' or 'calculators'. However, the development of the permanent institution of the *hisba* began in the great religious, social and economic and political urban centres, beginning with Abbasid Iraq and spread to other Islamic cities such as Cairo, Damascus and Jerusalem (Ghabin 2009: 54–7). However much of the evidence we have about the *muhtasib* institution in Palestine comes from the Mamluk and Ottoman periods (1260 to 1918). Theoretically our knowledge about the nature of *hisba* and the *muhtasib* institution comes from two main kinds of literature: The Islamic fiqh literature and the professional literature on *hisba* known as treatises (Ghabin 2009: 155). Although an Islamic institution with deep roots history in the social, economic and ethical history of Islamic trade, the *muhtasib* institution had remarkable equivalence in the pre-Islamic market regulations system of urban Palestine and the cities of the Levant. Its equivalence is the *agoranomos* system (*ἀγορανόμος*, plural: *agoranomoi*, *ἀγορανόμοι*) (Foster 1970: 128–44).

If the Greek term *agoranomos* ('market-overseer') is derived from the Greek term *agora*: marketplace, the Arabic term *hisba*, a marketplace, or souk – a name that applies to the historic markets in the Palestinian cities of Acre, Jerusalem, Nablus and others cities in Palestine – is derived from the Arabic term *muhtasib*. The *agora*, or marketplace, was a key feature in the city (*polis*) of urban Palestine the Romans and the Byzantines; a city in Palestine could have one or several *agronomoi* ('market-overseers'). These market-overseers were elected or appointed officials in the cities in Palestine under Byzantines who were responsible for order in the marketplace. The archaeological excavations and the discovery of hundreds of weights uncovered dating to Roman and Byzantine Palestine, with the seal of the *agoranomos*, serve as proof of the large-scale of economic activity in the cities of Palestine in Antiquity (Safrai 2003: 134).

The marketplaces (*agoras*) constructed in the cities of Palestine under the Romans and Byzantines were large and often with courtyards; they were supervised by the *agoranomos* who regulated the markets and supervised prices especially during the Byzantine period. The similarities in the duties of the *muhtasib and agoranomos* were remarkable, although there were also some differences. The duties of the *agoranomos* included setting prices for certain goods, certifying goods and weights and scales, controlling money exchange, and the important function of managing the supply of the *polis* with grain. In controlling unscrupulous merchants, an *agoranomos* also had the right to impose corporal punishment (and was often portrayed walking along the *agora* with a whip) on non-freeborn people, and fines on free citizens of the city. An *agoranomos* also kept an eye on temples and religious sites in the *agora*. Over time, *agoranomos* also became an honorary title for a public benefactor, who contributed significant amounts for public institutions (Chisholm 1911a: 381; Foster1970: 128–44).

As we have already seen in Chapter 6, during the Byzantine period, the church played a major part in the economy in Palestine and especially in key export-oriented industries such as wine and olive oil. Also major aspects of the economy and trade were controlled, to a large extent, by the state. Means of production and marketing were dependent on central government regulations; the market masters, or *agronomoi* were in charge of official state or local policies and regulating the economic affairs in the Byzantine cities in Palestine. The municipal government, or city council, occasionally regulated prices of foodstuffs as well as prices of wheat and bread. Subsidies for wheat and bread were also important means used by the authorities to prevent social unrest and to regulate prices of grain especially during periods of drought and famine. According to the available evidence from Byzantine Palestine the *agronomoi* dealt, largely, with weights and measures (Safrai 2003: 179).

The appointed official superintendent, inspectors and regulators of the urban markets and trade of Mamluk and Ottoman Palestine, the *muhtasibs,* dealt with many of the functions of the *agronomoi* – but they were also government's *tax collectors* in the urban market.

The institution of *muhtasib* and *hisba* have survived in the name of a leading Palestinian family from the city of al-Khalil (Hebron). The Muhtasibs in Al-Khalil were of the superintendents of the markets in the city. In fact the *muhtasibs' system* in Palestine and throughout the urban landscape of the Islamic world had little to do with socialism and more to do with the pre-capitalist conception of moral economy of trade and markets under Islam. Practically all Palestinian cities (Acre, Jerusalem, Nablus and Nazareth included) had their own *hisbas* and the *mutasibs* and *hisba* institutions in Palestine have survived in the fact that among ordinary Palestinians the term *hisba* is still being used today as an alternative term for the word market – the other word being *souq*. The quality of Palestinian products and produce (including glasswork, mosaics and crafts) was tightly regulated and this legacy of the Mamluk system of regulation has survived in modern Palestinian vernacular terms such as *Hisbe* and in Palestinian family names such as the *Muhtasib*, a leading Muslim family in the city of al-Khalil (Hebron). The quality of Palestinian glasswork, mosaics and crafts was tightly regulated and this legacy of the Mamluk system of economic regulation has survived in modern Palestinian vernacular terms such as *Hisbe* and in Palestinian family names. The *muhtasib* system in Islamic Palestine was part of the pre-capitalist 'moral economy' (to borrow an expression by English historian E. P. Thompson (1971)) influenced by sharia principles of social justice and the public good and widely promoted in the Near East.

In Palestine the *muhtasib* was an important official appointed by the Mamluk sultans; their duties included the regulation of prices and supervision and inspection of bazaars and trade in Palestine, Egypt and the Levant. The varied duties of the *muhtasibs* in Mamluk and Ottoman Palestine were much wider and more complex than those of the *agronomoi* in Byzantine Palestine. They included ensuring that public business was conducted in accordance with the ethical requirements of the *sharia* (Islamic law). Recurrent epidemics were a regular phenomenon in the urban centres of the Middle Ages and hygienic conditions and the continuous supply of clean water, for public baths and public drinking fountains in the cities, were major achievements of Islamic civil engineering in Palestine and throughout the Muslim world. Relying on written official manuals, the *muhtasib* supervised the regulation of hygienic conditions in the bazaars, weights and measures, money, prices of produce and manufactured goods, safety of public places and food sold publicly. They also ensured that craftsmen and builders adhered to the specification set for their craft and construction standards (Broadbridge 1999; Hill 1984; Ibn al-Ukhuwah 1976).

Although the functions of the *muhtasibs* varied from one period to another, overall the duties of the *muhtasibs* were much wider than those of the *agoranomos*. During the Abbasid period those who filled the post of *hisba* (and *muhtasibs*) were judges: *qadis*, versed in Islamic *fiqh* (jurisprudence), combing religious and moral duties together with the secular occupation of the market-overseers (*muhtasibs*) (Ghabin 2009: 56).

The *muhtasibs* in Islamic history also had a wide range of technical and professional duties. The Umayyad Caliphs established a major shipyard in the Palestinian port city of Acre and in this and other port cities of Islam such as Tyre and Sidon the muhtasib's technical expertise and inspections were extended to ships and shipyards and making sure that the shipyards operated correctly and there were no human or financial losses involved. The office of *muhtasib* determined the amount of cargo a ship can carry to prevent overloading (Khalilieh: 2006: 36). Unlike the Byzantine *agoranomos* but similar to the Byzantine *sekreton* of the sea, the office of Islamic *muhtasib* supervised *inter alia* shipbuilding and carriage by sea. The *muhtasib* had assistants called *urafaal-Sina'a* (inspectors of shipbuilding) whose main task was to observe that the shipwrights observed technical standards and did not use inferior or inadequate materials or methods (Khalilieh: 2006: 36).

Also the duties of *muhtasibs* in Mamluk Palestine were more complex and more varied from those of the *agronomoi* in Byzantine Palestine in the judicial sphere: the *muhtasib* was an important official appointed by the Mamluk sultan whose duties included not only the regulation of prices and supervision and inspection of urban *bazaars*, but they were the most influential judges and magistrates in urban Palestine (Ziadeh 1953: 122); they were powerful state agents and senior judges appointed by the state and this reinforced their powerful position in the economic affairs and the state as a whole.

The duties of the *muhtasibs* in Palestine were also more complicated than those of the *agronomoi* by the fact that the moral economy of Islam was influenced by the traditional Muslim prohibitions on usury. The inspection and regulation of the urban markets and control of prices by the *muhtasibs* were within the context of the pre-capitalist 'moral economy' of Islam – to borrow a concept by English historian E. P. Thompson (1971) – which were influenced by *sharia* principles of fairness, the greater good, social justice, mutual obligation, public services, the concept of a just price and the determination to regulate the quality and prices of commodities traded in the markets of urban Palestine against unscrupulous merchants and traders, aimed at providing a public service based on moral and charitable ethical principles and the greater good. This moral economy brought about the spread of Islamic endowments (*waqf* foundations) throughout the urban centres of the Islamic world. Urban *waqf* foundations were intended for the upkeep of hospitals, schools, libraries, public baths and religious buildings and hundreds of these *waqf* charities became central to the urban life of Palestine and drove the construction of urban institutions including mosques, sufi lodges, schools, hospitals, *merchant caravasais,* orphanages and urban soup kitchens for the urban poor.

The extensive powers of the *muhtasibs* included the appointments of heads of trades (*arifs*) in urban Palestine and the trades that middle-class people practised: rice and wheat merchants, water carriers, butchers, fish-friers, makers of sweetmeats, sausage-makers, weavers, potters, needle-makers, henna-sellers, workers in oil presses, sieve-makers, tanners, felt-makers, reed-mat makers and sellers of timber. Recurrent epidemics were a regular phenomenon in the urban centres of the Middle Ages and one of the earliest and best-known Palestinian hygienists – and physician, pharmacist and botanist – under classical Islam, Muhammad bin Aḥmad al-Tamimi al-Maqdisi (born in Jerusalem, died in Cairo in 990 or 1000) wrote a well-known text: 'Survival Substance for Removing Air Pollution and Prevention from the Suffering of Epidemics' (written 980). This is perhaps the first book written in Arabic about ecological pollution and how to deal with water pollution. In addition, hygienic conditions and the continuous supply of clean water, for public baths and public drinking fountains in the cities, were major achievements of Islamic civil engineering in Palestine and throughout the Muslim world. Relying on written official manuals, the *muhtasibs* supervised the regulation of hygienic conditions in the public baths (Ziadeh 1953: 123) and bazaars, weights and measures, money, prices of produce and manufactured goods, safety of public places and food sold publicly. They also ensured that craftsmen and builders adhered to the specification set for their craft and construction standards (Broadbridge 1999; Hill 1984; Ibn al-Ukhuwah 1976).

10

The Rise and Decline of a Trademark of Palestinian Identity

The Glassware and Ceramic Industries of Al-Khalil (Thirteenth to Twenty-First Centuries)

The glass-making crafts and industries of Islamic Palestine and Syria

Glassware is among the most exquisite products ever created by human beings and the glassware of al-Khalil, which began to flourish in the Middle Ages under Islam and was exported globally, was among the most important trademarks of historic Palestine. During Classical Islam the famed Islamic tradition of glass-making in Palestine, Syria and Egypt in the Middle Ages developed. The glass came in a variety of colours and was influenced by the advances made in sciences, metallics and the properties of glass, and the uses of colouring additives such as iron oxide and copper to produce colouring effects (Calvo 2008: 71). The Palestinian city of al-Khalil (Hebron) has manufactured exquisite glass and glass products that were characterized by elegance and exported internationally since the Middle Ages. In the modern period this old *glassware of al-Khalil* became, like *Jaffa Orange* and *Nablus Soap*, a trademark of Palestinian identity. Large amounts of glass and glass vessels have been recovered from the archaeological excavations of Islamic Jerusalem, in which according to the Palestinian Jerusalemite geographer al-Maqdisi included exquisite glass lamps made in the tenth century (Calvo 2008: 71).

This tradition of exquisite Islamic glass-making also benefited from multiple and diverse influences including the long tradition of glass-making in the region in Antiquity, especially in Roman and Byzantine Palestine, and the influences of the imported Chinese glass vessels on Islamic glass-making in the Middle Ages, especially the Chinese use of calligraphic and naturalistic ornaments in glass-making. Palestine's glassware and mosaics industries had their historic roots going back to Antiquity with cities such as Caesarea Maritima and Tiberias developing locally manufactured glassware. Palestine also developed an extensive mosaic industry in late Antiquity and had its own distinctive *Mosaic School of Gaza*. Mosaics are patterns or images made of small regular pieces of coloured glass or stones or ceramic, held in place by plaster, and covering a surface. Mosaics have a long history in the ancient Middle East, starting in Mesopotamia in the third millennium BCE. They were often used as floor and wall decorations, and were particularly popular in the urban centres of Roman Palestine and on the floors of Christian basilicas and churches in Byzantine Palestine. This extensive floor mosaic church tradition (and industry) can be seen in the modern archaeological excavations of the Gaza region and can also be found today in the great Constantinian basilica in the ancient city of Bethlehem: the Church of the Nativity; the original mosaic floor of this basilica, with its typical Byzantine geometric motifs of the fourth century has been partially preserved. Also the great Palestinian urban buildings of Justinian, the *Nea Church* in Jerusalem and the rebuilt Church of the Nativity in Bethlehem in the sixth century were decorated and embellished with mosaics. In the sixth century, the city of Gaza became the centre of mosaic-making in Palestine and the archaeological excavations of the Gaza region show floor mosaics and mosaic panels displaying a wide range of motifs including birds, sea-creatures, trees, fruits, flowers and abstracts patterns – all designed to celebrate a terrestrial paradise of God's creation. Furthermore the single most important piece of Byzantine mosaic art in the Near East is the Madaba Mosaic Floor Map made in the mid-sixth century as the floor of the church of Saint George at Madaba, in modern Jordan. Rediscovered in 1894, the Madaba Mosaic Map, enriched with flora and fauna and natural and social features, such as palm trees, birds, animals, boats, bridges and fishing, gives us some of the best depictions of great cities of Byzantine Palestine and is a great symbol of the golden age of the mosaic industry of Byzantine Palestine.

In the seventh century Islam inherited the classical art of mosaic-making and Arab craftsmen adapted and developed further the mosaic industry of Palestine making it their own. During the Umayyad period Palestinian Christians retained their own important role in the economy and arts and crafts of Palestine, and new Christian churches were built and repaired; some of the most important mosaics of the Eastern Christianity were made during the eighth century when the Levant was under Islamic rule. Islam also inherited the figurative mosaic traditions of Palestine and Syria, but mostly without using human figures. Mosaics were used widely on Umayyad Islamic religious buildings and secular palaces in early Islamic art. The most important early Islamic mosaic work is the decoration included in Islam's first great religious building in Palestine, the Dome of the Rock in Jerusalem, built by the Umayyads and in the Great Umayyad Mosque in Damascus. The best example of Umayyad mosaic works can be found in the bath house of Hisham's Palace near Jericho, was made around 744. The main panel depicts a large tree ('Tree of Life' mosaic) and underneath it a lion attacking a deer and two deer peacefully grazing. This style of Islamic art has also influenced the Palestinian modern ceramic industry of Jerusalem and al-Khalil (Hebron).

Under the Abbasids from the mid-eighth century onwards this Byzantine/Umayyad figurative-style of mosaics was discouraged, with an effective ban on figurative depiction. However the geometrical abstract patterns in designs and mosaic technique not only remained popular in many urban centres of Islam and in Palestine and the Levant but became one of the major forms of Islamic ornament, arts and architecture.

The rise and decline of the al-Khalil glassware

Beautiful stained glass windows produced in al-Khalil can be seen today in the Dome of the Rock in the Old City of Jerusalem.[1] Stained glass windows made in the city of al-Khalil dating to the twelfth century were also found in the Ibrahimi Mosque in the city, a mosque that was converted into a Christian church during the Latin Crusader period in Palestine (Comay 2001: 13).

However, the glassware industry of al-Khalil was already well-established during the Mamluk period in the thirteenth century like several other major Palestinian industries, such as the soap factories of Nablus and Jerusalem and the cotton industry of the Galilee, the glass industry of al-Khalil flourished in the fourteenth and fifteenth centuries. However, the roots of the glassware industry were in the much longer history of glass-making in Palestine, which had flourished in the urban centres of Palestine in Antiquity. Today the old city of al-Khalil still boasts a quarter named the 'Glass-Blowers Quarter' (*Haret al-Qazzazin*) and al-Khalil glassware continues to serve as a tourist attraction for this ancient and industrial city in Palestine. Today al-Khalil is also a top Palestinian industrial city, with more factories in it than in any other city in the West Bank. Like several other traditional industries in Palestine, the glass melted in al-Khalil benefited from using local raw materials, including sand from neighbouring villages and minerals: and sodium carbonate from the Dead Sea as their alkali.[2] The distance between al-Khalil and the Dead Sea is only about thirty kilometres. For colouring additives the glass factories of al-Khalil used iron oxide and copper oxide.

In the Middle Ages (thirteenth century) glass-making rose as a major industry in Syria, Palestine (al-Kalil) and Egypt:

> Glass-making was originally a Syrian craft, at least glassblowing had been invented there. The products of the Syrian and Egyptian glassmakers were renowned in the days of the caliphs; the transparency and thinness of the Syrian glass were proverbial. In the middle of the thirteen century a new period of growth began in the history of Levantine glass-making. The Egyptian and Syrian craftsmen produced excellent enamelled glass with fine red contours. The glass vessels produced in their workshops in the fourteen century show Chinese influences, mainly calligraphic and naturalistic ornaments. Moslem and European travellers who visited Syria and Palestine in that period praised the glass manufactured in Damascus and Hebron [al-Khalil]. Their products were exported to Asiatic and European countries, as far as China, on the one hand, and Germany, on the other. Documents referring to the Levantine trade of the south European trading nations contain data on the export of the Oriental glass to Europe at the end of the fourteen century.
>
> (Ashtor 2014: 211)

Apparently, at the time, Levantine glassware, from Damascus, Aleppo and al-Khalil, reached not only Germany but as far north as Sweden, southern Russia and even China (Calvo 2008: 71; Lamm 1941: 67). This Levantine international trade and export to the European markers of glass – as well carpets and bullion – was a major source of revenue for the Syrian city of Damascus as well as for the Palestinian city of al-Khalil (Burns 2007: 206). This global export led to the urban expansion of both cities during the Mamluk period; the city of al-Khalil, together with the cities of Jerusalem and Nablus, became the three most important industrial cities in Palestine during the Mamluk period (1260-1516) and early Ottoman period.

Indeed the medieval reputation of al-Khalil as a glass-making centre in Palestine is confirmed by some of the many European Christian pilgrims who visited the city over the centuries, Niccolò da Poggibonsi, an Italian Franciscan friar who made a famous pilgrimage to the Holy Land in 1345–1350, and visited Jaffa, Jerusalem, Nazareth, Gaza and al-Khalil, was the first of a long line of European pilgrims who testify to a flourishing glass production al-Khali. He described this in his *Libro d'oltramare*.[3] Poggibonsi's descriptions of glass factories of al-Khalil and the buildings and cities of Palestine are detailed, and the picture he paints of the city of Jerusalem was based on four months residence there. In the fifteenth century a Swiss Dominican theologian Felix Faber (1441–1502) wrote a detailed description of his pilgrimages to Palestine (Fabri 1848, 1893 Vols. 1-3). Faber and his companions also stopped in this 'exceeding ancient city', and he wrote the following:

> we came forth from our inn, and passed through the long street of the city, in which work-people of divers crafts dwelt, but more particularly workers in glass; for at this place glass is made, not clear glass, but black, and of the colours between dark and light.
>
> (Simmons 2013: 5)

In the sixteenth century merchants importing and selling al-Khalil glass were found in al-Karak in Transjordan and in Cairo, Egypt (al-Ju'beh 2008).

While in al-Khali the *Glass-Blower Quarter* (*Haret Kezazin*) has survived into the modern period, Niccolò da Poggibonsi reported that in Damascus a street near the Great Umayyad Mosque had been given the name '*the Street of the Glassmakers*'; the same street was also referred to by Muslim traveller and explorer Ibn Battuta in the fourteenth century (Lamm 1941: 67).

The high-quality of the glassware of Damascus, Aleppo and al-Khalil was exported in large quantities to the Italian cities and the rest of Europe at the height of the Mamluk period, contributing significantly, together with other Levantine products exported to Europe, to the prosperity of the two cities. The glass vessels of al-Khalil was also widely available in the markets of cities Jerusalem, Bethlehem and al-Khalil, cities that were visited by an increasing numbers of wealthy European pilgrims; the pilgrims would arrive in Venice and then be transported by the Venetian maritime merchants to the city of Jaffa; the pilgrims would then visit Jerusalem (Brennan 2022).

Inspired by the successes the glass-making industry of Palestine and Syria, the Italian city of Venice and its merchants and glassmakers, in the thirteen century, began importing Syrian alkali, which became 'indispensable raw material' for the development of the subsequent spectacular rise of the glass-making industry of Venice – an industry that would gradually present the toughest competitive challenge for the export-oriented glass vessels of Damascus and al-Khalil (Ashtor 2014: 212). The European glassmakers in Venice and Murano began to develop new methods of production and they used a new and better raw materials for the manufacturing of crystal and 'white Latino Latte Glass Clear' and for the colouring of glass they used cobalt imported from Germany; the outcome was of a high-quality new Murano glass being exported to the Levant (Ashtor 2014: 212) – a glass with which the al-Khalil glassware, who had failed to innovate and introduce new methods and techniques, could not compete. However, while exporting al-Khalil glass to Europe was effectively brought an end by the late Middle Ages by the phenomenal dominance of the Italian glass-making industry, the production of glass in al-Khalil for export to the Near Eastern market continued into the modern period.

Al-Khalil and Jerusalem as Islamic cities of pilgrimage

The urban environment of al-Khalil expanded and flourished during the Mamluk period (1260–1516) not only as an industrial city exporting glassware internationally, to many countries in Europe and as far as China, with profits being invested back in the city, but also as a site of key Islamic institutions and charitable foundations in Palestine. A mill at Artas, a village to the south of Bethlehem – abounding with many springs and water pools – was built in 1307, and the profits from its income were dedicated to a new hospital in al-Khalil (Sharon 1997, Vol. 1: 117–18).

From earliest centuries of Islam the Palestinian cities of Jerusalem and al-Khalil were closely connected and became part of the Muslim pilgrim (*hajj*) route and magnets for Muslim and Arab ascetics, Muslim Sufis and scholars, who either settled in the two holy cities or made extensive stays in them (Ephrat. 2006: 4–18; Masalha 2022). This Islamic tradition about the 'virtues' of these two holy cities was expanded in the post-Crusader period and under the Ayyubids and Mamluks. With their large mosques, madrasas and colleges and with the income generated from trade and the hospitality lodges for travellers and pilgrims, the urban renewal and renaissance of these two ancient cities in Palestine under the Mamluks made them pillars of the Holy Land/Palestine and its important pilgrimage traditions. Between 1318 and 1320, the construction of Jawli Mosque was carried out to enlarge the prayer space for worshipers at the Ibrahimi Mosque in the city (Dandis 2011), one of the most holy Muslim shrines in Palestine and a major Muslim pilgrimage site during this period. Pilgrimages certainly generated more income for the city. The expansion of the trade of and pilgrimage to the city led to the creation of a Muslim *waqf* (charitable) foundation near Ibrahim Mosque which distributed daily and freely some 1,200 loaves of bread to travellers and pilgrims of all faiths (Robinson and Smith 1856: 458).

Not surprisingly, during this Islamic age of intellectual renaissance and urban economic and social renewalism, prominent Palestinian judge and historian of Mamluk period Mujir al-Din al-'Ulaymi (1456–1522) chronicles the history of Jerusalem and al-Khalil, in a well-known work entitled: *The Glorious History of Jerusalem and al-Khalil*' (*al-Uns al-Jalil bi-tarikh al-Quds wal-Khalil*, c.1495), the most comprehensive and detailed source for the history of the two cities written in its time (Masalha 2018, 2022).

Regeneration of urban Palestine during the Mamluk period witnessed the construction of some the most spectacular architecture of Islamic Palestine, many of the structures survive today. The reconstructed monumental White Mosque of al-Ramla – originally an Umayyad Mosque – was located at the centre of the market of the city and showed the investment by the Mamluk rulers put into the economy, trade routes and bridges, sugar mills, schools, mosques and architecture of urban Palestine.

Also, after the expulsion of Muslims and Jews from Spain in 1492, many Arab Jews moved into the countries of the Ottoman empire, and a slow arrival of Jews to Palestine took place, with some Arab Jews settling in al-Khalil. Although the Spanish Inquisition ended centuries of Andalusian *convivencia* (coexistence), between Jews, Muslim and Christian, the arrival of Arab Jews in al-Khalil continued this tradition of *convivencia*.

The development of the sugar industry of Palestine under the Mamluks

Plagues were a recurrent feature of the Middle Ages, with often disproportionate impact on the densely populated walled cities in Europe and the Middle East. Originating in Asia the Black Death, often referred to as the bubonic plague pandemic, reached both Palestine and England around the same time in 1348 (Ring et al. 1994: 290), spreading along the trade routes across the Middle East and Europe; estimates of mortality vary and figures between 40 and 60 per cent of the population perished are cited. In England the plague returned in 1361–1363, this time causing the death of around 20 per cent of the population. In Palestine, key urban population centres including Jerusalem, al-Khalil, Nablus, Lydda and al-Ramla were badly affected; it also weakened the Mamluk central government, made the highways and trade routes of the country unsafe and generally created an environment of lawlessness and looting, including the looting of the sugar - processing factories of urban Palestine. The combination of Black Death, lawlessness, highway robberies, interruption of trade, bloodshed and looting of key factories in Palestine and killing of factory workers produced economic devastation with very high rate of death toll and impacted badly on the urban population of Palestine. This period of social, economic and urban decline lasted for nearly a decade and a half until law and order was restored and social and economic recovery began (Levanoni 2021: 179–81; Petry 2022: 183).

In England the Black Death of 1348–49 killed up to half of the population and brought about peasant uprisings and demands for higher wages by surviving workers who demanded higher pay due to the shortage of labour. In Palestine the Black Death led to the death of many factory workers. It is not entirely clear what the impact of this period was on the agricultural and industrial workers in Palestine in the post-pandemic period, but evidently the economy and urban centres of Palestine recovered fairly quickly and export-oriented industries such as the al-Khalil glassware and sugar industry experienced a boom.

In the tenth century Palestinian geographer al-Maqdisi describes sugar cane cultivated in the Tiberias region, especially the Jordan River valley, indigo, rice grown in Palestine and cotton cultivated in western Galilee and silkworm cocoons cultivated at Gaza (Le Strange 2011: 184). During the Ayyubid period (1187-1250) the Muslim geographer Yaqut al-Hamawi (1179–1229) describes Jericho as a town cultivating lots of dates, banana and having a sugar cane industry and producing the highest quality sugar in Palestine (Wa'ari 2023, Vol. 1: 33).

Farming and agriculture in Palestine during the Mamluk period benefited from the agricultural and industrial advances made during the Ayyubid period (Hawari 2007); but the Mamluks also improved on these advances and elevated the Palestine sugar industry to an industrial scale industry and they encouraged the cultivation of sugar cane in the Jordan valley on a scale bigger than any preceding period in the history of Palestine.

> Excellent examples of such [agricultural] systems have been found in the southern Dea Sea in Jordan where several aqueducts were apparently built originally by Mamluk technicians.
>
> Such water control made possible the introduction of a number of new crops into Palestine. One of these was sugar cane. The plants had been cultivated along the wet banks of the Nile Rover. It seems that it was under the Mamluks that the sugar cane industry was introduced into the southern Dead Sea valley and the northern Arabia. As archaeological study of the sugar mill advances, in understanding of the economics of Mamluk Palestine should increase.
>
> (Rast 1992: 199)

Family-owned industries: The modern glassware and ceramic industries of al-Khalil

During the Ottoman period al-Khalil remained famous throughout the Middle East and beyond for its glass production and glass export. The glass industry of al-Khalil was supported by Bedouin trade networks, which brought up minerals and sodium carbonate, from the Dead Sea. Despite its relative decline in the modern period, the glass industry of al-Khalil was still widely commended in the books of Western travellers and writers who visited Palestine in the eighteenth and nineteenth centuries. Count de Volney (Constantin François de Chasseboeuf), a French writer and orientalist who visited Palestine in the early 1780s, and wrote *Voyage en Egypte et en Syrie* (1787) noted on the al-Khalil glass:

> They make there great quantity of coloured rings, bracelets for the wrists and legs, and for the arm above the elbows, besides a variety of other trinkets, which are sent even to Constantinople [Istanbul].*
>
> (Volney 1788, Vol II: 325)

Two decades later the German explorer Ulrich Jasper Seetzen, who travelled and lived in Palestine in 1807–1809, wrote that 150 persons were employed in the glass industry of al-Khalil (Seetzen 1854, Vol. 3: 5-6; Schölch 1993: 161).

In 1799 the British Royal Navy positioned its ships in the port city of Acre and contributed to the failure of the Napoleonic siege of the city. Two decades later, in the early nineteenth century Charles Irby (1789–1845) and James Mangles (1786–1867), both officers in the British Royal Navy, left England in 1816 for a tour of the Near East; for two years they travelled from Egypt to Palestine and then Syria. They also visited a glass lamp factory al-Khalil in 1818, and were told the glass lamps were produced for export to Egypt (Irby and Mangles 1823: 344; Sears 1849: 260).

In the Middle Ages, as we saw in the case of the vast industries of the capital of *Jund Filastin*, al-Ramla (Chapter 8) there was a lack of strict separation between the industrial zone of the city and the residential areas. In the modern period the modern glass factories of al-Khalil have been family owned and are a family trade: the skills are passed down by a number of Palestinian families who owned operate the glass factories located just outside the city (al-Ju'bah 2008).

Al-Khalil glass products were still famous enough to be exhibited at the World Fair of 1873 in Vienna, held from 1 May to 2 October in the capital of the Austro-Hungarian Empire; a world fair for showing industry, culture and education and hosting over seven million visitors, and the French consul in Jerusalem reported in 1876 that glass-making remained an important source of income for al-Khalil with four factories making 60,000 franks per year (Schölch 1993: 161-2).

However since the late nineteenth century, the production of glassware at al-Khalil has continued to decline due to tough competition from Europe and the European export of high-quality glassware to both Egypt and Palestine. However, while the social elites of Palestine and Egypt could afford the more expensive European glass products, the more affordable glass and other related products of al-Khalil remained popular among ordinary people and the glass factories of al-Khalil continued to supply the households of Palestine with an immense amount of bottles and other glass products for everyday use. Also travelling Jewish salesmen from the city continued to market the glassware of al-Khalil (Schölch 1993: 161-2)

Al-khalil glass products, colourful bracelets and ceramics and the hand-blown bottles, cups and little jugs continued to be sold in large quantities to the growing number of Western and Russian pilgrims and tourists who flocked to the Holy Land from the second half of the nineteenth century as both international and local transport means and routes improved.

But this industry has also continued to decline sharply under the impact of the Palestinian-Zionist conflict. Today, the outcome of decades of Israeli settler-colonialism in al-Khalil is that most of the shops in the old city are barricaded and the doors of the Palestinian houses are sealed. A large area of the Palestinian old city is closed off to

Palestinians, and under Israeli apartheid policies, the city is divided into a Jewish and a Palestinian zone.

Also nowadays, in order to survive, the few remaining glass blowers in the city have adjusted their production and hand-blown glass today is made out of recyclable bottles, and is exported in modest quantities to Europe and overseas. In addition to stained glass windows, glass produced in the factories of al-Khalil was typically functional household items such glass oil lamps and eating and drinking vessels. The factories also produced jewellery and accessories, including glass jewellery, bracelets, rings, beads and souvenirs sold to tourists and pilgrims (Beard 1862: 19).

The long tradition of glassblowing in al-Khalil continues in the twenty-first century in three family-owned factories located outside of the traditional industrial quarter of the old city of al-Khalil; located to north of al-Khalil and south of the neighbouring Palestinian town of Halhoul these factories continue to produce functional household ceramics, traditional jewellery and nickels, amoles to ward off the evil-eye and souvenirs for tourists; two of these factories are owned by the Natsheh family. But the symbolism of this ancient glassware industry of al-Khalil as trademark of Palestinian identity has remained as powerful as the historical commercial importance of this industry to the city of al-Khalil.

11

Cities of Stone

Quarries and the Stone and Marble Industries of Palestine

Viewing Jerusalem from the Mount of Olives, one is faced with the city's apparently sculptural feel. Jerusalem's cobblestones, flying buttresses and vaulted roofs together summon a ubiquitous visual uniformity. Stone is what these elements have in common. However, stone is not merely the substance that grants Jerusalem its aesthetic identity: it is the material that has defined the city's trajectory since its earliest foundations. Every story of Jerusalem is also a story of its stone.[1]

The stone and marble industries of Nablus, Jerusalem and Beit Jibrin

The ancient stone and marble industry of Palestine evolved across millennia and witnessed a remarkable expansion in the process of extracting and refining stone-making during the Ottoman period, until it became one of the most important natural resources of Palestine exported to all parts of the country and to neighbouring countries. During the Ottoman period the cities of Nablus and Jerusalem and the town of Beit Jibrin, located to the west of Jerusalem, ranked among the top Palestinian cities in the extraction, manufacture and refinement of natural stone: in Nablus there were more than eighty-six stone quarries in and around the city. In the late Ottoman period (and according to the Ottoman census of 1905) among the five most common occupations in the city of Jerusalem were carpenters, master builders and stone cutters and blacksmiths (Büssow 2011: 140, 142).

Quarried from the hills surrounding the city of Jerusalem, as well as from other nearby mountainous regions of central Palestine, the limestone of the Jerusalem region and central Palestine has been a primary urban building material since Antiquity.[2] In the tenth century Palestinian geographer al-Maqdisi writes about the 'white stones and marble' industry of the Palestinian city of Beit Jibrin (also Beit Jibril) – (*Ahsan al-Taqasim* cited in Wa'ari 2023, Vol. 1: 118) – located twenty kilometres north-west of the city of al-Khalil.

Beit Jibrin was an ancient 'city of stone' and developed its own stone and marble industry early on. Its Arabic name, derived from Aramaic, literally means the 'House of the Mighty'. The city became officially known during the Roman period by its Greek name, Eleutheropolis (*Ἐλευθερόπολις*) 'City of the Free' and acquired the municipal title *polis*; coins minted on 1 January 200 CE during Roman Emperor Septimius Severus granting the city a municipal status and commemorating its new elevated status.[3]

Under the Romans the city became one of the largest cities in Palestine: its urban built-up space covered an area of 160 acres – an area then larger than the city of Aelia Capitulina (Jerusalem); Eleutheropolis had many public and civic buildings, a large amphitheatre for mass entertainment and aqueducts supplying the city with clean water; surrounding by farmed fields and located on the intersections of roads, the city also boasted an important market (Safrai 1994: 257) – its inhabitants were recognized by the Romans as 'free citizens' who were exempted from taxes in the province of *Syria-Palaestina*.

Located on the key route of Jerusalem-Gaza, the city became an early stronghold of Christianity and was described by its Christian clergymen in the fourth century as a 'City of Excellence' (Kloner 1999: 244-6). Under the Christian Byzantines Eleutheropolis became even more important and one of the largest and most important cities in *Palaestina*; it remained an important city in the Arab province of *Jund Filatin* under Islam. The Madaba Mosaic Map of the Byzantine period shows Eleutheropolis as a walled stone city with three towers, a curving street Beit Jibrin with a colonnade in the central part and an important basilica. Eleutheropolis, in the fourth century CE had a Christian bishop with the largest territory under his jurisdiction in the Byzantine province of *Palaestina Prima*. Today *Eleutheropolis in Palaestina* is a Titular See in the Roman Catholic Church.[4]

During the first four centuries of Islam in Palestine the extensive quarries of Beit Jibrin and its marble industry of the city and its central location in Palestine served a wide range of cities of *Jund Finlastin*, including the administrative capital al-Ramla and the two holy cities Jerusalem and al-Khalil (Hebron). Depopulated by Israel in 1948, today many of the Palestinian inhabitants of Beit Jibrin and their descendants are refugees in the camps of Fawwar and 'Azza in the southern West Bank.

The Palestinian marble and stone industry benefited from the geological fact that large parts of the country were rocky and idea for building stone structures, stones that were freely available and ready for quarrying and use as building material. Not surprisingly the Palestine stone mining and quarrying industry, which required organized skilled labour, goes back to the Bronze Age. Substantial quarries for the purpose of extracting build stones and the building of houses and walls and fortifications in the Jerusalem area can also be traced to the Iron Age; this stone industry continued during the Roman, Byzantine, Umayyad and Abbasid periods and had a major impact on the urban landscape of Palestine. Although during the Byzantine period cities such as Gaza imported marble from south-central Greece, in the Middle Ages, Palestine began developing its own marble industry. A significant part of the economy of the mountainous regions of Palestine was the proliferation of thousands of stone quarries and the development of an extensive marble and stone quarrying industry that supplied the local stone needs and other building material; Palestine also exported marble and quarried white stone to neighbouring countries (Masalha 2018).

The urban centres of Palestine were also known for the recycling of cultural objects and stone products from ancient Palestine into the modern period. For instance, some of the building materials, marble and granite components, for the spectacular White Mosque of Acre – whose name echoes the monumental White Mosque of the city of al-Ramla – one of the symbols of modern Palestine, famously known as al-Jazzar Mosque, was based on recycled ancient building stones. Constructed in 1781, with a complex that included an Islamic theological academy with student lodgings, an Islamic court and a public library, these stones and marble materials were taken from the ancient ruins and sites of medieval Acre and ancient *Caesarea Palaestina* (the great capital of Byzantine Palestine) and other urban sites and fortresses of ancient Palestine. Also the creation of the new capital city of the Arab province of Palestine (*Jund Filastin*), al-Ramla, during the first century of Islam, used recycled ancient building stones collected from various old sites and fortresses in the country.

The expansion of the soap industry of Jerusalem in the sixteenth century went hand-in-hand with the expansion of another Palestinian industry in the city: the Palestine stone industry during the early Ottoman period. The early Ottoman period was a period of urban building renewal and growth in the stone industry of the city; the Ottoman authorities during the reign of Sultan Suleiman the Magnificent invested heavily in the fortification of the holy city of Jerusalem, in its urban infrastructure and amenities and in the renovation of its key Muslim holy sites, the al-Aqsa Mosque and Dome of the Rock. Minarets were and still are great symbols of Islamic civilization and the Mamluk minarets of Jerusalem are part of the great architectural heritage of the city. Although the Ottomans preserved many of the Mamluk social and administrative institutions and great Mamluk architectural heritage of the city, they also introduced some urban architectural innovations that can still be seen in the new style Ottoman minarets in the city.

The construction, between 1537 and 1541, of the formidable walls of the Old City of Jerusalem – built from locally quarried stones after three centuries of the city of Jerusalem being 'without walls' under the Mamluks (a unique situation for a medieval city the size of Jerusalem to flourish for centuries without walls) was crucial. However, the city had a formidable Muslim fortress (Arabic al-*Qala'a*, the Citadel) built by the Mamluks in 1310 and located by present-day Jaffa Gate. The Ottomans renovated and strengthened the Citadel – a formidable model of Islamic military architecture radiating authority from miles around. Much of the Citadel that stand today dates from the Mamluk and Ottoman periods. The spectacular walls of the Old City whose stones were constructed by Palestinian labourers and craftsmen from the historic stone quarries of Palestine are 4,018 metres in length. In 1981 the formidable Ottoman walls were added, along with the Old City of Jerusalem as a whole, to the list of UNESCO World Heritage Sites. The Mamluk Citadel and the Ottoman walls of Jerusalem are part of the historic Islamic heritage of the Palestinian city and represent a key feature of the urban cityscape and beautiful architecture of Palestine and its historic *Cities of Stone*. They are also monuments to the millennia-old stone industry of Palestine.

Palestinian master stonemasons (Arabic: *hajjars*) were highly skilled craftsmen and they were usually better paid than ordinary labourers. In the Ottoman period the Palestine stone industry was a major contributor to the economy of the city of Jerusalem as well as other major cities such as Nablus and al-Khalil. Today this Palestinian stone and marble industry is still a major contributor to the Palestinian economy. Palestinian stonemasons utilized some of the best quality dolomitic limestone deposits in the world for quarrying, cutting, fabrication, and dressing of building and today Palestine's stone industry is among the largest employers and generators of revenue in the country, an industry which, unfortunately, also supplies Israeli settler-colonialism and occupation with stones (Ross 2019).

In Antiquity the urban centres of Palestine and the surrounding countries were affected by a large number of destructive earthquakes as a result of the tectonic movements of the Arabian plate and Jordan Rift Valley. Historic quakes from the Bronze Age to the modern period have damaged, and in some cases destroyed, these cities of stone in Palestine. For instance, the urban centres of Palestine and Syria rocked very heavily and were damaged by several large earthquakes during the Mamluk period in 1202, 1298 and 1302, and urban structures collapsed and the inhabitants of the towns and cities had to join together to repair and rebuild the destroyed neighbourhoods (Ziadeh 1953: 61). This mutual support has been a key feature of social and urban life in Palestine especially in times of catastrophe.

Today Palestine ranks twelfth globally in terms of stone production, with Palestinian quarries producing about twenty-two million square metres of stone products annually. The Palestine stone and marble industry, which has its roots in Antiquity, contributes a quarter of Palestine industrial revenue and about 5 per cent of the total Palestinians GDP (Abu Hanieh et al. 2012; Ross 2019: 272). However, today this ancient Palestine stone mining and quarrying industry faces new challenges, the greatest of which is the threat under Israel occupation. At present only seventy of about 300 Palestinian stone mining and quarrying operations are located in Area C (Niksic et al. 2014: 58), an area that is under direct Israeli control and from which Palestinians are facing the theatre of eviction by Israeli settler-colonialism in Palestine.

12

Cross-Weaving and Gauze from Palestine to Europe

The Silk and Linen Industries of Asqalan and Gaza Under the Mamluks

As for me, I will enter the mulberry trees
Where the silkworm makes me into a silk thread
Then I will enter a women's needle in one of the myths
Then I will fly like a shawl with the wind
Mahmoud Darwish, 'Enter the Melbury Tree and Fly Free', Unfortunately, It Was Paradise: Selected Poems (2003)

The Mamluk period (1260 to 1516) was one of the most spectacularly flourishing periods, commercially, economically, culturally, educationally and architecturally, in the medieval Islamic Palestine – a period in which the industry and foreign trade of Palestine and the role of Palestinian ports in trade expanded when the Mamluks dominated the land and maritime trade in the eastern Mediterranean. In addition to the establishment of dozens of schools and colleagues in Jerusalem (Masalha 2022), several Palestinian industries, including the textile industry and the production of natural indigo dye, used in Palestinian costumes, the soap industry of Jerusalem and Nablus (Chapter 15), the sugar industry of Palestine and the cultivation of sugar cane in the Jordan valley (Chapter 10) and the Palestine glassware industry of al-Khalil (Chapter 10) and the Palestine caravanserais and hospitality industry, expanded and reached unprecedented levels of sophistication. This expansion highlighted the key role played by Palestinian ports within the context of Mamluk dominance of maritime trade in the eastern Mediterranean and the growth of the production of natural indigo dye, used in Palestinian costumes, was seen in large plantations in Jordan valley and in Palestinian textiles exported to Europe.

European and American travellers to Palestine in late nineteenth and early twentieth centuries often commented on the rich variety of the costumes and exquisite embroidered clothing's worn by Palestinian women, both among the *fellaheen* (peasant) or village women and among the middle class urban women of Palestine. Images of

Palestinian women wearing a variety of embroidered clothings saturated what became known as Holy Land photography.

In the Middle Ages, during the Fatimid and Mamluk periods, Palestine produced and exported via its Mediterranean ports an extraordinary variety of fine and coarse silk fabrics – including one coarse type of silk fabric mixed with various types of wool and woven into coats. This type became known as *gazz* silk and was exported to Arabia and various Mediterranean and Europe countries (Gil 1997: 238; Goiten 1983: 403, note 141; Lewandowsky 2011: 243; Weir 1994: 288). Pure silk fabric was an expensive elite product, while coarse silk/wool clothing was widely affordable. Generally pure silk clothing was more expensive than linen fabric and high-quality linen more expensive than cotton fabric and cotton clothing more expensive than woollen garments.

Like *gazz silk*, *gauze* was another type of silk fabric attributed to Palestine. Both *gauze and Leno* fabrics were terms that designated varieties of woven fabrics concatenated under the generic term of 'cross-weaving', a style extensively used to the production of silk, cotton, and linen fabrics. When 'cross-weaving' was applied to fabrics of light, open and transparent texture, and produced from silk and cotton, they were described as *gauze* fabrics. For hundreds of years since the high Middle Ages, the fabric known in Europe, initially known in Latin as *gazzatum* (and subsequently as *gauze* fabric) of silk or cotton has been attributed by many European writers to the city of 'Gaza in Palestine' (Skeat 1882: 230; Taylor 2005: 288). Historically there were many types of horticulture in Palestine included *sericulture*: the cultivation of the mulberry tree and silkworms flourished in southern Palestine in the Middle Ages and the two southern cities of 'Asqalan and Gaza became major centres of the Palestine silk and cotton industries under the Mamluks. The attribution of *gauze* to 'Gaza in Palestine' was made by European writers in the thirteen century at the beginning of the Mamluk rule in Palestine (Garrison 2008: 261).

In the Middle Ages the *gauze* fabric was originally woven of silk and produced in the Middle East for clothing and exported widely to Europe. Islam developed an extensive silk industry in the Middle Ages and in the tenth and eleventh centuries the towns and cities of Syria and Palestine developed highly skilled specialisms in the textile industry with silk products being top of the list of these industries and the most profitable of the textile industries. Four cities in Syria: Damascus, Hims, Aleppo and Tyre, and four cities in Palestine: al-Ramla, Tiberias, 'Asqalan and Gaza became the most important centres for silk and textile production and textile export (Yusuf 1985: 127). As we have seen in Chapter 5, Christian monks and Christian missionaries brought silkworms to Byzantine Syria and Palestine from China in the sixth century and under Islam throughout the Middle Ages the cultivation of the mulberry tree and silkworms developed. The coastal cities of Lebanon and Syria and the southern cities of Palestine were among those places that silk production flourished in the Middle Age under Islam. In many of these Levantine cities, large silk-weaving mills were established. Gauze was also used in Europe in bookbinding which was called *mull*, and was used in case binding to adhere the text block to the book cover (Cambras 2004: 48).

Cross-weaving and the European Industrial Revolution: The modern French and Scottish gauze

The mechanization of the textile Industrial Revolution of modern Europe and the cross-weaving principle that was applied to fabrics of light and open textures resulted in the emergence of large-scale modern European gauze, especially the *French gauze* and *Scottish gauze*. Gauze is now made in Europe from both cotton and synthetic fibres and used for a variety of purposes, including *gauze* sponges for medical use. In fact today *gauze* is associated largely with a range of high-quality medical dressings and widely marketed as a *wound* care solution. In technical terms *gauze* was a thin, translucent fabric with a loose open weave; a weave structure in which the weft yarns were arranged in pairs and are crossed before and after each warp yarn keeping the weft firmly in place. The same weave structure was used to add stability to fabric, which is important when using fine yarns loosely spaced (Emery 1966: 180). In the modern European theatre and film industry gauze was often fashioned into a scrim, very light textile made from fibre-based materials. The multiple and extraordinary diverse uses, fashioning of *gauze* in Europe - and with the modern Industrial Revolution large-scale production of modern *French gauze* and *Scottish gauze*, produced in the town of Paisley in the nineteenth and twentieth centuries - over the centuries made it one of the most famous fabrics in history.

Theories and evidence about the origins of gauze

What is also remarkable is transformation of the term *gauze* from its Arabic origins in the Middle Ages into the medieval European Latin term of *gazzatum*, and then into the modern term *gauze*. However, there is uncertainty in the European literature about the historical origins of the term *gauze*. The conflation of some modern authors of the terms *gauze* and *gazz* (the medieval Arabic word for silk of any kind and of 'silkworm') added more confusion about the historical origins of the terms *gazzatum and gauze*. There are three distinct views of the origins of the term *gauze*, two of which are related to the textile industry of southern Palestine during the Mamluk period (1260 to 1516):

The most common view: the name *gauze* was derived from the name of the Palestinian city of *Gaza*. *The Fairchild Books Dictionary of Textiles* of 2013 states:

> Gauze: a thin, sheer, open weave fabric, usually made of cotton, silk or manufactured fibers in which some of the warp ends are interlaced with each other in a leno weave. There are also plain weave gauzes not made with a leno. The cotton fabric is used primarily for blouses and surgical dressings, the silk or rayon gauze for dress trimming. Sometimes applied to very sheer knitted fabric. Derivation: the city of Gaza (Tortora and Johnson 2013: 256); 'Gazzatum, a fine, sheer silk or linen gauze. Made during the Middle Ages, believed to have been made originally in Gaza, in what is now the Israeli-Palestinian Gaza Strip'.
>
> (Tortora and Johnson 2013: 257)

According to this view, the term *gauze* was derived from the name of the city of *Gaza*, because the city was a centre of a silk-weaving industry and the gauze silk fabric (Garrison 2008: 261). The US Webster's Dictionary of 1913, which supports this approach, states that the English word *gauze* is said to be derived from the name of the city of Gaza, which was a centre of weaving in Palestine in the Middle Ages (Taylor 2005: 288). Also in the *Encyclopedia of Antiquity and Elements of Archaeology: Classical and Medieval* of 1825, we find the following:

> Gauze: This stuff is similar to the *transparent* silk, dyed in purple, before weaving, which formed the famous *coavestis*, mentioned by Isaiah, as worn by Oriental females, and said by Pliny to be the invention of Pamphila. In the Middle Age, it is called *Gazzatum*, from Gaza in Palestine.
>
> (Fosbroke 1825, Vol. I: 396)

This encyclopeadia also says:

> The ristrum [summer garment]: A kind of very fine cotton or Gauze, which the women threw over the head and shoulders to keep off the sun. The Arabian women still wear it'.
>
> (Fosbroke 1825, Vols. I and II: 873)

The same idea can be found in *An Illustrated Dictionary of Historic Costume* (Planche 2013: 202). The Gaza local industry of cotton fabrics survived into the modern period and into the nineteenth century (Gilbar 2023: 76, Ritter 1866: 207).

This second view questions the Palestinian historical origins of the term *gauze* based and relies on the evolution of the *French gauze*. Gazz in medieval French, meant high-quality lightweight fabric having an aspect of transparency, very often made of silk but not necessarily silk. According to the French government's online etymological dictionary, the English form of the word derived from the French *gaze*, whose ultimate origin is uncertain, but is often attributed to the Arabic and Persian words *qazz*, or 'raw silk', which itself was obtained from the name of Gaza.[1] The same French source says the existence of 'an ancient textile industry in Gaza is not assured,' and it is not known how the word entered into widespread use in European languages, with examples of first usages cited being the Medieval Latin forms *garza* in Bologna in 1250 and *gazzatum* in Budapest in 1279.[2]

The third view centres on the idea that the Latin *gazzatum* (and later *gauze*) was a common trade name, conventionally assigned in medieval Europe to a silk textile type, and attributed to '*Gaza* in Palestine' not because the silk and cotton fabrics were exclusively produced Gaza, but because these fabrics were extensively produced in southern Palestine during the Mamluk period and then exported and largely shipped from the port of Gaza, which during this period was an important port on the Mediterranean for the export of goods and textile to Europe in the same way that *Vinum Gazetum* (Latin for *Gaza wine*), which was among the best favourite wines on European tables in late Antiquity, was produced in southern Palestine and the Naqab and then shipped from the port of Gaza to many countries in Europe and in the same way *Jaffa Orange* was cultivated in a large number of Palestinian villages and towns between Jaffa and Lydda and then shipped from the port of Jaffa to Europe in the modern period. This theory about the historical origins of the common trade name known as *gazzatum* can also finds echoes in the textile known as *silk damask* in Europe - which was different from *silk damask* which was stout compact, twilled fabric - that was produced widely in Syria and then exported from the city of Damascus, and in the way *calico* came to Europeans from the name *Calicut*, a city along the Malabar coast in India known as the 'City of Spices' because spices were shipped and exported from this port city. These historical common trade names in Europe simply referred to ports or 'market cities' from which such goods were exported and shipped to Europe, rather than to the original actual places of manufacture. In this sense, *gauze* was a fine type of silk fabric woven and manufactured in southern Palestine and shipped from Gaza to Europe as early as the thirteenth century and then widely popularized in the high Middle Ages of Europe under the trade name of *gazzatum*. We also have to keep in mind that Gaza was a global *emporium city* in late Antiquity and this perception of Gaza in Europe as a major *market city* at the centre of global trades routes in Antiquity persisted throughout the early Middle Ages.

This theory is backed by five factors: (1) the fact that Gaza and Jaffa were two key ports on the Mediterranean serving as entry points and exit points for goods coming from Europe and being exported to Europe and Africa; (2) that Mamluk rule in Palestine encouraged the production of crops like olives, grapes, wheat, and raw cotton in abundance and this raw cotton contributed to the flourishing of the local Palestine cotton fabric textile industry; (3) the fact that Mamluks Gaz became a major administrative centre in Palestine, becoming the capital of the 'Gaza province' of Palestine (*Mamlakat Ghazza*, the 'Governorship of Gaza'), a province that included the city of Asqalan, a major centre of linen and textile industries under the Mamluks. And like *Vinum Gazetum* (*Gaza wine*), which was highly popular on European tables in late Antiquity and during the Byzantine era (discussed in Chapter 6), the weaving and production of *gazzatum* fabric (or gauze) in Palestine was not confined to the city of Gaza; (4) the fact that the ancient harbour of the city of Ascalon – which was enlarged during the Crusaders wars and enabled Muslim Ascalon to receive supplies of corn from Egypt and thereby to protract its siege by the Crusaders – was effectively destroyed by the Mamluks after the defeat of the Crusaders in Palestine; under the Mamluks, Sultan Bibars filled up the port of Asqalan and cast stones into the sea in 1270 and he destroyed the remains of the fortifications, for fear of another Latin Crusader invasion of Palestine. With the destruction of the port of Asqalan, much of the manufactured silk and linen fabrics of Asqalan was shipped and transported to Egypt and Europe from Gaza; (5) at its height the Mamluk sultanate traded extensively with Europe and supplied Europe with vast quantities of raw materials and manufactured textiles, including silk, wool and linen fabrics as well as sugar, glass, soaps, paper and spices. The Papal restrictions on the importation of silk and *gazzatum* fabric from the countries of the Mamluk state were largely ignored in Europe; much of the Mamluk trade with Europe was shipped from the port cities in Palestine, Syria, including Acre, Jaffa and Gaza to Egypt or even directly to Europe and from Alexandria to Europe. Wealthy Italian merchants, primarily from the Italian city-states of Venice, Genoa and Pisa with each city-state having its own fleet of ships, traded gold and silver ducats, silk, wool and linen fabrics, furs, wax, honey and cheeses. In 1387 Sultan Barsbay (1422-1438) established control of Alexandria and a monopoly on luxury goods and the pricing of spices, then in 1429 he insisted the spice trade to Europe pass through medieval Cairo before reaching Alexandria. Also as we shall see in Chapter 13, throughout the Mamlūk period caravanserais were extensively constructed in Palestine and in the Gaza region and caravans and merchants from Palestine and Syria transported manufactured goods and silk and textile fabrics from Syria and Palestine to medieval Cairo and then to Alexandria to be shipped to Europe. The Arab-Venetian commercial preponderance lasted until the fifteenth century, however fifteenth and early sixteenth century Portuguese expansion into Africa and Asia cut into the Mamluk-Venetian monopoly on the trans-Mediterranean spice and silk trade contributing to the demise of the Mamluk sultanate.

However, whether the historical origins of the term *gauze* came from the silk fabric being shipped from *Gaza* and so became a Palestinian common trade name or whether the name comes the Arabic term *gazz*, 'silkworm' and 'raw silk', the explicit medieval prohibition on the importation of *gazzatum* fabric from the non-Christian Arab and Muslim regions of the Middle East by church authorities in Europe points clearly to the Arabic origins of the term *gauze*. Members of religious orders in Europe were forbidden by the church to wear *gazzatum*, then known as a fine type of silk fabric attributed to Gaza and Palestine as early as the thirteenth century (Garrison 2008: 261).

Encyclopaedia Metropolitana of 1845 states

> Gazzatus: flax or fine silk, commonly gazze, perhaps because first introduced from Gaza, a city of Palestine. If the Gazzatum of the medieval writers was Gauze (which there seems no reason to doubt), its use expressed forbidden by Ecclesiastics.

Du Cange continues the passage above by citing a Canon (the 61st of the Council of Buda), held in 1279, which said

> "We forbid a gazzatus and any other notably delicate cloth"
>
> (Planche 2013: 202; Smedley 1845: 496)

However, the ecclesiastical ban failed. Imported from the Middle East, subsequently this fabric became very fashionable in Europe and won a respectable place for itself in the international textile trade; gauze emerged as a distinct style and a fine fabric produced extensively in modern Europe (Garrison 2008: 261).

Al-Bazzazin: The linen weavers of Asqalan

As has already been shown in Chapter 5, the Palestinian flax cultivation and linen weaving industry of the city of Beisan and its surrounding villages was among the most prized industries in the Roman world. At the time Palestine also developed silk textile manufacturing based on raw silk imported from China. However by the time we get to the tenth century, the ancient Palestinian city of Asqalan emerges as the most important centre in the country for linen making and silkworms cultivation and silk manufacturing.

The renowned medieval textile and silk industry of the city of Asqalan, located under the Mamluks in the 'Gaza Province' of Palestine (*Mamlakat Ghazzah*), was first praised in the tenth century by prominent Palestinian geographer al-Maqdisi, who mentions cotton, sugar, indigo and rice as grown and the cultivation of silkworms in Gaza (Le Strange 2011: 184). Al-Maqdisi also praises the renowned silkworms and silk industry of the city of Ascalon (Conder 1887: 456), located a short distance from Gaza.

> Gaza is a large town on the main road to Egypt, on the border of the desert. The city stands far from the sea. There is here a beautiful mosque and the monument of [caliph] Umar Ibn al-Khattab. It is too the birthplace of [imam] al-Shafii, and possesses the tomb of Hahsim bin Abd Manaf [the great grandfather of the Prophet]. Maimas [ancient Maumas] on the sea, is a small fortified (*hasina*) town pertaining to Gaza. Askalan (Ascalon) is on the sea. A fine city, and a strongly garrisoned. Fruit is here in plenty, especially that of the Sycamore-tree (*Jummaiz*), of which all are free to eat. The great mosque stands in the market of the cloth-merchants, and is paved throughout with marble. The city is spacious, opulent, healthy, and well fortified. The silkworms of this place are renowned, its wares are excellent and life there is pleasant, and its markets are thronged, and its garrison alert.
>
> (Al-Maqdisi, *Ahsan al-Taqasim fi Ma'irifat al-Aqalim*; also Le Strange 1886: 53–64)

Asqalan (ancient Ascalon) was a city with a large textile bazaar, and for many centuries throughout the early Islamic period and subsequently during the Mamluk period the city and its surrounding villages became renowned for their breeding of high-quality silkworms and Asqalan was praised by Arab historians for its fine medieval silk and linen industries (Al-Dabbagh 1980: 325; Arraf 1992: 210; Hammudi et al. 2021: 57–8). Palestinian historian al-Maqdisi mentioned that in Asqalan there was a large textile bazaar area and implied that a considerable number of the inhabitants of the city worked in the silk industry, and the city was distinguished by its superior silkworm and its superior silk and this indicates that many people raised silkworms in the city and that this high-quality of silk was sold in Palestine and exported to neighbouring Arab countries. He also mentioned the linen industry of the city and that a neighbourhood in Asqalan was called the 'linen-makers': *al-Bazzazin* (Hammudi et al. 2021: 57–8).

Although Asqalan did develop large textile industry in the modern period and until the expulsion of its Palestinian inhabitants in the Nakba of 1948, all attempts at reviving the medieval silk industry of Palestine, and the cultivation of mulberry and breeding of silkworms, by the British Mandatory authorities in the 1930s met with limited success.

13

Caravanserais, Markets and Urban Life

The Urban and Rural Merchant Khans of Mamluk and Ottoman Palestine

Mamluk Palestine (1260-1516) was a golden age for the development of many rural and urban merchants' caravanserais in Palestine. The merchant caravanserais and traveller inns were not invented by Islam. In the iconic story of New Testament (Luke 2: 7), Jesus of Nazareth was born in a manger in the town of Bethlehem, in Roman Palestine, because there was 'No [guest] room at the inn' for Mary and Joseph. But is not entirely clear whether a small town like Bethlehem at the time, with a population of a few hundred people and not situated on a major trade route in Palestine, would have a public inn.

Over millennia the caravan systems in Palestine, which encompassed a variety of historical periods and contexts and diversity of merchandise, shared some basic features including the establishment of safe trade stations along the main highways for travellers, merchants and pilgrims and the provision of lodging, food and water for the consumption of humans and animals. As we have seen in Chapter 2, the earliest extensive trade system in Palestine was connected with the establishment of steady supplies and trade routes, established specifically for the copper trade (the copper was exchanged for other goods imported from the north during the Early Bronze Age). Also, as we have seen in Chapter 3, the Nabataean Arabs, who dominated the Trans-Arabian global trade in frankincense, aromatics and spices (from Asia and Yemen to the Mediterranean cities of Palestine) in Antiquity for centuries, long before the Roman conquest of Palestine, constructed the archetypal trade stations combined with military forts in southern Palestine (the Naqab) – trade stations that were supplied with the wells and cisterns and that evolved gradually into major cities of spice and aromatics and urban centres in the Palestinian Naqab. Palestine's geographic and strategic location at the crossroads of three continents (Asia, Africa and Europe) made it ideal for the Nabataean development of long-distance trade routes and a truly global trade system, which allowed Nabataean camel caravans and caravanserais in southern Palestine and facilitated the movement of large quantities of spices and aromatics, olive oil, henna, storax, asbestos, clothes, glass, gold coins and silver items and other luxurious goods across vast areas. This trade system of the Trans-Arabian caravans' and caravanserais' trade system in the Palestinian Naqab of Antiquity fits into a larger set of patterns of distant-travel, diversity of goods, technologies of transport, bulk of goods, social and economic frameworks for the trade and investment in infrastructures (Rosen 2019).

In Palestine the Romans and Byzantines inherited the Nabataean system of trade posts-cum-military forts and constructed new roads in Palestine, and Islam continued, transformed and expanded that tradition of global trade backed by a vast system of rural and urban caravanserais and an extensive system of covered marketplaces. The Islamic context of reshaping marketplaces and the expansion of the regional and global Islamic trade in the Middle Ages and the conversion of traditional inns into covered marketplaces is much in evidence from the late Umayyad period; in the early eighth century large caravanserai in Pella in Jordan were uncovered by archaeologists consisting of a double-story accommodation with rooms, porches and balconies around an open area:

> The unearthing of two male bodies carrying precious goods (a golden earning, a dagger, an iron ring, three dirhams, and a dinar from 712), seven camels, and a donkey, crushed by falling masonry during the earthquake of 749, supports the hypothesis that the building was used as a commercial hostelry in the first half of the eighth century.
>
> (Bessard 2020: 159)

The extensive Islamic caravanserai system was a system of roadside and urban inns that supported the flow of commerce, people and information across vast networks of trade routes used by merchants, travellers, pilgrims and Sufi preachers where merchants and travellers could rest, eat and recover from the day's journey or long-distance travel; this system of roadside and urban inns also accommodated camels, horses, donkeys and other pack animals as well as storage rooms for merchandise and public baths (*hammams*) (Chisholm 1911b). Built at intervals equivalent to a day's journey to facilitate land travel in stages, caravanserais were essential for long-distance trade and for the flow of regional, international and global commerce and for the movement of travellers, pilgrims, ideas and postal services across vast regions and the vast network of trade routes covering central Asia, the Middle East and North Africa. Also in the Middle Ages many caravanserais were dotted across central Asia and the global silk routes from China in the east to the Middle East and North Africa and southern Europe in the West.[1]

The global trade of Islam also necessitated the creation of specific commercial Islamic terminology and in Islamic Palestine the terms *khan* and *khan al-Tujjar* (*Merchants' Caravanserai*) referred to both urban and rural caravanserais. Historically other related terms were used in Arabic for the urban caravanserai: *wikala* (or *wakala: a* commercial agency) or *Khan al-Wakala*, an urban building that combined the functions of khan (caravanserai), warehouse and market – examples include *Khan al-Wikala*, which was built in the western parts of the city of Nablus at the beginning of the sixteenth century (Abujidi 2014: 90).

The Arabic term *wikala*, commercial agency, was used widely in connection with the urban caravanserai in Palestine and the term *wikala of soap* was also used to describe Palestinian merchants' caravanserais and commercial buildings in Cairo. As we shall in Chapter 15, under Islam the soap industry became a key export-oriented industry of the cities of Ramla, Nabus and Jerusalem, and *Wikalat Amir Qawsun* was a square-shaped caravanserai and commercial building in Cairo that was constructed by the Mamluk merchant Amir Qawsun (1302–1342), was used by Palestinian soap and coffee merchants during the seventeenth and eighteenth centuries, thus becoming known as the '*Wikala of Soap*'. The building was demolished in the 1960s to make way for a new school building, and only the gate of the original structure remains (Meinecke 1980; Warner 2005).

The urban caravanserai of merchants (*khan al-Tujjar*) were built within a city or a town while rural caravanserais were built along key traditional trade routes and the pilgrim route to Mecca. In Mamluk and Ottoman Palestine, the urban caravanserais were a main feature of urban life and numerous khans were located in the key cities of the country. Merchant khans were also built along the main highways of travel and rural trade routes and pilgrim routes to Mecca. Both rural Khan al-Tujjar near Mount Tabor and the urban Khan al-Tujjar of Nablus were *Souq al-Khan* (the Market Khan) and *Souq Khan al-Tujjat* (the Market of the Caravanserai) respectively. Both the urban and rural versions of the caravanserai provided lodging for travellers and merchants, their animals and their goods; they also served as shopping centres and markets for the storage and selling of goods and for trade transactions and other commercial activities. Also, as we have seen in the Introduction, important *gold markets* began to emerge in urban Palestine under Islam, and especially during the Mamluk period, top of which were the gold markets of Gaza, Nablus and Jerusalem.

Often located near the main markets (*bazaars*), the urban caravanserais became major hubs of economic and commercial activity in cities across Palestine, with many examples still standing in the historic and old cities of Nablus, Acre, Jerusalem and Nazareth. Some of the rural caravanserais in Palestine also held large weekly markets that attracted thousands of shoppers – as in the case of rural Khan al-Tujjar, near Mount Tabor, with its *Souq al-Khan* – and had permanent shops on site, catering for both local inhabitants and travellers and pilgrims – while many large urban caravanserais also housed shops inside the khans or in properties adjacent to them as in the case of the city of Nablus; in this city some of the largest textile merchants and their descendants were important proprietors in the Khan al-Tujjar (Merchant Caravanserai) of the city (Doumani 1995: 62).

In Palestine the combined urban caravanserais and markets were often managed through the Islamic *waqf* system as in many parts of the Muslim world, the revenues from urban caravanserais provided funds that were used to the support the maintenance of great mosques and *waqf* charitable foundations, schools and religious institutions. Originally constructed as a staging post on main highways, the Mamluk merchants' khans (both urban and rural) gradually added more functions including warehouses, shopping centres and markets (Luz 2014: 123):

> One of the changes to the *khan* under Islamic rule was the charitable [*waqf*] function it was assigned in cities throughout the Middle East ....[the Mamluk waqf deeds] not only attests to the connections between caravanserais and the religious activity of the *waqfs*, but also the complexity of endowments of their presence in many and manifold realms of urban life.
>
> (Luz 2014: 124)

The caravanserais of Islamic Palestine became key travel stations and enabled the journey and transport of merchandise within Palestine and across Palestine to be conducted in stages; these travel stations were fairly stable across centuries. Tenth- and twelfth-centuries Muslim geographers Ibn Hawqal (who travelled from AD 943 to 969) and Muhammad al-Idrisi (1100–1165) respectively mentioned the town of Isdud and Khan Isdud in his enumeration of the towns and cities located on the main Palestinian highway from Syria to Egypt; he recorded: from the city of al-Ramla to al-Fustat (medieval Cairo) in Egypt, there were eleven stages or stations. The first stage is from al-Ramla to the khan of Yubna and then from Yubna to the khan of Isdud, and then from Isdud to Gaza (Wa'ari 2023, Vol. 1: 38). The journey from Aylah (the Gulf of Aqaba) to Jerusalem was carried out in six stations (Wa'ari 2023, Vol. 1: 55).

In addition to the officially recognized caravanserais, travellers also used local mosques for sleeping and night rest. Describing his journey through the towns, villages and valleys of Palestine, Muslim scholar Abd al-Ghani al-Nabulsi – who visited Palestine in 1693: after leaving the town of Nazareth with his companions – mentioned sleeping in the mosque of the village of Iksal in Mar Ibn Amer and being treated very generously by the local villagers (Wa'ari 2023, Vol. 1: 46). Al-Nabulsi writes: we went through that overwhelmingly cultivated and lush plain full green and full things (Marj Bani Amer cited in Wa'ari 2023, Vol. 1: 46).

Regional trade, caravanserais and rural markets: Khan al-Tujjar (Near Mount Tabor) (1581 to late-nineteenth century)

Many urban caravanserais in Palestine also functioned as shopping centres and great urban markets. Although the majority of caravanserais/markets were located in the cities of Palestine, some pre-modern markets and annual fairs were located in rural areas, and these rural markets were centred on the rural caravanserais and merchants' khans of Palestine; these caravanserais were located on international highways of Palestine; examples of these rural merchants khans and rural markets are Khan al-Minya and Khan al-Tujjar, both were located in eastern Galilee and served nearby towns and villages (Petersons 2006: 479-80).

In the late nineteenth century the British Palestine Exploration Fund surveyed a list of sixteen caravanserais in Palestine many of which were constructed during the Mamluk period (1260-1516) – a golden age for the establishment of merchants' khans in Palestine; many of these caravanserais functioned for hundreds of years and survived into the Ottoman period. These included:

1. Khan Abu hajj Faris (Abu Faris caravanserai)
2. Khan Abu Heda
3. Khan al-Ahmar (the Red Caravanserai; Mamluk/Ottoman; Jerusalem-Jericho road)
4. Khan Bedaweyyeh
5. Khan al-Duweir (the caravanserai of the Little Convent)
6. Khan Esdud
7. Khan Hathrurah (caravanserai of Hathrurah)
8. Khan Jubb Yousif
9. Khan al-Qasimiya (the Qasimiyya caravanserai)
10. Khan Lubna (caravanserai of the town of Lubna)
11. Khan Minya (caravanserai of Minya near Tiberias)
12. Khan Miska (the Inn of the water works)
13. Khan al-Ram (caravanserai of al-Ram)
14. Khan al-Shawish
15. Khan al-Tujar (caravanserai of the Merchants) (Palestine Exploration Fund. 1888: 105).

Also called *The Market Khan* (*Souq al-Khan*), this merchants' caravanserai was built in lower eastern Galilee, near Mount Tabor, during the early Ottoman period on the instruction of the Ottoman Grand Vizier Sinan Pasha in 1581 (Sharon 1999, Vol 2: 230). Khan al-Tujjar combined both a caravanserai for lodging travellers and merchants and a fortress, garrisoned by local Ottoman forces. The site was built on the instruction of Sinan Pasha, the Albanian-born Ottoman military commander, who also served as governor of Damascus in 1580s. Sinan was famous as a builder of grand urban and rural caravanserais, urban public baths, grand mosques and bridges and military fortresses. The building of this fortress cum-rural caravanserai, which also became a major market centre in lower eastern Galilee for nearly three centuries, reflected the engineering ambitions for grand projects of Sinan Pasha during the early Ottoman period. The reasons given for the establishment of this caravanserai/fortress were that fortified building would secure this key trade route in Palestine and serve both merchants and pilgrims on their way to Mecca (Sharon, 1999, Vol. 2: 230).

As in the cases of the caravanserais of Jubb Yusuf and Minya, there was also a spring and a well in the vicinity of Khan al-Tujjar, with a perennial supply of water for the khan and its many customers (Conder and Kitchener 1881: 379).

This merchant caravanserai functioned for nearly three centuries and held a large weekly market, perhaps the largest fair in Palestine, which attracted thousands of customers and shoppers, not only from nearby towns such Nazareth, Tiberias and Jenin and the villages of eastern Galilee, but also merchants and shoppers from towns and cities across Palestine, including from the city of Nablus, as well as customers from neighbouring countries.

Like many rural caravanserais, this khan was equipped with a small mosque and a public bath (*hammam*). Many Western and Muslim travellers commented on the fact that the site was constructed as two large buildings, one a merchant caravanserai with shops, a mosque and a bath and the other building as a fortress. Ottoman explorer and traveller Evliya Çelebi, who visited Palestine twice, once in 1649 and once in 1670–1, describes in his travelogue, the *Seyahatname*, the caravansary as follows:

> It is a square, perfect fortress, built of masonry in the midst of a large, verdant meadow. It has a circumference of six hundred paces. The garrison consists of a warden and 150 men. It has a 'double' iron gate facing north. Inside the fortress are between forty and fifty rooms for the garrison ... Inside the fortress is the Mosque of Sinan Pasha, an artistically constructed work, with a lead roof, full of light. Its windows have light blue glass enamel fixed symmetrically with rock crystal and crystal(?). It measures eighty feet each side. The sanctuary has three graceful and lofty minarets—Praise be to the Creator, as if they were three young coquettish muezzons—and seven high domes. The wayfarers are lavishly given a loaf of bread and a tallow candle for each person, and a nosebag of barley for each horse—free of charge. On either side of the fortress is a caravanserai with eight shops.
>
> (Stephan, 1937: 84-5)

Several accounts by other western travellers described the caravanserai as two large buildings, one functioning as merchants' khan, with a mosque and a bath, and the other building looking more like a castle; the site also functioned as a shopping centre with permanent shops (Buckingham, 1821: 456-8; Egmont and Heyman 1759, Vol. 2: 27; Guérin 1880: 381-2; Robinson et al. 1841, Vol. 3: 236).

Some accounts from the early and mid-eighteenth century give the impression of a largely deserted khan, with no weekly market held on the site. But in *Travels through part of Europe, Asia Minor, the islands of the archipelago, Syria, Palestine, Egypt, Mount Sinai,* Egmont and Heyman (1759) noted two buildings, one with a mosque and bath inside the khan, and one of the buildings was being used for goods and cattle.

> a Kane [khan], called Ain Ettiiiari, the fountain of merchants. This Kane [khan] has a mosque and a bath, and near it is another square building, where the goods and cattle were kept, there being here formerly a very considerable weekly market; these parts being then well furnished with villages and houses; but at present totally desert[ed].
>
> (Egmont and Heyman 1759, Vol. 2: 27)

But one account from the early 1760s by the Italian traveller Giovanni Mariti, who visited Khan al-Tujjar, gives us a very different picture and notes the weekly market held on Monday:

> you arrive at El-Net-Tesgiar, or the Place of Merchants. I was very much struck with the elegance and magnificence of its walls. Incrusted with the most beautiful marble, which the hand of art has disposed with much taste ... El-Net-Tesgiar is

> enlivened by a very flourishing commerce. A fair is held here every Monday, which is resorted to by merchants from various countries. It is well furnished with cloth, cattle, and provisions of every kind; and in this respect it is, indeed, not inferior to the richest markets in Europe.
>
> (Mariti 1792, vol 1: 357)

British author, journalist and traveller James Silk Buckingham who visited the khan in 1816 and published his *Travels in Palestine* in 1821 also gives a picture of a thriving khan and a Monday market that attracts thousands of shoppers. He described how, on a Monday, he found four to five thousand merchants and shoppers assembled around the khan, in addition to numerous herds of cattle for sale (Buckingham, 1821: 456–8). Also American biblical writer Edward Robinson described his visit in 1838, a day after the weekly Monday market which had 'drawn away from their home a large portion of the people of Nazareth' (Robinson et al. 1841, Vol 3: 200, 236).

In the mid-1850s a colleague of Edward Robinson – William McClure Thomson, an American protestant missionary, who spent twenty-five years in Ottoman Palestine and Lebanon and initiated later what is now known as the American University of Beirut – vividly describes the weekly market day on Monday at Khan al-Tujjar:

> On Monday of each week a great fair is held at the khans, when, for a few hours, the scene is very lively and picturesque. These gatherings afford an excellent opportunity to observe Syrian manners, customs, and costumes, and to become acquainted with the character and quality of Syrian productions. Thousands of people assemble from all parts of the country, either to sell, trade or purchase. Cotton is brought in bales from Nablus; barley, and wheat, and sesamum, and Indian corn from Huleh, the Hauran, and Esdraelon [Mar Ibn Amer]. From Gilead and Bashan [Transjordan], and the surrounding districts, come horses and donkeys, cattle and flocks, with cheese, *leben, semen*, honey and similar articles. Then there are miscellaneous matters, such as chicken and eggs, figs, raisins, apples, melons, grapes and all sorts of fruits and vegetables in season. The pedlars open their packages of tempting fabrics, the jeweller is there with his trinkets; the tailor with his ready-made garments; the shoemaker with his stock, from rough, hairy sandals to yellow and red Morocco boots; the farrier is there with his tools, nails, and flat iron shoes, and drives a prosperous business for a few hours; and so does the saddler, with his coarse sacks and gaily-trimmed cloths. And thus it is with all the arts and occupations known to this people .... But long before sunset not a soul of this busy throng remains on the spot. All return home, or to take refuge in some neighbouring village.
>
> (Thomson 1859, Vol 2: 152–3)

The British Palestine Exploration Fund, which surveyed the two buildings on the site in 1881, described Khan al-Tujjar as no longer a working caravanserai, but it was still functioned as a large weekly market held there each Thursday (Conder and Kitchener, 1881: 394–6).

The caravanserais as large compounds

The Mamluk period in Palestine saw the revitalization of the trade system, the construction of many urban and rural caravanserais and the building of many new bridges along the road network of Palestine; the Mamluks also played a major part in improving the postal service of Palestine. While the Latin Crusader period (1099-1250) was characterized by insecurity, warfare and the establishment of many fortresses and castles in Palestine, the Mamluk period was a golden age for trade in Palestine and for the establishment of many rural and caravanserai and merchants' khan across the country. Both the caravanserai of Khan Yunis in the Gaza region and the khan of Jubb Yusuf in the eastern Galilee illustrates this golden age of the establishment caravanserais in Palestine.

Numerous caravanserais were built by the Mukluks along the main highways of Palestine, some of which constituted large compounds complete with a mosque and minaret. Impressive examples of large compounds can be seen in the urban caravanserais of Jerusalem and the caravanserai of Khan Yunis in the Gaza Strip. Khan Yunis was established in the fourteenth century by Mamluk rulers who built a large caravanserai for merchants and travellers travelling through the Mediterranean sea route in Palestine and between Damascus and Cairo. Also during the Mamluk period the Khan Yunis caravanserai was transformed into a permanent village (combined with a caravanserai) illustrating the impact of the Mamluk trade on the prosperity of the Gaza region (Filiu 2014). A further transformation Khan Yunis took place in the aftermath of the 1948 Nakba and the displacement of many Palestinian refugees who were driven out from their villages and towns in southern Palestine and forced into the Gaza Strip and today Khan Yunis is the largest second city in the Gaza Strip (after the city of Gaza) (Irving 2011: 270).

To repair trade routes, facilitate the movement of trade caravans and troops and speed up the postal service, many new bridges were also constructed by the Mamluks along the main highways of Palestine, such as Jisr Jindas ('Jindas Bridge') – which is flanked by two lions and sports Arabic inscriptions – and remains standing today (Petersen 2002: 232). Also known as Baybars Bridge – named after Mamluk Sultan Baybars – who brought an end to the Latin Crusaders in Palestine after recovering their last major stronghold in Acre in 1291 – Jisr Jindas was built in 1273. It crossed a small wadi on the old road leading to the south the towns of Lydda and al-Ramla. This was the most famous of the several bridges erected by Sultan Baybers in Palestine, which include the Yubna bridge and Isdud bridge (Clermont-Ganneau 1896, Vol. 2: 110-17).

Situated in rocky terrain northwest of Lake Tiberias, Jubb Yusuf was also established as a rural caravanserai during the Mamluk period in 1440 when the Mamluk Sultan Sayf al-Din Jaqmaq built a chain of merchants' khans in Palestine. The caravanserai evolved into a village and functioned as stopping place for several centuries. In 1470, the Belgian international merchant and traveller Anselm Adornes, with his family, was closely involved in international trade and in the administration of the city of Bruges and with the Mediterranean transactions with Genoese merchants. In 1470, Adornes undertook a pilgrimage to the Holy Land, accompanied by his son Jan Adornes. Jan wrote a memoir of their experiences. They also visited the Khan of Jubb Yussef and their travel account mentions 'a beautiful inn which was built not long ago, a stone's throw away from the city' (Adorno 1978: 323).

In the early eighteenth century, during the Ottoman period, 'Abd al-Ghani al-Nabulsi, the Muslim scholar and traveller and author on works on ethnography, agriculture and Sufism, mentioned the khan, the domed well, which still exists, and a nearby mosque. Both the village and Khan of Jubb Yusuf were built of basalt and limestone. There were a large number of springs in the vicinity of the caravanserais, which provided water for human and animal consumption. But Swiss traveller, geographer and Orientalist Johann Ludwig Burckhardt (who assumed the alias Sheikh Ibrahim Ibn Abdallah) in his travel in Palestine and the Middle East noted during his visit to the site in around 1816 that the khan was falling into ruin (Burckhardt 1822: 318).

An 1877 survey of the Galilee carried out by the Palestine Exploration Fund recorded:

> … Our next camp was at Khan Jubb Yusuf, where we arrived on the 4th of April. The Khan is a large building falling into ruins on the main road to Damascus.
>
> (Palestine Exploration Fund 1877: 124)

This Palestinian village of Jubb Yousif was depopulated and destroyed by Israel in 1948.

Another major caravanserai from the Mamluk period was Khan al-Minya, located west of the northern end of Lake Tiberias, was established during the Mamluk period near the site of a former Umayyad palace, which in modern times is known as Khirbet Minya. The Umayyad palace was erected as a qasr complex, with a palace and mosque one of the earliest to be built in Palestine. Subsequently, during the Mamluk period the site of the palace was reused and served as a caravanserai for merchants travelling from Palestine to Damascus and along the Sea of Galilee or northeast from the lake shore to the coast. Due to its location at a cross-road and the intersection between the main Damascus-Cairo route, and a secondary route to the Safad.

A Khan al-Minya was constructed 300 metres north of the site of the Umayyad palace by Mamluk governor of Syria Sayf al Din Tankaz (reigned 1312–40), one of Mamluk Sultan al-Nasir Muhammad bin Qalawoun's commanders. Parts of the Umayyad palace might have been used as building material for the new khan; baked bricks and a marble capital found during excavations of the khan were assumed to be taken from the palace (Petersen 2001, Vol 1: 220–2).

Urban caravanserais as centres of commercial and urban life in Palestine

Mamluk Jerusalem was the undisputed religious, commercial and architectural capital of Palestine. With dozens of schools and colleges established in Jerusalem during this period, the city became one of the most important 'learning cities' in the Near East and colleges and educational institutions began to attract some of the greatest Muslim scholars in the world and began rival the great colleges of Cairo and Damascus of this age (Masalha 2022).

While two other ancient cities in Palestine, Safad and Gaza (*Mamlakat Safad* and *Mamlakat Ghaza* respectively), became regional administrative capitals and two commercial centres under the Mamluks. Jerusalem attracted the greatest urban investment of resources in Palestine by the Mamluk state. The Mamluks were also behind some of the architecturally finest urban caravanserais in Palestine – merchants' khans were played a key role in the transformation of day-to-day in Jerusalem, Nablus, Gaza and other towns. For instance, Amir Tankaz was behind of the establishment of a famous urban caravanserai in Jerusalem, *Khan Tankaz*. This was a large area containing not only a caravanserai but two public baths (*hammams*), Al-'Ayn and Al-Shifa. Khan Tankaz, in the Old City of Jerusalem, was located in the central part of the 'Cotton Merchants' (*Souq al-Qattanin*). The Cotton Market and Khan Tankaz were built in proximity to the Muslim shrines of Haram al-Sharif in Jerusalem and as a commercial compound with Islamic *waqf* (charitable) connections and included lodgings for sufis and Muslim scholars because of its proximity to the Haram al-Sharif. This Mamluk period was not only the golden age of caravanserais in Palestine but is also considered the golden age of Islamic architecture in Jerusalem. Also architecturally designed public baths reached a new level of sophistication with Mamluk's urban design and planning becoming a major facet of urban Palestine during the Mamluk period – baths were also integrated with the social and religious life of the city. In Jerusalem al-Ayn *hammam* was established at the south-western entrance of the Cotton Market which leads to al-Aqsa Mosque and al-Shifa hammam was on the eastern side of Khan Tankiz.

While making the best use of the limited space in the crowded cities of medieval Palestine, most typically urban caravanserais in Palestine were buildings with a square or rectangular-walled exterior with a courtyard, which was almost always open to the sky. One impressive historic urban caravanserai in Jerusalem was *Khan al-Sultan*, a long rectangular structure in the Old City of Jerusalem. According to an inscription this Mamluk *khan* (and market *wikala*) was built by al-Malik al-Zahir Sayf ad-Din Barquq (1382 to 1399), who also founded the central caravanserai of the famous Cairo souq khan al-Khalili and whose reign was also marked by extensive international trade of the Mamluk empire with India and east Africa. *Khan al-Sultan*. this long rectangular complex, was aligned north-south, and was entered from a portal among shops on Tariq Bab al-Silsila Street. It is seventy-seven metres long and measures thirty metres at its widest.

The compounds consisted of three separate and distinct functions: it consisted of chambers, bays and cells designed to accommodate merchants, their animals and merchandise as well as permanent shops. The complex also provided water for human and animal consumption, and for washing and prayer ritual purification. The three areas were: (1) street market with seven mirror-vaulted bays that contained fourteen permanent shops; (2) a market hall that is a cross-vaulted corridor flanked by a total of nine rooms and archways among the four western rooms and opens into a large hall used as the stable for camels and other animals; twelve additional rooms were located on the upper floor of the market hall; (3) a caravanserai for merchants centred on a courtyard (north); merchants were logged in the upper story chambers while their goods were stored and sold in the cells below. The caravanserai complex now houses industrial workshops (Burgoyne 1987: 479–84; Najm 1983: 261–3).

The Mamluk period also witnessed the establishment of some of the architecturally finest caravanserais in Palestine, especially in the city of Nablus. This included *Khan al-Tujjat* and *Khan al-Wikala.* Khan al-Tujjar of Nablus is a fifteenth-century urban caravanserai situated at the heat of the old city of Nablus. While the Ottoman period rural *Khan al-Tujjrar* of lower Galilee was constructed as a formidable fortress, the urban *Khan al-Tujjar* of Nablus was built as a jewel of Islamic architecture and it was repeatedly noted by travellers as one of the finest caravansaries in Palestine and the Levant (Dumper and Stanley 2007: 267).

With the rise of Nablus as a premier commercial and industrial city in Palestine, a city with major industries, including textile and soap (see Chapter 15), *Khan al-Tujjar* also became central to the global trade of the city and the most prestigious commercial hub in the city; the caravanserai also became the expensive real estate area in Nablus (Doumani, 1995: 27). In the nineteenth century the largest textile merchants in Nablus, Tawfiq Arafat, and his modern-day descendants, continue to be important proprietors in Khan al-Tujjar. Shaykh 'Abdel-Ghani Arafat had his textile shop in the east end of Khan al-Tujjar (Doumani 1995: 62). Other merchant members of the Arafat family were also involved in the soap factories in Nablus.[2] Together with the other caravanserai in the city, *Khan al-Wikala*, *Khan al-Tujjar* constituted the most important commercial centre of Nablus for hundreds of years and was one of the most important hubs of commercial life in Palestine (Doumani, 1995: 27). Located at the centre of a long city, between its eastern and western parts Khan al-Tujjar became a hub of commercial activity in the city and permanent shops selling a variety of textile products and clothes imported from the Islamic and Arab worlds and merchants from Syria, Iraq and India were regular visitors to the khan and its market (Doumani, 1995: 68). Palestinian author Muhammad Izzat Darwaza of Nablus, (*b.* 1887), whose father, 'Abdel Hadi, was a cloth merchant, wrote in his memoirs that:

> In Nablus, shops were confined, or mostly confined, to a caravanserai called Khan al-Tujjar, in the middle of Nablus.

Architecturally and functionally Khan al-Tujjar was described as the finest caravanserai in Palestine, by Welsh author and Calvinist Methodist John Mills, who visited Palestine in 1855 and 1859 and resided in Nablus for three months and published two books: *Palaestina*, in Welsh (Mills 1858) and *Three Months' Residence in Nablûs, and an Account of the Modern Samaritans* (Mills 1864), wrote about *Khan al-Tujjar*:

> The principal bazaar is arched, and is very large and fine for Nablus. It is the finest, by far, in Palestine, and equals any, as far I observed, in the largest towns of the Turkish Empire.
>
> (Doumani, 1995: 59)

Khan al-Tujjar became central not only to the commercial life of the city, but also to its social, religious and spiritual life and its public holidays. In particular the caravanserai became at the centre of annual Muslim religious festivals, including the Muslim Sufi festival of Nabi Musa during the Ottoman and British Mandatory period and the Mawild (commemorating the birthday of Prophet Muhammad), when the city's textile merchants and other industrialists would decorate the floor of the khan with carpets and the walls with textiles, including silk. Flowers and sweets (with which Nablus is also famous, see Chapter 17) would be placed on tables brought from their homes on festive occasions (Doumani, 1995: 60). More recently Khan al-Tujjar was restored as a key architectural heritage site in the city and its current shops attract Palestinian shoppers from across Palestine[3] the current Yasmeen Hotel is adjacent to Khan al-Tujjar. Shaykh 'Abdel-Ghani Arafat had his textile shop in the east end of Khan al-Tujjar (Doumani, 1995: 62).

Key Palestinian trading cities such as Jerusalem, Nablus and Acre each boasted more than one caravanserai. The historic port city of Acre also developed some of the most important caravanserais in Palestine, many of which were linked to the rise of modern Acre in the second half of the eighteenth century as a key location for exporting Palestinian cotton and wheat to Europe. Many of the historic khans of Acre have survived into the modern period, although today they are used for multiple purposes. For hundreds of years caravans of merchants arrived from different parts of Palestine and Syria to sell spice, silk and merchandise to Genoese, Venetians and French merchants in Acre. In the large caravanserai the ground floor of the khan often provided stabling for animals, while the travellers and merchants could stay in safety upstairs (Irving 2011: 287).

The surviving historic caravanserais of Acre include:

Khan al-Shuna: built in the 1760s by Palestinian ruler of the Galilee Dhaher al-'Umar, it is located in the area adjacent to *Khan al-'Umdan*. Historically grain used to be stored on the site of the caravanserai and grain deals used to take place on site.

Khan al-Shawardeh. The current state of this caravanserai was described as follows:

> The space gives an idea about the scale of this important khan, but the buildings themselves-like many Ottoman monuments in Israel-are in a poor state of repair and much of the khan is taken up by a car park and a fast food joint. The Layaly Al-Sultan coffee shop, on your left as you entrance, seems a more appropriate use.
>
> (Irving 2011: 288)

Khan al-Franji (*Caravanserai of the Europeans*): Franjii is a generic term in Arab for Europeans. This is the oldest of the current khans in Acre, built around 1600, but incorporating parts of an older Franciscan nunnery that was established by Saint Francis of Assisi himself on his visit to the city in 1219 (Irving 2011: 288).

Khan al-'Umdan ('Caravanserai of the Pillars'). This is the best preserved of the caravanserais in the city. It was built by the Ottoman ruler of Acre, Ahmad Pasha al-Jazzar in the 1780s and is named for its many stone columns, brought by al-Jazzar from Caesarea and Atlit. Parts of the khan stand on the site of an older Dominican monastery and the city's original Genoese quarter (Irving 2011: 288). It is the largest and best preserved caravanserai in Acre and among the best preserved in Palestine. The modern recycling of the ancient material heritage of Palestine can also be seen in the construction of *Khan al-'Umdan*, aptly named the 'Caravanserai of the Columns': this beautiful caravanserai incorporated forty 'columns' that were taken from the ancient city of Caesaria-Maritima, which for hundreds of years had been the spectacular capital Palestine under the Romans and Byzantines, and some the ruins of ancient Crusader monuments in Acre itself.

Another well-known urban caravanserai is *Khan al-Basha* (Nazareth). Renovated in the nineteenth century, this imposing caravanserai was once the main resting place for merchants and traveller arriving in Palestine. Located at the bottom of the Casa Nova Street, it marked the main entrance to the city of Nazareth and is now home to the city's tourist information centre (Irving 2011: 278–9).

14

Palestine's Cottonopolis and Dhaher Al-ʿUmar

The Cotton Industry, Urbanization in Galilee and the Rise of Modern Acre

The Palestine cotton industry in historical perspective

As we have seen in Chapters 1-7 in Antiquity, the Palestinian Mediterranean coastal cities were among the most prosperous and most developed urban centres in the country; these coastal cities continued to flourish throughout early Islam. The traumatic Crusader period and defeat of the Latin Crusaders in the twelfth century, which brought about the re-establishment of Muslim rule in Palestine, did not lessen the threats of European invasion of Palestine from the Mediterranean Sea. This post-Crusader era brought about the reorientation of the country strategically and commercially and the reorientation of its urban centres away from the Mediterranean coast. This reorientation, which lasted for five centuries until the eighteenth century, was characterized generally by the decline of several coastal cities such as Acre and Jaffa, and by the rise of the interior urban centres of Palestine, with the re-focusing of the Palestinian trade on Bilad al-Sham (Greater Syria) and Egypt. However, in the eighteenth century we once again have economic, trade and political reorientation of Palestine towards Europe under the rule of Palestinian leader Dhaher al-ʿUmar, as well as during the Ottoman reforms of the second half of the nineteenth century; all these contributed to bringing Palestine into the modern era and revived the historic cities of Acre and Jaffa. In the eighteenth century the city of Acre rose again under the impact of the Palestine cotton and wheat trade with Europe caused by policies of Dhaher al-ʿUmar for one of the two wealthiest and most dynamic cities in Palestine. Trade with Europe and the European industrial and textile revolutions transformed the fortunes of the modern Mediterranean cities of Palestine and reoriented Palestine, beginning with the port city of Acre and the rise of modern Palestine cotton industry. Acre became the most important trading port in Palestine in the eighteenth century and, together with the city of Nablus, one of the wealthiest cities of the Levant.

For many centuries, since the Middle Ages, Palestine and the Galilee had been a major area of cotton cultivation (al-Maqdisi 1994; Le Strange 1890: 16-19; 2014: 18-19;

Quataert 2002: 27). In tenth century CE, Palestinian historian al-Maqdisi commented on the fact that cotton was one of the key agricultural products of Palestine (cited in Le Strange 2014: 18–19; also al-Maqdisi 1994; Le Strange 1890: 16–19). The use of cotton for fabric is known to date back to prehistoric times and cotton had been cultivated in ancient Egypt and Persia, and it was also known to the Arabs since Antiquity. Sizeable cotton cultivation and global trade with Palestine and the Levant continued in the course of the Mamluk period but flourished in late Ottoman Palestine, especially in the eighteenth century. Today *Souq al-Qattanin* ('Market of the Cotton Merchants') – also known as Souq of Amir Tankaz al-Nasiri, the Mamluk ruler of Palestine and Syria – in the Old City of Jerusalem is a monumental and toponymic testament to the long history and significance of this Palestinian cotton industry. *Souq al-Qattanin* is located on the west side of the Haram al-Sharif. The market dates from 1336 to 1337 CE and contains some of the most exquisite and richest Islamic architecture in Jerusalem. In the middle of the Souq there is the signature of one of the craftsmen who worked on its construction. Written in Arabic *naskhi* script, the inscription reads: 'May God have mercy on him, the work of Muhammad bin Ahmad bin' Alish'. The Suq has two entrances, one to the west and the other to the east, called *Bab al*-Qattanin ('Gate of the Cotton Merchants'), which opens on to the west side of the Haram. *Souq al-Qattanin* is considered to be one of the most complete and beautiful medieval markets not only in Palestine, but in the whole of the Near East (Burgoyne 1987; Burgoyne and Abu al-Hajj 1979: 128–9).[3]

The Ottoman tax register (*Tahrir Defterleri*) of 1595 gives us detailed information about Palestinian towns and villages in the Galilee and shows that many villages in Marj Ibn Amer and the Battof valley paid a fixed tax rate of 25 per cent on agricultural products, including cotton, olive, wheat, barley, fruit trees, summer crops as well as on goats and beehives and some on water mills and water buffaloes (Hütteroth and Abdulfattah 1977: 187–91). From the sixteenth to the early eighteenth centuries the chief commodity in Palestine's trade with Europe was processed cotton, mostly in its 'carded and spun forms'. During this period, France replaced Venice as the primary European importer of Palestinian cotton (Doumani 1995: 98).

Acre was at the centre of the Palestine cotton industry from the late Middle Ages to the Modern period and the city deserves the nickname of 'Palestine Cottonopolis' – a nickname that was given to the English city of Manchester in the nineteenth century as it evolved into a wealthy metropolis at the centre of the modern British cotton industry. The Palestine cotton industry is much older than the British cotton industry. The Palestine cotton industry and cotton foreign export to Europe flourished during the Mamluk period and this was facilitated through the Venetian maritime trading empire; Venetian cotton imports from the Acre region began in the late fourteen century; although at the beginning of the fifteenth century Acre was a small town, there was a Venetian vice-consul there and in Beirut and Hama in Syria, involved in the import of Palestine and Syrian cotton to Italy and Europe. Acre was mainly a cotton market and a small community of Venetian cotton merchants had resided in Acre as well as in other Palestinian cities such al-Ramla and Lydda (Ashtor 2014: 253–61).

From the time of the Crusades, the Levant and north Palestine had supplied both regional and European textile markets via port cities such as Acre. The cultivation of cotton in Palestine for the European markets flourished under the Mamluk and this was facilitated by the rise of Venetian maritime trade and Venetian merchants who imported Palestinians and Syrian raw cotton and marketed this cotton throughout Europe. The Ottomans in Palestine maintained this lucrative trade but it grew dramatically in the eighteenth century under the effective Palestinian leadership of Dhaher al-Umar al-Zaydani (1689–1775), who got involved in the world's most profitable commodity at the time: cotton. In the second half of the eighteenth and first half of nineteenth centuries, raw cotton and wheat shipments from the Palestinian port of Acre to Italy, southern France (Beheiry 1981: 67) and England helped save the growing population of France from famine and fuelled the English Industrial Revolution and the rise of commodity capitalism in Europe. This cotton and wheat trade and foreign export to Europe contributed to the rise of a local bourgeoisie in urban Palestine, in towns and cities such as Acre, Nazareth, Tiberias, Nablus, Jerusalem and Jaffa as well as the creation of a peasant economy directed towards cash crop export to Europe, as this foreign export became the more lucrative market. Echoing agricultural developments in Palestine in late Antiquity (see Chapter 6), this move during the second half of the eighteenth century transformed modern Palestinian agriculture and agri-industries from subsistence towards production for the international market, and brought about a new relationship between (larger) cities and towns, and the hundreds of villages where most people lived and worked. This increasing international trade with the rising modern capitalism of Europe, and the insatiable British demand, especially in the nineteenth century, for raw cotton for its mills, also ushered in early urban modernities in Palestine.

Furthermore the story of the rise of the modern port city of Acre shows, first, that the start of modernities was in the second half of eighteenth century Palestine; second, that the Napoleonic invasion of Palestine and failed siege of Acre in 1799 followed rather than led the European material culture and commodities (including European textiles), which became widely available in much of urban and rural Palestine throughout the rules of al-ʿUmar and al-Jazzar (Baram 2007a, 2007b); third, that the 'new' economy and new agricultural tools of Palestine in the second half of the eighteenth century had already been significantly integrated within the modern international trade and European capitalist economy, which had been ushered in by the British technological and industrial revolutions.

Albert Hourani's paradigm of 'urban notables', Palestinian agency and new approaches to urban Palestine

Much of the research on modern urban politics in the Near East in recent decades has been inspired by Albert Hourani's 1968 essay and paradigm of the 'urban notables' of the late Ottoman period (Hourani 1968: 41-68). Hourani's concept framed the politics of Arab social elites of the Middle East – elites who also exercised power on their countryside – as intermediaries between the imperial Ottoman capital of Istanbul and their Arab societies. These Arab cities were dominated by conservative elite groups of urban notables and aristocratic families who also competed with each other for power and influence. In Palestine, researchers applied this 'urban notables' paradigm to the politics of modern Nablus, Jerusalem, al-Khalil, Gaza, Jaffa, Nazareth, Acre and other Palestinian cities, but they failed to account for the spectacular rise to power of other forms of indigenous Palestinian agency notably the two most powerful leaders of the eighteenth- and nineteenth-centuries Palestine: Dhaher al-Umar (1689/90–1775) and Aqil Agha (*d.* 1870) (Mansour 2018). These two fiercely independent leaders who rebelled against the Ottomans had emerged from the 'margins' of Palestine and marginalized Palestinian countryside in the Galilee, not from the key urban centres of the country. They challenged both the 'urban notables' of the key cities of Palestine and the imperial Ottoman authorities of Istanbul. They also represented an alternative form of Palestinian agency, an agency different from that of the traditional 'urban notables' of Palestine, an agency that was more in tune with the mass majority of the Palestinian peasantry. Also the 'urban notables' paradigm, which centres on elite politics in Palestine, fails to account for people's history and for the spectacular rise of some modern urban metropoles, namely the Mediterranean cities of Acre, Haifa and Jaffa in the modern period (see also Chapter 18). Applying 'history from below' and 'history from the margins' approaches can enable us to explore new forms of Palestinian agency and new approaches to the urban history of Palestine.

Crucially unlike the constantly squabbling groups of 'urban notables' in Palestine, which exploited their countryside and the Palestinian peasantry and competed with each other for influence and favours from the Ottoman authorities in Istanbul, Dhaher al-ʿUmar not only challenged the Ottomans but also provided an alternative form of Palestinian indigenous and effective agency. The effective Palestinian administration of Dhaher al-ʿUmar in the eighteenth century brought about the considerable growth of cotton cultivation in Palestine in general, and in the Galilee, in particular, and paved the way for the growth of export of this cash crop to France and England. Although the European printing and educational revolutions did not catch up with Palestine until the late nineteenth century, the English Industrial Revolution of the late eighteenth century and rise of European capitalism impacted on the foreign trade and economy of Palestine directly and profoundly. The English Industrial Revolution was accompanied by the growing English trade with Palestine and the Levant and phrase 'a nation of shopkeepers' and merchants is an expression commonly used to refer to England in the late eighteenth century.

English merchants who imported raw cotton, olive oil and other merchandises from Palestine through the port city of Acre often employed Italian or French agents based in Acre. The Florence-born Italian scientist, traveller and historian Giovanni Filippo Mariti, who arrived in Acre in 1760, stayed in the French quarter of the city for two years as a commercial agent of the English merchant and shopkeeper Wasson. Mariti subsequently worked for the English consul T. Turner in the city of Larnaca (Cyprus) as chancellor of the consulate. Writing in *Travels Through Cyprus, Syria, and Palestine* about the effective administration of al-ʿUmar in Acre, Mariti also describes the swift response of the governor of Acre to the then raging plague that was affecting not only Palestine but also Egypt and Syria. Large and small epidemics (occasionally combined with famine) had been a recurrent feature of medieval Palestine with devastating effects in terms of the high death toll in the country. Small epidemics also occurred in the Mediterranean port cities of Palestine during the First and Second World War. Yet in 1760 the enlightened al-'Umar acted decisively, brushing aside religious superstitions and imposing precautionary measures including a strict quarantine in Acre and measures affecting traders entering and leaving the city; these measures helped to minimize the effect of the epidemic on the crowded city and saved many lives:

> The governor of Acre checked the progress of this plague, by giving the inhabitants the means of withdrawing from its ravages; and these means, though contrary to the dogmas of the Mohametan religion, were eagerly embraced. The Europeans became their models; and the governor, after deriving them from every necessary information, shut himself up, after their example, together with his numerous family. The Muphti [*mufti*, top religious judge of Acre] alone, born the protector of the Mohametan law, cannot imitate a conduct which that law condemns. Instead of shutting himself up with silence in a prudent confinement, he thundered forth against this new method; reproached the governor for his conduct ... The governor, however, only laughed at this pious folly of the Muphti and sent a detachment of soldiers to impose a fine on him of two hundred and fifty sequins.[6]
>
> (Mariti 1792: 200–1, 203–4)

These new economic and commercial forces unleashed by the administration of al-'Umar contributed to the reorientation of Palestine towards Europe and creation of a new political economy and statehood in mid-eighteenth century Palestine, a statehood that was effectively independent of the weakened Ottoman Empire. Natives of Safad, the Zaydanis, would have been familiar with the local traditions and social memories of the province of Safad under the Mamluks: 'Kingdom of Safad', and Dhaher al-'Umar became famous in Europe as 'King of the Galilee' (Nasrallah 2015: x). Al-'Umar's state has been referred to by its detractors as a *sheikhdom*, while the late Albert Hourani referred to it as a 'little kingdom' (cited in Heyd 1942; Joudeh 2015) but it would be more appropriate to describe it as a sovereign 'frontier state' in most of Palestine for decades. Backed by a professional modern army and most of the Palestinian peasantry, in the eighteenth century Dhaher al-'Umar stood up to and defeated the Ottoman army and created a statehood that managed to impose its power and practical sovereignty on much of modern Palestine (Masalha 2018). In 1774, at the height of his power, al-'Umar's statehood controlled the entire Palestinian coast and extended from Gaza in the south to Beirut in the north. Six years earlier, in 1768, the Ottoman authorities were forced into a humiliating position of having to recognize al-'Umar's administration in Palestine in the way the Ottomans had been forced to recognize the emirate of Mount Lebanon and the regime of Emir Fakhr-al-Din II a century earlier. The Ottomans granted al-'Umar the title of 'Sheikh of Acre, Emir of Nazareth, Tiberias, Safed, and Sheikh of all Galilee' (Philipp 2015). But in 1774 the Ottoman navy attacked Acre and in the summer of 1775 he was assassinated shortly outside of the walls surrounding the city of Acre. However for nearly half a century, faced with the Ottoman threat, al-ʿUmar's stature became such that he found it possible to forge temporary international alliances with the Russian government and to cooperate with the Mamluks in Egypt (Doumani 1995: 42). Whether or not the Palestinian raw cotton trade with Europe was conducted on equal terms is doubtful. In general, the incorporation of Palestine into the modern European markets and British-dominated global capitalist system and import of textiles from Lancashire to Palestine posed a major challenge to the locally produced textiles (Doumani 1995). By the mid-nineteenth century Ottoman government was coming under strong pressures from the English and European textile manufacturers, business associations and government officials to encourage the production of more raw cotton. The *Manchester Cotton Association*, for example, promoted exhibitions of commodities in Istanbul and Izmir and urged more landowners in the Levant to focus on growing more raw cotton for export to England (Doumani 1995: 286).

Indeed al-ʿUmar can easily qualify as the founding father of early Palestinian modernities and urban renewal, and the single most influential figure in the beginning of the modern reorientation of Palestine towards the Mediterranean region. In the early eighteenth century the majority of the Palestinian population in the Galilee (predominantly Muslim) were peasants who lived in villages or small towns, with a few large urban trading centres in the Galilee. Al-ʿUmar began the process of modern urban expansion in the Galilee with what he called urban *tajdid* (renewalism), a process of rebuilding, renovating and enlarging the ancient towns and cities of the Galilee that had suffered from centuries of neglect and decline. The enormous revenues al-ʿUmar accumulated through monopolizing Palestine's cotton, wheat and olive oil export to Europe financed his efficient administration and was reinvested in his urban expansion programme, civic projects and the fortification of towns and cities in the Galilee; also fair payment giving to Palestinian cotton and agricultural farmers and workers.

Often the story of modernization is associated with powerful political leadership and in modern Palestine powerful local leadership in eighteenth-century Galilee and modern urban renewalism and expansion manifested themselves in a variety of ways:

- The emergence of a new Palestine-based autonomous rule under both powerful leaders Dhaher al-ʿUmar and Ahmad Pasha al-Jazzar (1720–1804), a rule independent of both the Ottoman authorities in Istanbul and the intermediary conservative urban *notables* of Palestine–land-owning elites who claimed to be *patrician*, but had in fact traditionally collected taxes from the peasants and exploited them.
- New technological and agricultural innovations in Palestine that benefited the majority of Palestinian peasantry began in the eighteenth century – preceding and anticipating the rise of the local urban middle class merchants and urban bourgeois 'nationalists' by at least a century – and deeply affected the agricultural production of Palestine.
- The considerable growth of modern international and regional export of Palestinian agricultural produce and urban products was shown in the export of Palestinian cotton, olive oil, wheat and soap.

- Palestinian state monopoly on the flourishing cotton, wheat and olive oil exported to Europe and the international and regional export of Palestinian produce and products generated much-needed new capital for investment in the country.
- The expansions of small towns and villages and construction of 'new' urban spaces in Palestine in the second half of the eighteenth century and the beginning of a distinction between the 'old spaces' and 'new spaces' (*al-'Imarah al-Jadidah*) was noted by several authors.

Inspired by the model of the neighbouring and autonomous emirate of Mount Lebanon (1516–1841), al-'Umar's effective leadership, with popular backing by much of the Palestinian peasantry, and international trading relations with the French and British all brought about the creation of a new statehood in Palestine based on an indigenous agency, whose authority extended from Lebanon to Gaza, and whose modern capital was the port city of Acre, which he developed further and from which he exported cotton and wheat to Europe. 'New Acre' was the capital of Dhaher al-'Umar for nearly thirty years, from 1746 to 1775, and one of two most powerful trading cities in Palestine; the other one was Nablus. Building on the spectacular legacy of Dhaher al-'Umar, Acre remained the capital of al-'Umar's successor, Ahmad Pasha al-Jazzar, Governor of the Ottoman Pashalik – in reality, a 'province' – of Acre from 1776 until his death in 1804. The dominance of Acre continued well into the early nineteenth century. After the death of al-Jazzar the Ottoman Governors of Acre, Suleiman Pasha al-'Adil (*d.* 1819) and 'Abdullah Pasha (*d.* 1831) ruled much of Palestine and Lebanon and Damascus from their Palestinian capital of Acre. Several factors contributed to the urban transformation of 'new Acre' by Dhaher al-'Umar. One of these was due to:

> [new A]cre's exceptional status. Politically, it was an enclave–semiautonomous, if not completely independent of the center of empire and its administration. This began when a local chieftain, Daher al-'Umar, established himself as an independent ruler in the city. His self-declared sovereignty was expanded and interpreted on an even broader scale by his successor, Jazzar Pasha.
>
> (Rosen-Ayalon 1998: 519–20)

Ancient Acre (Greek: Ptolemais) had been an important Palestinian port city in Antiquity. The city, which had developed from a large town in the Middle Bronze Age, occupied a strategic location, sitting in a natural harbour on the Mediterranean coast of Palestine and flourishing from both maritime trading and the western Galilee coastal road. The city continued to flourish throughout early Islam and became hugely important during the Latin Crusades in the Middle Ages as a key maritime city connecting Europe with the Holy Land. The city was the last stronghold of the European Crusaders in Palestine prior to its final recovery by Islam at the hands of the Mamluks in 1291. Being a powerful Crusader stronghold and in view of the serious threats of new European Crusader invasion of Palestine from the sea, the Mamluks set about destroying the city, and re-orienting the urban and administrative centre of the Galilee to inland and mountainous old city of Safad. Under the Mamluks, Safad became the capital of the Galilee and *Mamlakat Safad*, a vast Palestine province extended from

Upper Galilee to the modern city of Jenin. In the immediate period after the defeat of the Crusaders in Palestine their capital city, Acre, slipped into oblivion and become a small fishing village (Philipp 2001: 1).

Acre began to recover slightly during the late Mamluk period under the impact of the Palestinian cotton trade in the fifteen century. By the time of the Ottoman conquest old Acre remained as a small town until its renewal and expansion by Dhaher al-ʿUmar in the eighteenth century. Al-ʿUmar not only transformed a small town into one of the most economically vibrant and wealthiest cities in the Levant; he also made it the modern capital of his statehood in Palestine and the leading export port city in Palestine and an international trading city.

Urban expansion and transformation of the towns and cities of the Galilee

The story of al-ʿUmar's administration in Galilee also illustrates not only the spectacular rise of modern Acre as the 'capital' of the Galilee and one of the wealthiest cities of the Levant but also the story of the transformation of urban centres of northern Palestine in the eighteenth century. The 'capitals' of al-ʿUmar's administration shifted westwards, from his first capital in the ancient city of Tiberias to the town of ʿAraabah in central Galilee, then to the town of Nazareth in lower Galilee, then to the large village Deir Hanna (also in central Galilee) and finally to the port city of Acre in 1746. Tiberias had been a major industrial and trading city in Roman Palestine and had retained its central urban centre throughout early Islam, becoming the 'capital' of the Palestine Arab province (*wilaya*) of Jund al-Urdun for four centuries; the other 'capital' of the province of Palestine: 'Jund Filastin' was the city al-Ramla, established by the Umayyads. In the early sixteenth century Tiberias had become a city of refuge for Andalusian Arab-Jewish survivors of the Spanish Inquisition and the mass expulsion of Jews and Muslims from Spain in 1492. These skilled Jewish migrants eventually contributed both to the expansion of Tiberias's silk industry and the growth of Tiberias's role as a major trade centre in Palestine connecting Damascus and the Hijaz in Arabia. Al-ʿUmar expanded and fortified Tiberias further, and built a spectacular mosque in the city; but he eventually made Acre his capital of the Galilee and the centre of his lucrative international trade with Europe. Acre remained the centre of his regime for nearly three decades and subsequently became the capital of another autonomous regime in Palestine, that of Ahmad Pasha al-Jazzar (the 'Butcher'), who lived in the palace built by al-ʿUmar for another two decades from 1776 until 1804. Al-ʿUmar's administration would also demonstrate once again the continuing interdependence of Palestine urban centres and their merchant communities with their rural contexts and with the Palestinian peasantry, an interdependence which ensured the success of the Palestinian agri-industries – a continuing feature of the history of Palestine, ancient, medieval and modern (Maqdisi 1994; Masalha 2018).

Al-ʿUmar's efficient administration ushered in a new dynamic era in Palestine, after a long period of Ottoman neglect, stagnation and rampant exploitation of the Palestinian peasantry, during which Palestine was turned into a frontier country and an imperial backwater. In this new dynastic period under al-ʿUmar, the Galilee and large parts of Palestine experienced effective and fair taxation, urban expansion and economic development.

Many public buildings, fortresses, fortifications, warehouses, *khans* (caravanserais) – the most spectacular of which is the exquisitely built *Khan al-Tujjar* of Acre and numerous places of worship were built throughout his domain. Many of these sites and monuments can still be seen today throughout the Galilee. Al-ʿUmar's state pursued religiously inclusive policies and encouraged the involvement of religious minorities (Christians, Jews and Shi'ites) in his administration, finance and economy. Statehood and early modernities in eighteenth-century Palestine were intertwined:

> Under the leadership of Dhaher al-ʿUmar al-Zaidani (1730–75), a powerful and protective state was formed in northern Palestine that fostered development. Security was ensured for agricultural production, mainly wheat and cotton for export, particularly to France whose agents resided in the Zaidani capital and port of Acre. Peasants and religious minorities were protected and thus had a stake in the success of the state. In 1764–65, al-ʿUmar established a new town [Haifa] and secured it with walls.
>
> (Seikaly 2002a: 97)

The political stability and effective and fair taxation system provided by al-ʿUmar in northern Palestine and the expansion and transformation of historic urban centres such as Acre, Tiberias and Safad also led to the founding of 'modern' Haifa and the transformation of Nazareth from a small village into a major town in Palestine. Modern Haifa, or the 'new Haifa' (*Haifa al-Jadidah*), was founded by al-ʿUmar in 1764–65. This was done by moving the 250 local inhabitants to the fortified village of Haifa 2.4 kilometres to the east of the old hamlet. This 'new/modern' Palestinian Arab village became the nucleus of the modern town of Haifa (Yazbak 1998), today the third largest city in Israel. The new village was originally named in Arabic *al-ʿImarah al-Jadidah* ('the New Construction'), a term applied to modern buildings in Palestine in the eighteenth century. Local Palestinians first called the village New Haifa and later simply Haifa. This new Arab village grew into an Arab town which in the twentieth century developed into the modern city of Haifa (Mariti 1792: 318; Seikaly 2002a, 2002b; Sharon 2013, Vol. 5: 262). In a similar vein, the 'new' era of al-ʿUmar's state symbolized the beginning of the modern history of Palestine.

The new agricultural economy and foreign trade of Palestine led to the transformation of Nazareth (al-Nasirah in Arabic, retaining the 'feminine' endings common to many Palestinian Arabic toponyms of Galilee) – by al-ʿUmar's state from a small hamlet into a large town by encouraging immigration to it. The 'new town' of Nazareth played important economic, religious and strategic roles under al-ʿUmar's rule.

Al-ʿUmar's fourth 'capital' was Nazareth and for this purpose he commissioned the construction of a new government house known as the Saraya (the 'Palace'). This historic building was constructed around 1740 and later in the nineteenth century served as the residence of the local Ottoman governor of Nazareth and its subdistrict and subsequently as the city's municipal headquarters until 1991. While using Nazareth to secure his control over the hugely fertile agricultural lands of central Galilee (Yazbak 1998: 15) and Marj Ibn ʿAmer, the rich granary of Palestine, al-ʿUmar encouraged religious toleration and protected the Christian communities in the town, which he also used to strengthen his international ties with France (Emmett 1995: 22). Al-ʿUmar also encouraged the Franciscans to purchase land and build a church in Nazareth in 1730, and enabled the Greek Orthodox community to build St Gabriel Church in 1767 (Emmett 1995: 220).

Beginning as a market town for the surrounding countryside under Dhaher al-ʿUmar, today Nazareth is the largest Palestinian city in Israel and the capital of the Palestinians inside Israel. Today the descendants of al-ʿUmar still live in Galilee and Nazareth and are known as the 'Dhawahri', in memory of Dhaher – along with the Fahoums, Zu'bis and ʿOnallas, the Muslim families which constituted part of Nazareth's urban traditional Muslim land-owning elite which first rose under al-ʿUmar's rule and continued to dominate the city's politics throughout the late Ottoman and British Mandatory periods and under Israel since 1948 (Srouji 2003: 187).

Throughout much of the eighteenth and early nineteenth centuries Acre, effectively and to all practical purposes, functioned as the second capital of modern Palestine. French cotton imports from Palestine and similar British imports following the European Industrial Revolution and the rise of 'new' British technologies, with their insatiable demand for cotton, together with the new regional and international trade in cotton, olive oil, silk and textiles, all helped transform Palestinian agriculture and urban spaces in much of the country. New urban spaces and neighbourhoods were created in key cities such as Acre and Nablus, making these cities not only the biggest and wealthiest centres in Palestine but also among the largest cities of the Levant (Doumani 1995; Philipp 2001). The newly expanded port of Acre (together with the smaller port of Jaffa) remained the main international gateway to and from Palestine throughout much of the eighteenth and nineteenth centuries. After the decline of the Palestine cotton industry, coastal Acre and Nablus, together with al-Quds/Jerusalem, were still the three most important 'new' urban centres in Palestine and were central to the Ottoman administrative reorganization of the country in the 1870s, and, as we shall see below, the '*Mutasarrifate* of Noble Jerusalem' and the Sanjaks of Acre and Nablus were central to the new (evolutionary) paradigm shift in the reconceptualization of late Ottoman Palestine.

Palestine's eighteenth century cotton trade pulled the country's economy into the orbit of the European Industrial Revolution and the world economy as a whole, but the reinvestment of revenues from this global trade also enabled Palestine, under the shrewd administration of Dhaher al ʿUmar, to instigate and speed up processes of modern urbanization (Yazbak 2012: 805–18). In particular, the expanding British textile industry fuelled demands for raw cotton from Palestine and the Levant. Spurred by the growing Palestine cotton industry and cotton export to Europe and the wealth accumulated from revolutionary technological and industrial developments in Europe, the urbanization policies of Dhaher al-'Umar in Acre and the Galilee benefited from the British Industrial Revolution and modern textile revolution in Europe directly and indirectly in the second half of the eighteenth century. In the second half of the eighteenth century modern Acre was the first of the major towns along Palestine's Mediterranean coast that quickly renewed its function as a 'new', dynamic, major port city following the sharp decline of the coastal cities in the post-Crusader period under both the Ayyubids and Mamluks (Philipp 2001: 1; Rosen-Ayalon 1998: 520). Within a few decades, the revenues from the Palestine cotton and wheat exports to Europe through the port city of Acre brought about a dramatic urban expansion of Acre: by 1785', new Acre had become one of the largest cities in Palestine and the third largest city in the Levant, after Damascus and Aleppo (Philipp 2001: 1).

Despite the massive technological developments in Europe in the nineteenth century and subsequent decline of the cotton economy of the Galilee (Heyd 1942), in the mid-nineteenth century the British Consul in Jerusalem James Finn would recall his journeys in central Palestine and the Nablus-Jenin-Tulkarem triangle, and note that the cotton plantations he visited were 'beautifully clean and orderly' (Kamel 2015). In fact, as a consequence of al-'Umar's policies, for over a century between the 1730s and 1860s cotton would remain the main export from Palestine to Europe.

Before 1852, Palestine exported its cotton mainly to the Levant region, Italy, France and, to a lesser extent, England. In 1859 it was reported by a British geographical gazetteer that

> Tobacco, lent[ils], olives, cotton and silk, are extensively produced in this pash[alik of Acre] ['a part of Palestine'] ... The only manufactures are silk and cotton fabrics. The situation of this district is highly favourable to commerce. The exports from Acre and Beirut, its principal ports, are wool, cotton, silk, tobacco, gums, dried fruits, gallnuts, madder-root, and skins. The export trade is principally carried on with France and Italy ... This pash[laik] is of modern creation. In 1749 it formed part of the pash[alik] of Saida or Sidon, when Dhahir, son of Omar, an Arab Sheikh, having invaded Acre, succeeded in subduing the whole pash[alik] to his way.[4]

However, after 1870 cotton lost its leading role as the key cash crop shipped to Europe, being largely replaced by the oranges of Palestine (the iconic Jaffa orange). Benefiting from new agricultural innovations and new tree grafting techniques, the Palestine Arab citrus fruits became the number one produce exported to Europe throughout the last quarter of the nineteenth century (Lucas 2003: 21-2). During the second half of the nineteenth century modern cotton-spinning machinery was also imported into Palestine and a small-scale cotton-spinning industry continued into the twentieth century. Also in the first half of the twentieth century and before 1948 many Palestinian villages in the Jaffa region continued to cultivate cotton alongside the main cash crop industry of Jaffa oranges (see Chapter 18).

Interestingly, in the eighteenth century the high-quality of Palestinian and Levantine cotton seeds led to its transferral to the soils of the colonies of North America. But unlike the settler-colonialism of North America, in which cultivating and harvesting cotton became the leading occupation of slaves, the Palestine cotton plantations were cultivated by ordinary farmers. Yet 'still, canton production in the Levant during the late eighteenth century exceeded, by a factor of nearly thirty, that in the American colonies' (Quataert 2002: 27). The expanded port city of Acre became the first 'modern' Palestinian city in the eighteenth century to be directly affected by the new foreign trade, the British Industrial Revolution and England's demand for raw cotton.

For a century between 1730 and 1831 the export of highly profitable cash crops – first cotton and then grain – made Acre the largest centre of trade and political power on the Palestinian/Lebanese coast. The city also began to play a role in international politics in the last quarter of the eighteenth century (Philipp 2001: 3). First under al-ʿUmar and later under al-Jazzar:

> [Modern] Acre was the key to the first region in the eastern Mediterranean that was tied into modern economy ... an important fortified city of perhaps 25,000 inhabitants [which] was closely connected with the ever-rising demand for cotton in Europe.
>
> (Philipp 2001: 1)

Under the impact of international trade during the rule of both al-ʿUmar and al-Jazzar:

> [W]ithin a very short period of time, [modern] Acre bloomed into a city possessing several mosques ... caravanserais ... [public] baths and markets. It also boasted fortified walls and an aqueduct to ensure its water supply. The [Galilee] villages further inland developed most of what was to become the basis of Palestine's agricultural economy.
>
> (Rosen-Ayalon 1998: 520)

Of modern creation, and perhaps the most monumental symbol of the culture of early modern Palestine is the White Mosque of modern Acre, famously known as al-Jazzar Mosque, which became the most powerful symbol of the modern capital of northern Palestine. Constructed in 1781, eighteen years before the Napoleonic invasion of Palestine and his failed siege of Acre, and influenced architecturally by the grand Ottoman mosques of Istanbul, its name (the White Mosque) evoked memories of the famous White Mosque of al-Ramla, the capital of *Jund Filastin*, the province of Palestine throughout early Islam. The compound of the White Mosque included an Islamic theological academy, the first college of its kind in Palestine. Modelled on the al-Azhar university college of Cairo, and departing from the traditional medieval Islamic schools (*madrasahs*) of Jerusalem, the mosque/college compound contained student lodging, an Islamic court and a major public library, all paid for by Palestinian local taxes and by the flourishing regional and international trade in cotton and other cash crops of Palestine. Spectacularly overlooking the Eastern Mediterranean Sea, al-Jazzar Mosque was also a statement of the reorientation of modern Palestine towards Europe under the impact of the international trade policies and the monumental building programmes pursued by the two powerful leaders, al-ʿUmar and al-Jazzar.

The encouragement of foreign trade, promotion of local agricultural innovations and export of profitable cash crops such as cotton, grain and olive oil to Europe, which began under al-ʿUmar in the 1730s, continued until 1830 and the legacy of this foreign trade stimulated the development in the Shamouti oranges (which became internationally known as the Jaffa orange). Developed by Palestinian farmers in the mid-nineteenth century, Shamouti oranges were an almost seedless variety of oranges with a tough skin that made them particularly suitable for international export (Gerber 1982; Issawi 2006: 127). Like the export of Palestine cotton and grain in the eighteenth and nineteenth centuries, much of the Shamouti orange crop was exported to France and England from the mid-nineteenth century onwards. This rising Palestinian citrus industry will be discussed in Chapter 18.

The international commercial position and wealth of the modern city of Acre attracted the ambitions of modern European colonial powers, especially the British and French. It is hardly a coincidence, therefore, that in 1799 Napoleon Bonaparte sought but failed to conquer the city after a siege of nine weeks. Seventy years later, in the early 1870s the Ottomans reorganized the administration of Palestine and created the autonomous *Mutasarrifate of Jerusalem* (with special administrative status) and the *sanjaks* of Nablus and Acre (Abu-Manneh 1999: 41–51). The importance of city of Acre was reaffirmed by these administrative reforms as one of the three most important cities and administrative regions in the country in the nineteenth century. Modern Acre can also be a case study of the impact of cash crop economy on the rise and decline of a modern Palestinian city. This beautiful and iconic capital of al-ʿUmar's state rose from the ashes to become one the most important modern Palestinian urban centres for nearly two centuries. This was less to do with imperial Ottoman calculations or the 'Ottoman heritage' of Palestine, and more the result of sheer indigenous determination and self-definition. However, by the end of the nineteenth century Acre's standing had declined to the advantage of the nearby coastal town of Haifa, as new powerful steam engines were developed in the West, powering bigger ships; new trade routes were opened up and the coast of Palestine became part of the regular route of the major European steamship companies (Seikaly 2002a: 97).

Although the Palestine cotton industry had a huge impact on the actual transformation of urban Palestine in the eighteenth and nineteenth centuries, especially of the towns and cities of Acre, Nazareth, Tiberias and Haifa, as we shall see in Chapter 15 in modern Palestinian *social memory*, the key commodity that gripped the *national imagination* and became a national symbol of agricultural production and international export in Palestine is *Jaffa Orange*.

15

The Soap Factories of Jerusalem and Nablus

Olive Oil and the Soap Industry of Palestine from the Middle Ages to the Modern Period

Food production and the olive economy of Palestine: Symbolism, social memory and popular culture

> If the olive tree remembered its planter,
> the oil would turn into tears!
> O wisdom of our ancestors,
> if we could give you a shield from our flesh!
> But the plain of the wind,
> does not give the slaves of the wind a crop!
> We will uproot with eyelashes the thorns and sorrows …
> uprooting them!
> And for what shall we bear our shame and our cross?
> While the universe strives …
> We will remain green in the olive tree,
> and a shield around the earth!
>
> (Palestinian national poet Mahmoud Darwish)

As we have seen in the Introduction, Palestine archaeology shows that the history of the olive tree extends back to 7,000 years ago, to the Chalcolithic Age, when the agricultural inhabitants of Palestine began domesticating it as an important source of Palestinian diet, with a huge impact on Palestinian culinary culture; olive trees longevity has become a major source of national pride and symbolism in Palestine and an element in the Palestinian struggle for self-determination against Zionist settler-colonialism in Palestine (Ababneh 2023: 55–65; Wilde 2022: 1–42). Becoming a major element in modern Palestinian identity, not only do olive trees represent the resilience of the Palestinian people under occupation, they are also one of the defining elements in the historic heritage of Palestine. Palestinian ancient agricultural and food producing practices of growing and harvesting olive trees and producing olive oil have continued for millennia but are now threatened by the Israeli occupation of Palestine.

The olive tree has been central to the poly-culture of Palestine and the agricultural economy and food production of the country since the Chalcolithic Age: 7,000 years ago. Palestinians have grown and farmed olive trees for millennia and these ever-green trees are an integral part of the landscape of the country. Considered the jewel in the Palestinian plants, the cultivation of the olive tree has been going on for millennia. It has already been shown in Chapter 6 that olives were an important and staple part of the peoples' diet and a source of wealth and prosperity for the country. Palestinian oil industries were at the centre of Palestinian agricultural industries and a major source export and of prosperity for the country. Olive tree cultivation and olive presses spread throughout Palestine. The scenes of harvesting olives in October and November were depicted in archaeological records in pottery and later on mosaic floors from the Roman period. Stone olive oil presses spread in Palestine during the Roman period and olive oil was stored in clay jars. Age tests carried out by Italian research institutions on samples of ancient olive trees in the grove of Jesus in the Church of Gethsemane (*Γεθσημανή*) in Jerusalem – a garden at the foot of the Mount of Olive with great resonance in Christianity, where, according to the New Testament, Jesus was arrested before his crucifixion and a place of great sacredness for Christianity and the site of a number of ancient olive presses – indicated that their history dates back to the tenth and eleventh centuries CE. It is worth noting that the name *Gethsemane* (*Gaḏ-Šmānê*) is a name derived from Syriac for an 'olive press' (Taha 2022). Indeed, olive oil production was pivotal to the Palestinian economy in Antiquity and during the Byzantine period Palestine had hundreds of olive presses – in fact, the country had the largest concentration of olive presses in the Byzantine world (Kingsley and Decker 2015a: 44–68).

The literature on the importance of the olive tree to modern Palestinian daily life, identity and historical heritage as well as struggles under Israeli occupation is extensive (Al Makadma and Bastian 2015; Doumani 1995; Rosenblum 1996; Sharkawi 2018; Simaan 2017; Taha 2022; Taxel 2013: 361–94).

The olive tree is a hugely important cultural and national symbol for modern Palestinians. Not only historically was the *olive branch* adopted as a global symbol of peace and hope, but the olive tree is a key symbol of Palestinian identity, an identity that is deeply-rooted in the ancient heritage of the Palestinians in Palestine. The sacredness of the olive tree is linked with the events of the ascension of Jesus of Nazareth on the Mount of Olives in Jerusalem (Palestine), and the Holy Qur'an mentioned the great oath: 'By the figs and the olives, and Mount Sinai, and this faithful country'. Also even today, despite the devastating effects of Israeli settler-colonial polices, with escalating settlers' attacks on Palestinian farmers, it is estimated that the olive farming industry supports the livelihoods of around 80,000 families in the occupied West Bank alone.[1] The great Palestinian poet Mahmoud Darwish summed up in an excerpt from his poem *Olive Leaves* the relationship between the Palestinians and the olive tree: 'If the Olive Trees knew the hands that planted them, Their Oil would become Tears'.

Olive oil and pickled olives are major food items in Palestine. It is consumed with bread and thyme (*za'atar*) and at the breakfast table. Olive oil is used as a cooking and frying material and is used in the preparation of a wide range of dishes, the most famous of which are '*musakhan*' and various types of pastries. Olive oil was also used as the main material for lighting, and since Antiquity people discovered the medicinal benefits of it. Olive wood and the material resulting from the pressing process, pomace, was used as a fuel and heating material. Crucially, as we shall see below, olive oil was used as a main material in the manufacture of soap and the important soap industries of Palestine from the Middle Ages to the modern period. The abounding goodness of the olive industries of Palestine is deeply ingrained in the popular culture and imagination of the Palestinians. This is evident in the way ordinary people celebrated the work associated with the ploughing, pruning and harvesting seasons, celebration evident in popular entertainments, songs and love stories.

There were more than twelve million trees in the occupied Palestinian territories between 1967 and 2015 (Al Makadma and Bastian 2015), and annual olive oil production in the Palestinian territories of the West Bank and Gaza ranges between twenty and twenty-two thousand tons, according to estimates by the Palestinian Oil Council.

Olive oil and the soap factories of Jerusalem, al-Ramla and Nablus: Medieval and modern

In the tenth century, Palestinian geographer al-Maqdisi (990) wrote:

> From Palestine, came olives, dried figs, raisins, the carob-fruit, stuffs of mixed silk and cotton, soap and kerchiefs'.
>
> (Le Strange 2014: 18–19; also Le Strange 1890: 16–19)

There is no exact date for the beginning of the soap industry of Palestine. The first recorded date of soap manufacturing in Palestine under Islam when soap-making was mentioned as one of the exports of Palestine by al-Maqdisi (990), although the latter did not identify the city, or cities, in which Palestinian soap was manufactured (Abu Khalaf 2013). In the Middle Ages the olive oil industry and soap plants were major parts of the economy of the city of Nablus and are described as such by the Arab historian Ibn Battuta in the fourteen century (Cohen 2002: 85). By the fourteen century Palestine had many soap factories and the soap plants of Nablus 'were well-known for their excellent products', which were produced for export (Ashtor 2014: 208). However, like the export-oriented Palestine wine industry of late Antiquity that had to compete with the Italian wine industry, in the Middle Ages (fourteenth to fifteenth centuries) the export of the soap industry of Palestine and the Levant faced tough competition from the Italian soap manufactures and by the fifteenth century the merchant fleets of the Italian cities (Venice and Genoa included) regularly sailed with their soap cargoes and other manufactured products such as glassware to Egypt and Syria, at a time when Nablus soap was also being exported to these two countries (Ashtor 2014: 209).

The soap industry of Jerusalem was already well-established during the Mamluk period (1260 to 1517). This is hardly surprising: Mamluk Jerusalem was one of the most developed urban centres and urban spaces in Palestine, a medieval Islamic city with a sophisticated system of clean running water and public hygiene, beautifully ornamented public drinking fountains (*sabils*) and spectacular public *hammams*, for both men and women – public baths that benefited from the sophisticated soap-making industry of the city. This spectacular improvement in medieval urban life also accompanied a period of public investment and civic building in the city. Islamic Jerusalem boasted the best and most sophisticated Islamic architecture in Palestine and masterpieces of Islamic ornamented vaulting known as the *muqarnas* architecture: the honeycomb architecture that adored places of worship and colleges across the city and touched the heavens. This artistic flouring of Islamic craftsmanship in the city was coupled with dozens of *madrasas* and colleges, large markets, public baths and drinking fountains, libraries, hospitals, Islamic *waqf* charitable foundations and soup kitchens for the urban poor (Masalha 2022). Cleanliness and public hygiene went hand-in-hand with the rise of the soap industry of the city and soap-making craftsmanship, so when the Ottomans occupied Palestine in 1516 the production of soap in the city of Jerusalem was already well-established and numerous soap factories existed (Cohen 2002: 61).

The soap factories of Jerusalem relied on the high-quality virgin olive oil produced in Nablus, the oil being a key agricultural product of the Nablus countryside. Not surprisingly under the impact of the public fame and collective memory of the modern soap industry of Nablus, much of the writing on soap-making in Palestine tends to focus, almost exclusively, on the spectacular rise of the soap factories of Nablus from the late Ottoman period until 1948. But social memory is always selective; in fact, throughout the Middle Ages, there were three soap-making centres in Palestine that centred on three key cities: Nablus, Jerusalem and al-Ramla. With the abundance of olive trees and olive oil in Palestine (and in the area of Nablus in particular) the olive oil and soap industry of the three cities of Jerusalem, Nablus and al-Ramla produced much of the soap output of Palestine throughout the late and early Ottoman period and their industries consumed much of the olive oil production in Palestine (Cohen 2002: 85–86).

Throughout much of the Ottoman period, Jerusalem, in particular, although remaining the premier religious capital of Palestine, did not straddle the main international trade route between Damascus and Cairo. The English reference book *Modern history or the present state of all nations*, written in 1744, stated that 'Jerusalem is still reckoned the capital city of Palestine, though much fallen from its ancient grandeur' (Salmon 1744: 461). However, early Ottoman Jerusalem did have an important and expanding soap-making industry and its soap was marketed throughout Palestine and exported to Egypt. In the early Ottoman period, in the middle of the sixteenth century, the population of Jerusalem was about 15,000, with about 2,500 to 3,000 families (Cohen 2002: 56). However, many powerful families in the city were involved in the olive oil soap factories and in 1584 a list of about fifty names was given for soap producers (who were referred to as 'merchants') including three who were identified as qadis (judges); the involvement in the soap-making factories was not excusive; they were also involved in other trading activities (Cohen 2002: 85).

Evidently the rise of the soap factories of Jerusalem under the Ottomans in the sixteenth century required large capital investments and this significant in soap factories followed the social, economic and political rise of the merchant community as a whole and the soap merchant in particular in the city. As we shall see below, the export-oriented soap industry of Nablus in the nineteenth century was also a *capital-intensive* industry, requiring intensive investments by the owners of the soap factories. To some extent this was also the case with the soap factories of Jerusalem in the sixteenth century. Many prosperous merchants and industrial entrepreneurs and wealthy members of the city establishment invested their money in soap-making factories of Jerusalem (Cohen 2002: 63–85).

Although soap-making was part of the economy of Nablus at the time, there is no evidence to suggest that the soap-makers of Nablus competed with the soap-makers of Jerusalem until the late Ottoman period, when Nablus soap, with its chief ingredient virgin olive oil, became the best and most internationally famous soap manufactured in Palestine (Cohen 2002: 85). In fact during the late Mamluk period, the soap factories of Jerusalem and al-Ramla consumed most of the olive oil of the Nablus region (Cohen 2002: 82–6). During the early Ottoman period, in the first half of the sixteenth century, twelve factories operated steadily in Jerusalem; by the end of the sixteenth century, the number of soap factories in the city had risen to eighteen.

> at least twelve soap-factories [*masbanas*] were operating steadily in Jerusalem ... In Jerusalem most soap-factories were known by name ... The overall number of soap-factories during the first fifty years of Ottoman rule might have been as high as fifteen or so. Most of them were located in two areas: the south-western part (the Jewish quarter, the Zion quarter better known as al-Risha) and the northern part (Bab al-'Amud and its vicinity) both inside the walled city. In other words, they were concentrated in the city's extremities, far from the densely populated environs ... all the materials used in the factories were imported in bulk from neighbouring, sometimes form distant areas so that the closer the *masbanas* were to the gate, the better it was for their owners.
>
> (Cohen 2002: 63)

Generally agricultural produce, olives included, and the soap factories of Jerusalem were a major source of taxation in early Ottoman Palestine and the rate levied was calculated as a certain percentage of the annual yield. When olives ripened, they were picked, pressed and the oil extracted, and certain percentage of the oil was delivered to the local tax collectors (Cohen 2002: 77–85). The large number of soap factories in Jerusalem and the systematic operation of these factories and proper maintenance and repairs in the exiting factories indicate a positive Ottoman policy and dynamic economic reality that existed at the time in the city (Cohen 2002: 63). More soap factories were built in the second half of the sixteenth centuries, bring the number to eighteen, thus increasing soap production and productivity (Cohen 2002: 63).

Olive oil had always been bought and sold in the markets of Jerusalem and the city had a specialist market called the 'Olive Oil Market': *Souq al-Zayt*. Olive oil merchants who specialized in the field of olive oil (*Jallabi al-Zyat*) were not allowed to sell at whatever prices they wished; olive oil had to be unloaded, weighed and sold at a *specialist olive oil market* in the city: *Khan al-Zayt* (the 'Caravanserai of the Oil Merchants') and the bulk was sold at the olive oil market either locally or abroad; camels usually transported the olive oil and soap into various cities in Palestine and Egypt and beyond (Cohen 2002: 77–85).

Olive oil, vineyards and general agricultural produce were major sources of taxation in early Ottoman Palestine and the rate levied was calculated as a certain percentage of the annual yield. The abundance of olive trees in Palestine put the olive trees and olive oil into a category by themselves for the purpose of state taxation. Grape trees and 'vineyards' were also a separate category for taxation (Cohen 2002: 72–85).

The guild of soap-makers in Jerusalem in the sixteenth century

In Jerusalem of the sixteenth century, the scale of soap productions and the professional expertise required for soap manufacturing enabled the emergence of the *guild of soap makers* – in the same way that the scale of the textile industry of Palestine in Antiquity, and specialist expertise required in this industry, encouraged the emergence of the ancient guilds of Roman and Byzantine Palestine. In sixteenth-century Jerusalem the entire soap production process was carried out by skilled soap-makers (*Sanii al-Saboun, or sabbans*) who had developed specialist expertise in the industry and whose services were hired by soap producers (*sabbans*), soap merchants and entrepreneurs who had invested in establishing or renting soap factories (*masbanas*) and had provided the raw materials for soap-making (Cohen 2002: 85). Furthermore, the professional qualifications of the expert soap-makers and members of the guild of soap-makers had to be checked and confirmed by the head of the guild: *Shaykh al-Mu'alliminfi Tabkh al-Sabun*, who was nominated by the Muslim Qadi (city of Jerusalem judge). The nominations were made at the request of the members of the guild. The experts of the guild of soap-makers were not permanently employed in one factory (Cohen 2002: 82–5). Jerusalem continued to have some soap factories during the late Ottoman period (Abu Manneh 1986: 93–107) but by this stage its soap factories could not compete with the soap factories of Nablus.

The commercial centrality of Nablus and the golden age of its soap factories: Mid-nineteenth century to 1948

Known in Palestine as 'mother of industries' (*Umm al-Sina'at*), historically the combined olive oil and soap industry of the country was one of the most iconic industries. Among the best accounts of the historical evolution and phenomenal expansion of the soap factories of Nablus from the mid-nineteenth century onwards and within the wider context of the late Ottoman reform period (*tanzmat*) and within the changing political and economic climate in the nineteenth century is found in Beshara Doumani's *Rediscovering Palestine: Merchants and Peasants in Jabal* (1995).

In Chapter 5, we saw how the textile industry of Nablus (ancient Neapolis) evolved in Antiquity to become a major component of the economy of the city. Under Islam the textile merchants of Nablus continued to flourish and exercise influence in a wide geographical area in the hinterland of Nablus and beyond (Doumani 1995: 185). Traditionally an industrial city, today Nablus boasts more factories than any other city in the West Bank with the exception of al-Khalil (Hebron). It had been a centre for the Palestinian textile industry and tanneries in Antiquity and had developed other manufacturing industries during the Ottoman period, including sweets (and especially *Kunafa*), *tahini*, grinding grains using water mills, goldsmithing, textiles, leather tanning, dyeing and blacksmithing, but none of these traditional industries could achieve the fame and reputation of its modern soap industry.

As we have already seen historically the district of Nablus had many olive presses and the city of Nablus was well-known for soap production at least as early as the fourteenth century. In the words of Shaykh Shams al-Din al-Ansari al-Dimashqi (*d.* 1326-27):

> The city of Nablus ... was bestowed by God Almighty with the blessed olive tree. Its olive oil is carried by the Bedouins to the Egyptian and Damascene lands, to the Hijaz and steppes. In it a superior soap is produced and sent to the above mentioned destinations and to the islands of the Mediterranean Sea.
>
> (cited in Doumani 1995: 185)

During the Mamluk and Ottoman periods, Egypt became a key destination for Palestinian soap merchants and the export-oriented soap industries of Jerusalem and Nablus. During the early Ottoman period, Syrian and Palestinian merchant communities and merchant families residing in Cairo played an important role in the trade and commercial life of the Egyptian capital and this can be seen in the names of wealthy merchants such as al-Nabulsi (from Nablus), al-Qudsi (from Jerusalem) and al-Safadi (from Safad). These rich merchants also played an important part in the social and religious life and 'guilds' associations of the city and they provided the commercial agency (*wikala*) for the large-scale imports of manufactured goods from Syria and Palestine. Some Palestinians in Cairo also achieved prominent position in the learning circles of Cairo. Al-Safadi (Salah al-Din al-Safadi), born and grew up in the city of Safad to a wealthy merchant family, left Safad for Cairo, became a distinguished author and historian of the Mamluk period and worked for some time in the Mamluk state bureaucracy of Cairo (Pomerantz and Shahin. 2015: 464-5).

Some Palestinian and Syrian merchants also achieved senior positions in the famous markets of Cairo and titles such as *Shaykh Khan al-Khalili* – head of the famous bazaar in the historic centre of Cairo, which was established in Mamluk era; other merchants carried titles such as head of guild of merchants of the *soap merchant agency* (*soap wikala*) (Hanna 1997: 17-18). Palestinian merchants' caravanserais and commercial buildings were also established in the markets of Cairo. For instance, *Wikalat Amir*

Qawsun (Cairo) was a square-shaped commercial building in Cairo – which was originally constructed by the Mamluk merchant Amir Qawsun (1302–42) – was used by Palestinian soap and coffee merchants during the seventeenth and eighteenth centuries – thus becoming known as the *Wikala of Soap*. The building was demolished in the 1960s to make way for a new school building, and only the gate of the original structure remains (Meinecke 1980; Warner 2005).

The chief ingredients of the high-quality Nablus soap were virgin olive oil (the main agricultural product of the Nablus region), water and an alkaline sodium compound – which was often supplied to the Bedouin communities of the Jordan valley who traded with Nablus. The finished product is ivory-coloured and has almost no scent. In Nablus, soap factories were renovated in the 1820s with financial investments by leading families in making soap production (Doumani 1995: 190).

The quantities of oil production in the Nablus region and in Palestine as a whole were enhanced in the mid-nineteenth century with the introduction of a large number of manual iron screw presses: This had an impact on the growth of the modern Nablus soap factories. One of the extraordinary things about the Nablus soap industry, at the time when the larger part of Ottoman manufacturing took place not in factories but in workshops and in domestic settings, the olive oil soap factories for Nablus became renowned not only in Palestine and other Arab countries but also perhaps was the most dynamic urban industry in the whole Ottoman region (Findley 2010). By the late 1830s John Bowring (Sir John Bowring (1792–1872), a British political economist and traveller, writer) noted that 'Nablus soap is highly esteemed in the Levant' (Doumani 1995: 195). At the time a significant number of urban properties in Nablus, including several soap factories and industrial mills in the city, were endowed Islamic family *waqf* charities (Mendelsohn 2020. 160). Statistics show that fifteen soap factories existed in Nablus by 1842, and that this number was increased to thirty in the early twentieth century (Abu Khalaf 2003). Others commented that during the Ottoman *tanzimat* period, especially of the second half of the nineteenth century, the number of soap factories at Nablus tripled and their production of soap quadrupled; once again the number of soap factories in the city rose from fifteen in 1890 to twenty-five in 1913. Some endowed (Islamic *waqf*) public baths (*hammams*) were also located close to some endowed (*waqf*) soap factories of Nablus, public baths which served also the needs of the soap workers; a *hammam* located close to the soap factory of the *waqf* of Mustafa Katkhuda in the old city:

> Nablus in Palestine offers another example of growth, based in this case on growing olives and making soap from the oil. During the Tanzimat, the number of soap factories at Nablus tripled, and their production quadrupled. Thus, an ancient manufacturing sector in a small interior city managed to grow and prosper without the introduction of new technology, the development of new techniques, the opening of new markets, or dependence on foreign investment capital.
>
> (Findley 2008: 34)

However, although the reputation of the soap factories of Nablus was established long before mid-nineteenth century, the evident expansion in these factories in the second half of the eleventh century followed the modernization of manufacturing technologies in Palestine and the improvement of the political atmosphere in the late Ottoman period (Doumani 1995: 190). The Ottoman *tanzimat* (literally 'reorganizations') – a period of major reforms 'from above' that began in 1839 and ended with the Ottoman First Constitutional era of 1876 – and their major impact on the economy of Palestine and the wider Arab East have been given most scholarly attention. Indeed the number and reputation of the soap factories of Nablus began to soar in the second half of the nineteenth century, in the aftermaths of the Ottoman *tanzimats*, reaching new heights in the early twentieth century and attracting large local capital investment in soap production. With a relatively low risk for these investments, the high-quality of Nablus soap and the demand for this product by foreign markets in Egypt, Syria, Arabia and further afield made this industry among the most famous and most profitable manufacturing industries of late Ottoman Palestine and the British Mandatory period (Doumani 1995: 185).

Nablus soap enjoyed such a high reputation in the Middle East that all similarly manufactured soap, whether produced in Egypt or Syria, came to be labelled 'Nablus soap' (Doumani 1995: 185). Even in the twentieth century, a modern oil factory established by Jewish settlers in Palestine during the British Mandatory period, Shemen Ltd advertised its premium brand of soap was 'of Nablus quality' (Doumani 1995: 185). The Syrian historian Muhammad Ali Kurd, writing in the 1930s, noted:

> Nablus soap is the best and most famous soap today for it has, it seems, a quality not found in others and the secret is that it is uncultured and well produced'.
>
> (Doumani 1995: 185)

In the nineteenth century, Nablus' most important economic sector in terms of income was commerce, and this sector had a direct impact on the urban life of the city and phenomenal rise of its manufacture and export of soap. A predominantly Muslim region in northern Palestine, the collaboration of peasants and merchants of Jabal Nablus ensured the production of high-quality olive oil, which was essential for the soap manufactured in factories of Nablus and became renowned from Damascus to Egypt (Beinin 2001: 32). Surrounded by a fertile countryside renowned for the quality of its olive oil, the city retained its paramount position as the centre for larger commercial transactions for central and northern Palestine, its merchants serving as suppliers and marketers for smaller towns, as well for the Bedoiun communities in the Jordan valley of Palestine. This commercial supremacy of Nablus made possible the accumulation of capital by the city's merchants capital, which was reinvested in the soap-making industry. The geographic and commercial location of the city with respect to the crossing of the Jordan River and trade with Transjordanian cities; and the new economic developments in the coastal plains of Palestine during the second half of the nineteenth century, in the aftermath of the Ottoman *tanzimat* were also crucial (Gilbar 1998: 282).

The economic wealth and prosperity of Nablus during the middle and late Ottoman period attracted fierce competition among its social elites and powerful families of the city, families such as the Tuqans and Jarrars, who competed with each other for the powerful and lucrative position of 'tax collector' (*mutassalem*) and other economic and religious positions in the city. At the beginning of the nineteenth century, the Tuqans were the dominant family in the city and held the position of *mutassalem* up to the Egyptian occupation of Palestine in the 1830s; Nablus became the centre of a largely Palestinian peasants' uprising against the new rulers' oppressive policies of taxation and military conscription. Under the short-lived Egyptian rule of Ibrahim Pasha in Palestine in the 1830s, a new family in the city, the 'Abdel-Hadi, became the strongest in the city.

From the mid-nineteenth century onwards, Nablus recovered its leading economic position in Palestine and the city became the capital of the soap and olive oil industries and its role in the cotton trade in Palestine also increased after the decline of the city of Acre. Not surprisingly, Nablus was also one of the great cities in Palestine to be granted modern municipality under the late Ottomans; its municipality was established in 1869 (Pappe and Mansour 2022: 313).

As modern trade and modern transport in goods and passengers increased through the Palestinian historic port city of Jaffa in the second half of the nineteenth century, with the result that port of Jaffa gradually replaced the port of Beirut as the main port for entry and outlet for central and southern Palestine, and with the Palestinian route between Nablus and Jaffa made shorter and more convenient than between Palestine and Beirut, the merchants of Nablus increasingly directed their international import and exports of goods through the port of Jaffa. These transport developments enhanced the centrality of Nablus as a convenient commercial hub and junction in northern Palestine. Another crucial development in the late nineteenth century was the introduction of the Palestine railway system and the inauguration of the rail road between the cities of Jaffa and Jerusalem in 1892; this further reinforced the commercial links between Nablus and Jaffa and the foreign export of Nablus soap through the port of Jaffa (Gilbar 1998: 281–92).

The rise and profitability of the soap industry of Nablus also spurred the development of the modern soap industry of Jaffa in the late nineteenth century. While Nablus was the dominant centre for soap-making in modern Palestine, and for making soap based on pure virgin olive oil, the other centres that produced oil in modern Palestine were the cities of Jaffa and al-Ramla. However, the modern soap industry of Jaffa and al-Ramla was of lower quality and its oils were produced from linseed, coconuts and peanut. However, during the 1930s the number of soap factories in Jaffa and al-Ramla began to decline. These were usually small factories employing on average eight persons each. In 1931 Egypt imposed customs tax on soap imported from Palestine. This was a major blow to the Jaffa and Ramla soap industry. By contrast, quality sells and the high-quality Nablus soap was able to retain its market in Egypt and even expand to Egypt because of the special qualities of its soap.

In terms of the impact of the commerce of Nablus, in general, and its soap industry, in particular, on the urban development and cityscape of Nablus, we can see that many of the civic and religious buildings and public baths in Nablus date from the Ottoman period with many religious and civic buildings in the city dating from this period of urban expansion. This urban flourishing of late Ottoman Nablus went hand-in-hand with the expansion of the commence of the city and the olive oil soap factories; by 1882 there were no fewer than thirty soap factories in the city (Dumper and Stanley 2007: 267), many of which were classed as Islamic *family waqf foundations*, including the *Al-Sha'arawiya Masbana*, the *Al-Sa'ariya Masbana* and the *Al-Masbana al-Othmaniyya.* Some of the most influential merchants who were involved in the soap industry of Nablus from the people of Nablus in the late Ottoman and early British Mandatory period were Muhammad Effendi Murtada Al-Ja'fari, Shaykh Yousef Zaid Al-Qadri, Hajj Mahmoud Tafaha Al-Husseini, Hashem Al-Jandali and As'ad Shamout, most of which belonged to the wealthy families and notable and religious elite in the city who were involved in Islamic waqf foundations in the city. Also a public bath (*hammam*) was located close to the soap factory (*masbana*) of the waqf of Mustafa Katkhuda and the Zawiya al-Mushbasiya (Weber 2010: 225).

In the late Ottoman period the administrative *Sanjaq Nablus* was established as one of three administrative urban centres in Palestine, cementing further the commercial and administrative centrality of Nablus in the history of modern Palestine. For many years under the Ottomans, members of the powerful Tuqan family had been the governors of Nablus, and several leading Nabulsi figures held senior positions in the Ottoman capital in Istanbul. One local official from the governing Tuqan family, Hafiz Tuqan, originally from the village of Tubas, located north-east of Nablus, who began as a local Ottoman tax collector, used the capital from that position to build a profitable soap factory in Nablus (Kimmerling and Migdal, 2003: 43).

Inspired by the successes of the Nablus soap factories and utilizing Palestinian local expertise, the German colony at the foot of Mount Carmel, which had been established by the German Templers in Ottoman Palestine in Haifa in 1868 (see also Chapter 18), set up a soap factory and in the late 1870s began to export Palestine-made soap to the US and Europe labelled 'Carmel Soap' produced by the 'German Mission Society in Palestine' and advertised extensively in US popular magazines, including *The Independent, the New York Observer,* and New York-based American magazine *Life* (originally launched in 1883 as a weekly publication), which featured contributions from many important writers, illustrators and cartoonists and played an important role in the history of photo journalism. They began to print commercials about 'Palestine-made pure olive soap', 'the Best Soap for Baby's Bath', 'the Superior Olive Oil Made in Palestine' … 'the Manufacture of Olive Oil Toilet Soap'.[2]

By 1907 modern Nablus had more than thirty soap factories that produced more than 5,000 tons of soap annually, a staggering quantity which constituted 23 per cent of the total annual soap production of both Syria and Palestine.[3] These factories supplied more than half the soap consumed in Palestine and the city's soap industry exported vast quantities of soap to Egypt, Syria, Iraq and Arabia (Doumani, 1995; Gilbar 1998: 281–92). By the early British Mandatory period, the number of soap factories in Nablus reached a record number of forty factories. In comparison the city of Jerusalem boasted eighteen soap factories at the height of its soap-making industry during the early Ottoman period, something which gives an indication, both quantitatively and qualitatively, about the superiority of the modern soap industry of Nablus over the Palestine soap-making industry of the Middle Ages.

Becoming the premier industrial city of Palestine, in addition of the export-oriented manufacture of soap, the city had developed a wide range of other industries including goldsmithing, textiles, leather tanning, dyeing, blacksmithing, sweets, tahini, lime and grinding grains using water mills. In the early twentieth century the commercial significance of the Palestine soap industry attracted the attention of the US Department of Commerce. Under the sub-heading: 'Soap Industry of Palestine', 'Commerce Reports' Compiled by the Near Eastern Division of Foreign and Domestic Commerce, the US Department of Commerce, dated 31 October 1921, the report contrasts the quality of the Nablus soap with the rest of the soap industry of Palestine. We find the following in the report:

> Olive-oil soap is the product of the most important industries which exist in Palestine. The center of the Palestine *soap* industry is at *Nablus*, 40 miles north of Jerusalem. There are about 40 small factories in Nablus, and all are engaged in making pure olive oil sop. There are almost as many factories at Jaffa (the port of Jerusalem), but the production as not as that great as that of the Nablus factories m is not exclusively of the pure oil verities of Nablus. Small factories are found in Jerusalem and elsewhere in Nablus and Jaffa are the most impotent centres. Nablus is also the centre of an olive oil district. Export figures as to the total quantity of sop produced in Palestine are not available. An estimate production of 8,000 tons annual is probably liberal. The Nablus soap makers estimate that they produce about 4,000 tons in a year, when olive oil is obtained in sufficient quantities. The value of the soap produced in Palestine varies with business conditions, but the *rotl* (6,349 pounds) has at present an average wholesale value of 20 Egyptian piasters, equal at current exchange rate to about 80 American cents. This wholesale rate maybe accepted as the value of the pure olive oil soap made in Palestine. The retail price locally averages 15 to 20 cents per rotl. The minor share of the total soap production, which contains fats, other than olive oil, sells a little cheaper. Considerably more than half of the total soap production in Palestine finds a market in Palestine, Syria and the Transjordan regions and maybe considered local trade. Palestine soap finds its principal export market in Egypt, which in normal times will take from $500,000 to $750,000 worth annually. Syria, Palestine and the Transjordan regions and Egypt consumes practically the entire soap production of this country, and there is important quantities exported to other markets. Generally no Palestine soap goes to the US And there is a small factory in Haifa which caters to a limited but pure American demand for pure olive oil soap. The quantity of this soap exported is comparatively unimportant.[4]

According to the Commerce Reports' Compiled by the Near Eastern Division of Foreign and Domestic Commerce, the US Department of Commerce, export figures as to the total quantity of soap produced in Palestine were not available; an estimate of the production of 8,000 tons of soap annually was given. Nablus soap-makers estimated that they produced about 4,000 tons in a year, when olive oil is obtained in sufficient quantities. The report says that value of the soap produced in Palestine varied with business conditions, but the *rotl* (6,349 pounds) had at present an average wholesale value of twenty Egyptian piasters, equal at current exchange rate to about eighty

American cents. The report added that this wholesale rate maybe accepted as the value of the pure olive oil soap made in Palestine; the retail price locally averages fifteen to twenty cents per *rotl*; a minor share of the total soap production, which contains fats, other than olive oil, sells a little cheaper.

The report by the US Department of Commerce added that the production of Nablus soap factories ranged in value from $500,000 to $750,000 annually and the soap of Nablus and other centres in the Levant such as Tripoli enjoy popularity in Egypt, Arabia, Iraq and other places; and that considerably more than half of the total soap production in Palestine finds a market in Palestine, Syria and the Transjordan regions and maybe considered local trade. Palestine soap finds its principal export market in Egypt, which in normal times will take from $500,000 to $750,000 worth annually. Syria, Palestine and the Transjordan regions and Egypt consume practically the entire soap production of this country, and there are important quantities exported to other markets. Generally no Palestine soap went to the US.[5]

Indigenous Nablus soap-making industry versus new Zionist settler soap industry

There are three celebrated cases mentioned below in which the Zionist colonial settlers in Palestine, who began to arrive in the late nineteenth century, sought to imitate the successes of the indigenous Palestinian industries and the Arab agri-industries of the region. The report by the US Department of Commerce above tells of a small factory in Haifa – without giving details – that catered to a limited American demand for pure olive oil soap. The quantity of this soap exported is comparatively unimportant.[6] This may be an indirect reference to the Zionist oil company in Haifa: Shemen. During the British Mandatory period, the Nablus soap industry competed effectively and successfully with this new Zionist soap factory. Shemen Industries Ltd is today the largest and leading company in Israel for the manufacture, development and marketing of edible oils for both home and industry. However, during the British Mandatory period, and especially before the Palestine Nakba in 1948 (Masalha 1992, 2012), Shemen, which had been established in 1906, sought to model itself on the successful Nablus soap industry, but could not compete effectively with the Palestinian soap industry. Nonetheless Shemen sought to imitate Nablus soap-making and bought some of its raw materials, mainly olive and olive waste for the extraction of additional oil from the Palestine Arab villages. It sold its products, soap and vegetable oil to the local Jewish and Arab markets (Bernstein 2000: 119). The Shemen soap was cheaper but was not a substitute for the famous Nablus oil. There is indication of direct completion and Shemen presented its oil as being 'refined as Nablus soap' and dyed it red to make it similar to the Palestinian-produced soap that was dyed with red dust that was left over from brickmaking (Bernstein 2000: 119–20).

In fact, this was not the only case in which the colonial settlers sought to imitate, but failed to compete with, indigenous agricultural industries of Palestine and the

Levant. The most celebrated of all of these cases of failure to compete with indigenous Palestinian industries of the Levant was the case of the mulberry and the silk industry of the region. This was part of the effort to adapt agricultural crops to industrialization in order to assist the Zionist *moshavot* (colonies) in Palestine. Inspired by the cultivation of mulberry trees and success of the silk industry of Lebanon and Syria, some Zionist settlements in upper Galilee began experimenting with mulberry tree cultivation and silk production in the early 1890s. At a tree nursery at the *moshav* colony of Yesud HaMa'ala, founded in 1883, mulberry trees were planted. Israeli historian Gad Gilbar explains that these experiments in Palestine were:

> inspired by the success of the cultivation of mulberry trees and silk manufacture in Syria and Lebanon. In the Upper Galilee similar natural conditions obtained and planation as well as a silk factory were established in Rosh Pina. The factory was a thread-spinning workshop which produced silk threads from coils gathered at the plantations. After several years of operation it became apparent that in this branch as well the main problem was market competition and in 1990 the J.C.A. [Jewish Colonisation Association] closed down the factory after it had accumulated a debt of Fr. 500,000.
>
> (Gilbar 1998: 281–92)

As we shall see in Chapter 18, the Zionist colonial settlers in Palestine also sought to imitate the Palestinian farmers and the successes of the Palestinian citrus industry – what became internationally known as Jaffa Orange – in the British Mandatory period.

Soap-making in Nablus as capital-intensive industries

The term *capital-intensive* refers to industries or business processes that require large amounts of capital investment to manufacture products and thus have a high percentage of fixed assets, such as lands, property and equipment. Capital-intensive industries tend to have high levels of operating leverage, which is the ratio of fixed costs to variable costs. As a result, capital-intensive industries need a high-volume of production to provide an adequate return on investment. The high-operating leverage makes capital-intensive industries much more vulnerable to international fluctuations in trade and foreign markets and economic slowdowns compared with labour-intensive industries. Also the operating costs of the capital investment soap factories of Nablus and regular repairs to these factories were a constant burden that had to be taken into account by investors (Singer 2002: 50). As we have seen in Chapter 6, with the rise to power of a new political elite, the land-owning church and monasteries in the fourth to sixth centuries the size of the Palestine wine industries grew significantly; also the available evidence suggests development of *capital-intensive* wine industries and high capital investment in the Palestinian wine industries by the land-owning church and Christian monasteries, with large and numerous manufacturing plants for processing wine being established in southern Palestine and the Naqab.

In the case of the rise of the soap factories of Jerusalem in the sixteenth century, and the soap factories of Nablus in the late Ottoman period, large capital investments followed the social, economic and political rise of new social and political groups and a new class of enterprising merchant communities. Significant capital investments in the Nablus soap factories accelerated in the late Ottoman period, especially following Ottoman *Tanzimat* of the mid-nineteenth century. The *Tanzimat* reforms had multiple effects (both positive and negative) on Palestinian economy. One effect was the agricultural diversification with an important impact on the structure of the manufacturing branch in Nablus city, which also resulted in increased commerce in Nablus. The second effect was the rise of a new commercial elite in the city, as merchants and merchant capital came to dominate ever-widening swathes of the hinterlands of Nablus and as administrative reorganization during the *Tanzimat* period increased the political weight of the new local political elite and the merchant community (both the oil merchants and soap factory owners) (Doumani 1995: 185).

Influential and powerful families always played a big part in the urban life, politics and economy of Palestine. Factory ownership in the various cities of Ottoman Palestine often operated as a family *waqf* (religious endowment) type of ownership. Ownership of soap factories in Nablus invariably began as family ownership; later – with the expansion of the soap industry and the requirement of massive capital investments in the nineteenth century – to be expanded into multiple forms of 'modern' ownership with multiple partnerships. The Yusufiyya soap factory was one of the oldest extant soap factories in Nablus and it was still being operated in 1994. It was named after Yusuf son of 'Abdulalh Pasha Nimr (*d.* 1685/1686). Yusuf was an Ottoman *sipahi* officer; his grandson Hajj 'Omar Agha (*d.* 1768/1769) the *mutasallim of Nablus* at the time – endowed one fourth of the factory as *waqf ahli* (family endowment) (Doumani 1995; 168–9). The Yusufiyya was later consolidated into a *single waqf*. The case of the Hallaqiyya soap factory in Nablus shows important social trends in the composition of the factory owners by the mid-nineteenth century (Doumani 1995: 185). Teams of workers from the cities Nablus and Ajlun (in Transjordan) produced and transported olive oil and lime (*sheed*) to the factory. Teams of artisans and workers cooked and packaged the soap. The soap merchants who acquired olive oil and commissioned cooked batches of soap, operated regional trade networks that allowed the merchant community in the city to gain access to local power and helped the merchant community to invest heavily in increasing and expanding soap factories (Doumani 1995: 187). The rise of the soap merchants of the city is evident from the fact that all the Muslim member of the newly established Nablus Advisory Council (*Majlis al-Shura*) were soap merchants and factory owners (Doumani 1995: 187).

A number of factors made Nablus soap a capital-intensive industry: the fixed assets are huge buildings, the wells where oil was stored, the large containers in which soap was cooked. Soap was cooked in large amounts, necessitating substantial investments in raw materials. It was anything from two to three years before the merchants in the soap factories could receive return on their investments.

The system of multiple ownerships of soap factories and partnerships was introduced in Nablus in the second half of the nineteenth century, enabling further financial investments and the expansion of the soap factories. Forming multiple partnerships enabled capital investments and enabled the owners to defray the high costs of soap production (Doumani 1995: 194). Soap factory workers were paid in cash and in kind (in olive and olive oil) and after each batch was made. There is no information on the wages for each type of job during the nineteenth century but the pay scale differed substantially within the hierarchy of work, and some skilled labour was imported from Egypt by one major soap factory in the early British Mandatory period rather to accede to local strikes and better wages for local workers (Doumani 1995: 200-1).

The Nablus soap industry began to decline during the mid-twentieth century; in 1927 a major earthquake destroyed large parts of the old city of Nablus in which the soap factories were located - but the industry recovered in the 1930s and Nablus soap continued to attract much praise throughout the Middle East. However, the decline was sharper after the Palestine Nakba of 1948 and later as a result of the disruption caused by the Israeli military occupation of the West Bank in 1967. Israeli military raids during the Second Intifada of 2000-2002 destroyed several soap factories in the historic city centre of Nablus. By 2008, only two soap factories had survived in Nablus. The general manager of a soap factory owned by the Tuqan family commented in 2008: before the Second Intifada of 2000, his factory used to produce 600 tons of soap annually. But due to the Israeli military checkpoints and roadblocks - creating problems in the transportation of supplies and material to and from the factory as well as making it difficult for workers to get from their homes to the factory - the factory produced barely half that amount in 2008.[7] Considered an important aspect of Nablus's material and cultural heritage, the old Arafat soap factory has been turned into a cultural heritage exhibition centre and a research centre with a small model soap factory that makes Nablus soap using methods of traditional soap-making.[8] Despite the sharp decline of the soap factories of Nablus, their products continue to be made and are currently sold primarily in Palestine and the Arab countries, with some fair-trade exports to Europe and sold at the charity shops of Oxfam (UK) and beyond.[9] Also considered an important aspect of Nablus's cultural an industrial heritage, the preservation of the soap-making industry of the city has been the focus of several local projects, including the restoration and conversion of the old Arafat soap factory into a Cultural Heritage Enrichment Centre for research and exhibition facilities.[10]

16

Tobacco, Coffeehouses and Popular Culture

The Transformation of the Urban Leisure Industries of Palestine

Popular entertainment in the ancient cities of Palestine

The leisure industry of urban Palestine began to flourish in Antiquity and was often linked to wine production and the ancient pleasurable habit of wine drinking. As we have already seen in Chapter 6, *Gaza wine* became an internationally famous brand under the Byzantines and under Christianity (fourth to early seventh centuries). Palestine became one of the most important wine-producing and wine-exporting countries in the world.

In Antiquity and throughout the Roman and early Byzantine period keeping the urban masses in Palestine entertained often meant cheap wine, horse chariot racing, public spectacles, competitions and athletic games, monumental urban theatres, hippodromes and amphitheatres dotted across Palestine and the Roman province of Arabia (Segal 2018; Weiss 2014). As we saw in Chapter 3, the former Nabataean Arab city of Kurnub of the Naqab, renamed Memphis under the Romans, began breeding Arabian horses for horse chariot racing and public spectacles – Arabian horses were prized for their stamina and endurance (Culbertson 2014; Negev 1988: 8).

Cheap wine remained the key beverage of the masses under the Byzantine Palestine, but cruel sports and the excesses of the Roman public spectacles were drastically curtailed in the sixth century by the Christian emperor Justinian, while wine production declined under Islam and was effectively banned under the Abbasids. However, throughout Antiquity several 'cities of leisure' evolved in Palestine, mostly to do with sunbathing and the Mediterranean Sea, and with the socially relaxed atmosphere and 'wine festivities' and the cult of Dionysus (Bachus) of Mediterranean cities such as Jaffa, Ascalon and Gaza. Although the excesses of public spectacles and cruel sports in Roman urban Palestine were curbed under Byzantine rule, Christianity encouraged wine drinking and luxurious *Gaza wine* was earmarked for export. The availability of a variety of cheap wine in Palestine made wine-consumption, sanctified by religion, an important daily pleasure not only in the hundreds of monasteries dotted across Palestine but also affordable for most ordinary people in the thriving towns and cities of Palestine.

Some continuities in the leisure industries of urban Palestine, with a huge impact on the quality of urban life across millennia, can be seen in the way the famous bathhouses of Roman and Byzantine Palestine metamorphosed into the great and exquisite bathhouses of urban Palestine under Islam (Chapter 6). However, in the Middle Ages wine drinking was banned under Islam and the world-famous wine industry of Palestine dramatically declined, with the exception of small-scale wine-making by Palestinian monasteries. But new forms of urban leisure activities began to emerge under Islam and the ancient sea-side city of Jaffa often functioned as a summer holiday retreat and recreation area for the inhabitants of Jerusalem (Masalha 2022). Most importantly the Palestinian city of Tiberias (*Τιβεριάς*, Arabic: *Tabariyyah*), founded in Roman Palestine, had become the regional capital of Galilee under Islam and remained a key Palestinian centre of trade, silk industry and leisure activities for several centuries to come. Under Islam the reputation of Tiberias as a multicultural, hedonistic and leisure city – located a long distance from the conservative sacred city of Jerusalem and situated in the proximity of many natural thermal springs and hot health baths – became so great that the Sea of Galilee became known in Arabic as the 'Sea of Tiberias' (*Bahr Tabariyyah* and later *Buhayrat Tabariyyah*) (Masalha 2018).

The urban bathhouses as key leisure institutions

The leisure industry of Palestine was not confined to the urban coffeehouse. For hundreds of years under Islam the public bath, or the *hammam* – whose Arabic name is derived from heated water – like the coffeehouse, was an essential institution and central to urban leisure and everyday life in the cities of Palestine. As we have already seen in Chapter 6, the urban public baths were a common feature of urban life in Roman and Byzantine Palestine and the bath houses of the monasteries of Byzantine Palestine maintained the 'three chambers' tradition of the classical Roman bath: *frigidarium* (cold room), *tepidarium* (warm room), and *caldarium* (a hot room). However Islam introduced adaptations to the classical Roman/Byzantine bath houses:

> It is not surprising that the Umayyads drew upon earlier baths while introducing adaptations such as large audience halls and few immersion pools. Dressing rooms were enlarged and the domed hot rooms expanded, while the tepid rooms gradually and evenly declined in size.
>
> (Peteet 2024: 92)

Furthermore under the Mamluks, the booming economy and trade of Jerusalem contributed to the establishment of some of the most architecturally complex *hammams* in Palestine (Chapter 13). Also some urban *hamamms* established during the Mamluk period, such as Hamman al-Wikala in Nablus, were established by, or attached to, local commercial agencies and served local and travelling merchants.

In Islam cleanliness, clean water and the Islamic ritual of purification, ablution (*wudu*), procedure for cleansing parts of the body before prayer is an article of faith. This belief and the requirement of urban hygiene contributed to the spread and flourishing of *hammams* – often built with Islamic architecture in mind – throughout the urban centres of Islam and historic cities of Palestin. These urban *hammams* were often adjacent to, and an integral part of, the urban markets. Also linked to the urban markets were the *sabeels*: small fountains built in the Islamic architecture tradition where clean drinking water is available freely to members of the public and travellers. These became permanent structures of urban civic and religious importance in the cities of Palestine and the Levant.

However, historically the urban *hamamms* acquired multiple meanings and multiple functions: a pleasurable space, the *hammams* were places of health, cleanliness, spirituality and sociability and part of everyday urban life and urban pleasure. Dr Charles Shepard, who opened the first Ottoman-style *hammam* in Brooklyn Heights in 1863, wrote:

> The hammam is a *majlis mudaris*—a place to gather with others, to learn things and exchange information. We used to go to hammam in Lydda [Palestine] not as a luxury like today but as part of normal life'
>
> (cited in Peteet 2024: 2)

Public baths were a common feature of the urban landscape in Nablus, Jerusalem, al-Khalil, Acre, Gaza, Lydda, al-Ramla, Jaffa and Haifa (Peteet 2024: 162). And these urban *hammams* benefited from the fact that the cities of Nablus and Jerusalem developed some of the best and most famous soap industries in the Islamic world.

> Nablus is well known for its soap production and its hammams. Of thirty-two baths operative in 1920s Palestine, Nablus had the largest share of eight, followed by Hebron [al-Khalil] with five … A Nabulsi proverb captures their centrality to everyday life. When pandemonium prevails, Nablus quips: What happened? Did they turn off the water in the hammam"?
>
> (Peteet 2024: 161)

Of the old city of Nablus's eight historic *hamamms*, two working historic *hammams* have survived in the city: Hammam al-Hana ('Delight Bath') and Hammam al-Shifa ('Healing Bath') (Irving 2011: 219), while some other historic *hammams* have changed their function and usages or have fallen into ruins (Abujidi 2014: 114).

The urban coffeehouse and everyday life in Palestine

> *Coffee should not be drunk in a hurry. It is the sister of time, & should be sipped slowly, slowly. Coffee is the sound of taste, a sound for the aroma. It is a mediation & a plunge into memories & the soul.*
>
> (Palestinian poet Mahmoud Darwish, *Memory for Forgetfulness*: August, Beirut, 1982, University of California Press. 1995)

The urban coffeehouse, with its *shisha* (*nargila*) smoking and its social custom of coffee-drinking, is the epitome of popular culture in Palestine. There are also Palestinian folk stories about Palestinian coffee merchants and sellers in Jerusalem who sought to refine and elevate the roasting of coffee beans and the refinement of the taste and aroma of coffee to an art from. Drinking sweet and aromatic coffee and smoking tobacco shisha are closely associated with the famous urban coffeehouses and urban culture of Palestine and the Middle East. As cultural institutions, with multiple meanings in the history of the region and urban life, the coffeehouses are associated with the daily life of ordinary people, their leisure life and modern pleasure habits and their social abilities. But ideas of the urban coffeehouse in the Levant also evolved across time and were adapted by different people in different contexts to suit their understanding of entertainment and leisure time.

Coffee and tobacco are also at the forefront of modern global commodities and modern leisure industries and the pleasures of these two commodities constitute habits of modernity. Cultivated and consumed widely, today coffee is one of the highest value commodities traded worldwide. Consumption of tobacco in the Levant begins after the sixteenth century and coffee was virtually unknown in the Middle East until the fourteenth century. Tobacco was brought to the Arab world and Ottoman empire by Spanish merchants in the wake of the 'discovery' and colonization of the America by the Europeans. Coffee-drinking and the Middle Eastern coffeehouse culture spread Europe in the sixteenth century and eventually to Britain in the seventeenth century and in so doing coffee reshaped the commercial and consumer revolutions in Britain and Europe (Cowan 2005).

In London the most famous eighteenth-century coffeehouse was the 'Jerusalem Coffee-House', established in 1770s, which was a rendezvous of owners of ships engaged in the commerce with India and so a favoured place to gather of members of the East India Company. Today coffee and tobacco are globally traded and consumed top commodities across the world; these commodities have also been central to the urban coffeehouse and everyday life of Palestine and the Arab world.

The histories of the spread of the consumption of both coffee and tobacco are connected to the early modern period. Coffee (known in Arabic as *qahwah*) is based on *Coffea arabica* which is believed to be the first species of coffee to have been cultivated in Ethiopia and Yemen and generally the Red Sea basin. Today *Coffea arabica* is the worlds' dominant coffee bean, representing more than 60 per cent of the global production of coffee. The first written record of roasting and brewing Arabica coffee beans comes from Arab scholars and it was Arab merchants who spread Arabica coffee first among the Ottomans and later to Europe in the early sixteenth century and early Ottoman rule in the Near East. Also during the early Ottoman period, Spanish merchants were the first to introduce the modern trade in tobacco to both Europe and the Ottoman empire. The terms *coffee* and *tobacco* in European languages are also related to the historical origins and spread of these two globally traded modern commodities. The term *tobacco* in European languages is derived from the Spanish *tabaco* and in return the Spanish word is possibly derived from the Arabic *ṭubbaq*, which refers to a type of plant. While the modern Arabic word *tabgh* is derived from the Spanish for *tabaco*, the word for *coffee* in major European languages is derived from Ottoman Turkish which is derived from Arabic for *qahwah* (or *qahweh*).

Unlike sugar and tobacco, coffee was never produced in Palestine, but its impact on modern life in the country is no less significant. Coffee was imported into Ottoman Palestine and became widely available in the country in the seventeenth and eighteenth centuries and this can be seen from the fact that Palestinian soap and coffee merchants established a commercial agency (*wikala*) in Cairo for marketing both soap and coffee in Egypt (Meinecke 1980; Warner 2005).

Women worked side by side with men and played a big and equal part to men in the rural and agricultural economy of Palestine. Historically, however, the use of urban coffeehouse as public spaces was largely confined to men; women in the towns and cities of Palestine were largely confined to private spaces and their agency, influence and power were often exercised most effectively within the context of the family-oriented Palestinian society. Of course women were legally entitled to own property and commercial businesses and some wealthy Muslim women in Jerusalem went on found schools, colleges and many charitable (*waqf*) foundations (Masalha 2022), but their access to the public domain and positions of power in society were severely restricted.

However drinking sweet and aromatic coffee was not confined to the urban public coffeehouses in the Middle East or to men; aromatic coffee (spiced with cardamom which had long been imported since Antiquity from the Indian subcontinent and Indonesia) was consumed in large quantity in private and domestically by Palestinians and by Palestinian women in villages and towns across Palestine. Palestinian women's social traditions included morning gatherings called *subhiyya*: derived from the word *sabahah*, morning, *subhiyya* was a morning gathering of women that took place in villages and towns (and in Palestinian refugee camps after the 1948 Nakba) among friends, family members and neighbours for slow-drinking of morning coffee by women and for socializing for a couple of hours with a different hostess each time (Wari 2017: 189).

Tobacco is a global industry and tobacco-related products have become central to modern leisure industries around the globe, Palestine included. Historically the versatility of consumption of tobacco related products in Palestine and the Levant as a whole is evident in the fact these were consumed in three different ways:

- *Snuff tobacco* (known in Arabic as *su'out*): it is a type of smokeless tobacco product made from finely ground or pulverized tobacco leaves; it was widely consumed in both rural and urban Palestine until recently. It was widely snorted in Palestine with a flavoured or scented blended tobacco products by users;
- *Nargila* (or *shisha*) pipe tobacco: it is waterpipe though which tobacco has long been smoked in Palestine and the Middle East;
- *Cigarette smoking:* as we shall see below the manufacturing of cigarettes in Palestine began in the British Mandatory period and cigarette smoking began to spread widely in Palestine since this Mandatory period.

Within the social history of tobacco, *shisha* smoking tied up with the unique institution of the coffeehouse in urban Muslim society and Palestine, and the coffeehouses became a distinctive feature of urban life in Ottoman Palestine and the Levant. The urban coffeehouses began in the mid-sixteenth century with the spread of coffee-drinking and the coffee trade, which originated in Arabia and was spread to the Levant and Egypt and then throughout the Ottoman Empire by Syrian and Palestinian merchants. In the Ottoman capital Istanbul the first coffeehouses were founded in 1555 by two Syrian merchants, one from Damascus and the other from Aleppo, under the name of *Qahveh Khaneh* (coffee shop), derived from the Arabic name *qahuwa* for coffee. Introduced by Arab merchants, this social institution was readily adapted to Ottoman customs and urban culture (Asli 2001; Beeley 1970: 475–93; Hattox 1982; Yılmaz et al. 2017: 213–20).

English travel writer Richard Pococke, who visited Syria, Palestine and Egypt from 1737 to 1741 and published his *Description of the East* in 1745, wrote:

> The Coffee-houses in Damascus are remarkably pleasant; many of them are large rooms, and the ceilings of them are supported with rows of pillars, round which they have their sophas; there is generally a court behind them with a basin of water, and a fountain in the middle, and the seats round the courts either shaded with trees or covered over; one in particular on the Barraday [river] which runs through the city has an island behind it, planted with trees. and the place is accommodated in a very convenient manner, which renders it one of the most delightful places one can imagine in the midst of a great city; in these coffee houses they have concerts of musick at certain hours every day, and in some, a person paid by the house tells at a fixed hour Arabian stories in a very grateful manner, and with much eloquence. These coffee-houses answer the end of public house with those, who openly drink nothing but coffee, water and sherbets; where all idle people, strangers, and others, who are not of the first rank, pass their leisure hours, send to the shops for their provisions …,the people from without [the coffee-houses] carrying about their different sorts of sherbets, which the place is famous.
>
> (Pococke 1743–45: 122)

As a space of urban leisure and an institution of social and public entertainment, with a relaxed social environment, the Damascus-style coffeehouse evolved and was adapted in different urban contexts of the Ottoman empire, Palestine included. The Ottoman authorities were content to derive great revenues by taxing these popular urban leisure institutions. Subsequently, following the introduction of tobacco into Europe and the Ottoman Empire by Spanish merchants, the Ottoman state maintained its monopoly on the tobacco trade, deriving additional state revenues from both coffee and tobacco and the popular coffee houses which also introduced *shisha* smoking. In *The Early History of Coffee Houses in England* (1893), Edward Forbes Robinson gave an account of the early history of the Ottoman coffee houses in Istanbul and commented that under the name of 'Kahweh Khaneh' (coffee shop) coffee lounges, with richly carpeted and provided with luxurious cushions, were the resorts of all manners of society; to these 'schools of the wise' also came young students and professors; other persons who came from the countryside to seek employment in the city also frequented them; also lovers of chess and backgammon spent time in them; also acquaintances who wanted to pass time with others frequented them; all found entertainments in the coffeehouse for modest sums:

> After a while when court officials and persons of distinction began to come hither, the suspicion of the authorities, both religious and civil, was aroused.
>
> (Robinson 1893: 37–8)

Unlike coffee, tobacco is not an indigenous Near East industry. It was first cultivated, produced and used in religious and social ceremonies by the indigenous peoples of the Americas. This product became widely traded and lucrative after it was introduced to Europe and subsequently to the Ottoman Empire by the Spaniards following their conquests in Latin America. Fuelling colonization and fuelling the African slave labour, the European Industrial Revolution and modern capitalism of the eighteenth and nineteenth centuries brought about the mass production of cigarettes and the lucrative glamorization of cigarette smoking across the world. In the Levant (especially in Lebanon and Palestine) tobacco also became a lucrative industry and was a heavily traded commodity to support the growing popular habit of smoking. Today around 1.3 billion people use tobacco across the world.

Tobacco is one of the most widely used addictive substances in the world. Until the middle of the twentieth century little was known or produced about the ill-effects on health of cigarette smoking and other tobacco-related products. This began to change since and medical research began to show the severe negative health impact of tobacco smoking, which was linked to lung and throat cancer. This led many governments to adopt new policies designed to reduce sharply the use of tobacco. The World Health Organization has suggested that tobacco affect both smokers and non-smokers and kills more than eight million people each year worldwide.[1] Although these public health policies have brought about a global decline in cigarette consumption over the past decade, the two geographical regions that have continued to demonstrate remarkable growth have been the Middle Eastern and African markets – regions with young and growing population – with an annual growth rate over the past decade of about 5 per cent. Despite global public health concerns regarding the use of tobacco, shisha smoking, which in the Arab world had long preceded the modern cigarette, continues to be highly popular in the coffeehouses of urban Palestine.

Unlike most modern indigenous Palestinian trade and industries, the tobacco trade in late Ottoman Palestine was controlled by foreign companies. Tobacco trade in the Ottoman empire was a government monopoly until the early 1880s, after which this trade was handed to a European company formed by several European states and banks associated with European Ottoman Public Debt Administration (OPDA) (Akarli 1993: 118–19). The OPDA was a vehicle by which the European colonial powers maintained their financial grip on some important sectors of the Ottoman economy. The OPDA represented European powers such as the British, French, Germans, Austrians, Italians and the Dutch, and this company was provided monopolies on the trade of tobacco and salt in the Ottoman empire. The company was also afforded taxes on silk, fishing, stamps and alcohol in some regions of the Ottoman empire.

As we have already seen for hundreds of years under Islam, and long before modernity, Palestine produced and exported sugar, olive oil, soap, cotton, textile, wheat and barley. However, by the late Ottoman period Palestine begins to import sugar – in addition to coffee and tobacco. As the standard of living and the average real income in Palestine continued to grow during the late Ottoman period, the consumption of coffee and tobacco in the country continued to grow and the value of the import of coffee, sugar and tobacco – three commodities which often went hand in hand – through the port of Jaffa rose from £58,970 in 1900 to £172,800 in 1913 (Gilbar 2023: 188–210). The centrality of coffee-drinking to Palestinian social and cultural life meant that Palestinians (men and women) consumed large qualities of coffee both at home and in the numerous coffeehouses dotted across urban Palestine; wealthy Palestinian merchants, in particular, often kept a large number of domestic items related to coffee brewing and coffee consumption at home; when Shaykh 'Abdel-Razzaq 'Arafat, a wholesale textile merchant from Nablus, passed away bankrupt in 1810, leaving behind a wife and thirteen children and a large debt, eighty-two coffee cups were registered in his home by the Islamic Muslim Court in the city (Doumani 1995: 53).

Also as the coffeehouses became numerous in Palestine and the Levant, they began to function not only as popular community hubs and leisure spaces for ordinary, but they began offering more than coffee and tobacco shisha smoking; they began vending sweets and various beverages (Tokman 2001). By the late Ottoman period Palestinian cities were full of coffeehouses, a lucrative leisure industry that became an essential part of everyday life for ordinary people. Men from all walks of life frequented the coffeehouse, which became popular spaces for social entertainment, local gossip and exchange of information. At a time of relatively low literacy rates and with no modern forms of communication or accessibility of print news until the late Ottoman period, the urban coffeehouses were important hubs of news and exchange of information:

> In his social history of coffeehouses, Ralph Hattox offers a rather different reading of the origins of café society in the Middle East. He rejects this distinction between 'respectable' and "ill-reputed" cafés, which is implied by Hanssen, and suggests the main divide to be between bars and cafés. While the former were associated with gambling and drunkenness, 'the coming of the coffeehouse signalled the beginning of an entirely new phenomenon. Perfectly respectable people went out at night for purposes other than piety'. But in Cairo and Istanbul, the public café tradition had a much earlier pedigree. Jabarti chronicled the co-existence of wine taverns and coffeehouses in Cairo during the late eighteenth century, before the French Expedition. During Ramadan, coffeehouses were major centres for public entertainment and arghileh-smoking. What seems to have given cafés an aura of respectability was their patronage by Al-Azhar scholars and sheikhs, who supported their own coffeehouses'
>
> (cited in Tamari 2003)

Spanning over four decades, the memoirs of Palestinian musician and ethnographer Wasif Jawhariyyeh, '*the Storyteller of Jerusalem*', are a remarkable treasure trove of writings on the popular culture, coffeehouses, music, communitarian ethos and the transformation of daily life of Jerusalem from the late Ottoman period to 1948 (Tamari and Nassar 2014). Modern technology also had a major impact on the urban coffeehouses and popular culture of Jerusalem. The phonograph, later known as gramophone, became a trademark in Europe in 1887 and by 1910 Palestinians in Jerusalem began listening to gramophones (which later developed into record players) in the coffeehouses in Jerusalem.[2] This shows that coffeehouses were far from being bastions of tradition in Palestine and continued to evolve as other aspects of modernity affected ordinary urban life in late Ottoman Palestine. The impact of modern technology on the daily leisure activity of late Ottoman Palestine created new forms of recreation and cultural activity at the urban coffeehouse. This took many forms including the introduction of the printing press and newspapers, which can now be read the coffeehouses of the cities. Also the European gramophone was imported into the coffeehouses of Palestine in addition to the musical concerts that were combined with drinking coffee and having shisha sessions (Ghosheh 2013).

Palestinian Jerusalemite writer Subhi Ghosheh in his book *Jerusalem: Arab Social Life, Traditions, and Everyday Pleasures in the 20th Century*, a compendium of 'social life, traditions and everyday pleasures' in Jerusalem, a city packed urban cultural and religious festivals, cuisine and even the everyday simple pleasures, he also notes the appearance of the gramophone in Jerusalem coffeehouses for the first time in 1910, remarks on its use in several coffeehouses to attract customers: 'I remember how funny it was when the song used to fade away, indicating that the phonograph needed to be wound up again, by turning its handle clockwise' (Ghosheh 2013; Johnson 2014: 31-5). Also both Palestinian Arab coffeehouses and the Arab-Jewish coffeehouses of urban Palestine began to play gramophone music and offer domino and backgammon boards to their clientele. Arab neighbours frequently visited Arab-Jewish coffeehouses and there were some joint coffeehouse in the cities (Klein 2014: 134-53).

From *Leisure Coffeehouses* to *Cultural Coffeehouses* and *Modern Theatres*: Sakakini's philosophy of pleasure and the urban coffeehouse as a space of radical thought

From the late Ottoman period onwards, and especially during the British Mandatory period, some urban coffeehouses began to transform themselves into a combination of coffeehouse and urban theatre. This can be seen in the first coffeehouses-theatres that appeared in the city of Jaffa in the late nineteenth century such as *al-Zarafiyya theatre*, the theatre of the *al-Bannur coffeehouse*, the *Parisana Theatre* and the *theatre of the al-Halawani Coffeehouse.* New types of modern urban theatres and cinemas also emerged in the first half of the twentieth century. Also *conceptually distinct* urban *coffeehouse* and modern *theatre/music hall* of Jaffa began to overlap in the same way that the modern urban *soap factories* of Nablus (discussed in Chapter 15) began to overlap with the public baths (*hammams*) in the city and in the same way that the great Muslim colleges of Jerusalem in the Middle Age also functioned as urban lodges for travelling *sufi* preachers and in the way the colleges of Byzantine Palestine (discussed in Chapter 6) combined 'gown and town' and were overlapping with other civic urban institutions in the country (Masalha 2022).

During the British Mandatory period, in particular, many combined urban coffeehouses-theatres in Palestine became key venues for holding musical concerts; in Acre the Glass Coffeehouse became a famous venue for hosting not only local singer but also famous Egyptian and Lebanese singers (Nassar 2023: 495). Also during the British Mandatory period another new form of popular social entertainment arrived in Palestine: the modern cinema. The Hamra Cinema in Jaffa was a 1937 art deco building and one of the largest and most luxurious popular entertainment cinemas in the country. While classical music concerts were held in the cities and appealed to the Palestinian urban middle class,[3] Al-Hamra Cinema in Jaffa and other urban cinemas in Jerusalem and Haifa began hosting some of the most popular women and men singers of the Arab world. The concerts at the al-Hamra Cinema by Umm Kulthum, Farid al-Atrash and Leila Murad attracted audiences from all corners of Palestine (Yazbak 2024: 8-25).

With the spread of mass education, literacy and political activism in the late Ottoman period and the first half of the twentieth century the coffeehouses of Jerusalem, Nablus, Jaffa, Acre, Lydda and al-Ramla became sites of newspapers reading and hubs of political and intellectual activity (Masalha 2022). Especially during the British Mandatory period more and more urban coffeehouses became the sites of political, cultural and intellectual activity, and Arabic newspapers and periodicals became widely available in the urban coffeehouses of Palestine and some educated readers would visit coffeehouses to read the main news of the day. In early 1920, during the independent Arab government at Damascus, local leaders in the city of Lydda were reported 'reading the papers out in the cafes and telling the public about the heroic deeds of their brethren in Syria and their war with the French', while newspapers and journals publishers began complaining about people 'who tried to get the paper from friends who had already read it, or to read it in a cafe' (Ayalon 2010: 105). But the 'coffeehouse and the press cohabited in a kind of symbiosis: when the editor and reporters were sitting in a cafe engaged in a discussion, the content of their exchanges occasionally found its way to the next issue. Reportedly, some pieces were written actually on the spot [in the coffeehouse]' (Ayalon 2010: 105). Also the post-Nakba period, some urban coffeehouses in the Galilee, especially in Acre and Nazareth, were used as venues for political activity and holding protest meetings against Israeli discrimination policies against the Palestinian citizens of Israel (Pappe 2011: 84).

The modern coffeehouses of the old city of Jerusalem evolved to serve not only coffee and tea but also some of them developed into cultural venues and began holding cultural events and the old city of Jerusalem became famous for its *cultural coffeehouses*. They began holding cultural events in which the old city of Jerusalem became well-known for its *cultural coffeehouses*, the most famous of which was the 'Vagabond Coffeehouse'. This cultural coffeehouse opened in 1918 and was located near Bab al-Khalil (Jaffa Gate). It attracted Jerusalem's Palestinian intellectuals, including some famous writers, most notably Khalil Sakakini, Khalil al-Khalidi, Said Jarallah, Najib Nassar and Bandali al-Jawzi. The coffeehouse also holds a weekly literary symposium called the 'Wednesday Circle', which was attended by many Palestinian and Arab literary figures. Subsequently the patrons of this cultural coffeehouse formed what became known as the 'Vagabond Coffeehouse' (*Maqha al-Sa'alik*) from 1921 onwards (Al-Badri and Abu Harb 2018). The cultural manifesto of this coffeehouse was published by al-Sakakini in 1925 and contained eighteen articles, the manifesto reflected the 'philosophy of pleasure' of al-Sakakini himself (Tamari 2003; Willson 2013: 200). The concept of *sa'aleek* refers to pre-Islamic Arab bandits and rebel poets who fought for social justice and is deeply rooted in Arab mythology, folklore and literature, and the term finds echoes in Eric Hobsbawm's *Bandits* (1969) and *Primitive Rebels* (1959) – the coffeehouse near Jaffa Gate of the Old City of Jerusalem became associated with Sakakini's circle of 'vagabonds' and 'bandits' (local Muslim, Christian and Jewish intellectuals) in Jerusalem, before, during and immediately after the First World War (Tamari 2003); he also later gathered around him a group of like-minded rebels at Piccadilly Café on Mamilla Street (Klein 2014a: 52; 2014b: 134–53).

The most influential Palestinian intellectual and educator of the modern era which became the centre of this new radical cultural coffeehouses of Jerusalem and at the centre of the 'Vagabond Coffeehouse' was Khalil Sakakini (1878–1953) of Jerusalem (Beška 2015: 40–53; Masalha 2022; Othman 2016: 184) whose educational career began in the late Ottoman period and ended in the post-Nakba period. Sakakini was the epitome of the scholar-writer essayist-activist educationist and a great champion of humanist Arab renaissance (*nahda*) education (Masalha 2022). Sakakini's approaches to modernity, education and urban leisure also reflected the new revolutionary spirit of the rising Palestinian middle class of the late Ottoman and British Mandatory periods and the impact of this enterprising class on the transformation of modern urban life in Palestine (see Chapter 18).

Sakakini's modern and enlightened position against corporal punishment in schools can be seen from the Arabic tradition of Aristotelian philosophy of education of Ibn Miskawayh, a librarian-intellectual and a secretary in the enlightened courts of several wazirs and sultans in Abbasid Baghdad during classical Islam, which influenced Sakakini's philosophy of pleasure, of minimizing emotional harm and maximizing emotional intelligence and the pleasures in learning practices, emphasized the importance of children being encouraged to 'read for pleasure' – an approach that was influenced by what became widely known in classical Islam as 'philosophy of pleasure' (*falsafar al-surur*). Inevitably this Islamic medieval 'philosophy of pleasure' was often criticized by the conservative religious authorities in the way the urban modern popular coffeehouses were viewed with deep suspicion by many Islamic clergy in modern times.

Sakakini's philosophy of pleasure was interpreted by Palestinian scholar Salim Tamari as a hedonistic 'philosophy of pleasure' (Tamari 2003). Sakakini's philosophy of pleasure was influenced by a medieval Islamic work of ethics written by the moral philosopher and educationalist Ibn Miskawayh (932–1030 CE): Tahdhib al-Akhlaq (Cultivation of Morals), translated into and published in English under the title Refinement of Character. Sakakini himself rightly attributed this 'philosophy of joy' to Ibn Miskawayh, who stated: 'Sorrow [unhappiness] is neither necessary nor natural. We should immerse ourselves in life and cherish it with celebrating our nights … we should indulge in music and singing. If disasters come our way, we should receive them courageously and prevent grief from consuming us' (Tamari 2003; Willson 2013: 200).

Sakakini's own involvement and delight in urban social leisure, shisha smoking and the urban coffeehouse sought to break the distinction between the high culture of learning and urban intellectual life and the popular mass culture of the urban coffeehouse. The famous extensive diary of Sakakini is one of the most important records of the evolution of Sakakini's philosophy of life as well as, crucially, of the concrete educational experiences of a highly influential Palestinian teacher. Salim Tamari cites Sakakini's entry of his diary of 13 April 1918 in which Sakakini describes what looks like an action strategy in pursuit of happiness – with a list of joyous activities and experiences all aimed at achieving 'happiness':

> I have the greatest pity for those who do not experience pleasure [surur] in their lives… I woke up having had the greatest joy during my sleep; I start my exercises with a great deal of sensuality; I bathe my body and find the greatest bliss engulfing my body in cold water; I eat as if the greatest reward comes from eating - even if it is a dry piece of bread. I smoke my arghileh [shisha] and think that happiness lies in smoking; I read and write and enjoy what I have recorded; I take a walk and find great delight in walking; I sit and talk with my friends and find contentment in socialising with them. Even when I have problems, I find a great enjoyment in overcoming my travails. I face catastrophes with fortitude and experience a strange satisfaction from confronting them (Tamari 2003).

The pursuit of all kinds of joie de vivre - emotional, physical, sensual, social and intellectual - and delighting in emotional pleasure and the delight in (secular and church) music, Arabic poetry, listening to the melodic recitation of the Quran and all kinds of pleasures was Sakakini's take on Ibn Miskawayh's philosophy of pleasure. Sakakini's rebellious streak, his love of shisha smoking and music and hedonistic lifestyle fitted perfectly into the coffeehouses of Jerusalem of the Ottoman period and British Mandatory period. Coupled with pleasure and daily leisure activities, Sakakini's philosophy of pleasure and shisha smoking and socializing caused him to spend a great deal of time in Jerusalem's coffeehouses, the centre of café culture in late Ottoman and British Mandatory Palestine.

From shisha smoking to the modern cigarette industry: Arab women and the tobacco factory of Nazareth

Much of the consumption of tobacco in late Ottoman Palestine was through shisha smoking rather than cigarette smoking. Also, in Ottoman Palestine tobacco cultivation was a relatively small-scale industry. This tobacco industry began to grow during the British Mandatory period and this can be seen in the city of Nazareth, in which a relatively large foreign-owned tobacco factory was established in 1931: the biggest and most thriving modern industry was the tourism and hospitality sector associated with Holy Land pilgrims and travellers who flocked to the city associated with the birth of Christianity and Jesus of Nazareth. The Nazareth cigarette factory was located in the city because tobacco was primarily cultivated during the late Ottoman period in the Galilee region. The Report of the British Palestine Government's

Department of Agriculture and Forests for the year 1931-32 (Jerusalem) commented about the growth in the cultivation and production of tobacco in Palestine in the early 1930s and the demands of cigarette manufacturers for a better tobacco leaf: in 1930, 28,457 *dunnams* were cultivated, which produced 953 tons of tobacco; in 1931, 23,479 dunams were cultivated, which produced 504 tons; while in 1934, 19,948 *dunams* were cultivated producing 1,012 tons of tobacco:

> The area of 9,328 dunams in 1933 has grown to 19,948 [dunams in 1934 producing 1012 tons], probably due to the opening of a new cigarette factory in Nazareth, the very favourite climate conditions obtaining in the spring and the increase in the numbers of [tobacco cultivation] licences issued in the Samarian distinct. Gradually but surely the areas on which Turkish tobacco are grown are being limited to the ranges of Acre and Galilean hills. While it is indisputable that the northern hills produce the finest quality leaf, there certainly are other districts where the crop might be profitably grown ...The yield [in 1934] per dunam was a good deal in excess of tat of the previous year in addition to the area being double that in 1933.
>
> (Government of Palestine 1936: 31-2)

The report also shows the import of tobacco and foreign cigarettes into Palestine was on the increase.

Almost everywhere female factory workers were largely the product of the modern Industrial Revolution. While historically most Palestinian urban industries employed predominantly men, with the growing foreign capitalist investment in Palestine during the British Mandatory period the tobacco factory of Nazareth began to employ local urban women. This was also the case in modern Lebanon in which the tobacco industry, as this work shows (Abisaab 2001), attracted cheap women labour. The foreign-owned cigarette companies in Palestine engaged in the growth, preparation for sale, shipment, advertisement and distribution of cigarettes and tobacco-related products.

However in Palestine during the British Mandatory period, this tobacco industry (and tobacco leaf sorting) was highly exploitative with notoriously low wages and appalling working conditions. Evidence from the British-owned tobacco company in Nazareth during 1931–38 suggests this factory employed some 400 workers, the overwhelming majority of whom were Arab women, children and the elderly. Arab women in this industry worked on average thirteen hours per day and were paid low wages both in absolute terms and in comparison with Jewish women in the same industry; their working conditions were also appalling (Abdo 2013). The Nazareth cigarette factories continued to function in Israel into the 1970s.

17

Sweets as a Modern Trademark

Urban Life, Sweet Bakeries and the Confectionary Culture of Palestine

Known by the biblical metaphor as 'the Land of Milk and Honey', honey was produced in Palestine millennia before the biblical stories were put together, and both milk and honey have greatly influenced the culinary and confessionary culture of Palestine. Influenced by the rich and multilayered culinary traditions of the country and ancient history of trade in spices and incense, Palestinian sweets and pastries, like other Middle Eastern desserts, have used common ingredients such as spices, nuts and natural sweeteners like locally produced honey. By the Bronze Age the locally produced ancient honey of Palestine had acquired an international reputation and was mentioned in connection with the Palestine campaigns of Pharaoh Thutmose III, whose imperial army besieged and defeated the army of the Canaanite city-state of Megiddo in Palestine, at the Battle of Megiddo, one of the most famous battles of the middle Bronze Age. After this battle the city-states of Palestine came under Egyptian domination and their chiefs were obliged to pay tribute to the Egyptian empire – a tribute which included 823 vessels of incense and 1,781 vessels of honey, wine and ivory (Budge 2013: 37).

Honey-based desserts and confectionary in general have continued to play an important role in the modern culinary cultures of the Middle East and often heavily sweetened mint tea is served in Palestinian and Arab homes. The sugar cane industry of Palestine developed significantly under the Mamluks, and part of this sugar industry was aimed at exporting its products to Egypt but as historian 'Abdel-Qader al-Juzairi remarked, the trade in sugar and sweetened goods in Palestine continued to grow during the late Mamluk period (Wa'ari 2023, Vol. 1: 60). Furthermore in the fourteenth century Muslim traveller Ibn Battuta mentioned the horticultural factories of olive oil and the great carob factories of Nablus that produce jams and confectionary and 'sweets made of carob', which was exported to Damascus (Ibn Battuta 2024, part 1).

While exporting sweet products, the demand for imported luxury items, spices and baked sweetened goods, bread and sweets have existed in the urban centres of the Mediterranean since Antiquity and baked goods and sweets became a key feature of urban life and urban pleasure in Palestine. Consequently urban bakers became an important skilled profession in Antiquity and the first *bakers' guild* was established in Rome, to protect skilled professional bakers, in 168 BCE. In urban Roman Palestine bakers would often bake bread more than once a day in a *polis* (city). It is possible that there was a guild of bakers in some cities (Safrai 2003).

The history of sweets is partly to do with the history of sugar cane cultivation and production. Sugar cane cultivation and sugar production, consumption as sweeteners and trade played an important part in the social, economic and day-to-day life of medieval Islamic societies (Sato 2014). In the tenth century, Palestinian geographer al-Maqdisi wrote about the cultivation of sugar cane in Palestine and development of a sugar industry and the export of sugar syrup, grape syrup, grapes and raisins to Egypt and other countries in the region (Shahin 2005: 375). As we saw in Chapter 10, the Palestinian export-oriented sugar industry and sugar syrup developed significantly during the Mamluk period. In the Middle Ages, sugar was produced in Palestine in the form of *sugar syrup*. Furthermore the use of sugar syrup can be seen today in sweets products of the Zalatimo's bakery in Jerusalem (see below).

Also, as we have already seen the *spice markets* also became a key feature of the urban markets in Palestine in the Middle Ages and the modern period, and spices such as cinnamon, like the medieval *sugar syrup*, played an important part in the development of the sweets industry of modern Palestine. Spices and nuts became essential ingredients for garnishing and filling Arab and Middle Eastern sweets and desserts including the sweet, crispy and cheesy Palestinian Kunafa. Both the Palestinian sugar and syrup industries of the Middle Ages and urban spice markets played an important part in the historical evolution of the Palestinian Kunafa.

There are two distinct modern Palestinian brands of sweets manufacturers: Nablus Kunafa and Zalatimo Sweets of Jerusalem. In addition to Nablus and Jerusalem the cities of Nazareth and Acre, in the Galilee, are also known for their modern manufacturing of high-quality *baklava* and other sweet products and for being culinary centres in Galilee.

Nablus Kunafa

Nabulsi Kunafa is part of the folk tale of the ancient Palestinian city of Nablus and one of the several trademarks of modern Palestinian identity (trademarks that include *Jaffa Orange*, *al-Khalil Glassware* and *Nablus Soap*) both in Palestine and among the millions of Palestinians in the post-Nakba *shatat*.

The Kunafa is a delicious Palestinian and Middle Eastern dessert with layered crispy pastry and sweet cheese soaked in syrup. The Kunafa is crunchy on the outside, cheesy and gooey on the inside; its hot and rich pastry made with shredded fill dough and baked with a stretchy sweet cheese stuffing and topped with a drizzle of orange blossom syrup.

Originating in the Palestinian city of Nablus several centuries ago, and becoming one of the most famous dessert dishes in the Arab world, Kunafa was made using local white Nabulsi cheese; today delicious Kunafa is also produced in Nazareth, Jerusalem and other Palestinian cities as well as by Palestinians bakers across the world. Today Palestinians view the Kunafa as a traditional culinary gem and a symbol of Palestinian culinary dishes (Abu Shihab 2012: 74; World Health Organization 2009: 44).

Zalatimo sweets: From a bakery in Jerusalem in the 1860s to an international brand

Zalatimo is a dynasty of modern pastry and cake makers from Jerusalem. In 1860 Zalatimo bakery of sweets, located in the heart of the old city of Jerusalem, was founded by Muhammad Zalatimo, who had served in the Ottoman army and rose to become sergeant, and who started making a deliciously unique Palestinian dessert named *mutabbaq* ('folded' in Arabic) using the finest ingredients. The bakery also made sweet loaves (Nuseibeh 2009: 143).

As we have seen in the glassware industry of al-Khalil (Hebron) and the soap industry of Nablus, the vast majority of the Palestinian traditional industries were family-owned factories and in these family-owned businesses *succession planning* is crucial for the continuation and thriving of family-owned industries (Muna 2012).

After six generations of succession and 165 years of history, Zalatimo sweets manufacturers have expanded from the original location as a small bakery in the old city of Jerusalem, then located next to the Church of the Holy Sepulchre, to become an internationally recognized chain of bakeries and shops, operating in several countries and an officially registered global brand. The Zalatimo sweets manufactures offer a taste of Palestinian sweets that is steeped in the history and long traditions of the country. Today the Zalatimo family carries on the same tradition in the city of Jerusalem using the same original recipe of producing *mutabbaq* as well as other Arab and Western pastries. Its products include delicious *baklava*, assortments of pastries and individually wrapped *ma'amoul* cookies:

> Hidden in a vault underneath the Ethiopian monastery, Zalatimo is famous for its *mutabbaq*, created using a family recipe finessed over 150 years ... pastry is stuffed with clarified butter, cinnamon, walnuts or sheep's cheese, baked and drizzled with sugar syrup.
>
> (Robinson 2022)

Despite the restrictions imposed by the Israeli occupation, 'Zalatimo Brothers for Sweets' have achieved a huge success with products of exceptional quality; indeed the name 'Zalatimo' is one of several modern Palestinian common brands – a brand of exceptional quality; 'A trademark ... Zalatimo manufacturer [is] the special oriental sweets of exceptional quality' (Khoury 2010: 14; Zalatimo 2018). The *Zalatimo Sweets*

Since 1860 and *Zalatimo Sweets Company* are listed in the *Official Gazette of the United State Patent and Trademark Office.*[1]

As of 2018 'Zalatimo Brothers for Sweets' employed 250 people in outlets in Palestine, Jordan and across the Middle East and with a worldwide distribution system and a global brand; they took in 15 million dollars:

> so recognisable is the name [Zalatimo Sweets] that in 2014 a rogue outfit in Dubai started to sell pastries using Zalatimo branding.
>
> (Teller 2022)

18

City of Oranges

Jaffa Orange, Palestine's Citrus Industry and the Transformation of Jaffa into a Modern Metropolis (1845–1948)

The birth of a modern Palestinian icon and dramatic rise of modern Jaffa

In the Middle Ages under Islam the port city of Jaffa was one of Palestine's main mercantile centres, and the key port for the city of Jerusalem surviving catastrophis upheavals caused by wars, the Napoleonic invasion of Palestine of Jaffa in 1799 included, and epidemics. The city of Jaffa (like the city of Acre) had been surrounded by high walls, and extensive fortifications, which had been constructed by Ahmad Pasha al-Jazzar, the Ottoman governor of Acre. But unlike Acre, Jaffa fell after a short French siege. When the French army occupied Jaffa in spring 1799 the city's harbour provided vital shelter for the French fleet (Falk 2015: 185). The French invasion of Palestine was short-lived but Jaffa, and generally the Palestine coastal towns, did not develop in the first half of the nineteenth century like the cities of the Palestine hinterland; Jaffa's modern development began rather late (Büssow 2011: 216, 220) and its dramatic rise began in the mid-nineteenth century following the establishment of the Palestine citrus industry from the middle of the nineteenth century onwards. In the year following the French invasion:

> Around 1800, the city [of Jaffa] had not been more than a fortified village of 500 inhabitants and the outpost of a few traders. But by about 1900, Jaffa had grown into the second-largest Palestinian city and had become the main port along the southern part of the Levant between Beirut and Alexandria.
>
> (Büssow: 2011: 216)

The spectacular economic and demographic growth of Jaffa in the second half of the nineteenth century under the impact of the rise of the Palestine citrus industry and the introduction of modern education and modern health services by various

European missionary groups was remarkable (Masalha 2022). What drew these diverse population groups to Jaffa and the surrounding areas of Jaffa was the attraction of its extraordinary agricultural potential, advantageous climate, its abundant water resources and the proximity of the port of Jaffa, which made the local orange groves and vineyards highly productive assets (Büssow 2011: 216).

> The greatest single driver of economic growth in the region was the trade in citrus fruits, especially the famous Jaffa oranges.
>
> (Büssow 2011: 220)

The Palestinians often refer to Jaffa, a key port city in medieval Palestine, as 'city of oranges'. A famous global trademark of modern Palestine, Jaffa oranges are not just oranges; they are a key symbol of Palestinian modernity and an icon of global Palestine. The rise of the citrus industry of Jaffa was a product of the modern period. In the twelfth century Arab geographer Muhammad al-Idrisi (1100–1165) described three coastal cities of Palestine, Jaffa and Arsuf and Asqalan (ancient Ascalon) as follows: these are all cities whose sizes, characteristics and the conditions of their people are similar, even though they are pleasant. There are many fortified buildings, many olive trees and vines, and Jaffa is a city in itself. It is the coastal and port city for Jerusalem (Wa'ari 2023, Vol. 1:25).

Jaffa (Joppa) was one of the ancient and most spectacular port cities in Palestine; the site has been settled since the early Bronze Age. Renowned since Antiquity for its beauty, Jaffa was often described by indigenous Palestinians in modern times (before and after the 1948 Nakba) as the 'Bride of the Sea' (*'Arus al-Bahr*) and the 'Bride of Palestine' (*'Arus Filastin*) (Monterescu 2015: 103).

The relaxed sea-side social setting of modern Jaffa echoed the famous relaxed social settings of other Palestinian Mediterranean cities of Antiquity, Gaza and Ascalon included (see Chapter 6). Jaffa's location and topography on the Mediterranean coastline at the top of a naturally elevated outcrop on the coast made it one of the most beautiful cities in Palestine. Also, for many centuries under Islam in the Middle Age the city functioned as a port city for Jerusalem and as a summer holiday resort for Palestinians. In the modern era Jaffa was often called 'the Gateway to Palestine' (*Bawwabat Filastin*) and as Palestine's main transit port the city of Jaffa became the primary entryway for merchants, travellers, pilgrims who arrived to Palestine by sea in the second half of nineteenth and early twentieth centuries. Unlike the historic harbour of Acre, the local conditions of the harbour of Jaffa were hazardous and large modern vessels and merchant ships were forced to dock half-a-mile away from the rocky reef, offloading their passengers and cargo onto small boats that carried them to the city of Jaffa.[1]

Although in Palestinian *collective and social memory* Jaffa oranges existed from time immemorial, there is no evidence to suggest that orange cultivation in Palestine existed before the modern period. Furthermore there was no mention of orange cultivation in Jaffa, and in Palestine as a whole, by Muhammad al-Idrisi in the twelfth century or by Palestinian geographer al-Maqdisi in the tenth century. Unlike all local

Palestinian industries (textile, silk, cotton, tenancies, olive oil, wine, glass, mosaics and leather) whose historic roots can be traced to Antiquity or the Middle Ages, the Palestine citrus industry is a modern industry. It began in the mid-nineteenth century and flourished for about a century until the Palestine Nakba of 1948. The rise of this citrus industry in Palestine began after the Crimean War (1853–56), and was spurred by important innovations in local agriculture and the rapid expansion of citrus cultivation of what is known as the Shamouti orange, which was mentioned as being exported to Europe in British consular reports in the 1850s shortly after the Crimean War. Of all modern Palestinian industries, the Jaffa citrus industry became the most iconic. Moreover, in many ways the modern international trademark and spectacular rise of the Palestine citrus industry from the mid-nineteenth century mirrored the rise of the Nablus soap-making factories in the second half of the nineteen century. However, while the soap factories of Nablus centred on the city of Nablus itself, the citrus industry of modern Palestine, like the wine industry of Palestine in Antiquity, came from a wide region of citrus gardens (or *bayyarat*) in coastal Palestine and the cultivated lands surrounding the cities of Jaffa, Lydda and al-Ramla. As we shall see below, *Jaffa Orange*, like *Gaza Wine* in Antiquity, was simply named after the port of export.

Although the citrus industry was introduced in Palestine by indigenous Palestinian farmers in the 1840s, the actual label *Jaffa Orange* was coined by the Christian German Templers settlers in Palestine in the late nineteenth century. German Templers established the first colony in Ottoman Palestine in Haifa, the German Colony, in 1868, which was the first of several colonies established by the Christian group in Palestine (the Holy Land). The second German colony (Sarona) was established outside Jaffa (in what is later became the modern Zionist-Jewish city of Tel Aviv) in 1871. These German 'Templars colonies' were often located in the vicinity of key Palestinian cities (Jaffa, Haifa, Jerusalem, Lydda). Although benefiting from the power and prestige of Germany, these colonies were established by Christian evangelical religious-messianic settlers rather than merchant settlers or imperial colonists. Relying on the emerging modern banking sector in Palestine (including Deutsche-Palastina Bank), modern postal services and other amenities of modernizing Palestinian cities of the late nineteenth century, the ethos of these German colonists emphasized agricultural labour and self-sufficiency. During and shortly after World War Two, these German colonies were depopulated and their residents deported to Australia. Numerically the Templars colonies were too small to make an enormous impact on the overall economy of Palestine – at their height they numbered about 2,200 people – but they introduced modern carriage transport into Palestine and set up modern hotels in several cities in Palestine (in Jaffa, Haifa, Tiberias, Jerusalem, al-Ramla, Nazareth) and their seven German colonies in Palestine became an inspiration and model for local organizational methods and the construction of international connections for subsequent European Zionist-Jewish colonies in Palestine. These models applied to agricultural modes of farming, housing styles of building, local industrial workshops and above all the German Templar colonists provided the Zionist colonists with a template for international financial backers of local financial investment and agricultural and industrial experimentation; no wonder the German Templars were considered by some historians as 'pro-Zionist' colonial settlers (Yazbak 1999: 40–54).

The German Templars, being Europeans, also fully appreciated the importance and power of modern popular European branding; hence the export label of *Jaffa Orange* – a label that gradually, during the late nineteenth century, was transformed into a global brand of Palestine. While *Jaffa Orange* became the global trademark for the Palestine citrus industry from the late nineteenth century until 1948, the indigenous Palestinian name was known to the local Palestinian farmers, who began cultivating orange groves from the early 1840s, by its Arabic name, *Shamouti Orange*. Also the exports of the Shamouti orange grew phenomenally from 200,000 oranges in 1845 to thirty-eight million oranges by 1870 (Gerber 1982: 250–64).

As in the case of the 'soap factory' of the Templars in Haifa, whose 'pure olive oil soap' production was literally modelled on the famous soap industry of Nablus (discussed in Chapter 15), the Templars involvement in 'Jaffa Oranges' was based on an already highly successful, export-oriented indigenous Palestinian citrus industry. In 1872, a European traveller through Jaffa noted:

> Surrounding Jaffa are the orange gardens for which it is justly extolled, and which are a considerable source of wealth to the owners. The annual value of fruits grown in Jaffa was said to be 10,000 pounds.
>
> (LeVine 2005: 34)

In view of the fact that it takes several years for the orange grove to yield fruit, when the actual label: *Jaffa Orange*, was initially marketed by the German Templer colony Sarona – established outside Jaffa in 1871 – the colony was marketing Shamouti oranges in Europe under this label, oranges which were being cultivated by Palestinian farmers; therefore the label was introduced long after the Shamouti export to Europe was already well-established.

In addition to Shamouti oranges, the region of Jaffa cultivated a range of citrus fruits including clementines, mandarins as well as other fruit groves such as apples and red and white guavas. However Shamouti orange was the most successful of Jaffa agricultural plantations. Shamouti is a sweet orange variety with few seeds and a tough thick skin that made the citrus fruit particularly suitable transporting for export to foreign markets. These qualities contributed to making Shamouti orange Palestine's most important export in the second half of the nineteenth century and first half of the twentieth centuries. Britain became the first major importer of Jaffa oranges before and after the British occupation of Palestine in 1918; the orange was also exported to Europe and then the US and globally. Capitalizing on the international success of Jaffa orange, in May 1926 the British Empire Marketing Board began advertising Jaffa oranges by commissioning and issuing an art deco style poster for Jaffa oranges design by prominent English poster artist Frank Newbould; the poster featured Jaffa's on the Mediterranean coastline at the top of its naturally elevated outcrop on the coast and camels carrying Jaffa oranges in boxes along the beach of Jaffa.[2]

The Shamouti citrus industry of Palestine (like its contemporary soap industry of Nablus was capital intensive: see Chapter 15) requiring large capital investments with no yield for investors for several years; therefore this citrus industry could have only been developed in the mid-nineteenth century and primarily owned by wealthy Palestinian farmers and merchants and notables, rather than small farmers (Krämer 2008; LeVine 2005: 34, 91).

However, despite the large capital investments in Jaffa's expanding citrus industry, overall this industry remained labour-intensive requiring an army of wage labourers and migrant workers who flocked to this industry from both Egypt and rural Palestine. By the time of the British Mandatory period there were tens of thousands of wage labourers, including men, women and children, who were involved in the indigenous Palestinian citrus industry, making it the largest single employer in country. This army of workers were at the centre of the cultivation of plantations and the harvest, storage and delicate wrapping of oranges in boxes and then transporting the boxes to the port area of Jaffa where they were loaded onto small boats to take them to the large ships anchored in the sea to be shipped to Europe. By 1939 fifteen million of orange boxes were shipped annually through the port of Jaffa to foreign shores.[3] This army of labourers – which is rarely credited by historians – made the citrus industry the most successful industry of modern Palestine and in the process contributed to the transformation of Jaffa into a modern commercial and industrial metropolis of Palestine.

This phenomenal international success of the export of the sweet Shamouti variety – with its global trademark of *Jaffa Orange* – was now being exported from the port city of Jaffa to all European cities (Basan 2007: 83; Issawi 2006: 127). The *Shamouti Orange* became, along with the navel and bitter orange, one of three main varieties of the citrus fruit grown in the Mediterranean region, southern Europe and the Middle East. Developed originally in Palestine, the cultivation of *Jaffa Orange* spread to Lebanon, Syria, Cyprus, Iraq and Turkey (Basan 2007: 83; Ladaniya 2008: 48–9).

The global success of Jaffa Orange also attracted the attention of international businessmen and international orange growers. In the 1880s an American businessman and diplomat Henry Shelton Sanford – known for founding the city of Sanford, in Florida – who had become the owner of the largest orange grove in Florida after the American Civil War and had begun experimenting with varieties of citrus plantings, introduced the cultivation of the 'Jaffa, Mediterranean Sweet Orange' to Florida (Derr 1989: 79).

Although modern trademarks display the names of producers and traders as a guarantee that the goods were of a certain quality, in Palestine the label *Jaffa Orange*, like the label *Gaza Wine* in Antiquity (discussed in Chapter 6) the name *Jaffa Orange* was given after the port of export: Jaffa. By the middle of the British Mandatory period many new commercial enterprises and industrial sectors, including soap factories, were established in Jaffa and the city had developed into a key metropolitan cultural centre in Palestine; but the Shamouti Orange and citrus industry remained the primary foreign export from the port city of to Europe and beyond. Practically seedless, the flavour of Shamouti Orange was described as 'sweet and fine' (Basan, 2007: 83; Krämer 2008: 91, 99; Page 2008). It is distinguished by its oval shape and thick peel, which is deep orange in colour and normally very easy to remove from the fruit. Its tough skin made it 'especially suitable for export' (Krämer 2008: 99; Page 2008). The Shamouti orange variety as foremost among the citrus varieties cultivated and exported to Europe was mention by British consular reports as early as the 1850s – nearly a decade before the arrival of the German Templars in Palestine (Issawi 2006: 127; Krämer 2008: 91).

Six major factors contributed to this rapid growth of the Palestinian citrus industry, and especially the export of the Shamouti orange variety to Europe in the second half of the nineteenth century:

(1) the wider *modernization* context in Palestine and developments in modern technology and infrastructure of the late Ottoman period brought about a rapid rise of the Palestinian port city of Jaffa as a leading modern urban centre in the country and a powerhouse of social, economic, industrial, intellectual and cultural activities. The modernization processes of the Ottoman *tanzimat* ('reorganizations') and the changing political and economic climate of Palestine and the significant improvement of its transport system from the nineteen century attracted large local capital investment in new industries and contributed to the growth of several Palestinian industries including the soap factories of Nablus and Jaffa and the emerging citrus industry of Palestine. As modern trade and modern transport in goods and passengers increased through the city of Jaffa in the second half of the nineteenth century, with the result that port of Jaffa effectively replaced both the ports of Acre and Beirut (in Lebanon) as the main port for entry and outlet for central and southern Palestine, and with the Palestinian route between Jaffa on the one hand, and Jerusalem, Nablus, Lydda, al-Ramla, on the other hand, made more convenient and more efficient than between Palestine and Beirut, Palestinian merchants directed increasingly their exports of goods through the port of Jaffa. A key development in the late nineteenth century Jaffa was the development of the Palestine railway system and the inauguration of the railway line between the cities of Jaffa, Haifa and Jerusalem in 1892 (Gilbar 1998: 281–92).

By and large the effects the *tanzimat* reforms in Palestine were mixed. On the negative side, the 1858 Ottoman land privatization codes brought about the alienation of many peasants from their lands and altered the urban-rural relations in Palestine adversely; historically and until the first half of the ninteenth century the urban-rural relations were symbiotic and relations between the urban and rural leaders were characterized by both completion and cooperation, but the privatization of lands slowly shifted the balance of power in favour of the rich urban elites, who acquired tax farms (*iltizams*) and further enriched themselves by buying more lands, while leading to the increasing pauperization of the Palestinian peasants; on the positive side, however, the establishment of modern urban municipalities in the second half of the nineteenth century allowed these modern municipalities to exercise control over key resources such as roads and water conduits (Büssow 2011: 138).

(2) the quality and popularity of this sweet variety of orange with its few seeds and its tough skin made the orange ideally suitable for export and as a cash crop attracting major investment and in the crop grown to sell in Europe for significant profits.

(3) as in Antiquity, when the export-oriented Palestine wine industry benefited from technological innovation in local agriculture in Palestine (Chapter 6), the rapid expansion of the export-oriented Palestinian citrus cultivation, and Shamouti variety, in particular, also benefited from the most important modern innovation in local agriculture from the mid-nineteenth century onwards (Krämer 2008: 91).

(4) the rapid development of steamships, which led to the further globalization of trade and the expansion of global markets. The development in fast steam engine-powered ships began in the first half of the nineteenth century and accelerated in the second half of the century. These ships were less dependent on wind patterns and opened up new trade routes, and ships were described a 'major driver of the first wave of trade globalization (1870–1913) and key contributors to an increase in international trade that was unprecedented in human history (Pascali 2017).

While in Antiquity it took weeks for the Palestine wine produce to arrive at the shores in Europe, now the steamships enabled the export of Shamouti oranges to the European markets in days (Gerber 1982: 250-64). Normally crates of Jaffa oranges would be loaded on boats and ferried to a waiting cargo ship for export to Europe.

(5) the growing importance of the port of Jaffa as the main port of Jerusalem and Christian holy sites in the second half of the nineteenth century as a result of growing tourism and pilgrims by American, French, British and Italian and generally European nationals (LeVine 2005: 34).

(6) the relative lack of European control over the cultivation of oranges in Palestine in comparison with the cotton industry of Palestine. As we saw in Chapter 14, cotton was a primary cash crop export commodity of Palestine in the eighteenth century and second half of the nineteenth century, but gradually, following the assassination of Palestinian leader Dhaher al-'Umar, cotton came under the control of European powers. However by the late nineteenth century the Shamouti orange cultivation and export to Europe had overtaken the cotton foreign export (Croil 1898: 54; Masalha 2018).

Indigenous versus settler, cooperation versus competition: The Zionist-Jewish citrus sector during the Mandatory Period (1918-1948)

During the British Mandatory period, more than half a century after the rise of the Palestine citrus industry, European Zionist settlers in Palestine began to move into this internationally successful industry. The Austro-Hungarian Empire was the birthplace of Theodore Herzl, the founder of modern political Zionism. Herzl, who sought the patronage of the Great Western Powers for Zionism, visited Palestine in 1898 to meet the German Keiser Wilhelm II. On his way back to Europe, he sailed from Jaffa to Alexandria taking the *Dundee*, a British cargo ship of 350 tons shipping Jaffa Oranges to Alexandria and then to Europe (Rozenblum 2001: 312).

Four years later, in 1902, two decades before the beginning of Zionist orange cultivation in Palestine, an extensive study of the growth of the international export of the Palestinian-Arab orange industry (and Jaffa Orange trade) by two Zionist officials was carried out possibly under the instruction of Herzl himself. The study, while deriding the local 'primitive' farming methods, pays tribute to the growth of this Arab industry and details the various Arab owners of Shamouti orange groves and the wide reach of the Palestinians citrus export with England, Turkey, Egypt and the Austro-Hungarian Empire as primary markets (LeVine 2005: 34).

Evidently, however, Zionist settlers in late Ottoman Palestine did not play any role in the Palestine citrus industry in the period 1845–1918. Furthermore although European (Ashkenazi) Jewish immigrants began to have some presence in the shops and markets of Jaffa (including money-changers and jewellery businesses) and during the late Ottoman period before the First World War,

> Jews did not play a significant role in the citrus industry and Jewish accounts complained that the citrus orchards were mostly owned by Arab Muslims and Christians.
>
> (Dierauff 2020: 146; LaBor 2007: 20–30)

But, as we shall see below, and as a challenge to the 'Urban Notables' paradigm discussed in Chapter 14, this new enterprising and revolutionary middle-class of Palestinian-Arab merchants and citrus plantation owners were different from the old land-owning conservative urban 'notables' of Palestine.

As we have already seen, the Palestinian Shamouti citrus industry, like many industries of ancient, medieval and modern Palestine, was an indigenous industry. It was developed by Palestinian farmers and merchants in the 1840s and gained global reputation under the trademark *Jaffa Orange* by the early 1870s. However, the global successes of this citrus industry has attracted more attention from recent writers than any other modern Palestinian industry – partly because of the Zionist settlers subsequent involvement in this industry. As we have already seen, the global export successes of this indigenous Palestinian industry had already taken roots long before the birth of modern political Zionism and at least half a century before the First Zionist Congress in Basel in 1897, organized by Theodor Herzl, the founder of the modern Zionism movement. In a recent publication of a research project funded by Israeli official funding institutions, the authors attributed the successes of this industry largely to Palestinian-Zionist settlers 'cooperation'. Ascribing the success of the Palestine citrus industry – an industry which was almost totally confiscated stolen by Israel the 1948 Nakba – in pre-Nakba to the so-called 'Zionist-Palestinian collaboration' was recently claimed by Mustafa Kabha and Nahum Karlinsky in their book: *The Lost Orchard: The Palestinian-Arab Citrus Industry, 1850 – 1950* (2021).

But as we have already seen in Chapter 15, the Zionist settlers in Palestine also attempted – rather successfully – to imitate the high-quality and commercial successes of the indigenous Palestinian soap industry of Nablus during the Mandatory period. The two cases were not the only time that the European Zionist colonial settlers sought to imitate and compete with indigenous agricultural industries of Palestine and the Levant. One of the best-known cases was the instance of the mulberry tree and the silk industry of the region. Inspired by the cultivation of mulberry trees and successes of the silk industry of the Levant, Zionist settlers in Galilee planted mulberry in the early 1890s.

This was part of the effort to adapt agricultural crops to industrialization in order to assist the Zionist *moshavot* (colonies) in Palestine. Inspired by the cultivation of mulberry trees and success of the silk industry of Lebanon and Syria, some Zionist settlements in Upper Galilee began experimenting with mulberry tree cultivation and silk production in the early 1890s with the support of the Jewish Colonization Association – an experiment which ended up in failure (Gilbar 1998: 281–92).

Although European Jewish settlers did not play any significant part in the Palestine citrus industry until the British occupation of Palestine in 1918, things began to change during the British Mandatory period and the Zionist settlers began to imitate the achievements of an indigenous Palestinian industry with some considerable success during the British Mandatory period (1918–48). This was in part due to several factors: (1) the increasing European Jewish immigration to Palestine during this period; (2) the active British support for Zionism and Zionist settler-colonization of Palestine; (3) the scale of Zionist activity and demographics in Palestine during this period began to change significantly due to mass European immigration; the Jewish population in Palestine grew from about 5 per cent of the total population in the country in the 1870s, to about 10 per cent in 1918, and then to about one third of the population in 1948; (4) the arrival of highly skilled middle-class European Jewish immigrants and settlers during the 1920s and 1930s also began to have an impact on both the growth of Zionist settlers' agricultural industries in Palestine and Palestinian land dispassion. The October 1930 British 'Report on Immigration, Land Settlement and Development' – commonly referred to as the Hope Simpson Enquiry – noted:

> The cultivation of the orange, introduced by the 'Arabs before the commencement of Jewish settlement, has developed to a very great extent in consequence of that settlement. There is no doubt that the pitch of perfection to which the technique of plantation and cultivation of the orange and grapefruit have been brought in Palestine is due to the scientific methods of the Jewish agriculturist.[4]

By 1939, the joint orange orchards in Palestine covered 75,000 acres and employed over 100,000 (Arab and Jewish) workers and there were also cases of joint Palestinian-Arab-Jewish cooperation in this sector (Kabha and Karlinsky 2021).

Despite the massive Zionist investment during the Mandatory period in the European Jewish Yishuv's (Settlement's) sector of the citrus industry of Palestine, the indigenous Palestinian-Arab sector of this industry maintained its primacy – in the way the Nablus soap factories maintained their quality and primacy over the Zionist Shemen oil industry during the Mandatory period – and by the end of the Mandatory period the total area of Palestinian-Arab-owned and cultivated orange orchards exceeded that was cultivated by Zionist settlers. As in the case of the maintenance of the superior quality of *Nablus Soap*, the new enterprising merchant class of Palestine, which dominated the Palestine citrus industry, ensured – until the 1948 Nakba – the primacy of the indigenous of Palestinian orange industry.

The new merchants and middle classes and transformation of modern Jaffa

It has already been suggested that the army of wage labourers made the citrus industry of Palestine the most successful industry in the country, a highly lucrative export-oriented industry that also transformed Jaffa into one of the most important and dynamic commercial centres in Palestine. But the phenomenal international success of the Palestine citrus industry in second half of the nineteenth century and first half of the twentieth century also benefited from the emergence of a new breed of enterprising Palestinian middle-class merchants, who differed significantly from the historically conservative landed notable elites and traditional urban leadership of urban Palestine. This new breed of middle-class merchants, in addition to their interest in the introduction of new technologies and new innovative export skills, was prepared to invest heavily in citrus orchards and managed to transform the citrus industry and trade into Palestine's largest economic sector. This class of Palestine's new powerful urban merchants also played an important role as 'the modern agents of change' in Jaffa and beyond (Yazbak 2012: 805–18).

There is a romantic perception of Jaffa Orange among Palestinians – perception which developed in the post-Nakba period – that the rise of the iconic Jaffa Orange of the late Ottoman and British Mandatory periods took place within the context of Jaffa being an agricultural 'market town' surrounded by belts of orange plantations and dominated by an agricultural economy. In fact from the 1880s onwards Jaffa – spurred by the successful citrus industry – began to emerge as a pioneering industrial city in Palestine and became best known in Palestine for its modern soap factories (Kark 1990: 256–7). The soap factories and citrus industry also gave rise to other factories in the city that produced orange-crates, paper rapping for orange, seltzer, alkali and cosmetics. The city also developed factories for olive oil, leather, wine, ice, barrels, corks, candy and ink. Other successful modern factories in the city were the metalworking factories, which were machine workshops run by the German Templars employing over 100 workers in 1910 (Kark 1990: 256–7).

The German Templars also reintroduced modern wine-making industry in Jaffa and Haifa (Gilbar 2023: 140) and Jaffa also became known for its silversmiths, watchmakers and shoemakings.

Historically Jaffa had been an important holiday resorts for Jerusalemites. In the modern period Jaffa developed its extensive hospitality sector and its famous leisure industry and the city acquired a reputation of being a city of fun, sunbathing and pleasure. Palestinian author Ghada Karmi, who grew up in Jerusalem during the British Mandatory period, wrote:

> Families [from Jerusalem] often went to the new garden cafes outside Jerusalem in Ramallah and around the village of Beit Jala. We went for outings to the Grand Hotel in Ramallah … But well-to-do Palestinians still preferred to go to Jaffa for picnics, to swim and saunter about. This had traditionally been Palestine's major city, where the best families lived, where the first Palestinian newspapers were

established, and where the intelligentsia met. "The bride of the sea", people called it: bride in Arabic used to denote a thing of great beauty.

Jaffa had wide roads, big houses, picturesque views over the Mediterranean, and a lovely, busy harbour. It was a place of fun, for business, and, as Palestine's major port, for travel. Before Jerusalem livened up, people went there to get away from the fusty religious atmosphere. Whenever my father went to Jaffa to work at the Near Eastern Broadcasting station established by the British, he would take [my sister] Siham and [my brother] Ziad along with him. As soon as they saw the sea, they would beg to go swimming and then my father would leave them trustingly in the care of one of the men who looked after the beach.

(Karmi 2004: 38-9)

Public timekeeping and urbanism: From the ancient water clock of Byzantine Gaza to the urban tower clocks of modern Palestine

The speedy economic and industrial growth and urban transformation of Jaffa into a key metropolis in Palestine in the second half of the nineteenth century and early twentieth centuries fuelled demands for migrant skilled and unskilled manpower spurred by the expansion of the global trade, local industries and financial sector of the city. By the beginning of the twentieth century the population of the city had swelled considerably by migrant workers (both internal Palestinian and regional workers), who worked in the growing factories of the city and on the orange plantations and lived in densely populated neighbourhoods in growing Jaffa.

Like other medieval walled 'old cities' in Palestine – such as Jerusalem and Acre – Jaffa was a walled city until the late nineteenth century. In the city, in the 1870s, a second gate was opened in the city's walls to 'meet the city's development, its expanding trade sector, its doubling number of its inhabitants, and its increasing density.'[5] However, within a few years, the demographic expansion of the city brought down the historic city walls, the establishment of new neighbourhoods, to the north and south; the new northern suburb of Manshiyyeh – a working-class neighbourhood was created, attracting workers from across Palestine; and the city's market was widened.[6] New modern avenues were created and a monumental modern administrative buildings to house the city's new civic institutions were all built in the late Ottoman period.

As we have already seen in Chapter 6, since late Antiquity urban Palestine was familiar with the public clocks situated at the centre of urban public spaces. The development of the Water Clock of Gaza was a case in point: this was a key treasure of Palestine in late Antiquity, a clock which symbolized the immense commercial and technological progress of urban Palestine in late Antiquity – a water clock which had also a major impact on the historical development of clocks, in general and the water clocks of medieval classical Islam and the Levant in the Middle Ages.

However modernity and modern technological developments introduced new forms of urban public clocks. Symbolizing the rapid urban modernization of Jaffa, the Jaffa clock tower, a limestone tower, was constructed in 1900 with financial contributions from the merchants and local inhabitants of a multicultural growing city. Constructed in the centre of the city to commemorate the silver jubilee of the reign of the Ottoman Sultan Abdel-Hamid II – and as one seven clock towers built in seven cities across Palestine (Jaffa, Jerusalem, Nablus, Acre, Haifa, Nazareth and Safad) – the Jaffa clock tower ushered in the idea modern public time keeping in urban life in Palestine and the transformation into a thriving modern metropolis. As well as being the historic headquarters of the most influential modern Palestinian newspaper, *Falastin* (Palestine), Jaffa became the de factor 'cultural capital of Palestine' (Muamar 2022).

The transformation of cultural life and art deco architecture in the city

New middle-class suburbs began to spring up in modern Jaffa. To the south of the city, the new wealthy middle-class Ajami neighbourhood was built, with a hybrid of local and European architectural styles of buildings.[7] From the late Ottoman period onwards the social urban and cultural life in the city began to change rapidly and new forms of urban entertainment began to emerge. Also several urban coffeehouses in the city began to combine elements of the old coffeehouse with the new urban theatres and music halls. This form of social entertainment and cultural hybridity can be seen in the way several coffeehouses also began to function as modern urban theatres and music halls for mass social entertainment: *al-Zarafiyya theatre*, the theatre of the *al-Bannur coffeehouse*, the *Parsiana Theatre*, the *theatre of the al-Halawani Coffeehouse.*

In Europe new revolutionary art deco styles in the inter-war period represented a beautiful fusion of elegant modernity and transformative modern architecture. Emerging in the 1920s, this design movement combined geometric shapes – which had characterized traditional Islamic arts and architecture – with luxurious materials and vivid colours. Its influence extended to many artistic fields, leaving a huge mark on urban architecture in Europe and some great urban buildings in Jaffa and Jerusalem.

These styles of modern architecture were also introduced in Palestine the 1920s and 1930s and can be seen in the Palestine Archaeological Museum in Jerusalem (later renamed the Rockefeller Archaeological Museum), which opened in 1938. Situated in East Jerusalem, it is a magnificent white limestone structure whose stones were quarried by the famous stone industry of Palestine (see Chapter 11). Today the museum houses a unique collection of Palestine antiquities unearthed in excavations conducted in the country mainly during the time of the British Mandatory period. The impact of the art deco styles on modern urban Jaffa was even greater than its impact on modern Jerusalem, as the urban planning authorities of the British Palestine Government generally insisted on the 'antiquation' of modern buildings in the holy city. Jaffa, by contrast, boasted many new art deco buildings in the inter-war period including the Al-Hamra cinema, a 1937 art deco style building on Jerusalem boulevard in Jaffa, a building designed by Lebanese architect Elias al-Mor, and named after the famous Andalusia Islamic palace in Grenada, Spain. A symbol of modern Jaffa, the Al-Hamra cinema was one of the largest and luxurious buildings in Palestine and one of the most important cultural and popular entertainment venues in the country, hosting famous Arab artists and popular singers such as Umm Kulthum, Leila Murad and Farid al-Atrash (Yazbak 2024: 8–25). Emerging as a modern metropolitan city and a major leisure and entertainment centre in Palestine during the Mandatory period, Jaffa also boasted more modern cinemas than any other Palestinian city: these included Nabil Cinema; Apollo Cinema; Al-Shaq Cinema, al-Rashid Cinema; Farouk Cinema; Al-Salahi Cinema; Al Tobji Cinema; Fanqal Cinema; and Aden Cinema.

All these modern social developments and new social urban and architectural innovations in Jaffa reflected the revolutionary social and economic changes taking place not only in Jaffa but in the coastal city of Haifa and other cities in Palestine; they also embodied the enterprising, modernizing and industrializing spirit of the new middle-class merchants and found expression in many aspects of the urban life and new building styles in the city and in the ornate architecture of the houses of the wealthy class and in the new patterns of consumption in the city and generally in the rising living standards in Jaffa. The powerful merchant middle-class were also the first actors to import new technologies to Palestine, technologies required to develop new businesses and new industries (Yazbak 2012: 805–18).

By the end of the late Ottoman period this ancient/modern city of Jaffa had become a leading modern city in Palestine, with a thriving economy, based on global trade and local industries and with an educated middle-class merchant community whose influence grew with the establishment of a range of modern (mostly European) banks; the city was transformation into a financial centre in the country. With the rise of literacy in the country in the late Ottoman and Mandatory period (Masalha 2022), the city also became an intellectual hub in Palestine with many excellent modern schools and a centre for the introduction of modern technology in Palestine. Jaffa was also at the centre of the printing press revolution of the late Ottoman period, and the city also became the headquarters of the leading modern Palestinian Arabic language newspaper, *Filastin* ('Palestine') which was founded in 1911 by 'Issa al-'Issa and his cousin Yousif al-'Issa (Masalha 2022). In fact the vast majority of the printing shops of late Ottoman Palestine were set up in the cities of Jaffa, Haifa and Jerusalem (Ayalon 2004: 59; Masalha 2022) and most newspapers and books that were printed in late Ottoman Palestine were published in Jaffa.

The economy, trade and services industry of Jaffa – together with its citrus and soap industries – continued to expand rapidly during the British Mandatory period. By the 1940s the phenomenal urban transformation of the city led the local municipal council to commission a new ambitious urban development plan for the further expansion of the city and the improvement of its social infrastructure. The plan included new transport system and new housing projects and public parks as well as improvements to the city's naturally beautiful waterfront. But the occupation and depopulation of Jaffa by Zionist forces in the 1948 Nakba brought an end to one of the most iconic cities in the country and one of the most dynamic and fast-growing urban centre in modern Palestine.[8] The traumatic events of the Palestinian Nakba were compounded by the loss of one of the most iconic cities of historic Palestine (Masalha 1992, 2012). A 'lost paradise', this historic Palestinian city and modern metropolis Jaffa was transformed by Israel into a backyard of neighbouring Tel Aviv and subsumed under the modern Hebrew title: 'Tel Aviv-Yafo' (Monterescu 2015: 103).

While Palestinian Jaffa existed since the Bronze Age, Tel Aviv is a large Israeli metropolitan city founded by the Zionist movement in 1909 and a city that epitomized the European Zionist settler-colonial ideology of creating Jewish-only settlement in Palestine.

The continuing commercial and emblematic struggle over the Jaffa Orange trademark

In the post-Nakba period many of the Palestinian refugees from the teeming working-class neighbourhoods of Jaffa ended up in the crowded and poverty-stricken refugee camps in Gaza and there was a common saying among these refugees: 'We will go back to Jaffa, eat oranges and have dessert with guava'.

Also in the post-Nakba period – following the ethnic cleansing of Palestine and expulsion of the Palestinians, Israel expropriated much of the Palestinian citrus plantations and today Israel is a key provider of citrus fruits to the European Union; much of this Israeli citrus industry is based on the appropriation of indigenous Palestinian lands and Palestinian orange plantations. Also in 1950s and 1960s the Israeli state sought to make *Jaffa Orange* an international emblem of the Israeli state; but these attempts were faced with limited success. But generally the decline in the importance of agriculture to the Israeli economy brought about a decline in the citrus industry of Israel and overall productivity in Jaffa oranges. Also by the 1960s several countries, including Spain and South Africa, were cultivating and exporting widely their own varieties of Jaffa Orange.

Internationally, however, the struggle for the Jaffa Orange trademark has continued. During the Mandatory period the commercial success of *Jaffa Orange* in Britain spurred the creation of the *Jaffa Cake* with supermarkets selling bright blue packets of McVitie's *Jaffa Cakes*, a cake made of chocolate-and-citrus flavoured confections, introduced by McVitie and Price in 1927 and named after Jaffa Oranges. However because McVitie's did not register the name *Jaffa Cakes* as a trademark, other biscuit manufacturers and supermarkets have made similar products under the same name (Wallop 2012).

The product's classification as a cake or biscuit was part of a VAT tribunal in 1991, with the court finding in McVitie's favour that Jaffa Cakes should be considered cakes and not biscuits for tax purposes. In 2012, they were ranked the best-selling cake or biscuit in the United Kingdom.[9]

McVitie's entire line of Jaffa Cakes is produced at the McVitie's factory in the British city of Stockport and the Jaffa cake production area covers an acre (4,046 m^2) and includes a production line over a mile (1.6 km) long. In June 2024, McVitie's launched Cola Bottle flavour Jaffa Cakes.

Notes

Introduction

1 Eaz Swgal, 'A Textbook Case of Genocide', 13 October 2023. https://jewishcurrents.org/a-textbook-case-of-genocide (accessed 15 November 2025).

2 David Gritten and Imogen Foulkes, 'Israel has committed genocide in Gaza, UN commission of inquiry says', *BBC*, 16 September 2025. https://www.bbc.co.uk/news/articles/c8641wv0n4go (accessed 15 November 2025).

3 Indlieb Farazi Saber, 'A "cultural genocide": Which of Gaza's heritage sites have been destroyed?' *Aljazeera*, 14 January 2024. https://www.aljazeera.com/news/2024/1/14/a-cultural-genocide-which-of-gazas-heritage-sites-have-been-destroyed (accessed 15 November 2025).

4 Malak A. Tantesh and Jason Burke. "I will spend my life rebuilding": Gaza's heritage sites destroyed by war', *The Guardian*, 27 August 2025. https://www.theguardian.com/world/2025/mar/17/i-will-spend-my-life-rebuilding-gaza-heritage-sites-destroyed-by-war (accessed 15 November 2025); Saber, 'A "cultural genocide": Which of Gaza's heritage sites have been destroyed?'

5 Saber, 'A "cultural genocide": Which of Gaza's heritage sites have been destroyed?'

6 'Ancient Jericho/Tell es-Sultan', World Heritage Sites. https://whc.unesco.org/en/list/1687 (accessed 15 November 2025).

7 On indigenous Palestinian toponymy, retrospective Zionist colonization and renaming Israeli strategies, see Masalha (2023: 37–71).

8 Maissoun Sharkawi, 'Olive Oil Production in the Late Ottoman Rule'. https://www.palquest.org/en/highlight/36858/olive-oil-production-late-ottoman-rule (accessed 15 November 2025).

9 The *Gezer calendar* is a small limestone tablet with an early Canaanite inscription commonly dated to the tenth century BCE – although there is still uncertainty about its dating – currently displayed at the Museum of the Istanbul Archaeology Museum.

10 The Greek term *Phoinike,* which shares roots with the word *phoenix* a term that to the ancient Greeks connoted blood-red or purple; 'The Development of Dyes by the "Purple People," the Phoenicians'. https://www.encyclopedia.com/science/encyclopedias-almanacs-transcripts-and-maps/development-dyes-purple-people-phoenicians (accessed 15 November 2025).

11 The Greek original, composed between 350 and 362 CE, was lost, but survived through Latin translations made during the sixth century (Grüll 2014: 629–42).

12 The whole region which includes Beqaa Valley to Damascus was known in classical Antiquity as Coele-Syria.

13 See, for instance, 'Appropriating the Past: Israel's Archaeological Practices in the West Bank'. https://emekshaveh.org/en/wp-content/uploads/2017/12/Menachsim-Eng-Web.pdf (accessed 15 November 2025).

14 Details of this battle come primarily from Egyptian sources in the Temple of Amun-Re at Karnak in Luxor, Egypt.

15 The Greek term *mouseion* gave us the modern word *museum.*
16 The text was discovered during British excavations at Nineveh in the library of the Assyrian king Ashurbanipal, in the mid-nineteenth century. British Museum in London with numbers K 3500, 4444, 1023
17 See J. Clack, 'Dioscorides and Antipater of Sidon: The Poems': 6–10. http://www.attalus.org/poetry/antipater1.html#16.178 (accessed 15 November 2025).
18 'Spice Trade', *Encyclopædia Britannica,* 2016. https://www.britannica.com/money/spice-trade (accessed 15 November 2025).
19 'Spice Trade', *Encyclopædia Britannica.*
20 Official Gazette of the United States Patent and Trademark 2003, p. 43. https://www.uspto.gov/learning-and-resources/official-gazette/trademarks/tmog-archive-2003 (accessed 15 November 2025); The Directory of U.S. Trademarks, 1993. Volume 5 (Thomson Corporation, 1993): 5692.

Chapter 1

1 The Philistines and Philistia 57 invocations. A large collection of the inscriptions is assembled in the multi-volume *Corpus Inscriptionum Arabicarum Palaestina* (Sharon 1997–2013). Furthermore Arabic-language epigraphic evidence from Palestine east of the Jordan River is extensive, with some Arabic inscriptions dating from the Roman era and as early as 150 CE. In fact, Palestine is extremely rich in Arabic inscriptions, most of which date from the early Islamic and Umayyad periods. Already in early Islam Palestine acquired particular religious, economic and strategic importance. The historical importance of Filastin (Palestine) is shown in the hundreds of Palestine Arabic inscriptions that cover a huge variety of topics: architecture, Islamic religious (waqf) endowments, epitaphs, construction, markets, dedication, Quranic texts and Arabic inscriptions found in Palestine.
2 In the Egyptian al-Amarana letters.
3 A 7,000 year-old site inhabited continuously until 1948.
4 https://www.google.co.uk/books/edition/Roads_in_the_Deserts_of_Roman_Egypt/I3zKDwAAQBAJ?hl=en&gbpv=1&dq=Gaza+Petra+trade&pg=PT118&printsec=frontcover (accessed 16 November 2025).

Chapter 2

1 Archae Solenhofen, 'Ancient Egyptian Copper Slabbing Saws', 10 December 2002. http://www.hallofmaat.com/unforbiddengeology/ancient-egyptian-copper-slabbing-saws (accessed 16 November 2025).
2 Greek: δρομάςκάμηλος (*dromaskamelos*), literally 'running camel'.
3 Smithsonian magazine, January–February 2021.

Chapter 3

1 'Petra Lost and Found', *National Geographic*, 2 January 2016

2 'Frankincense', *The Oxford English Dictionary*. Volume IV: F–G, reprint 1978 (Oxford: Oxford University Press, 1933): 512; Groom (1981).
3 UNESCO, 'Incense Route – Desert Cities in the Negev', UNESCO World Heritage Centre. https://whc.unesco.org/en/list/1107 (accessed 17 November 2025).
4 https://web.archive.org/web/20160305131754/http://www.christusrex.org/www1/ofm/mad/discussion/109discuss.html (accessed 17 November 2025).
5 'Vita Sancti Hilarionis', 25, in *Patrologia Latina*, XXIII, col. 41
6 https://web.archive.org/web/20160305131754/http://www.christusrex.org/www1/ofm/mad/discussion/109discuss.html (accessed 17 November 2025).
7 https://web.archive.org/web/20160305131754/http://www.christusrex.org/www1/ofm/mad/discussion/109discuss.html (accessed 17 November 2025).
8 'Elusa' Catholic Encyclopedia (New York: Robert Appleton Company, 1913).
9 Renamed by Israel Shivta.
10 The new Israeli name Shivta is a Hebrewization of the original Palestinian name given by the Negev Naming Committee in the early 1950s. Be'er-Sheva'. Ḳiryat-sefer. 1992. p. 61. The Arabic name of the site is A-Sbaita and is associated with the Sobata mentioned in the Nessana papyri. A. Negev assumes that the name originated from the Nabatean name Shubitu. The Hebrew name, Shivta, was awarded by the Governmental Commission of Names. Negev, Avraham; Gibson, Shimon (2001). Sobota; Shivta. New York: Continuum. p. 474.
11 'Shivta National Park', at: https://en.parks.org.il/reserve-park/shivta-national-park (accessed 17 November 2025).
12 Adam Montefiore, 'Deep in the desert', *The Jerusalem Post*, 16 August 2012.
13 Deborah Rubin Fields, 'No sour grapes', *The Jerusalem Post*, 17 February 2011, at https://www.jpost.com/magazine/lifestyle/no-sour-grapes (accessed 17 November 2025).
14 Ariel David, 'How volcanoes and plague killed the Byzantine Wine Industry in Israel', *Haaretz*, 29 July 2020. https://www.haaretz.com/israel-news/2020-07-29/ty-article/.premium/israeli-archaeologists-reveal-secrets-of-ancient-desert-wine-industry/0000017f-f4f4-d460-afff-fff64bb90000 (accessed 17 November 2025).
15 David, 'How volcanoes and plague killed the Byzantine Wine Industry in Israel'.
16 Customs Letter About a Long-Lost Suitcase Leads to Artifacts from Desert with Early 'Jesus' Painting, 19 February 2019. https://www.livescience.com/64798-lost-artifacts-shivta.html (accessed 17 November 2025).

Chapter 4

1 The Greek original, composed between 350 and 362 CE, was lost, but survived through Latin translations made during the sixth century (Grüll 2014: 629–42).
2 Ancient Greek: στάδιον: *stádion*, a 600 foot racetrack.

Chapter 5

1 Latin: *Edictum de Pretiis Rerum Venalium,* an edict concerning the sale price of goods issued by of Roman Emperor Diocletian in 301 CE.

Chapter 6

1 CHURCH FATHERS: City of God, Book XV (St. Augustine) (newadvent.org).
2 The limestone massif is the highlands on the western part of the Aleppo plateau in northwestern Syria.
3 A poet, diplomat and bishop. Sidonius is 'the single most important surviving author from fifth century Gaul'.
4 Lyaeus was a member of the pantheon of Greek gods, is known as the 'Deliverer from care'. He is an epithet of Dionysus as the god of wine who freed people from care and anxiety.
5 N. Wiener, 'Tel Kabri: The 2013 Excavations', Bible History Daily, Biblical Archaeology Society, 12 September 2013. https://www.biblicalarchaeology.org/daily/biblical-sites-places/biblical-archaeology-sites/tel-kabri-the-2013-excavations (accessed 18 November 2025).
6 Eudoxia (Εὐδοξία), a feminine name which originally meant 'good fame or judgement'.
7 In Greek mythology Medusas (*Μέδουσα*'guardian, protectress') is generally described as winged human females with living venomous snakes in place of hair. Medusa was beheaded by the Greek hero Perseus who then used her head, which retained its ability as a weapon. The mythological image of the head of Medusa appeared in the evil-averting device.
8 In Greek and Roman architecture, a *tympanum* is the semi-circular or triangular decorative wall surface over an entrance, door or window, which is bounded by an arch and often contains a sculpture or ornaments.
9 In Greek mythology Hercules was famous for his strength and for his numerous far-ranging adventures including the 'Twelve Labours'.
10 'Tell Umm Amer', UNESCO World Heritage Centre. https://whc.unesco.org/en/list/1749 (accessed 18 November 2025).
11 Evagrius Ponticus (345–399 CE) was an influential Christian theologian and writer in the late fourth century church; he travelled to Jerusalem, where in 383 he became a monk at the monastery of Rufinus and Melania the Elder.
12 Basil of Caesarea in Cappadocia (330 -January 1 or 2, 379).
13 Shenoute of Atripe (347-465 or 348-466) was the abbot of the White Monastery in Egypt.
14 Some early rules for Syrian monks introduced by a Nestorian clergyman Rabbula in the fifth century.
15 Juridical texts transmitted within the Syrian Christian traditions of the fifth century.

Chapter 7

1 Porphyry was born in Thessalonica and he lived in Egypt and Palestine and was bishop of Gaza from 395 to 420.

Chapter 10

1 'Vases', *Holy Land Handicraft Cooperative Society*. https://handmadepalestine.com/en-gb/collections/holy-land-handicraft-cooperative?srsltid=AfmBOopXLGMbCSYHgkieGt-7-g4jsz_A3AVPEf7Q38plS5qHn39xboig (accessed 19 November 2025).

2 https://web.archive.org/web/20121011074210/http://www.dphjewelry.com/art-n0809-131.html (accessed 19 November 2025).

3 *Ancient Testimonies: Fra Niccolò di Poggibonsi. Custodia Terrae Sanctae: Sanctuary Capernaum*, noting that 'they make great works of art in glass'. Readings in Glass History – Volumes 1-2: 24.

Chapter 11

1 Nadi Abusaada, 'Jerusalem stone: The history and identity of Palestinian stereotomy', *The Architectural Review*, 12 April 2022. https://www.architectural-review.com/essays/city-portraits/jerusalem-stone-the-history-and-identity-of-palestinian-stereotomy (accessed 19 November 2025).

2 Nadi Abusaada, 'Jerusalem stone: The history and identity of Palestinian stereotomy'.

3 'Eleutheropolis', *New Advent*. https://www.newadvent.org/cathen/05380a.htm (accessed 19 November 2025).

4 http://www.catholic-hierarchy.org/diocese/d2e22.html (accessed 19 November 2025).

Chapter 12

1 Centre National de Resources Textuelles et Lexicales: GAZE. https://www.cnrtl.fr/lexicographie/gaze (accessed 19 November 2025).

2 https://www.cnrtl.fr/lexicographie/gaze (accessed 19 November 2025).

Chapter 13

1 'Caravanserais: Cross-roads of commerce and culture along the Silk Roads', *Silk Roads Programme UNESCO*. https://en.unesco.org/silkroad/content/caravanserais-cross-roads-commerce-and-culture-along-silk-roads (accessed 19 November 2025).

2 'The Heritage of Soap Factories in Nablus', 15 July 2021, https://palestiniansoap.coop/blogs/news/soap-factories-in-nablus-palestinian-heritage-turath-at-the-local-level (accessed 19 November 2025).

3 http://www.shahincomputer.com/nablus/nablus/history.htm (accessed 19 November 2025).

Chapter 15

1 https://www.tumblr.com/interpaluk/101339541014/if-the-olive-trees-knew-the-hands-that-planted (accessed 20 November 2025).

2 https://www.google.co.uk/books/edition/The_Independent/hMsxAQAAMAAJ?hl=en&gbpv=1&dq=MISSIONARY+SOCIETY+Haifa+Carmel+soap+factory&pg=RA9-PA19&printsec=frontcover (accessed 20 November 2025).
3 *Asian and African Studies*, 25 (1): 49.
4 https://www.google.co.uk/books/edition/Commerce_Reports/of4RosT3SK0C?hl=en&gbpv=1&dq=Nablus+soap&pg=PA557&printsec=frontcover
5 https://www.google.co.uk/books/edition/Commerce_Re-ports/of4RosT3SK0C?hl=en&gbpv=1&dq=Nablus+soap&pg=PA557&printsec=frontcover
6 Commerce Reports - Volume 4, Issue 9.31 October 1921: 557. https://www.google.co.uk/books/edition/Commerce_Re-ports/of4RosT3SK0C?hl=en&gbpv=1&dq= Nablus+soap&pg=PA557&printsec=frontcoverhttps://www.google.co.uk/books/edition/Commerce_Re-ports/of4RosT3SK0C?hl=en&gbpv=1&dq=Nablus+soap&pg=PA557&printsec=frontcover (accessed 20 November 2025).
7 Michael Phillips, 'Nablus' olive oil soap: A Palestinian tradition lives on', Institute for Middle East Understanding (IMEU), 11 March 2008.
8 Phillips, 'Nablus' olive oil soap: A Palestinian tradition lives on'.
9 On the continuing problems both in terms of the soap's manufacture and its export, Rich Wiles, 'Crafting traditional olive oil soap in Palestine', 8 April 2016.
10 Phillips, 'Nablus' olive oil soap: A Palestinian tradition lives on'.

Chapter 16

1 'Tobacco'. https://www.who.int/news-room/fact-sheets/detail/tobacco (accessed 20 November 2025).
2 Everett Collection / Bridgeman Images: https://www.bridgemanimages.com/en/noartistknown/coffee-shop-with-gramophone-jerusalem-c-1910s/black-and-white-photograph/asset/2928640 (accessed 20 November 2025).
3 Rima Nasir Tarazi, 'Music in Palestine During the Mandatory Period'. https://www.comunicazionearezzo.com/wp-content/uploads/2017/08/Music-in-Palestine.pdf (accessed 20 November 2025).

Chapter 17

1 U.S. Department of Commerce. 2003. Official Gazette of the United States Patent and Trademark Office: Trademarks, p. 431.

Chapter 18

1 Nada Abusaada, 'Jaffa: The Rise and Fall of an Agrarian City', 20 September 2020. https://www.palestine-studies.org/en/node/1650539 (accessed 20 November 2025).
2 https://www.meisterdrucke.ie/fine-art-prints/Frank-Newbould/1466891/Jaffa,-from-the-series-%27Buy-Jaffa-Oranges%27.html (accessed 20 November 2025).
3 Nada Abusaada, 'Jaffa: The Rise and Fall of an Agrarian City'.

4 PALESTINE, 'Report on Immigration, Land Settlement and Development' by Sir John Simpson, 1930: https://www.un.org/unispal/document/auto-insert-194707/ (accessed 20 November 2025).
5 Nada Abusaada, 'Jaffa: The Rise and Fall of an Agrarian City'.
6 Nada Abusaada, 'Jaffa: The Rise and Fall of an Agrarian City'.
7 Nada Abusaada, 'Jaffa: The Rise and Fall of an Agrarian City'.
8 Nada Abusaada, 'Jaffa: The Rise and Fall of an Agrarian City'.
9 https://www.telegraph.co.uk/finance/newsbysector/retailandconsumer/9249366/Jaffa-Cakes-definitely-not-biscuits-prepare-to-take-on-imitators.html (accessed 20 November 2025).

Bibliography

Ababneh, Mohammad Daher. 2023. 'Olive Symbolism in Palestinian and Spanish Poetry: A Comparative Study', *International Journal of Linguistics, Literature and Translation*, 6(4): 55–65.

Abbasi, Mustafa. 2023. *Arab Tiberias Under British Rule, 1918–1948* (Doha: Arab Centre for Research and Policy Studies).

Abdo, Nahla. 2013. *Women in Israel: Race, Gender and Citizenship* (London: Zed Books).

Abdulkarim, M., M. Al Maqdissi and G. Meucci. 2003. *Apollodorus of Damascus and Trajan's Column: From Tradition to Project* (Rome: L'Erma Di Bretschneider).

Abisaab, Malek Hassan. 2001. *A History of Women Tobacco Workers: Labor, Community and Social Transformation in Lebanon, 1895–1997* (Binghamton: University of New York).

Abu Hanieh, Ahmed Mohammed et al. 2012. Stone and Marble Industrial Sector in Palestine: Model for Sustainability. Conference: 10. The Global Conference on Sustainable Manufacturing – Towards Implementing Sustainable Manufacturing, Istanbul, Turkey, October.

Abujidi, Nurhan. 2014. *Urbicide in Palestine: Spaces of Oppression and Resilience* (London: Routledge).

Abu Khalaf, Marwan. 2013. 'Soap Manufacture', in Mahmoud Hawari, Yusuf Natsheh and Nazmi Al-Ju'beh (eds.), *Pilgrimage, Sciences and Sufism: Islamic Art in the West Bank and Gaza* (Vienna: Museum with No Frontiers (Museum Ohne Grenzen)).

Abu Manneh, Butris. 1986. 'The Husaynis: The Rise of a Notable Family in 18th Century Palestine', in David Kushner (ed.), *Palestine in the Late Ottoman Period: Political, Social and Economic Transformation* (Jerusalem: Yad Izhak Ben-Zvi Press): 93–107.

Abu-Manneh, Butrus. 1999. 'The Rise of the Sanjak of Jerusalem in the Late Nineteenth Century', in Ilan Pappé (ed.), *The Israel/Palestine Question* (London: Routledge): 41–51.

Abu Shihab, Sana Nimer. 2012. *Mediterranean Cuisine* (AuthorHouse).

Achi, Andrea Myers. 2023. *Africa and Byzantium* (New York: Metropolitan Museum of Arts).

Adams, J. N. 2003. *Bilingualism and the Latin Language* (Cambridge: Cambridge University Press).

Adkins, Lesley and Roy A. Adkins. 1994. *Handbook to Life in Ancient Rome* (New York: Facts on File).

Adorno, Jean. 1978. '*Itinéraired*', *Anselme Adornoen Terre sainte (1470–1471)*, Jacques Heers and Georgette Groër (eds.) (Paris: Editions du Centre national de la recherche scientifique).

Al-'Arif, 'Arif. 1943. *A Brief History of Asqalan* (Jerusalem: Bayt al-Maqdis Press [Arabic]).

Al-Badri, Ishaq and Qasim Abu Harb. 2018. *The Urban Scene in the City of Jerusalem* (Jerusalem: Jami'yyat al-Dirasat al-Arabiyya [Arabic]).

Album, Stephen. 1998. *A Checklist of Islamic Coins*, 2nd edition (Santa Rosa, CA: S. Album).

Al-Dabbagh, Mustafa Murad. 1965 and 1972–1986. *Biladuna Filastin* [Our Country, Palestine], 11 vols. (Beirut: Dar al-Taliah and Dar al-Huda).

Alexander, Wayne M. and Violet, William. 2012. 'Trade and Traders of Mesopotamian Ur'. Proceedings of ASBBS (American Society of Business and Behavioral Sciences) 19: 12–17. http://asbbs.org/files/ASBBS2012V1/PDF/A/AlexanderW.pdf (accessed 20 November 2025).

al-Hiyal al-Handasiya, manuscript (London: British Library [Arabic]).

Al-Hroub, Ishaq. 2015. *Atlas of Palestinian Rural Heritage* (Bethlehem: Diyar Publisher [Arabic]).

al-Jazri, Ismail Ben Razzaz. 1206; 1700/1799. *Book in Knowledge of Engineering Tricks (Kitab fi Ma'rifat)* (Alphen aan den Rijn, Netherlands: Kluwer Academic Publishers).

Al-Ju'beh, Nazmi. 2008. 'Hebron Glass: A Centuries-old Tradition', *This Week in Palestine*, 25 January.

al-Ju'beh, Nazmi and Yusuf Natsheh. 2010. 'Islamic Palestine: History, Politics and Religion', in Mahmoud Hawari, Yusuf Natsheh and Nazmi Al-Ju'beh (eds.), *Pilgrimage, Sciences and Sufism: Islamic Art in the West Bank and Gaza* (Vienna: Museum with No Frontiers (Museum Ohne Grenzen).

Akarli, Engin. 1993. *The Long Peace: Ottoman Lebanon, 1861–1920* (Berkeley, CA: University of California Press).

Al-Ayedi, Abdul Rahman. 2006. *The Inscriptions of the Ways of Horus* (Exeter: Obelisk Publications).

Alda, Ángel del Río. 2014. 'One Elephant and Two Giraffes on the Incense Route', in Ana de Francisco Heredero, David Hernández de la Fuente and Susana Torres Prieto (eds.), *New Perspectives on Late Antiquity in the Eastern Roman Empire* (Cambridge: Cambridge Scholars Publishing): 191–200.

Al-Dabbagh, Mustafa Murad. 1980. *A Hrief History of Arab Countries and Their Eras in Our Country Palestine* (Beirut: Dar al-Tali'a li-Tiba'a wan-Nashr [Arabic]).

Al Makadma, Abdulkarim and Wid Bastian. 2015. *The Tears of Olive Trees: An Autobiographic Story Featuring Poems from Mahmoud Darwish* (South Carolina: Createspace Independent Publication).

Al-Maqdisi (al-Muqaddasi), Muhammad ibn Ahmad Shams al-Din. 1866. *Description of Syria, Including Palestine* (Bengal: Asiatic Society of Bengal).

Al-Maqdisi. 1994. *The Best Divisions for Knowledge of the Regions* [Ahasan al-Taqasim Fi Ma'rifat al-Aqalim] (Reading: Garnet Publishing).

Al-Maqdisi. 2002. *Ahsan al-Taqasim fi Ma'rifat al-Aqalim* [The Best Divisions for Knowledge of the Regions] (Beirut: Dar al-Kutub al-'Ilmiyya).

Amar, Z. 2003. 'The Ancient Trade in Incense, Perfumes and Spices', *Michmanin*, 25: 61–6.

Ameling, Walter, Hannah M. Cotton, Werner Eck, Avner Ecker, Benjamin Isaac, Alla Kushnir-Stein, Haggai Misgav, Jonathan Price, Peter Weiß and Ada Yardeni (eds.). 2014. *Corpus, Corpus inscriptionum Iudaeae/Palaestinae*, Vol. III: South Coast, 2161–2648 (Berlin and Boston: De Gruyter): 409–42.

Anderson, John Kinloch. 1961. *Ancient Greek Horsemanship* (Berkeley, CA: University of California Press).

Arraf, Shukri. 1992. *The Junds [Provinces] of Palestine and Jordan in Islamic Geographical Literature* (Beirut: Dar Shafaq [Arabic]).

'Arraf, Shukri. 2024. *Bread in Palestine: It Became Bread and Salt Among Us* (Haifa and Sharija: Dar Raya for publication and Translation [Arabic]).

Arteca, Richard N. 2015. *Introduction to Horticultural Science*, 2nd edition (Stamford, CT: Cengage Learning).

Aslı, Tokman. 2001. *Negotiating Tradition, Modernity and Identity in Consumer Space: A Study of a Shopping Mall and Revived Coffeehouse* (Thesis). Bilkent University.

Ashtor, Eliyahu. 2014. *Levant Trade in the Middle Ages* (Princeton: Princeton University Press).

Athenaeus. 1941. *The Deipnosophists*. Translated by Gulick Charles Barton (Cambridge, MA: Harvard University Press).

Atkinson, Kenneth. 2012. *Queen Salome: Jerusalem's Warrior Monarch of the First Century B.C.E.* (Jefferson, NC: McFarland & Co).

Avi-Yonah, M. 1932. 'Mosaic Pavements in Palestine', *Quarterly of the Department of Antiquities* of *Palestine*, 2: 136–181.

Avi-Yonah, M. 1933. 'Mosaic Pavements in Palestine', *Quarterly of the Department of Antiquities* in *Palestine*, 3: 26-47; 49-73.

Avi-Yonah, M. 1936. 'Mosaic Pavements at El Hammam, Beisan', *Quarterly of the Department of Antiquities in Palestine*, 5: 11-30.

Avni, Gideon. 2014. *The Byzantine-Islamic Transition in Palestine: An Archaeological Approach* (Oxford: Oxford University Press).

Ayalon, Ami. 2004. *Reading Palestine: Printing and Literacy, 1900–1948* (Austine: University of Texas Press).

Baram, Uzi. 2007a. 'Archaeological Surveys, Excavations and Landscapes of the Ottoman Imperial Realm: An Agenda for the Archaeological Modernity of the Middle East', in Sauro Gelichi and Mauro Librenti (eds.), *Constructing Post-medieval Archaeology in Italy: A New Agenda* (Lorenzo: Edizioni All' Insegna del Giglio): 11-18.

Baram, Uzi. 2007b. 'Filling a Gap in the Chronology: What Archaeology Is Revealing About the Ottoman Past in Israel', in Sandy Sufian and Mark LeVine (eds.), *Reapproaching Borders: New Perspectives on the Study of Israel-Palestine* (Lanham, MD: Rowman & Littlefield): 17-40.

Bard, Kathryn A. 2005. *Encyclopedia of the Archaeology of Ancient Egypt* (London: Routledge).

Barisitz, Stephan. 2017. *Central Asia and the Silk Road: Economic Rise and Decline over Several Millennia* (Berlin: Springer).

Barjamovic, Gojko, Thomas Chaney, Kerem Coşar and Ali Hortaçsu. 2019. 'Trade, Merchants, and the Lost Cities of the Bronze Age', *The Quarterly Journal of Economics*, 134 (3) (August): 1455–503.

Barnes, Timothy D. 1981. *Constantine and Eusebius* (Cambridge, MA: Harvard University Press).

Basan, Ghillie. 2007. *The Middle Eastern Kitchen* (New York: Hippocrene Books).

Beard, John Relly. 1862. *The People's Dictionary of the Bible*, Vol. 2 (Oxford: Oxford University Press).

Beeley, Brian W. 1970. 'The Turkish Village Coffeehouse as a Social Institution', *Geographical Review*, 60 (4): 475-93.

Beheiry, Marwan R. 1981. 'The Agricultural Exports of Southern Palestine, 1885-1914', *Journal of Palestine Studies*, 10 (4): 61-81.

Beinin, Joel. 2001. *Workers and Peasants in the Modern Middle East* (Cambridge: Cambridge University Press).

Beit-Arieh, Itzhaq. 1996. 'Edomites Advance into Judah: Israelite Defensive Fortresses. Inadequate', *Biblical Archaeology Review*, 22 (6): 28–36.

Belayche, Nicole. 2004. 'Pagan Festivals in Fourth-Century Gaza', in Brouria Bitton-Ashkelony and Aryeh Kofsky (eds.), *Christian Gaza in Late Antiquity* (Leiden: Brill): 5–22.

Ben David, H. 2005. 'The Paved Roman Road from Petra to the Arava', *Cathedra*, 116: 31–48 [in Hebrew].

Ben-Dov, Meir. 1977. 'Found After 1400 Years – The Magnificent Nea', *Biblical Archaeology Review*, 3(4), December. https://www.biblicalarchaeology.org/daily/biblical-sites-places/jerusalem/found-after-1400-years-the-magnificent-nea (accessed 20 November 2025).

Benzaquen, John. 2012. 'A Hop, Skip and a Iump into the Past', *The Jerusalem Post*, 26 August. https://www.jpost.com/travel/around-israel/a-hop-skip-and-a-jump-into-the-past (accessed 20 November 2025).

Berkey, Jonathan Porter. 2014. *The Transmission of Knowledge in Medieval Cairo: A Social History of Islamic Education* (Princeton, NJ: Princeton University Press).

Berkoff (Engle), Anita. 1973. *Readings in Glass History*, Volumes 1–2 (Jerusalem: Phoenix Publications).

Bernstein, Deborah S. 2000. *Constructing Boundaries: Jewish and Arab Workers in Mandatory Palestine* (New York: State University of New York Press).

Beška, Emanuel. 2015. 'Khalil al-Sakakini and Zionism Before WWI', *Jerusalem Quarterly* (63/64): 40–53.

Bessard, Fanny. 2020. *Caliphs and Merchants: Cities and Economies of Power in the Near East (700–950)* (Oxford: Oxford University Press).

Billé, Franck, Sanjyot Mehendale and James W. Lankton. 2022. *The Maritime Silk Road: Global Connectivities, Regional Nodes, Localities* (Amsterdam: Amsterdam University Press).

Bitton-Ashkelony, Brouria and Aryeh Kofsky (eds.). 2004. *Christianity in Gaza in Late Antiquity* (Leiden: Brill).

Bitton-Ashkelony, Brouria and Aryeh Kofsky. 2006. *The Monastic School of Gaza* (Leiden: Brill).

Black, Jeremy and Anthony Green. 1992. *Gods, Demons and Symbols of Ancient Mesopotamia: An Illustrated Dictionary* (London: The British Museum Press).

Blanchard, Ian. 2001a. *Mining, Metallurgy and Minting in the Middle Ages: Asiatic Supremacy*, Vol. 1, 425–1125 (Wiesbaden: Franz Steiner Verlag).

Blanchard, Ian. 2001b. *Mining, Metallurgy and Minting in the Middle Ages: Afro-European Supremacy*, Vol. 2, 1125–225 (Wiesbaden: Franz Steiner Verlag).

Blanchard, Ian. 2005. *Mining, Metallurgy and Minting in the Middle Ages: Continuing Afro-European Supremacy*, Vol. 3, 1250–450 (Wiesbaden: Franz Steiner Verlag).

Blankinship, Khalid Yaya. (1994). *The End of the Jihad State: The Reign of Hisham Ibn Abd Al-Malik and the Colla: Reign of Hisham Ibn 'Abd Al-Malik and the Collapse of the Umayyads* (New York: State University of New York Press).

Bough, Jill. 2012. *Donkey* (London: Reaktion Books).

Bowersock, Glen W. 1994. *Roman Arabia* (Cambridge, MA: Harvard University Press).

Bowersock, Glen W. 2007. 'Hellenism and Islam', in Eva R. Hoffman (ed.), *Late Antique and Medieval Art of the Mediterranean World* (Malden, MA: Blackwell): 85–96.

Bowersock, Glen W. 2019. 'The Many Lives of Palestine', *New York Times*, 18 April. https://www.nybooks.com/articles/2019/04/18/nur-masalha-many-lives-palestine/?srsltid=AfmBOoqvWFK5tkCaQbEyf488S-g9hB0vzrlX_XNP1M3VNAM_OVHDfBGw (accessed 20 November 2025).

Breasted, James Henry (trans. and ed.). 2001. *Ancient Records of Egypt: The Twentieth Through the Twenty-sixth Dynasties*, Vol. 4 (Urbana: University of Illinois Press).

Brennan, Michael G. 2022. *English Travellers to Venice 1450–1600* (London: Routledge).

Broadbridge, Anne F. 1999. 'Academic Rivalry and the Patronage System in Fifteenth-Century Egypt', *Mamluk Studies Review*, 3: 85–107.
Brockliss, Laurence (ed.). 1989. *History of Universities*, Vol. VIII (Oxford: Oxford University Press).
Broshi, Magen. 2001. *Bread, Wine, Walls and Scrolls* (London: Bloomsbury).
Broshi, Magen and Ram Gophna. 1985. 'Middle Bronze Age II Palestine: Its Settlements and Population', *Bulletin of the American School of Oriental Research*, 261 (February): 73–90.
Brostrom, Geralyn G. and Jack Brostrom. 2008. *The Business of Wine: An Encyclopedia* (Westport, CT: Greenwood Press).
Brunello, Franco. 1973. *The Art of Dyeing in the History of Mankind* (Vincenza: Neri Pozza Editore).
Brunning, Sue, Luk Yu-ping, Elisabeth R. O'Connell and Tim Williams. 2024. *Silk Roads* (London: British Museum).
Bruyère, Bernard. 1929–1930. *Mert Seger à Deir el Médineh* [The Egyptian Deity Mertseger at al-Medina] (Cairo: Institut Français d'Archéologie Orientale).
Bucking, Scott, Daniel Fuks, Zachary C. Dunseth, Lior Schwimer and Tali Erickson-Gini. 2022. 'The Avdat in Late Antiquity Project: Uncovering the Early Islamic Phases of a Byzantine Town in the Negev Highlands', *Antiquity*, 96 (387): 754–61.
Buckingham, James Silk. 1821. *Travels in Palestine Through the Countries of Bashan and Gilead, East of the River Jordan, Including a Visit to the Cities of Geraza and Gamala in the Decapolis* (London: Longman).
Budge, E. A. Wallis. 2013. *A History of Egypt from the End of the Neolithic Period to the Death of Cleopatra VII B.C. 30* (London: Routledge).
Burckhardt, John Lewis. 1822. *Travels in Syria and the Holy Land* (London: J. Murray).
Burgoyne, Michael Hamilton. 1987. *Mamluk Jerusalem: An Architectural Study* (London: British School of Archaeology in Jerusalem and the World of Islam Festival Trust).
Burgoyne, Michael Hamilton and Amal Abu al-Hajj. 1979. 'Twenty-Four Medieval Arabic Inscriptions from Jerusalem', *Levant*, 11: 128–9.
Burns, Ross. 2007. *Origins of the Colonnaded Streets in the Cities of the Roman East* (Oxford: Oxford University Press).
Burns, Ross. 2019. *Damascus: A History* (London: Routledge).
Burns, Thomas S. and John W. Eadie (eds.). 2001. *Urban Centers and Rural Contexts in Late Antiquity* (East Lansing, MI: Michigan State University Press).
Burrows, Leah. 2013. 'Archaeologists Discover Largest, Oldest Palatial Wine Cellar', *BrandeisNOW*, 22 November. https://www.brandeis.edu/now/2013/November/winestory.html (accessed 20 November 2025).
Bury, John Bagnell. 2019. *The Rise and Decline of the Roman Empire* (Prague: e-artnow).
Büssow, Johann. 2011. *Hamadan Palestine: Politics and Society in the District of Jerusalem, 1872–1908* (Leiden: Brill).
Butt, Gerald. 1995. *Life at the Crossroads: A History of Gaza* (Limasso: Rimal Publications).
Calvo, Emilia 2008. *A Shared Legacy: Islamic Science East and West: Homage to Professor J.M. MillàsVallicrosa* (Barcelona: University of Barcelona)
Cambras, Sosep. 2004: *The Complete Book of Bookbinding* (Lincoln: Lark Books)
Cameron, Averil. 1976. *Flavius Cresconius Corippus: In laudem Iustini Augustiminoris (in Praise of Justin II)* (Translation and commentary). (London: The Athlone Press).
Cameron, Averil. 1985. *Procopius and the Sixth Century* (London: Duckworth).

Cameron, Averil, Bryan Ward-Perkins and Michael Whitby. 2000. *The Cambridge Ancient History: Late Antiquity: Empire and Successors, A.D. 425–600*, Vol. XIV (Cambridge: Cambridge University Press).

Canar, Daniel E. 2010. *History and Hagiography from the Late Antique Sinai* (Liverpool: Liverpool University Press).

Caritas Internationalis. 2023. 'Caritas Mourns Colleague's Death in Israeli Airstrike on Gaza church, 20 October. https://www.caritas.org/2023/10/caritas-mourns-colleagues-death-in-an-attack-in-gaza (accessed 20 November 2025).

Carriker, Andrew James. 2003. *The Library of Eusebius of Caesarea* (Leiden: Brill).

Casson, Lionel (eds.). 1989. *The Periplus Maris Erythraei*: Text with Introduction, Translation, and Commentary (Princeton: Princeton University Press),

Casto, E. Ray. 1937. 'Economic Geography of Palestine', *Economic Geography*, 13 (3): 235–59.

Caswell, F. Matthew. 2015. *The Khamriyyat of Abu Nuwas: Medieval Bacchic Poetry* (Market Harborough, Leicestershire: Troubador Publishing).

Catholic Encyclopedia. n.d. 'Elusa'. https://www.newadvent.org/cathen/05395a.htm (accessed 20 November 2025).

Chisholm, Hugh (ed.). 1911a. 'Agoranomi', *Encyclopædia Britannica*. 11th edition. (Cambridge: Cambridge University Press): 381.

Chisholm, Hugh (ed.). 1911b. 'Caravanserai', *Encyclopaedia Britannica*. 11th edition. (Cambridge: Cambridge University Press).

Chisholm, Hugh (ed.). 1911c. 'Cassiodorus', *Encyclopædia Britannica*. 11th edition. (Cambridge: Cambridge University Press): 459–60.

Clackson, J. James, Patrick James, Katherine McDonald, Livia Tagliapietra and Nicholas Zair (eds.). 2020. *Migration, Mobility and Language Contact in and Around the Ancient Mediterranean* (Cambridge: Cambridge University Press).

Clermont-Ganneau, C. E. 1896. *Archaeological Researches in Palestine During the Years 1873–1874*, Vol. 2 (London: Committee of the Palestine Exploration Fund).

Cline, Eric H., Alexandra Ratzlaff and Assaf Yasur-Landau (eds.). 2023. *Excavations at Tel Kabri III* (The 2013 to 2019 Seasons) (Leiden: Brill).

Cohen, Amnon (ed.). 1984. *Egypt and Palestine: A Millennium of Association* 868–1948 (New York: St. Martin's Press).

Cohen, Amnon. 2002. *Economic Life in Ottoman Jerusalem* (Cambridge: Cambridge University Press).

Cohen, R. 1982. 'New Light on the Date of the Petra-Gaza Road', *Biblical Archaeologist*, 45: 240–7.

Colt, Harris Dunscombe. 1962. *Excavations at Nessana I* (London: British School of Archaeology in Jerusalem).

Comay, Joan. 2001. *Who's Who in the Old Testament* (London: Routledge).

Conan, Michel. 2007. *Middle East Garden Traditions: Unity and Diversity Questions, Methods, and Resources in a Multicultural Perspective* (Washington, DC: Dumbarton Oaks).

Conder, Claude Reigner. 1887. *Syrian Stone-Lore; or, The Monumental History of Palestine* (London: Watt).

Conder, Claude Reignier. 2018 [1878]. *Tent Work in Palestine* (*Frankfort*: Outlook Verlag).

Conder, Claude Reigner and H. H. Kitchener. 1881. *The Survey of Western Palestine: Memoirs of the Topography, Orography, Hydrography, and Archaeology*, Vol. 1. (London: Committee of the Palestine Exploration Fund).

Contenau, Georges, 1954. *Everyday Life in Babylon and Assyria* (Hodder: London).

Cook, S. A., E. E. Advock and M. P. Charlesworth (eds.). 1930. *The Cambridge Ancient History: Volume 8, Rome and Mediterranean* (Cambridge: Cambridge University Press).

Corippus. 1976. *In Praise of Justin*, edited Averil Cameron. *Flavius Cresconius Corippus: In laudem Iustini Augustiminoris (in Praise of Justin II).* (Translation and commentary) (London: The Athlone Press).

Cornelius, Izak. 2008. *The Many Faces of the Goddess: The Iconography of the Syro-Palestinian Goddesses Anat, Astarte, Qedeshet, and Asherah c. 1500–1000 BCE*, 204 (Fribourg: Academic Press/Göttingen, Germany: Vandenhoeck & Ruprecht).

Cowan, Brian. 2005. *The Social Life of Coffee: The Emergence of the British Coffeehouse* (New Haven: Yale University Pres).

Croil, James. 1898. *Steam Navigation: And Its Relation to the Commerce of Canada and the United States* (Toronto: William Briggs).

Crone, Patricia with Adam Silverstein. 2016. 'The Ancient Near East and Islam: The Case of Lot-Casting', in Hanna Siurua (ed.), *Islam, The Ancient Near East and Varieties of Godlessness*, Vol. 3 (Leiden: Brill).

Crown, Alan David (ed.). 1989. *The Samaritans* (Tübingen: J.C.B. Mohr).

Culbertson, Cynthia. 2014. *The Arabian Horse of Egypt* (Illustration by Marei Nasr) (Cairo: The American University in Cairo Press).

Dalby, Andrew. 2003. *Food in the Ancient World, from A to Z* (London: Routledge).

Dandis, Wala. 2011. *History of Hebron.* https://www.scribd.com/document/71913073/History-of-Hebron (accessed 20 November 2025).

Darwish, Mahmoud. 2003. *Unfortunately, It Was Paradise Selected Poems*, translated and edited by Munir Akash, Carolyn Forché, Sinan Antoon and Amira El-Zein (Berkeley, CA: University of California Press).

David, Ariel. 2017. 'Ancient Egyptian Records Indicate Philistines Weren't Aegean Pirates After All', *Haaretz*, 23 July. https://www.haaretz.com/archaeology/2017-07-23/ty-article-magazine/ancient-records-indicate-philistines-werent-aegean-pirates/0000017f-eef9-ddba-a37f-eeff03cd0000 (accessed 26 January 2026).

David, Ariel. 2020. 'How Volcanoes and Plague Killed the Byzantine Wine Industry in Israel', *Haaretz*, 29 July. https://www.haaretz.com/israel-news/2020-07-29/ty-article/.premium/israeli-archaeologists-reveal-secrets-of-ancient-desert-wine-industry/0000017f-f4f4-d460-afff-fff64bb90000 (accessed 20 November 2025).

Decker, Michael. 2006. 'Agriculture and Agricultural Technology', in Elizabeth Jeffreys, John Haldon and Robin Cormack (eds), *The Oxford Handbook of Byzantine Studies* (Oxford: Oxford University Press): 400–1.

Decker, Michael. 2008a. 'Water into Wine: Trade and Technology in Late Antiquity', *Late Antique Archaeology*, 4 (1): 63–92.

Decker, Michael J. 2008b. 'The Political Geography of the Byzantine World. Production, Manufacture and Technology. Agriculture and Agricultural Technology,' in Elizabeth Jeffreys, John F. Haldon and Robin Cormack (eds), *The Oxford Handbook of Byzantine Studies* (Oxford: Oxford University Press): 397–406.

Decker, Michael J. 2009. 'Ancient Mediterranean', in Geralyn Brostrom and Jack Bronstrom (eds), *The Business of Wine: An Encyclopedia* (Westport: Greenwood Press): 5–7.

Delpuget, David. 1866. *Les juifsd'Alexandrie, de Juffu et de Jérusalemen 1865* (Bordeaux).

Demetriou, Denise. 2023. *Phoenicians Among Others: Why Migrants Mattered in the Ancient Mediterranean* (Oxford: Oxford University Press).

De Romanis, Federico. 2020. *The Indo-Roman Pepper Trade and the Muziris Papyrus* (Oxford: Oxford University Press).
Derr, Mark. 1989. *Some Kind of Paradise. A Chronicle of Man and the Land of Florida* (New York: William Morrow and Company).
De Vaux, Roland. 1966. 'Palestine in the Early Bronze Age', in John Chadwick (ed), *The Cambridge Ancient History*, Vol. 1, Part 15 (Cambridge: Cambridge University Press).
De Vaux, Roland. 2008. 'Palestine in the Early Bronze Age', in I. E. S. Edwards, C. J. Gadd and N. G. L. Hammond (eds), *The Cambridge Ancient History* (Cambridge: Cambridge University Press): 208–37.
Diaconus, Marcus. 1913. *The Life of Porphyry, Bishop of Gaza* (Oxford: Clarendon Press).
Diaconus, Marcus. 2010. *The Life of Porphyry, Bishop of Gaza*, trans. Fr George Francis Hill (Charleston, SC: Nabu Press).
Dierauff, Evelin. 2020. *Translating Late Ottoman Modernity in Palestine: Debates on Ethno-Confessional Relations and Identity in the Arab Palestinian Newspaper Filasn … Filasṭīn (1911–1914)* (Göttingen: V & R Unipress GmbH).
Dignas, Beale and Englebert Winter. 2007. *Rome and Persia in Late Antiquity: Neighbours and Rivals* (Cambridge: Cambridge University Press).
Di Rocco, Gabriella Di. 1988. 'Julian of Ascalon', *Journal of Hellenic Studies*, 112: 31–43.
Di Segni, Leah. 2022. *An Introduction to Late Antique Epigraphy in the Holy Land: A Thorough Study on Greek and Latin Epigraphy in the Holy Land* (Jerusalem: Edizioni Terra Santa).
Donaghy, Thomas. 2014. *Horse Breeds and Breeding in the Greco-Persian World: 1st and 2nd Millennium BC* (Cambridge: Cambridge Scholar).
Doughty, Dick. 2006. 'Gaza: Contested Crossroads', *This Week in Palestine*, November. https://web.archive.org/web/20110907165624/http://www.thisweekinpalestine.com/details.php?id=1958&ed=133&edid=133 (accessed 20 November 2025).
Doumani, Beshara. 1995. *Rediscovering Palestine: Merchants and Peasants in Jabal Nablus, 1700–1900* (Berkeley, CA: University of California Press).
Doumani, Beshara. 2017. *Family Life in the Ottoman Mediterranean: A Social History* (Cambridge: Cambridge University Press).
Dow, Martin. 1996. *The Islamic Baths of Palestine* (Jerusalem: British School of Archaeology in Jerusalem).
Drory, Joseph. 2004. 'Founding a New Mamlaka: Some Remarks Concerning Safed and the Organization of the Region in the Mamluk Period', in Michael Winter and Amalia Levanoni (eds), *The Mamluks in Egyptian and Syrian Politics and Society* (Leiden: Brill): 163–90.
Dumper, Michael and Bruce E. Stanley (eds.). 2007. *Cities of the Middle East and North Africa: A Historical Encyclopedia* (Santa Barbara, CA: ABC-CLIO).
Dukes, Hunter and Adam Green (n.d.). *Photographs of Life in Palestine (ca. 1896–1919)*. https://publicdomainreview.org/collection/photographs-of-palestinian-life (accessed 15 November 2025).
Edwards, E. S., C. J. Gadd and N. G. L. Hammond (eds.) 1971. *The Cambridge Ancient History*, Vol. I, Part I: Prolegomena and Prehistory. 3rd edition (Cambridge: Cambridge University Press).
Egmond van der Nijenburg, J. Aegidius van and Johannes Heyman, 1759. *Travels Through Part of Europe, Asia Minor, the Islands of the Archipelago, Syria, Palestine, Egypt, Mount Sinai, &c. Giving a Particular Account of the Most Remarkable Places*, Vol. 2. (London: L. Davis and C. Reymers).

El-Badawi, Emran. 2024. *Female Divinity in the Qur'an: In Conversation with the Bible and the Ancient Near East* (London: Palgrave Macmillan).

Elliott, Jack D. 1996. 'The Nabatean Synthesis of Avraham Negev: A Critical Appraisal', in Joe D. Seger (ed.), *Retrieving the Past: Essays on Archaeological Research and Methodology in Honor of Gus W. Van Beek* (Winona Lake, IN: Eisenbrauns): 47-60.

Emery, Irene. 1966. *The Primary Structure of Fabrics* (Washington, D.C.: Thames and Hudson).

Emmett, Chad F. 1995. *Beyond the Basilica: Christians and Muslims in Nazareth* (Chicago: University of Chicago Press).

Ephrat, Daphna. 2006. 'The Genesis of the *wali Allah* in Mamluk Jerusalem and Hebron', in David Wasserstein and Ami Ayalon (eds.), *Mamluks and Ottomans: Studies in Honour of Michael Winter* (London: Taylor & Francis): 4-18.

Eshel, Hanan. 2008. *Dead Sea Scrolls and the Hasmonean State* (Grand Rapids, MI: Wm. B. Eerdmans Publishing).

Etheredge, Laura S. 2011. *Historic Palestine, Israel, and the Emerging Palestinian Autonomous* (Buffalo, NY: Rosen Publishing).

Etheredge, Laura (ed.). 2011a. *Saudi Arabia and Yemen* (New York: Rosen Education Service).

Eusebius. 1861. *The History of the Martyrs in Palestine* (*De Martyribus Palaestina*), translated by William Cureton (London: Williams and Norgate). http://www.tertullian.org/fathers/eusebius_martyrs.htm (accessed 20 November 2025).

Eusebius. 1971. *Onomasticon* (*On the Place Names in Holy Scripture*) (Washington, DC: Catholic University of America Press).

Eusebius Pamphilus. 2011. *The Ecclesiastical History of Pamphilus Eusebius* (Boulder, CO: Merchant Books).

Evans, James Allan. 2005. *The Emperor Justinian and the Byzantine Empire* (Westport, CT: Greenwood Press).

Evian, Shirly Ben-Dor. 2017. 'Ramesses III and the "Sea-peoples": Towards a New Philistine Paradigm', *Oxford Journal of Archaeology* (July): 267-85.

Fabian, P. 1996. 'Evidence of Earthquake Destruction in the Archaeological Record – The Case of Ancient Avdat', in *Big Cities World Conference on Natural Disaster Mitigation in Conjunction with the Tenth International Seminar on Earthquake Prognostics, Abstracts*, January 5-10 (Cairo, Egypt).

Fabri, Felix. 1848: *Fratris Felicis Fabri Evagatorium in Terrae sanctae, Arabiae et Aegypti peregrinationem*: 3 vols in Latin, Vol 1.

Fabri, Felix. 1893a. *Felix Fabri* (c. 1480–1483 A.D.), Vol. II, part I (London: Palestine Pilgrims' Text Society).

Fabri, Felix. 1893b. *The Wanderings of Felix Fabri* (c. 1480-1483 AD), Vol. 1-3 (London: The Library Palestine Pilgrims' Text Society).

Falk, Avner. 2015. *Napoleon Against Himself: A Psychobiography* (Durham: North Carolina: Pitchstone Publishing).

Farina, Fiorella Festa. 2003. 'Forward', in M. Abdulkarim, M. Al Maqdissi and G. Meucci (eds), *Apollodorus of Damascus and Trajan's Column: From Tradition to Project* (Rome: L'Erma Di Bretschneider).

Feldman, Louis H. 1996. *Studies in Hellenistic Judaism* (Leiden: Brill).

Fields, Deborah Rubin. 2020. 'No Sour Grapes: 1,500 Years Ago Residents of Shivta Used Intensive Runoff Agriculture and Harvested Dew to Irrigate Their Vineyards', *The Jerusalem Post*, 17 February. https://www.jpost.com/magazine/lifestyle/no-sour-grapes (accessed 20 November 2025).

Fiema, Zbigniew T., Ahmad Al-Jallad, Michael C. A. Macdonald and Laïla Nehmé. 2015. 'Provincia Arabia: Nabataea, the Emergence of Arabic as a Written Language, and Graeco-Arabica', in Greg Fisher (ed.), *Arabs and Empires Before Islam* (Oxford: Oxford University Press): 373–433.

Filfil, Rania and Barbara Louton. 2008. 'The *Other Face of Gaza*: The *Gaza Continuum*', *This Week in Palestine*, (September). https://web.archive.org/web/20090207121431/http://www.thisweekinpalestine.com/details.php?id=2564&ed=157&edid=157 (accessed 18 November 2025).

Filiu, Jean-Piere. 2014. *Gaza: A History* (Oxford: Oxford University Press).

Findley, Carter Vaughn. 2008. 'The Tanzimat', in Resat Kasaba (ed.), *The Cambridge History of Turkey*, Vol. 4 (Cambridge: Cambridge University Press): 11–37.

Findley, Carter Vaughn. 2010. *Turkey, Islam, Nationalism, and Modernity: A History* (New Haven, CN: Yale University Press).

Finkelstein, Israel. 1988. 'Arabian Trade and Socio-Political Conditions in the Negev in the *Twelfth-Eleventh Centuries B.C.E.*', *Journal of Near Eastern Studies*, 47(4): 241–52.

Finkelstein, Israel. 2007. *David and Solomon: In Search of the Bible's Sacred Kings and the Roots' of the Western Tradition* (Florence, MA: Free Press).

Finney, Paul Corby. 2017. *The Eerdmans Encyclopedia of Early Christian Art and Archaeology* (Grand Rapids, MI: Wm. B. Eerdmans Publishing).

Fischer, Moshe, Itamar Taxel and David Amit. 2008. 'Rural Settlement in the Vicinity of Yavneh in the Byzantine Period: A Religio-Archaeological Perspective', *Bulletin of the American Schools of Oriental Research*, 350 (May): 7–35.

Fisher, Greg (ed.). 2015. *Arabs and Empires Before Islam* (Oxford: Oxford University Press).

Flood, Finbarr. 1997. 'Umayyad Survivals and Mamluk Revivals: Qalawunid Architecture and the Great Mosque of Damascus', in Gülru Necipoglu (ed.), *Muqarnas XIV: An Annual on the Visual Culture of the Islamic World* (Leiden: Brill): 57–79.

Flood, Finbarr. 2001. *The Great Mosque of Damascus: Studies on the Makings of an Umayyad Visual Culture* (Leiden: Brill): 129–30.

Flusser, David and Shua Amorai-Stark. 1993. 'The Goddess Thermuthis, Moses, and Artapanus', *Jewish Studies Quarterly* 1 (3): 217–33.

Forbes, Robert J. 1964. *Studies in Ancient Technology*, Vol. 1 (Leiden: Brill).

Forbes, Robert J. 1965. '*The Coming of the Camel*', in Robert J. Forbes (ed.), *Studies in Ancient Technology*, Vol. 2. 2nd edition (Leiden: Brill): 193–213.

Fosbroke, Thomas Dudly. 1825a. *Encyclopedia of Antiquity and Elements of Archaeology: Classical and Medieval*, Vol. I (London: John Nichols).

Fosbroke, Thomas Dudly. 1825b. *Encyclopedia of Antiquity and Elements of Archaeology: Classical and Medieval*, Vol. II. (London: John Nichols).

Foster, Benjamin R. 1970,'Agoranomos and Muhtasib', *Journal of the Economic and Social History of the Orient*, 13 (2) (April): 128–44.

Foster, Zachary J. 2016. 'Was Jerusalem Part of Palestine? The Forgotten City of Ramla, 900–1900', *British Journal of Middle Eastern Studies*, 43 (2): 1–15.

Fotopoulos, John (ed.). 2006. *The New Testament and Early Christian Literature in Greco-Roman Context* (Leiden: Brill).

French, Carole. 2012. *Jordan* (Buckinghamshire: Bradt Travel Guides).

Fritz, V. 1981. 'The Israelite "Conquest" in Light of Recent Excavations at Khirbet elMeshâsh', *Bulletin of the American Schools of Oriental Research*, 241: 61–73.

Gangal, Kavita, Graeme R. Sarson and Anvar Shukurov. 2014. 'The Near-Eastern Roots of the Neolithic in South Asia', *PLOS One*, 9 (5). https://journals.plos.org/plosone/article/file?id=10.1371/journal.pone.0095714&type=printable (accessed 20 November 2025).

Garrison, Webb B. 2008. *Why You Say It* (Redditch: Read Books).

Geiger, Joseph. 1992. 'Julian of Ascalon', *The Journal of Hellenic Studies*, 112: 31–43.

Geiger, Joseph. 2010. 'Lawyers in Late Antique Palestine'. https://www.openstarts.units.it/server/api/core/bitstreams/f258eda7-ddc8-4913-b64f-4a7c88ff17b7/content (accessed 20 November 2025).

Gerber, Haim. 1982. 'Modernization in Nineteenth-Century Palestine: The Role of Foreign Trade', *Middle Eastern Studies*, 18 (3): 250–64.

Ghabin, Ahmad. 2009. 'Hisba, Arts and Craft in Islam', *Journal of Islamic Studies*, 22 (2): 252–4.

Ghosheh, Subhi S. 2013. *Jerusalem: Arab Social Life, Traditions, and Everyday Pleasures in the 20th Century* (New York: Olive Branch Press).

Gibbon, Edward, 1875. *The History of the Fall and Decline of Roman Empire*, Vol.1 (Philadelphia: JB Lippincott).

Gibson, Dan. 2002, 2022. 'The History of Nabataea'. https://nabataea.net/explore/history/history (accessed 20 November 2025).

Gil, Moshe. 1997. *A History of Palestine, 634–1099* (Cambridge: Cambridge University Press).

Gilbar, Gad G. 1998. 'Economic and Social Consequences of the Opening of New Markets: The Case of Nablus, 1870–1914', in Thomas Philipp and Birgit Schäbler (eds.), *The Syrian Land: Processes of Integration and Fragmentation: Bilād al-Shām from the 18th to the 20th Century* (Stuttgart: Franz Steiner Verlag): 281–92.

Gilbar, Gad G. 2023. 'The Growing Economic Involvement of Palestine with the West, 1865–1914', in Gad G. Gilbar (ed.), *Ottoman Palestine 1800–1914: Studies in Economic and Social History* (Leiden: Brill): 188–210.

Glucker, Carol A. M. 1987. *The City of Gaza in the Roman and Byzantine Periods* (Oxford: BAR Publishing).

Goitein, S. D. 1983. *A Mediterranean Society: Daily Life*, Vol. IV (Berkeley: University of California Press).

Goldsworthy, Adrian Keith. 2016. *Pax Romana: War, Peace, and Conquest in the Roman World* (New Haven: CN: Yale University Press).

Gonen, R. 1984. 'Urban Canaan in the Late Bronze. Age', *Bulletin* of the *American Schools* of *Oriental Research*, 253: 61–73.

Goodwin, Tony. 2004. 'The Arab-Byzantine Coinage of Jund Filastin: A Potential Historical Source', *Byzantine and Modern Greek Studies*, 28 (1): 1–12.

Government Offices of Israel. 1966. *The Directory of Israeli Merchants and Manufacturers* (Commercial & Industrial Directory) (Israel: N.A. Etrogy).

Government Offices of Israel. 1972. *Israel Directory* (Jerusalem).

Government of Palestine. 1931. Report Palestine. Department of Agriculture and Forests (Jerusalem).

Government of Palestine. 1936. Palestine: Report Department of Agriculture and Forest (Jerusalem).

Graf, David F. 2019. *Rome and the Arabian Frontier from the Nabataeans to the Saracens* (London: Routledge).

Graf, David F. and contributors. 2022. 'Arabia Eudaemon', a Pleiades place resource. https://pleiades.stoa.org/places/746710 (accessed 20 November 2025).

Grainger, John D. 2016. *Syria: An Outline History* (Barnsley: Pen & Sword Books).

Grigson, Caroline. 2013. 'Camels, Copper and Donkeys in the Early Iron Age of the Southern Levant: Timna Revisited', *The Journal of the Council for British Research in the Levant*, 44: 82–100.

Grillmeier, Alois. 1975. *Christ in Christian Tradition*: Vol 1. (Louisville, KY: Westminster/ John Knox Press).

Groom, Nigel. 1981. *Frankincense and Myrrh: A Study of the Arabian Incense Trade* (New York: Longman).

Groom, Nigel. 2012. *The Perfume Handbook* (Berlin: Springer).

Grüll, Tibor. 2014. 'Expositiototius mundi et gentium. A Peculiar Work on the Commerce of Roman Empire from the Mid-fourth Century – Compiled by a Syrian Textile Dealer?' in Zoltán Csabai (ed.), *Studies in Economic and Social History of the Ancient Near East in Memory of Péter Vargyas, Ancient Near Eastern and Mediterranean Studies* 2 (Pécs–Budapest: Department of Ancient History, L'Harmattan): 629–42.

Gualtieri, Sarah M. A. 2009. *Between Arab and White: Race and Ethnicity in the Early Syrian American Diaspora* (Berkeley: University of California Press).

Guérin, Victor 1880. *Description Géographique Historique et Archéologique de la Palestine*, Vol. 3: Galilee, pt. 1 (Paris: L'Imprimerie Nationale).

Guérin, Victor. 1868–1880. *Description géographique, historique et archéologique de la Palestine*, 7 vols. (Paris: Imprimé par autorisation de l'empereur à l'Impr. Impériale).

Guérin, Victor. 1881–1883. *La Terre Sainte: Son histoire, ses souvenirs, ses sites, ses monuments*, 2 vols. (Paris: Imprimeurs-Éditeurs).

Gutwein, Kenneth C. 2000. *Third Palestine: A Regional Study in Byzantine Urbanization* (Bloomington, IN: iUniverse).

Hadas, Moses. 2007. *Aristeas to Philocrates: (Letter of Aristeas)* (Eugene, OR: Wipf and Stock): 46–7.

Hadjittofi, Fotini. 2019. 'Town and Gown in the Orations of Choricius of Gaza', in Jan R. Stenger (ed.), *Learning Cities in Late Antiquity: The Local Dimension of Education* (London: Routledge): 145–63.

Hakim, Besim S. 2001. 'Julian of Ascalon's Treatise of Construction and Design Rules from Sixth-Century Palestine', *Journal of the Society of Architectural Historians*, 60 (1 March): 4–25.

Hammudi, Muhammad, Ashraf Salih Muhammad Sayyid and 'Adel-Hamid Jamal al-Furani. 2021. *Civilizational Studies in Islamic history: (Industry – Medicine – Life)* (Cairo: Arab Administrative Development Organization [Arabic]).

Hanfmann, George M. A. 1939. 'The Seasons in John of Gaza's Tabula Mundi', *Latomus*, T. 3, Fasc. 2 (Avril-Juin): 111–18.

Hanna, Nelly. 1997. *Making Big Money in 1600: The Life and Times of Isma'il Abu Taqiyya, Egyptian Merchant* (New York: Syracuse University Press).

Harding, G. Lankester. 1965. '*Inside Arabia Felix*', *Saudi Aramco World*, 16 (1): 24–7.

Harmless, William. 2004. *Desert Christians: An Introduction* to the *Literature* of *Early Monasticism* (Oxford: Oxford University Press).

Hart, George. 2005. *The Routledge Dictionary of Egyptian Gods and Goddesses* (London: Routledge).

Hasel, Michael G. 1998. *Domination and Resistance; Egyptian Military Activity in the Southern Levant ca. 1300–1185 B. C.* (Leiden: Brill).

Hattox, Ralph S. 1982. *Coffee Houses and Urban Society in the Mamluk and Ottoman Lands in the Fifteenth and Sixteenth Centuries* (Ann Arbor, MI: University Microfilms).

Hattox, Ralph S. 1985. *Coffee and Coffeehouses: The Origins of a Social Beverage in the Medieval Near East* (Seattle: University of Washington Press)

Hawari, Mahmoud. 2007. *Ayyubid Jerusalem (1187–1250): An Architectural and Archaeological Study* (Oxford: British Archaeological Reports).
Hawari, Mahmoud, Yusuf Natsheh and Nazmi Al-Ju'beh (eds.). 2010. *Pilgrimage, Sciences and Sufism: Islamic Art in the West Bank and Gaza* (Ramallah: Ministry of Culture and Museum with No Frontiers).
Healey, John F. 2001. *The Religion of the Nabataeans: A Conspectus* (Leiden: Brill).
Hendy, Michael F. 2008. *Studies in the Byzantine Monetary Economy c. 300–1450* (Cambridge: Cambridge University Press).
Herodotus. 1836. *History*, Vol. 1, Book II, translated by William Beloe (New York: Harper & Brothers).
Herodotus. 1841. *Egypt of Herodotus*, with notes by John Kenrick (London: B. Fellowes).
Herodotus. 1858. *The Histories* (Book I to Book IX), translated by George Rawlinson, edited by E. H. Blakeney (London: J. M. Dent & Sons). https://archive.org/stream/herodotus00herouoft/herodotus00herouoft_djvu.txt (accessed 20 November 2025).
Herodotus. 1904. *The History of Herodotus*, Vol. III. Translated by George Campbell Macaulay (London: Macmillan and Company)..
Herodotus. (5c BC) 1920. *The Histories*. Translation by A. D. Godley (ed.), Ιστορίαι (Ηροδότου) (Cambridge, MA: Harvard University Press).
Hevelone-Harper, Jennifer L. 2005. *Disciples of the Desert: Monks, Laity, and Spiritual Authority in Sixth-Century Gaza* (Baltimore, MD: The Johns Hopkins University Press).
Heyd, Uriel. 1942. *Dhahir al-Umar, Ruler of the Galilee in the 18th Century* (Jerusalem: Rubin. Mass) [Hebrew].
Hezser, Catherine. 1997. *The Social Structure of the Rabbinic Movement in Roman Palestine* (Tübingen: Mohr Siebeck).
Hidary, Richard. 2017. *Rabbis and Classical Rhetoric: Sophistic Education and Oratory in the Talmud and Mishna* (Cambridge: Cambridge University Press).
Hildebrandt, Berit. 2017. *Silk: Trade and Exchange Along the Silk Roads Between Rome and China in Antiquity* (Barnsley: Oxbow Books).
Hill, Donald. 1984. *A History of Engineering in Classical and Medieval Times* (London: Routledge).
Hill, George F. 1914. 'Catalogue of the Greek Coiuns of Palestine (Galilee, Samaria and Judaea)'. https://www.forumancientcoins.com/numiswiki/BMC/BMC_Palestine.pdf?srsltid=AfmBOop98yqzX7PFoW9XTzTlLGvZlK Nna0lpIeLvgCnglEOmozuDmWvn (accessed 23 January 2026).
Hirschfeld, Yizhar. 2004. 'The Monasteries of Gaza: An Archaeological Review', in Brouria Bitton-Ashkelony and Aryeh Kofsky (eds.), *Christian Gaza in Late Antiquity* (Leiden: Brill): 67–9.
Hodges, Richard. 1983. *Mohammed, Charlemagne, and the Origins of Europe* (New York: Ithaca).
Hölbl, Günther. 2001. *A History of the Ptolemaic Empire* (London: Routledge).
Hollander, David B. 2007. *Money in the Late Roman Republic* (Leiden: Brill).
Hollis, Susan Tower. 2019. *Five Egyptian Goddesses: Their Possible Beginnings, Actions, and Relationships in the Third Millennium BCE.* (London: Bloomsbury Academic).
Houdaille, Clémence. 2018. 'Isaïe de Gaza'. *La Croix*. https://www.la-croix.comAbonnes/Isaie-Gaza-2018-03-23-1700925792 (accessed 20 November 2025).
Hourani, Albert. 1968. 'Ottoman Reform and the Politics of Notables', in William R. Polk and Richard L. Chambers (eds), *Beginnings of Modernization in the Middle East* (Chicago: University of Chicago Press): 41–68.

Howell, Jeremy. 2010. 'Frankincense: Could It Be a Cure for Cancer?', *BBC World News*, 9 February. http://news.bbc.co.uk/1/hi/world/middle_east/8505251.stm (accessed 20 November 2025).
Hoyland, Robert G. 2015. 'The Earliest Attestation of the Dhimma of God and His Messenger and the Rediscovery of the P. Nessana', in Asad Q. Ahmed, Behnam Sadeghi, Robert G. Hoyland and Adam Silverstein (eds), *Islamic Cultures, Islamic Contexts* (Leiden: Brill): 51–71.
Humbert, Jean-Baptiste. 2000. *Gaza Méditerranéenne: Histoire et archéologieen Palestine* (Paris: Editions Errance).
Hütteroth, Wolf-Dieter, and Kamal Abdulfattah. 1977. *Historical Geography of Palestine, Transjordan and Southern Syria in the Late 16th Century* (Erlanger: Vorstand der Fränkischen Geographischen Gesellschaft).
Ibn al-Ukhuwah. 1976. *Kitab Ma'alim al-Qurba fi Ahkam al-Hisba* [Guide for the Enforcement of the Rules of Accounting] (Cairo: Al-Hai'a al-Misriyya).
Ibn Battuta. 2005. *Travels in Asia and Africa 1325–1354*, translated and edited by H. A. R. Gibb (New Delhi: Asian Educational Services).
Ibn Battuta (Abu 'Abdullah Muhammad Al-Tanji). 2024. *A Masterpiece for the Observer of the Curiosities of Cities and the Marvels of Travel*, Part One (Alexandria: Hindawi [Arabic]).
Irby, Charles Leonard and J. Mangles, 1823. *Travels in Egypt and Nubia, Syria, and Asia Minor; During the Years 1817 & 1818.* (London: Printed for Private Distribution by T. White & Co).
Irving, Sarah. 2011. *Palestine* (The Vale, Chalfont St. Peter: Bradt Travel Guides).
Isaac, Benjamin. 2003. 'The Eastern Frontier', in Averil Cameron and Peter Garnsey (eds.), *The Cambridge Ancient History*, Vol. XIII: *The Late Empire A.D. 337–425* (Cambridge: Cambridge University Press): 437–60.
Issawi, Charles. 2006. *An Economic History of the Middle East and North Africa*, reprint edition (London: Routledge).
Israel Antiquities Authority. 2014. Excavators and Excavations Permit for Year 2014, Survey Permits # G-67 and # G-69. https://www.antiquities.org.il/m_digs_eng.aspx?shana=2014 (accessed 20 November 2025).
Jerome, Saint. 1913. *'Vita Sancti Hilarionis', 25, in Patrologia Latina*, XXIII, col. 41. http://www.documentacatholicaomnia.eu/02m/0347-0420,_Hieronymus,_Vita_Sancti_Hilarionis,_MLT.pdf (accessed 20 November 2025).
Jacoby, David. 1992. 'Silk in Western Byzantium Before the Fourth Crusade', *Byzantinische Zeitschrift*, 85 (1–2): 452–500.
Jacoby, David. 1997. *Trade, Commodities and Shipping in the Medieval Mediterranean* (London: Routledge).
Johnson, A. C. and L. C. West 1949. *Byzantine Egypt: Economic Studies* (Princeton: Princeton University Press).
Johnson, Penny. 2014. 'Idylls of Jerusalem', review of Issa Boullata, Bells of Memory: A Palestinian Boyhood in Jerusalem, *Jerusalem Quarterly*, 60: 31–5.
Jones, A. H. M. 1970. 'Asian Trade in Antiquity', in D. S. Richards (ed.), *Islam and the Trade of Asia: A Colloquium* (Philadelphia, PA: University of Pennsylvania): 1–10.
Jones, Horace Leonard (ed.) and John Robert Sitlington Sterrett (trans.) 1917 (1961). *The Geography of Strabo*, 8 Vols, Loeb Classical Library, 49, 50, 182, 196, 211, 223, 241, 267 (London: William Heinemann).

Jones, Michael Rice. 2007. 'Oxhide Ingots, Copper Production, and the Mediterranean Trade in Copper and Other Metals in the Bronze Age', Metadata. https://oaktrust.library.tamu.edu/handle/1969.1/5957 (accessed 18 November 2025).

Joudah, Ahmad Hasan. 1987. *Revolt in Palestine in the Eighteenth Century: The Era of Shaykh Zahir Al-ʿUmar* (Princeton, NJ: Kingston Press).

Joudah, Ahmad Hasan. 2015. 'Zahir al-ʿUmar and the First Autonomous Regime in Ottoman Palestine (1744–1775)', *Jerusalem Quarterly* (63–4): 72–86.

Josephus, Flavius. 1930. *Jewish Antiquities* (iv.vii.§1). Translated by H. St. J. Thackeray. (Cambridge, MA: Harvard University Press).

Josephus, Flavius. 2004. *Antiquities of the Jews* (Boston: Digireads.com Publishing).

Josephus, Flavius. 2006. *Jewish Antiquities* (London: Woodsworth Classics).

Jung, Dinah. 2011. *An Ethnography of Fragrance: The Perfumery Arts of 'Adan/Laḥj: 84* (Leiden: Brill).

Kabha, Mustafa and Nahum Karlinsky. 2021. *The Lost Orchard: The Palestinian-Arab Citrus Industry, 1850–1950* (Syracuse, NY: Syracuse University Press).

Kamel, Lorenzo. 2014. 'The Impact of "Biblical Orientalism" in Late Nineteenth and Early Twentieth Century Palestine', *New Middle Eastern Studies*, 4: 1–5.

Kamel, Lorenzo. 2015. *Imperial Perceptions of Palestine: British Influence and Power in Late Ottoman Times* (London: I. B. Tauris).

Kark, Ruth. 1990. *Jaffa: A City in Evolution* (Jerusalem: Yad Yitzhak Ben-Zvi).

Karkov, Catherine E. (ed.). 2013. *The Archaeology of Anglo-Saxon England: Basic Readings* (London: Routledge).

Karmi, Ghada. 2004. *In Search of Fatima: A Palestinian Story*, new edition (London: Verso Books).

Kassinger, Ruth G. 2003. *Dyes: From Sea Snails to Synthetics* (Minneapolis, MN: Twenty First Century Books).

Khalilieh, Hassan Salih. 2006. *Admiralty and Maritime Laws in the Mediterranean Sea (ca. 800–1050): The KitābAkriyat Al-Sufun Vis-a-vis the Nomos Rhodion Nautikos* (Leiden: Brill).

Khoury, Amir H. 2010. *The Intellectual Property and You Series* (Arlington, VA: US Patent & Trademark Office).

Khusrau, Nasir. 1888. *Diary of a Journey Through Syria and Palestine*, Vol. IV, translated from Persian and annotated by Guy Le Strange (London: Palestine Pilgrims' Text Society; first published 1047).

Killion, Ulric. 2006. *A Modern Chinese Journey to the West: Economic Globalisation and Dualism* (New York: Nova Science Publishers).

Kimmerling, Baruch and Joel S. Migdal. 2003. *The Palestinian People: A History* (Cambridge, MA: Harvard University Press).

Kimberling, Charley. 2021. *Through the History of Monks and Wine: How Have Monks Cultivated and Developed Wine Culture: The Relationship Between Monks and Wine* (Independently published).

Kingsley, Sean A. 2003. 'Late Antique Trade: Research Methodologies and Field Practices', in Luke A. Lavan and William Bowden (eds.), *Theory and Practice in Late Antique Archaeology* (Leiden and Boston: Brill): 113–38.

Kingsley, Sean A. 2004. *Shipwreck Archaeology of the Holy Land: Processes and Parameters* (London: Bloomsbury).

Kingsley, Sean A. and Michael Decker. 2015a. 'New Rome, New Theories of Inter-Regional Exchange: An Introduction to the East Mediterranean Economy in Late Antiquity', in Sean A. Kingsley and Michael Decker (eds.), *Economy and Exchange in the East Mediterranean During Late Antiquity* (Oxford: Oxbow Books): 1-27.

Kingsley, Sean A. and Michael Decker. 2015b. '*The Economic Impact of the Palestinian Wine Trade in Late Antiquity*', in Sean A. Kingsley and Michael Decker (eds.), *Economy and Exchange in the East Mediterranean During Late Antiquity* (Oxford: Oxbow Books): 44-68.

Klein, Menachem. 2014a. *Lives in Common: Arabs and Jews in Jerusalem, Jaffa and Hebron* (Oxford: Oxford University Press).

Klein, Menachem. 2014b. 'Arab Jew in Palestine', *Israel Studies*, 19 (3): 134-53.

Kletter, Raz, Irit Ziffer and Wolfgang Zwickel. 2010. 'Yavneh I: The Excavation of the "Temple Hill" Repository Pit and the Cult Stands', *Orbis Biblicus et Orientalis*, Series Archaeologica (OBOSA), Book 30 (Switzerland: Academic Press and Göttingen: Vandenhoeck & Ruprecht).

Klimscha, Florian. 2011. 'Long-Range Contacts in the Late Chalcolithic of the Southern Levant. Excavations at Tall Hujayrat al-Ghuzlan and Tall al-Magass Near Aqaba, Jordan', in Jana Mynářová (ed.), *Egypt and the Near East-the Crossroads. Proceedings of an International Conference on the Relations of Egypt and the Near East in the Bronze Ages* (Berlin: Topoi, Freie Universität Berlin and Humboldt-Universität zu Berlin): 177-210.

Kloner, Amos. 1999. 'The City of Eleutheropolis', in *The Madaba Map Centenary 1897-1997*, Piccirillo Michele and Eugenio Alliat (eds.), *Travelling Through the Byzantine Umayyad Period* (Collection Maior 40) (Jerusalem: Studium Biblicum Franciscanum): 244-6.

Komar, Paulina. 2021. *Eastern Wines on Western Tables: Consumption, Trade and Economy in Ancient Italy* (Leiden: Brill).

Kopf, L. 1956. 'The Zoological Chapter of the Kitab al-Imta' wal-Mu'anasa of Abu Hayyan al-Tauhidi (10th Century)', *Osiris*, 12: 390–466.

Korjenkov, A. M., P. Fabian, and P. Becker, 1996. 'Evidence for 4th and 7th Century AD Earthquakes, Avdat Ruins (Israel): Seismic and Historical Implications', *Annual Meeting of the Israel Geological Society*, Eilat, March 18–21, 1996: 52.

Kowalewska, Arleta. 2021. *Bathhouses in Iudaea, Syria-Palaestina and Provincia Arabia from Herod the Great to the Umayyads* (Oxford: Oxbow).

Krämer, Gudrun. 2008. *A History of Palestine: From the Ottoman Conquest to the Founding of the State of Israel* (Princeton, NJ: Princeton University Press).

Kruk, Remke. 2008. 'Zarafa: Encounters with the Giraffe, from Paris to the Medieval Islamic World', in Beatrice Gruendler and Michael Cooperson (eds.), *Classical Arabic Humanities in Their Own Terms: Festschrift for Wolfhart Heinrichs on His 65th Birthday* (Leiden: Brill): 568-92.

Kucukdogan, Bilge. 2021. Current Excavations at Çatalhöyük, UNESCO World Heritage site. https://www.catalhoyuk.com (accessed 20 November 2025).

Kudlien, Fridolf. 1970. 'Alexander of Tralles', in *Dictionary of Scientific Biography*, Vol. 1. (New York: Charles Scribner's Sons).

Kushner, David (ed.). 1986 [2023]. *Palestine in the Late Ottoman Period: Political, Social and Economic Transformation* (Jerusalem: Yad Izhak Ben-Zvi Press).

Ladaniya, Milind S. 2008. *Citrus Fruit: Biology, Technology and Evaluation* (Atlanta: Elsevier Inc.).

Laden, Jonathan. 2021. 'Byzantine Tombstone Discovered in Negev', *Bible History Daily*, 11 January. https://www.biblicalarchaeology.org/daily/ancient-cultures/ancient-near-eastern-world/byzantine-tombstone-discovered-in-negev (accessed 20 November 2025).

La Gerarchia Cattolica. 2013. *Annuario Pontificio* (Rome: Libreria Editrice Vaticana).

Lamm, Carl Johan. 1941. *Oriental Glass of Mediaeval Date Found in Sweden and the Early History of Lustre Painting* (Kungl. Vitterhets historie och antikvitets akademiens handlingar, del 50:1) (Stockholm: Wahlström & Widstrand).

Langslow, D. R. 2006. *The Latin Alexander Trallianus: The Text and Transmission of a Late Latin Medical Book* (London: Society for the Promotion of Roman Studies).

Lapin, Hayim. 2001. *Economy, Geography, and Provincial History in Later Roman Palestine* (Tübingen: Mohr Siebeck).

Lawson, Russell M. 2004. *Science in the Ancient World: An Encyclopedia* (Santa Barbara, CA: ABC-CLIO).

LeBor, Adan. 2007. *City of Oranges: An Intimate History of Arabs and Jews in Jaffa* (New York: W. W. Norton & Company).

Lefebvre, Henri. 2011. *The Production of Space* (Hoboken, NJ: Wiley-Blackwell).

Leiwo, Martti. 1989. 'Philostratus of Ascalon, His Bank, His Connections and Naples in c. 130–90 B.C', *Athenaeum* (Pavia, Italy), 67 (January): 575–84.

Lemche, Niels Peter. 1998. *The Israelites in History and Tradition* (Westminster: John Knox Press).

Lepinski, Nadav. n.d. *'Tell Maresha'*, in Sefi Ben-Yosef (ed.), Israel Guide – Judaea (A useful encyclopedia for the knowledge of the country), Vol. 9 (Jerusalem: Keter Publishing House [in Hebrew]).

Le Strange, Guy. 1886. *A Description of Syria Including Palestine by Mukaddasi* (London: Committee of the Palestine Exploration Fund).

Le Strange, Guy. 1890. *Palestine Under the Moslems: A Description of Syria and the Holy Land from A.D. 650 to 1500* (London: Committee of the Palestine Exploration Fund).

Le Strange, Guy. 2011 [1905]. *The Lands of the Eastern Caliphate: Mesopotamia, Persia, and Central Asia from the Moslem Conquest to the Time of Timur* (New York: Cosimo Classics).

Le Strange, Guy. 2014. *Collected Works of Guy Le Strange: Medieval Islamic World*, Vol. 1 (London: I. B. Tauris).

Lev, Yaacov. 2006. 'Palestine', in Josef W. Meri (ed.), *Medieval Islamic Civilisation: An Encyclopedia*, Vol. 2 (London: Routledge): 590–2.

Levanoni, Amalia. 2021. *A Turning Point in Mamluk History: The Third Reign of Al-Nasir Muḥammad Ibn Qalawun (1310–1341)* (Leiden: Brill).

Levin, Yigal. 2020. 'The Religion of Idumea and Its Relationship to Early Judaism', *Religions*, 11 (10): 487.

Levine, Lee I. 1975. *Caesarea Under Roman Rule* (Leiden: Brill).

LeVine, Mark. 2005. *Overthrowing Geography: Jaffa, Tel Aviv, and the Struggle for Palestine, 1880–1948* (Berkely, CA: University of California Press).

Levy-Rubin, Milka. 2000. 'New Evidence Relating to the Process of Islamization in Palestine in the Early Muslim Period: The Case of Samaria', *Journal of the Economic and Social History of the Orient*, 43 (3): 257–76.

Levy, T., R. Adams and M. Najjar. 2002. 'Early Bronze Age Metallurgy: A Newly Discovered Copper Manufactory in Southern Jordan', *Antiquity*, 76 (June). https://levlab.ucsd.edu/resources/ELRAP-Publications/Ant0760425.pdf (accessed 20 November 2025).

Lewandowsky, Elizabeth. 2011. *The Complete Costume Dictionary* (Lanham, MD: Scarecrow Press).

Library of Congress. 1940. *Galilee Trip. Nazareth, the Arab Cigarette & Tobacco Co. Ltd. 'Tatli-Sert' Cigarette Factory. Group of Women Separating Tobacco Leaves for Drying.* Photographer's logbook: Matson Registers, Vol. 2, 1940-1946, 9-11 July. https://www.loc.gov/item/2019711477 (accessed 20 November 2025).

Lieberman, S. 1970-1971. 'A Few Words on the Book by Julian the Architect of Ascalon', *The Laws of the Palestine and Its Customs. Tarbiz*, 40 (Jerusalem [Hebrew]): 409-17.

Liu, Li, Maureece J. Levin, Florian Klimscha and Danny Rosenberg. 2022. 'The Earliest Cotton Fibers and Pan-regional Contacts in the Near East', *Research Topic Frontiers in the Study of Ancient Plant Remains*, 13. https://www.frontiersin.org/journals/plant-science/articles/10.3389/fpls.2022.1045554/full (accessed 20 November 2025).

Liu, Xinru. 1998. *Silk and Religion: An Exploration of Material Life and the Thought of People, AD 600-1200* (India: Oxford University Press),

Live Science. 2019. Customs Letter About a Long-Lost Suitcase Leads to Artifacts from Desert with Early 'Jesus' Painting, 19 February. http://innovatorscorner.blogspot.com/2019/02/customs-letter-about-long-lost-suitcase.html (accessed 20 November 2025).

Lucas, Catherine. 2003. *Palestine, la dernièrecolonie?* (Berchem: EPO).

Luz, Nimrod. 1997. 'The Construction of an Islamic City in Palestine. The Case of Umayyad al-Ramla', *Journal of the Royal Asiatic Society*, 7 (April) (1): 27-54.

Luz, Nimrod. 2014. *The Mamluk City in the Middle East: History, Culture and Urban Landscape* (Cambridge: Cambridge University Press).

Maeir, Aren M., Itzhaq Shai and Liora Kolska Horwitz. 2011. '"Like a Lion in Cover": A Cylinder Seal from Early Bronze Age III Tell Eṣ-Ṣafi/Gath, Israel', *Israel Exploration Journal*, 61 (1): 12-31.

Magness, Jodi. 2003. *The Archaeology of the Early Islamic Settlement in Palestine* (Winona Lake, IN: Eisenbrauns).

Maloney, George A. 1997. *Gold, Frankincense, and Myrrh: An Introduction to Eastern Christian Spirituality* (New York: Crossroads Publishing Company).

Mango, Marlia Mundell (ed.) 2016. Byzantine Trade, 4th-12th Centuries The Archaeology of Local, Regional and International Exchange. Papers of the Thirty-eighth Spring Symposium of Byzantine Studies, St John's College, University of Oxford, March 2004 (London: Routledge).

Manimanis, Vassilios N., Efstratios Theodosiou1 and Milan S. Dimitrijevic. 2012. 'The Geographers of the Early Byzantine Period', *European Journal of Science and Theology*, 8 (4): 23-40.

Mansour, Johnny. 2018. *Aqila Agha Al-Hassi: The Man and His Era* (Nablus: Al-Nasr Press [Arabic]).

Mariti, Giovanni. 1792. *Travels Through Cyprus, Syria, and Palestine; with a General History of the Levant.* Translated from the Italian, Vol. 1 (Dublin: P. Byrne).

Masalha, Nur. 1992. *Expulsion of the Palestinians: The Concept of 'Transfer' in Zionist Political Thought, 1882-1948* (Washington, DC: Institute for Palestine Studies).

Masalha, Nur. 2012. *The Palestine Nakba: Decolonising History, Narrating the Subaltern, Reclaiming Memory* (London: Zed Books).

Masalha, Nur. 2018. *Palestine: A Four Thousand Year History* (London: Zed Books).

Masalha, Nur. 2022. *Palestine Across Millennia: A History of Literacy, Learning and Educational Revolutions* (London: I.B. Tauris).

Masalha, Nur. 2023. 'Indigenous Versus Colonial-Settler Toponymy and the Struggle over the Cultural and Political Geography of Palestine: The Appropriation of Palestinian Place-Names by the Israeli State', in Sa'adi H. Ahmad and Nur Masalha (eds),

Decolonizing the Study of Palestine: Indigenous Perspectives and Settler Colonialism After Elia Zureik (London: I.B. Tauris): 37–71.
Matar, Nabil. 2013. 'Palestine', in Jennifer Speake (ed.), *Literature of Travel and Exploration: An Encyclopedia*, Vol. 1 (London: Routledge): 913–6.
Mayerson, Philip. 1985. 'The Wine and Vineyards of Gaza in the Byzantine Period,' *Bulletin of the American Schools of Oriental Research*, 257: 75–80.
Mayerson, Philip. 1992a. 'The Gaza "Wine" Jar (Gazition) and the "Lost" Ashkelon Jar (Askalônion)', *Israel Exploration Journal*, 42 (1/2): 76–80.
Mayerson, Philip. 1992b. 'The Island of Iotabê in the Byzantine Sources: A Reprise', *Bulletin of the American Schools of Oriental Research*, 287 (August): 1–4.
Mayerson, Philip. 1993. 'The Use of Ascalon Wine in the Medical Writers of the Fourth to the Seventh Centuries', *Israel Exploration Journal*, 43 (2/3): 169–73.
Mazzawi, Nisreen and Amalia Sa'ar. 2018. 'Hawakir of Nazareth: The History and Contemporary Face of a Cultural Ecological Institution', *International Journal of Middle East Studies*, 50 (3): 537–55.
McLaughlin, Raoul. 2010. *Rome and the Distant East: Trade Routes to the Ancient Lands of Arabia, India and China* (London: Continuum).
McLaughlin, Raoul. 2014. *The Roman Empire and the Indian Ocean: The Ancient World Economy & the Kingdoms of Africa, Arabia & India* (Barnsley: Pen & Sword).
McNeil, Ian (ed.). 1990. *An Encyclopedia of the History of Technology* (London: Routledge).
Meerzon, Yana and S. E. Wilmer (eds.). 2023. *The Palgrave Handbook of Theatre and Migration* (New York: Palgrave Macmillan).
Meinecke, Michael. 1980. *Islamic Cairo: Architectural Conservation and Urban Development of the Historic Centre: Proceedings of a Seminar*, 39 (London: Art and Archaeology Research Papers).
Mellaart, James, 1962. Excavations at Çatal Hüyük: First Preliminary Report, 1961, *Anatolian Studies*, 12: 41–65.
Mendelsohn Rood, Judith. 2020. *Sacred Law in the Holy City: The Khedival Challenge to the Ottomans as Seen from Jerusalem, 1829–1841* (Leiden: Brill).
Meyboom, P. G. P. 2016. *The Nile Mosaic of Palestrina: Early Evidence of Egyptian Religion in Italy* (Leiden: Brill).
Meyer, Martin A. 1907. *History of the City of Gaza: From the Earliest Times to the Present Day* (New York: Columbia University Press).
Meyer, Martin Abraham. 1907. *History of the City of Gaza: from the Earliest Times to the Present Day* (New York: Columbia University Press).
Meyers, Eric M. 1997. *The Oxford Encyclopedia of Archaeology in the Near East* (New York: Oxford University Press).
Mills, John. 1858. *Palaestina*, in Welsh (Llanidloes).
Mills, John. 1864. *Three Months' Residence at Nablus: And an Account of the Modern Samaritans*, 2 vols. (London: John Murray).
Mommsen, Theodor and William Purdie Dickson. 1886. *The Provinces of the Roman Empire from Caesar to Diocletian*, Vol. 1 (London: R. Bentley).
Montefiore, Adam. 2012. 'Wine Talks: Deep in the desert', *The Jerusalem Post*, 21 August. https://www.jpost.com/arts-and-culture/food-and-wine/wine-talk-deep-in-the-desert (accessed 20 November 2025).
Montefiore, Adam. 2025. 'Wine Tourism: Visit the Historic Wineries of the Galilee in Israel's North', *The Jerusalem Post*, 11 January. https://www.jpost.com/food-recipes/article-836804 (accessed 20 November 2025).

Monterescu, Daniel. 2015. *Jaffa Shared and Shattered: Contrived Coexistence in Israel/ Palestine* (Bloomington, IN: Indiana University Press).

Moors, Annelies. 1998. 'Wearing Gold', in Patricia Spyer (ed.), '*Border Fetishisms: Material Objects in Unstable Spaces* (London: Routledge): 208-23.

Moran, William L. (ed.). 1992. *The Amarna Letters* (Baltimore: Johns Hopkins University Press).

Muamar, Muhammad. 2022. *An Image of the City of Jaffa Through the newspaper Palestine* (Nablus: Dar al-Shamel [Arabic]).

Mukaddasi, Muḥammad ibn Aḥmad. 1886 [*c.* 985]. *Description of Syria, Including Palestine*. Translated by Guy Le Strange (London: Palestine Pilgrims' Text Society).

Muna, Farid and Grace C. Khoury. 2012. *The Palestinian Executive: Leadership Under Challenging Conditions* (London: Routledge).

Murphy-O'Connor, Jerome. 2008. *The Holy Land: An Oxford Archaeological Guide from Earliest Times to 1700* (New York: Oxford University Press).

Murphy-O'Connor, Jerome. 2010. *Keys to Second Corinthians: Revisiting the Major Issues* (Oxford: Oxford: Oxford University Press).

Najm, Yusuf. 1983. *Kunuz al-Quds* (Milano: Sagdos).

Nashif, Khaled. 2009. *Olive Presses in Palestine* (Irbid: Yarmouk University [Arabic]).

Nasrallah, Ibrahim. 2015. *The Lanterns of the King of Galilee: A Novel of 18th Century Palestine* (Cairo: The American University in Cairo Press).

Nassar, Hala Khamis. 2023. 'Chronicles of Refugee Foretold', in Meerzon Yana and S. E. Wilmer (eds.), *The Palgrave Handbook of Theatre and Migration* (London: Palgrave Macmillan): 487-97.

National Geographic. 2016. 'Petra Lost and Found'. 2 January. https://www.nationalgeographic.com/history/history-magazine/article/petra (accessed 20 November 2025).

Natsheh, Yusuf. 2010a. 'Desert Monasticism', in Mahmoud Hawari, Yusuf Natsheh and Nazmi Al-Ju'beh (eds.), *Pilgrimage, Sciences and Sufism: Islamic Art in the West Bank and Gaza* (Vienna: Museum with No Frontiers).

Natsheh, Yusuf. 2010b. 'Jerusalem as Centre for Religious Study and Knowledge', in Mahmoud Hawari, Yusuf Natsheh and Nazmi Al-Ju'beh (eds), *Pilgrimage, Sciences and Sufism: Islamic Art in the West Bank and Gaza* (Vienna: Museum with No Frontiers).

Natsheh, Yusuf. 2010c. 'The Daily Life of a Student in a Madrasa', in Mahmoud Hawari, Yusuf Natsheh and Nazmi Al-Ju'beh (eds), *Pilgrimage, Sciences and Sufism: Islamic Art in the West Bank and Gaza* (Vienna: Museum with No Frontiers).

Natsheh, Yusuf. 2016. 'Muslim Women Patrons in Jerusalem', in Barbara Drake Boehm and Melanie Holcomb (eds.), *Jerusalem: 1000–1400: Every People Under Heaven* (New York: Metropolitan Museum of Art): 242–70.

Negev, Avraham. 1988. 'The *Architecture of Mampsis'*, *Qedem*: vols. 26–7.

Negev, Avraham. 1991.'The Temple of Obodas: Excavations at Oboda in July 1989 Avraham Negev', *Israel Exploration Journal*, 41 (1-3): 62-80.

Negev, Avraham and Shimon Gibson (eds). 2001a. 'Edom: Edomites', in *Archaeological Encyclopedia of the Holy Land* (New York and London: Continuum): 149-50.

Negev, Avraham and Shimon Gibson (eds). 2001b. 'Nessana; Auja el-Hafir', in *Archaeological Encyclopedia of the Holy Land* (London: Continuum): 367–8.

Negev, Avraham and Shimon Gibson. 2005. *Archaeological Encycopedia of the Holy Land* (London: Continuum International Publishing Group).

Neuwirth, Angelika, Nicolai Sinai and Michael Marx. 2009. *The Qur'an in Context: Historical and Literary Investigations into the Qur'ānic Milieu* (Leiden: Brill).

Nicholson, Oliver (ed.). 2018. *The Oxford Dictionary of Late Antiquity*, Vol. 2 (Oxford: Oxford University Press).

Nicolle, David. 1996. *Medieval Warfare Source Book: Christian Europe and Its Neighbours* (Leicester: Brockhampton Press).

Niksic, Orhan, Nur Nasser Eddin and Massimiliano Cali. 2014. *Area C and the Future of the Palestinian Economy* (Washington, DC: World Bank Publications).

Nuseibeh, Hazem Zaki. 2009. *Jerusalemites: A Living Memory* (Limassol: Rimal Publications).

Ochsenwald, William and Sydney Nettleton Fisher. 2004. *The Middle East: A History* (New York: McGraw-Hill).

Ornit, Ilan and Michael Sebbane. 1989. 'Copper Metallurgy, Trade and Urbanization of Southern Canaan in the Laccolithic and Early Bronze Age 1', *British Archaeological Reports*, 1: 139-62.

Othman, Enaya Hammad. 2016. *Negotiating Palestinian Womanhood: Encounter Between Palestinian Women and American Missionaries, 1880s–1940s* (Lanham, MD: Lexington Books).

Owen-Crocker, Gale R. 2004. *Dress in Anglo-Saxon England* (Martlesham: Boydell & Brewer).

Page, Martin. 2008. *Growing Citrus: The Essential Gardener's Guide* (Portland, OR: Timber Press).

Pahlitzsch, Johannes. 2001. 'The Concern for Spiritual Salvation and Memoria in Islamic Public Endowments in Jerusalem (XII–XVI C) as Compared to the Concepts of Christendom', in Urbain Vermeulen and Jo van Steenbergen (eds.), *Egypt and Syria in the Fatimid, Ayyubid and Mamluk Eras III* (Leuven: Peeters): 329–44.

Pahlitzsch, Johannes. 2009. 'Christian Pious Foundations as an Element of Continuity Between Late Antiquity and Islam', in Frenkel Miriam and Yaacov Lev (eds.), *Charity and Giving in Monotheistic Religions* (New York: Walter de Gruyter): 125-52.

Palestine Exploration Fund. 1877. *Quarterly Statement for 1877* (London: Society's Office Palestine Exploration Fund).

Palestine Exploration Fund. 1888. The Survey of Western Palestine: A General Index to 1. The Memoirs, Vols. I.-III.; 2. The Special Papers; 3. The Jerusalem Volume; 4. The Flora and Fauna of Palestine; 5. The Geological Survey; and to The Arabic and English Name Lists, Vol. 1 (London). https://books.google.co.uk/books?id=H6A_AAAAYAAJ&printsec=frontcover&source=gbs_ge_summary_r&cad=0#v=onepage&q&f=false (accessed 21 November 2025).

Pappe, Ilan. 2011. *The Forgotten Palestinians: A History of the Palestinians in Israel* (New Haven, CN: Yale University Press).

Pappe, Ilan and Johnny Mansour. 2022. *Historical Dictionary of Palestine*, 22nd edition (Lanham, MD: Rowman & Littlefield Publishers).

Pascali, Luigi. 2017. 'Globalisation and Economic Development: A Lesson from History', 24 August. https://web.archive.org/web/20200801045951/https://ehsthelongrun.net/2017/08/24/globalisation-and-economic-development-a-lesson-from-history (accessed 21 November 2025).

Patel, Ismail, Adam Patel and 'Arwa Aburawa. 2016. *Huma's Travel Guide to Palestine* (London: Turath Publishing).

Patrich, Joseph. 2001a. *Studies in the Archaeology and History of Caesarea Maritima* (Leiden: Brill).

Patrich, Joseph. 2001b. 'Urban Space in Caesarea Maritima, Israel', in Thomas S. Burns and John W. Eadie (eds.), *Urban Centers and Rural Contexts in Late Antiquity* (East Lansing, MI: Michigan State University Press): 77–110.

Patrich, Joseph. 2011. *Studies in the Archaeology and History of Caesarea Maritima: Caput Judaeae, Metropolis Palaestinae* (Leiden and Boston: Brill).

Peacock, D. P. S. 1975. 'A Petrological Note on Certain Amphoras from Caesarea', The Pottery from the first session of Excavation in the Caesarea Hippodrome, *Bulletin of the American Schools of Oriental Research*, 218: 30.

Peacock, D. P. S and D. F. Williams. 1986. *Amphorae and the Roman Economy: An Introductory Guide* (London: Longman).

Peacock, Matthew. 2013. 'The "Romanization" of Petra', *Bulletin of the Institute of Classical Studies*, 120: 169–93.

Pearlstine, Elise Vernon. 2022. *Scent: A Natural History of Fragrance* (New Haven: CN: Yale University Press).

Peskowitz Miriam. 2004. 'Gender, Difference and Everyday Life: The Case of Weaving and Its Tools', in Douglas R. Edwards (ed.), *Religion and Society in Roman Palestine: Old Questions, New Approaches* (London: Routledge): 129–45.

Peteet, Julie. 2024. *The Hammam Through Time and Space* (Syracuse, NY: Syracuse University Press).

Petersen, Andrew. 2001. *A Gazetteer of Buildings in Muslim Palestine* (British Academy Monographs in Archaeology). Vol. 1 (Oxford: Oxford University Press).

Petersen, Andrew. 2002. *Dictionary of Islamic Architecture* (London: Routledge).

Petersen, Andrew. 2005. *The Towns of Palestine Under Muslim Rule, AD 600–1600* (Oxford: British Archaeological Reports).

Peterson, Andrew. 2006. 'Markets', in Josef W. Meri and Jere L. Bacharach (eds.), *Medieval Islamic Civilization: An Encyclopedia L–Z* (London: Routledge): 479–80.

Peterson, Andrew. 2010. 'Bridges in Medieval Palestine', in U. Vermeulen and K. D'Hulster (eds.), *Egypt and Syria in the Fatimid, Ayyubid and Mamluk Eras* VI (Leuven: Uitgeverij Peeters): 147–56.

Petersen, Andrew. 2021. *Ramla: City of Muslim Palestine, 715–1917: Studies in History, Archaeology and Architecture* (Oxford: Archaeopress Archaeology).

Petra National Foundation, Madain project. 2017. 'City of Petra: A Short History', Archived from the original on 4 December. https://madainproject.com/petra_(city) (accessed 21 November 2025).

Petry, Carl F. 2022. *The Mamluk Sultanate: A History* (Cambridge: Cambridge University Press).

Philipp, Thomas. 1992. *The Syrian Land in the 18th and 19th Century: The Common and the Specific in the Historical Experience* (Stuttgart: F. Steiner).

Philipp, Thomas. 2001. *Acre: The Rise and Fall of a Palestinian City, 1730–1831* (New York: Columbia University Press).

Philipp, Thomas. 2015. 'Ẓāhir al-'Umar al-Zaydānī', *Encyclopaedia of Islam*, 2nd edition, P. Bearman, Th. Bianquis, C. E. Bosworth, E. van Donzel and W. P. Heinrichs (eds), BrillOnline. https://referenceworks.brill.com/display/entries/EIEO/SIM-8083.xml (accessed 21 November 2025).

Philipp, Thomas and Birgit Schäbler (eds). 1998. *The Syrian Land: Processes of Integration and Fragmentation. Bilad Al-sham from the 18th to the 20th Century* (Wiesbaden: Franz Steiner Verlag).

Piéri, Dominique, 2005. *Le commerce du vin oriental à l'époque Byzantine* (Beirut: Bibliothèque d'Archéologie et d'Histoire. InstitutFrançais du Proche Orient).

Pinault, D. 1998. 'Sinbad', in Julie Scott Meisami and Pual Starkey (eds), *Encyclopedia of Arabic Literature*, Vol. 2 (London: Taylor & Francis): 721–3.

Pinch, Geraldine. 2003a. *Egyptian Mythology: A Guide to the Gods, Goddesses, and Traditions of Ancient Egypt* (New York: Oxford University Press).

Pinch, Geraldine. 2003b. *Votive Offerings to Hathor* (Oxford: Griffith Institute).

Planche, James R. 2013. *An Illustrated Dictionary of Historic Costume* (New York: Dover Publications).

Pococke, Richard. 1743-1745. *A Description of the East, and Some Other Countries* (London: W. Bowyer).

Pomerantz, Maurice A. and ʿAram Shahin (eds). 2015. *The Heritage of Arabo-Islamic Learning: Studies Presented to Wadad Kadi* (Leiden: Brill).

Porphyry of Gaza. *Oxford Dictionary of Byzantium*. https://www.oxfordreference.com/display/10.1093/acref/9780195046526.001.0001/acref-9780195046526-e-4423 (accessed 21 November 2025).

Power, Timothy. 2012. *The Red Sea from Byzantium to the Caliphate: AD 500–1000* (Cairo: The American University of Cairo).

Preece, John E. and Paul E. Read. 2005. *The Biology of Horticulture: An Introductory Textbook* (Hoboken, NJ: John Wiley & Sons).

Procopius. 1999 [1888]. *Of the Buildings of Justinian*. Translated by Aubrey Stewart and Annotated by C. W. Wilson and Professor Hayter Lewis (London: Palestine Pilgrims' Text Society and Adegi Graphics LLC).

Prokopios (Procopius). 1940. *On Buildings* (Cambridge, MA: Harvard University Press).

Prokopios (Procopius). 2005. *History of the Wars*, bks 1 and 2 (of 8) (Salt Lake City, UT: Project Gutenberg eBook; first published *c.* 560). http://www.gutenberg.org/files/16764/16764-h/16764-h.htm (accessed 18 November 2025).

Prokopios (Procopius). 2014. *The Wars of Justinian* (Cambridge, MA: Hackett Publishing). 'Publisher's Note: Church Missionary Society Archive: Section IX: Middle East Missions'. n.d. Adam Matthew Publications. http://www.ampltd.co.uk/digital_guides/cms_section_ix_part_1/publishers-note.aspx (accessed 21 November 2025).

Procopius of Caesarea. 2022. *The Persian Wars a Historical Commentary*, translated by Geoffrey Greatrex (Cambridge: Cambridge University Press).

Pryor, John H. 2016. *Logistics of Warfare in the Age of the Crusades* (London: Routledge).

Quataert, Donald. 2002. *Ottoman Manufacturing in the Age of the Industrial Revolution* (Cambridge: Cambridge University Press).

Ramadan, Tareq. 2010a. 'The Standing Caliph Coins of Aylah Filastin', *Journal of the Oriental Numismatic Society*, 203 (Spring): 3–6.

Ramadan, Tareq. 2010b. 'An Umayyad Post-Reform Coin of Aylah, a Concise Commentary', *Journal of the Oriental Numismatic Society*, 205 (Autumn): 10–12.

Rast, Walter E. 1992. *Through the Ages in Palestinian Archaeology: An Introductory* (London: Continuum).

Ray, Himanshu Prabha and Jean-François Salles (eds.). 1996. *Tradition and Archaeology: Early Maritime Contacts in the Indian Ocean* (New Delhi: Manohar Publishers).

Redford, Donald B. 1992. *Egypt, Canaan, and Israel in Ancient Times* (Princeton: Princeton University Press).

Remiisen, Sofie. 2015. *The End of Greek Athletics in Late Antiquity* (Cambridge: Cambridge University Press).

Renfrew, Colin. 2006. 'Inception of Agriculture and Rearing in the Middle East', *Human Palaeontology and Prehistory*, 5 (1): 395–404.

Retso, Jan. 2003. *The Arabs in Antiquity: Their History from the Assyrians to the Umayyads* (London: Routledge).
Reynolds, Paul. 2005. 'Levantine Amphorae from Cilicia to Gaza: A Typology and Analysis of Regional Production Trends from the 1st to 7th Centuries, LRCW I. Late Roman Coarse Wares, Cooking Wares and Amphorae in the Mediterranean: Archaeology and Archaeometry', *British Archaeological Reports International Series*, 1340: 563–612.
Rhode, H. 1979. The Administration and Population of the Sancak of Safad in the Sixteenth Century. PhD thesis. Columbia University, New York.
Richard, Suzanne. 1987. 'Archaeological Sources for the History of Palestine: The Early Bronze Age: The Rise and Collapse of Urbanism', *Near Eastern Archaeology*, 50 (1): 22–43.
Ring, Trudy, Noelle Watson and Paul Schellinger (eds.). 1996. *Middle East and Africa International Dictionary of Historic Places* (London: Routledge).
Ritter, Carol. 1866. *Comparative Geography of Palestine and the Sinaitic Peninsula* (New York: D. Appleton).
Robertson, Kristel and Jan A. Swanepoel. 2015. The Economics of Metrology. RESEARCH PAPER 6/2015. Department of Industry Science and Resources. https://www.industry.gov.au/publications/economics-metrology (accessed 21 November 2025).
Robinson, Daniel. 2022. *Israel & the Palestinian Territories (*Melbourne: Lonely Planet).
Robinson, Edward. 1841. *Biblical Researches in Palestine, Mount Sinai and Arabia Petraea: A Journal of Travels in the Year 1838* (London: J. Murray).
Robinson, Edward. 1865. *Physical Geography of the Holy Land* (Boston: Crocker & Brewster).
Robinson, Edward, Eli Smith and Others. 1841 [2023]. *Biblical Researches in Palestine and the Adjacent Regions: A Journal of Travels in the Years 1838 & 1852 by Edward Robinson, Eli Smith and Others*; Vol. 3 (London: Legare Street Press).
Robinson, Edward, Eli Smith and Others. 1860. *Biblical Researches in Palestine and Adjacent Regions: A Journal of Travel in the Years 1838 & 1852* (Boston: Crocker and Brewster).
Robinson, Edward Forbes. 1893. *The Early History of Coffee Houses in England: With Some Account of the First Use of Coffee and a Bibliography of the Subject* (London: K. Paul, Trench, Trübner).
Robinson, E. and E. Smith. 1856. *Biblical Researches in Palestine*, 1848–52, vol.2 (Boston: Crocker and Brewster).
Röhl, Constanze. 2010. Shivta, Architektur und Gesellschaft einer byzantinischen Siedlungim Negev (PhD thesis); [Shivta, Architecture and Society of a Byzantine settlement in the Negev]. Cologne, Germany: University of Cologne.
Romeny, Bas Ter Haar. 2007. 'Procopius of Gaza and His Library', in Hagit Amirav, |R. B. Ter Haar Romeny (eds.), *From Rome to Constantinople: Studies in Honour of Averil Cameron* (Leuven: Peeters): 173–90.
Rose, John. 2010. 'In Praise of the Sun: Zodiac Sun-Gods in Galilee Synagogues and the Palestinian Heritage', *Holy Land Studies*, 9 (1): 25–49.
Rosen-Ayalon, Myriam. 1998. 'Between Cairo and Damascus: Rural Life and Urban Economics in the Holy Land During the Ayyubid, Mamluk and Ottoman Periods', in Thomas Evan Levy (ed.), *Archaeology of Society in the Holy Land* (London: Continuum): 512–23.
Rosen-Ayalon, Myriam. 2006. *Islamic Art and Archaeology of Palestine* (Walnut Creek: CA: Left Coast Press).

Rosenberg, Danny. 2024. Tel Tsaf, a Middle Chalcolithic Site in the Jordan Valley: A Preliminary Report on the 2013-2022 Excavation Seasons, January. https://www.researchgate.net/publication/377414590_Tel_Tsaf_a_Middle_Chalcolithic_Site_in_the_Jordan_Valley_A_Preliminary_Report_on_the_2013-2022_Excavation_Seasons (accessed 21 November 2025).

Rosenblum, M. 1996. *Olives: The Life and Lore of A Noble Fruit* (New York: Macmillan).

Rosen, Steven A. 2019. 'Trade Through the Desert: A Long-Term Perspective on Goods, Animals, and Polities in the Negev', *Chungara Revista de Antropología Chile*, 51 (1): 71-84. https://www.scielo.cl/pdf/chungara/2019nahead/0717-7356-chungara-00401.pdf (accessed 15 November 2025).

Ross, Andrew. 2019. *Stone Men: The Palestinians Who Built Israel* (London: Verso Books).

Ross, Jon., Haskel J. Greenfield, Kent D. Fowler and Aren M. Maeir. 2020. 'In search of Early Bronze Age potters at Tell es-Safi/Gath: A New Perspective on Vessel Manufacture for Discriminating Chaines Operatoires', *Archaeological Review from Cambridge*, 35: 74-89. https://api.repository.cam.ac.uk/server/api/core/bitstreams/0abe673d-4670-4c3e-a040-333ebb81ccd8/content (accessed 14 November 2025).

Rougé, Jean (ed.). 1966. *Expositiototius mundi et gentium* (Paris, Éditions du Cerf).

Rozenblum, Serge-Allain. 2001. *Theodor Herzl* (Paris: Editions du Félin).

Runciman, Steven. 1987. *A History of the Crusades*, Vol. 3: *The Kingdom of Acre and the later Crusades* (London: Penguin).

Sadeq, Moain. 2015. 'Christian Topography of Byzantine Gaza', *International Journal of Humanities and Social Science*, 5 (12) (December): 47-54.

Safrai, Zeev. 1994. *The Economy of Roman Palestine* (London: Routledge).

Safrai, Zeev. 2003. *The Economy of Roman Palestine* (London: Routledge).

Saint Augustine. 2017. *The City of God*, translated by Marcus Dod (Digireads.com Publishing). https://files.romanroadsstatic.com/materials/romans/nicene-christianity/City%20of%20God.pdf (accessed 14 November 2025).

Salmon, Thomas. 1744. *Modern History, or, the Present State of All Nations: Describing Their Respective Situations, Persons, Habits, and Buildings, Manners, Laws and Customs ... Plants, Animals, and Minerals*, Volume 1 (London: T. Longman).

Sapir-Hen, Lidar and Erez Ben-Yosef. 2013. 'The Introduction of Domestic Camels to the Southern Levant: Evidence from the Aravah Valley' (Tel Aviv), *Journal of the Institute of Archaeology of Tel Aviv University*, 40 (2): 277-85.

Sartre, Maurice. 2005. *The Middle East Under Rome* (Cambridge, MA: Harvard University Press).

Sato, Tsugitaka. 2014. *Sugar in the Social Life of Medieval Islam* (Leiden: Brill).

Scarborough, John. 2005. *Oxford Dictionary of Byzantium* (Oxford: Oxford University Press).

Schaeublin, Emanuel. 2023. *Divine Money: Islam, Zakat, and Giving in Palestine* (Bloomington, IN: Indiana University Press).

Schäfer, Peter. 2003. *The History of the Jews in the Greco-Roman World: The Jews of Palestine from Alexander the Great to the Arab Conquest*. 2nd revised edition (London: Routledge).

Scheidel, Walter. 2019. *The Ancient Economy: Recent Approaches* (Edinburgh: Edinburgh University Press).

Schmid, Stephan G. and Michel Mouton. 2013. *Men on the Rocks: The Formation of Nabataean Petra* (Berlin: Logos Verlag).

Schmitz, Leonhard. 1870. '*Alitta*', in William Smith (ed.), *Dictionary* of *Greek* and *Roman Biography* and *Mythology*, Vol. 1 (Boston: Little, Brown and Company).

Schoff, Wilfred H. 2021. *The Periplus of the Erythraean Sea: Travel and Trade in the Indian Ocean by a Merchant of the First Century, with Expandable Map of The Periplus Maris Erythraei* (Delhi: Dev Publishers & Distributors).

Schölch, Alexander. 1992. 'Britain in Palestine, 1838-1882: The Roots of the Balfour Policy', *Journal of Palestine Studies*, 22 (1): 39-56.

Schölch, Alexander. 1993. *Palestine in Transformation, 1856-1882: Studies in Social, Economic, and Political Development* (Washington, DC: Institute for Palestine Studies).

Schurer, Emil. 2014. *The History of the Jewish People in the Age of Jesus Christ*, Vol. 2 (London: Bloomsbury).

Schuster, Ruth. 2021. 'Biggest Winemaking Facility in Entire Byzantine World Found in Central Israel', *Haaretz*, 11 October. https://www.haaretz.com/archaeology/2021-10-11/ty-article-magazine/biggest-winemaking-facility-in-entire-byzantine-world-found-in-central-israel/0000017f-f0a9-d497-a1ff-f2a9292b0000 (accessed 21 November 2025).

Schwartz, Glenn M., Hans H. Curvers, Sally S. Dunham, Barbara Stuart and Jill A. Weber. 2006. 'A Third-Millennium B.C. Elite Mortuary Complex at Umm El-Marra, Syria: 2002 and 2004 Excavations', *American Journal of Archaeology*, 110 (4): 603-41.

Scott, Michael. 2012. *Space and Society in the Greek and Roman Worlds* (Cambridge: Cambridge University Press).

Sears, Robert. 1849. A New and Complete History of The Holy Bible as Contained in the Old and New Testaments: From the Creation of the World to the Full Establishment of Christianity, Vols. 1-2 (New York).

Seeher, Jurgen. 2005. 'Ma'adi and Wadi Digla', in Kathryn A. Bard (ed.), *Encyclopedia of the Archaeology of Ancient Egypt* (London: Routledge).

Seetzen, U. J. 1854. *Ulrich Jasper Seetzen's Reisen durch Syrien, Palästina, Phönicien, die Transjordan-länder, Arabia Petraea und Unter-Aegypten*, Vol. 3 (Berlin: G. Reimer).

Segal, Arthur. 1988. *Town Planning and Architecture in Provincia Arabia: The Cities Along the Via Traiana Nova in the 1st-3rd centuries C.E.* (Oxford: BAR publishing).

Segal, Arthur. 2018. *Theatres in Roman Palestine and Provincia Arabia* (Leiden: Brill).

Segreteria di StatoVaticano. 2013. *Annuario Pontificio 2013* (Rome: Libreria Editrice Vaticana).

Seikaly, May. 2002. *Haifa: Transformation of an Arab Society 1918-1939* (London: I. B. Tauris).

Seikaly, May. 2002a. 'Haifa at the Crossroads: An Outpost of New World Order', in Leila T. Fawaz, C. A. Bayly with Robert Ilbert (eds.), *Modernity and Culture from the Mediterranean to the Indian Ocean* (New York: Colombia University Press): 96-111.

Sergeant, R. B. and Ronald Lewcock (eds.). 1983. *San'a: An Arabian Islamic City* (London: World of Islam Festival Trust).

Shaddel, Mehdy. 2017. Studia Onomastica Coranica: Al Raqim, Caput Nabataeae', *Journal of Semitic Studies*, 62 (2): 303-18.

Shahid, Irfan. 1984a. *Rome and the Arabs: A Prolegomenon to the Study of Byzantium and the Arabs* (Washington, DC: Dumbarton Oaks Research Library and Collection).

Shahid, Irfan. 1984b. *Byzantium and the Arabs in the Fourth Century* (Washington, DC: Dumbarton Oaks Research Library and Collection).

Shahid, Irfan. 1986. 'The Jund System in Bilad al-Sham: Its Origins', in M. A. Bakhit and M. Asfour (eds.), *Proceedings of the Fourth International Conference on the History of Bilad al-Sham: Bilad al-Sham During the Byzantine Period*, Vol. 2 (Amman: University of Jordan/Yarmouk University): 45-52.

Shahid, Irfan. 1989. *Byzantium and the Arabs in the Fifth Century* (Washington, DC: Dumbarton Oaks Research Library and Collection).
Shahid, Irfan. 1995. *Byzantium and the Arabs in the Sixth Century*, Vol. 1 (Washington, DC: Dumbarton Oaks Research Library and Collection).
Shahid, Irfan. 2006. *Byzantium and the Arabs in Late Antiquity*, Vol. 3 (Washington, DC: Dumbarton Oaks Research Library and Collection).
Shahid, Irfan. 2009. *Byzantium and the Arabs in the Sixth Century*, Vol. 2, Part 2 (Washington, DC: Dumbarton Oaks Research Library and Collection).
Shahid, Irfan. 2010. *Byzantium and the Arabs in the Sixth Century*, Vol. 2, Part 2 (Cambridge, MA: Harvard University Press and Dumbarton Oaks Research Library and Collection).
Shahin, Mariam. 2005. *Palestine: A Guide* (Northampton, MA: Interlink Books).
Sharkawi, M. 2018. Iron Screw Presses With Manual Activation of the 19th Century as an Object of Heritage, in the Context of the Palestinian Cultural Heritage'. Doctoral dissertation. Nancy: University of Lorraine.
Sharon, Moshe. 1997. *Corpus Inscriptionum Arabicarum Palaestinaem*, Vol. 1 (Leiden: Brill).
Sharon, Moshe. 1999. *Corpus Inscriptionum Arabicarum Palaestina*, Vol. 2 (Leiden: Brill).
Sharon, Moshe. 2013. *Corpus Inscriptionum Arabicarum Palaestina*, Vol. 5 (Leiden: Brill).
Shaw, Ian. 2002. *A Dictionary of Archaeology* (London: John Wiley & Sons).
Sidonius Apollinaris. 1936. *Poems and Letters*. With an English translation, introduction and notes by W. B. Anderson. Cambridge, MA: Harvard University Press.
Simaan, Juman. 2017. 'Olive Growing in Palestine: A Decolonial Ethnographic Study of Collective Daily-Forms-of-Resistance', *Journal of Occupational Science*, 24 (4): 510–23.
Simla, Basar. 2005. *Phytochemical Investigations on Boswellia Species* (Thesis). Universität Hamburg.
Simmons, Alan H. 2007. *The Neolithic Revolution in the Near East: Transforming the Human Landscape* (Tucson, AZ: University of Arizona Press).
Simmons, Gail. 2013. 'Hebron's Glass History', *Saudi Aramco World* (January/February): 5.
Singer, Amy. 2002. *Constructing Ottoman Beneficence: An Imperial Soup Kitchen in Jerusalem* (Albany: State University of New York Press).
Singh, Ram J. and Prem P. Jauhar (eds.). 2011. *Genetic Resources, Chromosome Engineering, and Crop Improvement*: Grain Legumes, Vol. I (Boca Raton, FL: CRC Press).
Sivan, Hagith. 2008. *Palestine in Late Antiquity* (Oxford: Oxford University Press).
Skeat, Walter William. 1882. *An Etymological Dictionary of the English Language* (Oxford: The Clarendon Press).
Smedley, Edward. 1845. *Encyclopaedia Metropolitana; or, Universal Dictionary of Knowledge* (London: J. J. Griffin).
Smith, Paul. 2010. Translation Introduction. *The Wine Poems of Abu Nuwas (Khamriyyat)*, Kindle Edition (London: New Humanity Books).
Smith, Richard L. 2008. *Premodern Trade in World History* (London: Routledge).
Smith, William (ed.). 1870. *Dictionary* of *Greek and Roman Biography and Mythology*, Vol. 1 (Boston: Little, Brown and Company).
Sogno, Cristiana, Bradley K. Storin and Edward J. Watts (eds). 2019. *Late Antique Letter Collections: A Critical Introduction and Reference Guide* (Oakland: University of California Press).

Solenhofen Archae. 2002. 'Ancient Egyptian Copper Slabbing Saws', 10 December. http://www.hallofmaat.com/unforbiddengeology/ancient-egyptian-copper-slabbing-saws (accessed 21 November 2025).

Sperber, Daniel. 1976. 'Objects of Trade Between Palestine and Egypt in Roman Times', *Journal of the Economic and Social History of the Orient*, 19 (2): 113–47.

Srouji Elias S. 2003. *Cyclamens from Galilee: Memoirs of a Physician from Nazareth* (New York: iUniverse).

Stark Carl Bernhard. 1852. *Gaza und die PhilistäischeKüste* [Gaza and the Philistine Coast] (Jena: Mauke).

Stenger, Jan R. (ed.). 2019. *Learning Cities in Late Antiquity: The Local Dimension of Education* (London: Routledge).

Stephan, Stephan Hanna. 1937. 'Evliya Tshelebi's Travels in Palestine, IV', *The Quarterly of the Department of Antiquities in Palestine*, 6: 84–97.

Stern, Sasha. 2012. *Calendars in Antiquity: Empires, States and Societies* (Oxford: Oxford University Press).

Stroumsa, Rachel. 2014.*'Greek and Arabic in Nessana'*, in Alexander T. Schubert and Petra M. Sijpesteijn (eds.), *Documents and the History of the Early Islamic World*, Vol. III (Leiden: Brill): 143–57.

Suburban Emergency Management Project. 2006. Nablus Soap: Cleaning Middle Eastern Ears for Centuries. Biot # 402, 20 September. https://web.archive.org/web/20080111095241/http://www.semp.us/publications/biot_reader.php?BiotID=402 (accessed 21 November 2025).

Su-il, Jeong. 2016. *The Silk Road Encyclopedia* (Honolulu: University of Hawai'i Press).

Sukenik, Naama, David Iliz, Zohar Amar Alexander Varvak, Orit Shamir and Erez Ben-Yosef. 2021. 'Early Evidence of Royal Purple Dyed Textile from Timna Valley (Israel)', *PLOS One*, 1: e0245897.

Taha, Hamdan. 2017. 'Palestine: A Fascinating History', *Palestine*, No. 232 (August): 6–11.

Taha, Hamdan. 2018. 'Ancient Schools in Palestine', *This Week in Palestine*, 246, October. https://www.comunicazionearezzo.com/wp-content/uploads/2014/07/Palestine-A-Fascinating-History.pdf. (accessed 26 January 2026); https://www.comunicazionearezzo.com/wp-content/uploads/2018/10/Ancient-Schools-in-Palestine.pdf (accessed 26 January 2026).

Taha, Hamdan. 2022. *On the Dialectical Relation Between Palestinians and the Olive Tree'*, Institute for Palestine Studies, 25 October. https://www.palestine-studies.org/ar/node/1653353?fbclid=IwAR1jeYWLkJwSv0QR-pvbakyLYOVuIVk3x5LyxDqo7ge7pX3GCFmU1K_6j4o (accessed 21 November 2025).

Taha, Hamdan and Gerrit van der Kooij. 2014. *Tell Balata Archaeological Park Guidebook* (Ramallah), published by Department of Antiquities and Cultural Heritage, the Palestinian Ministry of Tourism and Antiquity. http://unesdoc.unesco.org/images/0023/002319/231930e.pdf (accessed 21 November 2025).

Talgamm, Rina. 2004. 'The Ekphrasis Eikonos of Procopius of Gaza and the Depiction of Mythological Themes in Palestine and Arabia During the Fifth and Sixth Centuries', in B. Bitton-Ashkelony and A. Kofsky (eds.), *Christianity in Gaza in Late Antiquity* (Leiden: Brill): 209–34.

Talgam, R. and Z. Weiss, 2004. *The Mosaics o f the House o f Dionysos at Sepphoris*, excavated by E. M. Meyers, E. Netzer and C. L. Meyers. Qedem 44 (Jerusalem: Institute of Archaeology, the Hebrew University).

Tamari, Salim. 2003. 'The Vagabond Café and Jerusalem's Prince of Idleness', *Jerusalem Quarterly*, 19. https://www.palestine-studies.org/sites/default/files/jq-articles/19_Vagabond_3_0.pdf (accessed 21 November 2025).

Tamari, Salim. 2008. *Mountain Against the Sea: Essays in Palestinian Society and Culture* (Berkeley, CA: University of California Press).

Tamari, Salim and Issam Nassar (eds.). 2014. *The Storyteller of Jerusalem: The Life and Times of Wasif Jawhariyyeh, 1904-1948* (Northampton MA: Olive Branch Press).

Taxel, Itamar. 2013. 'The Olive Oil Economy of Byzantine and Early Islamic Palestine: Some Critical Notes', *Liber Annuus*, 63: 361-94.

Taylor, Isaac. 2005. *Words and Places or Etymological Illustrations of History, Ethnology and Geography* (Whitefish: Montana Publishing).

Taylor, Jane. 2001. *Petra and the Lost Kingdom of the Nabataeans* (London: I.B Tauris).

Tebes, Juan Manuel. 2008. 'el Negev y sus interacciones con Egipto, Asiria y elLevanteen la Edad de Hierro (1200-586 a.C.)' [*Core and Periphery in the Ancient World: The Negev and Its Interactions with Egypt, Assyria, and the Levant in the Iron Age (1200-586 BC)*], Society of Biblical Literature and Centro y periferiaenelmundoantiguo. https://repositorio.uca.edu.ar/handle/123456789/8014#:~:text=Centro%20y%20periferia%20en%20el,Tebes%2C%20Juan%20Manuel (accessed 26 January 2026).

Teixidor, Javier. 2015. *The Pagan God: Popular Religion in the Greco-Roman Near East* (Princeton, NJ: Princeton University Press).

Teller, Matthew. 2022. *Nine Quarters of Jerusalem: A New Biography of the Old City* (London: Profile Books).

Temin, Peter 2013. *The Roman Market Economy* (Princeton, NJ: Princeton University Press).

Terpstra, Taco. 2019. *Trade in the Ancient Mediterranean: Private Order and Public Institutions* (Princeton, NJ: Princeton University Press).

The Encyclopaedia of Islam. 1965. Vol. II, new edition (Leiden: Brill).

The Oxford English Dictionary. 1933 [1978]. 'Frankincense', Vol. IV: F–G. (Oxford: Oxford University Press): 512.

The Silk Road Encyclopedia. 2016 (Cambridge: University of Hawai'i Press).

Thompson, E. P. 1971. *The Moral Economy of the English Crowd in the Eighteenth Century* (Oxford: Oxford University Press).

Thompson, Thomas L. 2016. 'Ethnicity and a Regional History of Palestine', in Ingrid Hjelm and Thomas L. Thompson (eds), *History, Archaeology and the Bible Forty Years After 'Historicity': Changing Perspectives* 6 (London: Routledge): 159-73.

Thomson Corporation. 1993. *The Directory of U.S. Trademarks*, Vol. 5 (Stamford, CT: Thomson & Thomson).

Thomson, William M. 1859. *The Land and the Book: Or, Biblical Illustrations Drawn from the Manners and Customs, the Scenes and Scenery of the Holy Land*, Vol. 2 (New York: Harper & Brothers).

Timotheus. 1949. *Timotheus of Gaza on Animals*: Fragments of a Byzantine paraphrase of An Animal-Book of the 5th Century A.D., translated and edited by F. S. Bodenheimer and A. Rabinowitz (Paris: Academie Internationale D'histoire des Sciences).

Tokman, Aslı 2001. Negotiating Tradition, Modernity and Identity in Consumer Space: A Study of a Shopping Mall and Revived Coffeehouse. Master's thesis. Bilkent University.

Tortora, Phyllis G. and Ingrid Johnson. 2013. *The Fairchild Books Dictionary of Textiles* (New York: Fairchild Books).

Toussaint-Samat, Maguelonne. 2009. *A History of Food* (London: John Wiley & Sons).

Trigger, B. G., B. J. Kemp, D. O'Connor and A. B. Lloyd. 1983. *Ancient Egypt: A Social History* (Cambridge: Cambridge University Press).

Tristram, Henry Baker. 1884. *The Survey of Western Palestine: The Fauna and Flora of Palestine* (London: The Committee of the Palestine Exploration Fund).

Trombley, Frank R. 1995. *Hellenic Religion and Christianisation: c. 370–529*, Vol. 1, Part 1, second edition (Leiden: Brill).

Twede, Diana. 2002. 'Commercial Amphoras: The Earliest Consumer Packages? *Journal of Macromarketing*, 22 (1): 98–108.

UNESCO. 2005a. 'Incense Route – Desert Cities in the Negev', Incense Route – Desert Cities in the Negev – UNESCO World Heritage Centre. https://whc.unesco.org/en/list/1107 (accessed 21 November 2025).

UNESCO. 2005b. Israel National Commission for UNESCO 2005: Report on Activities 2004–2005. https://unesdoc.unesco.org/ark:/48223/pf0000159995 (accessed 21 November 2025).

UNESCO. 2024. 'Saint Hilarion Monastery/*Tell Umm Amer*', *UNESCO World Heritage Centre*. https://whc.unesco.org/en/list/1749 (accessed 21 November 2025).

United States Patent and Trademark Office, 2003. Official Gazette of the United States Patent and Trademark. https://www.uspto.gov/trademarks/trademark-updates-and-announcements/trademark-official-gazette-notices-2003 (accessed 21 November 2025).

Unwin, Tim. 2005. *Wine and the Vine: And the Historical Geography of Viticulture and the Wine Trade* (London: Routledge).

Usher, Abbot Payson. 2003. *A History of Mechanical Inventions*, revised edition. (New York: Dover Publications).

Vivian, Cassandra. 2008. *Western Desert of Egypt: An Explorer's Handbook* (Cairo: American University in Cairo Press).

Volney, C. – F. 1788 [2006]. *Travels Through Syria and Egypt, in the Years 1783, 1784, and 1785: Containing the Present Natural and Political State of Those Countries, Their Productions, Arts, Manufactures, and Commerce; with Observations on the Manners, Customs, and Government of the Turks and Arabs. Illustrated with Copper Plates*, Vol. 2 (Leiden: Brill).

von Hagen, V. W. 1957. *The Ancient Sun Kingdoms of the Americas* (Ohio: The World Publishing Company).

Vroom, Joanita. 2018. 'Gaza, Amphorae and Gaza Wine', in Oliver Nicholson (ed.), *The Oxford Dictionary of Late Antiquity*, Vol. 2 (Oxford: Oxford University Press): 648.

Wa'ari, Naila. 2023. *Palestine in the Books of Arab and Muslim Geographers and Travelers*, Vol.1 (Amman: Dar Ward al-Urduniyya Li-Nashr wa-Tawzi'a [Arabic]).

Wallop, Harry. 2018. 'Jaffa Cakes – Definitely Not Biscuits – Prepare to Take on Imitators', *The Daily Telegraph*, 6 May. https://www.telegraph.co.uk/finance/newsbysector/retailandconsumer/9249366/Jaffa-Cakes-definitely-not-biscuits-prepare-to-take-on-imitators.html (accessed 21 November 2025).

Walmsley, Alan. 1996. 'Byzantine Palestine and Arabia: Urban Prosperity in Late Antiquity,' in N. Christie, and S. T. Losseby, (eds.), *Towns in Transition: Urban Evolution in late Antiquity and the Early Middle Ages* (Aldershot: Scholar Press): 126–58.

Walmsley, Alan. 2000. 'Production, Exchange and Regional Trade in the Islamic East Mediterranean: Old Structures, New Systems,' in Inge Lyse Hansen and Chris Wickham (eds.), *The Long Eighth Century: Production, Distribution and Demand* (Leiden: Brill): 265–343.

Walter, Christopher. 1995. 'The Origins of the Cult of Saint George', *Revue des études byzantines*, 53 (1): 295–326.

Ward, Walter David. 2008. *From Provincia Arabia to Palaestinae Tertia: The Impact of Geography, Economy, and Religion on the Sedentary and Nomadic Communities in the Later Roman Province of Third Palestine*. PhD dissertation, UCLA.

Ward-Perkins, Bryan, 2008. 'Specialized Production and Exchange', in Averil Cameron, Bryan Ward-Perkins and Michael Whitby (eds.), *The Cambridge Ancient History: Late Antiquity: Empire and Successors, A.D. 425–600* (Cambridge: Cambridge University Press): 346–91.

Wari, Shahd. 2017. *Palestinian Berlin: Perceptions and Use of Public Space* (Berlin: LIT Verlag).

Warner, Nicholas. 2005a. *The Monuments of Historic Cairo: A Map and Descriptive catalogue*, 88 (Cairo: American University in Cairo Press).

Warner, Nicholas. 2005b. *The Monuments of Historic Cairo: A Map and Descriptive Catalogue*, 88 (Cairo: American University in Cairo Press).

Weber, Stefan. 2010. 'The Making of an Ottoman Harbour Town: Sidon/Saida from the Sixteenth to the Eighteenth Centuries', in Peter Sluglett and Stefan Weber (eds.), *Syria and Bilad al-Sham Under Ottoman Rule*: Essays in Honour of Abdul Karim Rafeq (Leiden: Brill): 179–240.

Webster. 1971. *New Geographical Dictionary* (Springfield, MA: Merriam-Webster).

Weingarten, Susan. 2015. 'Markets in Israel: Traditions and Transformations', in Mark McWilliams (ed.), *Food and Markets: Proceedings of the Oxford Symposium on Food and Cookery 2014* (Sheffield: Prospect Books): 399–408.

Weir, Shelagh. 1994. *Palestinian Costume* (London: British Museum).

Weiss, Ze'ev and Ehud Netzer. 1998. *Promise and Redemption: A Synagogue Mosaic from Sepphoris* (Jerusalem: The Israel Museum).

Weiss, Zeev. 2014. *Public Spectacles in Roman and Late Antique Palestine* (Cambridge, MA: Harvard University Press).

Westberg, David. 2009. 'The Rite of Spring: Erotic Celebration in the Dialexis and Ethopoiiai of Procopius of Gaza', in Ingela Nilsson (ed.), *Plotting with Eros: Essays on the Poetics of Love and the Erotics of Reading* (Copenhagen: Museum Tusculanum Press, University of Copenhagen): 187–211.

Westberg, David. 2017. 'The Letter Collection of Procopius of Gaza', in Cristiana Sogno, Bradley K. Storin and Edward J. Watts (eds.), *Late Antique Letter Collections: A Critical Introduction and Reference Guide* (Berkeley, CA: University of California Press): 394–417.

Westberg, David. 2019. 'Ideals of Education and Sophistic Realities in Late Antique Gaza', in Jan R. Stenger (ed.), *Learning Cities in Late Antiquity: The Local Dimension of Education* (London: Routledge): 164–86.

Whately, Conor. 2016. *Battles and Generals: Combat, Culture, and Didacticism in Procopius' Wars* (Leiden: Brill).

Wheatley, Paul. 2001. *The Places Where Men Pray Together: Cities in Islamic Lands: Seventh Through the Tenth Centuries* (Chicago: University of Chicago Press).

Wickham, Chris (ed.). 2000. *The Long Eighth Century: Production, Distribution and Demand* (Leiden: Brill): 265–343.

Wickham, Chris. 2005. *Framing the Early Middle Ages: Europe and the Mediterranean, 400–800* (Oxford: Oxford University Press).

Wiener, Noah. 2013. 'Tel Kabri: The 2013 Excavations: Storage Magazine Sheds Light on Canaanite', 12 September, *Bible History Daily*. https://www.biblicalarchaeology.org/daily/biblical-sites-places/biblical-archaeology-sites/tel-kabri-the-2013-excavations (accessed 21 November 2025).

Wiener, Noah. 2016. 'Early Bronze Age: Megiddo's Great Temple and the Birth of Urban Culture in the Levant', *Bible History Daily, Biblical Archaeology Society*, 10 September. https://www.biblicalarchaeology.org/daily/news/early-bronze-age-megiddos-great-temple-and-the-birth-of-urban-culture-in-the-levant (accessed 21 November 2025).

Wigoder, Geoffrey. 2005. *The Illustrated Dictionary and Concordance of the Bible* (New York: Sterling Publishing Company).

Wilde, Ralph. 2022. 'Tears of the Olive Trees: Mandatory Palestine, the UK, and Reparations for Colonialism in International Law,' *Journal of the History of International Law*, 25 (2): 1-42.

Wilkinson, Richard H. 2003. *The Complete Gods and Goddesses of Ancient Egypt* (London: Thames & Hudson).

Willson, Rachel Beckles. 2013. *Orientalism and Musical Mission: Palestine and the West* (Cambridge: Cambridge University Press).

Wimmer, Stefan J., and Aren M. Maeir. 2007. '"The Prince of Safit?": A Late Bronze Age Hieratic Inscription from Tell Eṣ-Ṣāfi/Gath', *Zeitschrift des Deutschen Palästina-Vereins*, 123 (1): 37–48.

Woodman, Earle Jess. 1964. *The Expositio Totius Mundi et Gentium*: Its Geography and Its Language. MA Thesis. Ohio University.

World Health Organization. 2009. *Hazard Analysis and Critical Control Point Generic Models for Some Traditional Foods: A Manual for the Eastern Mediterranean Region.* https://iris.who.int/handle/10665/119885 (accessed 21 November 2025).

Wright, G. R. H. 1985. *Ancient Building in South Syria and Palestine*, Vol. 1 (Leiden: Brill).

Yazbak, Mahmoud. 1998. *Haifa in the Late Ottoman Period, 1864-1914: A Muslim Town in Transition* (Leiden: Brill).

Yazbak, Mahmoud. 1999. 'Templars as Proto-Zionists? The "German Colony" in Late Ottoman Haifa', *Journal of Palestine Studies*, Vol. 28, No. 4 (Summer): 40–54

Yazbak, Mahmoud. 2012. 'Palestinian Commercial Networks in Transformation', *Sociology Study*, 2 (11): 805-18.

Yazbak, Mahmoud. 2024. 'Jaffa Before the Nakba: Palestine's Thriving City, 1799–1948', in Sarah Irving (ed.), *The Social and Cultural History of Palestine: Essays in Honour of Salim Tamari* (Edinburgh: Edinburgh University Press): 8-25.

Yılmaz, Birsen, Nilüfer Acar-Tek and Saniye Sözlü. 2017. 'Turkish Cultural Heritage: A Cup of Coffee', *Journal of Ethnic Foods*, 4 (4): 213–20.

Young, Gary K. 1997. *The Customs-Officer at the Nabataean Port of Leuke Kome ("Periplus Maris Erythraei' 19) Zeitschrift für Papyrologie und Epigraphik Bd. 119*: 266-8.

Yusuf, Muhsin M. D. 1985 *Economic Survey of Syria During the Tenth and Eleventh Centuries* (Berlin: Klaus Schwarz Verlag).

Zalatimo, Salah Akram. 2018.*The Magical Hands Of Zalatimo: How a Resilient Young Man Created the World's Tastiest Treats* (South Carolina: CreateSpace Independent Publishing Platform).

Zeiner, Noelle K. 2005. *Nothing Ordinary Here: Statius as Creator of Distinction in the Silvae* (London: Routledge).

Ziadeh, Nicola A. 1953. *Urban Life in Syria Under the Early Mamluks* (Westport, CN: Greenwood Press Greenwood Press).

Index